CITE THIS BOOK

THUS:

first tuesday

Real Estate
Practice

4th Edition

Cutoff Dates:
Legal editing of this material was
completed January 2006

Copyright ©2006 by first tuesday
P.O. Box 20069, Riverside, CA 92516

Editorial Staff

Legal Editor/Publisher:
Fred Crane

Managing and Project Editor:
Ai M. Kelley

Contributing Editors:
Melissa L. Clayton
Connor P. Wallmark
Sheena Wong

Senior Editorial Assistant:
Joseph Duong

Editorial Assistant:
Sylvia Rodemeyer

Comments or suggestions to:
first tuesday, P.O. Box 20069, Riverside, CA 92516
e-mail: editorial@firsttuesday.us
www.firsttuesdayonline.com

Table of Contents

Section A

**Agency
Issues**

Section B

**Listings:
Employment
by the public**

Section C

**Property
Conditions &
Disclosures**

Section D

Contract Law

Table of Forms

Introduction

Real Estate Practice is part of the **first tuesday** series of California-specific real estate study materials. Each title in the series has a different topic as its primary content. As part of a comprehensive real estate education program, the series includes Principles of Real Estate, Real Estate Finance, Legal Aspects of Real Estate and Real Estate Property Management.

first tuesday's real estate series uses plain language and eliminates the extensive overlap of identical course material commonly offered by other publishers. Issues arising in more than one factual setting are referenced as necessary, but are dealt with fully in only one **first tuesday** title.

Real Estate Practice is written for real estate licensees, lenders, attorneys, title officers, buyers and sellers. This course material is designed to be an educational tool to provide an agent with the guidance needed to prepare the forms used to solicit employment, disclose property and transactional facts and to enter into contracts to buy and sell real estate. The scope of the material presented extends beyond a minimum acceptable level of knowledge and professional development.

The objective of this material is to fully develop the real estate professional's understanding of the use and preparation of forms typically used in general brokerage services, ranging from employment agreements and purchase contracts to disclosures and worksheets. **Real Estate Practice** also discusses the effect provisions in the forms will have on different parties involved in a transaction, as well as the advice and counsel to be given to a client when reviewing the forms.

Included, with an explanation for their use, are all the forms and notices required when bringing a buyer and seller together as a match in a real estate sales transaction. Forms are treated as itemized checklists of disclosures and provisions to be considered by an agent and reviewed with buyers and sellers of real estate.

These forms fully reflect the relevant codes, judicial decisions and practices in effect on the date of this publication. The forms referenced are developed and published by **first tuesday**.

SECTION A

Agency Issues

Chapter 1

Brokerage activities: agent of the agent

This chapter introduces the concept of a licensed real estate sales agent being an agent of a licensed real estate broker and classified as either an employee or independent contractor.

For, on behalf of and in place of

Historically, as brokerage services in the mid-20th century became more prevalent in California and the public demanded greater consistency and competence in the rendering of these services, the state legislature began standardizing and regulating:

- who could become licensees and offer brokerage services;

- the duties and obligations owed by the licensees to members of the public; and

- the procedures for soliciting and rendering services while conducting licensed activities on behalf of clientele.

The resulting legislation and regulations which now control the brokerage services provided on the sale and purchase of real estate are straightforward and uncomplicated. Collectively, the standards set the minimum level of conduct expected of a licensee when dealing with the public, such as **competency and honesty**. The key to implementing these professional standards is the **education and training** of the licensees.

Individuals who wish to become real estate brokers are issued a broker license by the **Department of Real Estate (DRE)** only after completing extensive, additional real estate related course work and meeting minimum on-the-job experience requirements. On receiving the license, a broker is presumed to be competent in his skill and diligence, with the expectation that he will conduct himself in a manner which rises above the minimum level of duties owed to clientele and other members of the public.

Therefore, the individual or corporation which a buyer or seller, landlord or tenant, or borrower or lender retains to represent them in a real estate transaction may only be a licensed real estate broker.

To retain a broker to act as his real estate agent, the buyer or seller enters into an employment contract with the broker, called a *listing agreement*.

Broker vs. sales agent

Brokers are in a distinctly different category from sales agents. Brokers are authorized to deal with **members of the public** to offer, contract for and render brokerage services for compensation, called *licensed activities*. Sales agents are not. [Calif. Business and Professions Code §10131]

A real estate salesperson is strictly an agent of his employing broker. An agent **cannot contract in his own name** or on behalf of anyone other than his employing broker. Thus, an agent cannot be employed by any person who is a member of the public. This is why an agent's license must be handed to his employing broker, who must retain possession of the license until the agent leaves the employ of the broker. [Bus & P C §10160]

Only when acting as a representative of his broker may the sales agent perform brokerage services which only the broker is authorized to contract for and provide to others, called *clients*. [**Grand** v. **Griesinger** (1958) 160 CA2d 397]

Further, a sales agent can only receive compensation for his real estate related activities from

3

his employing broker. An agent cannot receive compensation directly from anyone else, e.g., the seller or buyer, or another licensee. [Bus & P C §10137]

Thus, brokers are the *agents* of the members of the public who employ them, while a broker's sales agents are the *agents of the agent* who render services for the broker's clients as the broker's representatives. [Calif. Civil Code §2079.13(b)]

As a result, brokers are responsible for all the activities their agents carry out **within the course and scope** of their employment. [**Gipson** v. **Davis Realty Company** (1963) 215 CA2d 190]

Responsibility for continuous supervision

When a broker employs a sales agent to act on behalf of the broker, the broker must **exercise reasonable supervision** over the activities performed by the agent. The broker who does not actively supervise his agents risks having his broker license suspended or revoked by the DRE. [Bus & P C §10177(h)]

Here, the employing broker's responsibility to the public includes:

- on-the-job training for the agent in the procedures and practice of real estate brokerage; and

- continuous policing by the broker of the agent's compliance with the duties owed to buyers and sellers.

The sales agent's duties owed to the broker's clients and others in a transaction are equivalent to the duties owed them by the employing broker. [CC §2079.13(b)]

The **duties owed** to the various parties in a transaction by a broker, which may be carried out by a sales agent under the employing broker's supervision, oversight and management, include:

- the *utmost care, integrity, honesty and loyalty* in dealings with a **client**; and

- the use of *skill, care, honesty, fair dealing and good faith* in dealings with **all parties** to a transaction in the disclosure of information which adversely affects the value and desirability of the property involved. [CC §2079.16]

To insure that his agents are diligently complying with the duties owed to clientele and others, the employing broker must establish **office policies, procedures, rules and systems relating to:**

- *soliciting* and obtaining buyer and seller listings and *negotiating* real estate transactions of all types;

- the *documentation* arising out of licensed activities which might affect the rights and obligations of any party, such as agreements, disclosures, reports and authorizations prepared or received by the agent;

- the *filing, maintenance and storage* of all documents affecting the rights of the parties;

- the handling and safekeeping of *trust funds* received by the agent for deposit, retention or transmission to others;

- *advertisements*, such as flyers, brochures, press releases, multiple listing service (MLS) postings, etc.;

- compliance by his agents with all federal and state laws relating to *unlawful discrimination*; and

- the receipt of regular *periodic reports* from agents on their performance of activities within the course and scope of their employment. [Department of Real Estate Regulations §2725]

One method for implementing the need for supervision is for a broker employing agents to develop a **business model**. With it, the broker establishes the means and manner by which listings are produced and serviced, and how purchase agreements are negotiated and closed by his agents. The development of a plan of operations logically starts with an analysis of the conduct required of an agent by establishing categories of administrative and licensed activities. [See Figure 1 accompanying this chapter]

Categories of business and licensed activities include:

- **administrative rules**, covering a description of the general business operations of the brokerage office, such as office routines, phone management, sign usage, budgetary allocations for agent-support activities (advertising, farming, etc.), agent interviews, goal setting and daily work schedules;

- **procedural rules**, encompassing the means and methods to be used by agents to obtain measurable results (listings, sales, leases, loans, etc.);

- **substantive rules**, focusing on the documentation needed when producing listings, negotiating sales, leases or loans and fulfilling the duties owed by the broker to clientele and others;

- **compliance checks**, consisting of periodic (weekly) and event-driven reports (a listing or sale) to be prepared by the agent, and the review of files and performance schedules by the broker, office manager or assistants, such as listing or transaction coordinators; and

- **supervisory oversight**, an ongoing and continuous process of training agents and managing their activities which fall within the course and scope of their employment.

The rules and procedures established by the broker to comply with his responsibility to manage and oversee the conduct of his agents when they are acting in his place in dealings with clientele and other members of the public must be agreed to in writing with the agents he employs. A **written employment contract** sets forth the duties of the sales agent and the agent's need to comply with an office manual which contains the broker's policies, rules, procedures and other conduct the broker deems necessary to control the fulfillment of his responsibility for supervision.

Also, the written employment agreement must spell out the **compensation** the agent is to receive for representing the broker in soliciting and negotiating listings, purchase agreements, leases and financing. [DRE Regs. §2726]

The (not so) independent contractor

Most sales agents receive compensation from their brokers based on a negotiated percentage of **contingency fees** received by the brokers for completed sales, leases or loans solicited or negotiated by the agents.

Whether state and federal income tax is withheld depends on the type of employment agreement the broker and agent enter into, i.e., an **independent contractor** (IC) or **employee-employer** (EE) agreement.

A sales agent licensed by the DRE and employed by a broker under an independent contractor agreement, who is paid based on the broker's receipt of a contingency fee, **will not be treated as an employee** for purposes of income tax withholding or contributions. [Internal Revenue Code §3508]

The chief advantage for a real estate broker who uses an IC agreement is the simplification of the bookkeeping process. An IC agreement avoids withholding for income taxes or medicare and social security benefits from the agent's fee, while also avoiding employer contributions.

In turn, the broker files a 1099 report with the Internal Revenue Service (IRS) naming each agent and stating the fee amount each received as an employee of the broker under a contingent-fee, IC agreement.

To further simplify disbursement of the agent's share of the fee due from the broker, some brokers instruct and authorize escrow to disburse to the agent, from fees accruing to the broker on the close of a sales escrow, the amount of the fee due the agent from the broker. However, this system of payment leaves the broker without adequate records for 1099 and workers' compensation reporting.

For sales agents entering into an IC agreement, they report their fees received from their broker as business income (Schedule C). In turn, the agent expenses all his business-related costs of operation incurred while acting within the course and scope of his employment with the broker, no matter the degree of control the broker actually exercises over the agent's activities.

However, even though the agreement is called an "independent contractor" agreement, the agent is still an agent of his employing broker.

When testing the conduct of an agent while engaged in real estate related activities, the IC provision in his broker-agent employment agreement cannot and will not change the agent's classification as an agent of his broker under California real estate law. [Gipson, *supra*]

Thus, brokers who use an IC agreement must not be mislead or believe that somehow the agent may permissibly act independent of the broker, or that the DRE will treat the relationship as devoid of control and assertiveness by the broker over the agent's conduct.

Agent imposes liability on broker

Consider a sales agent who is employed by a broker under an IC agreement. The broker gives the agent *total discretion* in his handling of clientele and documentation of listings and sales.

However, the IC agreement includes a provision calling for the agent to deliver to the broker a binder for liability insurance on the agent's car which names the broker as an insured. The IC agreement also requires all documents and funds received on listings and sales to be entered into and taken in the name of the broker, and all advertising and business cards to identify the agent as acting for the broker as an associate licensee.

One day, while the sales agent is driving his car to list a property, he collides with another vehicle, injuring the driver. The driver makes a demand on the agent's broker to pay for the driver's money losses incurred due to the agent's negligence.

The broker rejects the demand, claiming the agent is an independent contractor, not an agent (much less an employee) of the broker, and thus the broker has no (vicarious) liability for the losses inflicted on the driver by the agent.

The driver claims the broker is liable for his losses since the agent is a representative of the broker, acting within the *course and scope* of his employment when the injuries occurred.

Can the driver injured by the agent's negligence recover his money losses from the agent's broker?

Yes! The sales agent is the *agent of the broker* as a matter of law, without concern for the type of employment agreement they have entered into.

Further, and in spite of the IC employment agreement allowing total discretion to the agent in the conduct of his handling of listings and sales, the agent is subject to supervision by his broker who is required by law to actively conduct his brokerage business. Since the sales agent is an agent of the broker, without regard to their employment agreement, and at the time of the injury was acting within the course and scope of the agency with the broker, the broker cannot escape liability for his agent's negligence. [Gipson, *supra*]

Figure 1

Forming a business model

Within each category of activity covering the broker's management of his agents' conduct for producing, servicing and negotiating listings and sales, is a list of items to be considered.

Administrative	Organizational Procedures	Substantive Activities	Compliance	Supervision
• E & O insurance • workers' compensation insurance • automobile insurance binder • general comprehensive business insurance • agent policy manual (on procedural, substantive and compliance activities) • new agent qualifications and interview procedures • institutional advertising franchise affiliation • trade organization membership • MLS subscriptions • employment contracts with sales agents • agent pay, advances, and escrow disbursements • production goals • phone/floor-time coverage • hours/agents' work schedules • business cards • storage of documents (3 years) • office meetings/attendance • agent contribution to expenses • bank trust accounts • general business bank accounts	• forms to be used • use of coordinators • use of office equipment • use of affiliated services • use of controlled businesses • attorney inquiry/referral to broker • trust fund handling (deposit and log) • e-mail content • public record inspection • servicing property listings (MLS, signs, ads, property profiles, open houses, correspondence, showings, checklists, rents, etc.) • servicing buyers (listings, property profiles, broadcasts, wants, showings, qualifying, checklists, etc.) • client lists and follow up	• taking property listings (addenda and disclosure checklists, deposits, property profiles, further approvals, fee setting, seller profiles, etc.) • preparing offers (documents/disclosures and addenda checklists, duty checklists, advice on use of arbitration, forfeiture, escrow, title, misc. provisions, fee provisions, etc.) • FSBO submission of offers (fee arrangements, listings, dual agency, etc.) • preparation of documents, use of attorneys, added provisions	• pay contingent on file audit and completeness • listing logs • transaction logs • trust fund logs • periodic reports • listing reports • sales reports • schedule of report due dates • other events which trigger notices or reports to management	• continuous daily oversight • constant follow-up on compliance with procedures and substantive activities • instructions on propriety of acts within the course and scope of employment • degree of enforcement being tight and disciplined, or lax and allowing great discretion • use of assistants to provide oversight

The broker hiring agents who use their own cars to conduct brokerage activities by going to and from appointments, meetings and properties not only needs to be a named insured on the agent's car insurance policy, but also needs to maintain general comprehensive business liability insurance and professional liability coverage (errors and omissions insurance) since tortious conduct of all sorts can arise out of listings and sales transactions solicited and negotiated by their agents.

Thus, supervision is critical to the reduction of the broker's exposure to liability for their sales agents' failure to inspect, disclose, advise and care for clients.

Unemployment insurance benefits

For the purposes of administering real estate law, a sales agent is considered both an *agent and an employee* when acting within the course and scope of employment with a broker. [Grand, *supra*]

However, as with state and federal income tax withholding, an agent is not always treated as an employee.

For example, licensed real estate sales agents, as well as real estate brokers, are **excluded employees** for purposes of the California Unemployment Insurance Law. Even though a sales agent is considered both an agent and an employee under California real estate law, a broker does not have to contribute to the state unemployment insurance fund on behalf of the agent. In turn, the agent cannot collect unemployment benefits from the state when he is terminated from the employ of the broker.

Receipt of compensation by a licensed real estate agent under an employment agreement, paid as a *contingency fee* for closing transactions and not based on a per hour amount, is the **only test required** for the broker to avoid paying into and for the agent to be denied unemployment benefits, regardless of the degree to which the broker supervises and controls the agent's real estate related activities. [Calif. Unemployment Insurance Code §650]

Minimum wage exclusion

A sales agent is entitled to payment of minimum hourly wages from a broker if the agent is classified as an *employee* under California labor laws, a technical condition requiring **constant supervision** and **total control** by the broker over the agent's **means, manner and mode** of engaging in activities requiring a real estate license.

However, as *agents* of their broker, most agents have a high level of discretion and control in the setting of their schedules, especially during the hours spent outside of their broker's office.

Typically, the agents' time in the office spent at the updesk, or on the phones or floor, rarely take up more than one day a week, usually less than 20% of the time spent on real estate related listings and sales. Little additional time is spent in the office at staff meetings. As a result, agents are rarely considered employees, except for the purpose of judging their conduct as a licensee under California real estate law.

As an *outside salesperson* who regularly works **more than half** of his time **away** from his place of employment, selling items or obtaining contracts for services, a real estate sales agent is **excluded from collecting a minimum wage** from his broker. [Calif. Labor Code §1171]

Consider an agent who is employed by a broker under an IC agreement. The broker does not have a policy manual, training program or any requirements as to what forms to use and what duties are to be fulfilled by the agent (a dereliction of the broker's duties of supervision). Once a month, the agent reports to the broker by preparing and presenting a transaction log noting the listings and sales activity the agent has been involved in during the month.

After several months of employment and no sales, the broker terminates the agent. During the employment, the broker disbursed funds to the agent as an advance draw against fees yet to be earned by the agent. Any amounts not reimbursed are payable on termination. Thus, by agreement, the broker calls due the amounts advanced and unpaid, and makes a demand on the agent for payment.

The agent claims he is entitled to an offset since he is an employee of the broker and thus entitled to a minimum wage in amounts which exceed the advances received from the broker. The agent makes a demand on the broker for unpaid wages at the minimum rate per hour worked.

Here, the agent demanding a minimum wage must demonstrate that his actual working relationship with his broker was more than just that of an independent contractor or an agent of his broker, but that of an employee under the labor code.

Accordingly, the agent must demonstrate that the relationship he actually experienced while employed by the broker included total control by the broker over every **means, manner and mode of conduct** used by the agent to carry out licensed activities on behalf of the broker, such that the agent was nearly without discretion to operate on his own.

Here, the broker's supervision and management of the agent by implementing policies and procedures for the negotiation of real estate transactions were nearly nonexistent.

While the sales agent was an agent of the broker, the sales agent was not under the *common law control* of the broker as required to establish the agent as a *servant* hired to perform under continuous direction. Thus, the sales agent was not an *employee* for the purposes of the labor law, and therefore could not receive a minimum wage. [CC §2079.13(b); **Grubb and Ellis Company** v. **Spengler** (1983) 143 CA3d 890]

The issue of being excluded from collecting a minimum wage based on the agent being classified as an *outside salesperson* never arose in the *Grubb and Ellis Company* case.

However, even if the broker had controlled the agent's activities, hours, scheduling and production of listings and sales, the agent still would most likely have been outside the office more than half of the hours spent working for the broker. Thus, the agent most likely would have been classified as an employee under the labor law, but would definitely have been **excluded** from collecting a minimum wage due to his status as an outside salesperson.

Workers' compensation coverage for employees

For purposes of workers' compensation insurance, the relationship between a broker and his agents is that of an employer and his employees. As a consequence, all real estate brokers in California **must provide workers' compensation insurance** coverage for their sales agents. [Lab C §§3200 et seq.; Department of Real Estate Bulletin, Fall 2004, Page 10]

A broker who is illegally uninsured or forces his agents to carry their own workers' compensation insurance may face:

- a **stop order** from the Department of Industrial Relation's Division of Labor Standards Enforcement (DLSE), preventing the broker from conducting business until proof of insurance is offered up;

- **civil penalties and fines** up to $100,000; and

- **claims** from current and former agents seeking reimbursement for premiums they paid. [Lab C §§3700 et seq.]

For a broker who employs one or more agents, he must, by necessity, be covered by workers' compensation insurance, along with business, vehicle and professional liability insurance (errors and omissions coverage). The coverage provides the broker with a financial safety net against agent-imposed liability by shifting the risk of loss to the insurance companies, whether the sales agents are mere agents or also employees.

Thus, the well supervised real estate brokerage business, as owned and managed by a broker who runs a properly conducted operation, provides an enduring professional environment in which their sales agents should flourish.

Chapter 2

An agent's perception of riches

This chapter presents a worksheet for use by sales agents to analyze the income and expenses they will share or incur during their employment with a broker.

The broker avoids deception

An individual receives an original salesperson license from the Department of Real Estate (DRE). The newly licensed agent contacts a real estate broker in response to an advertisement soliciting agents to join his office. The agent will interview this broker, and others, in an effort to find a suitable office in which to work.

Eventually, the agent will select the office he feels is most able to provide the training and guidance he will need to earn a living in real estate sales.

During an interview, the question of earnings is addressed. The agent is told his employment relationship with the broker will be under an independent contractor (IC) agreement with workers' compensation coverage provided by the broker, but no income tax withholding or employer contributions for social security, Medicare or unemployment insurance.

Further, the broker explains the agent will need cash reserves or income from other sources to meet his living and business expenses for six to nine months. Several months will pass before income will be forthcoming from closings in which the agent will have participated. The brokerage office does not make monthly advances against future fees.

To assist the agent in an analysis of his potential earnings, an income and expense data worksheet is prepared by the agent. The agent enters the approximations made by the broker for the various expenses a typical agent should experience during his first year with the brokerage office. [See Form 504 accompanying this chapter]

The agent uses the worksheet to further analyze income, expenses, cash reserves and the sales goal he believes must be met in order to provide an acceptable after-tax income to cover his personal living expenses.

Data underlying an income analysis

As a prerequisite to an agent's use of an income and expense data worksheet, the agent must collect data during his interview with a prospective broker, including:

- the **price range** of property the agent is most likely to list and sell;

- the **number of sales** the agent will likely close in that price range during his first year;

- the **gross brokerage fees** generated by the number of sales during the first year; and

- the **share of the gross brokerage fees** the agent will receive under the fee-sharing schedule proffered by the broker.

The likely gross fees the broker will receive and the agent's share of those fees are entered on the worksheet as a result of the interview. [See Form 504 §§1 and 2]

Ultimately, the **sales goal** set by the agent reflects the amount of after-tax income the agent seeks for himself. [See Form 504 Annual Gross Fee Projection section]

Until the worksheet is filled out accurately, projecting fees to be received by the agent, estimating expenses to be incurred and attempting to set sales volume goals or probable after-tax earnings is an uneducated guess.

AGENT'S INCOME DATA SHEET

Date prepared: _____, 20_____
Brokerage office:_____

> **Note:** This Income and Expense Worksheet is used to assist an Agent or Associated Broker in an analysis of the income and expenses now experienced or likely to be experienced with a brokerage office for coming one-year period and to estimate the entry or change-of-office costs.

ANNUAL INCOME AND EXPENSES:

1. **Gross Brokerage Fees:**. . . . . $_____   100 %

   1.1   Franchise fee disbursement (_____% of § 1.) . – $_____

      a. Subtotal . . . . $_____

   1.2   Broker retains _____% of ☐ §1., or ☐ §1.1a. . . – $_____

2. **Gross Fees due Agent:**. . . . . $_____   _____%

3. **Transaction Deductions by Broker:**

   3.1   Less:

      a. E & O premium ($_____ per closing) $_____

      b. Prior client promotion (_____% of fee) . . . . . $_____

      c. Listing/Transaction coordinator . . . . $_____

      d. _____ . . . $_____

   3.2   Total charges withheld . . . . – $_____   _____%

4. **Office Expenses:**

   4.1   Equipment rent . . . . $_____

   4.2   Forms & manuals. . . . . $_____

   4.3   Desk space and parking charges . . . . $_____

   4.4   Membership:

      a. Trade association. . . . . $_____

      b. MLS fees. . . . . $_____

      c. Affiliations . . . . $_____

   4.5   Supplies/software updates . . . . $_____

   4.6   Postage/delivering services . . . . $_____

   4.7   Library/subscriptions. . . . . $_____

   4.8   Photocopies. . . . . $_____

   4.9   Equipment use charge . . . . $_____

   4.10 Total office expenses: . . . . – $_____   _____%

5. **Agent's Business Expenses:**

   5.1   Telephone:

      a. Phone/fax . . . . $_____

      b. Cell phone. . . . . $_____

   5.2   Auto:

      a. Gas/oil. . . . . $_____

      b. Repairs and maintenance/carwash . . . . $_____

      c. Insurance . . . . $_____

      d. Loan/lease payment. . . . . $_____

      e. Registration . . . . $_____

   5.3   Printing:

      a. Farm letters. . . . . $_____

      b. Postage. . . . . $_____

   5.4   Licensing fees and education . . . . $_____

   5.5   Internet service . . . . $_____

   5.6   Legal and accounting. . . . . $_____

5.7   Marketing sessions . . . . $_____   ⇧

5.8   Travel/hotel . . . . $_____

5.9   Entertainment . . . . $_____

5.10   Insurance (business and health) . . . . $_____

5.11   Total Business Expenses: . . . . − $_____   _____%

6.   **Marketing and Sales Expenses:**

6.1   Printing flyers/mailer for listings. . . . . $_____

6.2   Property ads:

       a.   Newspaper/magazine. . . . . $_____

       b.   TV/radio/web . . . . $_____

6.3   Postage (marketing) . . . . $_____

6.4   Property preparation. . . . . $_____

6.5   Open house (food/drinks). . . . . $_____

6.6   Gifts on closing . . . . $_____

6.7   Transactional expenses . . . . $_____

6.8   Total marketing and sales expenses: . . . . − $_____   _____%

7.   **Agent's Net Income:**. . . . . $_____   _____%

7.1   Income, SS & medicare taxes. . . . . − $_____   _____%

8.   **Agent's After-Tax Income** . . . . $_____   _____%

9.   **Other Income Sources:**

9.1   Draw/Advance . . . . $_____

9.2   Other:_____. . . . . $_____

9.3   Other:_____. . . . . $_____

10.   **Cost-of-Entry/Change-of-Office Analysis:**

10.1   Marketing course . . . . $_____

10.2   Lock boxes . . . . $_____

10.3   Open house signs . . . . $_____

10.4   Stationary/cards . . . . $_____

10.5   Computer/programs/printer . . . . $_____

10.6   Office furniture . . . . $_____

10.7   Photocopier . . . . $_____

10.8   Phone/fax equipment . . . . $_____

10.9   Phone installation . . . . $_____

10.10 Camera/printer . . . . $_____

10.11 Vehicle . . . . $_____

10.12 Other:_____ . . . . $_____

10.13 Other:_____ . . . . $_____

10.14 **Total Entry/Relocation Costs:**. . . . . $_____

11.   **GROSS BROKERAGE FEE PROJECTION/FORECAST:**

11.1   Annual after-tax income desired by agent: . . . . $_____

11.2   DIVIDE by percentage of after-tax income at §8: . . . . ÷_____

11.3   Annual Gross Brokerage Fee needed at §1.
       to earn the desired after-tax income at §11.1:. . . . . =_____

11.4   Analyze the source of Gross Brokerage Fees at §1 by setting the price of the typical transaction the agent
       will close, the dollar amount the broker will receive as the gross brokerage fee on the typical transaction,
       and the number of typical transactions the agent must close within one year to attain the gross Brokerage
       fees set as the goal at section 11.3.

_____

_____

_____

_____

_____

FORM 504   06-05   ©2006 **first tuesday**, P.O. BOX 20069, RIVERSIDE, CA 92516 (800) 794-0494

The agent's personal role

Since the volume of real estate sales closed by new agents during their first year in the business is a "numbers game," with only a percentage of all sales efforts coming to fruition in the form of fees received from closings, the type of person attracted to real estate sales must have an innate curiosity and enthusiasm for estimating and forecasting income and expenses if he is to succeed.

If a prospective agent is discouraged or daunted by the exercise of completing a worksheet, that individual is unlikely to be a prime candidate for employment in the real estate brokerage business.

The broker steps forward

Brokers, by experience, tend to be more organized than agents. Also, brokers who employ agents tend to be better able to anticipate the income and expenses an agent will incur than recently licensed agents. It is the broker who can best draw a conclusion about an agent's future with the broker's office, not the agent who is new to the world of real estate sales or who is now languishing in another office due to inadequate or nonexistent planning.

A broker's primary objective when hiring agents is to increase the gross brokerage fees received by his office without a disproportionate increase in his operating expenses. For the broker to make hiring a productive endeavor, the broker must strive to avoid the constant turnover of agents who remain with the office for only a short period of time.

Long-term employment of agents not only contributes to a favorable industry-wide reputation about the broker, but also provides a return to the broker for his time and energy invested with each agent during the employment process and the agent's start-up period. Energy, money, time and enthusiasm all wane fast when the turnover of agents in an office is due to the failure of unrealistic expectations held by the agents.

A broker's full disclosure, upfront and prior to employment, covering the agent's likely income and expenses, and why the sharing and allocations are reasonable, will lead to a realistic expectation of income by the agent. Monthly and quarterly sales goals can then be set at levels designed to meet projected earnings should the agent be employed by the broker.

To control the agent's interview and get long-term results, the broker should initiate the income and expense discussion himself, not wait until the prospective agent takes charge by raising the question of earnings.

To be ready for an interview with a prospective agent, the broker should himself prepare a worksheet by estimating the expenses the agent is most likely to incur. Also, the broker needs to estimate the initial cash investment the prospective agent will be required to make to cover one-time, nonrecurring expenditures and carrying costs necessary to get a proper start in real estate sales. [See Form 504 §10]

Once the operating expenses, nonrecurring costs and carrying costs incurred by the typical agent have been established — based on the broker's history with his present agents — what remains is the difficult task of anticipating an agent's gross fees from sales which will close during the first year of employment.

Forecasting gross fees

A couple of approaches for estimating future fees are apparent. For one, the broker can project a range of gross brokerage fee amounts, varying from the earnings generated by a high producer to those of a low producer during their first year with the office. The various gross brokerage fee projections, ranging from low, medium to high, could be entered on separate but duplicate copies of the income and expense worksheet. The agent's expenses estimated for the first year would also be included in the worksheets.

Thus, the prospective agent's after-tax income can be calculated based on various levels of sales.

Another approach for the interview is to discuss the range of gross brokerage fees an agent can generate, without the broker first entering any fees on the income and expense worksheet he hands to the agent. Thus, the agent is left to enter and calculate the income he either believes he can produce or wants to produce to attain the after-tax income he seeks.

Reviewed by the broker and the prospective agent under either approach, or a combination of approaches, the worksheet becomes both a **budget and a sales goal** for the agent. With an open-minded review of the pros and cons of income sharing and expense allocation, the broker encourages the agent to set attainable production goals.

At the same time, the broker confirms whether the prospective agent has the financial capacity to carry his personal and business expenses during the start-up period with the office before the fees from closings come rolling in.

A failure to inform

The failure of an employing broker to inform a prospective agent about the operating expenses the agent will most likely incur, the investment by the agent which is necessary for trappings such as a vehicle, equipment, multiple listing service (MLS) fees, instruments and materials to enter real estate sales, and the net operating income (NOI) from sales is an oversight by the broker. Without these disclosures, an analysis of the agent's long-term potential with the office has not taken place.

At worst, the failure to advise a prospective agent is an omission of facts known to the broker, which, when discovered by the sales agent, will lead to either a termination of employment or dissatisfaction over lost expectations.

Thus, a realistic and relatively accurate disclosure of income, expenses and the initial investment an agent will incur in the employ of the broker will:

- reduce the office turnover of agents;

- reduce the broker's investment of time and energy hiring and training agents; and

- produce a sales staff whose income expectations will be met due to their ability to most likely attain the sales goals each have set for themselves.

Selecting a broker by comparison

After a few years of employment in the business of real estate sales, efficient agents generally want to earn more for the time they spend listing properties, locating buyers and engaging in all the activities surrounding the sale of a parcel of real estate.

Before walking into the broker's or manager's office with a demand for the office to cover more expenses and give the agent a larger share of the brokerage fees, the agent should first do a little **comparative shopping** to determine how other brokers share expenses and fees with their agents.

The first step for the agent interested in renegotiating his current employment arrangement with his broker or moving to another broker's office, is to prepare a worksheet on his current operating conditions. Just what fees the agent has generated, the share of the fees the agent received, the operating expenses paid by the agent and the net income, as well as the after-tax income experienced during the past 12-month period, is a requisite for any comparison.

If the exercise goes no further, the worksheet can act as a **budget** or a basis for forecasting the next 12 months. Further, the variables controlling the amount of income and expenses can be analyzed, adjusted and projected to set sales goals the agent would like to attain during the next 12 months.

The second step is to distinguish the agent's current arrangement with his broker from the earning opportunities available to him with other acceptable brokerage offices. The comparative analysis is accomplished by preparing a worksheet for each prospective office. Information for the worksheet may be gathered from interviews with those brokers or their managers, or agents in those offices who have a handle on their income and expense arrangements with their broker.

On completion of the worksheet for each office, a comparison shows up the distinctions and parallels between the different offices.

Armed with comparisons reflected by the data developed on the worksheets, the agent seeking to renegotiate fee splits and the allocation of expenses with his current broker can structure his request for specific changes based on the market place.

Alternatively, the agent seeking to change offices uses the worksheet to make the same comparisons and size up prospective brokerage offices. Ultimately, the agent hopes to negoti-ate an income and expense sharing arrangement which satisfies the agent and provides a better opportunity for greater earnings — expectations realized based on comparison shopping and the agent's past sales history.

However, timing is important. The period during which the agent begins negotiations with his current broker or schedules interviews with other brokers can effect his results.

For instance, at the height of a booming market, a broker will be more willing to increase a productive agent's share of the fees since the broker's current overhead is already covered without the fees from additional sales. The agent's advantage of a better fee split and cost allocation would carry over into the inevitable slowdown in sales which follows every boom.

Conversely, a new agent entering an office during a recessionary period just prior to an upswing in sales will benefit from the broker's attention to the care and training of new agents, and the invaluable assistance of experienced agents in the office who will have a little extra time on their hands. All have time in a slower market to assist others, a bonding process important for a successful future in real estate sales in the coming years.

Chapter 3

Real estate's low-level management of human resources

This chapter comments on the rapid and seemingly wasteful turnover of entrants into the real estate profession.

The entry and exit of agents

In 1999, the Department of Real Estate (DRE) issued original real estate salesperson licenses to 20,410 individuals. By the end of 2003, four years after newly acquiring their licenses, 58% (11,868) of the originally licensed agents in 1999 **no longer participated** as licensees rendering services in real estate transactions on behalf of brokers.

This group of nonparticipating agents either failed to renew (9,203) or renewed as inactive, unemployed licensees (2,665). Thus, of all the agents originally licensed in 1999, **only 42% remain active** in the practice of real estate brokerage.

Now consider the 21,450 original real estate salesperson licenses issued in 2001 by the DRE. By July 2003, only 18 months after the last of the 2001 group of agents received their licenses, 21% (4481) were suspended and no longer engaged in real estate related services. They had failed to complete the basic DRE-mandated educational requirements to retain the use of their sales licenses.

In addition, another 18% (3,805) of this group of licensees from 2001 were inactive by January 2004.

When this 2001 group of newly licensed agents completes their first four-year renewal in 2005, the attrition will likely produce a total dropout rate of 60%. This nearly equals the 65% dropout rate at the end of four years for those agents who came into the real estate business in 1998, and slightly more than the 58% four-year dropout rate for 1999.

In 2003, 40,479 individuals received original real estate salesperson licenses. By the end of 2003, 27% (10,867) were inactive and unemployed as real estate agents.

Thus, when the agents who were originally licensed in 2003 complete their first four-year renewal in 2007, approximately 40% will likely remain active as agents participating in real estate transactions. Some will have become brokers. Another 15% will likely renew their license in an inactive, nonparticipating status, for a total fallout rate anticipated for the licensees from 2003 of 60%.

Solving the dropout problem

The rate of attrition for agents entering the real estate profession suggests that fully one third of the new licensees are not qualified by education, temperament and/or experience. They should not have been licensed or hired in the first place.

Possibly, the attrition is due to the brokerage community's inability or unwillingness to give new licensees the administrative oversight, technical training, structured routine and organizational support necessary to attract and retain individuals seeking to enter the business of real estate services as a life-long profession.

Also, the cyclical nature of boom and bust within the real estate industry, reflected in the number of entrants from year to year, is a factor which only aggravates the turnover rate.

Alternatively, the DRE guidelines may be too permissive, i.e., the threshold to obtain a license may be too low.

Becoming licensed as a real estate agent borders on being a "no-brainer," especially for individuals with a little tenacity. A certificate of completion for a principles course, needed to qualify to take the state exam for licensing, is attained by either attending classes at a real estate school or community college for the requisite 45 hours of attendance, or by completing an equivalent homestudy course and passing a final exam.

However, passing the state licensing exam may require more instruction. Thus, a "boot-camp" style, weekend cram course (or some other equally intense program) designed solely to pass the state exam is needed to supplement the principles course in order for most individuals to pass the state exam. This preparatory course for the state exam is not treated as education since it does not contribute to the competence of the individual for purposes of being a real estate agent.

Therefore, new real estate agents come to the real estate brokerage world without any practical experience and insufficient effective education to assist, much less advise, the clients who retain the services of their broker.

A step in the right direction would be on-the-job training for a new agent as an assistant, sometimes called a "runner," to his broker or an experienced agent in the office. The agent then learns the ropes under a high-volume agent in the office or with the office's transaction coordinator until the agent completes the courses required to receive an **unconditional** sales license. Industrial and commercial brokers tend to follow this course of action.

It would also be productive, by a measurable degree, for the DRE to take steps to rid the industry of under-educated new licensees by eliminating the conditional sales license. This would force the completion of at least three college-level courses (including a practices course) **before receiving a license.** Alternatively, brokers could insist on the completion of the education before employment.

The entry hurdle for new agents would be raised by the prerequisite of three courses for original licensing. Those individuals possessing a lack of enthusiasm for formal education before soliciting or rendering services on behalf of a broker would then be eliminated before licensing, not 18 months later as are the 20% to 25% of the new agents who fail to complete this education and are suspended.

The broker takes charge

To operate a successful brokerage office, the broker must employ viable agents.

It is the quantity and quality of agents that produce the end result sought by brokers to be successful, i.e., brokerage fees.

As in all service businesses, the lynchpin for achieving success is the ability of management to orchestrate the efforts of qualified agents.

However, most brokers employing agents tend not to dedicate much energy to the supervision of their agents. A level of seemingly deliberate neglect prevails in most single-family residential brokerage offices. Thus, agents are left to learn the trade by observation and to hone their skills by trial and error, an empirical result based more on the agents' good instincts than on training, procedural policy and constant supervision.

Brokers need to be more than distant observers limited to providing remote oversight for the agents. They or their administrative assistants and managers must learn to supervise and police the business-related conduct of their agents.

Such conduct includes:

- setting the production goals to be attained (listings and sales);

- an analysis of the agent's income and expenses;

- the setting of fees needed for the agent to become financially viable as a real estate agent;

- establishing the personal routines and activities which will likely make the agent productive, i.e., overseeing the agent's management of time spent working for the broker; and

- the insistence that compliance reports be prepared and delivered periodically to management.

Further, the broker must be actively involved in the agent's fulfillment of the duties owed by the broker to those clients with whom the agent has contact.

Thus, the agent knows from the beginning just what level of production is expected of him by the broker as a requirement for remaining with the office. Also, the broker will be demonstrating his expectation that the sales agent is to maintain a competitive attitude about producing listings and buyers. Further, an environment will have been created with a greater probability of producing purchase agreements and closings, which spells success for all involved.

The myth of "too much control"

A dilatory broker employing sales agents in his residential brokerage business frequently uses as an excuse for his lack of supervision the old, pre-1979 myth that a broker cannot tell an agent what to do, when or where to do it, and the amount of time the agent will spend doing it. As the myth goes, the agents are not employees; they are independent contractors who must operate free from the broker's direction, otherwise some adverse financial, legal or tax result will be visited on the broker.

Agents are employees as a matter of California real estate law. They and their brokers are excluded as *exceptions* from benefits and contributions for unemployment insurance and income tax withholding on the employment of real estate agents.

Minimum wages are only an issue if the agents are desk-bound in the office more than half the time spent working for the broker. The only other employer/employee concern is workers' compensation insurance which every broker employing a sales agent is required to carry. [See Chapter 1]

Should all of the broker's efforts during the apprenticeship and start-up period fail to develop agents who remain in the business, the broker should review why the agents should not have been hired, and if they should have been hired, what would have made them successful real estate agents.

With adjustments by employing brokers in hiring, training and managing their agents, the broker's human resources will become a long-term asset — the arms and legs of his business — not just bodies occupying cubicles and floor space in the office.

Chapter 4

The MLS environment

This chapter presents the role multiple listing services (MLSs) have had, and continue to have, on the residential brokerage community.

An industry-wide misconception

In everyday practice, sales agents who work with buyers on behalf of their brokers are commonly referred to as "buyer's agents" or "selling agents." However, in legal terms, it is the brokers employed by the buyers who are the **real buyer's agents**. [Calif. Civil Code §2079.13(n); see **first tuesday** Form 305 §3]

Historically, and incorrectly, the broker and his agent who represented a buyer in a sales transaction have been referred to as *subagents* within the residential multiple listing service (MLS) brokerage community. The misnomer was a product of the pre-1980s MLS environment, which held that all brokers (and their agents) who were members of a trade union's MLS were automatically "seller's agents."

The basis for the rationale rested on the premise that the sole purpose of the MLS was to **locate a buyer** for those sellers whose properties were posted in the MLS. Thus, all MLS members were said to be working either as the listing agent or a "subagent" of the seller, **employed to sell** the property listed in the MLS.

Therefore, the MLS member who produced the buyer was improperly viewed as having been **appointed** by the listing agent to act on behalf of the seller by virtue of the MLS membership and the authority granted by a **subagency provision** in the listing agreement of the day. Thus, the buyer of a property published in the MLS was without representation since no member of a trade union MLS could theoretically represent a buyer.

The MLS subagency concept was perpetuated by peer pressure amongst MLS residential brokers to conform to "industry trade standards." Thus, buyers were unable to employ brokers who were MLS members, a situation which often led to an undisclosed dual agency by their agent.

However, the MLS subagency approach to marketing real estate had begun to wane by the early 1980s. By then, brokers who sought to openly represent the best interests of buyers began to classify themselves as *single-agency* brokers. In fact, this single-agency activity was the predecessor of today's openly acknowledged buyer's agent.

The cooperating broker's subagency dilemma

Today, some two decades later, the buyer's broker and the broker's agents still sometimes improperly refer to themselves as the cooperating office or cooperating agents in a sales transaction. The term "cooperating" arose out of the old MLS subagency concept whereby the listing broker shared the fee paid by the seller with the buyer's broker, which is still authorized by the broker cooperation clause in listing agreements today. [See **first tuesday** Form 102 §4.2]

Originally, under the old MLS application of subagency, the existence of the cooperation clause was **essential to the receipt of fees** by those brokers and sales agents who "produced" a buyer since the agent was without a retainer agreement with the buyer and had to get "cooperation" under a fee-sharing arrangement with the seller's broker in order to get paid.

MLS brokers under the MLS subagency theory were not employed to act as an agent for a buyer. The purchase agreement forms used were devoid of fee arrangement provisions in the buyer's offer. Yet, a fee provision in the offer is needed to provide the buyer's broker with the ability to independently set his fee and, if accepted or some other arrangement is concluded, enforce collection of the fee.

All MLS subagency arrangements came to a stop by the mid-1980s when the real estate agency law was enacted and buyer's listings began to be generally used.

Under a buyer's listing, MLS brokers and their agents could now effectively act on behalf of buyers without negotiating a fee-sharing arrangement with the seller's broker, who is the **adversary** of the buyer and the buyer's broker. As a result, buyer's agents began to set the amount of the fee they were to receive (paid by sellers) without the listing agents dictating, managing or controlling negotiations over the amount of the fee buyers were willing to allow their agents to receive.

Selling agent or buying agent

The term "selling agent" also has its roots in the old subagent/cooperating agent MLS environment. At the time, listings published in MLS books were reviewed by members with the intent of "helping to sell" the properties to buyers.

Thus, the nonlisting broker/agent, under prior MLS logic, was the one "selling the property" to a prospective buyer "produced" by the selling agent. However, the buyer's agent was, and still is, **selling nothing at all**. A selling agent acting on behalf of a buyer is locating property and representing his buyer in the purchase of real estate as a "buying agent."

Today, the term "selling agent" has been codified in real estate agency law, as has the term "buyer's agent."

However, use of the term "selling agent" does not always mean the selling agent is the buyer's broker.

For instance, the buyer's agent is **always defined** as a selling agent. However, the selling agent is **not always the equivalent** of the buyer's agent. The term selling agent is also legally defined to include a listing broker or his agent who is in direct contact with a buyer, whether or not the listing agent has obligated himself as a dual agent to act as the representative of the buyer.

Representing the buyer requires the agent to locate suitable property and to carefully and diligently advise the buyer on the nature of the property. Also, if an agent represents a buyer, he must seek the most advantageous price and terms available to the buyer when negotiating the acquisition of property.

Thus, when no other broker is involved in a sales transaction, the **listing broker** is also legally referred to as the *selling agent*, a situation referred to in practice as "double ending" the sale.

The listing broker who double ends a transaction is not the buyer's agent at all. However, the listing agent may undertake the representation of the buyer to locate and advise on the acquisition of suitable property, in which case the broker is also a dual agent. A buyer's agent absolutely represents the best interests of a buyer. This is not always so when classified as a selling agent.

In a real estate sales transaction, the agent identified and referred to as the **buyer's broker** or buyer's agent is known to all persons, be they judges, legislators, sellers, buyers, lenders, escrow officers or even fellow licensees, as the **agent exclusively representing the buyer**.

The title "buyer's agent" is now, but has not always been, conceded by the real estate profession to be an appropriate reference to the buyer's representative. However, the clarity and ease of its use is both undeniably generic and persuasive, and indicates the *special agency duties* owed by a buyer's agent to the buyer in a sales transaction. This attitude is lost by use of the nebulous and multifaceted term, selling agent.

Competition vs. price fixing

In 1955, a group of California residential MLS brokers agreed the fee to be charged a seller on all home sales was to be 6% of the price paid by a buyer. This 6% rate of compensation met little resistance from anyone for the next 20 years, even though the price fixing scheme of "same-percentage, same-split" arrangements had already been ruled a violation of federal antitrust laws.

However, the unionized residential MLS brokers did not comply with court orders. To enforce the price fixing 6%/50:50 fee split, the residential brokers used the MLS they controlled to require brokers who published listing information on the MLS to include the total fee agreed to by the seller (and it was to be 6%), with a share (3%) to be retained by the listing broker and a share (3%) to be paid to the buyer's broker.

In this fashion, the seller's broker submitting a listing to the MLS was policed by all other brokers and agents for conformance to the 6%/50:50 policy of fixed fees and sharing. If a seller's agent did not comply, all the other (fee-fixing) MLS brokers and their agents were instructed by the trade union to either refuse to deal with the nonconforming office or to unilaterally refuse to share fees (50:50) on the sale of their listings with the offending, nonconforming listing broker.

More financially persuasive, the residential broker's trade union arbitration board would (and did) enforce the 6%/50:50 rule. Thus, after a short period of fellow-broker inflicted financial injury, the fee-cutting (and successfully competitive) listing office would eventually capitulate to the 6%/50:50 routine or go out of business. [**People** v. **National Association of Realtors** (1981) 120 CA3d 459]

Enforcement by residential brokers of the 6%/50:50 rule was made possible through binding arbitration. The local trade union owned or controlled the MLS and compulsory membership in one (the trade association with its binding arbitration agreement) was then a requisite to admission to the MLS. Thus, if a broker using the MLS violated its price-fixing policies regarding fees, the trade association became the instrumentality used by conforming brokers to enforce the patently illegal price fixing activity (by a money award in arbitration, followed by a automatic court-ordered judgment for enforcement against the competitive fee-cutting, discount broker).

In California, MLS subscribers no longer need to become members of a trade association in order to post listings and access the MLS database, even if the MLS is owned by the association. Thus, the MLS subscriber avoids the suppressive instrumentality of trade association membership. [**Marin County Board of Realtors, Inc.** v. **Palsson** (1976) 16 C3d 920]

MLS fees fixed and competition banned

Consider a group of local real estate trade associations who each operate their own multiple listing service (MLS). Each association provides their own MLS support services to their subscribers. They also set the price for these support services independently, based on cost. Some are efficient and very successful at providing these services, incurring less than $10 in total costs per subscriber monthly. Others are inefficient and incur costs of $50 per subscriber monthly to provide their MLS support services.

The associations then form a separate corporation in which they are shareholders in order to create and operate a county-wide MLS. Each association is independently contracted by the corporation to provide MLS support services for the subscribers to the new regional MLS.

To assure the continued financial viability of those associations with disproportionately higher operating costs for their inefficient servicing of their MLS subscribers, the associations collaborate to set the minimum fee all associations will charge at $25 per subscriber monthly. The less efficient associations are paid a fixed monthly cash subsidy on top of the support services fee since they are providing these services at a loss. With the **fee fixed** for services, the efficient associations agree not to charge less and compete to deprive the less efficient associations of subscribers.

However, the question arises, when competitive organizations **join together** to eliminate their separate MLS database operations in favor of a single county-wide MLS which is more effective (greater regional coverage) and efficient (reduced need of brokers to subscribe to two or more MLS database services), can they then *collude* to set the fee charged for the MLS services each will provide, and **ban any discounting or rebates** by the efficient and more competitively operated associations?

The simple answer is no. Price fixing is illegal!

The fee which reimbursed the associations for the cost of their MLS support services cannot be legally set by agreement between the competing associations, especially when the larger, more efficient associations received millions of dollars in excess MLS support services fees over the actual cost they incurred to provide those services. This arrangement provided the large associations with huge financial rewards at the improper expense of their subscribers. [**Freeman** v. **San Diego Association of Realtors** (9th Cir. 2003) 322 F3d 1133]

It was the likelihood that some of the associations would go out of business under an efficient county-wide MLS which led to the price being fixed at a *supracompetitive* and illegal level in the first place. This led to the banning of competitive pricing for MLS services provided to subscribing brokers by agreeing to no discounts or rebates to their broker-subscribers (which would have reflected the actual costs of an association).

However, if competition or *economic darwinism* had been properly allowed to occur, by the process of *creative destruction*, the more efficient associations would have brought about the demise of the less productive associations to the financial benefit of all the MLS users.

Chapter 5

Subagency and dual agency

This chapter examines the conduct of a subagent in contrast to the conduct of a dual agent, and distinguishes fee-sharing/broker-cooperation arrangements from both.

Agency and fee sharing misconceptions

Payment by a seller or listing broker of the brokerage fee earned by a buyer's broker in a real estate transaction in no way determines the agency relationship of the buyer's broker and his agents to either the buyer or the seller.

Thus, neither a *subagency* nor a *dual agency* relationship is created between the seller and the buyer's broker simply because the seller pays the buyer's broker a fee. This fee-agency rule applies whether the seller pays the fee directly to the buyer's broker, or it is paid to him indirectly from the fee received by the seller's/listing broker. [Calif. Civil Code §2079.19]

Conversely, the buyer's broker does become a dual agent should the wording of the seller's acceptance provision in a purchase agreement state the seller **employs** the buyer's broker as part of the seller's provisions for payment of fees.

However, in practice, brokers and agents working for buyers to locate suitable property rarely consider themselves agents of the seller when they show their buyers properties listed with other brokers. They also do not normally conduct themselves as *subagents* of the seller or as *dual agents* representing both seller and buyer.

Subagency: MLS membership myth

The mere membership of a buyer's broker in a multiple listing service (MLS) never creates a dual agency or subagency relationship with any of the sellers represented by other broker-members who publish listings of property for sale in the MLS. Agency, whatever the type, is created by the **conduct of each broker (and his agents)** when interacting with a buyer or seller in a transaction, not by trade memberships or the seller's payment of the fee. [CC §2307]

Subagency duties differ greatly from misleading MLS subagency concepts. "MLS subagency" arose out of notions held about the nature of *cooperation* between brokers in fee-sharing arrangements. The focus within the MLS for determining agency relationships was improperly placed on the relationship between the brokers, which overlooked the principal-to-broker relationships in transactions.

For example, when an MLS selling broker (erroneously) believes he is a "subagent" in a transaction on property listed in the MLS by another broker, the critical brokerage facts include:

- the broker working with the buyer is an MLS member;

- the buyer has been assisted by the broker (or the broker's agents) to locate qualifying properties for the purpose of purchasing one which is suitable;

- the buyer has signed a purchase offer prepared by the broker to buy property listed with another broker who is also an MLS member; and

- the brokerage fee due the broker will be paid from funds accruing to the seller based on an agreement made by the listing broker in MLS publications to share his fee with any broker-member who submits an offer from a buyer at the listed price.

Again, the buyer's broker does not become a subagent of the seller due to the sharing of the fee, unless he **conducts himself** as the seller's representative in negotiations without undertaking any agency duties to represent and negotiate on behalf of the buyer.

It is instructive to observe that a buyer's broker shares fees with the listing broker, not duties. The buyer's broker is not mandated to perform a visual inspection and disclose his observations on behalf of the seller as required of listing agents, legal subagents and dual agents.

Subagent vs. fee-sharing broker

A seller's listing agreement authorizes the listing broker to cooperate with other brokers and to divide with them any brokerage fee due under the listing. [See **first tuesday** Form 102 §4.2]

Today, listing agreements no longer include wording which also authorizes the seller's listing broker to delegate to other brokers the authority to **also act** on behalf of the seller as the seller's agent to **locate buyers** and obtain offers to purchase, an activity legally establishing a subagency with the seller.

However, should a provision in a listing agreement actually authorize the listing broker to **create a subagency**, the listing broker may then act on behalf of the seller to employ another brokerage office as a *subagent* to help market the property.

It is beneficial to understand the circumstances under which a buyer is handled when a subagency exists so the multiplicity of real estate agency roles available in California can be better appreciated.

Subagency facts in a purchase agreement setting typically include:

- two separate brokers, one being a seller's listing broker and the other broker referred to legally as a "selling broker" (since he has contact with a buyer);

- a seller who is exclusively represented by the listing broker; and

- a buyer who is not represented by the selling broker (and may or may not be represented by yet another broker.

Dual agency as an authorized practice

Simply put, a *dual agent* is a broker who is acting as the agent for the **opposing parties** in a transaction, e.g., both the buyer and the seller. [CC §2079.13(d)]

The problem with dual agents is not that dual agency is improper. Dual agency has always been and is proper brokerage practice. However, what is improper is failing to confirm the existence of a dual agency in the agency confirmation provision of a purchase agreement for a one-to-four unit residential property. [CC §2079.17]

Further, a broker on any type of real estate transaction who fails to promptly disclose his dual agency at the moment it arises is subject to:

- the loss of his brokerage fee;

- liability for his clients' money losses; and

- disciplinary action by the Department of Real Estate (DRE). [Calif. Business and Professions Code §10176(d)]

For example, a buyer's agent locates property his buyer is interested in purchasing. The agent then negotiates and receives a written listing agreement from the seller without first disclosing his agency relationship with the buyer. The buyer then makes an offer, which the seller accepts. In the offer, the seller agrees to pay the broker a fee. Again, there is no disclosure of the agency relationship with the buyer.

Before closing, the seller discovers the broker's prior relationship with the buyer and cancels payment of the brokerage fee. The broker demands his fee for locating the buyer.

Here, the broker cannot recover a brokerage fee. The broker intentionally failed to disclose his dual agency to the seller at the moment it arose, i.e., at the time he entered into the listing with the seller. [**L. Byron Culver & Associates** v. **Jaoudi Industrial & Trading Corporation** (1991) 1 CA4th 300]

Also, once a broker becomes a dual agent, he (and his agents) too often do not know how to perform as a dual agent, usually due to a lack of training.

A rule of sorts for disclosure of relevant facts about the transaction, which are known or come to the dual agent's attention either before or after acceptance of an offer, is to advise both parties of the facts by written memorandum, and keep a copy of the memo in the client's file.

However, when a dual agency is established in a one-to-four unit residential sales transaction, and both parties are represented by the same broker, the broker (and his agents) may not pass on any information relating to the **price or terms of payment** from one party to the other. What price the buyer may be willing to pay, or the seller may be willing to accept, must remain the undisclosed knowledge of the dual agent, unless authorized to release the information in a writing signed by the principal in question. [CC §2079.21]

Thus, without authorization, the dual agent is now a "secret agent." He must keep secret the minimum pricing sought by the seller and the maximum pricing obtainable from the buyer.

The decision not to release pricing information must be made and maintained from the moment the dual agency arises, typically occurring when the buyer who is an existing client is exposed to property listed by the broker — a moment which always occurs before the purchase agreement is prepared and the agency confirmed.

The written authority needed to advise the seller of the buyer's willingness to pay more, or the seller's willingness to accept less, is best documented on a **modification of listing** form signed by the client whose confidential pricing information is to be released to the other client. The authority would be given to the broker who would retain the document in his file. [See **first tuesday** Form 120]

Dual agency and diminished benefits

Generally, the clients of a dual agent do not receive the full range of benefits they would have obtained from an exclusive agent. The conflicts which exist in a broker's dual representation rule out aggressive negotiations to obtain the best business advantage for either party. This holds true even if different (listing and selling) agents employed by the **same broker** each work with different parties to the same transaction.

While a broker owes his client the duty to pursue the best business advantage legally and ethically obtainable through negotiations and agreements, the dual agent is foreclosed from achieving this advantage for either client. The dual agent cannot take sides with one or the other during negotiations.

Thus, a natural inability exists to negotiate the highest and best price for the seller, and at the same time, negotiate the lowest and best price for the buyer. Further, the broker and his agents, while acting as dual agents, are precluded in sales transactions on one-to-four unit residential property from discussing pricing without prior written approval.

The *legal agent* for a buyer or seller in a transaction is the broker, not the broker's agents or brokers employed by the broker who are in contact with the principal. Inhouse transactions which involve the broker as a dual agent make it particularly difficult for the broker to oversee and supervise dual agency negotiations.

Typically, one agent employed by the broker acquires the listing from a seller while another agent in the broker's employ works separately with a buyer to locate qualifying properties listed with other brokers.

The broker becomes a dual agent the moment the buyer is then shown an in-house listing.

However, an improper tendency in transactions involving only one broker and two of his agents who are separately working with a seller and buyer in a sale is to automatically designate the broker as a dual agent.

In fact, the buyer may well be a party to whom no agency duties are owed by any broker or agent. The buyer may have simply responded to the broker's "For Sale" sign, open house or ads marketing the listed property. And without being shown unlisted properties or properties listed with other brokers, the buyer may make

an offer on an "in-house" listing through an agent employed by the broker who is not the listing agent.

When the buyer's inquiry and review of properties is limited to properties listed with the broker, the sale of an in-house listing directly to a buyer who has not retained a broker to represent him does not, without more, create an agency relationship with the buyer. [**Price** v. **Eisan** (1961) 194 CA2d 363]

However, there remains, as always, the listing broker's *general nonfiduciary duty* to disclose material facts about the listed property to all parties, including the non-client buyer. Facts to be disclosed include the condition of the property's physical aspects, hazards and location that may have an adverse effect on its value or might affect the buyer's decision to purchase the property, subject to even further disclosures by the agents in response to any inquiry by the buyer.

Chapter 6

The agency law disclosure

This chapter examines the use of the statutorily mandated Agency Law Disclosure form and its timely presentation to sellers and buyers in order to perfect the brokers' right to collect the agreed fee.

Legislated order

As the practice of real estate brokerage developed and matured, rules and regulations were created to keep transactions running smoothly and to channel agency activities toward a broader public good.

However, when the professional misconduct of real estate licensees was overlooked and mishandled by the brokerage community, legislative and judicial forces felt compelled to step into the "power vacuum" created by the lack of proper internal policing. Thus, an agency disclosure law to cure some of these deficiencies was enacted by the California legislature.

The real estate agency law requires two different sets of agency-related disclosures:

- an **Agency Law Disclosure form** setting out the "rules of agency" controlling the conduct of real estate licensees in a transaction; and

- an **agency confirmation provision** in purchase agreements to disclose the agency of each broker involved in the transaction.

The legislation created an agency scheme in an attempt to cure a number of previously misleading brokerage practices. In doing so, it established uniform real estate terminology and brokerage conduct covering targeted transactions on one-to-four unit residential property. The Agency Law Disclosure form is a succinct restatement of existing agency codes and codified case law on agency relationships.

Additionally, the legislated real estate agency scheme made changes in how and when each broker must proceed to **confirm** his agency relationship with the principals in targeted one-to-four unit residential sales transactions.

Uniform jargon and agency law

Basically, the Agency Law Disclosure form was created by the legislature for use by brokers and their agents to educate and familiarize clientele (as well as the brokers and their agents) with:

- a uniform jargon for real estate transactions; and

- the various agency roles licensees may undertake on behalf of their principals and other parties in a real estate related transaction.

This information is presented in a two-page form, sometimes referred to as the *Rules of Agency* or the *Agency Law Disclosure*. The exact wording of its entire content is dictated by statute. [Calif. Civil Code §2079.16; see Form 305 accompanying this chapter]

The Agency Law Disclosure defines and explains, in general terms, many of the words and phrases commonly used in the real estate industry to express:

- the agency relationships of brokers to the parties in the transaction;

- broker-to-broker relationships; and

- the relationship between brokers and their agents.

DATE:_____, 20_____, at _____, California

To Seller/Buyer: _____

> **NOTICE:** This agency disclosure complies with agency disclosures required with property listings and offers to buy, sell, exchange or lease one-to-four residential units and mobile homes. [Calif. Civil Code §§2079 et seq.]

1. **FACTS:** When you enter into a discussion with a real estate agent regarding a real estate transaction, you should, from the outset, understand what type of agency relationship or representation you wish to have with the agent in the transaction.

2. **SELLER'S AGENT:** A Seller's agent under a listing agreement with the Seller acts as the agent for the Seller only. A Seller's agent or a subagent of that agent has the following affirmative obligations:

   2.1 To the Seller:

   a. A fiduciary duty of utmost care, integrity, honesty and loyalty in dealings with the Seller.

   2.2 To the Buyer and the Seller:

   a. Diligent exercise of reasonable skill and care in performance of the agent's duties.

   b. A duty of honest and fair dealing and good faith.

   c. A duty to disclose all facts known to the agent materially affecting the value of desirability of the property that are not known to, or within the diligent attention and observation of the parties.

   2.3 An agent is not obligated to reveal to either party any confidential information obtained from the other party which does not involve the affirmative duties set forth above.

3. **BUYER'S AGENT:** A selling agent can, with a Buyer's consent, agree to act as agent for the Buyer only. In these situations, the agent is not the Seller's agent, even if by agreement the agent may receive compensation for services rendered, either in full or in part, from the Seller. An agent acting only for a Buyer has the following affirmative obligations:

   3.1 To the Buyer:

   a. A fiduciary duty of utmost care, integrity, honesty and loyalty in dealings with the Buyer.

   3.2 To the Buyer and the Seller:

   a. Diligent exercise of reasonable skill and care in performance of the agent's duties.

   b. A duty of honest and fair dealing and good faith.

   c. A duty to disclose all facts known to the agent materially affecting the value or desirability of the property that are not known to, or within the diligent attention and observation of the parties. An agent is not obligated to reveal to either party any confidential information obtained from the other party which does not involve the affirmative duties set forth above.

4. **AGENT REPRESENTING BOTH SELLER AND BUYER:** A real estate agent, either acting directly or through one or more associate licensees, can legally be the agent of both the Seller and the Buyer in a transaction, but only with the knowledge and consent of both the Seller and the Buyer.

   4.1 In a dual agency situation, the agent has the following affirmative obligations to both the Seller and the Buyer:

   a. A fiduciary duty of utmost care, integrity, honesty and loyalty in the dealings with either Seller or Buyer.

   b. Other duties to the Seller and the Buyer as stated above in their respective sections.

   4.2 In representing both Seller and Buyer, the agent may not, without the express permission of the respective party, disclose to the other party that the Seller will accept a price less than the listing price or that the Buyer will pay a price greater than the price offered.

5. The above duties of the agent in a real estate transaction do not relieve a Seller or Buyer from the responsibility to protect their own interests. You should carefully read all agreements to assure that they adequately express your understanding of the transaction. A real estate agent is a person qualified to advise about real estate. If legal or tax advice is desired, consult a competent professional.

6. Throughout your real property transaction, you may receive more than one disclosure form depending upon the number of agents assisting in the transaction. The law requires each agent with whom you have more than a casual relationship to present you with this disclosure form. You should read its contents each time it is presented to you, considering the relationship between you and the real estate agent in your specific transaction.

7. This disclosure form includes the provisions of Sections 2079.13 to 2079.24, inclusive, of the Civil Code set forth on the reverse hereof. Read it carefully.

Buyer's Broker	Date	Buyer's Signature	Date
Associate Licensee's Signature	Date	Buyer's Signature	Date
Seller's Broker	Date	Seller's Signature	Date
Associate Licensee's Signature	Date	Seller's Signature	Date

— *PAGE ONE OF TWO — FORM 305* —

§2079.13. As used in sections 2079.14 to 2079.24, inclusive, the following terms have the following meanings:

(a) "Agent" means a person acting under provisions of Title 9 (commencing with Section 2295) in a real property transaction, and includes a person who is licensed as a real estate broker under Chapter 3 (commencing with Section 10130) of Part 1 of Division 4 of the Business and Professions Code, and under whose license a listing is executed or an offer to purchase is obtained.

(b) "Associate licensee" means a person who is licensed as a real estate broker or salesperson under Chapter 3 (commencing with Section 10130) of Part 1 of Division 4 of the Business and Professions Code and who is either licensed under a broker or has entered into a written contract with a broker to act as the broker's agent in connection with acts requiring a real estate license and to function under the broker's supervision in the capacity of an associate licensee.

The agent in the real property transaction bears responsibility for his or her associate licensees who perform as agents of the agent. When an associate licensee owes a duty to any principal, or to any buyer or seller who is not a principal, in a real property transaction, that duty is equivalent to the duty owed to that party by the broker for whom the associate licensee functions.

(c) "Buyer" means a transferee in a real property transaction, and includes a person who executes an offer to purchase real property from a seller through an agent, or who seeks the services of an agent in more than a casual, transitory, or preliminary manner, with the object of entering into a real property transaction. "Buyer" includes vendee or lessee.

(d) "Dual agent" means an agent acting, either directly or through an associate licensee, as agent for both the seller and the buyer in a real property transaction.

(e) "Listing agreement" means a contract between an owner of real property and an agent, by which the agent has been authorized to sell the real property or to find or obtain a buyer.

(f) "Listing agent" means a person who has obtained a listing of real property to act as an agent for compensation.

(g) "Listing price" is the amount expressed in dollars specified in the listing for which the seller is willing to sell the real property through the listing agent.

(h) "Offering price" is the amount expressed in dollars specified in an offer to purchase for which the buyer is willing to buy the real property.

(i) "Offer to purchase" means a written contract executed by a buyer acting through a selling agent which becomes the contract for the sale of the real property upon acceptance by the seller.

(j) "Real property" means any estate specified by subdivision (1) or (2) of Section 761 in property which constitutes or is improved with one to four dwelling units, any leasehold in this type of property exceeding one year's duration, and mobilehomes, when offered for sale or sold through an agent pursuant to the authority contained in Section 10131.6 of the Business and Professions Code.

(k) "Real property transaction" means a transaction for the sale of real property in which an agent is employed by one or more of the principals to act in that transaction, and includes a listing or an offer to purchase.

(l) "Sell," "sale," or "sold" refers to a transaction for the transfer of real property from the seller to the buyer, and includes exchanges of real property between the seller and buyer, transactions for the creation of real property sales contract within the meaning of Section 2985, and transactions for the creation of a leasehold exceeding one year's duration.

(m) "Seller" means the transferor in a real property transaction, and includes an owner who lists real property with an agent, whether or not a transfer results, or who receives an offer to purchase real property of which he or she is the owner from an agent on behalf of another. "Seller" includes both a vendor and a lessor.

(n) "Selling agent" means a listing agent who acts alone, or an agent who acts in cooperation with a listing agent, and who sells or finds and obtains a buyer for the real property, or an agent who locates property for a buyer or who finds a buyer for a property for which no listing exists and presents an offer to purchase to the seller.

(o) "Subagent" means a person to whom an agent delegates agency powers as provided in Article 5 (commencing with Section 2349) of Chapter 1. However, "subagent" does not include an associate licensee who is acting under the supervision of an agent in a real property transaction.

§2079.14. Listing agents and selling agents shall provide the seller and buyer in a real property transaction with a copy of the disclosure form specified in Section 2079.16, and, except as provided in subdivision (c), shall obtain a signed acknowledgment of receipt from that seller or buyer, except as provided in this section or Section 2079.15, as follows:

(a) The listing agent, if any, shall provide the disclosure form to the seller prior to entering into the listing agreement.

(b) The selling agent shall provide the disclosure form to the seller as soon as practicable prior to presenting the seller with an offer to purchase, unless the selling agent previously provided the seller with a copy of the disclosure form pursuant to subdivision (a).

(c) Where the selling agent does not deal on a face-to-face basis with the seller, the disclosure form prepared by the selling agent may be furnished to the seller (and acknowledgment of receipt obtained for the selling agent from the seller) by the listing agent, or the selling agent may deliver the disclosure form by certified mail addressed to the seller at his or her last known address, in which case no signed acknowledgment of receipt is required.

(d) The selling agent shall provide the disclosure form to the buyer as soon as practicable prior to execution of the buyer's offer to purchase, except that if the offer to purchase is not prepared by the selling agent, the selling agent shall present the disclosure form to the buyer not later than the next business day after the selling agent receives the offer to purchase from the buyer.

§2079.15. In any circumstance in which the seller or buyer refuses to sign an acknowledgment of receipt pursuant to Section 2079.14, the agent. or an associate licensee acting for an agent, shall set forth, sign, and date a written declaration of the facts of the refusal.

§2079.17. (a) As soon as practicable, the selling agent shall disclose to the buyer and seller whether the selling agent is acting in the real property transaction exclusively as the buyer's agent, exclusively as the seller's agent, or as a dual agent representing both the buyer and the seller and this relationship shall be confirmed in the contract to purchase and sell real property or in a separate writing executed or acknowledged by the seller, the buyer, and the selling agent prior to or coincident with execution of that contract by the buyer and the seller, respectively.

(b) As soon as practicable, the listing agent shall disclose to the seller whether the listing agent is acting in the real property transaction exclusively as the seller's agent, or as a dual agent representing both the buyer and seller and this relationship shall be confirmed in the contract to purchase and sell real property or in a separate writing executed or acknowledged by the seller and the listing agent prior to or coincident with the execution of that contract by the seller.

(c) The confirmation required by subdivisions (a) and (b) shall be in the following form:

_____ is the agent of (check one):
(Name of Listing Agent)

( ) the seller exclusively; or

( ) both the buyer and seller.

_____ is the agent of (check one):
(Name of Selling Agent if not same as above)

( ) the buyer exclusively;

( ) the seller exclusively; or

( ) both the buyer and seller.

(d) The disclosures and confirmation required by this section shall be in addition to the disclosure required by Section 2079.14.

§2079.18. No selling agent in a real property transaction may act as an agent for the buyer only, when the selling agent is also acting as the listing agent in the transaction.

§2079.19. The payment of compensation or the obligation to pay compensation to an agent by the seller or buyer is not necessarily determinative of a particular agency relationship between an agent and the seller or buyer. A listing agent and a selling agent may agree to share any compensation or commission paid, or any right to any compensation or commission for which an obligation arises as the result of a real estate transaction, and the terms of any such agreement shall not necessarily be determinative of a particular relationship.

§2079.20. Nothing in this article prevents an agent from selecting, as a condition of the agent's employment, a specific form of agency relationship not specifically prohibited by this article if the requirements of Section 2079.14 and Section 2079.17 are complied with.

§2079.21. A dual agent shall not disclose to the buyer that the seller is willing to sell the property at a price less than the listing price, without the express written consent of the seller. A dual agent shall not disclose to the seller that the buyer is willing to pay a price greater than the offering price, without the expressed written consent of the buyer. This section does not alter in any way the duty or responsibility of a dual agent to any principal with respect to confidential information other than price.

§2079.22. Nothing in this article precludes a listing agent from also being a selling agent, and the combination of these functions in one agent does not, of itself, make that agent a dual agent.

§2079.23. A contract between the principal and agent may be modified or altered to change the agency relationship at any time before the performance of the act which is the object of the agency with the written consent of the parties to the agency relationship.

§2079.24. Nothing in this article shall be construed to either diminish the duty of disclosure owed buyers and sellers by agents and their associate licensees, subagents, and employees or to relieve agents and their associate licensees, subagents, and employees from liability for their conduct in connection with acts governed by this article or for any breach of a fiduciary duty or a duty of disclosure.

A *buyer's agent* and a *seller's agent* are mentioned but not defined. A "single agent," which is typically a buyer's agent who is paid by the buyer, is not even mentioned.

Legally, an **agent** is a licensed real estate broker. Thus, the word agent, when used in the disclosure, is not a reference to the broker's agents who in fact call themselves "agents." Ironically, in practice, a broker rarely, if ever, refers to himself as an agent, which in law, he is.

However, two sections on the face of the Agency Law Disclosure, entitled "seller's agent" and "buyer's agent," address the duties owed to the seller and buyer in a real estate transaction by these otherwise undefined brokers.

The seller's listing broker is correctly noted as being an agent for the seller. Peculiar to real estate brokerage, the buyer's broker is referred to as the *selling agent*.

One then wonders who is the "buying agent" — an unmentioned phrase, but one more plainly descriptive of the activities undertaken by a broker acting as an agent exclusively on behalf of the buyer.

The Agency Law Disclosure does not mention, much less define, the broker's role as an *exclusive agent* for either the buyer or seller. Yet the separate agency confirmation provision mandated to be included in all purchase agreements used on targeted transactions provides the broker with options to characterize himself as the agent of the "seller exclusively" or the "buyer exclusively."

It is certain these exclusive characterizations of agency have absolutely no relationship to exclusive (employment) listings to sell or to buy property. The listing agent with an exclusive right-to-sell listing needs to understand the prospective buyer may well turn out to be one of his clients, making the broker a dual agent.

However, the two sections on the first page of the Agency Law Disclosure entitled "seller's agent" and "buyer's agent" do state, in broad legal terms, generally accepted principles of law governing the conduct of brokers who are acting as agents solely for a seller or a buyer in a transaction, as well as the general duty of fairness owed the other party and broker in the transaction.

Two categories of **broker obligations** arise in a sales transaction and are properly emphasized in the Agency Law Disclosure:

- the **special agency duties** of an agent which are owed by a broker (and his agents) to his client — being the fiduciary duties of a trustee to his beneficiaries; and

- the **general duties** owed by each broker to all parties in the transaction — to be honest and avoid misleading or deceitful conduct.

Agencies confirmed in the purchase agreement

As part of the same agency disclosure scheme, a separate **agency confirmation provision** is mandated for inclusion in purchase agreement forms used to memorialize targeted transactions. The agency confirmation provision located in a purchase agreement advises the buyer and seller, at the time they sign the purchase agreement or its counteroffer, of any agency relationships each broker has with the parties in the transaction.

The Agency Law Disclosure contains the agency confirmation provision which is required to be included in purchase agreements. However, the provision in the Agency Law Disclosure is **not to be filled out or used in lieu of** the agency confirmation provision contained in a purchase agreement since the agencies to be confirmed by each broker in the purchase agreement provisions are not even known at the listing stage when the seller is first required to be presented with the Agency Law Disclosure form. [CC §2079.17(d)]

The agency confirmation provision in a purchase agreement is filled out to disclose each broker's actual agency relationship, established by the broker's conduct and the conduct of their agents with the buyer and/or seller. The agency relationship confirmed is the broker's **legal determination** of the actual agency created by his and his agent's prior conduct with the parties.

When two brokers are involved in a targeted transaction, each broker must disclose whether he is acting as the agent for the buyer or the seller. Alternatively, when only one broker is involved, he must confirm whether he and his agents are acting as the exclusive agent for one party or as a dual agent for both the buyer and seller. [See **first tuesday** Form 150 Signature section]

A broker (or his agents) should include the agency confirmation provision and attach the Agency Law Disclosure form to all purchase agreements used in the sale of all types of property, not just as mandated for targeted one-to-four unit residential sales or leases exceeding one year. Written disclosures tend to eliminate later disputes over agency, which can become the basis for cancelling a purchase agreement, the payment of a brokerage fee, or both. [**L. Byron Culver & Associates** v. **Jaoudi Industrial & Trading Corporation** (1991) 1 CA4th 300]

Use of the Agency Law Disclosure

The Agency Law Disclosure form is mandated to be presented to all parties, by brokers or their agents, when listing, selling, buying or leasing (for over one year) property containing:

- one-to-four residential units; or

- mobilehomes. [CC §§2079.13(j), 2079.14]

However, not all transactions involving one-to-four unit residential properties are **targeted** to require the attachment of the Agency

Law Disclosure or the inclusion of the agency confirmation provision in purchase agreement forms. Arranging the secured interests of lenders and borrowers under trust deeds or as collateral loans, for example, are not targeted transactions.

The sale, exchange or creation of interests in residential property transactions targeted by the agency disclosure law include transfers of:

- fee simple estates in real estate or registered ownerships for mobilehomes;

- life estates;

- existing leaseholds with more than one year remaining, such as ground leases; and

- leases created for more than one year. [CC §2079.13(l)]

The Agency Law Disclosure must be attached to the following documents and signed by all parties in targeted transactions:

- a seller's listing;

- a purchase agreement offer and acceptance;

- an exchange agreement;

- a counteroffer, by attachment or by reference, to a purchase agreement containing the disclosure as an attachment;

- a landlord's authorization to a broker to lease property on his behalf for more than one year; and

- a residential lease agreement for a period exceeding one year. [CC §2079.14]

Negotiations and agreements on one-to-four residential units concerning buyers' listings, property management (unless entry into leases for periods exceeding one year are authorized), purchase options, financing arrangements, one-year leases and month-to-month rental agreements **do not yet require** statutory disclosure of the broker's agency.

Agency rules for a seller's listing

A seller's listing, open or exclusive, employing a broker and his agents to sell a one-to-four unit residential property is a targeted transaction requiring the inclusion of the Agency Law Disclosure as an addendum to the seller's listing agreement. [CC §2079.14(a)]

Failure of the listing agent to provide the seller with the Agency Law Disclosure prior to his entering into the listing agreement will result in the broker's loss of his fee on a sale, if challenged by the seller. The loss of the fee is not avoided by a later disclosure made as an addendum to a purchase agreement or escrow instructions. [**Huijers** v. **DeMarrais** (1992) 11 CA4th 676]

The Agency Law Disclosure is also required to be used by agents listing and submitting offers regarding leasehold estates involving one-to-four unit residential property. These transactions occur when a long-term ground lease is being conveyed to a buyer and will be security for any purchase-assist financing. [CC §§2079.13(j), 2079.13(l), 2079.14]

Also, **the seller's signature is required on the Agency Law Disclosure to acknowledge receipt of a copy at both:**

- the listing stage, as an addendum to the listing; and

- on presentation of a buyer's offer, as an addendum to the purchase agreement. [CC §2079.14]

Thus, the Agency Law Disclosure is to be treated by the listing agent as a preliminary and compulsory listing event since the listing broker expects to collect a brokerage fee on a later sale. The Agency Law Disclosure should be signed by the seller and handed back to the broker (or his agent) before settling down to finalize the listing to which it will be attached.

Should the broker (or his sales agent) fail to hand the seller the Agency Law Disclosure at the listing stage, the listing, and thus the agency, can be cancelled by the seller at any time, even after the transaction sought under the listing agreement is in escrow and the brokerage fee has been further agreed to in the purchase agreement and escrow instructions, which contain the Agency Law Disclosure.

On the other hand, the buyer's broker *perfects* his right to collect his portion of any brokerage fee, if the fee is payable directly to the buyer's broker by the seller, by including the Agency Law Disclosure as a signed addendum to his purchase agreement offer.

However, the buyer's broker might erroneously agree to let the seller's broker receive the entire fee from the seller and then be paid his share of the fee by the seller's broker under a fee-sharing agreement. Should the seller's broker fail to obtain a signed Agency Law Disclosure as an addendum to the listing, the seller may legally avoid payment of the agreed fee to the listing broker. In turn, this refusal leaves the buyer's broker without a fee to be received as agreed from the seller's broker.

For the buyer's broker to protect his fee, the seller must agree in the body of the purchase agreement offer signed by the buyer that the seller will pay both brokers himself. The buyer's broker always takes control over the payment and collection of his fee when the buyer's agent includes a fee provision in the purchase agreement offer made by his buyer.

Documenting a refusal to sign

On occasion, a seller may accept a purchase agreement offer or enter into a counteroffer without signing an Agency Law Disclosure form as requested. If the seller should refuse to return a signed copy of the Agency Law Disclosure, the broker or his agent must document the refusal to preserve the right to receive his fee from the seller. [CC §2079.15]

34

No particular method of documenting the refusal is given by legislation or regulations. However, the facts of the refusal are to be **written, dated** and **signed** by the broker or his agent. What is to be done with the broker's documentation of the refusal is not mentioned.

However, the objective of these disclosures seems to be to eliminate disputes which might later arise over legal information contained in the Agency Law Disclosure regarding the conduct a seller or buyer might expect of a broker and his agents. Also, if a party claims they were never handed the Agency Law Disclosure, the broker's written documentation, created at the time of the refusal, would dispel such a claim — and preserve the fee.

Accordingly, documentation of the facts surrounding any refusal to sign a **timely presented** Agency Law Disclosure should be prepared on a memorandum form and a copy retained in the broker's records. [See **first tuesday** Form 525]

Further, a copy of the refusal memorandum should be mailed to all parties — including the party refusing to sign — together with a copy of the Agency Law Disclosure.

Examples of other refusals to sign the Agency Law Disclosure, which do not have an effect on the collectibility of a brokerage fee, but require receipt and acknowledgement of the Agency Law Disclosure, might occur when:

- an owner refuses to sign a seller's listing after the interview soliciting the listing;

- a "For Sale by Owner" (FSBO) seller refuses, on presentation of the purchase agreement offer, to accept or counter, or otherwise rejects an offer to purchase; or

- a buyer refuses to sign a purchase offer which is prepared and presented to the buyer by a selling broker for consideration.

Should a refusal to sign the Agency Law Disclosure be based on an earlier failure to timely present it as an addendum to the listing or purchase agreement, the refusal is justified and cannot be overridden by later documentation.

SECTION B

Listings:
Employment
by the public

Chapter 7

Types of listings

This chapter introduces the listing agreement as an employment contract and reviews the various types of listing agreements available to the real estate industry.

Listings as employment contracts

A listing agreement is a written employment contract between a client and a licensed real estate broker. On entering into a listing agreement, the broker and his sales staff are retained and authorized to perform real estate related services on behalf of the client in exchange for a fee. [Calif. Civil Code §1086(f)]

The client retaining a broker might hold an ownership interest in real estate, which he seeks to sell, lease or use as collateral to obtain trust deed financing.

Conversely, the client soliciting the services of a broker might be seeking to acquire an interest in real estate as a buyer, tenant or trust deed lender.

The individual employed by a client to provide real estate services in expectation of compensation will **always be** a licensed real estate broker. Likewise, if a dispute arises with a client over the client's failure to pay a fee, only the broker employed in a writing (listing) signed by the client may pursue collection.

A real estate agent employed by the broker may have obtained the listing, but the agent did so on behalf of the broker and has no independent right to enforce the listing agreement. An **agent's right to a fee** arises under the agent's written employment agreement with the broker, not a listing agreement with the client. Through the broker-agent employment agreement, the agent is entitled to a share of the fees actually received by the broker on listings or sales in which the agent participated.

A licensed agent represents a broker as an *agent of the broker*. As the broker's agent, the agent performs on behalf of the broker (as well as the client) all of the activities the broker has been retained by the client to provide. Conversely, an agent providing real estate related services on behalf of a client may not do so independent of his broker. Thus, an agent employed by a broker is referred to as "the agent of the (client's) agent." [CC §2079.13(b)]

The listing agreement sets the **scope of the services** the broker is authorized to undertake while representing the client. Also, the listing authorizes the broker to perform brokerage services and to serve as the client's representative in the negotiation of a real estate transaction.

Further, the listing contains the client's promise to pay a fee, a promise given in exchange for the broker's **promise to use diligence** in his efforts to meet the objectives sought by the client in the employment.

The relationship created between the client and the broker by a listing agreement has two distinct legal aspects:

- an **employment relationship**; and

- an **agency relationship**.

The *employment relationship* established on entering into a listing agreement specifies the **scope of activities** the broker and his agents are to undertake in the employment and authorizes the broker to carry them out.

On the other hand, the *agency relationship* is imposed on the broker by law as arising out of the representation authorized by the employment. Agency carries with it the *fiduciary duties* of loyalty and full disclosure owed by the broker (and his sales agents) **to the client**.

As a **fiduciary**, the broker's conduct and the conduct of his agents under the employment are equated to the conduct required of a trustee acting on behalf of his beneficiary. This fiduciary duty, also called *agency*, survives the termination of the employment relationship. [CC §2079.16]

While an oral agreement to perform brokerage services on behalf of a client imposes an agency law obligation on the broker and his agents to act as fiduciaries, the client's oral promise to pay a fee does not entitle the broker to enforce collection of the fee due from his client. A fee agreement employing a broker to purchase or sell real estate, lease a property for over one year or arrange trust deed financing is controlled by the rules of contract law which require the fee agreement to be in a writing signed by the client before the broker can enforce his right to collect a fee. [CC §1624(a)(4)]

Types of listing agreements

A variety of listing agreements exist, each employing and authorizing a broker to perform real estate related services under different conditions. The variations usually relate to the extent of the representation and type of services to be performed by the broker and his agents, or the event which triggers payment of a fee.

Most listing agreements are for the sale or purchase of single-family residential property. Others are for residential-income and nonresidential-income properties, such as industrial, motel/hotel, commercial, office, farm or unimproved properties.

Despite the application of various agreements to the type of property listed, all listings fall into one of two general categories: *open* or *exclusive*.

Open listings

An **open listing**, sometimes called a *nonexclusive listing*, does not grant exclusive rights to the listing broker and his agents to be the **sole representative** of the client, be he a buyer, tenant or borrower, or a seller, landlord or lender. The client can enter into open listings with as many brokers as he wants to without becoming obligated to pay more than one fee.

A brokerage fee under an open listing to sell real estate is due a broker only if the broker or his agent *procures* a ready, willing and able buyer and *presents* the owner with an offer from the buyer to purchase the listed property. The terms contained in the offer must be substantially the same as the terms sought by the owner under the listing, called a *full listing offer*, unless other terms offered by a buyer are accepted by the owner.

For a broker to be entitled to a fee under an open listing, the broker or his agents must present the offer to the owner before the property is sold to some other buyer located by another broker or by the owner directly. The offer must be submitted before the listing expires or is revoked by withdrawal of the property from sale or by the termination of the agency. [CC §1086(f)(3)]

The broker employed under an open listing is not obligated to use diligence in his efforts to locate a buyer. The broker only has a *best-effort obligation* since the broker does not "accept" the employment until he produces a buyer for the property. Thus, an open listing is legally classified as an *unilateral contract*. However, the **agency duties** of a fiduciary exist at all times under an open listing, and on locating a buyer the broker must commence his due diligence effort to make disclosures and close the transaction.

The first broker to submit an offer during his open listing period from a ready, willing and able buyer to purchase property on the listed terms, or on other terms accepted by the owner, has earned the agreed fee, unless the property has already been sold. None of the other brokers holding open listings from the owner are entitled to a fee.

Also, an open listing allows the owner to market the property himself. Thus, the owner may compete against the listing brokers to locate buyers himself. If he does, the owner does not become obligated to pay a fee under any open listing he may have agreed to.

A broker may also **represent a buyer** to locate property under an open listing agreement. A broker assisting a buyer to locate a suitable property among multiple listing service (MLS) listings held by other brokers should at least consider asking the **buyer to sign** an open listing should the broker be too reticent to solicit an exclusive representation.

An open listing does not need to contain an expiration date, unlike an exclusive agency or exclusive right-to-sell/buy listing which must have an **expiration date**.

However, the owner revoking an open listing that contains an expiration date owes a fee to the broker should the owner personally consummate a sale with a prospective buyer located by the broker during the listing period, or should the owner revoke the listing for the mere purpose of escaping payment of the agreed fee. [**Heffernan** v. **Merrill Estate Co.** (1946) 77 CA2d 106]

Conversely, an open listing without an expiration date may be terminated by the owner at any time without becoming obligated to pay a fee. No fee is due under an open listing for an unlimited time on the *good-faith withdrawal* of the property from the market or on the premature *termination* of the employment before the broker has submitted a full listing offer. [**Tetrick** v. **Sloan** (1959) 170 CA2d 540]

However, an open listing may contain a provision calling for the owner to pay the listing broker a set amount, at an agreed time, for services other than procuring a buyer, such as the preparation of disclosure documents needed by the owner to sell the property, including:

- property disclosures (transfer disclosure statements, natural hazard disclosures, annual property operating data, etc.);

- carryback financing disclosures;

- multiple listing service publications;

- property profiles;

- termite/well/septic clearances; and

- occupancy certificates. [CC §1089]

Although the broker does not have a due diligence requirement under an open listing, the listing broker owes a **duty to prospective buyers** to make a full disclosure of the property's condition, as known to the broker, based on the broker's **visual inspection** of the property prior to the buyer and seller entering into a purchase agreement.

Exclusive listings

Under the category of **exclusive listings**, a broker receives the **sole right**:

- to represent an owner by marketing the listed property and locating a buyer or tenant; or

- to represent a buyer or tenant by locating property sought by the buyer or tenant.

The sole right to represent an individual or entity does not exist in an open listing.

Exclusive listings require an agent to **use diligence** in his efforts to fulfill his client's objectives to locate a buyer for the property. An exclusive listing must also provide for a **specified period of employment** by including a date for the expiration of the employment, such as 90 or 180 days after its commencement. If an expiration date is not included in an exclusive listing, the broker faces suspension or revocation of his license by the California Department of Real Estate (DRE). [Calif. Business and Professions Code §10176(f)]

Two types of exclusive employment agreements exist:

- an *exclusive agency agreement* for a seller or buyer; and

- an *exclusive right-to-sell* or *right-to-buy* listing agreement.

Both types of exclusive listings establish the broker and his agents as the **sole licensed real estate representatives** of the client (seller or buyer). However, the types are distinguished by whether or not the broker has any right to a fee when the property is sold or located solely by the efforts of the client.

Under the fee provision in an **exclusive agency agreement**, the broker does not earn a fee when the client, acting independently of any other broker or the listing broker, accomplishes the objective of the employment himself, i.e., selling the listed property or locating and buying the property sought.

Conversely, under the fee provision in an **exclusive right-to-sell/buy agreement**, the broker earns a fee no matter who produces the buyer or locates the property sought under the listing, be it the client, another broker or other representative of the client, or the listing broker.

Exclusive agency variations

The **exclusive agency listing** is a hybrid of the open and the exclusive listings. The variation is rarely used by brokers as a practical matter and seems best suited to academic discussion.

Under an exclusive agency listing, the client employs the broker as his sole agent, as he does in an exclusive type of listing. Also, the broker is entitled to a fee on any transaction in which he, a finder or another agent produces a buyer. (A finder is an unlicensed agent with no authority to negotiate.)

However, under the exclusive agency listing, an **owner retains the right** to sell the property

to any buyer he locates without becoming obligated to pay the broker a fee. Likewise for a buyer under an exclusive agency listing who finds the property sought on his own.

As with open listings, brokers are reluctant to spend much time and energy under exclusive agency circumstances. The bottom line is an obstructed brokerage effort with diminished benefits to both the client and broker.

Exclusive right-to-sell listings

An **exclusive right-to-sell listing** affords a real estate broker the greatest fee protection. This type of listing makes the broker the sole agent of the owner to market the property and negotiate with all potential buyers and their agents to sell the property. The broker is entitled to a fee **regardless of who procures the buyer**. Under an exclusive right-to-sell agreement, the owner relinquishes his right to list the property with other agents and to defeat the broker's entitlement to compensation by selling the property himself.

An owner of real estate, on entering into an exclusive right-to-sell listing agreement, grants a broker the **right to locate a buyer** for the property prior to the expiration of the period of employment specified in the listing agreement. The broker is entitled to the agreed-to fee in the listing if, during the listing period:

- the property is sold on any terms, no matter who produced the buyer; or

- the broker or his agent presents the seller with a bona-fide offer from a ready, willing and able buyer on terms sought by the seller under the listing, or on other terms accepted by the seller. [CC §1086(f)(1)]

Exclusive right-to-sell listings give a broker and his agents the greatest incentive to work toward attaining the client's goal of locating a buyer. The seller's broker does not compete with his client to sell the property; they work together to achieve the sale.

Buyer's brokers know that sellers who enter into exclusive right-to-sell listings have committed themselves to working with brokers. Also, listed sellers usually have been counseled on prices of comparable properties and current market conditions. Thus, the listed seller is more likely to accept a reasonable offer. Sellers who employ brokers under an exclusive right-to-sell listing are not reserving the right to make their own deal with a buyer and avoid payment of a fee, as is usually the case under exclusive agency or open listing arrangements.

Buyer's brokers are quite comfortable exposing their clients to properties that are listed exclusively. The exchange of information is greater between brokers when the listing broker is authorized to share fees, another primary reason the exclusive right-to-sell listing is the variation most widely used by brokers.

Exclusive right-to-buy listings

For brokers and their agents, an **exclusive right-to-buy listing** creates a positive and contrasting activity from listing and marketing property. A buyer's listing employs the broker to locate qualified properties to be purchased by a potential buyer the broker exclusively represents.

As with an exclusive right-to-sell listing, the right-to-buy variation provides for a brokerage fee if the buyer acquires property during the listing period of the type sought as described in the buyer's listing.

Also, the exclusive right-to-buy listing provides greater incentive for brokers and their agents and imposes a duty to work **diligently and continuously** to meet their buyers' objectives of locating and purchasing suitable real estate.

The buyer as a client benefits under an exclusive right-to-buy listing due to the greater likelihood the broker will find the particular type of property sought. Brokers have continuous access to all available properties and will in-

vestigate and qualify properties as suitable before they are presented to the buyer, and will advise the buyer on the pros and cons of each property presented.

A buyer's broker locating properties listed by other brokers does not become a dual agent or lose his status as the buyer's exclusive agent merely because he works with listing brokers and his fee is paid by the seller.

A broker who seeks out and locates properties at the request of the buyer negotiates the purchase terms as the **buyer's agent** regardless of who pays the fee, which is nearly always paid by the seller from the proceeds of the sales price paid by the buyer.

Net listings

A **net listing** is used only with sellers, not buyers, and can be structured as either an open or an exclusive type of listing. The net listing has more to do with the way compensation is calculated than with whether it is exclusive or open.

The broker's fee is not predetermined by, or based on, a percentage of the selling price.

Instead, the seller's net sales price, excluding brokerage fees and closing costs, is established in the listing agreement. As his brokerage fee, the broker will receive whatever amount the buyer pays in excess of the seller's net figure and closing costs.

However, the broker must disclose to the seller the full sales price paid by the buyer and the amount of the broker's residual fee **before** the seller accepts an offer on a net listing. Failure to disclose the benefits the broker receives on any transaction leads to the loss of the entire fee. [Bus & P C §10176(g)]

For example, if the seller enters into a net listing agreement with a real estate broker for a net sale price of $200,000, the broker will not receive a fee if the property sells for $200,000 or less.

On the other hand, if the property sells for $220,000, the broker's fee is $20,000.

Net listings tend to be unpopular with DRE and consumer protection organizations. They have been outlawed in some states.

By their nature, net listings are particularly prone to claims from buyers and sellers that the broker has been involved in misrepresentations and unfair dealings based on an improper valuation of the property at the time of the listing or a failure to disclose the fee received by the broker when the property sells.

If the seller thinks the broker's fee is excessive, the seller is likely to complain he was improperly advised about the property's fair market value when employing the broker.

Net listings should be used very sparingly, if at all. If a net listing is used, complete disclosures as to the property's value, the price paid by a buyer and the resulting amount of the fee must occur.

Option listing variation

An **option listing** is normally a variation of the exclusive right-to-sell listing.

Its unique feature is the additional element of a grant to the broker of an **option to buy** the property at a predetermined price if the property does not sell during the listing period.

The broker wears two hats when holding an option listing: one as an agent, the other as a principal.

The temptation for misrepresentation is quite apparent. The concurrent status of agent and principal is a conflict of interest for the broker. As a result, the seller's broker might fail to market the property aggressively, with a view toward buying it himself and reselling it at a profit. Likewise, the broker might neglect to inform the seller about all inquiries into the listed property.

As always, brokers are required to disclose any outstanding offers or other factors affecting the seller's decision to sell when the broker exercises the option. [**Rattray** v. **Scudder** (1946) 28 C2d 214]

The broker's exercise of a purchase option contained in a listing agreement requires the broker to disclose to the seller the full amount of the broker's earnings (profit) and obtain the seller's written consent to the earnings prior to or at the time the broker exercises the option. [Bus & P C §10176(h)]

Should market prices rapidly increase after the listing broker exercises his option to purchase, allowing a quick resale by the broker at a substantial profit, the seller might claim the profit should be his and resort to litigation to recover it under the belief he has been cheated by his agent.

As with net listings, option listings should be used with great care, if at all. Only after full disclosure by the broker about all material facts relating to the property and the identity of all potential buyers and their offers should the option be exercised and the property acquired by the broker from the client.

Guaranteed sale variation

A **guaranteed sale listing** is also usually a variation of the exclusive right-to-sell listing. Brokers have been known to use the guarantee feature to boost sales activity during recessionary periods.

A guaranteed sale listing is distinct from a regular, exclusive right-to-sell listing in that it is the broker who grants the option to his seller. The **seller** is given the right to call on the broker to buy the property at a predetermined price if the property does not sell during the listing period. In this respect, the guaranteed sale listing establishes a reverse role for the seller from the option listing should the property fail to sell during the listing period.

The difference with the guaranteed sale listing is that the seller, not the broker, has the right to exercise the option by accepting the broker's irrevocable offer (promise) to buy the listed property.

The guaranteed sale variation can be attractive to sellers who, on account of job transfers, sudden unemployment or other financial factors, must sell at all costs. The benefit to the seller is the assurance of a back-up, last-resort sale during recessionary periods of market uncertainty, a risk some brokers are willing to take.

As with the option listing, the broker may tend not to work the listing vigorously if the price he will pay under the guarantee is much lower than the amount the seller would net on a sale at current market prices. Thus, the broker would stand to acquire the property at a bargain price if it does not sell during the listing period.

In practice, if a buyer is not produced during the listing period, a desperate seller may have no choice but to sell to the broker since the seller delegated complete control to the broker to locate a buyer.

The broker's advantage, however, is lessened by a DRE regulation which disallows the inclusion of advance fees in a guaranteed sale listing. [Department of Real Estate Regulations §2970(b)(5)]

As always, the broker must disclose all offers and the status of potential offers during the listing period and at the time the seller exercises his option to sell to the broker.

Other listings

Other listing variations contain provisions for the broker to obtain a tenant for a landlord, lease a property for a tenant, arrange a loan on behalf of a borrower who owns real estate or holds a trust deed note, or find a borrower for a lender seeking to make such a loan. Unimproved real estate, business opportunities and mobile homes can also be the subject of the employment. All of these employment variations can be used with the open or exclusive type of listing agreements.

Chapter 8

The exclusive right-to-sell listing agreement

This chapter presents the seller's exclusive right-to-sell listing agreement along with instructions for an agent's use of the form.

When the fee is earned

A broker's right to a fee for representing his client originates with a written employment agreement, commonly called a *listing*, entered into by the client who employs the broker. [**Crane** v. **McCormick** (1891) 92 C 176]

By entering into an exclusive right-to-sell listing agreement, an owner of real estate employs a broker to act on his behalf to locate a buyer for his property.

The right-to-sell listing agreement grants the broker sole authority to market the property, locate a buyer and negotiate a sale. It also specifies the fee amount the seller agrees the broker is to receive and the conditions which must be met by the broker or acted on by the seller for the broker to earn the fee.

For example, an exclusive right-to-sell listing entitles a broker to a fee from a seller in several instances, including when:

- the broker locates a ready, willing and able buyer and submits the buyer's **full listing offer** to the seller [See Form 102 §3.1(a) accompanying this chapter];

- the seller **accepts an offer** submitted by the broker [See Form 102 §3.1(a)];

- **anyone purchases** the property during the listing period [See Form 102 §3.1(a)];

- the seller **withdraws the property** from the market or interferes with the broker's performance [See Form 102 §3.1(b); see Chapter 10];

- the seller **terminates the agency** of the broker prior to expiration of the listing period [See Form 102 §3.1(c); see Chapter 10];

- a prospective buyer with whom the broker negotiates during the listing period recommences negotiations to purchase the property during the **safety period** following the expiration of the listing. [See Form 102 §3.1(d); see Chapter 11]; or

- the seller **acquires replacement real estate** in a transaction negotiated by the broker. [See Form 102 §3.2]

Analyzing the exclusive employment

The exclusive right-to-sell listing agreement, **first tuesday** Form 102, is used by brokers and their agents to solicit employment by a prospective seller of real estate. It is prepared and submitted as the broker's offer to act as the seller's **exclusive real estate agent** to market the seller's property, locate a ready, willing and able buyer and negotiate a sale. In exchange, the seller promises to pay a fee on **any sale** of the property entered into during the period of employment.

Formal documentation of an obligation to pay a fee — a written agreement signed by the seller — is the legislatively enacted and judicially mandated requisite to the right to enforce collection of a brokerage fee from the seller.

For the listing agent, the seller's listing agreement and its addenda serve as a **checklist** for the contents of a listing package or marketing package on the property to be handed to prospective buyers for review. The package contains information about the property known to the seller or the broker and his listing agent. The marketing process requires information about the property to be handed to prospective buyers before they enter into a purchase agreement with the seller.

Each section in Form 102 has a separate purpose and need for enforcement. The sections include:

1. *Brokerage services*: The employment period for rendering brokerage services, the broker's due diligence obligations and any advance deposits by the seller are set forth in sections 1 and 2.

2. *Brokerage fee*: The seller's obligation to pay a brokerage fee, the amount of the fee and when the fee is due are set forth in section 3.

3. *Conditions*: The broker's authority to receive a purchase offer, accept a good-faith deposit, enter into fee-splitting arrangements with other brokers and enforce the listing agreement is set forth in section 4.

4. *Property description and disclosures*: Identification of the listed real estate and personal property, the terms of existing financing and the conditions of the property are set forth in sections 5, 6 and 7.

5. *Sales terms*: The price and terms sought by the seller for the sale, exchange or option of the property are set forth in sections 8, 9, 10 and 11.

6. *Signatures and identification of the parties*: On completion of entries on the listing form and any attached addenda, the seller and the broker (or his listing agent) sign the document consenting to the employment.

Preparing the seller's listing agreement

The following instructions are for the preparation and use of the Seller's Listing Agreement,

first tuesday Form 102, with which a seller employs a broker as his exclusive agent to market a property for sale and locate a buyer.

Each instruction corresponds to the provision in the form bearing the same number.

*Editor's note — **Check** and **enter** items throughout the agreement in each provision with boxes and blanks, unless the provision is not intended to be included as part of the final agreement, in which case it is left unchecked or blank.*

Document identification:

Enter the date and name of the city where the listing is prepared. This date is used when referring to this listing agreement.

1. **Retainer period**:

   1.1 *Listing start and end date*: **Enter** the date the brokerage services are to commence.

   Enter the expiration date of the employment period. The expiration must be set as a specific date on which the employment ends since an exclusive listing is being established.

   1.2 *Broker's/agent's duty:* **States** the broker and his agents promise to use diligence in their effort to locate a buyer for the listed property. The agency duties a broker and his agents owe the seller are always implied, if not expressed in writing.

2. **Seller's deposit**:

   2.1 *Advance fees and costs*: **Enter** the amount of deposit negotiated to commence the brokerage services.

SELLER'S LISTING AGREEMENT
Exclusive Right to Sell, Exchange or Option

DATE:_____, 20_____, at _____, California

Items left blank or unchecked are not applicable.

FACTS:

1. RETAINER PERIOD:

1.1 Seller hereby retains and grants to Broker the exclusive right to market, solicit and negotiate for the disposition of the property, through sale, exchange or option, for the period beginning on _____, 20_____ and terminating on _____, 20_____.

1.2 Broker agrees to use diligence in the performance of this employment.

2. SELLER'S DEPOSIT:

2.1 Seller hands $_____ to Broker for deposit into Broker's trust account for application to Seller's obligations under this agreement and the following attachments:

    a. ☐ Advance Fee Addendum [**ft** Form 106]

    b. ☐ Listing Package Cost Sheet [**ft** Form 107]
       (Also see §§7j, 7.1b and 8.2)

3. BROKERAGE FEE:

NOTICE: The amount or rate of real estate fees is not fixed by law. They are set by each Broker individually and may be negotiable between Client and Broker.

3.1 Seller agrees to pay Broker _____ of the price sought or obtained, IF:

    a. Anyone procures a buyer, exchanger or optionee on the terms stated in this agreement or on any other terms accepted by Seller during the period of the listing.

    b. The property is withdrawn from sale, transferred or leased without Broker's consent, which will not be unreasonably withheld, or otherwise made unmarketable by Seller during the period of the listing.

    c. Seller terminates this employment of Broker during the period of the listing.

    d. Within one year after termination of this agreement, Seller or his agent enter into negotiations, which later result in a transaction contemplated by this agreement, with a prospective buyer whom Broker or a cooperating broker negotiated with during the period of this listing. Broker to identify prospective buyers by written notice delivered personally or electronically, or mailed to Seller within 21 days after termination of this agreement. [**ft** Form 122]

3.2 Should Seller acquire replacement property in a transaction in which Broker negotiates, Seller to further compensate Broker on acquisition of the replacement property based on the fee amount stated in §3.1.

3.3 Should this agreement terminate without Seller becoming obligated to pay Broker a fee, Seller to pay Broker the sum of $_____ per hour of time accounted for by Broker, not to exceed $_____.

4. GENERAL PROVISIONS:

4.1 Broker is authorized to place a For Sale sign on the property, inspect the property's condition, verify any operating income or expenses and publish and disseminate property information to meet the objectives of this employment.

4.2 Seller authorizes Broker to cooperate with other brokers and divide with them any compensation due.

4.3 Broker is authorized to accept, on behalf of any buyer, an offer and deposit.

4.4 Offers to purchase received by Broker may be submitted to Seller personally or electronically, or by USPS postage-prepaid mail.

4.5 The buyer shall not have possession of the property before: _____.

4.6 In any action to enforce this agreement, the prevailing party shall receive attorney fees.

4.7 This listing agreement will be governed by California law.

5. REAL ESTATE:

5.1 Type: _____

    Described as: _____

    Vesting: _____

5.2 Encumbrances of record:

    a. A first loan in the amount of $_____ payable $_____ per month until paid, including interest at _____%, ☐ ARM, type _____, impounds being $_____ monthly.

    Lender: _____

    b. A second loan in the amount of \$_____ payable \$_____ per month, including interest at _____%, due _____, 20_____.

        Lender: _____

    c. Other encumbrance, bond, assessment or lien in the amount of \$_____.

        Description of debt: _____

6. PERSONAL PROPERTY INCLUDED:
   6.1 Described as: _____

   6.2 Encumbered for the amount of \$_____ payable \$_____ monthly, including interest at _____%, due _____, 20_____.

        Lender: _____

7. ADDENDA attached to this agreement regarding the listing package include:
    a. ☐ Agency Law Disclosure (mandated on one-to-four residential units) [**ft** Form 305]
    b. ☐ Federal Residency Declaration [**ft** Form 301]
    c. ☐ Condition of Property (Transfer) Disclosure [**ft** Form 304]
    d. ☐ Local Ordinance (Option) Disclosure [**ft** Form 307]
    e. ☐ Natural Hazard Disclosure [**ft** Form 314]
    f. ☐ Lead-based Paint Disclosure [**ft** Form 313]
    g. ☐ Residential Earthquake Hazards Report [**ft** Form 315]
    h. ☐ APOD (Annual Property Operating Data) [**ft** Form 352, or 562 for a SFR]
    i. ☐ MLS property profile
    j. ☐ Listing Package Cost Sheet [**ft** Form 107] (Also see §2.1b)
    k. ☐ Criminal activity and security statement
    l. ☐ _____

   7.1 Additional addenda not part of the listing package include:
    a. ☐ Seller's Net Sheet [**ft** Form 310]
    b. ☐ Work Authorization [**ft** Form 108] (Also see §§2.1b and 8.2)
    c. ☐ _____

8. SALE TERMS:
   8.1 Price sought is \$_____, payable:
    a. ☐ In cash, or cash to a new loan obtained by the buyer;
    b. ☐ Cash to the existing loan(s) and the buyer to assume the loan(s) with the lender(s);
    c. ☐ Cash down payment of no less than \$_____. The buyer to assume the existing loan(s) with the lender(s) in the amount of \$_____, and execute a \$_____ note and trust deed to Seller bearing _____% interest with monthly amortization over _____ years, all due _____, 20_____.

   8.2 Seller agrees to pay for the following costs on a sale:
        (Also see §§2.1b, 7j and 7.1b)
    a. ☐ Property inspection report
    b. ☐ Natural hazard disclosure report
    c. ☐ Pest control clearance
    d. ☐ CLTA title insurance
    e. ☐ FHA/VA appraisal fee
    f. ☐ Non-recurring loan costs of the buyer
    g. ☐ Home warranty policy
    h. ☐ Smoke detector and water heater anchor installation
    i. ☐ Local ordinance sale or occupancy compliance
    j. ☐ Well water quality and quantity reports
    k. ☐ _____
    l. ☐ _____

9. EXCHANGE TERMS:
   9.1 Seller will exchange the property for or reinvest the sales proceeds in the following property:
        Type: _____
        Location: _____
        Assume or originate financing up to \$_____.

10. OPTION TERMS:
   10.1 For option money in the amount of \$_____, Seller will grant an option to purchase on any of the sale terms stated above, for a period of _____ months.

11. OTHER TERMS:

_____
_____
_____
_____

I agree to render services on the terms stated above.

Date:_____, 20_____

Seller's Broker : _____

By: _____

Address: _____

_____

Phone:_____

Fax: _____

E-mail: _____

I agree to employ Broker on the terms stated above.

Date:_____, 20_____

Seller's Name:_____

Seller's Name:_____

Signature: _____

Signature: _____

Address: _____

_____

Phone:_____

Fax: _____

E-mail: _____

Check the box for each form to be attached as an addendum and **fill out** and **attach** the forms detailing the services to be rendered or costs to be incurred and charged against the deposit. [See **first tuesday** Forms 106 and 107]

3. Brokerage fee:

3.1 *Fee amount:* **Enter** the fee amount negotiated to be paid as a percentage of the sales price or a fixed dollar amount. This amount will be paid when any one of the following conditions occur triggering payment:

a. *Fee on any sale:* **States** the brokerage fee is earned and due on 1) presentation during the listing period of an offer for the price and terms sought under the listing, or 2) any sale, exchange or option of the property agreed to by the seller during the listing period. [See Form 102 §3.1(d) for fee due on post-listing period sales]

b. *Fee on withdrawal:* **States** the brokerage fee is earned and due if the seller, without the broker's consent, withdraws the property from the market or significantly interferes with the broker's ability to market the property.

c. *Fee on termination:* **States** the brokerage fee is earned and due if, during the listing period, the seller terminates this employment.

d. *Safety clause fee:* **States** the brokerage fee is earned and

due if, within one year after the listing expires, a prospective buyer whom the broker or his agent negotiated with during the listing period and whose name the broker registered with the seller on expiration of the listing, negotiates to buy, exchange for or acquire an option to buy the listed property, and the negotiations culminate in a binding agreement with the seller. Within 21 days after expiration of the listing period, the broker must provide the seller with a list of the prospective buyers. [See **first tuesday** Form 122]

3.2 *Replacement property fee:* **States** an additional fee is earned and due, based on the same terms as the fee for a sale of the listed property if, through negotiations involving the broker, the seller acquires replacement property, such as occurs in a IRS §1031 tax-exempt transaction.

3.3 *Hourly fee:* **Enter** the negotiated dollar amount for the broker's per hour fee. The hourly fee is earned for time spent on behalf of the seller if the property is not sold, exchanged or optioned after a diligent effort is made to market the property and locate a buyer.

4. General provisions:

4.1 *For Sale signs:* **Authorizes** the broker to place *For Sale* signs on the property and publish information (in multiple listing services (MLSs), classified ads, broadcasts, fliers, etc.) regarding the property described in the listing.

4.2 *Authority to share fees*: **Authorizes** the broker to cooperate with other brokers and share with them any fee paid on any transaction.

4.3 *Authority to accept deposits*: **Authorizes** the broker to work with buyers to obtain offers and receive good-faith deposits.

4.4 *Handling offers*: **Authorizes** the broker to deliver offers from buyers to the seller in person, by electronic transmission (fax or email) or by mail.

4.5 *Vacating the property*: **Enter** the date or event on which the seller (or a tenant) will vacate the premises, such as "the close of escrow."

4.6 *Attorney fees*: **Entitles** the prevailing party to attorney fees if litigation results from the seller's failure to pay fees or the broker's breach of an agency duty.

4.7 *Choice-of-law provision*: **States** California law will apply to any enforcement of this employment.

5. **Real estate:**

5.1 *Type of real estate*: **Enter** a brief description of the type of real estate to be sold, such as apartment, commercial, office, industrial, land or single-family residence (SFR), its legal description or common address, and the vesting of its title.

5.2 *Encumbrances of record*: **Enter** all financing of record which are liens on the real estate, including information on amounts, payments, interest rates, impounds, due dates and type of lenders. [See Form 102 §§5.2(a), 5.2(b) and 5.2(c)]

Loan information submitted to the MLS or included in a marketing (listing) package gives a prospective buyer the alternative of making an offer which includes the existing loan as part of the purchase price.

6. **Personal property included:**

6.1 *Description*: **Enter** a brief description of any personal property included in the price. If numerous items or inventory are included in the sale, **prepare** and **attach** an exhibit for inventory/personal property and refer to it by **entering** "See attached Personal Property Exhibit." [See **first tuesday** Form 250]

6.2 *Encumbrances*: **Enter** the balance, terms of payment, interest rate, due date and the name of the lender on any financing secured by the personal property.

7. **Listing package addenda**: **Check** the appropriate boxes and **attach** each addendum to be prepared or reviewed by the seller for inclusion in the listing package. The addenda will contain the seller's representations about the property needed by the broker to properly market the property to locate and induce prospective buyers to purchase the property.

Editor's note — The Agency Law Disclosure is mandated to be included in the seller's listing agreement regarding one-to-four unit residential property under penalty of a lost fee on the resulting sale. The applicable federal and California residency and withholding disclosures are also most prudently presented at the listing stage since the information is known to the broker and might be of financial concern to the seller.

The other addenda listed are disclosures about the property which are prepared by the seller and received by the broker to be included in the listing package for delivery to prospective buyers so they will be informed of the property's condition before the seller accepts an offer or makes a counteroffer.

7.1 **Check** the appropriate boxes and **attach** each addendum prepared by the broker and reviewed with the seller to disclose the costs the seller will incur on the sale of the property.

8. Sale terms:

8.1 *Price/terms sought*: **Enter** the dollar amount of the price sought for the property by the seller.

a. *Cash price*: **Check** the box to provide for the price to be paid in cash on closing. The seller is to discharge and clear all liens from title, either himself or through escrow.

b. *Loan assumption*: **Check** the box if the seller will allow a buyer to pay a cash down payment (to cash out the seller's equity) and assume the loan(s) referenced in section 5.2.

c. *Carryback financing*: **Enter** the amount of the down payment the seller will accept. **Enter** the amount of any existing financing the seller will allow a buyer to assume. **Enter** the amount, terms of payment, interest rate, the number of years for monthly amortization payments and the due date for carryback financing the seller will accept from a creditworthy buyer.

8.2 *Sale and closing costs*: **Check** the box for each item of expense the seller will incur to market the property. Prudent practice dictates

the seller proceed to promptly prepare disclosures and authorize the inspections, reports or clearances needed for the broker to properly market the property and inform prospective buyers about its condition before the seller enters into an agreement to sell the property.

9. Exchange terms:

9.1 *Acquisition property*: **Enter** the type of property, its location (city, county or state) and the dollar amount of equity and debt on replacement property the seller is willing to acquire with the net proceeds from a sale of the listed property or by an exchange of its equity.

10. Option terms:

10.1 *Seller will option*: **Enter** the amount of option money the seller would accept to grant an option to a buyer. **Enter** the period during which the option may be exercised.

11. Other terms: **Enter** any special provision to be included in the listing.

Signatures

Broker's/Agent's signature: **Enter** the date the listing is signed and the broker's name. **Enter** the broker's (or agent's) signature. **Enter** the broker's address, telephone and fax numbers, and his email address.

Seller's signature: **Enter** the date the seller signs the listing and the seller's name. **Obtain** the seller's signature. If additional sellers are involved, prepare duplicate copies of the listing agreement and enter their names and obtain their signatures until all sellers are individually named and have signed. **Enter** the seller's address, telephone and fax numbers, and his email address.

Chapter 9

This chapter discusses the exclusive aspect of a broker's employment as established by the fee provision in a seller's listing agreement.

A fee earned on any sale

An exclusive right-to-sell listing agreement documents the employment of a broker by an owner of real estate. In its fee provision, the owner agrees to pay the broker a fee if his property is sold, exchanged or optioned during the listing period, regardless of whether the broker's or his agent's activities brought about the transaction. [**Carlsen** v. **Zane** (1968) 261 CA2d 399]

Consider a broker who is employed under an exclusive listing agreement to locate a buyer for a property. The broker and his listing agent diligently investigate and market the property, but have not located a qualified buyer willing to make an offer.

During the listing period, the property owner enters into a purchase agreement (or an exchange or option to sell agreement) with a buyer represented by another broker. Later, after the listing expires, an escrow is opened and the property is acquired by the other broker's buyer.

On discovery of the sale, the listing broker demands a fee from the owner. The owner claims the listing broker is not owed a fee since another broker **procured the buyer** and the property could not be considered sold until escrow closed — a date after the listing period expired.

Here, an exclusive right-to-sell listing, due to the *exclusive representation clause* in its fee provision, requires the owner to pay the listing broker a fee on any sale, exchange or option of the property entered into during the listing period, regardless of who produced the buyer or when escrow closed. [See **first tuesday** Form 102 §3.1(a)]

However, a broker employed under an exclusive listing must himself, or through his agents, *exercise due diligence* in gathering data on the condition of the property, marketing the property and locating a buyer. The broker will **lose his right to a fee** under the exclusive representation clause should the owner cancel the listing due to the broker's (or his agent's) failure to exercise due diligence.

Due diligence

Consider an agent who obtains a listing on a form which contains an exclusive representation clause in the listing's fee provision. No effort is made to market the property. Instead, the agent chooses only to place a "For Sale" sign on the property and a listing of the property's availability in a multiple listing service (MLS).

The agent limits his activities to acquiring listings and refuses to assist buyers or their agents, except to make the listed property available for inspection through a lock-box arrangement.

The agent does not prepare disclosures or provide a listing package regarding the condition of the property, hazards, operating cost or other releases of information on the property. He also does not obtain property profiles, inspection reports or pest control reports. All these items are left to a buyer's agent to obtain or for a buyer to demand in escrow. The listing agent plans to have a "transaction coordinator" (TC) prepare the documents and obtain the seller's signature prior to close of escrow — at an extra charge to the seller for the TC's services.

None of these limitations on the marketing services provided by the agent are disclosed to the seller, except for the cost of the TC to close a sale.

No potential buyers are produced by the agent.

The seller, dissatisfied with the agent's marketing efforts, cancels the listing without the agent's consent. Another broker is employed by the seller to market the property. The property is sold under the new listing, but during the listing period remaining on the canceled listing.

The listing agent's broker makes a demand on the seller to pay a fee since the property was sold during the original listing period. The seller claims the agent's lack of *due diligence* in marketing the property and locating buyers bars the broker from collecting a brokerage fee.

Is the listing broker entitled to the fee called for in the exclusive listing agreement?

No! The listing agent's efforts to market the property and locate buyers were insufficient to entitle his broker, and thus himself, to a fee on any sale after the seller canceled the listing.

When employed under an **exclusive listing agreement**, a broker and his agents are obligated:

- to inform the seller about the brokerage services which will and will not be rendered; and

- to diligently perform the agreed-to services in pursuit of buyers who are ready, willing and able to purchase the listed property.

Agents are expected to work in cooperation with other agents who represent buyers and to engage those buyers who are not represented by an agent. Listing agreements authorize the agent to prepare offers and accept deposits from buyers. [See **first tuesday** Form 102 §4.3]

A diligent effort is required on the part of the agent to fulfill his agency duty owed under an exclusive listing by making a **concerted** and **continuing effort** to locate a buyer and do so while performing at a level which meets the owner's reasonable expectations. Otherwise, the owner has *good cause* to terminate the agency and cancel the listing without becoming obligated to pay a fee on cancellation or on a later resale. [**Coleman** v. **Mora** (1968) 263 CA2d 137]

An agent's written (and if not written, implied) promise on entering into an exclusive listing is to diligently perform his **agency obligations**, which includes applying his abilities to investigate, market and negotiate a sale of the listed property.

The *diligent effort* of a broker under an exclusive listing is measured by the conduct and actions taken by the broker and his agents, which include:

- **analyzing the property**, a responsibility imposed on the broker or his agent to gather at the earliest opportunity — before marketing begins — as much information about the listed property as a competent broker would include in a listing package to be handed to prospective buyers, ranging from inspecting the property, obtaining third-party reports on the property and reviewing a title profile, to reporting its income, expenses and any local information about the surrounding area [**Jue** v. **Smiser** (1994) 23 CA4th 312]; and

- **marketing the property**, which includes advertising in MLSs or other broker-associated publications, making phone calls, putting up "For Sale" signs, distributing fliers, holding open house events if appropriate, broadcasting the property at pitch sessions, etc., and advising prospective buyers and their agents about the property by handing them the information package (disclosures) previously prepared.

An agent must keep records to provide proof he has exercised *due diligence* in his analysis and marketing of a property if he is to avoid unwarranted cancellation of the listing. Records of all solicitations, contacts, money spent, advertisements placed, buyers contacted, etc., should be maintained on worksheets in a file on the listed property. [See **first tuesday** Forms 520 and 525]

A ready, willing and able buyer

Occasionally, during a period of rising real estate prices, a seller who employs an agent to locate a buyer will *reject* a full listing offer submitted by the agent.

Rejection occurs by either:

- the seller's **refusal to accept** the offer; or

- the seller's **counteroffer** on different terms.

Consider an agent under a listing who locates a buyer who makes an offer to buy property on substantially the same terms sought by the seller in the listing, called a *full listing offer*.

The offer is submitted to the seller, who refuses to accept the offer. Instead, the listing agent is instructed to prepare a counteroffer at a higher price, which the seller signs, believing the buyer should pay more for the property than the listed price.

The counter to the full listing offer is submitted to the prospective buyer, who rejects it and terminates negotiations.

The listing agent's broker demands payment of a fee, which the seller refuses to pay. The seller claims a fee is not due the broker since the

counteroffer was rejected and a sale of the property did not occur.

Here, the broker has **earned a fee** under any type of listing agreement, open or exclusive, since the broker or one of his agents:

- **located a** financially qualified (able) buyer who was also ready and willing to purchase the property on the terms of sale stated in the listing; and

- brought the buyer and seller together by **submitting** the buyer's offer to the seller and handing the seller a copy of the offer. [**Barnes** v. **Osgood** (1930) 103 CA 730]

The fact the seller rejected the offer by way of a counteroffer (which was not accepted) has no effect on the broker's right to a fee under the listing agreement.

However, to earn a fee for obtaining and submitting a full listing offer, the prospective buyer, on making the offer, must be *ready, willing and able*. Specifically, the buyer must:

- **make an offer** on substantially the same terms as the seller's listed terms, called *ready*;

- **intend to enter** into a binding purchase agreement with the seller, called *willing*; and

- **qualify financially and legally** to perform on the offer, called *able*.

Once the listing agent has submitted a full listing offer from a buyer who meets each of the ready, willing and able criteria, the listing agent's broker is entitled to a fee from the seller. [**Woodbridge Realty** v. **Plymouth Development Corporation** (1955) 130 CA2d 270]

For example, an owner of real estate enters into a listing agreement employing a broker to locate a buyer who will agree to purchase the property. The price and terms of payment the owner seeks for his property are contained in the listing agreement, as is a brokerage fee provision.

During the listing period, the broker's listing agent locates a financially qualified buyer who makes a written offer to purchase the property on substantially the same terms sought by the owner in the listing agreement. When the offer is submitted to the owner, the owner rejects the offer, opting not to sell his property on the terms listed. The listing agent's broker promptly makes a demand on the owner for his fee based on the brokerage fee provision in the listing agreement. The owner refuses to pay, claiming the broker did not earn his fee since a sale was never completed.

However, the broker did earn his fee. During the listing period, the broker's agent located a financially qualified buyer who offered to purchase the property on the owner's listed terms for a sale.

The broker may enforce collection of his fee at the moment the **opportunity to accept** a full listing offer, oral or written, is presented to the owner. Whether the offer is accepted or a sale is ever consummated is not a condition of the broker's employment under a listing agreement. Upon fully performing his employment under the listing by producing a ready, willing and able buyer on the listed terms, the broker's recovery of his fee is not barred by the owner's refusal to now sell the property. [**Twogood** v. **Monnette** (1923) 191 C 103]

However, if a buyer offers to purchase the property on terms different from those in the listing agreement, the owner must first accept the buyer's offer before the broker is entitled to a fee, no matter how reasonable the buyer's offer may be. [**Seck** v. **Foulks** (1972) 25 CA3d 556]

Fee for purchase of other property

Often, the property listed for sale is held by an owner as an investment, such as rental income property or vacant land, or for use in the owner's trade or business. Thus, the listed property is Internal Revenue Code (IRC) §1031 *like-kind property*. It is not the owner's residence or dealer property, such as lots held by a developer.

If the listed price is greater than the owner's remaining cost basis in the property, the owner is selling the property at a profit, called a *capital gain*.

The listing agent who is alert to an opportunity to render additional services for an additional fee should know the owner can avoid payment of any profit tax on a sale. If the owner **acquires replacement property** which has equal-or-greater *equity* and equal-or-greater *debt*, profit taxes are avoided on the property sold as an exempt (tax-free) transaction.

Thus, the agent should bring to the owner's attention the advantageous §1031 tax exemption treatment available on the sale. Further, the agent should recommend implementation of a §1031 reinvestment plan by the timely acquisition (through the agent) of other *like-kind* property using the net proceeds from the sale of the listed property.

As in any employment engaging a broker to act on behalf of a client, the authorization to locate replacement property and receive payment for doing so must be in writing to enforce collection of the fee. An exclusive right-to-sell listing accomplishes this objective by containing a replacement property provision. [See **first tuesday** Form 102 §3.2]

The type of replacement property to be acquired and the amount of debt the owner is willing to incur to purchase the property should be entered in the appropriate places on the listing agreement. [See **first tuesday** Form 102 §9.1]

A fee is earned if the broker or his agent is involved in negotiations which lead to the owner's purchase of replacement property. The fee for assisting in the purchase of replacement property is based on the same formula or dollar amount used to set the fee due on the sale of the listed property.

However, to fully protect a listing broker's right to a fee when replacement property is to be purchased, a **buyer's exclusive right-to-buy listing** should also be entered into.

The right-to-buy listing, being more specific, would supersede the replacement property provision in the exclusive right-to-sell listing. The exclusive right-to-buy listing assures the broker that he will receive a fee should the owner acquire replacement property during the right-to-buy listing period, regardless of who brings the property to the owner's attention.

Granting an option

Consider a broker who is employed by a seller under a listing agreement which states the broker will receive a fee if he negotiates a sale, exchange or the grant of an **option to purchase** the seller's property. [See **first tuesday** Form 102 §10]

An agent of the broker locates a qualified buyer. The seller grants the buyer, also called an *optionee,* an option on the receipt of *option money* paid by the buyer. The broker receives

no fee on the grant of the option, although he is entitled to a fee under the listing. Also, the option does not contain a fee provision.

After the listing expires, the buyer exercises the option and acquires the property.

The broker makes a demand on the seller for a fee under the listing agreement. The seller refuses, claiming the broker is not entitled to a fee since the buyer exercised the option after the listing agreement expired and the option did not provide for a fee on its exercise.

Here, the broker did earn a fee. During the listing period, the seller granted the buyer an option to buy the property, which the buyer later exercised to acquire the property. [**Anthony** v. **Enzler** (1976) 61 CA3d 872]

Thus, when an option is exercised, the sale relates back to the **time the option was granted**, i.e., during the listing period. This *relation back* is roughly comparable to entering into a purchase agreement or opening an escrow during the listing period, and closing the transaction after the listing expires.

Alternatively, consider a seller who agrees to pay a broker a partial fee on the granting of an option without any reference to payment of a further fee on the exercise of the option. To avoid the lost expectations of the payment of a further fee on exercise, the broker or his agent must then include a fee provision in the body of the option. [See **first tuesday** Form 160 §6]

Chapter 10

A fee due on withdrawal or termination

This chapter examines the events which trigger the withdrawal-from-sale and termination-of-agency clauses in the fee provision of an exclusive listing.

Exercising an alternative

An owner of real estate enters into an exclusive right-to-sell listing agreement, employing a broker to locate buyers and sell the property. The broker's compensation for his and his listing agent's services is set forth in a fee provision in the listing agreement. The fee provision contains both a *withdrawal-from-sale* and a *termination-of-agency* clause. [See **first tuesday** Form 102 §3.1]

The **withdrawal-from-sale** clause entitles the broker to be paid a full listing fee if, during the listing period, the property is:

- withdrawn from the market;

- transferred to others;

- further leased without the broker's consent; or

- made unmarketable by the owner. [See **first tuesday** Form 102 §3.1(b)]

Further, the separate **termination-of-agency** clause entitles the broker to collect a full listing fee if the owner cancels the broker's employment during the listing period, with or without the intent by the owner to continue marketing the property for sale.

Withdrawal from sale

On undertaking the obligation of employment imposed by a listing, a listing agent gathers available information about a seller's property and organizes it into a listing package. The package is reproduced and handed to those most likely to make a offer, called *prospective buyers*.

On completing the listing package, multiple listing service (MLS) and newspaper advertisements are placed, and a "For Sale" sign is erected on the property with a box for distribution of informational fliers to interested parties.

Before the listing period expires, the seller withdraws the property from sale. Further, the agent is instructed to remove his "For Sale" sign and lock box, and to cease marketing the property.

The agent confirms the seller's withdrawal in writing and immediately complies with the seller's request. The listing agent's broker then makes a demand on the seller for payment of a full listing fee, claiming the withdrawal-from-sale clause in the listing agreement entitles him to a fee earned at the moment the seller removes the property from the market during the unexpired listing period.

The seller refuses to pay, claiming the broker is not due a fee since the broker's agent failed to produce a buyer due to the lack of a diligent effort to market the property. The seller also claims the provision for payment of the brokerage fee on the seller's withdrawal of the property from the market is unenforceable as an unfair and **unenforceable penalty** since the property did not sell.

Is the broker entitled to a full listing fee under the withdrawal-from-sale clause?

Yes! The seller became obligated to pay the broker the fee agreed to in the listing when:

- the broker, through his listing agent, at all times exercised diligence in the marketing of the property; and

- the seller **exercised his right** under the withdrawal-from-sale clause to voluntarily remove the property from the marketplace during the listing period.

Further, the brokerage fee the seller agreed to pay on a withdrawal from sale prior to the expiration of the listing period is not a penalty payment or forfeiture. The fee due the broker on the seller's withdrawal from the market is a fair amount since the agreed amount preserves the earnings the broker **expected to receive** by ultimately selling the property. When the seller entered into the listing agreement, the broker and the listing agent commenced their due diligence efforts to locate a buyer.

On withdrawal, the fee due the broker compensates him for his **lost opportunity**. When the broker loses his authority to market the property and locate a buyer, he has lost his ability to accomplish the objective of the employment, which was to sell the property and earn a fee.

Thus, instead of leaving the property on the market for the entire listing period (and paying a fee if it sells), the seller has exercised one of his **alternative performance options** allowing the seller to either:

- remove the property from the market, in which case a fee is earned and due; or

- terminate the agency by canceling the listing while leaving the property on the market, in which case a fee is also earned and due.

A withdrawal of the property from the market always results in a termination of the broker's agency relationship with the seller. However, a termination of the agency by the seller is not always due solely to a withdrawal of the property from sale.

Termination of agency by seller

A seller of real estate enters into a listing agreement with a broker to sell a property within a three-month period. The listing includes a fee provision which contains a *termination-of-agency* clause entitling the broker to a full fee should the seller terminate the broker's employment, without good cause, prior to expiration of the listing period. [See **first tuesday** Form 102 §3.1(c)]

The broker's listing agent promptly commences a diligent marketing effort to properly present the property for sale and locate a buyer who is willing to acquire the property. However, during the listing period and before a buyer is located, the seller terminates the agency by canceling the listing.

The broker makes a demand on the seller for a full listing fee, claiming the termination-of-agency clause in the fee provision of the listing calls for payment of a fee as earned when the seller prematurely terminates the agency. The seller claims the broker is not entitled to a full brokerage fee, but only to money losses based on an accounting for his time, effort and costs incurred to market the property, called *quantum meruit*, since a seller may legally terminate a broker's agency at any time.

Is the broker entitled to collect a full fee from the seller upon the seller's exercise of his legal right to terminate the agency?

Yes! While a seller may terminate the broker's agency at any time, the seller cannot terminate the agency during the listing period and avoid payment of a fee if a termination-of-agency clause exists. The termination-of-agency clause in the listing couples the canceling of the listing with the payment of a fee.

The seller has chosen between:

- continuing to work with the broker under the listing and paying a fee if a buyer is located before expiration of the listing period; and

RELEASE AND CANCELLATION OF EMPLOYMENT AGREEMENT
Waiver of Rights

DATE:_____, 20_____, at_____, California.

> This agreement is used to both terminate a listing employment and eliminate any claims which may have arisen during its existence.

Items left blank or unchecked are not applicable.

1. FACTS:

1.1 This mutual release and cancellation agreement with waiver of rights pertains to the following employment agreement:

a. ☐ Seller's Listing Agreement [**ft** Form 102]　　e. ☐ Buyer's Listing Agreement [**ft** Form 103]

b. ☐ Loan Broker Listing [**ft** Form 104]　　f. ☐ Note Resale Listing [**ft** Form 112]

c. ☐ Exclusive Authorization To Lease [**ft** Form 110]　　g. ☐ Exclusive Authorization To Locate Space [**ft** Form 111]

d. ☐ Property Management Agreement [**ft** Form 590]　　h. ☐ _____

1.2 Dated _____, 20_____, at_____, California.

1.3 Entered into by (Broker) _____

and (Client) _____

1.4 Regarding property referred to as: _____

_____

2. AGREEMENT:

2.1 Broker and Client hereby cancel and release each other and their agents from all claims and obligations of any kind, known or unknown, arising out of the employment agreement.

2.2 In consideration of Broker's acceptance of this cancellation, Client to pay Broker a brokerage fee of $_____.

2.3 In consideration of Broker's acceptance of this cancellation, Client to pay the brokerage fee set forth in the employment agreement if Client enters into an agreement for any of the following checked events within _____ months after the date of this cancellation agreement:

a. ☐ The property is sold, exchanged or otherwise transferred.

b. ☐ An option to buy or sell the property is created.

c. ☐ The property is relisted with another broker.

d. ☐ The property is refinanced or further financed.

e. ☐ The property is leased.

f. ☐ The property is acquired.

g. _____.

3. WAIVER:

The parties hereby waive any rights provided by Section 1542 of the California Civil Code which states:

"A general release does not extend to claims which the creditor does not know or suspect to exist in his favor at the time of executing the release, which if known by him must have materially affected his settlement with the debtor."

I agree to the terms stated above.	I agree to the terms stated above.
Date:_____, 20_____	Date:_____, 20_____
Broker:_____	Client's Signature:_____
By: _____	Client's Signature:_____

FORM 121　　10-01　　©2006 **first tuesday**, P.O. BOX 20069, RIVERSIDE, CA 92516 (800) 794-0494

- terminating the broker's agency and paying the broker his full listing fee, whether or not the property is removed from the market.

No alternatives to breach

Occasionally, both the withdrawal-from-sale and the termination-of-agency clause are excluded from a listing agreement. Without these provisions, a broker will be unable to collect a full brokerage fee on a withdrawal or termination since no amount was agreed to be paid on the occurrence of either event.

Thus, only a *breach* of the listing occurs for lack of **alternative performance provisions** in the exclusive listing agreement. [See **first tuesday** Form 102 §§3.1(b) and 3.1(c)]

On a breach by the seller of a listing which does not contain a termination-of-agency clause, the terminated broker will only be entitled to recover:

- the out-of-pocket costs incurred to service the listing; and

- the value of the time and effort expended under the listing, called *quantum meruit* recovery. [**Hedging Concepts, Inc.** v. **First Alliance Mortgage Company** (1996) 41 CA4th 1410]

Documenting the cancellation

An agent needs to be certain the seller intends to withdraw his property from sale or terminate the agency before ceasing all efforts to market the property and locate a buyer. Marketing efforts should be continued until the seller makes his decision known directly to the agent.

When a seller, by word or by conduct, clearly indicates he no longer desires to sell the property, the agent should prepare a **Release and Cancellation of Employment Agreement** form for the seller to review and sign. [See Form 121 accompanying this chapter]

Editor's note — This release and cancellation agreement is a new contract between the agent's broker and the seller, effectively replacing the listing agreement.

The release and cancellation agreement may call for immediate payment of the full brokerage fee agreed to in the listing in exchange for mutual cancellation of the listing agreement. Alternatively, it may call for payment at a later date should the property be sold, placed on the market, exchanged, optioned, refinanced (if the broker was retained to arrange new financing) or leased to anyone within a specified time period (for example, one year) after the date of the agreement. A compromise could be the payment of a partial fee with the balance due should the property be sold within the cancellation period.

This release and cancellation agreement is also used when a buyer wants to cancel an exclusive right-to-buy listing. On cancellation, the broker is deprived of the opportunity he acquired under the listing to earn a fee. Thus, he has the right to receive compensation.

In this case, the agreement entitles the broker to a fee if, within the cancellation period, the buyer purchases property similar to that which the broker was retained to locate.

In short, if the client accomplishes on his own what he retained the broker to do, and the client does so during the cancellation period, the broker is entitled to his fee.

Editor's note — The broker cannot require the client to relist with him if he decides to buy or sell within the cancellation period. This coupling of the cancellation to future employment would be an illegal tying arrangement. [Calif. Business and Professions Code §16727]

Reimbursement on cancellation

A cancellation agreement can also call for a client to pay a broker cash compensation for his and his agent's time, effort and expenses expended during the employment under the listing. The client and broker can negotiate an appropriate hourly rate at the time of settlement.

The broker will not later be able to collect a fee should the property sell after the listing is canceled since the broker settled for a lump sum amount to end the relationship and eliminate all claims under the listing agreement.

However, by entering into a settlement on cancellation, the broker would be compensated immediately rather than waiting for a transaction that might not happen. With this agreement, the broker ensures he will not be out-of-pocket on this listing.

If the broker believes the client may use his services in the future, or will refer other clients, this is a fair alternative.

By being reasonable, both about the client's decision to cancel and about the value of his professional services, the broker is bargaining for continued good will.

At the same time, the client obtains his objective — cancellation of the listing agreement — while the broker remains protected just in case the property is relisted or sold.

Chapter 11

The safety clause

This chapter demonstrates the use of a safety clause in a listing to earn a fee after the listing has expired for the time and effort spent with prospective buyers during the listing period.

A fee earned after the listing expires

A broker is retained to represent a seller under an employment agreement, commonly called a *listing*. The listing, whether open or exclusive, contains a *safety clause* entitling the broker to the agreed fee, if:

- a person has contact with the broker (or his agent) regarding the property during the listing period, called *solicitations*;

- the broker treats the person as a **prospective buyer** by providing the person with information about the property, legally called *negotiations*;

- negotiations with the person terminate without resulting in a sale;

- on expiration of the listing period, the broker registers the person by name with the seller as a **prospective buyer**; and

- the person and the seller, with or without involving the broker, later commence negotiations within a specified time period following the expiration of the listing, called the *safety period*, and ultimately complete a sale of the property.

For example, during the listing period, a broker's listing agent has contact with prospective buyers. All of the buyers are **handed a listing package** fully disclosing the property's condition.

The listing agent's discussions with each buyer and the property information given to each buyer, as well as to any buyer's agent, is noted on an Activity Report Sheet in the agent's listing file. [See **first tuesday** Form 520]

Also, each prospective buyer's name, address or phone number are added to the list of prospective buyers for the property on a registration form also maintained in the listing file. [See Form 122 accompanying this chapter]

After "follow-up" conversations with the prospective buyers, the listing agent does not have any further contact with any of them.

The listing period expires and the property remains unsold. After the listing expires, the listing agent sends the seller the list of prospective buyers he has entered on the registration form and closes his file on the property. The list includes all those buyers who, during the listing period, were in contact with, and **received information** about the property from, the broker, his agents or through the buyer's broker. [See Form 122]

Within the safety period after the listing agreement expires, a buyer registered by the agent on the list of prospective buyers **enters into negotiations** with the seller to purchase the property. Negotiations ultimately result in a completed sale. Neither the broker nor his listing agent are involved in the renewed negotiations in any way.

On the listing agent's discovery of the completed sale, the broker makes a written demand on the seller for his fee as earned under the safety clause in the expired listing.

The seller refuses to pay the broker a fee, claiming the broker has no right to a fee since neither the broker nor his agent was the *procuring cause* of the sale, i.e., the broker did not obtain and submit the offer.

The broker claims he does not need to be the procuring cause to be entitled to a fee since a prospective buyer who was provided information about the property during the listing period acquired the property as a result of **negotiations commenced during the safety period**.

Is the broker entitled to a fee from the seller?

Yes! The seller owes the broker a fee under the safety clause in the listing agreement's fee provision. A prospective buyer, who reviewed information about the property with the broker's agent during the listing period, was **registered with the seller**. After the listing expired, the registered buyer acquired the property as a result of negotiations commenced during the safety period, either directly with the seller or through another broker. Payment of a fee in the listing agreement's fee provision was not limited solely to *procuring* a buyer. [**Leonard** v. **Fallas** (1959) 51 C2d 649]

Contrary to the claims of the seller, a broker will never be the *procuring cause* of a sale when the brokerage fee is earned under the safety clause. The safety clause is always triggered by negotiations which have a "fresh start" after the listing expires.

Negotiations initiated during the listing period, **which continue**, with or without the broker, beyond the expiration date on the listing and result in a purchase agreement being entered into with the seller, are the essence of procuring cause.

The safety net for due diligence

A safety clause in the fee provision of a listing agreement provides an additional period after the listing expires for a broker to earn a fee for the time and money the broker and his listing agent invest during the listing period in their effort to market the listed property and locate a buyer. The clause preserves the broker's and listing agent's expectations of earnings for reviewing the property with prospective buyers during the listing period should the prospective buyer become disinterested, break off negotiations, and then later reappear after the listing expires to buy the property.

Thus, the broker is assured a fee under the safety clause if:

- **information** about the property is provided to prospective buyers during the listing period by his listing agent;

- the **seller is notified** of the identification of the prospective buyers as soon as possible after termination of the listing; and

- a **prospective buyer from the list acquires** the property as a result of negotiations commenced during the safety period.

Theoretically, an agent's knowledge of prospective buyers is information the seller is entitled to on expiration of the listing should the seller request the information, with or without a safety clause.

The terms of the safety clause

A safety clause is usually included in the fee provision of a listing agreement. Both the open and exclusive types of seller's and buyer's listing agreements typically contain safety clause provisions. [See **first tuesday** Forms 102 §3.1(d) and 103 §5.1(c); see Chapter 14 for safety clause in a buyer's listing]

The safety clause imposes an obligation on the seller to pay a fee on a sale which resulted from negotiations with registered prospective buyers commenced by anyone within the safety period.

Like an exclusive listing agreement, the safety clause also contains an expiration date, establishing a time period during which the clause is in effect. Typically, safety clauses are drafted to cover a sufficient and reasonable period of time needed to protect the agent's time and ef-

DATE:_____, 20_____, at _____, California.

TO: _____

Your employment agreement calls for payment of a brokerage fee on transactions with these prospective buyers or tenants resulting from negotiations commenced within the one-year period following termination of the agreement.

If you employ another broker to provide similar services for the same property during the one-year period, bring this document and the expired agreement to the broker's attention.

Items left blank or unchecked are not applicable.

1. **FACTS:**

    1.1   This is an addendum to the following agreement:

        a. ☐ Exclusive Right to Sell Listing [**ft** Form 102]

        b. ☐ Exclusive Authorization to Lease [**ft** Form 110]

        c. _____

    1.2   Dated _____, 20_____, at_____, California

    1.3   Entered into by you and the undersigned broker regarding real estate referred to as:

    _____

2. **IDENTIFICATION:**

    2.1   This addendum registers with you the identities of prospective buyers or prospective tenants the undersigned, directly or through other brokers, solicited and negotiated with for the purchase or lease of the real estate under the above agreement.

    2.2   You are obligated under the above agreement to pay a brokerage fee if, within one year after expiration of the agreement, you enter into negotiations which result in the sale or lease of the real estate to any of the following prospective buyers or prospective tenants:

        Name:_____   Address: _____

        Name:_____   Address: _____

        Name:_____   Address: _____

        Name:_____   Address: _____

        Name:_____   Address: _____

        Name:_____   Address: _____

        Name:_____   Address: _____

        Name:_____   Address: _____

        Name:_____   Address: _____

        Name:_____   Address: _____

        Name:_____   Address: _____

        Name:_____   Address: _____

        Name:_____   Address: _____

        Name:_____   Address: _____

        Name:_____   Address: _____

        Name:_____   Address: _____

3. **This addendum consists of _____ page(s). (Add a page to name additional prospective buyers.)**

This is a true and correct statement.

Broker: _____

By: _____

Address: _____

_____

Phone: _____

fort spent with prospective buyers on behalf of the seller. The safety clause period **commences on termination** of the listing period.

The listing is terminated, commencing both the safety clause period and the period for putting the seller on notice of prospective buyers, upon:

- the seller's **withdrawal** of the property from the market during the listing period;

- the seller's **termination** of the agency before expiration of the listing period; or

- **expiration** of the listing agreement by its own terms.

The seller's premature termination of the broker's agency relationship does not also terminate the listing period in an exclusive listing agreement which fails to contain a termination-of-agency fee provision. **[Century 21 Butler Realty, Inc.** v. **Vasquez** (1995) 41 CA4th 888]

Whether or not the listing contains a termination-of-agency clause, premature termination should be treated as an act which commences the safety clause period. Thus, on premature termination of the agency, withdrawal or expiration of the listing period, the agent should send the seller his list of prospective buyers to *perfect his right* to earn a fee under the safety clause should a prospective buyer commence negotiations during the safety period and later buy the property.

Perfecting the safety clause

A broker has the burden of *perfecting* his right to a fee under the safety clause.

Several crucial activities must be performed by the listing agent to establish his broker's right to a fee under the safety clause, including:

- **providing information** about the listed property to any prospective buyers he or buyer's brokers have contact with;

- **documenting** dealings with prospective buyers by maintaining an Activity Report Sheet in a listing file [See **first tuesday** Form 520]; and

- **registering** the prospective buyers with the seller on termination of the listing by providing the seller with a List of Prospective Buyers in a timely manner (e.g., within 21 days). [See Form 122]

Most listing agreements contain **broker cooperation provisions** which authorize brokers to work with and share fees with other brokers who represent buyers interested in the listed property. [See **first tuesday** Form 102 §4.2]

Thus, when registering prospective buyers with the seller, the broker whose listing contains a broker cooperation provision should be sure to include any buyers with whom buyer's brokers dealt. If a sale covered by the safety clause occurs, both brokers will be protected and will share the fee.

The disclosure of the prospective buyers by registration with the seller is required to "arm" the safety clause. Thus, by registration, the broker *perfects* his right to earn a fee under the clause. If a prospective buyer registered by the broker or his agent enters into negotiations during the safety period, and as a result acquires the listed property, the broker has earned a fee.

Negotiations which result in a sale do not need to be concluded during the safety clause period to qualify the broker for a fee. Escrow also does not need to be closed prior to the expiration of the safety period. Once negotiations are commenced during the safety clause period, which leads to a sale of the listed property to a registered prospective buyer, the broker has earned his fee. An acceptance of a purchase offer or the close of a sales escrow **relates back** to the date negotiations commenced, a date which, if it falls within the safety clause period, entitles the broker to a fee. [Leonard, *supra*]

Contact with prospective buyers

The **degree of involvement** a broker or his agents must have with a buyer during the listing period in order to qualify the buyer as a *prospective buyer* is set by the terms of the safety clause.

For example, a fee provision may state the broker or his agents are required to **personally introduce** the property to a buyer to qualify the buyer as a prospective buyer, not merely conduct negotiations over the phone. [**Korstad** v. **Hoffman** (1963) 221 CA2d Supp. 805]

For all listings, a buyer is not a prospective purchaser under the safety clause if the buyer's only relationship with the broker is the buyer's observation of a "For Sale" sign on the property or of a published advertisement regarding the property placed by the broker or his agent. [**Simank Realty, Inc.** v. **DeMarco** (1970) 6 CA3d 610]

At the very least, a broker or his listing agent is required to provide the buyer with **information regarding the property** to qualify as having commenced negotiations. The agent does not need to produce a written offer from a buyer for the buyer to be a prospective purchaser.

Consider a broker who is retained by a seller under an exclusive right-to-sell listing agreement which contains a safety clause requiring prospective buyers to have *negotiated* with the broker or his listing agent. [See **first tuesday** Form 102 §3.1(d)]

During the listing period, the agent has contact with and provides property information to several individuals. The list of prospective buyers is prepared and delivered to the seller. The listing agent includes the names of people who were not contacted or were not provided with any information about the listed property.

During the safety clause period, a person who was registered, but had no contact with the broker or the listing agent, negotiates to purchase the property directly from the seller (or through another broker). The negotiations result in a sale.

The broker makes a demand on the seller for a fee since a person registered as a prospective buyer acquired the property through negotiations which commenced during the safety period.

The seller refuses to pay a fee, claiming the broker's listing agent never treated the person as a prospective buyer since the listing agent never exposed the person to the property in any way.

Has the broker earned a fee under the safety clause?

No! For the broker to earn a fee under this safety clause, the broker, his listing agent or another agent employed by the broker must have entered into negotiations with the likely buyer. For the listing agent's contact with the buyer to be **equated with negotiations**, the listing agent or another agent of the broker must have handed the buyer information regarding the property, such as its income and expenses, title conditions, property conditions or operating conditions. At no time during the listing period did the listing agent review any aspect of the property with the buyer or the buyer's agent. [**Hobson** v. **Hunt** (1922) 59 CA 679]

Price paid

Now consider a listing agent who markets a property for a seller under a listing which contains a safety clause requiring negotiations with the buyer as one condition for receiving a fee. The listing agent provides detailed information on the property to a likely buyer, including water availability and an estimate of assessments on the property. The agent has several follow-up conversations with the prospective buyer about the property.

The buyer becomes disinterested in the property due to his interest in another property. On expiration of the listing period, the listing agent registers the buyer with the seller by delivering the agent's list of prospective buyers as required by the safety clause.

During the safety clause period, the buyer is contacted by the seller regarding the property. Negotiations result in the prospective buyer's purchase of the property for less than the listed price.

The listing agent's broker learns of the sale and makes a demand on the seller for a fee.

The seller refuses to pay a fee, claiming the broker is not entitled to a fee since the price paid for the property was less than the full listing price.

The broker claims he has earned a fee since the sale was to a registered buyer who negotiated to purchase the property during the safety clause period and acquired it.

Here, the broker is entitled to the agreed fee under the safety clause since the buyer:

- reviewed the property with the listing agent during the listing period;

- was registered with the seller on expiration of the listing;

- negotiated with the seller (or an agent of the seller) during the time period covered by the safety clause; and

- ultimately purchased the property due to the negotiations.

Based on the price paid for the property, the broker earns the percentage of the price paid (or the fixed fee) stated in the listing agreement. [**Delbon** v. **Brazil** (1955) 134 CA2d 461]

Dual liability on relisting

A properly worded and perfected safety clause **remains enforceable** even when a seller relists the property for sale with another broker after the original listing expires. [See **first tuesday** Form 102 §3.1(d)]

Thus, a broker or his agent who enters into a listing must first inquire into the existence of an unexpired safety clause in a prior listing the seller may have had with another broker.

The seller is exposed to multiple fees when the property is sold by a new broker to a prospective buyer registered with the seller under the safety clause in an expired listing.

If a safety clause is still in effect, the new listing agent should obtain a copy of the list of prospective buyers registered with the seller. Since solicitations or negotiations by the new listing agent with these buyers would expose the seller to liability under the prior broker's safety clause, the broker should negotiate a *fee-sharing agreement* with the prior broker and document the arrangement as part of the listing process. [See **first tuesday** Form 105]

A fee-sharing agreement, also improperly called a *cooperating broker agreement,* allows for both the prior broker and the present broker to share fees, usually 50-50. The fee-sharing agreement broadens the pool of prospective buyers for the new listing agent and clarifies the opportunity of both brokers to earn a fee — for the duration of the safety period.

On expiration of a listing, the seller may avoid the dual liability situation altogether by relisting with the same broker, rather than listing with another broker, a *relisting advantage* held by the original broker. The relisting should be by way of a modification of the expiration date (and any other terms) of the listing. Modification eliminates the need to register prospective buyers until the listing expires under the extension. [See **first tuesday** Form 120]

For the seller, re-listing with the same broker avoids any overlap of the prior broker's safety clause period and the new broker's listing period. Re-listing with the same broker also preserves the original listing agent's efforts spent educating the seller while marketing the property.

Safety clause vs. procuring cause

Sellers often confuse the workings of the safety clause with the open-listing or full-listing-offer theories of *procuring cause*. A broker is the procuring cause of a buyer and entitled to a fee when the broker holds an **open listing** and he or his agent is either:

- the *direct cause* of a sale to a buyer; or

- the cause of a *series of events* which result in a sale to the buyer.

Consider a broker who enters into an employment agreement with a lender to locate a person who will syndicate the purchase of trust deed loans *warehoused* by the lender, a process called *securitization*.

The agreement contains a fee provision calling for payment of a fee only if the broker or his agent **initiates a transaction** which is successfully completed. The agreement also contains a ten-year safety clause.

On expiration of the listing, the broker's agent hands the lender a list of several securities firms who create or represent trust deed investment pools which purchase trust deed notes in the secondary money market. None of the investment firms listed as prospective trust deed buyers enter into negotiations with the agent, much less complete a transaction with the lender which was initiated by the agent.

Later, an investment firm registered by the agent buys trust deeds from the lender.

The agent's broker discovers the transaction and demands a fee from the lender. The broker claims he is entitled to a fee since his agent **in-troduced the lender** to the firm which eventually purchased the loans within the ten-year safety period.

The lender claims the broker is not entitled to a fee since the broker was hired to **initiate and complete** a successful transaction, and he did not do so by merely registering the names of investment firms.

Is the broker entitled to a fee?

No! The broker is not entitled to a fee for merely registering the names of firms which his agent knew bought trust deed notes. The fee provision required the broker or his agent to be the *procuring cause* of a sale, not just naming, soliciting or negotiating with prospects. Payment of a fee is contingent on the broker's **initiation** of a transaction which is **successfully completed**. [**Hedging Concepts, Inc.** v. **First Alliance Mortgage Company** (1996) 41 CA4th 1410]

A fee agreement calling for a broker to be paid only if he is the *procuring cause* of the sale **automatically voids** any safety clause contained in the fee provision of a listing agreement. Thus, recovery under a safety clause and a procuring cause clause are inconsistent provisions — one or the other, but not both in the same document. [Delbon, *supra*]

Now consider a seller who employs a broker under a listing agreement which entitles the broker to a fee if he **locates a buyer** who eventually acquires the property.

During the listing, the broker or his listing agent has contact with a buyer resulting in the delivery of information on the listed property. The buyer has difficulty arranging purchase-assist financing. After several discussions, the listing agent no longer follows up on the buyer and they engage in no further negotiations.

On expiration of the listing, the property remains unsold. Three months later, the seller contacts the buyer to see if he is still interested in purchasing the property. Negotiations are resumed when the buyer ultimately arranges financing and is able to acquire the property. The listing agent discovers the sale and alerts his broker.

The broker then makes a demand on the seller for a fee, claiming he was the procuring cause of the sale since he presented the property to a buyer who remained interested in the property and eventually purchased it when financing became available.

The seller claims the broker is not entitled to a fee since the buyer acquired the property through negotiations commenced by the seller after the listing expired.

However, the broker is entitled to a fee. He was the **procuring cause** of the sale since the broker's contact with the buyer **set into motion** an uninterrupted chain or series of events, separated only by time, which eventually resulted in a sale. [**E. A. Strout Western Realty Agency, Inc.** v. **Lewis** (1967) 255 CA2d 254]

Editor's note — A safety clause in the listing agreement and registration of the prospective buyer would have avoided this dispute.

Chapter 12

Preparatory costs for marketing

This chapter reviews the marketing assistance a seller provides a listing agent by authorizing investigative reports regarding the listed property before it is marketed.

Greater transparency in a sale

An owner of a single-family residence (SFR) wants to list the property for sale with the brokerage office of an agent known to the owner.

The agent prepares an exclusive right-to-sell listing agreement form for review with the owner.

The agent also prepares an addendum (among others) in which he estimates the cost of third-party **investigative reports** needed to provide prospective buyers with information on the property. The reports are those which are always demanded by prudent buyers and careful buyer's agents for confirmation and approval by the buyer before closing escrow on a purchase of property.

The listing agent will present this listing package cost sheet addendum to the owner as a "seller's budget," also called an *authorization for preparatory charges*. As a disclosure, it sets the costs of those third-party reports the owner will most likely incur on a sale.

The cost sheet prepared by the agent estimates the cost of investigative reports prepared by other professionals or government agencies which will help put a face on the property so it can be better **evaluated by prospective buyers**. The recommended reports include an occupancy (transfer) certificate (by local ordinance), natural hazard disclosure (NHD), structural pest control report (and possible clearance), home inspection report, well water report and a septic tank report. [See Form 107 accompanying this chapter]

The reports will become part of the listing agent's **marketing package** for the sale of the listed property. The agent is aware the best way to market property and expose it to a prospective buyer who will actually enter into a purchase agreement without further negotiations prior to the close of escrow is to fully disclose the condition of the property when first dealing with the buyer.

Also, a **buyer's expectations** about the property are legally established based on his impression of the property at the time he enters into a purchase agreement, not later after the price has been set, escrow opened and the true condition of the property revealed to the buyer for the first time due to an in-escrow delivery of the reports. [**Jue** v. **Smiser** (1994) 23 CA4th 312]

Here, the owner has to make a choice as to when he will incur the expense of third-party reports, be it:

- **now,** when he lists the property for sale, so a purchase agreement entered into with a prospective buyer has a greater likelihood of closing due to the prior delivery of the reports to avert claims of deception about the property's existing condition; or

- **later,** after entering into a purchase agreement with a buyer who has already developed expectations about the property which will probably differ from the reports and, unless the owner repairs the defects or adjusts the price, will likely result in the buyer canceling the purchase agreement or closing escrow and demanding a return of the overpayment in price or the cost incurred for repairs. [Jue, *supra*]

The listing agent meets with the owner to review the listing agreement and its addenda.

DATE:_____, 20_____, at_____, California.

Items left blank or unchecked are not applicable.

1. FACTS:

1.1 This is an addendum to an employment agreement referred to as a Seller's Listing Agreement [ft Form 102]

1.2 Dated_____, 20_____, at _____, California

1.3 Entered into by:
Broker:_____
Seller: _____

1.4 Regarding property described as:_____

1.5 For a period beginning on _____, 20_____ and expiring on _____, 20_____.

2. BROKER'S DISCLOSURE AND PERFORMANCE:

2.1 The items listed below with estimated costs constitute a disclosure of the reports and activities Seller can reasonably expect will be required to either bring about or close a transaction under the employment agreement, and if acquired early, will assist Broker to provide prospective buyers with property information Broker anticipates he will need to effectively perform under the employment agreement.

   a. Natural hazard disclosure report . . . . $_____

   b. Local ordinance compliance certificate . . . . $_____

   c. Structural pest control report and ☐ clearance . . . . $_____

   d. Smoke detector and water heater anchor installation . . . . $_____

   e. Property (Home) inspection report . . . . $_____

   f. Association (CID) documents charge . . . . $_____

   g. Lead-based paint report . . . . $_____

   h. Mello Roos assessment notice . . . . $_____

   i. Listing (transaction) coordinator's fee . . . . $_____

   j. Well water quality and quantity report . . . . $_____

   k. Septic/sewer report . . . . $_____

   l. Soil report . . . . $_____

   m. Survey of property (civil engineer) . . . . $_____

   n. Appraisal report . . . . $_____

   o. Architectural (floor) plans . . . . $_____

   p. Title report: ☐ property profile, ☐ preliminary report, ☐ abstract . . . . $_____

   q. MLS and market session input fees . . . . $_____

   r. Sign deposit or purchase, installation and removal . . . . $_____

   s. Advertising in newspapers, magazines, radio or television . . . . $_____

   t. Information flyers and postage (handout or mailing) . . . . $_____

   u. Open house — food and spirits . . . . $_____

   v. Photos or video of the property . . . . $_____

   w. Credit report on prospective buyer . . . . $_____

   x. Travel expenses . . . . $_____

   y. _____ . . . . $_____

   z. _____ . . . . $_____

2.2 **TOTAL ESTIMATED COSTS** . . . . $_____

2.3 ☐ Broker is hereby authorized and instructed to incur on behalf of Seller the cost estimated above.

3. PAYMENT OF COSTS:

3.1 ☐ Seller agrees to pay, on presentation of a billing, those costs estimated above and incurred by Broker.

3.2 ☐ Broker agrees to incur the expenses of the estimated costs set out and authorized in section 2.3 during the first 21 days of the employment and to timely pay the charges. Seller agrees to reimburse Broker for the costs Broker incurs, if:

    a. Seller closes a transaction which is the subject of the employment agreement;

    b. Seller terminates the employment agreement by cancellation or by conduct before it expires; or

    c. Seller retains another Broker on the expiration of the employment agreement to pursue a transaction which is the subject of the employment agreement with Broker.

3.3 ☐ Costs paid by Seller under this addendum shall be credited toward any contingency fee earned by Broker upon closing a transaction which is the subject of the employment agreement.

3.4 Seller herewith hands Broker a deposit of $_____ as an advance for the payment of costs incurred by Broker on behalf of Seller as estimated above.

4. TRUST ACCOUNT: (To be filled out only if a deposit is entered at §3.4 above.)

4.1 Broker will place the advance cost deposit received under §3.4 above into his trust account maintained with _____
at their _____ branch.

4.2 Broker is authorized and instructed to disburse from the trust account deposit those amounts required to pay and satisfy the obligations incurred as agreed.

4.3 Within 10 days after each calendar ☐ month, or ☐ quarter, and upon termination of this agreement, Broker will deliver to Seller a statement of account for all funds withdrawn from the advance cost deposit handed Broker under §3.4 above.

4.4 Each statement of account delivered by Broker shall include no less than the following information:

    a. The amount of the advance cost deposit received.

    b. The amount of funds disbursed from the advance cost deposit.

    c. An itemization and description of the obligation paid on each disbursement.

    d. The current remaining balance of the advance cost deposit.

    e. An attached copy of any advertisements paid from the advance cost deposit since the last recorded accounting.

    f. _____

4.5 On termination of this agreement, Broker will return to Seller all remaining trust funds.

I agree to the terms stated above.

Date:_____, 20_____

Broker's name: _____

By: _____

I agree to the terms stated above.

Date:_____, 20_____

Seller's name: _____

Seller's Signature:_____

Seller's Signature:_____

The cost sheet is presented as an integral part of the agent's **marketing plan** to attract buyers willing to buy the property based on their full knowledge of its condition. The disclosures provide a competitive sales advantage over other apparently qualified properties which are marketed without reports to corroborate their condition.

Also, agents representing buyers are attracted to properties offered with all investigative third-party reports handed to them in a complete **listing package** (marketing package). With this package, property disclosures made to buyers through the use of third-party reports help reduce:

- the seller's exposure to liability under his duty to fully disclose his actual knowledge of the property's condition [Calif. Civil Code §1102.4]; and

- the listing agent's exposure to liability under his duty to personally inspect, observe and report his findings about a property's condition. [CC §2079]

Also, closing escrow on the purchase agreement will not be subject to the buyer's further-approval of the property conditions when all reports are delivered to the prospective buyer prior to entering into a purchase agreement.

The primary marketing advantage for the owner who provides prospective buyers with third-party reports is that the sale of the property is *transparent* at its inception since the price is based on property conditions "as disclosed" by the reports.

Avoided is the undisclosed (and prohibited) "as is" sale which leads inevitably to price renegotiations, repairs, or worse yet for all, cancellation of the purchase agreement or litigation for failing to disclose facts about material defects known when the purchase agreement was accepted. [CC §§1102.1, 2079]

Owner's motivation to sell

An owner's reaction to a listing agent's request for the owner to participate in an advantageous marketing plan by incurring the costs of property reports upfront offers the agent an insight into the extent of the owner's **motivation** to sell the property. The agent's goal, besides getting a listing, is to encourage and receive maximum cooperation from the owner in the sales effort.

An owner can "dress up " the property and enhance its "curb appeal" by cosmetic painting, landscaping and clean up. However, it is the **fundamentals about the property** which generate firm offers to purchase. It is to this end the owner is asked not only to list the property, but to be enthusiastic about disclosing the property's fundamentals to prospective buyers at the **earliest opportunity**.

However, the owner's motivation to sell may have more to do with his lack of available cash for loan payments than his desire to incur the cost of the reports needed to properly market the property. In the case of a financially distressed owner who is unwilling or unable to obtain expert third-party reports, the listing comes with a significant increase in the listing agent's risk of losing a sale due to a buyer's disapproval of contingencies involving in-escrow disclosures.

Also, an owner may not want to disclose the condition of the property until after he accepts a purchase agreement offer from a buyer. He will then make only those concessions necessary to keep the transaction together, or resell the property to a competing back-up buyer who has been fully informed about the property's condition. Such conduct by an owner is deceitful.

Here, the owner knows something fundamental about the property which negatively affects its value and he does not want to tell the buyer before entering into a purchase agreement. He would rather wait to make disclosures after the buyer has committed himself to purchase the property, a type of intentional seller fraud.

The best time for the listing agent to present the owner with the cost sheet is when the listing in entered into. If the owner really wants to sell and not just "test his price" in the market, he will respond in a positive manner to the agent's advice. If the owner's response is negative, the owner's intentions to quickly enter into a sales transaction with a likelihood of closing are probably suspect.

The owner's negative response to making property disclosures at the **earliest opportunity** is an indicator of the level of future cooperation in marketing, contracting to sell and closing an escrow which the agent can expect to encounter from the owner.

Brokerage fee considerations

The amount of the brokerage fee sought by a listing agent on a property is implicitly related to:

- the price sought by the owner of the property;

- the time and effort the agent will spend servicing the listing; and

- the probability of actually locating a buyer and closing a sale.

After analyzing these implications, it is the likelihood the property will sell and the broker receive a fee that causes a broker and his listing agent to agree to a listing in the first place, on terms and for a fee which are reasonable under the circumstances.

Consider a broker who requires his agents to attach a cost sheet to all listings. By including the addendum, the owner will (or will not) authorize the listing agent to order out reports needed to more effectively market the property and screen prospective buyers. The broker requires the cost sheet addendum to increase the productivity of his agents. Property reports reduce the time spent closing a purchase agreement since the purchase agreement has been **preceded by disclosures**, rather than the reverse order of events.

As part of the listing agent's negotiations to set the fee for a commissionable event, the agent is instructed by his broker to first attempt to get the owner to authorize the immediate purchase of the necessary reports. If the owner concedes the reports are necessary, but wants to wait until a buyer is located, the listing agent, to overcome the objections, might then negotiate terms to acquire the immediate authority to order reports.

As an economic inducement, the broker, through his agent, might offer to **offset the fee** earned on a sale by the amount of the cost of the reports (but not for the amount of any corrective work undertaken on the owner's property). [See Form 107 §3.3]

Alternatively, a reduction in the brokerage fee by one-quarter to one percent, or more, might be offered to induce the owner to assist in the marketing process by paying for the reports now. The reduced fee would reflect the greater likelihood of a successful closing of a sale, devoid of complications before or after closing.

Thus, the fee ultimately agreed to reflects:

- the reduced time and effort necessary to service the listing;

- the reduced risk of loss of the time, effort and money invested in the listing by the broker and the listing agent; and

- a more effective marketing plan, which, on average, will produce more transactions annually for the broker.

Making a sales transaction more transparent for buyers always rewards the brokers and agents for their professionalism in this and future transactions.

Requesting authority

When preparing the cost sheet authorizing the agent to incur the cost of preparatory reports, cost estimates will be entered on items which will ultimately be required to close a sale. If an owner should refuse to incur the cost of third-party reports on the sale of his property, then a prudent buyer will incur them (on the advise of his agent). In turn, the buyer will inevitably use the reports against the owner as a "punch list" for demanding repairs and replacements to be completed before the buyer will close escrow.

Thus, for an owner selling property, it is best to get the reports sooner rather than later. The same holds true for implementing the listing agent's marketing plan for the property.

It is worth noting that none of the listed items on the cost sheet are part of the broker's overhead for maintaining a brokerage office. All the costs listed, if incurred, are related solely to the condition of the property listed, marketed and sold. They are incurred to **establish the condition** of the owner's property, not to pay for the services of the broker and the listing agent. Thus, the cost rightly should be paid by the owner and not borne by the broker or the listing agent.

Further, since the reports are of assistance to the listing agent in the marketing of the property, the costs should be incurred by the owner at the time of the listing. Thus, the reports would be received before the listing agent puts the property on the market. It is always helpful to know the nature and condition of the property you are marketing since the knowledge reduces omissions and misstatements. [Jue, *supra*]

Occasionally, a reticent broker or agent will entertain the thought that some brokers do not ask owners for authority to order reports before a property is sold. And since the competition doesn't ask, why should they ask, lest they lose listings to other brokers by asking owners to spend money on property reports. One supposes these reticent brokers and listing agents should then themselves advance the cost of these reports in the hope the property will sell and they receive a fee to cover their advances.

Business cycles in real estate sales may also influence a broker's desire to request authorization to obtain property reports for a listing package. During periods of rising prices, disclosures seem less likely to occur as sellers become greedy and demanding while buyers are anxious and permissive. Both sellers and buyers drop their guard in a deliberate effort to meet their objectives. Brokers and their agents are too often accommodating of the lax environment. The failures only lay dormant until the next recession when the inevitable drop in property values bring some of the failures to litigation.

Conversely, during periods of decreased sales volume with buyers more selective and buyer's agents increasingly more protective of their clients, the owner will have to step forward to fund the cost of reports in order to "sell" the property. The listing agent with property reports in hand has a better listing package, and thus a better disclosed and more certain set of property conditions than competing, under-disclosed properties.

When to pay

When filling out the cost sheet, an owner has choices as to when and how he will pay for the cost of the reports.

The owner may agree to pay the charges directly to the third-party vendors when billed, in which case the agent coordinates the arrangements for payment with the vendors. While the owner's check is payable to the vendor, not the broker, if it is handed to the listing agent for delivery to the vendor, the check constitutes *trust funds* which require an entry in the trust fund ledger maintained by the listing agent's broker. [See Form 107 §3.1]

On the other hand, the owner may deposit the estimated cost of the reports with the broker by making the check payable to the broker, called *advance costs*. The broker would then pay the charges from the deposit when billed by the reporting service. [See Form 107 §3.2]

Advance costs as trust funds

Funds advanced by a client directly to a broker belong to the client.

The broker must place all advance deposits received in the broker's name in a trust account, whether they are advances for future costs or fees. [Calif. Business and Professions Code §10146]

The cost sheet authorizes the broker to disburse the client's funds from the trust account **only** as costs are incurred.

When the listing terminates, the broker must return all remaining trust funds to the client. The broker **cannot** use trust funds to offset any fees the client still owes him.

At least every calendar quarter, the broker must give the client a statement accounting for all funds held in trust. A monthly mailing of a copy of the client's trust account ledger would create a better business relationship.

A final accounting must be made when the listing agreement expires. Again, if any funds remain in trust, they must be returned to the client with this accounting. [Bus & P C §10146]

The **statement of account** for the trust funds must include the following information:

- the amount of the deposit toward advance costs;

- the amount of each disbursement of funds from the trust account;

- an itemized description of the cost obligation paid on each disbursement;

- the current remaining balance of the advance cost deposit; and

- an attached copy of any advertisements paid for from the advance cost deposit.

Lastly, the broker must keep all accounting records for at least three years and make them available to the Department of Real Estate (DRE) on request. [Bus & P C §10148]

A broker who fails to place those advance deposits payable to the broker in his trust account, or who later fails to deliver proper trust account statements to his client, is **presumed** to be guilty of embezzlement. [**Burch** v. **Argus Properties, Inc.** (1979) 92 CA3d 128]

Chapter 13

"For Sale" sign regulations

This chapter discusses a property owner's right to display signs advertising his property "For Sale."

Property owners can display

Consider an owner of a residential unit in a common interest development (CID), such as a condominium project, who places a "For Sale" sign in the window of his unit.

A neighbor in the project complains about the sign to the homeowners' association (HOA) which manages the project. In response, the HOA makes a demand on the owner to remove the sign claiming the sign is a violation of the conditions, covenants and restrictions (CC&Rs) controlling conduct in the project.

Can an owner place a "For Sale" sign in the window of his unit where it can be seen by others when the display is in violation of the HOA's CC&Rs or policy statements?

Yes! Owners of real estate and their brokers have the right to display "For Sale" signs of reasonable dimension and design on their property, or on property owned by others if they have their **consent**, in spite of title restrictions in the CC&Rs. [Calif. Civil Code §712]

The "For Sale" sign displayed on the property being sold by the owner or his agents, or displayed on other private property with that owner's consent, may contain:

- advertising stating the property is for sale, lease or exchange;

- directions to the property;

- the owner's or agent's name; and

- the owner's or agent's address and telephone number.

However, the sign or location of a "For Sale" sign must not adversely affect public safety or impede the safe flow of vehicular traffic.

Further, any local governmental ordinance which attempts to **bar or unreasonably restrict** the placement of a real estate "For Sale" sign on the property for sale, or private property owned by others who have consented to the placement of a directional "For Sale" sign on their property, is unenforceable. [CC §713]

Reasonably located on-site signs

"For Sale" signs may be reasonably located in plain view for the public to observe. [CC §§712, 713]

For example, in a CID, the boundaries of a unit owned as the separate interest of a member of the CID are the walls, windows, floors and ceilings. If the CC&Rs of the CID do not state otherwise, the interior surface of the perimeter walls, floors, ceilings, windows, doors, outlets and airspace located within a unit are considered the owner's separate interest. All other portions of the walls, floors, ceilings and real estate are part of the common area maintained and managed by the HOA. [CC §1351(l)]

Thus, the owner is entitled to display a "For Sale" sign on the **interior side** of the window of his condominium unit. The interior side of the window belongs to the owner and placing of the sign in the window is reasonable.

However, if the owner seeks to display the sign on the exterior wall or ground area surrounding his unit, the owner must obtain the permission of the HOA since the exterior walls and ground area are part of the common area, **owned by others**, specifically, the undivided ownership interest held by all the owners of units in the CID or the HOA. [CC §712]

Reasonable restrictions

Now consider a city which prohibits the display of all "For Sale" signs to stop perceived white-flight from a racially integrated city.

A property owner and his listing agent claim the ban is an unconstitutional interference with real estate sales, called a *restraint on alienation,* and violates the owner's freedom of speech.

The city claims the sign prohibition is constitutional since it does not prohibit other ways in which to advertise property for sale, only those advertisements located on the property.

Is the city ordinance a reasonable restriction on the display of "For Sale" signs?

No! Prohibiting the display of "For Sale" signs is a violation of the First Amendment freedom of speech right since other methods of advertising real estate for sale are less effective and the ordinance prohibits the free flow of truthful commercial information. [**Linmark Associates, Inc.** v. **Township of Willingboro** (1977) 431 US 85]

Further, cities and counties may not prohibit the placement of "For Sale" signs on private property, be it the property to be sold or property owned by others who consent to a directional sign being placed on their property. However, government agencies may determine the location, shape and dimensions of "For Sale" signs to ensure the signs do not affect public safety, including traffic safety. [CC §713]

Cities and counties restrict the display of "For Sale" signs on private property through ordinances, nuisance laws or building requirements. Restrictions may vary between residential and industrial zones, and among cities. Copies of "For Sale" sign ordinances controlling their use on private property are available through the city and county planning departments.

Additionally, HOAs cannot prohibit owners of units in a CID from displaying "For Sale" signs within the owner's separately owned land areas if the sign complies with state law and local ordinances. [CC §712]

A copy of a HOA's governing documents and CC&Rs controlling the dimensions and design of "For Sale" signs are available from the HOA.

Signs on right-of-ways and alongside public highways

The display or placement of a "For Sale" sign on a private or public right-of-way, such as roadways, may be limited or regulated by local government agencies. [CC §713]

Further, a directional sign advertising real estate for sale, lease or exchange that is located on property other than the property advertised for sale and visible from a highway which is subject to the federal Highway Beautification Act requires a **special permit** be obtained from the Director of Transportation of the State of California before the sign may be erected. [Calif. Business and Professions Code §§5200 et seq.]

Locating signs off-site

Consider an agent who, on behalf of a seller of real estate, advertises the seller's property by placing a directional "For Sale" sign on a neighbor's property without first obtaining the neighbor's permission.

The neighbor discovers the "For Sale" sign on his property and removes it. However, the seller's agent continues to replace the sign on weekends without permission from the neighbor.

Does the neighbor have recourse against the broker?

Yes! Placing a sign on private property without the **property owner's permission** is a misdemeanor public nuisance. Preventing a public nuisance is the responsibility of local government authorities on a complaint from the owner who does not consent to the placement of directional signs. [Calif. Penal Code §§556.1, 556.3]

Further, if a property owner or a real estate agent places a "For Sale" or a directional sign on public property without permission, such as on a sidewalk right-of-way or at the curbside, the placement is also a misdemeanor public nuisance. [Pen C §556]

Cities and counties often refuse or severely limit the granting of permission for placement of "For Sale" signs on public property, such as street corners, choosing to strictly enforce the penalties allowed by the California Penal Code. [Pen C §556]

When government agencies do allow "For Sale" signs, they are usually by a special permit and payment of use fees, and allowed only for the sale of parcels in a subdivider's development.

Mobilehomes

A mobilehome owner can place a "For Sale" sign:

- in the window of his mobilehome; or

- outside the mobilehome facing the street.

Signs posted outside of the mobilehome can be of an H-frame or A-frame design and must face the street, but cannot extend into the street. [CC §798.70]

Signs in mobilehome parks may be up to 24 inches wide and 36 inches high, and may contain the name, address and telephone number of the mobilehome owner or the owner's agent.

The right to display mobilehome "For Sale" signs extends to brokers, joint tenants, heirs or a representative of a mobilehome owner's estate who acquires ownership of a mobilehome on the owner's death.

Also, mobilehome owners and their agents can display an "open house" sign in the same locations as "For Sale" signs, if the mobilehome park does not prohibit open house signs.

Tubes or holders for leaflets with information on the mobilehome being advertised may be attached to either the "For Sale" sign or to the mobilehome. [CC §798.70]

Chapter 14

Operating under a buyer's listing

This chapter reviews the benefits accruing to a buyer and his broker when they enter into an employment agreement authorizing the broker and his agents to act on behalf of the buyer to locate property.

A prerequisite to representation

Most brokers have come to the realization that a signed buyer's listing agreement is the minimum commitment necessary from a buyer to produce the maximum financial return for the time, effort and money brokers and their agents invest when assisting buyers as their representative in negotiations.

A buyer's agent need not and should not require a lesser commitment from a buyer than a listing agent requires from a seller for his services. A buyer's brokers needs to assure himself he will be paid a fee for his services before commencing efforts to locate qualifying properties for a buyer. To accomplish this level of financial certainty, a buyer's broker must enter into a written employment agreement with a prospective buyer, called a *buyer's exclusive right-to-buy listing agreement.* [See **first tuesday** Form 103]

A buyer who refuses to enter into a written listing agreement provides the broker and his agent with a clear understanding that this buyer does not want a representative. What this unlisted buyer wants is someone to act as a **locator** or **finder** of properties without any entitlement to the collection of compensation for the assistance.

An agent who actually assists a buyer who refuses the agent's solicitation to enter into a listing agreement will soon discover the buyer has turned to a friend or relative who is licensed to submit an offer on the property. Alternatively, the buyer may simply submit an offer directly to the listing agent or seller himself.

Without the buyer's written promise to pay a fee, the buyer's broker will not be entitled to receive a fee should the buyer acquire property by "going around" the broker. No fee has been earned which is collectable from anyone, unless a fee-sharing agreement exists with the listing broker registering the buyer's name. [See **first tuesday** Form 105]

More importantly, it is unreasonable for a broker and his agent to expect to receive a fee, no matter who is to pay it, for working with a buyer who acquires property located and presented to him by them, unless the broker has been retained under a written employment agreement with the buyer. [**Phillippe v. Shapell Industries, Inc.** (1987) 43 C3d 1247]

The fee-payment bargain

When an agent solicits employment by a prospective buyer of real estate with the intent of generating fees for his broker, and in turn for himself, various working relationships and compensation arrangements may be struck with the buyer.

Some arrangements for the payment of fees are at best tenuous, especially when the buyer's agent fails to obtain any fee commitment from the buyer, oral or written. Others are astutely built on written promises, signed by the buyer and broker, which call for payment of a fee should the buyer acquire property. Writings, by their nature, are intended by all who enter into them to be enforced, such as a signed buyer's listing calling for payment of a fee when the buyer's objective of acquiring property is met.

Here are several situations which demonstrate the various likelihoods of collecting a fee for assisting a buyer:

1. **No listing exists.** Neither the seller nor the buyer have employed a broker. Typically, the real estate involved is other than an owner-occupied residential property. Also, the seller is usually an experienced real estate investor, subdivider, land speculator, REO lender or other well-seasoned owner who is capable of negotiating a real estate transaction without representation.

   The buyer is usually as experienced as the seller, being a builder, developer, syndicator, professional real estate investor or speculator, but may also be an inexperienced buyer of real estate who believes he possesses the business acumen needed to handle the real estate negotiations by himself. Thus, all the principals feel they do not need a broker to represent them and negotiate the sale or purchase of properties. However, they do need someone or some medium to bring them together as a match.

   Editor's note — It is this class of buyer who occasionally induces a broker or sales agent to bring properties to their attention. What the buyer lacks, and seeks to get from anyone willing to act, is a locator or finder who will bring him qualifying properties. If asked, the buyer will always orally assure the broker or sales agent their fee will be protected. Unlisted sellers are more blunt, telling the agent to simply bring them offers.

2. **"A one-shot" seller's listing exists.** A buyer is willing to make an offer through the agent who brought a property to the buyer's attention. Both the seller and buyer are typically sophisticated principals.

Here, the agent fails to ask the buyer to enter into an exclusive right-to-buy listing. Obliquely, the agent solicits and obtains a "one-shot" right-to-sell listing from the seller before the agent will submit the buyer's offer to the seller. The seller's listing contains a promise to pay a fee. Sometimes the separate fee agreement is the one intended to accompany the offer, which is neither identified nor yet submitted.

This brokerage situation comes about primarily because the purchase agreement the agent is told to use does not include a fee provision requiring someone to pay a fee should the buyer eventually acquire the property.

Here, the buyer is not solicited to agree to pay a fee under a buyer's listing and the broker has mistakenly instructed his agent to list the seller before submitting an offer.

3. **Customer turned client.** An agent of a broker with several listed properties is contacted by a prospective buyer. The buyer is exposed to all the "in-house" listings, none of which are suitable or of interest to the buyer. Having exhausted the in-house inventory of listings, the agent can either see the buyer off or make arrangements with the buyer to look into qualifying properties listed by other brokers or into unlisted properties For Sale By Owners (FSBOs), and when located, present them to the buyer.

   If the buyer agrees to allow the agent to locate qualifying properties, the agent **must ask** the buyer to sign a buyer's listing agreement if his broker is to be assured payment of a fee when the buyer acquires property. If the buyer refuses to enter into a buyer's listing, the agent might still proceed to assist the buyer to locate property.

Should the buyer later make an offer prepared by the agent, a purchase agreement form must be used which places the fee provision in the **body of the buyer's offer** if the agent is to protect his fee.

On failing to obtain a signed listing, the buyer's agent should enter into a fee-sharing arrangement with the listing office for the property specifically naming (registering) the prospective buyer so the time and effort of the buyer's agent is protected should the buyer "go around" the agent and acquire the property. [See **first tuesday** Form 105]

4. **A buyer's listing agreement exists.** An agent's broker is employed in writing under a signed exclusive right-to-buy listing agreement to represent the buyer by locating and negotiating the purchase of suitable property of the type sought by the buyer. A seller of suitable property may or may not have signed a seller's listing agreement with another broker. Either way, the buyer's broker controls the amount and destiny of the fee he is to be paid when his buyer buys.

Providing expertise without a writing

One should sense, on a review of the four basic fee arrangements available to buyer's brokers and their agents, that the lack of a written fee agreement with a buyer when representing the buyer is a failure to exercise prudent judgment in the management of a brokerage business.

Yet many buyer's agents fail to ask their buyer for a written commitment to assure payment of a fee on the buyer's purchase of property. Occasionally, buyer's agents are inexplicably willing to work for a buyer who, when asked, refuses to enter into a buyer's listing agreement.

Consider a real estate agent who is fairly knowledgeable about subdividable and developable land for the construction and sale of single-family residences. Most of the parcels of land known to the agent are not listed since the sellers are experienced speculators and investors who will not enter into employment contracts with brokers, be they open, exclusive agency or exclusive right-to-sell employment agreements.

The agent contacts prospective buyers. One is a builder who expresses an interest in acquiring land for development. The agent tells the buyer he expects a 10% fee should the buyer acquire any of the properties the broker presents to him. The buyer agrees he will pay the fee, or see to it that the seller pays the fee. When asked, the buyer refuses to sign a buyer's listing agreement.

Undeterred, the agent exposes the builder to numerous parcels, one of which the builder would like to acquire. The agent assists in the builder's due diligence investigation, gathering significant portions of the data on the property. Correspondence during the due diligence investigation, signed and sent by the agent, reminds the builder of his obligation to pay or protect the 10% brokerage fee if he acquires the property. The builder never once mentions the fee in any of his correspondence to the agent (or in writings to anyone else).

The builder, having had contact with the seller during the initial due diligence investigation, prepares his own purchase agreement offer and submits it directly to the seller. A fee provision is not included in the purchase agreement. The transaction is closed and the agent's broker does not receive a fee.

The broker makes a demand on the builder for payment of the promised fee, which the builder now refuses to pay. The builder claims the broker cannot enforce a promise to pay a brokerage fee unless the buyer who made the promise has signed a writing evidencing his promise to do so.

The broker claims a writing is not necessary to document the builder's promise to pay a fee since the builder induced the broker's agent to enter into an agency relationship with the builder, which the agent faithfully and fully performed. Further, the builder relied on the agent's services with the deceitful intent of benefitting from the services and acquiring the property without payment of a fee.

Can the broker enforce collection of the fee?

No! All **promises to pay** or assurances of the payment of a brokerage fee on a real estate transaction are required by the Statute of Frauds to be reduced to a writing signed by the person who agreed a fee would be paid, regardless of whether the fee would be paid by that person or by another party to the transaction. [Phillippe, *supra*]

Here, the dilemma the broker and his agent face when a buyer refuses to sign a buyer's listing agreement, be it an open or exclusive listing, is the decision to either:

- **terminate the solicitation** of employment by this buyer and locate other buyers willing to agree in writing to pay a fee for the broker's and agent's valuable services; or

- **undertake the representation** of the buyer and hope to finesse the inclusion of a fee provision in a purchase agreement offer should one be prepared by the broker and signed by the buyer.

The agent chose the second approach and lost. The unlisted buyer prepared his own offer and "went around" the agent and his broker.

Buyer's agent lists the property

In an example of a "one-shot" listing, an agent for a broker assists a prospective buyer who wants to acquire nonresidential income property. The agent does not ask the buyer to sign an employment agreement since the agent (mistakenly) believes he may only contract with sellers or listing brokers regarding the payment of his fee. Also, the agent's broker requires the agent to use purchase agreement forms which fail to include fee provisions in the buyer's offer. Thus, the buyer's agent is left to negotiate the fee arrangements with the seller (or the seller's broker), rather than arranging with the buyer to set the amount the seller will pay in the buyer's offer.

A seller of real estate who has not listed his property for sale has released information on the property's income and physical condition with the understanding he will "cooperate with brokers" by paying a brokerage fee to any broker who **produces a prospective buyer** who purchases the property.

The buyer's agent brings the property to the attention of his prospective buyer, along with several other properties available for purchase. After further investigation on behalf of the buyer, the seller's property appears suitable for acquisition by the buyer.

However, before preparing a purchase offer for the buyer to sign, the agent believes (or is instructed by his broker) that before submitting an offer, he must first obtain a written fee agreement signed by the seller which employs the broker (and thus himself) so payment of a fee is assured.

As a result, the buyer's agent solicits the seller to sign a "one-day" or "one-shot" listing. The agent does not inform the seller of his efforts as a buyer's agent spent locating property on behalf of the prospective buyer, although an agency law disclosure is attached to the listing.

The seller agrees to the "one-shot" listing and signs a listing agreement prepared by the agent. On obtaining the listing, the agent prepares an offer which his prospective buyer signs. On submission to the seller, the offer is accepted forming a binding purchase agreement. Again, the agency relationship with the buyer is not disclosed to the seller.

Prior to closing the transaction, the seller discovers the prospective buyer was represented by the agent as a client of the broker at the time of the listing.

The seller immediately cancels the supplemental escrow instructions, unsigned by the buyer, which authorizes escrow to pay the agent's broker a fee. The sales escrow is closed and the buyer acquires the property. No fee is received by the broker. In turn, the sales agent receives no fee.

At no time did the buyer agree in writing to the payment by anyone of a fee to the broker. Thus, the buyer does not owe a fee since he did not make a written commitment or interfere with payment of the fee.

The broker makes a demand on the seller for payment of a fee, claiming the broker and his agent had fully performed under the listing. The seller claims he does not owe a fee since, prior to entering into the listing agreement, the broker's agent failed to disclose the **pre-existing agency relationship** with the buyer which was established when the agent assisted the buyer to locate suitable property.

In this situation, can the broker enforce collection of the fee agreed to by the seller in the listing, the purchase agreement and the escrow instructions?

No! Before becoming employed by a seller to negotiate the sale of property with a prospective buyer who is already represented by the broker, the existence of the agency relationship previously created (by conduct) with the prospective buyer to locate suitable property must be disclosed to the seller. It is a fact which might alter the seller's decision to sell or his negotiations with the buyer if he decides to sell.

Here, the seller thought the agent (and his broker) represented only the seller, not both the seller and the buyer. Accordingly, the minimum liability of the broker to the seller for the **undisclosed dual agency** is the loss of his fee for failure to faithfully represent the seller due to an undisclosed conflict of interest. [**L. Byron Culver & Associates** v. **Jaoudi Industrial & Trading Corporation** (1991) 1 CA4th 300]

The proper structuring of a provision and documentation of the brokerage fee by a broker and his agent who are already assisting a prospective buyer to locate and acquire property is to either:

- **enter** into a written employment agreement with the buyer, called a buyer's listing, then **prepare** a purchase agreement offer on a form which places the fee provision within the terms of the buyer's offer, stating the exact amount of the fee and who will pay it, and **submit** the purchase agreement offer to the seller for acceptance without ever entering into an employment agreement under any type of listing with the seller; or

- if the buyer refuses to sign a buyer's listing agreement, **prepare**, at the earliest opportunity, an offer to buy on a purchase agreement formatted with the fee provision located within the body of the buyer's signed offer, and **submit** the offer without ever entering into a listing agreement with the seller.

Converting a prospect into a client

A brokerage office which has been marketing its inventory of listed properties is contacted by a buyer who is interested in properties of the type they offer for sale. The properties were listed by several different agents in the office, each called the *listing agent* when referring to the listing they took. The broker's agent contacted by the buyer is referred to as the *selling agent* by the other agents in the office. The selling agent loosely refers to the unlisted buyer as his "customer."

Editor's note — Even though the agent who will provide the prospective buyer with information on "in-house listings" is called the "selling agent," neither the agent nor the broker have yet conducted themselves in a manner which raises the legal stature of their relationship with the buyer to that of the buyer's agent.

The buyer is furnished information on various properties listed by the office. None of the properties attract the buyer's interest. In the process of reviewing data on listed properties with the buyer, the agent has developed a good understanding of the type, price range, price-to-earnings ratios and location desired for property sought by the buyer. Also, the agent has determined the prospective buyer is financially capable of acquiring property and has not yet employed a broker to locate properties and negotiate a purchase on his behalf.

The agent, having made a diligent effort to provide information and sell property listed with his broker, now has to choose between:

- soliciting and establishing a continuing working relationship with the buyer as a *buyer's agent* to locate qualifying properties and assist with the investigation and determination as to whether the property meets the buyer's acquisition standards; or

- restricting his brokerage activities to advising the prospective buyer that he will be contacted when property which fits the parameters of his investment objectives is listed with the agent's broker.

The broker and agent opt to undertake an **agency relationship** with the buyer in order to work diligently to locate and investigate available properties on behalf of the buyer.

The buyer, who has until now been treated as a customer, is now asked to become a **client**. As a client, he authorizes the agent to act on behalf of the buyer to locate and look into properties unlisted, but known to be on the market or listed with other brokers. The buyer agrees.

The agent explains the brokerage office needs written authorization employing them as the buyer's agent in order to contact listing brokers and sellers on the buyer's behalf. Again, the buyer agrees. An exclusive right-to-buy listing agreement is prepared by the agent and signed by the buyer, who now becomes a client entitled to the agent's *utmost care and diligence* in the locating and analyzing of properties for purchase.

Thus, the agent converted a prospective buyer from a **customer** who contacted the office inquiring about property they had listed, into a **client** on whose behalf the entire office of agents can act (under their broker) as the **buyer's agent**. Thus, the office is assured payment of a fee should the buyer acquire property during the listing period or the following safety clause period, whether the property purchased is located by agents in the office or by anyone else (including the buyer).

Agency duties owed to buyers

The special agency duties owed to a buyer when a broker and his agents undertake to locate property on behalf of the buyer first arise when the broker:

- enters into an exclusive right-to-buy agreement with the buyer; or

- presents property information to an unlisted buyer who they have agreed to assist by locating qualifying properties.

When representing a buyer under a written exclusive right-to-buy employment agreement, the broker (and his agents) have entered into a *bilateral employment agreement*. Such an employment obligates the broker, through his agents, to exercise *due diligence* by way of a constant and continuing search to locate qualifying properties, while keeping the buyer informed of their progress.

Without an exclusive right-to-buy listing, the brokerage duties which exist to locate properties for a buyer are *best-effort obligations* created by an oral (or written) open listing, called a *unilateral employment agreement*. A **best-effort obligation** requires no affirmative action (diligence) on the part of the broker's office to locate property.

However, under a buyer's listing, be it exclusive or open, the act of **delivering property information** to the buyer they are assisting obligates the broker and his agents to use due diligence in their efforts to:

- **gather readily available data** on the property under review;

- **assist in the analysis** of the property data gathered; and

- **advise the buyer** regarding the property and any proposed transaction in a conscientious effort to act honestly, care for and protect the buyer's best interests.

When acting as the buyer's agent regarding the acquisition of a particular property, due diligence includes disclosing facts about the integrity of the property and recommending investigative activity which the agent knows might influence the buyer's conduct in negotiations.

Without an exclusive employment with a buyer on whose behalf the agent is locating properties, the agent is reduced to a mere "locator" or "finder." Worse yet, the agent is burdened with the affirmative agency duties of utmost care and protection owed the buyer when undertaking a review of data on a property with the unlisted buyer.

Provisions for payment of a fee

An exclusive right-to-buy agreement contains the same operative provisions as are found in exclusive right-to-sell agreements. [See **first tuesday** Form 103]

In exchange for the broker's promise to use *due diligence* while rendering services to comply with his end of the employment bargain, the buyer promises in the exclusive right-to-buy listing agreement to pay the broker a specific fee — either a fixed dollar amount or a percentage of the price paid. The fee is earned when the buyer enters into a binding purchase agreement during the (buyer's) listing period to acquire the type of property described in the buyer's listing.

However, buyers, like sellers, often do not enter into a purchase agreement during the period of employment. Thus, on expiration of the listing, the buyer's broker has not earned a fee. An event triggering payment of the promised fee has not yet occurred.

However, the fee provision of a buyer's listing agreement contains a *safety clause*. The clause provides protection to the broker and his agent after the employment expires from the loss of their time, effort and money "invested" during the employment period to assist the buyer. [See **first tuesday** Form 103 §5.1(c); see Chapter 11]

Thus, the broker of the buyer's agent will be entitled to a fee if, within an agreed-to period after the expiration of the buyer's listing:

- information specific to the property was provided to the buyer by the buyer's agent during the listing period;

- on expiration of the buyer's listing, the buyer is handed an itemized list which identifies those properties the buyer's agent brought to the buyer's attention, as required to *perfect* the broker's right to a fee [See **first tuesday** Form 123];

- the buyer entered into negotiations with the owner of a registered property; and

- the safety-period negotiations ultimately resulted in the buyer acquiring an interest in the property.

Buyer's liability for the brokerage fee

While the buyer under a listing agreement promises to pay a full brokerage fee on the acquisition of property (typically 6% of the purchase price), the buyer will nearly always close the purchase without directly paying the promised brokerage fee. Further, the buyer's broker will typically **accept a fee** equal to no less than one-half of the fee the buyer agreed to pay under the buyer's listing when the property purchased by the buyer is listed with another broker (who it is presumed has done his half of the work).

Can the broker enforce the fee arrangement in the buyer's listing and recover the remaining 3% from the buyer when the seller pays a lesser fee than the buyer agreed to pay?

No! The buyer's obligation to pay the brokerage fee is **fully satisfied** when the buyer's broker agrees to accept a fee from the seller or the seller's broker, which is nearly always the case. [See **first tuesday** Form 103 §5.2]

Benefits for the listed buyer

Like sellers, buyers may resist making a written commitment to exclusively employ one brokerage office as their agent to locate and negotiate the purchase of real estate on their behalf. However, listed buyers reap benefits unavailable to those buyers who are not exclusively represented by a broker and his agents. Without representation, the unlisted buyer is on his own to conduct a random search among available properties to locate a suitable property.

However, brokers and their agents have access to data which is often not made publicly available to buyers, such as multiple listing service (MLS) printouts, new listings, database searches for qualifying properties, property profiles and comparable sales data provided to brokers and agents by title companies and other brokers.

The activities of a buyer's agent also include pre-qualifying their buyer with a capable lender and advising the buyer on the location of qualifying properties, the socio-economic mix of neighborhoods, schools and their reputations, local bus lines, religious facilities, zoning, and subdivision and common interest development (CID) restrictions on property usage. Also, agents attend numerous marketing sessions and trade meetings for the sole purpose of sharing information on listed properties and properties sought by buyers.

All this general information is centrally controlled, channelled and best understood by brokers and agents. It is their business. Thus, when entering into a buyer's listing agreement employing a broker and his agents, a buyer bargains for this insider information to help make decisions which will make the ownership of real estate more viable.

Chapter 15

The buyer's listing agreement

This chapter presents the buyer's exclusive right-to-buy listing agreement with instructions for an agent's use of the form.

Analyzing the buyer's listing

The exclusive right-to-buy listing agreement, **first tuesday** Form 103, is used by a broker and his agents to prepare and submit the broker's offer to act as a prospective buyer's *exclusive real estate agent* employed to locate property sought by the buyer in exchange for the buyer's **assurance a fee will be paid** the broker if the buyer acquires the type of property sought during the listing period. [See Form 103 accompanying this chapter]

Formal documentation of an obligation to pay a fee — a written agreement signed by the buyer — is the legislatively enacted and judicially mandated requisite to the right to enforce collection of a brokerage fee through or from the buyer.

Each section in Form 103 has a separate purpose and need for enforcement. The sections include:

1. *Brokerage services*: The employment period for rendering brokerage services, the broker's due diligence obligations and any advance deposits are set forth in sections 1, 2 and 3. General provisions for enforcement of the employment agreement and broker fee-splitting arrangements are included in section 4.

2. *Brokerage fee*: The buyer's obligation to either pay a brokerage fee or assure payment of the brokerage fee by the seller or a listing broker, the amount of the fee and when the fee is due are set forth in section 5.

3. *Property sought*: A general description of the type of property to be located for the buyer is set forth in section 6.

4. *Signatures and identification of the parties*: On completion of entries on the listing form and any attached addenda, the buyer and the broker (or his agent) sign the document consenting to the employment.

Preparing the buyer's listing agreement

The following instructions are for the preparation and use of the Buyer's Listing Agreement, **first tuesday** Form 103, with which a buyer employs a broker as his exclusive agent to locate suitable property for the buyer to acquire.

Each instruction corresponds to the provision in the form bearing the same number.

*Editor's note — **Check** and **enter** items throughout the agreement in each provision with boxes and blanks, unless the provision is not intended to be included as part of the final agreement, in which case it is left unchecked or blank.*

Document identification:

Enter the date and name of the city where the listing is prepared. This date is used when referring to this listing agreement.

1. **Retainer period**:

   1.1 *Listing start and end date*: **Enter** the date the brokerage services are to commence.

   Enter the expiration date of the employment period. The expiration must be set as a specific date on which the employment ends since an exclusive listing is being established.

2. Broker's obligations:

2.1 *Broker's/agent's duty*: The broker and his agents promise to use diligence in their effort to locate the property sought by the buyer. The agency duties a broker and his agents owe the buyer are always implied, if not expressed in writing.

2.2 *Agency Law Disclosure*: **Check** the box if an Agency Law Disclosure is to be attached as an addendum to this agreement, and if so, **fill out** and **attach** the form.

3. Buyer's deposit:

3.1 *Advance fees and costs*: **Enter** the amount of deposit negotiated to commence the brokerage services.

Check the box for each form to be attached as an addendum and **fill out** and **attach** the forms detailing the services to be rendered or costs to be incurred and charged against the deposit. [See **first tuesday** Forms 106 and 107]

4. General provisions:

4.1 *Attorney fees*: **Entitles** the prevailing party to attorney fees if litigation results from the buyer's failure to pay fees or the broker's breach of an agency duty.

4.2 *Authority to share fees*: **Authorizes** the broker to cooperate with other brokers and share with them any fee paid on any transaction.

4.3 *Choice-of-law provision*: **States** California law will apply to any enforcement of this employment.

5. Brokerage fee:

5.1 *Fee amount*: **Enter** the fee amount negotiated to be paid as a percentage of the sales price or a fixed dollar amount. This amount will be paid when any one of the following conditions occur triggering payment:

a. *Fee on any sale*: **States** the brokerage fee is earned and due if the buyer acquires, exchanges for or options property during the listing period. [See Form 103 §5.1(c) for fee due on post-listing period sales]

b. *Termination fee*: **States** the brokerage fee is earned and due if, during the listing period, the buyer terminates this employment or withdraws from pursuing the purchase of real estate.

c. *Safety clause fee*: **States** the brokerage fee is earned and due if, within one year after the listing expires, the buyer enters into negotiations for the purchase, option or exchange of property the broker exposed him to during the listing period. Within 21 days after expiration of the listing period, the broker must provide the buyer with a list of the qualifying properties reviewed with the buyer during the listing period. [See **first tuesday** Form 123]

5.2 *Fees paid by seller*: The buyer will not owe any fees if the seller pays a fee or the seller's broker shares a fee in an amount acceptable to the broker. If the seller or the seller's broker do not agree to pay or share a fee with the broker, the buyer pays the brokerage fee in addition to the purchase price.

BUYER'S LISTING AGREEMENT
Exclusive Right to Buy, Lease or Option

DATE:_____, 20_____, at_____, California.

Items left blank or unchecked are not applicable.

1. RETAINER PERIOD:

1.1 Buyer hereby retains and grants to Broker the exclusive right to locate real property of the type described below and to negotiate the terms and conditions for its purchase, lease or option, acceptable to Buyer, for the period beginning on _____, 20_____ and terminating on _____, 20_____.

2. BROKER'S OBLIGATIONS:

2.1 Broker to use diligence in the performance of this employment.

2.2 ☐ See attached Agency Law Disclosure. [**ft** Form 305]

3. BUYER'S DEPOSIT:

3.1 Buyer hands $_____ to Broker for deposit into Broker's trust account for application to Buyer's obligations under this agreement and the following attachments:

a. ☐ Advance Fee Addendum [**ft** Form 106]

b. ☐ Listing Package Cost Sheet [**ft** Form 107]

4. GENERAL PROVISIONS:

4.1 In any action to enforce this agreement, the prevailing party shall receive attorney fees.

4.2 Buyer authorizes Broker to cooperate with other brokers and divide with them any compensation due.

4.3 This agreement will be governed by California law.

5. BROKERAGE FEE:

NOTICE: The amount or rate of real estate fees are not fixed by law. They are set by each Broker individually and may be negotiable between Client and Broker.

5.1 Buyer agrees to pay Broker _____ of the purchase price of the property sought, IF:

a. Buyer, or any person acting on Buyer's behalf, purchases, leases, exchanges for or obtains a purchase option on real property sought under this agreement during the retainer period.

b. Buyer terminates this employment of the Broker during the listing period.

c. Within one year after termination of this agreement, Buyer enters into negotiations which result in Buyer's acquisition of an interest in any property Broker has solicited information on or negotiated with its owner, directly or indirectly, on behalf of Buyer prior to this agreement's termination. Broker to identify prospective properties by written notice to Buyer within 21 days after termination. [**ft** Form 123]

5.2 Buyer's obligation to pay Broker a brokerage fee is extinguished on Broker's acceptance of a fee from Seller or Seller's Broker of property acquired by Buyer.

5.3 In the event this agreement terminates without Broker receiving a fee under §5.1 or §5.2, Buyer to pay Broker the sum of $_____ per hour of time accounted for by Broker, not to exceed $_____.

6. TYPE OF PROPERTY SOUGHT:

GENERAL DESCRIPTION: _____

SIZE: _____

LOCATION: _____

PRICE RANGE AND TERMS: _____

_____

I agree to render services on the terms stated above.

Date:_____, 20_____

Buyer's Broker: _____

By: _____

Address: _____

_____

Phone:_____

Fax: _____

Email: _____

I agree to employ Broker on the terms stated above.

Date:_____, 20_____

Buyer's Name: _____

Signature: _____

Signature: _____

Address: _____

_____

Phone:_____

Fax: _____

Email: _____

FORM 103   09-03   ©2006 **first tuesday**, P.O. BOX 20069, RIVERSIDE, CA 92516 (800) 794-0494

5.3 *Hourly fee*: **Enter** the negotiated dollar amount of the broker's per hour fee. The hourly fee is earned for time and effort spent on behalf of the buyer should property not be optioned or acquired by purchase or exchange after a diligent effort is made to locate property.

6. Type of property sought:

Property description: **Enter** a description of the type of real estate sought by the buyer, including its size, general location, purchase terms and property requirements.

Signatures

Broker's/Agent's signature: **Enter** the date the listing is signed and the broker's name. **Enter** the broker's (or agent's) signature. **Enter** the broker's address, telephone and fax numbers, and his email address.

Buyer's signature: **Enter** the date the buyer signs the listing and the buyer's name. **Obtain** the buyer's signature. If additional buyers are involved, prepare duplicate copies of the listing agreement and enter their names and obtain their signatures until all buyers are individually named and have signed. **Enter** the buyer's address, telephone and fax numbers, and his email address.

This chapter reviews the history and current status of fee sharing between seller's agents and buyer's agents on the sale of a home.

Buyer's agent or cooperating agent?

The characterization of a buyer's agent, in practice, as a cooperating agent is improper. The word "cooperating" lacks descriptive value if its purpose is to label the agent or broker involved as the representative of a buyer.

The **plain meaning** of the adjective "cooperating" is of no help in determining any activity other than a collaboration by two brokers to pair their respective clients to make a match for the transfer of property.

For the buyer's agent to tell a buyer, "Oh yes, we cooperate with other brokers on their listings," conveys no thought of fee sharing or the establishment of an agency. The buyer logically only understands that the brokers are **sharing information** in a joint effort to assist the buyer in a decision as to which, of all the prospective properties available, he should buy.

However, at the judicial level and based on legislation, the *cooperating agent* has been established as the title for a **subagent of the seller**, never a buyer's agent acting exclusively and in the best interests of his buyer. Thus, any use of the title "cooperating (selling) broker" is a legal reference to a subagent acting on behalf of the seller, and if a dual agent, then also on behalf of the buyer.

The codified agency law scheme defines a *cooperating broker* as one acting as a subagent with specific affirmative duties of care **owed the seller**, not the buyer. However, any cooperating broker must deal fairly and in a nondeceitful manner with the buyer, as must also the seller's primary agent. No such severe limitations exists on the duties owed to buyers by a buyer's agent. [Calif. Civil Code §2079.16]

Further, a **subagent** is identified by code as the agent in the sales transaction who *cooperates* with the listing agent **to sell** the property or **to locate** a buyer on behalf of the seller. The real estate agency scheme also labels the subagent as a *selling agent* if, while acting on behalf of the seller, he deals directly with the prospective buyer, there presumably being no buyer's agent. The scheme separates the seller's subagent from any buyer's agent who is engaged by the buyer to locate property. [CC §2079.13(n)]

Thus, the "cooperation" contemplated by the legislature is not the fee-sharing structure employed in the fee-sharing addendum attached to purchase agreements still demanded by multiple listing service (MLS) residential listing brokers. Brokers and their agents who act exclusively as agents for the buyer and share fees, simply put, are not cooperating brokers.

Unbundled, off-form fee provisions

For a buyer's broker to have equal ability to negotiate and collect a fee as a seller's broker:

- the buyer's broker must enter into an employment agreement with their buyer, called a buyer's listing, to be assured the buyer will have legal incentive to back up any fee demands which the buyer's agent may make on the seller;

- a fee provision must be written into the buyer's purchase agreement offer, stating the seller will pay a brokerage fee in an amount set by the buyer's broker and the buyer;

- the fee earned and payable by the seller to the buyer's broker must be payable directly to the buyer's broker by the seller, through escrow;

- the seller must agree to pay the fee earned by the brokers should the seller wrongfully fail to close the sale so the buyer's broker can pursue collection of his share, no matter the action or inaction to do so by the seller's broker; and

- the buyer must agree to pay the fee earned by the brokers if the buyer unjustifiably fails to close, allowing both the seller's broker and the buyer's broker to enforce collection of their respective share of the fee from the buyer.

The payment by the seller of the fee earned by the buyer's broker in no way establishes or indicates an agency with the seller. Thus, no rationale exists to take the payment of the brokers' fees due on the acceptance of a purchase agreement offer "off form," placing it in a separate agreement calling for the seller to pay only the seller's broker. [CC §§2079.16, 2079.19]

However, the buyer's broker may wish to abide by the off-form scheme for payment of his brokerage fee by the listing broker and not the seller directly. If the fee offered by the listing broker is less than the amount the buyer's broker feels he is entitled to on the transaction, the buyer's broker can then negotiate with the listing broker, agree to a different fee schedule than the one offered in the MLS publication and reduce the agreement to a writing.

Thus, on acceptance of the buyer's purchase agreement offer (which is devoid of a fee provision), the buyer's broker is assured that the "off-form" fee agreement will actually provide for the listing broker to pay the agreed share to the buyer's broker. [See **first tuesday** Form 105]

If the buyer's broker does acquiesce to the off-form fee agreement in which he receives his fee from the listing broker, the covert aspect of not letting the buyer know what fees are paid the buyer's broker is a direct violation of the agency rule stating the client is to be informed of all compensation received from all sources by his agent as a result of the representation.

Had the buyer's agent actually been only a *cooperating agent* negotiating the sale of the property to the buyer on behalf of the seller (as a statutory subagent), then the off-form fee arrangement and the nondisclosure to the buyer of the subagent's compensation is of no concern to the buyer. The buyer has no agent, or has his own agent. The seller, as the client of the cooperating (selling) broker, is fully aware of his subagent's compensation since he is agreeing to it.

All distortions and shortcomings in fee arrangements are avoided and the buyer's broker's fee is protected when the buyer's agent simply includes the fee arrangements as a provision in the purchase agreement offer agreed to by the buyer.

Chapter 17

The breaching buyer pays

This chapter highlights the collection of a brokerage fee from a buyer under various fee provisions when the buyer breaches the purchase agreement.

Brokerage fee protection

A buyer contacts a real estate sales agent to locate suitable properties for review with the intent to buy. The agent agrees to do so. However, the agent does not discuss or obtain an oral or written commitment from the buyer regarding the payment of a fee to his broker for services provided by him as the buyer's agent.

The agent locates a property suitable for the buyer's purposes. The agent prepares an offer to purchase, which the buyer signs. The offer is prepared on a purchase agreement form which does not contain a brokerage fee provision in the body of the offer above the buyer's signature. However, the seller's acceptance provision following the buyer's signature at the end of the form, outside the buyer's offer, does contain a reference to a separate fee agreement between the seller and his listing agent.

The seller signs the acceptance provision. Concurrently, the seller agrees, directly or indirectly, to pay both brokers a fee on completion of the sale. Should the buyer breach the purchase agreement, the seller's fee provision limits the brokerage fee to one-half of any money damages awarded to the seller in litigation or otherwise collected from the buyer.

Nowhere does the buyer agree to any aspect of the fee arrangement or to pay a fee if he breaches the purchase agreement by failing to close escrow.

The acceptance is returned to the buyer.

The separate fee agreement between the seller and his listing agent is retained by the listing broker. The brokers have or will enter into yet another and separate agreement to share the fee to be paid to the listing broker by the seller.

The buyer, without justification or excuse, later fails to complete the purchase. The seller, due to the buyer's breach of the purchase agreement, makes a demand on the buyer for money losses he has incurred due to the buyer's breach.

However, the seller's money losses, if any exist to be recovered, **may not include** the amount of the brokerage fee lost by the brokers. The seller did not incur a loss on the sale by paying the brokerage fees.

Only the buyer's broker collects

Continuing with the above example, the buyer's broker then makes a demand directly on his buyer to pay his fee. The buyer's broker does not wait for the seller to litigate with the buyer, recover his money losses and share them with the brokers. The listing broker does not (and may not) participate in the fee demand made on the buyer by the buyer's broker.

The buyer's broker claims the purchase agreement offer signed by the buyer is subject to an *implied promise* from the buyer to close the transaction so his broker will receive his fee.

The buyer claims his broker is not entitled to a fee from the buyer. The only fee provision which exists merely entitles the brokers to half the money losses recovered by the seller should the seller pursue collection of losses he incurred due to the buyer's breach. However, the seller's losses on the failed sale do not include the brokerage fee which went unpaid. Thus, the seller cannot recover the fee for the brokers on a claim against the buyer since the seller did not incur a loss by paying the fees.

Can the buyer's broker collect a fee from the defaulting buyer who never agreed, orally or in writing, to pay any fees?

Yes! The buyer **orally retained** the services of the broker, but did not *expressly promise*, orally or in writing, to pay a brokerage fee should the buyer's agent locate suitable property for the buyer to purchase. However, on entering into a purchase agreement, the **buyer knew** the seller promised to pay the buyer's broker a fee on closing. Thus, the buyer's offer to purchase the property contained an *implied promise* by the buyer to his broker not to **wrongfully interfere** with the payment of the brokerage fee, part of the client's obligation to his broker due to the principal/agent relationship.

Here, the buyer owes his broker the fee which the seller does not now owe. The payment of the fee by the seller was contingent on the close of escrow, which did not occur. [**Chan** v. **Tsang** (1991) 1 CA4th 1578]

Conversely, the seller's broker has no contractual right to collect a fee from the breaching buyer. The listing broker lacks:

- a client relationship with the buyer which carries with it the *implied promise* to avoid interference with the payment of a fee; and

- a *written agreement* signed by the buyer to pay the fee in lieu of the seller on the buyer's breach.

A **fundamental rule** of real estate practice for judicial enforcement of fee arrangements requires brokerage fee agreements to be **in writing and signed** by the parties responsible for payment.

However, a **common flaw** in the placement of brokerage fee provisions in some purchase agreement forms is the failure to include the fee provision in the body of the buyer's purchase agreement offer, i.e., **above the buyer's signature**, sometimes referred to as *"within the four corners of the contract."*

The fee provision placed within the buyer's offer usually states the seller will pay the fee if the transaction closes, and if it does not close due to a breach, the **breaching party will pay** the fee. Thus, all parties to the purchase agreement have agreed on what amount they owe, when they owe it and to whom it will be paid. [See **first tuesday** Form 150 §13]

Brokers as beneficiaries

When a buyer and seller both agree in writing to the payment of a brokerage fee, their brokers, by contract, become *third party beneficiaries* to the purchase agreement. Should either the buyer or the seller enforce the purchase agreement contract against the other by *specific performance*, the brokers will be paid on closing as part of the terms contained in the purchase agreement.

However, when the fee provision is located outside the buyer's offer and agreed to only between the seller and the brokers, the transaction can be closed without payment of the fee. The brokers are then left with a claim against a (bankrupt) seller for breach of the **separate fee agreement**. [**In re Munple, Ltd.** (9th Cir. 1989) 868 F2d 1129]

A **third party beneficiary** is a person for whose benefit two other individuals place provisions in an agreement — such as when a buyer and seller under a purchase agreement or escrow instructions mutually provide for the payment of a brokerage fee by the **seller or defaulting party**.

A brokerage fee provision written into the purchase agreement gives both brokers an **enforceable contract right** to collect their entire fee, either as part of the closing or from the breaching party on a failure to close. The shift in assurance is due to the location and wording of the fee provision. [Calif. Civil Code §1559]

Chapter 18

The seller's interference with fees

This chapter discusses a seller's responsibility for payment of a brokerage fee when the seller wrongfully interferes with the close of escrow.

The breaching seller pays

A buyer's agent, agreeing on behalf of his broker to take on the task of locating suitable real estate for a buyer, fails to enter into an exclusive right-to-buy listing agreement with his buyer before starting his search for qualifying properties.

The agent locates a suitable property for sale which is not listed with a broker. An offer to purchase the unlisted property is prepared by the buyer's agent, signed by his buyer and submitted to the seller.

A provision in the purchase agreement form used to prepare the buyer's offer sets the amount of the brokerage fee the buyer agrees the seller will pay the agent's broker should the buyer acquire the property. The fee provision calls for a fixed (or variable) fee, payable on the close of escrow. [See **first tuesday** Form 150 §13]

The seller rejects the buyer's offer and refuses to sign a counteroffer, stating he will not pay a brokerage fee.

Later, the buyer contacts the seller directly, without involving the buyer's agent. The buyer is willing to pay the seller's price, but feels the agent deserves to be paid something for having brought the transaction to this point.

The buyer expresses concern about the non-payment of a brokerage fee. The seller points out that neither the buyer nor the seller agreed to pay the broker a fee. The buyer's offer called only for the seller to pay a fee, not the buyer, and the seller rejected the offer.

The seller and buyer eventually enter into a purchase agreement without providing for the payment of a fee to the broker employing the buyer's agent. The transaction closes and the broker is not paid a fee.

On the agent's discovery of the buyer's purchase of the property, the agent's broker makes a **demand on the seller** for immediate payment of the fee set out in the buyer's offer previously rejected by the seller. The broker claims the seller is liable for payment of the fee since the seller **knew** the buyer agreed to the fee and then **induced** the buyer to abandon efforts to assure payment of a fee. Thus, the seller has *unlawfully interfered* with the broker's contractual relationship with the buyer and the broker's *prospective economic advantage* as evidenced by the fee provision in the purchase agreement offer submitted.

The seller claims he cannot be held responsible for the payment of any brokerage fee since he rejected the purchase offer containing the fee provision which, if he had accepted, would have required him to pay a fee.

Is the fee provision in the rejected purchase agreement offer enforceable **against the seller** who never agreed to it?

No! However, the broker can enforce the contract provision in the rejected offer to collect his fee from the **buyer**. The buyer did sign a writing (the purchase offer) providing for the payment of a brokerage fee on the buyer's purchase of the property, which the buyer did do.

Even though the buyer is obligated to pay the fee, the seller is also responsible for payment of the amount the buyer agreed would be paid.

Here, the seller **wrongfully induced** the buyer to breach a provision calling for the payment of a fee contained in a writing signed by the buyer.

Thus, the seller also owes the brokerage fee specified in the buyer's offer since the seller:

- **knew** the fee provision existed in the offer signed by the buyer; and

- **induced** the buyer to exclude the brokerage fee with the unjustified and improper intent of interfering with an existing agreement between the buyer and the broker. [**Rader Company** v. **Stone** (1986) 178 CA3d 10]

Editor's note — The legal basis for the broker's recovery against the seller is a tort theory called **intentional interference with contractual relations***. It is not a recovery based on the* **seller's breach of a provision** *in the purchase agreement offer, which is a contract theory. The seller never became a party to the purchase agreement contract in which the broker was a third-party beneficiary for the fees provided for in the contract.*

Conversely, the buyer owes the fee under a contract theory. The buyer breached his written promise that the broker would be paid as called for in the unaccepted purchase agreement offer signed by the buyer. However, the broker, while obtaining a money judgment for his fee against both the buyer and the seller, can only collect the amount of the fee once.

Oral fee agreements

An oral agreement between an agent and a buyer or seller involving the payment of a brokerage fee on the purchase or sale of property is unenforceable by the agent's broker against the buyer or seller promising to pay the fee. However, if the oral fee arrangement is later formalized in a writing signed by the buyer or seller who earlier orally agreed to pay the fee, the broker can enforce the signed written agreement and collect his fee from the person who signed it.

Oral fee agreements are unenforceable even when mentioned in the agent's written correspondence he delivers to the buyer or seller. It is not enough that the agent signs the correspondence containing the oral fee arrangement. The person who agreed to pay the fee must sign the writing which sets the fee before collection of a fee from the person making the oral promise can be enforced. [**Phillippe** v. **Shapell Industries, Inc.** (1987) 43 C3d 1247]

However, a buyer's broker and his agent need only have an *oral fee agreement* with a buyer for the broker to recover his fee from a seller when:

- the seller is **aware** of the oral fee agreement between the broker and the buyer; and

- the seller, without proper cause or privilege, **acts to interfere** with the fee agreement and causes the broker not to receive his fee on the buyer's acquisition of the property.

Thus, when the buyer has arranged for payment of a brokerage fee, either by a signed writing or by an oral agreement, and then the seller knowingly interferes with that arrangement by inducing the buyer to **breach** his written or oral promise to provide for payment of a fee, the **seller owes** the broker the promised fee. [**Della Penna** v. **Toyota Motor Sales, U.S.A., Inc.** (1995) 11 C4th 376]

The contingency fee

Fee provisions in purchase agreements and escrow instructions typically state the fee earned is payable out of the sales proceeds due a seller on the close of escrow, called a *contingency fee provision.*

However, escrows do not always close. Thus, a brokerage fee which has been earned might not be paid. However, the contingency fee may be due the broker based on the seller's conduct, even when escrow does not close.

Consider a seller who refuses or is unable to remove liens on the real estate in order to convey title as agreed. No contingency provision exists allowing the seller to cancel for his failure to obtain a release of the liens.

Escrow does not close due to the liens. The broker makes a demand on the seller for payment of his fee, claiming the fee was earned and is now unpaid due to the seller's failure to close escrow as agreed.

The seller claims the broker is not entitled to receive a fee since no sales proceeds were received from which escrow could pay the fee.

Here, the seller cannot avoid paying the brokerage fee by relying on provisions calling for the fee to be paid from funds the seller is to receive on closing. The **seller breached** the purchase agreement by preventing the close of escrow and his receipt of sales proceeds, the events triggering payment of the fee.

The contingency fee provision in the purchase agreement and the escrow instructions merely **designates the time** for payment of a fee already earned. It does not defeat the broker's right to compensation he has fully earned simply because the event allowing escrow to pay the fee does not occur due to the seller's unexcused failure to perform on the purchase agreement. [**Steve Schmidt & Co.** v. **Berry** (1986) 183 CA3d 1299]

In a listing agreement, a broker and seller may agree to any legally enforceable condition which must first occur or be satisfied before the broker **earns his fee,** such as locating a ready, willing and able buyer to purchase on the listed terms or any other terms of an offer accepted by the seller.

However, when the condition for earning the fee occurs as called for in the listing, such as the seller's acceptance of an offer, the fee is immediately due and payable to the broker.

However, most purchase agreements used to write up a buyer's offer include a boilerplate contingency fee provision. The wording of the provision shifts the time for payment of the fee the broker has already earned under the listing agreement from the acceptance of the purchase agreement offer to the time of closing.

Method of payment

Unless altered, fee provisions in purchase agreements set a fixed-dollar or calculable dollar amount which is payable by the seller and due on the close of escrow. Escrow instructions are drawn to provide for the payment of this agreed-to fee.

However, sellers who are given the unilateral ability in escrow instructions to change the terms of the fee they owe brokers and still close escrow, will occasionally try to alter the amount, time or method of payment, or worse, cancel escrow's authorization to pay the fee.

For example, a broker consents to fee arrangements by including a fee provision in the purchase agreement calling for payment in full on closing. Here, the seller cannot enforce contradictory escrow instructions (or cancel instructions) calling for the brokerage fee to be paid in installments, unless the broker consents to the change (or cancellation). [**Seck** v. **Foulks** (1972) 25 CA3d 556]

Escrow instructions for paying the fee

Escrow instructions are the final arrangements for the payment of a brokerage fee. It does not matter which agent dictates instructions, or if they do so by use of a transaction coordinator. Their paramount, co-existing objective is to eliminate the risk that the brokers will not be paid on the close of escrow.

The brokerage fee has already been earned on the acceptance of a purchase agreement offer. However, payment of the earned fee is usually delayed and made contingent on the close of the sales escrow, a 30- to 60-day period after the brokers have already earned their fees.

It is during the period of time necessary to close escrow that sellers who have committed themselves to pay the fee sometimes decide they no longer want to pay the fee.

The ability of the seller to interfere with payment of the fee and still close escrow depends totally on the nature of the fee provision dictated by the agents and contained in the escrow instructions.

When dictating escrow instructions regarding the payment of the fee, brokers and their agents have several options which provide various degrees of assurance that their fee will be paid. **Payment arrangements** for brokerage fees include:

- **instructions signed only by the seller,** called *unilateral fee instructions*, which authorize escrow to pay the brokerage fee from the net proceeds due the seller on closing;

- an **assignment accompanied by unilateral fee instructions** from the seller which authorize escrow to pay the brokerage fee from the seller's net proceeds;

- a **lien** on the seller's net proceeds to secure payment of the brokerage fee which is **accompanied by unilateral fee instructions** signed by the seller;

- **instructions signed by the seller and brokers,** but not entered into by the buyer, which authorize escrow to pay the brokerage fee from the seller's net proceeds; and

- **mutual instructions signed by the seller and buyer,** whether or not entered into or approved by the brokers, which authorize escrow to pay the brokerage fee from the seller's net proceeds.

When the agent dictating the instructions fails to specify the type of payment-of-fee provision to be used by escrow, the typical fee provision used by escrow services is a "default fee provision." In it, the seller alone instructs escrow, by way of supplemental (and unilateral) escrow instructions, to pay the brokers from funds accruing to the seller on close of escrow.

Mutual vs. unilateral instructions

Of all the various fee arrangements available to brokers for payment of their fees, the unilateral fee instructions (signed only by the seller) leave the brokers with the least assurance the fee will be paid on close of escrow.

Unilateral fee instructions give the seller the sole and absolute ability to cancel, revoke or alter the brokerage fee instructions and still close escrow. When unilateral instructions are canceled, no conflict arises which would interfere with the escrow officer's ability to close escrow under the mutual instructions.

For example, should a seller cancel his unilateral fee instructions, escrow must close and pay all net proceeds to the seller — including funds originally intended for payment of the brokerage fee. Thus, no funds remain in escrow as a source of recovery by the brokers. **[Contemporary Investments, Inc.** v. **Safeco Title Insurance Co.** (1983) 145 CA3d 999]

The addition of the broker's consent to or approval of the seller's unilateral fee instructions adds no assurance that the seller will not act to cancel, revoke or alter the fee instructions.

When the seller's unilateral fee instructions, whether or not joined in by the brokers, call for either an **assignment** of an amount equal to the brokerage fee or a **lien** on the seller's net proceeds in the amount of the fee, the seller can still cancel, revoke or alter the fee instructions and close escrow without payment of the agreed-to brokerage fee.

The best protection a broker has against cancellation, revocation or alteration of the brokerage fee instructions is to dictate **mutual instructions** as the seller's agreement to pay the brokerage fee, signed by both the buyer and the seller. Escrow should not be allowed to relegate the fee to separate, unilateral fee instructions signed only by the seller (and possibly the broker).

Then, for the seller to cancel payment of the brokerage fee payable under mutual instructions, the buyer would have to collaborate with the seller, making the buyer (as well as the seller) responsible for the wrongfully withheld fee.

Further, mutual instructions should call for any change in the fee provision agreed to by the seller and the buyer to be subject to the broker's approval. Thus, the broker "locks in" the payment of his fee by *triangulation*, should escrow close.

Chapter 19

Finders: a nonlicensee referral service

This chapter discusses a broker's or his agent's use of finders to locate sellers, buyers or borrowers, and presents the finder's fee agreement along with instructions for an agent's use of the form.

Agency relationships in real estate transactions

Three classes of real estate "agents" have been established in California:

- licensed brokers;

- licensed sales agents; and

- unlicensed agents, called *finders*.

Licensed brokers and agents owe *fiduciary duties* to the principals they represent. Fiduciary duties require licensees to perform on behalf of their client with utmost care and diligence.

A finder has no such agency duty. A finder's function as an agent is limited to soliciting, identifying and referring potential real estate clients or participants to brokers, agents or principals in exchange for the promise of a fee.

A finder working for a principal is distinguished from a licensed broker working for a principal. Limitations are placed on the conduct of a finder. A finder lacks legal authority to participate in any aspect of property information dissemination or other transactional negotiations. [Business and Professions Code §§10130 et seq.]

Although not licensed by the California Department of Real Estate (DRE) or admitted as members of a real estate trade association, finders are authorized by statute *to solicit* prospective buyers, sellers, borrowers, lenders, tenants or landlords *for referral* to real estate licensees or principals. Thus, they **provide leads** about individuals who may becomes participants in real estate transactions.

A finder is entitled to a fee as an unlicensed individual if he solicits, locates, places, introduces or delivers up names of prospective clients to a broker or principal. It is the one and only service he provides. [**Tyrone** v. **Kelley** (1973) 9 C3d 1]

Implementing the finder relationship

Finders are often individuals who are employed by large companies. Their work makes them privy to information on other employees who are relocating and will most likely need to sell or buy a home. They, in turn, pass this information on to a broker or an agent employed by the broker.

A finder is, in essence, a type of "middleman." He locates or has knowledge of potential buyers, sellers and other prospective clients or participants in real estate transactions and **places** them with an agent either by referring them to the agent or providing the agent with the lead. Once brought together by placement or referral, the parties are left to negotiate their real estate related arrangements apart from the finder. [Tyrone, *supra*]

For example, an individual employed in a corporate personnel department agrees to provide a loan broker with a list of people moving into the area. The broker believes many of the referrals will be purchasing a new home and will likely need financing. The list is not a trade secret of the individual's employer and the release is not in conflict with company policy.

In exchange, the loan broker will pay the individual a percentage of the fee the broker receives from each loan closed with any of the leads developed from the referrals.

The individual referring potential clients to the broker is not licensed by the DRE to render brokerage services for a fee.

Can an individual who is not licensed by the DRE earn a fee when a loan transaction results from his referral?

Yes! The nonlicensee is a **finder**, exempt from real estate licensing laws as long as he restricts his solicitation activities to the single act of **placing (introducing) or referring** a borrower or a trust deed investor to the loan broker. [Tyrone, *supra*]

Since the finder is performing a *single act* (the referral) in a transaction which requires financing, no Real Estate Settlement Procedures Act (RESPA) violation has occurred by the payment of a fee.

Conversely, the same loan referral fee paid by a lender to a licensee participating as an agent in a single-family residence sale would be a violation of RESPA since the referral is not the only service the agent provides the borrower.

The finder's fee bargain

Generally, a **finder's fee** is a lump sum amount or a percentage of the fee received by the broker on a transaction which is closed due to the finder's referral. Only sound economics controls the amount of the fee a broker, agent or principal should pay a finder for a lead. Also, no limit is placed on the volume of referral business conducted by a finder.

For instance, a loan broker can compensate his finder with:

- a salary;

- a fee based on a percentage of the loan; or

- a lump sum basis per closing. [**Zalk v. General Exploration Company** (1980) 105 CA3d 786]

Also, while brokers may, finders may not collect advance fees from principals. **Advance-fee**

operators, masking themselves as finders for principals, sometimes collect fees "up front," a prohibited activity for an unlicensed individual. [Bus & P C §10131.2]

Who qualifies as a finder?

Anyone can be a finder, unless barred by professional regulations or code-of-ethics or conflict-of-interest policies controlling an individual's conduct.

For instance, a licensed agent registered with the DRE as an employee of a broker cannot be a finder. The agent is employed to solicit clients on behalf of his broker, not others. In turn, only his broker can receive a fee generated by the agent's real estate licensed activities. On the employing broker's receipt of a fee, the fee is split with the agent under their written employment agreement. [Bus & P C §10132; Department of Real Estate Regulations §2726]

CPAs are barred by regulation from being finders and receiving a fee for the referral of their clients to others. [16 Calif. Code of Regulations §56]

A finder who advertises to locate leads he will place or refer to a broker or principal must not hold himself out as also rendering services which require a broker's license. [Bus & P C §10139]

Thus, a finder may advertise as a "referral service." He may state he will **place** an interested party with a broker or principal, or **refer** a principal to a match sought for a real estate transaction.

Soliciting to place or refer a match

A finder providing referral services for a fee may:

- find and introduce parties;

- solicit parties for referral to others [Tyrone, *supra*]; and

- be employed by principals or brokers.

A finder may not:

- take part in any negotiations [Bus & P C §10131];

- discuss the price;

- discuss the property; or

- discuss the terms or conditions of the transaction. [**Spielberg** v. **Granz** (1960) 185 CA2d 283]

A finder who steps over into any aspect of negotiations which lead to the creation of a real estate transaction needs a real estate license for he is both **soliciting and negotiating**. Unless licensed, an individual who enters into negotiations (supplying property or sales information) cannot collect a fee for services rendered — even if he calls it a finder's fee. Also, he is subject to a penalty of up to $10,000 for engaging in brokerage activities without a license. [Bus & P C §§10137, 10139]

In addition, a broker who permits a finder or anyone else in his employ (or his agents' employ) to perform any type of "licensed" work beyond solicitation for a referral, may have his license suspended or revoked. [Bus & P C §§10131, 10137]

Entitlement to a fee

A finder's fee agreement entered into between a finder and a **principal** regarding the finder's referral services must be evidenced in a writing signed by the principal who employed the finder. If not, the finder cannot enforce his fee agreement with the principal. [Calif. Civil Code §1624(a)(4)]

However, the principal's **use and benefit** of a finder's referral under an oral finder's fee agreement, such as closing a sale with an individual referred by the finder, will substitute for a written agreement. [**Tenzer** v. **Superscope, Inc.** (1985) 39 C3d 18]

Likewise, oral fee agreements between a broker (or his agents) and a finder are enforceable. No written agreement is required between a broker (or his agents) and a finder. However, a writing memorializes the agreement as documentation against memories to the contrary. [See Form 115 accompanying this chapter]

Consider a nonlicensed individual who enters into an oral agreement with a broker to introduce the broker to prospective buyers or sellers in return for 10% of the broker's earnings on any transaction put together with the "lead."

The finder introduces the broker to prospects who close transactions with the broker. The broker refuses to pay the finder the agreed-to compensation since the oral agreement is not evidenced in a writing signed by the broker who retained him.

However, the finder can enforce the broker's oral fee agreement. Oral fee-sharing agreements between brokers or finders are enforceable. [**Grant** v. **Marinell** (1980) 112 CA3d 617]

Analyzing the finder's fee agreement

The finder's fee agreement, **first tuesday** Form 115, is used by brokers and their agents, as well as principals, who seek to contract with an unlicensed individual by entering into a finder's agreement. The agreement calls for the individual (finder) to identify prospective clients, be they sellers or buyers, lenders or borrowers, or landlords or tenants, in exchange for a fee on the closing of one or more transactions between the broker and the prospective client.

Finders, unlike licensed real estate agents, are true independent contractors. Also, finders are authorized by statute to collect a fee directly from a principal; licensed sales agents are not.

If a principal uses the finder's fee agreement to contract with a finder, the party named as broker in the form is merely re-identified as the principal (be he an owner, buyer, lender, etc.).

Each section in Form 115 has a separate purpose and need for enforcement. The sections include:

1. *Service to be rendered*: A broker (or an agent acting on behalf of the broker) contracts with an individual as a finder to locate and refer prospective real estate clients to the broker. The services of the finder are limited to the referral of prospective client(s) while the broker retains control over the gathering and handling of all property information, client confidentialities and negotiations as set forth in sections 1 and 2.

2. *Identification of potential clients*: The finder identifies the prospective client and the property involved, if applicable, as set forth in sections 3 and 4.

3. *Finder's fee*: The amount of the fee due the finder and when the fee is earned and payable is established by negotiations between the broker/agent and the finder as set forth in sections 5 and 6.

Editor's note — No limits exist and no formula is prohibited in the setting of the fee or when the fee will be paid. However, brokers tend to set a time period for the expiration of the finder's right to earn further referral fee(s) on future transactions entered into between the client the finder located and the broker. Conversely, the finder usually seeks to be paid on all deals with the prospective client, forever.

4. *Signatures*: The broker (or his agent) and the finder sign the agreement consenting to the contracted employment.

Preparing the finder's fee agreement

The following instructions are for the preparation and use of the Finder's Fee Agreement, **first tuesday** Form 115, by a broker to employ a finder who agrees to refer prospective clients to the broker.

Each instruction corresponds to the provision in the form bearing the same number.

*Editor's note — **Check** and **enter** items throughout the agreement in each provision with boxes and blanks, unless the provision is not intended to be included as part of the final agreement, in which case it is left unchecked or blank.*

Document identification:

Enter the date and name of the city where the agreement is prepared. This date is used when referencing this agreement.

1. *Type of client sought*: **Check** the box for the type of prospective client the finder is to refer to the broker.

2. *Participation in negotiations*: The finder agrees not to participate in any negotiations or to solicit loans. If he does, the finder may not enforce collection of the agreed-to compensation since a broker's license is required to collect a fee for providing property information, collecting information from the client or negotiating a transaction.

   2.1 The finder acknowledges he is not a real estate licensee.

3. *Identification of prospective clients*: **Enter** the name, address and telephone number of the prospective client the finder is referring to the broker.

   3.1 If additional prospective clients are to be covered by the agreement, such as buyers who are now known or will be located in the future, use an addendum to add names now or to include others later. [See **first tuesday** Form 250]

4. *Information on property*: **Enter** the common street address of any real estate in question.

FINDER'S FEE AGREEMENT

DATE:_____, 20_____, at_____, California.

> This form is used by brokers and their agents to employ an unlicenseed individual to locate, solicit, and refer or identify persons who need the services of the broker and his agents. [Business and Professions Code §§10130, 10139]

Items left blank or unchecked are not applicable.

1. In consideration for services to be rendered by Finder, Broker hereby contracts with Finder to refer to Broker a prospective client in need of services as a:

   ☐ Buyer   ☐ Lender   ☐ Borrower
   ☐ Owner/Seller   ☐ Tenant   ☐ Landlord

2. Finder agrees not to participate in or conduct any negotiations with the prospective client, or solicit loans on behalf of the prospective client.

   2.1 Finder is not licensed by the California Department of Real Estate.

3. The prospective client is identified as:
   Name: _____
   Address:_____
   Telephone:_____

   3.1 Further referrals of other prospective clients may be included in this agreement by an addendum signed by both Broker and Finder. [**ft** Form 250]

4. The real estate involved, if any, is referred to as:
   Common address: _____

   Legal description/Assessor's parcel number: _____
   _____
   _____
   _____

5. As compensation for each referral by Finder, Broker agrees to pay Finder the following amount:

   a. $_____ for each prospective client.

   b. _____% of the Broker's fee received on the first transaction with each prospective client.

   c. _____% of the purchase price paid on the first transaction with each prospective client on which Broker receives a fee.

   d. Other payment: _____

6. Finder's compensation is earned and payable:

   a. ☐ On close of the first transaction involving each prospective client.

   b. Other time of payment: _____

   c. Should the prospective client not enter into a commissionable transaction through Broker within _____ months after the date that prospective client is identified in writing to Broker, Broker shall owe Finder no compensation.

7. Additional terms and conditions: _____
   _____
   _____

I agree to the terms stated above.	I agree to the terms stated above.
Date:_____, 20_____	Date:_____, 20_____
	Finder's name: _____
Broker:_____	Signature: _____
By: _____	Social Security #: _____
Address: _____	Address: _____
Phone:_____ Cell:_____	Phone:_____ Cell:_____
Fax: _____	Fax: _____
Email: _____	Email: _____

FORM 115   09-01   ©2006 **first tuesday**, P.O. BOX 20069, RIVERSIDE, CA 92516 (800) 794-0494

Enter the legal description or assessor's number for the property, information which can be obtained from a copy of a recorded deed or a title insurance policy on the property, or from any title company on request.

5. *Payment of finder's fee*: **Enter** the dollar amount or percentage in the appropriate blank which establishes the finder's fee. The amount of the fee may be set as a fixed dollar amount (§5a), a percentage of the broker's compensation from the client (§5b), a percentage of the purchase price (§5c) or some other agreed-to method of determining payment (§5d).

Editor's note — No limit exists on the amount to be paid or the number of referrals a finder can be paid for.

6. *Fee earned and payable*: **Check** the box indicating when the fee has been earned by the finder and when it is due and payable by the broker. If box **a** is checked, a transaction brought about by this agreement must close before the broker is liable to the finder for payment of a fee. If box **b** is checked, **enter** in the blank the event other than closing which triggers payment of the finder's fee.

6.1 *Expiration of finder agreement*: **Enter** the number of months after which the finder will not be entitled to receive a fee for subsequent transactions with the prospective client(s).

7. *Additional terms*: **Enter** any additional terms agreed to between the finder and the broker.

Signatures:

Broker's/Agent's signature: **Enter** the date the agreement is signed and the broker's name. **Enter** the broker's (or agent's) signature. **Enter** the broker's address, telephone and fax numbers, and his email address.

Finder's signature: **Enter** the date the finder signs the agreement and the finder's name. **Obtain** the finder's signature. **Enter** the finder's social security number, address, telephone and fax numbers, and his email address.

SECTION C

Property Conditions and Disclosures

Chapter 20

Due diligence obligations

This chapter discusses the due diligent conduct owed a seller or buyer on the exclusive employment of a broker and his agents.

The duty owed to clients

Every exclusive listing agreement entered into by an agent on behalf of his broker is an employment which creates a client relationship. The employment imposes *special agency* (fiduciary) duties on the broker and the agent, owed to the client, to use "due diligence" in a continuous effort to meet the objective of the employment, be it to buy, sell, lease or finance an interest in real estate. [See **first tuesday** Form 102 §1.2]

The promise of **due diligence** is the consideration a broker and his agents give their client to render services in exchange for employment as the *exclusive representative* of the client to locate the "match" sought by the client. If the promise to use diligence in the employment is not stated in the exclusive listing agreement, it is implied as existing in the relationship.

The broker with authority to be the exclusive representative of a client must take reasonable steps to promptly gather all *material facts* about the property in question which are *readily available* to the broker or the broker's agent. After gathering factual information about the integrity of the property, the broker's agent proceeds to do every reasonable and ethical thing to pursue, with utmost care, the purpose of the employment.

In contrast to an exclusive listing, a broker and his agents entering into an open listing are not committed to render any services at all. The broker and his agents only have a *best-effort obligation* to act on the employment.

However, when an agent holding an open listing enters into preliminary negotiations, such as an exchange of property data, a due diligence obligation arises to provide the utmost care and protection of the client's best interests. Having **acted on the open listing**, the agent must now inspect the property and gather all readily available information on the property under consideration. Further, the agent is obligated to advise the client on the nature of the information and any ramifications the transaction might have on the client which are unknown to the client.

Once the agent actually begins to perform services under an open listing entered into by a buyer or seller, the agent has **acted on the employment** and the due diligence standards of duty owed to the client apply to his future conduct.

Diligence includes the advice and counsel the agent gives the client about the property, the market pressures, impending negotiations and their consequences, which affect the client's position.

Maintaining the client file

Typically, the agent who produces a listing (and thus his broker's right to a fee) becomes the agent in the broker's office who is responsible to the broker for the care and maintenance of the client's file.

On entering into a listing, a **physical file** must be set up to house information and document all the activity which arises within the broker's office due to the existence of the listing. For example, the file on a property listing should at least contain the original listing agreement, its addenda and all the property disclosure documents the seller and listing agent provide to a prospective buyer before the seller accepts an offer to buy.

The file needs an **activity sheet** for entry of information on all manner of file activity. Any paperwork, notes, messages, billings, correspondence, email printouts, fax transmissions, disclosure sheets, worksheets, advertising copy, tear sheets, copies of offers/counteroffers and rejections, and all other related documentation are to be kept in the file. Nothing occurs as a result of the client employment which is not to be put in and retained in the file.

The file is the **broker's file**, not the listing agent's file, although it will likely remain with the listing agent until close of a sale on the listed property or the listing expires unrenewed. The agent hands the broker the completed file on close of escrow, usually a *condition precedent* to payment of the agent's share of the fee received by the broker.

Guidelines and checklists

Guidelines used to build a file's content are available in the many forms, such as checklists prepared by a broker or his listing coordinator, a transaction coordinator's (TC's) closing checklist, escrow worksheets, work authorization forms, advance fee and advance cost checklists, or income property analysis forms. [See **first tuesday** Form 403]

Checklists belong in the file to be reviewed periodically by the agent, office manager, TC or employing broker for work which can be done to better service the listing and earn a fee.

This chapter discusses some — but certainly not all — steps a broker and his agent might undertake to fulfill their employment responsibilities owed to the client.

For example, information to be gathered, activities to be performed, events to be arranged and advice to be given to a seller by a listing agent when listing and marketing a property **for sale** include:

1. A **property profile** of the seller's title from a title company in order to identify all owners needed to list, sell and convey the property.

2. A **condition of property** disclosure sheet (Transfer Disclosure Statement) filled out and signed by the seller. [See **first tuesday** Form 304]

3. A **home inspection report** (by a home inspector) paid for by the seller and attached to the condition of property statement (TDS) before the listing agent signs the TDS.

4. A **natural hazard disclosure** (NHD) on the property from a local agency or a vendor of NHD reports, paid for by the seller, and reviewed and signed by the seller and the listing agent. [See **first tuesday** Form 314]

5. An **annual property operating disclosure** (APOD) statement covering the expenses of ownership and any income produced by the property, filled out and signed by the seller, together with a rent roll and copies of lease forms which the owner uses, to be included in the listing package only after reviewing the seller's data. [See **first tuesday** Forms 352 and 562]

6. Copies of all the Covenants, Conditions and Restrictions (CC&Rs), disclosures and assessment data from any **homeowners' association** involved with the property. [See **first tuesday** Form 150 §11.8]

7. A **termite report** and clearance paid for by the seller.

8. Any replacement or **repair of defects** noted in the home inspection report or on the TDS, as authorized and paid for by the seller.

9. An occupancy **transfer certificate** (including permits or the completion of retrofitting required by local ordinances) paid for by the seller.

10. A statement on the amount and payment schedule for any special district property **improvement bonds** which are liens on the property (shown on the title company's property profile).

11. A **visual inspection** of the property and a survey of the surrounding neighborhood by the listing agent to become informed about readily available facts affecting the marketability of the property.

12. **Advising** the seller about the marketability of the listed property based on differing prices and terms for payment of the price, and for property other than one-to-four residential units, the financial and tax consequences of various sales arrangements which are available by using alternative purchase agreements, options to buy, exchange agreements and installment sales.

13. A **marketing (listing) package** on the property compiled by the listing agent and handed to prospective buyers or buyer's agents before the seller accepts any offer to purchase the property, consisting of copies of all the property disclosures required to be handed to prospective buyers or the buyer's agent by the seller and listing broker.

14. A **marketing plan** prepared by the listing agent and reviewed with the seller for locating prospective buyers, such as by distributing flyers, disseminating property data in multiple listing services, newspapers and periodicals, broadcasts at trade meetings attended by buyer's agents, press releases to radio or television, internet sites, posting "For Sale" signs on the premises, hosting open house events, posting on bulletin boards, mailing to neighbors and using all other advertising media available to reach prospective buyers.

15. A **seller's net sheet** prepared by the listing agent and reviewed with the seller each time pricing of the property is an issue, such as when obtaining a listing, changing the listed price, reviewing the terms of a purchase offer or when substantial changes occur in charges or deductions affecting the net proceeds from a sale since the net sheet discloses the **financial consequences** of the seller's acceptance of a purchase agreement offer. [See **first tuesday** Form 310]

16. Informing the client of the listing agent's **sales activities** by weekly communications advising what specifically has been done during the past several days and what the listing agent expects to do in the following days, as well as what the seller can do in response to comments taken by the listing agent from buyers and their agents, and to changes in the real estate market.

17. Keeping records in a client file of all activities and documents generated due to the listing.

Duty to DRE to keep records

All records of an **agent's activities** on behalf of a buyer or seller during the listing period must be retained by the agent's broker for three years. [Calif. Business and Professions Code §10148]

The **three-year period** for retaining the buyer's or seller's activity file for Department of Real Estate (DRE) review begins to run from the closing date of a sale or, if a sale does not occur, from the date of the listing.

The records must be available for inspection by the Commissioner of Real Estate or his representative, or for an audit the Commissioner may order.

Advising the seller

An agent, on behalf of his broker, solicits an owner of a run-down (depreciated) single-family residence to list the property for sale.

After gathering and analyzing data on comparable sales, the agent advises the seller that the present condition of the property justifies a listing price of no more than $230,000.

However, the agent believes the property will sell for $300,000, an additional $70,000 in price, if the seller is willing to spend $15,000 to $20,000 to correct deferred maintenance and eliminate some obsolescence.

Also, the agent is aware the current demand by buyers of a residence in this price range consists mostly of individuals who are looking for a ready-to-occupy home, with few speculators looking for "fixer-uppers" they can restore and resell at a profit.

The agent determines the seller has the funds needed to correct the defects and appearance of the property. Based on market demands and housing prices, the agent advises the seller to invest the time, effort and money to fix up the property. However, the seller is not now willing to invest funds to fix up the property.

Rejecting the agent's advice, the seller agrees to list the property for sale at $230,000 and sell it in its present condition, after full disclosure of the property's condition by including a home inspection report.

Since the client has rejected the agent's advice, does the agent now need to explain the reasoning behind his advice?

Yes! Professionals are liable for their failure to explain the **rationale** behind their advice and the **consequences** which can result when ad-

vice is rejected. Here, the agent needs to advise the seller (and confirm in a memo) that the resale value of the property after the property has been fixed up for sale will increase. So, when it is fixed up by a buyer and resold at a far greater price, the broker and his agent have evidence they advised the client about the consequences (costs) of this inaction. [**Truman** v. **Thomas** (1980) 27 C3d 285]

Advice and consequences

In a real estate transaction, brokers and their agents must be certain who is their **client**. Likewise, they must determine who is not their client, but is a **customer** with whom the broker is directly negotiating or who is represented by another broker. Only a general duty to deal fairly and honestly is owed to a customer.

For example, the *general duty* owed a perspective buyer by a listing agent regarding property disclosures does not include advice on what investigations, audits or additional reports on the disclosed defects are available, or what reasons the agent may have to believe they should be obtained by a prudent buyer. Further, a listing agent does not owe a duty to the prospective buyer to explain the consequences of the customer's **failure to further investigate** or analyze adverse facts disclosed by the agent. Investigations and inquiries are the **customer's duty of care** owed to himself to exercise concern for the protection of his own interests.

Also confusing for customers is the purpose behind the brokerage community's use of pre-printed suggestions, recommendations, and disclaimers of responsibilities, few of which are relevant to any one transaction. They are typically handed to each person in a sales transaction by the listing agent with a demand the parties acknowledge receipt of the preprinted, boilerplate and mostly irrelevant advice, called *advisory disclaimers*.

When a listing agent hands these advisory disclaimers to a third-party customer, such as a prospective buyer, the advisory provides a disclosure of the services available to the customer (by other than the listing agent). The advisory disclaimers **recommend** that the buyer independently check out and determine the consequences of the property information disclosed by the listing agent and undertake efforts to protect his interests in the transaction (whether or not he has retained a broker to do so).

Advising the buyer

However, a buyer is entitled to far more assistance from his agent than the naked suggestions or recommendations contained in **advisory disclosures** about the availability of services. The duty of the buyer's selling agent goes well beyond the listing agent's limited disclosure obligations.

If these boilerplate advisory services were contracted for, the buyer would be provided with an independent analysis of the property and the transaction.

Here, the buyer's broker and his agent, acting on behalf of a buyer, must use the advisory statement of recommended investigations as a **checklist** of activities from which the buyer's agent will select those services he believes his buyer should undertake to protect the buyer's interests.

More importantly, services the buyer's agent has **reason to believe** the buyer should engage must be made the subject of *contingency provisions* in the purchase offer. Thus, the buyer's agent allows the buyer (and himself) an opportunity and the time needed to investigate and analyze the agent's concerns prior to closing.

Going beyond mere notice about available activities and services the client should consider by including contingencies in an offer is imperative when an agency relationship exists with the client.

For example, a buyer's agent has an affirmative duty of care to protect his buyer by pointing out why a recommended activity or inquiry needs to be undertaken in a transaction when the activity may uncover a situation which, if it exists, must be dealt with prior to closing. If it were otherwise, the conditions suspected by the buyer's agent to exist would interfere with the buyer's use and successful ownership of the property after closing.

A residential broker and his agents nearly always know more about one-to-four unit residential property conditions and the transactional aspects (legal, financial and tax) which will affect the client than the client does. With this knowledge of facts and inclinations about the property, the parties, available services, the documents involved and the provisions they contain, agents have insight into the need for a particular investigative report. The reports would address problems the agent suspects might exist which would have an adverse impact on the client's sale or use of the property.

The buyer's agent using an advisory statement of recommended activities as a checklist will:

- determine which of the itemized activities his buyer should undertake before closing;

- help the buyer weigh the probability of discovering undisclosed defects or conditions which would have consequences adverse to the buyer's objectives; and

- help the buyer analyze the risk of loss should defects of the type suspected be discovered after closing.

Chapter 21

The listing agent and the prospective buyer

This chapter focuses on a listing agent's limited, nonfiduciary general duty owed to all prospective buyers as distinguished from a buyer's agent's special fiduciary agency duties owed to these buyers.

General duty to voluntarily disclose

A listing broker and his agents have a special *fiduciary agency duty*, owed solely to a seller who has employed the broker, to diligently market the listed property for sale. The objective of this employment is to locate a prospective buyer who is ready, willing and able to acquire the property.

On locating a prospective buyer, either directly or through a buyer's agent, the listing agent owes the prospective buyer, and thus also the buyer's agent, a limited, nonclient *general duty* to **voluntarily provide** information on the listed property, called *disclosures*. What is limited about the duty is not the extent or detail to which the listing agent may go to provide information, but the **minimal quantity of fundamental information** and data about the listed property which must be handed to the prospective buyer or the buyer's agent.

The information disclosed need only be sufficient enough in its content to place the buyer on notice of facts which may have an **adverse affect** on the property's value.

Thus, the disclosure obligations of the listing agent to voluntarily inform prospective buyers about the fundamentals of the listed property acts to limit the listing agent's ability to employ any conduct or means at hand to exploit the prospective buyer. The listing agent may not:

- deliver up less than the minimum level of information to put the buyer on notice of the property's fundamentals;

- give unfounded opinions or deceptive responses in response to inquiries; or

- stifle inquires about the property while in the vigorous pursuit of the best financial advantage obtainable for the seller.

Gathering facts on adverse features

The gist of a listing agent's limited general duty owed to a nonclient prospective buyer is to put the prospective buyer or the buyer's agent on notice of facts which might, if known to the prospect, **adversely affect his valuation** of the listed property.

The **methods for gathering** adverse facts about the property's fundamental characteristics, as well as those facts which enhance value, which the listing agent is specifically required to use on a **one-to-four unit residential property** include:

- conducting a **visual inspection** of the property to observe conditions which might adversely affect the market value of the property and entering any observations on the seller's Condition of Property (Transfer) Disclosure Statement (TDS) if not already noted on the TDS by the seller or if inconsistent with the seller's disclosures, regardless of whether a home inspector's report has been or will be obtained by the seller [Calif. Civil Code §2079];

- assuring compliance by the seller with the **seller's duty** to deliver statements to prospective buyers as soon as practicable, i.e., disclosing a variety of facts about natural hazards (NHD), the condition of the property (TDS), the local environment (TDS), Mello-Roos liens, lead-based paint, neighborhood industrial zoning, occupancy and retrofit ordinances, military ordnance locations, condo documents, etc., **by providing the seller** with statutory forms at the listing stage to be filled out by the seller, and picking up the seller prepared and signed documents for inclusion in the marketing/listing package to be handed to prospective buyers;

- **reviewing and confirming**, without further investigation or verification by the listing agent, that all the information and data in the disclosure documents received from the seller are consistent with the listing agent's knowledge about the information and data, and if not, correct the information and data, or if the listing agent has reason to believe the information might not be accurate, either investigate and clarify the information or disclose his uncertainty about the information to the seller and the prospective buyer;

- advising the seller on **risk avoidance procedures** by recommending the seller obtain third-party inspections of the property's condition and its components (roof, plumbing, septic, water, etc.), to **reduce the exposure** to claims by a buyer who might discover deficiencies in the property not known to the seller or the listing agent or, worse yet, were known and not disclosed prior to entry into a purchase agreement, and then make a demand on the seller (and the broker) to correct the defects or reimburse the buyer for the costs incurred to correct them; and

- **responding to inquiries** by the prospective buyer or buyer's agent into conditions relating to any aspect of the property with a full and fair answer of related facts known to be or which might be considered detrimental to the value of the property without suppressing further investigation or inquiry by the buyer or the buyer's agent since the inquiry itself makes the subject matter a *material fact* about which the prospective buyer needs more information before completing negotiations or acquiring the property.

The pass-through of filtered information

A listing agent's statutory duty owed to prospective buyers to disclose facts about the integrity of the physical condition of a listed one-to-four unit residential property is limited to his prior knowledge about the property and the observations he made while conducting his **mandatory visual inspection**. To complete the disclosure process, the listing agent serves as a conduit through which property information provided by the seller is filtered before it is passed on to the prospective buyer.

Accordingly, all property information received from the seller must be reviewed by the listing agent for any inaccuracies or untruthful statements **known or suspected to exist** by the listing agent. Corrections or contrary statements by the listing agent must be included before the information may be used to market the property and induce prospective buyers to purchase.

Unless asked on an inquiry by a prospective buyer or buyer's agent, the listing agent need only comply with minimal disclosure requirements.

The extent to which disclosures about the physical condition of the property must be made is best demonstrated by what the listing agent is **not obligated** to provide.

Of concern to buyer's agents is the fact listing agents have **no duty to investigate** any of the information or data provided by the seller in an effort to authenticate its accuracy or truthfulness before passing it on to the prospective buyer.

However, before handing a prospective buyer information received from the seller, the listing agent must:

- **review the information** received from the seller;

- **include comments** about the agent's actual knowledge and observations he made during his visual inspection of the property which reflect the inaccuracies, inconsistencies, false nature or omissions in the seller's statements; and

- **identify the source** of the information as the seller.

The dumb agent rule

A listing agent on a one-to-four unit residential property **owes no affirmative duty** to a prospective buyer to gather or voluntarily provide the prospect with any facts about:

- the property's **title conditions**, consisting of encumbrances which a preliminary title report would disclose, such as easements, Covenants, Conditions and Restrictions (CC&Rs), legal descriptions, trust deed provisions, etc., other than assuring compliance by the seller with disclosures about liens for improvement district bonds, such as Mello Roos bonds;

- the **operating expenses** for the property (and any tenant income) the buyer will experience during ownership, such as utilities, sanitation, property taxes, yard and pool maintenance, insurance, etc., except the statutory disclosures the seller must make about any fire hazard clearance requirements which exist due to the property's location (NHD);

- the **zoning** or other **use restrictions** which may affect the buyer's future use of the property, except for the existence of industrial zoning, which affects the property, and nearby ordnance locations;

- the **income tax aspects** of the buyer's acquisition (or seller's disposition) of the property, such as limitations on interest deductions, avoidance of profit tax by exclusion or exemption on the sale of other property (on which the purchase of the listed property may be contingent);

- the **suitability of the property** to meet the buyer's objectives in the acquisition, be they financial, legal, possessory, etc.; and

- information or data on any **mixed use** of the property, such as acreage included in the purchase for use as subdividable lands, groves or other farming operations, or for use for tenant income or as a vacation rental.

Further, the listing agent owes no duty to prospective buyers to give advice, make recommendations, offer suggestions, comment on the extent of the adversity of the (adverse) facts disclosed, offer assistance (locate boundaries), investigate (due diligence), state an opinion or explain the effect on the buyer of any facts about the property's physical, natural or environmental conditions which have been provided by the listing agent.

However, **when asked** by the prospective buyer or a buyer's agent about any aspect, feature or condition which relates to the property or the transaction in some way, the listing agent is duty-bound to respond fully and fairly to the inquiry. The response must include material facts known to the listing agent about the subject matter of the inquiry and be free of half-truths and misleading statements.

Conversely, it is the buyer or the buyer's agent on his behalf who has a **duty to care for and protect** the buyer's best interests in the purchase of property. The buyer's agent, not the listing agent, must determine what due diligence efforts are first required before allowing the buyer to make the decision to purchase or close escrow.

Opinions in lieu of investigations

Consider a listing agent of a residence who is asked by a prospective buyer to point out the location of the boundaries for the lot on which the home is located. The listing agent does not provide the buyer with the metes and bounds description contained in subdivision maps or tell the buyer to investigate the location of the boundaries himself. Instead, the listing agent says the boundaries are represented by a fence which surrounds the property.

The listing agent does not indicate the source of this opinion, such as the seller, a surveyor or himself. He also does not conditionalize his statement with words such as "the boundaries in this subdivision are usually where the fence has been placed." The listing agent did not even say, "in my opinion" or "I believe" to state any uncertainty he may have about the location of the boundaries. His statement of the boundary location was absolute — it is the fence.

The buyer further indicates he intends to have a pool built for the use of his family if he acquires the property. The listing agent does not respond to the buyer's statement about the intent to build a pool. The listing agent has no actual knowledge of easements or zoning ordinances which could **adversely affect** implementation of the buyer's intended future use of the property.

Further, the buyer asks the seller to confirm whether the fences are the outside parameters of the property. The seller indicates the fences demarcate the division line between the properties.

Without further investigation, a purchase agreement is entered into by both the prospective buyer and the seller. In preparation of the purchase agreement offer, the listing agent does not include a contingency provision to provide the buyer with an opportunity to verify the location of the boundaries or to confirm his ability to obtain a permit to build a pool as a condition for closing escrow.

Prior to closing, the title company is not asked nor is a surveyor brought in to establish the boundaries. Neither the local planning department nor a pool contractor was consulted about the ability to obtain a permit to build a pool.

The actual facts place the location of the rear fence several feet beyond the property line, giving the rear yard the actual appearance of having sufficient room to accommodate a pool, which it will not. Also, an easement for water lines and a sewer line runs across the entire rear of the property, as well as along one side of the home allowing these services to be supplied to a rear, uphill property.

Here, the buyer acted in reliance on the listing agent's (and seller's) opinion about the location of the boundaries to close escrow. As a result, liability for the boundary discrepancy will be imposed on the listing agent for his failure to **conditionalize his statement** about the location of the boundaries. Without qualifying his statement, it was a misrepresentation about the actual location of the boundaries.

Further, the listing agent, due to his lack of actual knowledge of the easements, has no liability exposure for his failure to disclose the easements which further interfered with meeting the announced interest of the buyer to build a pool. The listing agent did not owe the buyer a duty to advise him of the need to check title for any easements or restrictions which might interfere with the construction of a pool.

The listing agent did conduct a visual inspection of the property and observed nothing which indicated the existence of an easement. Further, he knew nothing about any such easement and, importantly, had no duty to investigate the condition of title or zoning since they are public records and go beyond observations resulting from a visual inspection.

Since the buyer made an inquiry (boundaries) and announced an intended use of the property (build), the information about the subject matter of the inquiries and the announced use became *material facts*. When a listing agent responds, as he must, to an inquiry by a prospective buyer and gives information without conditionalizing his statement, **the buyer may rely** on the information and proceed to acquire the property without further confirmation of the accuracy or truthfulness of the information.

Here, due to the inquiry, the listing agent should have included a **contingency provision** in the purchase agreement. Then, the buyer would have been required as a condition of closing to further investigate. Thus, if the results of the due diligence investigation into the feasibility of constructing a pool (and the location of the boundaries) were not satisfactory to the buyer, he could have cancelled the transaction.

Without the inquiry from the buyer, the listing agent would not have volunteered his opinion about the location of the boundaries. Thus, without the inquiry he would not have gone beyond his minimum required disclosures about the physical condition of the property. Once he did respond to the request of the buyer, a contingency provision for further approval of the condition included in the purchase agreement would have avoided the dispute (and possibly the sale).

In response to an inquiry

A listing agent owes no duty to a prospective buyer to address the existence, much less the nature, of an easement located on the listed property. However, when the listing agent responds to an inquiry by the prospective buyer by providing information on the easement, he must state fully and fairly, without deceptive or misleading wording, his knowledge about the easement. Further, he must **identify the source** of his information if he has not confirmed its accuracy or correctness, or **condition his response** in such a way as to prevent the prospective buyer from justifying any reliance on the information without further investigation.

Consider a prospective buyer who has no experience in real estate matters. The prospective buyer deals directly with the listing agent of a property which seems suitable to the buyer. The prospective buyer observes a 30-foot easement on the subdivision map running the entire width of the frontage to the property. He asks the listing agent what the easement is about. The listing agent responds, explaining it is "for those water lines you find on the curb of the street, it is nothing to worry about."

The prospective buyer decides to buy the property and build a home on it. In escrow, the preliminary title report also reflects the easement. On further inquiry by the buyer, the listing agent again assures the buyer the easement is on the front side of the lot and is not a problem due to the large setbacks.

After close of escrow and commencement of construction of a residence, the local water company digs a ditch 16 feet deep and installs a major waterline. The interference of the easement causes the buyer to relocate his driveway to the side street entrance since placing the driveway over the easement would require the buyer to remove it at his expense should the water company again need to access the easement in the future.

The buyer makes a demand on the listing agent for lost value paid for the property. The buyer had relied on the listing agent's representation that the easement presented no problem to his use of the property, when in fact it did.

Here, the listing agent, having responded to an inquiry from the prospective buyer on the nature of the easement, must be candid in his explanation. The buyer must be informed about the significance of the buyer's limited ability to use the portion of the lot burdened by the encumbrance of the easement. Instead, the listing agent gave evasive answers calculated to stifle and avoid the buyer's further investigation into the true facts about the burden placed on the property by the easement.

Since a material fact is involved, the buyer's inquiry is entitled to a response based on the listing agent's working knowledge of the underlying facts or by identifying the source of the information given. If the listing agent lacks sufficient knowledge to comment, he is duty-bound to say so.

Ads based on seller information

A listing agent may use information obtained from a seller concerning the size of a property in an **advertisement** offering property for sale, such as stating a parcel contains more than one acre or a home contains 5,000 square feet. The listing agent does not need to investigate whether this information is accurate as long as it is not known to the agent to be false. Further, the agent does not need to identify the seller as the source of the data in his advertisement.

As for the advertisement used to locate buyers, the figure given must be consistent with the **observations** made by the listing agent while conducting his visual inspection of the property, e.g., does the property look like it contains more than one acre or look like a 5,000 square foot improvement? However, the listing agent is not required to measure the property or check the public records.

Conversely, in **response to an inquiry** from a prospective buyer expressing an interest or concern about the size of a parcel or improvement, the listing agent must either confirm the accuracy of the area or size, or attribute the information to a source.

For income-producing property, the operating income and expense data received from the seller can be passed on to the buyer or the buyer's agent by the listing agent by providing the buyer with the figures without either confirming its accuracy or disclaiming any responsibility for its correctness. However, no matter how presented to the prospective buyer, the listing agent is the conduit for information received from the seller. The listing agent must first **review it** and, if he has no knowledge the

data might be suspect, inaccurate or a misrepresentation, provide it to the prospective buyer and indicate the seller is the source of the data.

By giving the source of the information, the listing agent demonstrates the information **does not constitute the opinion** of the listing agent.

Sufficient notice to alert the buyer

Consider a listing agent of a condominium unit who is aware other units in the project have suffered water intrusion damage. Also, he is aware the homeowners' association (HOA) has filed a lawsuit against the developer to recover the cost of repair for the water intrusion damage in the affected units.

The agent conducts his statutorily mandated visual inspection of the unit, but finds no visible signs of water damage in the unit. The seller claims none exist.

A prospective buyer is located who is not represented by a broker. The seller's Condition of Property (TDS) disclosure on the property's physical condition, which includes the listing agent's observations, is handed to the buyer.

The TDS discloses the seller and the listing agent know of no water intrusion damage in the seller's unit. Further, the listing agent advises the prospective buyer about the existence of HOA litigation over water intrusion damage in other units within the project. The buyer does not further inquire or comment on the HOA litigation or water damages to the project.

The buyer then makes an offer to purchase the property as prepared by the listing agent. The offer contains wording acknowledging the buyer's awareness of the HOA's water intrusion lawsuit and receipt of the TDS, as well as other mandated disclosures.

Later, the listing agent receives newsletters and minutes from the HOA's meetings which further discuss the previously disclosed water intrusion problems. The listing agent also reads the HOA's complaint against the developer.

The documents contain no new information and are not brought to the attention of the buyer.

Escrow closes and the buyer moves into the unit. Later, the buyer discovers pre-existing water intrusion damage to the unit.

The buyer claims the listing agent owed him a **general duty** to pass on all documents known to exist concerning the **extent** of the water intrusion damage in the development, such as the newsletters, minutes from the HOA meetings and a copy of the lawsuit filed by the HOA.

Did the seller's listing agent sufficiently inform the buyer about the water intrusion problem to **place the buyer on notice** that a water intrusion problem existed?

Yes! The listing agent disclosed the essential facts necessary to notify the buyer about the water intrusion damage. Once informed of the potential problem within the project, it was the buyer's duty (or the buyer's agent's duty) to exercise reasonable care to protect the buyer.

With notice of the problem, any further details concerning the extent or nature of the water intrusion were **readily ascertainable** by the buyer on request of the listing agent, the HOA or a third-party investigator. It was not the duty of the listing agent to also advise the prospective buyer to investigate the consequences of the facts disclosed before deciding to buy. [**Pagano** v. **Krohn** (1997) 60 CA4th 1]

Minimum level of disclosure

A listing agent locating a prospective buyer for his client's one-to-four unit residential property owes a duty to the prospective buyer to conduct a reasonably diligent **visual inspection** of the property for defects which adversely affect the value of the listed property. On completing the inspection, the listing agent must note on the (seller's) TDS any defects **observable or known** to the listing agent which are not al-

ready noted by the seller or are inconsistent with the seller's disclosures. The TDS is to be handed to prospective buyers *as soon as practicable*. [CC §§2079 et seq.]

However, the visual inspection and investigation of one-to-four unit residential property by the listing agent and the disclosure of his knowledge and observations excludes other readily available information, such as:

- the inspection of areas reasonably and normally **inaccessible** to the broker;

- the investigation of **off-site areas** and areas surrounding the property; and

- the inquiry into or review of **public records** or permits concerning title or use of the property. [CC §2079.3]

However, the minimum disclosure rule does not apply to a buyer's broker or his agents, much less limit the buyer's agent's duty to fully and fairly inform and advise on what investigation the buyer should undertake.

Further, the minimum one-to-four unit inspection and reporting requirements imposed on listing agents excludes the **common law duty** still imposed on listing agents of other types of property to further investigate and disclose to buyers or sellers any material facts he discovers regarding:

- title conditions;

- the financial consequences of owning the property, such as the property's operating costs; or

- the tax aspects of the transaction (seller only).

Purpose of inspection

The one-to-four unit disclosure limitation on listing agents serves to set a minimum level of information and data to be disclosed to put the buyer and the buyer's agent on **notice of physical defects** in the property which are **observable or known** to the seller or the listing broker and his agents.

For example, an agent lists a residence located on a hillside. The property is subject to natural geological hazards including a high groundwater level, landslides and a fault line.

A prospective buyer for the property is located by the listing agent. The buyer is informed a neighboring owner has had problems with underground water on his property and that he installed a pump to manage the high water level. The listing agent also tells the buyer the neighbor's property previously suffered landslide damages.

The listing agent provides the buyer with a geological report the seller had acquired regarding the property. The report indicates the property lies within a geological hazard area and is susceptible to landslides and groundwater buildup.

The buyer is also informed a back fence was removed since erosion caused it to slide down the hillside. When asked by the buyer, the seller also discloses the pool is located in the front yard since a fault line runs through the backyard.

After a review of the disclosures, the buyer makes an offer to purchase the property.

The listing agent prudently includes a **further-approval contingency provision** in the purchase agreement. The contingency provision calls for the buyer to further investigate the hazards by obtaining his own geological report and approving it as a condition of closing.

Before closing, the buyer obtains a report which states the property shows signs of instability and confirms that a high groundwater level exists. The report also states the house does not show signs of cracking or distress.

During the escrow period, the listing agent attends a meeting between area homeowners and county officials in which the geological hazards of the properties in the area and possible solutions are discussed.

The listing agent does not inform the buyer of the occurrence of the meeting or the topics discussed since no information previously unknown to the agent and undisclosed to the buyer was released.

Later, after escrow closes, the residence slides down the hillside and is condemned by the county as uninhabitable.

On a complaint filed by the buyer, the Department of Real Estate (DRE) attempts to revoke the listing agent's license claiming the subject matter of the meeting held by county officials was itself a fact which should have been disclosed to the buyer by the listing agent since the mere occurrence of the town hall meeting might have affected the buyer's decision to buy.

However, the listing agent was the **exclusive representative of the seller** of one-to-four residential units and only had a general nonfiduciary duty of disclosure to the buyer, which is limited to:

- providing the buyer with all existing geological reports held by the seller or the agent; and

- disclosing groundwater and landslide problems known to the listing agent which occurred on the property or in the neighboring area.

Here, the listing agent properly disclosed the geological hazards of the property by alerting the buyer to the potential problems. The homeowners' meeting was not required to be brought to the buyer's attention since the meeting was a review of the same geological hazards already known to the agent and disclosed to the buyer. Also, the buyer's independent investigation under the further-approval contingencies did not deter the buyer from proceeding with the purchase of the residence.

Thus, the listing agent did not violate the limited general nonfiduciary duty he owed to the nonclient buyer to disclose sufficient information on adverse property conditions to put a prospective buyer on notice so he (or the buyer's agent) could take steps to protect and care for the buyer's best interests. Thus, the DRE cannot revoke the listing agent's license for limiting his disclosures to the initial notice of the defect in the property without further elaboration. [**Vaill** v. **Edmonds** (1991) 4 CA4th 247]

Chapter 22

Opinions with erroneous conclusions

This chapter discusses how an opinion formed by a broker or his agent, given to a prospective buyer to predict a future event or activity regarding the use and operation of a property, might impose liability should the opinion prove to be erroneous.

When an opinion becomes a guarantee

Occasionally, a buyer will ask either a listing agent or his own agent what the agent "believes, contemplates, anticipates or projects" will occur based on the agent's greater knowledge about the condition of a property.

The response of the **buyer's agent** to the buyer's questions about disclosures made by the listing agent will naturally be limited to the agent's knowledge and expertise on the subject. However, the opinion given in response will speculate, based on the observations, knowledge and beliefs of the agent, on the likelihood an event or condition will occur in the future. These statements by the buyer's agent to his buyer are either:

- couched in words of anticipation, estimation, prediction or projection, denoting it is a **mere opinion** about an uncertain future event; or

- worded as an assurance the events and conditions, as presented, will occur, a response reaching the level of a **guarantee**.

The difference between the wording used by an agent to express either an opinion or a guarantee creates the liability the agent is exposed to when:

- the buyer **acts in reliance** on the information by making an offer to buy or eliminating a contingency and acquiring the property; and

- **the event or condition fails to occur**.

An **opinion** is a statement by a broker or his agent, given as his contemplation concerning an event or condition which has not yet occurred. To be classified as an opinion, the statement must be developed by the agent based on **readily available facts** and his **knowledge** and **expertise** on the subject.

It is the nature of an opinion that the event or conditions speculated to come about need not actually occur. The **speculation** is about an uncertain future event or condition.

In an opinion, the event or condition expressed is not a factual representation. The event or condition expressed has not occurred and does not exist at the time the opinion is given. A **fact** is an existing condition, presently known or knowable by the agent due to the ready availability of data or information. Facts are the subject of disclosure rules, not the rules of opinion.

Special circumstances impose liability

A statement made to a buyer by any agent which **predicts** the future occurrence of an event, activity or condition is an *opinion*. The general rule is that the agent and his broker cannot be held responsible when the prediction given in an opinion does not come to fruition.

However, several **special circumstances** may surround an agent's giving of an opinion and raise his statement to the status of a *misrepresentation*.

If special circumstances exist, the broker and his agent are **exposed to liability** for the losses caused by the failure of the predicted event, activity or condition to occur.

Special circumstances which may cause a failed prediction to be an actionable misrepresentation include:

- an opinion which is given by an agent acting as the representative of the person who relies on the opinion, such as occurs between the listing agent and his seller or the buyer's agent and his buyer, called a *fiduciary agency relationship* [**Ford** v. **Cournale** (1973) 36 CA3d 172];

- an opinion which is given to a buyer by a listing agent who holds himself out as **specially qualified** or possessing **expertise** about the subject matter of the transaction [**Pacesetter Homes, Inc.** v. **Brodkin** (1970) 5 CA3d 206];

- an opinion which is given by a listing agent (or his seller) who has **superior knowledge** on the subject matter of the opinion under circumstances implying the agent (or the seller) has **inside information** not available to the buyer which makes the prediction worthy of reliance [**Borba** v. **Thomas** (1977) 70 CA3d 144]; or

- an opinion which is given to a buyer by a listing agent who **could not honestly hold or reasonably believe** the truth of his opinion due to facts known or readily available to him. [**Cooper** v. **Jevne** (1976) 56 CA3d 860]

An opinion based on facts

An **opinion** is an honestly held belief based on a reasonable (although sometimes faulty) analysis of property information known or readily available to the agent giving the opinion. However, the opinion does not by itself create any liability should the event not occur. A special condition needs to envelope the opinion to impose liability.

Consider a prospective buyer who is interested in acquiring a lot within a subdivision track and building a home on it.

The subdivider's listing agent, based on subdivision maps and discussions with the subdivider, advises the buyer all the lots in the entire tract of land are going to be the same size and subject to the same use restrictions requiring all homes built on the lots to be worth at least $400,000.

The buyer purchases the lot and builds his home in accordance with the use restrictions.

Due to an economic downturn at the end of the current business cycle, the subdivider resubdivides the remaining unsold lots and removes the use restrictions. The resubdividing is intended to increase the marketability of the unsold lots in the tract.

The buyer now seeks to rescind the purchase and recover his entire investment claiming the subdivider's agent made false representations about the subdivision which the buyer relied on to purchase the lot.

The listing agent claims he honestly believed in the truth of his representations that the subdivider would not in the future alter the lots remaining to be sold.

Here, the listing agent's representations about the lot size and the Covenants, Conditions & Restrictions (CC&Rs) the subdivider would require in the future were made truthfully, with no intent to deceive the buyer. Both the buyer and the subdivider had a reasonable basis for believing changes would not be necessary at the time of the purchase. However, a later shift in the economy warranted the changes as necessary to prevent the tract from deteriorating in its marketability.

The agent's statements about the future were **honestly entertained**. Thus, his statements qualify as an expression of his opinion.

Further, the buyer **did not reasonably rely** on the listing agent's opinion when he agreed to purchase the property. The buyer did not require the deed from the seller to include a grant of the promised rights that all the lots would be the same size with the same restrictions on minimum value. [**Meehan** v. **Huntington Land & Improvement Co.** (1940) 39 CA2d 349]

Conditional opinions

Special circumstances surrounding the giving of an opinion may create an environment in which the buyer, with good reason, **may rely** on the agent's opinion to make decisions.

Consider a developer of a residential duplex subdivision who provides his listing agent with a schedule of **projected rents**. The agent is instructed to inform prospective buyers these rents are estimates of the amounts obtainable from the duplexes should they buy one.

The developer has not developed properties in the area prior to this project. Also, he has no actual knowledge of the rents a duplex might obtain in the area.

A buyer with minimal investment property experience in the area contacts the listing agent for information about the duplexes being built.

The buyer is advised by the listing agent that "if you receive the rents we contemplate, it will be a good investment."

The buyer purchases a duplex, but is unable to locate tenants willing to pay the rental amounts the listing agent gave in his opinion. Ultimately, the buyer loses the property to foreclosure.

The buyer makes a demand on the listing agent and the listing agent's broker for the loss of his invested funds. The buyer claims the listing agent's statements about the property's future rental income were misrepresentations, which the buyer relied on to purchase the duplex,

since the listing broker, his agent and the developer had **superior knowledge** about rental conditions in the area.

The listing broker claims the statement his agent made about rental amounts was a mere opinion since it **conditioned success** on collecting these amounts.

Here, the listing agent's statement was only an estimate or opinion he held about future anticipated rental income for a new development since no operating history existed to draw on when making the projections. Thus, his opinion was based on **all readily available information.**

Also, the buyer's lack of experience as an owner of investment property, the agent's choice of words, i.e., "if" and "contemplate," and the developer's lack of prior rental experience in the area or knowledge of rents actually attainable by the duplexes made the statement an opinion. Thus, the buyer could not rely on the rent projections given by the adversarial listing agent as a fact which could reasonably motivate his decision to buy. [Pacesetter Homes, Inc., *supra*]

Conclusions drawn from opinions

An opinion given by a listing agent predicting the future occurrence of an event or condition concerning the buyer's use or management of a property does not impose liability on the listing agent for erroneous conclusions when the buyer is or has been made **aware of all the relevant facts** on which the agent's opinion is based.

Also, a buyer who has knowledge of and **equal access** to the same information and documents relied on by the listing agent to form his opinion, and has sufficient **time to conduct** his own independent investigation to ascertain the accuracy of the agent's opinion, cannot later claim he acted in reliance on the listing agent's opinion. This is especially true for buyers who possess the expertise needed to analyze the facts and make their own determination about the likelihood the agent's predictions will occur.

Thus, the buyer cannot ignore his own knowledge of the same facts used by the listing agent to develop the agent's opinion and then claim he relied on the listing agent's opinion as an assurance the prediction would occur.

Consider a leasing agent acting on behalf of a prospective tenant in lease negotiations with an experienced commercial landlord who has not retained the services of a real estate agent.

The leasing agent tells the landlord that "in my opinion" the tenant's annual gross sales receipts will be in excess of $5,000,000. After several months of negotiations conducted between the tenant's leasing agent and the seller's attorney, both of whom are very experienced practitioners, a lease agreement is entered into. The lease rent is a base monthly amount plus a percentage of annual gross sales receipts over $5,000,000. The landlord pays the leasing agent's fee.

A dispute erupts between the landlord and the tenant. The landlord now wants to recover the fee he paid the tenant's agent, claiming the agent actually represented the potential gross sales receipts as $7,500,000, an amount much higher than the sales the tenant would ever experience during the leasing period. Thus, the landlord would receive very little if any percentage rent above the fixed minimum rent.

Here, the tenant's agent prefaced his statements with the words "in my opinion." Also, a landlord cannot reasonably rely on or treat the representation of future gross sales as an event which will actually occur.

Thus, the landlord should have known the gross receipts prediction was just an estimate honestly made by the agent who represented the buyer. He could not treat the estimates of the adversarial agent as fact.

Further, the landlord had ample time and the means to make his own inquiries and analyze his findings. Since the landlord was not represented by a real estate agent, he should have conducted his own due diligence investigation if he intended to eliminate the uncertainties of estimates an agent made on behalf of the tenant. [**Foreman & Clark Corporation** v. **Fallon** (1971) 3 C3d 875]

Opinions of the buyer's broker

A **seller's broker** and listing agent, acting exclusively on behalf of a seller, have only a *general non-agency duty* to deal honestly and in good faith with a prospective buyer. As for a buyer, the listing agent's opinions are those of an adversary.

Thus, a listing agent's opinion cannot be reasonably relied upon by a prospective buyer as having a high probability of occurring, unless **special circumstances** surround the agent's act of giving an opinion.

In contrast, a **buyer's broker** and his agent have a *special fiduciary (agency) duty* to handle a buyer with the same level of care and protection a trustee would exercise on behalf of his beneficiary.

This **special agency duty** owed to a buyer raises an opinion given to a buyer by the buyer's broker or his agent to a higher level of reliability than had the same opinion been expressed by a listing agent acting solely on behalf of a seller. Thus, as a fiduciary, the opinion of the buyer's agent becomes an **assurance** that the condition or event which was the subject of the opinion will occur, unless the buyer's agent *conditionalizes* his opinion.

For the buyer's agent to give his opinion to his buyer and keep it from rising to an actionable assurance, the advice given with the opinion must include a **recommendation** to investigate and expertly analyze relevant information in order to confirm the agent's opinion. Further, a **contingency provision** covering the condition or event that is the subject of the opinion needs to be included in any offer the buyer makes and the contingency must be eliminated before closing. [Borba, *supra*]

Consider a buyer's agent who represents a prospective buyer looking for rental income property.

The buyer's agent is aware that the buyer's primary purpose for acquiring property is to receive a minimum amount of spendable income from the investment.

The agent locates a multi-unit apartment complex. The agent assures his buyer that:

- monthly vacancies will only be three or four units since the apartment complex is the only complex in the area which allows children and pets;

- the complex will require very little expense to maintain; and

- the buyer will receive the amount of spendable income sought from the investment.

Even though the seller's books and records are **readily available** for inspection, the buyer's agent does not verify the accuracy of the seller's income and expense statements, or confirm the maintenance costs. Without doing so, the agent fills out and hands his buyer an Annual Property Operating Data (APOD) sheet restating the representations already made to the buyer about the agent's projections of future income. [See **first tuesday** Form 352]

The buyer, in reliance on his agent's predictions about the property's future operations, enters into a purchase agreement with the seller as prepared by his agent. No **contingency provisions** are included to confirm the integrity of the improvements or investigate the income and expenses experienced by the seller.

After the buyer acquires the property, the buyer encounters higher maintenance costs and significantly lower rental income than represented by his agent. Also, the property has a high turnover rate and a large number of tenants are constantly delinquent in the payment of rent.

The buyer does not receive the sought-after minimum spendable income projected by his agent. Soon, due to persistent negative cash flow, the property is lost to foreclosure.

The buyer makes a demand on his agent for his lost investment, claiming the agent misrepresented the operations of the property. The buyer's agent rejects the demand, claiming his comments on the property's performance were opinions, not guarantees.

Here, the buyer had the **right to rely** on his agent's unconditional statements of facts about the property and treat them as true without concern for their verification since a fiduciary relationship existed between the buyer and his agent.

Thus, the buyer's agent's **predictions were misrepresentations**, the basis for the buyer's recovery of the value of the lost investment. The unfounded and careless predictions of the buyer's agent, given in an opinion as fact, constituted *deceit*, a form of misrepresentation. [Ford, *supra*]

Expertise of the broker or agent

Agents are known to be specialists and often properly hold themselves out as experts with **superior knowledge** about a particular type of transaction, such as high-end residential properties, apartment projects, industrial buildings or land. Prospective buyers, aware of a listing agent's specialty, often ask the agent for his opinion about some anticipated future use or operation of the property.

However, due to their experience, special training and education in a particular aspect of a property or type of transaction, listing agents may find that when they give their opinion to a buyer, their special qualifications suddenly become *reasonable justification* for the buyer to rely on their opinion as an **assurance** that the predicted event, activity or condition will actually be experienced as stated.

Thus, an agent's wording of his opinion needs to express that the opinion is **only his belief** or his thought on the matter. Having expressed an opinion, the agent then needs to include a further-approval contingency calling for the buyer to confirm information given in the opinion.

Consider a developer who controls a homeowners' association (HOA) which governs a subdivision of homes he is marketing to prospective buyers as having a panoramic view of the countryside.

The developer and his listing agent hold themselves out as experts in the establishment and administration of HOAs when questions about HOA operations and the Covenants, Conditions and Restrictions (CC&Rs) are received from prospective buyers.

The listing agent assures prospective buyers that the subdivision's CC&Rs protect the view from each lot, that any future landscaping or fencing requires approval from a special architectural committee, and that the committee will not approve fences or landscaping which interfere with the view. The recorded CC&Rs contain provisions for the committee and view protection which confirm the agent's statements.

However, an architectural committee is never setup. Further, all proposals for fences are reviewed and approved by the developer himself, a fact known to his agent, but not to prospective buyers. A prospective buyer pays a premium for a view lot improved with a home which has a panoramic view.

After acquiring the property, a neighbor erects a fence as approved by the developer. The fence blocks the buyer's view. The buyer makes a demand on the listing agent for his money losses brought about by a loss in value suffered by his property since the agent's statement on view rights failed to come true.

The listing agent claims his statement about the view rights was his opinion, given as a representative of the seller, a statement which could not be reasonably relied on by the buyer when making a decision to purchase the property.

Here, the listing agent held himself out as **an expert** on association management and CC&Rs enforcement. The agent then stated the CC&Rs and architectural committee would maintain the view provided by the development.

However, the listing agent knew the committee required to make such decisions had not been created and that the developer himself had full control. Thus, the buyer could pursue the agent to recover his lost value, i.e., the view, due to his false opinion about the HOA's ability to protect the buyer's view rights in the future.

When an agent holds himself out to be specially qualified and informed in the subject matter expressed in his opinion regarding future expectations, his opinion becomes a **positive statement of truth** on which a buyer or seller of lesser knowledge can rely. [**Cohen** v. **S & S Construction Co.** (1983) 151 CA3d 941]

Inducing reliance by assurances

All agents give opinions to buyers predicting all sorts of events or conditions the buyer will experience after acquiring a property. However, when the opinion is **coupled with advice** expressing no further need for the buyer, or others on behalf of the buyer, to investigate and confirm the prediction, the opinion is elevated to the level of a *guarantee*.

The level of assurance equivalent to a guarantee also arises out of a **buyer's indication** to any agent that the buyer is relying on the agent to analyze a qualifying property to determine the property's ability to be used or operated as the buyer has indicated, and to advise on whether the property is suitable and will meet the buyer's expectations.

Also, any affirmative activities or statements of any agent designed to **suppress the buyer's inspection** of the property, his inquiries of the owner or the owner's manager or agents, or the employment of other experts when the agent knows the buyer will rely on the agent's representations about a property's future performance, are considered assurances which make the conclusion drawn in the opinion the equivalent of a fact.

If the predicted event or condition does not come to pass and it was the **buyer's agent** who suppressed the buyer's due diligence activities, the buyer's agent is liable for the lost *benefit of the bargain* he predicted would occur, including projected net spendable income, not just the loss of the price paid.

As for the **listing agent's** liability to the buyer under the same circumstances, liability is limited to the loss of the price paid and no future losses are collectable.

Facts not supporting the conclusion

An agent's opinion must be a belief honestly held by the agent if the agent is to avoid liability when the predicted event or condition does not occur. For an agent to hold an **honest belief,** the opinion must be formed based on a due diligence investigation and knowledge of all readily available facts which have a bearing on the probability of the event or condition occurring.

When facts affecting the conclusion drawn by the agent in his opinion are known or readily available to the agent, the test of an *honestly held opinion* is whether the agent giving the opinion **should have known better** than to give such an opinion.

Thus, an agent who fails to conduct a due diligence investigation to determine the facts before expressing an opinion which the investigation would have influenced will be liable for his opinion as a misrepresentation should the event or condition fail to occur, no matter his wording to limit the prediction to a mere speculative opinion.

Without first having the facts on which to base an opinion, the agent's opinion is either an *unfounded guess* or an *unreasonable assumption* about events and conditions he predicts will occur in the future.

Consider a listing agent for a condominium project who advertises "luxury" condos for sale. The listing agent knows the condos are poorly constructed and that the defects are unobservable to someone not knowledgeable in the field of construction.

A buyer contacts the agent for more information.

The listing agent tells the buyer that the condos are an "outstanding" investment opportunity. Unaware of the defects, the buyer purchases a condo.

The buyer soon discovers that the building housing the condos is in danger of falling down.

Here, the listing agent (and his broker) are guilty of both *affirmative* and *negative fraud*.

By telling the buyer that the condos were an outstanding investment opportunity, an opinion the broker could not have honestly held in light of his knowledge of the construction defects, the broker's representation is an **affirmative fraud,** also called an *intentional misrepresentation*. The listing agent should have known better than to give such an opinion.

Also, the significant defects in the "luxury" project were **material facts** since they adversely affected the present value and desirability of the condos. Accordingly, the listing broker is liable for damages caused by his nondisclosure (omission) of the defects which were known to him, but unknown and unobservable by the buyer, an example of a representation which is a **negative fraud**, also called *deceit*. [Cooper, *supra*]

Predicting the conduct of others

The transfer of real estate to a buyer typically involves **third parties** who are not principals or agents in the transaction. Approval, consent, administrative review and other like-type **conduct by others** regarding some event or condition which is to occur before or after closing, cause buyers to be concerned about whether the third party will respond favorably to the proposed transaction. As a result, buyers ask agents what they believe might be the **reaction of others**, such as a HOA, water authority, landlord, contractor, lender, attorney, accountant, planning agency or redevelopment agency.

Consider agricultural land listed for sale. For a buyer to receive water from the Bureau of Reclamation, the buyer must obtain approval of the purchase price from the Bureau, a third party.

The listing agent locates a buyer.

A purchase agreement is drawn up contingent on the Bureau's approval of the purchase price. The agent estimates the approval process will take 30 to 60 days.

The buyer, concerned with meeting the planting deadline for this season, asks the listing agent about the probability of the Bureau's approval.

The agent consults with his seller as to whether the transaction would be approved by the Bureau since the seller has dealt with the Bureau over water issues before.

The seller says "he believes" it would.

The listing agent tells the buyer of the seller's opinion on Bureau approval. The buyer waives the Bureau-approval contingency, stating he will get the approval later. Escrow is closed.

The buyer files for Bureau approval of the sale when the property's natural well caves in.

The Bureau refuses to approve the transaction. Thus, the Bureau will not provide water.

The buyer seeks to recover his losses from the seller, claiming the seller's prediction of a future event (approval by the Bureau) was a fact on which he could rely in his purchase of the property.

However, nothing suggests the seller or the listing agent held themselves out to be **specially qualified** on the subject of Bureau approval. Thus, the seller's erroneous prediction about the approval was not a misrepresentation of fact, but a mere expression of his opinion.

The seller's access to and awareness of facts concerning the Bureau's approval process or likelihood of approval were either **known or equally available** to the buyer. If the buyer is curious about the details and paperwork needed for the approval, the buyer (or his agent) is duty bound to contact the Bureau himself.

Furthermore, unless a **special relationship** exists between the seller and buyer, the buyer is not entitled to rely on the opinion of the seller (or the listing agent) concerning the future decisions of a public body, in this case, the Bureau of Reclamation. [Borba, *supra*]

When the buyer has ready access to the third party, the **buyer's reliance** on the opinion of the seller's listing agent is *unjustified*. All the buyer need do to answer his own inquiry is contact the person involved and inquire himself.

As for a buyer's agent, his response to his buyer's inquiry may be an opinion on the probability of a positive or negative reaction by the third party, but must be accompanied with the advice to make the offer to purchase conditioned on getting the approval. If the contingency already exists, then get the approval to satisfy the contingency or be disapproved and cancel.

Estimates as projections or forecasts

Estimates presented to prospective buyers by agents are labelled with many titles and arise in a variety of real estate transactions. Every transaction offers agents the opportunity to provide estimates for their clients or the other principals involved. Estimates include approximations, predictions, pro-forma statements, anticipated expenditures and contemplated charges.

Estimates relate to income and/or expenditures, such as exist in:

- seller's net sheets;

- buyer's cost sheets;

- operating cost sheets for owner-occupied properties;

- APODs on income properties;

- loan origination or assumption charges;

- lender impounds;

- rent schedules (rolls);

- repair costs for clearances; and

- any other like-type predictions of costs or charges.

Estimates by their nature are not facts. The amounts estimated have not yet actually occurred. The amount estimated will become certain only by its occurrence in the future. The amount actually experienced may or may not equal the amount estimated.

A document entitled an "estimate" is typically based on the actual amount which would currently be experienced. Thus, estimates are expected to be quite accurate in amount, not just a guess. Words used in titles such as contemplated, pro-forma, anticipated or predicted indicate something less than an accurate estimate and provide less basis for a client to rely on them as an assurance they will occur.

Opinions voiced by agents about an income property's future performance fall into one of three general categories:

- *projections*;

- *forecasts*; or

- *unfounded opinions*.

A **projection** is prepared by a listing agent on a property's annual operations using an APOD sheet which will be handed to prospective buyers to induce them to purchase the property. The data entered on the APOD by the agent is a projection based exclusively on the income and expenses **actually incurred** by the owner/seller of the property during the preceding 12-month period.

The amounts experienced by the owner/seller during the past year are **projected to occur** (again) over the next year, adjusted by the agent for any trends in income and expenses reflected by information currently available or presently known to the owner or the agent.

Trend information is used in a projection to make mathematical adjustments to income and expenses based on market conditions or implementable rent control increases, and to operating costs known to be increasing (or decreasing) by prior announcements of the providers.

Thus, the past year's operations experienced by the property are anticipated to be repeated, as adjusted, and occur again during the first 12 months of operation by a new owner. No estimations, contemplations or use of figures other than those experienced by the owner are used to prepare a projection, except for adjustments to reflect changed conditions known (or should be known due to readily available facts). If these adjustments are not included in the projection, the opinion is not honestly held since it would be an opinion not actually held or not reasonably held by the agent or seller preparing the projection.

A **forecast** is an entirely different opinion from a projection, although both are based on beliefs about events and conditions which are honestly believed will likely occur in the future.

A forecast requires the knowledge and analysis of an anticipated change in circumstances (other than trend factors used for projections) which will influence the future income, expenses and operations (use) of a property and produce **forward changes** in income and expense the preparer of the forecast believes will probably occur under new or developing circumstances.

Changes in circumstances which might affect the income, expenses and debt servicing the buyer **should experience** during the 12-month period following the close of escrow and would be considered in a forecast include:

- new management;
- rent increases up to current market rates;
- elimination of deferred maintenance and replacement of obsolete fixtures/appliances (renovation);
- changes in rent control ordinances;
- new construction adding to the supply of competing income properties;
- commodity market prices (natural gas, water, fuel oil, electricity, etc.);
- local and state government fiscal demands for revenue and services (taxes);
- federal monetary policy effects on short-term and long-term rates (controlling any ARM loans encumbering the property or refinancing);
- demographics of increasing/decreasing population density in the area immediately surrounding the property (age and appreciation for the location);
- traffic count changes anticipated (due to traffic buildup or diversions);
- zoning changes reducing, altering or increasing the availability of comparable competitive properties;
- government condemnation, relocation or redevelopment actions;
- changes in the local employment base of employed and unemployed individuals;
- on-site security measures for the prevention of crime;
- the age and condition of the major components of the structure;
- local socio-economic trends; and
- municipal improvement programs affecting the location of the property.

Chapter 23

Condition of property: the owner's disclosures

This chapter explains the affirmative duty of a seller and his listing agent to disclose their awareness and knowledge about the property's condition to a prospective buyer.

Mandated on four-or-less residential units

A seller of a one-to-four unit residential property must **complete and deliver** to a prospective buyer a statutory form called a *Transfer Disclosure Statement* (TDS), generically called a Condition of Property Disclosure Statement. [Calif. Civil Code §§1102(a), 1102.3; see Form 304 accompanying this chapter]

The seller must prepare the mandatory TDS with **honesty and in good faith**, whether or not a broker and listing agent is retained by the seller to assist in its preparation. [CC §1102.7]

When preparing the TDS, the seller sets forth any property defects **known or suspected** to exist by the seller.

Any conditions known to the seller which **negatively affect** the value and desirability of the property must be disclosed, even though they may not be preprinted on the TDS. Disclosures to the buyer are not limited to the items preprinted on the form. [CC §1102.8]

Any attempt to have the buyer **waive delivery** of the statutorily-mandated TDS, such as by use of an "as-is" provision in the purchase agreement, is *void* as against public policy. The words "as is" should never be used. The words imply a failure to disclose something known to the seller or the listing agent. [CC §1102.1(a)]

Delivery of the disclosure statement

While it is the seller who must prepare the TDS, it is the agent who obtains the purchase agreement offer from the buyer who must hand the buyer the seller's Condition of Property Disclosure Statement. If the sales transaction is directly between the seller and buyer, without the participation of an agent in negotiations, the seller has the obligation to deliver the TDS to the buyer. [CC §1102.12]

The failure of the seller or any of the agents to **deliver** the seller's TDS to the buyer will not invalidate a sale of property which has closed. However, the seller and the listing broker will be liable to the buyer for the amount of actual monetary losses caused by an undisclosed defect known to them, a point of law which has always existed. [CC §1102.13]

For the seller's disclosure statement to be an effective pronouncement, **material defects** in the integrity of the property must be disclosed to the buyer before the price of the property is agreed to by acceptance of an offer or counteroffer.

If the seller's statement is delivered to the buyer of a one-to-four unit residential property after the seller enters into a purchase agreement, the buyer has the right to:

- **cancel** the purchase agreement on discovery of undisclosed defects known to the seller and unobserved by the buyer or the buyer's agent prior to acceptance [CC §1102.3];

- **make a demand** on the seller to correct the defects or reduce the price accordingly before escrow closes [See **first tuesday** Form 150 §11.2]; or

- **close escrow** and make a demand on the seller for the costs to cure the defects known to the seller and not disclosed prior to acceptance. [**Jue** v. **Smiser** (1994) 23 CA4th 312]

Buyer's right to cancel

The Condition of Property Disclosure Statement is to be delivered to a buyer as soon as practicable, and in any event, before closing a sale. **Delivery** of the seller's TDS to the buyer is deemed to have been met if the TDS is attached to the purchase agreement offer made by the buyer or the counteroffer made by the seller. [CC §1102.3]

If the TDS is belatedly delivered to the buyer — after he enters into a purchase agreement — the buyer may, among other remedies, **elect to cancel** the purchase agreement under a statutory three-day right to cancel. The buyer's statutory cancellation right runs for three days following the day of the in-escrow delivery of the disclosure statement. [CC §1102.3]

However, buyers are not required to cancel the purchase agreement and "go away" on their in-escrow receipt of an unacceptable TDS.

As an alternative to canceling the purchase agreement on receipt and review of the seller's disclosure statement, the buyer may **make a demand** on the seller to cure any material defect (affecting value), which was known to the seller and not disclosed or known to the buyer prior to entering into the purchase agreement. The same rule holds for the listing agent who has knowledge of defects and does not disclose the facts to the buyer before the buyer enters into the purchase agreement. [See **first tuesday** Form 269]

If the seller will not cure the defects, the buyer may close escrow and recover the cost incurred (or valuation lost) to correct the defect. The defects must be known and undisclosed, or inaccurately disclosed, by the seller at the time of acceptance of the purchase agreement. [Jue, *supra*]

Another alternative for the buyer is to complete the purchase by tendering a **price reduced** by the cost to repair or replace the defects known to the seller and undisclosed (or unconditionally misrepresented) on the date the purchase agreement was entered into. [See **first tuesday** Form 150 §11.2]

Reliance limited to seller's awareness

On listing his home for sale, a seller of a one-to-four unit residential property signs and hands his listing agent a completed Condition of Property Disclosure Statement.

A preprinted disclaimer contained in the TDS states the disclosures made by the seller on the form:

- **may not be relied on** by a buyer as a warranty of the actual condition of the property; and

- are **not part of the terms** of the purchase agreement (even though the disclosure statement may be attached).

On the disclosure statement, the seller indicates he is **unaware** of any building code violations on the property. The listing agent adds nothing as he has no knowledge to the contrary and his visual inspection brought nothing to his attention as a violation.

A buyer is located, a purchase agreement entered into and escrow opened. During the escrow period, the buyer is handed the TDS, which he approves. Prior to closing escrow, a county building inspector contacted by the buyer advises the buyer that building code violations exist on the property.

After closing, the buyer makes a demand on the seller to pay the cost of correcting the code violations, claiming the seller misrepresented the condition of the property since the seller failed to disclose in the Condition of Property Disclosure Statement that building code violations existed on the property.

CONDITION OF PROPERTY
Transfer Disclosure Statement — TDS

This disclosure statement is prepared for the following:

☐ Seller's listing agreement

☐ Purchase agreement

☐ Counteroffer

☐ _____

dated_____, 20_____, at _____, California,

entered into by _____,

and _____.

REAL ESTATE TRANSFER DISCLOSURE STATEMENT

THIS DISCLOSURE STATEMENT CONCERNS THE REAL PROPERTY SITUATED IN THE CITY OF

_____, COUNTY OF _____, STATE OF CALIFORNIA,

DESCRIBED AS _____

_____

_____

_____

_____

_____

_____

_____.

THIS STATEMENT IS A DISCLOSURE OF THE CONDITION OF THE ABOVE DESCRIBED PROPERTY IN COMPLIANCE WITH SECTION 1102 OF THE CIVIL CODE AS OF _____, 20_____. IT IS NOT A WARRANTY OF ANY KIND BY THE SELLER(S) OR ANY AGENT(S) REPRESENTING ANY PRINCIPAL(S) IN THIS TRANSACTION, AND IS NOT A SUBSTITUTE FOR ANY INSPECTIONS OR WARRANTIES THE PRINCIPAL(S) MAY WISH TO OBTAIN.

COORDINATION WITH OTHER DISCLOSURE FORMS

This Real Estate Transfer Disclosure Statement is made pursuant to Section 1102 of the Civil Code. Other statutes require disclosures, depending upon the details of the particular real estate transaction (for example: special study zones and purchase-money liens on residential property).

Substituted Disclosures: The following disclosures and other disclosures required by law, including the Natural Hazard Disclosure Report/Statement that may include airport annoyances, earthquake, fire, flood or special assessment information, have or will be made in connection with this real estate transfer, and are intended to satisfy the disclosure obligations on this form, where the subject matter is the same:

☐ Inspection reports completed pursuant to the contract of sale or receipt for deposit.

☐ Additional inspection reports or disclosures:_____

_____

_____

_____

_____

_____

_____

SELLER'S INFORMATION

Seller discloses the following information with the knowledge that even though this is not a warranty, prospective Buyers may rely on this information in deciding whether and on what terms to purchase the subject property. Seller hereby authorizes any agent(s) representing any principal(s) in this transaction to provide a copy of this statement to any person or entity in connection with any actual or anticipated sale of the property.

THE FOLLOWING ARE REPRESENTATIONS MADE BY THE SELLER(S) AND ARE NOT REPRESENTATIONS OF THE AGENT(S), IF ANY. THIS INFORMATION IS A DISCLOSURE AND IS NOT INTENDED TO BE PART OF ANY CONTRACT BETWEEN THE BUYER AND SELLER.

Seller ☐ is, ☐ is not, occupying the property.

A. The subject property has the items checked below **(read across):**

☐ Range   ☐ Oven   ☐ Microwave
☐ Dishwasher   ☐ Trash Compactor   ☐ Garbage Disposal
☐ Washer/Dryer Hookups   ☐ Rain Gutters
☐ Burglar Alarms   ☐ Smoke Detector(s)   ☐ Fire Alarm
☐ TV Antenna   ☐ Satelite Dish   ☐ Intercom
☐ Central Heating   ☐ Central Air Conditioning ☐ Evaporator Cooler(s)
☐ Wall/Window Air Conditioning ☐ Sprinklers   ☐ Public Sewer System
☐ Septic Tank   ☐ Sump Pump   ☐ Water Softener
☐ Patio/Decking   ☐ Built-in Barbecue   ☐ Gazebo
☐ Sauna
☐ Hot Tub ☐ Locking Safety Cover*   ☐ Pool ☐ Child Resistant Barrier*   ☐ Spa ☐ Locking Safety Cover*
☐ Security Gate(s)   ☐ Automatic Garage Door Opener(s)* Number of Remote Controls:_____
Garage: ☐ Attached   ☐ Not Attached   ☐ Carport
Pool/Spa Heater: ☐ Gas   ☐ Solar   ☐ Electric
Water Heater: ☐ Gas   ☐ Anchored, Braced or Strapped*   ☐ Private Utility or
                                                            Other:_____

Water Supply: ☐ City   ☐ Well
Gas Supply: ☐ Utility   ☐ Bottled
☐ Window Screens   ☐ Window Security Bars
                               ☐ Quick Release Mechanism on Bedroom Windows*

Exhaust Fan(s) in_____
220 Volt Wiring in_____
Fireplace(s) in _____
Gas Starter _____
Roof(s): Type_____
Age:_____ (approx.)
☐ Other:_____
_____
_____
_____
_____
_____
_____

Are there, to the best of your (Seller's) knowledge, any of the above that are not in operating condition?
☐ Yes ☐ No
If yes, then describe (attach additional pages if necessary): _____
_____
_____
_____
_____ ☐ Addendum attached

B. Are you (Seller) aware of any significant defects/malfunctions in any of the following: .... ☐ Yes ☐ No
If yes, check appropriate boxes below.
☐ Interior Walls   ☐ Ceilings   ☐ Floor   ☐ Exterior Walls ☐ Insulation ☐ Roof(s)   ☐ Windows
☐ Doors   ☐ Foundation ☐ Slab(s) ☐ Driveways   ☐ Sidewalks ☐ Walls/Fences
☐ Electrical Systems   ☐ Plumbing/Sewers/Septics
☐ Other Structural Components (describe): _____
_____
_____
_____

If any of the above is checked, explain (attach additional pages if necessary): _____

_____

_____

_____

_____

_____

_____

_____ ☐ Addendum attached

*This garage door opener or child resistant pool barrier may not be in compliance with the safety standards relating to automatic reversing devices as set forth in Chapter 12.5 (commencing with Section 19890) of Part 3 of Division 13 of, or with the pool safety standards of Article 2.5 (commencing with Section 115920) of Chapter 5 of Part 10 of Division 104 of, the Health and Safety Code. The water heater may not be anchored, braced or strapped in accordance with Section 19211 of the Health and Safety Code. Window security bars may not have quick-release mechanisms in compliance with the 1995 edition of the California Building Standards Code.

C. Are you (Seller) aware of any of the following:

1. Substances, materials or products which may be an environmental hazard, such as, but not limited to, asbestos, formaldehyde, radon gas, lead-based paint, mold, fuel or chemical storage tanks, and contaminated soil or water on the subject property . . . . ☐ Yes ☐ No

2. Features of the property shared in common with adjoining landowners, such as walls, fences and driveways, whose use or responsibility for maintenance may have an effect on the subject property . . . . ☐ Yes ☐ No

3. Any encroachments, easements or similar matters that may affect your interest in the subject property . . . . ☐ Yes ☐ No

4. Room additions, structural modifications or other alterations or repairs made without necessary permits . . . . ☐ Yes ☐ No

5. Room additions, structural modifications or other alterations or repairs not in compliance with building codes . . . . ☐ Yes ☐ No

6. Landfill (compacted or otherwise) on the property or any portion thereof . . . . ☐ Yes ☐ No

7. Any settling, from any cause, or slippage, sliding or other soil problems . . . . ☐ Yes ☐ No

8. Flooding, drainage or grading problems . . . . ☐ Yes ☐ No

9. Major damage to the property or any of the structures from fire, earthquake, floods or landslides . . . . ☐ Yes ☐ No

10. Any zoning violations, nonconforming uses or violations of "setback" requirements . . . . ☐ Yes ☐ No

11. Neighborhood noise problems or other nuisances . . . . ☐ Yes ☐ No

12. CC&Rs or other deed restrictions or obligations . . . . ☐ Yes ☐ No

13. Homeowners' Association which has any authority over the subject property . . . . ☐ Yes ☐ No

14. Any "common area" (facilities, such as pools, tennis courts, walkways or other areas co-owned in undivided interest with others) . . . . ☐ Yes ☐ No

15. Any notices of abatement or citations against the property . . . . ☐ Yes ☐ No

16. Any lawsuits by or against Seller threatening to or affecting this real property, including any lawsuits alleging a defect or deficiency in this real property or "common areas" (facilities, such as pools, tennis courts, walkways or other areas co-owned in undivided interest with others) . . . . ☐ Yes ☐ No

If the answer to any item in Section C is yes, explain (attach additional pages if necessary): _____

_____

_____

_____

_____

_____

_____

_____ ☐ Addendum attached

Seller certifies that the information herein is true and correct to the best of Seller's knowledge as of the date signed by Seller.

Seller:_____ Date:_____, 20_____

Seller:_____ Date:_____, 20_____

SELLER'S AGENT'S INSPECTION DISCLOSURE
(To be completed only if the Seller is represented by an agent in this transaction):

THE UNDERSIGNED, BASED ON THE ABOVE INQUIRY OF THE SELLER(S) AS TO THE CONDITION OF THE PROPERTY AND BASED ON A REASONABLY COMPETENT AND DILIGENT VISUAL INSPECTION OF THE ACCESSIBLE AREAS OF THE PROPERTY IN CONJUNCTION WITH THAT INQUIRY, STATES THE FOLLOWING:

☐ Agent notes no items for disclosure.

☐ Agent notes the following items: _____

_____

_____

_____

_____

_____

_____

_____

_____

_____

_____

_____

_____

_____

_____

Listing Broker: _____
(Broker representing Seller — Please print)

By: _____ Date:_____, 20_____
(Associate Licensee or Broker Signature)

BUYER'S AGENT'S INSPECTION DISCLOSURE
(To be completed only if the agent who has obtained the offer is other than the agent above):

THE UNDERSIGNED, BASED ON A REASONABLY COMPETENT AND DILIGENT VISUAL INSPECTION OF THE ACCESSIBLE AREAS OF THE PROPERTY, STATES THE FOLLOWING:

☐ Agent notes no items for disclosure.

☐ Agent notes the following items: _____

_____

_____

_____

_____

_____

_____

_____

_____

_____

_____

_____

_____

_____

Selling Broker: _____
(Broker obtaining the offer — Please print)

By:_____ Date:_____, 20 _____
(Associate Licensee or Broker Signature)

BUYER(S) AND SELLER(S) MAY WISH TO OBTAIN PROFESSIONAL ADVICE AND/OR INSPECTIONS OF THE PROPERTY AND TO PROVIDE FOR APPROPRIATE PROVISIONS IN A CONTRACT BETWEEN BUYER(S) AND SELLER(S) WITH RESPECT TO ANY ADVICE/INSPECTIONS/DEFECTS.

I/We acknowledge receipt of a copy of this statement.	I/We acknowledge receipt of a copy of this statement.
Date:_____, 20_____	Date:_____, 20_____
Buyer: _____	Seller: _____
Buyer: _____	Seller: _____
Buyer's Broker:	**Seller's Broker:**
Date:_____, 20_____	Date:_____, 20_____
Agent: _____ (Broker obtaining the offer — Please print)	Agent: _____ (Broker representing Seller — Please print)
By: _____ (Associate Licensee or Broker Signature)	By: _____ (Associate Licensee or Broker Signature)

SECTION 1102.3 OF THE CIVIL CODE PROVIDES A BUYER WITH THE RIGHT TO RESCIND A PURCHASE CONTRACT FOR AT LEAST THREE DAYS AFTER THE DELIVERY OF THIS DISCLOSURE IF DELIVERY OCCURS AFTER THE SIGNING OF AN OFFER TO PURCHASE. IF YOU WISH TO RESCIND THE CONTRACT, YOU MUST ACT WITHIN THE PRESCRIBED PERIOD.

A REAL ESTATE BROKER IS QUALIFIED TO ADVISE ON REAL ESTATE. IF YOU DESIRE LEGAL ADVICE, CONSULT YOUR ATTORNEY.

FORM 304   01-04   ©2006 **first tuesday**, P.O. BOX 20069, RIVERSIDE, CA 92516 (800) 794-0494

The seller claims the buyer is not entitled to recover the cost of curing the code violations. The TDS disclosed that the seller **possessed no knowledge** of any code violations when he prepared the disclosure statement received and approved by the buyer.

Here, the seller **disclosed his lack of actual knowledge** of any code violations in the TDS. The disclosure in the statement enables the seller to avoid liability for building code violations which actually existed and were unknown to the seller.

A seller completes the mandatory Condition of Property Disclosure Statement only as a disclosure of the seller's **state of awareness** (actual knowledge) regarding the condition of the property. Thus, the statement does not itself disclose the **actual conditions** which may exist on the property. In a word, it is not a *warranty* of the actual state of the property's condition. Instead, it is a statement of the seller's **awareness** of the property's condition.

The buyer's alternative remedies include:

- canceling the transaction under the statutory seller's disclosure scheme;

- requiring the violations be cured before escrow can close; or

- reducing the price by the cost to cure the violations.

Excuse my state of awareness

Serving as a **lack-of-awareness** disclosure, the statutory Transfer Disclosure Statement has become discredited as the buyer's primary source of information about the integrity of the physical condition of the property being purchased.

In practice, a listing agent hands the seller's TDS to a prospective buyer (or the buyer's agent) to **induce reliance** on its content to establish the integrity of the property's condition. With the TDS in hand, the buyer establishes the price, terms and conditions on which he will make an offer to purchase the property or close escrow.

The disclosure is not presented to the buyer by the listing agent as a "red flag warning" accompanied by instructions to the buyer to confirm the condition of the seller's state of awareness by obtaining a home inspection report to determine the actual condition of the property before entering into a purchase agreement or closing escrow.

However, the buyer's agent, mindful of the lack-of-awareness limitation on the effectiveness of the TDS, cannot in good faith allow his buyer to give any weight to the seller's disclosure statement, except for the defects actually disclosed.

Thus, the "not-a-warranty" disclaimer in the disclosure statement puts everyone on notice that the TDS is not a part of the purchase agreement. The fact the TDS is an addendum to the purchase agreement to evidence its delivery to the buyer does not make it a representation of the actual condition of the property. The question remains as to just what role the disclosure should play, other than to get the seller on record as to the defects he will disclose.

Buyers and their agents will learn not to use the disclosure handed them by the listing agent as a basis for setting a definitive price and terms of purchase. To everyone's benefit, the well-informed buyer will be induced to rely on home inspection reports, whether obtained by the seller or the buyer, to advise the buyer about the actual physical condition of the property and not on the seller and listing agent.

Include a home inspector

A competent listing agent will aggressively recommend to his sellers that they retain a **home inspector** at the earliest opportunity to conduct a physical examination to determine the condition of the property and issue a report on his findings before the property is marketed. [See Chapter 25]

A home inspector often detects and reports property defects overlooked by the seller and not observed during a visual inspection by the listing agent. Significant defects which remain undisclosed tend to surface after closing as claims against the listing broker for deceit. A home inspector troubleshoots for defects not observable to the untrained eye of a broker and his listing agent. [Calif. Business and Professions Code §7195]

Listing broker's mandatory inspection

A **seller's broker** (or the broker's listing agent) is obligated to personally carry out a visual inspection of the property. The seller's disclosures on the Condition of Property Disclosure Statement are then reviewed by the broker or the listing agent for discrepancies. They then add any information about their knowledge of material defects which have gone undisclosed by the seller (or the home inspector) and are known to the listing agent or observed during the agent's inspection.

A buyer has **two years** to pursue the seller's broker and listing agent to recover losses caused by the broker's or his agent's **negligent failure** to disclose observable and known defects affecting the physical condition and value of the property. Undisclosed defects permitting recovery are those which would have been observed by a reasonably competent broker during a visual on-site inspection. A listing agent is expected to be as competent in an inspection as his broker would be. [CC §2079.4]

However, the buyer will be unable to recover money from the seller's broker if the seller's broker or listing agent inspected the property and would not have observed the defect and did not actually know it existed. [CC §1102.4(a)]

Following their mandatory visual inspection, the seller's broker or his listing agent might make some of their disclosures on the seller's TDS by relying on **specific items** covered in a home inspector's report. Should the items relied on later be contested by the buyer as incorrect or inadequate, the broker and his agent are entitled to indemnification from the home inspection company issuing the report. [**Leko** v. **Cornerstone Building Inspection Service** (2001) 86 CA4th 1109]

Unconfirmed seller representations

Consider a broker who is acting as a relocation agent for a property owner's employer. The broker takes title to the owner's one-to-four unit residential property since it did not sell during the listing period. After taking title, a buyer is located for the property.

The prospective buyer is handed the previous owner's Condition of Property Disclosure Statement. The statement does not disclose night-time noise conditions which affect the property's value and were known to the owner. The broker does not know of the noise conditions and observes none during his day-time visual inspection of the property. Thus, he does not note the adverse condition on the owner's TDS in the space provided for an agent's comments.

The buyer, on occupying the property, discovers the undisclosed noise conditions. Due to the intensity of the noise, the value of the property is less than the price paid.

The buyer seeks to recover the lost value from the listing broker. The broker claims he is not liable for the lost value since he was unaware of any noise conditions and could not have observed the noise during his day-time visual inspection of the property.

The buyer claims the broker is liable for the lost value since he owed a duty to the buyer to

investigate and **verify** the prior owner's representations on the TDS for accuracy, not just visually inspect the property.

However, the seller's broker and his listing agent on the sale of a one-to-four unit residential property do not owe a duty to the buyer to investigate and confirm the truthfulness of the owner's representations. The broker does not represent the buyer. Thus, the listing broker is not liable for the lost value resulting from the undisclosed noise, unless known to the listing broker or his agent.

A listing broker's duty to the buyer is limited to conducting a visual inspection of the property and disclosing any **observations and actual knowledge** the listing broker or listing agent may have of the conditions on or about the property. The listing broker's awareness of conditions did not include the existence of night-time noise. [**Shapiro** v. **Sutherland** (1998) 64 CA4th 1534]

Nondisclosure by the seller

Now consider a residence which has a defect in its foundation. The defect affects the value of the property and is known to the seller, but not readily observable by a buyer.

The seller's Condition of Property Disclosure Statement does not reflect the seller's knowledge of the defective foundation.

A purchase agreement is entered into between the seller and buyer. The TDS is attached to the purchase agreement to acknowledge the buyer's receipt and avoid contingencies. Escrow is opened and the property is conveyed to the buyer on closing.

Within four years after escrow closes, the defective foundation worsens and becomes obvious to the buyer. The buyer makes a demand on the seller for his costs incurred to cure the defect.

Is the seller liable to the buyer for the cost incurred to repair the defective foundation?

Yes! Any seller, whether or not he is represented by a listing broker, has a duty to the buyer to disclose on the statutory Transfer Disclosure Statement all facts **known to the seller** about the condition of the property, which:

- are **not readily observable** by the buyer on an inspection of the property; and

- **affect the value and desirability**, and thus the integrity, of the property in the hands of the buyer. [**Prichard** v. **Reitz** (1986) 178 CA3d 465]

The broker's illegal "as-is" sale

Consider a listing agent who, on conducting his visual inspection of a property, has reason to believe the property fails to conform to building and zoning regulations.

The listing agent knows a prospective buyer interested in making an offer is not aware of the possible violations, and might view the property's value differently if he learns the violations may exist.

The buyer submits a purchase agreement offer. The listing agent prepares a counteroffer and includes an "as-is" disclaimer provision which the seller signs. The provision states the agent "makes no representations regarding the property and incurs no liability for any defects, the buyer agreeing to purchase the property 'as is.'" The counteroffer is submitted to the buyer and accepted.

After closing, the city refuses to provide utility services to the residence due to building code and zoning violations.

The buyer makes a demand on the seller's broker and listing agent for the buyer's money losses due to overpricing and the cost of corrective repairs. The buyer claims the seller's broker and listing agent breached their *general agency duties* owed the buyer. They failed to disclose material defects in the property **known** to the listing agent, but not the buyer.

The broker claims the buyer waived his right to collect money damages when he signed the purchase agreement with the "as-is" disclaimer.

Does use of an "as-is" disclaimer provision shield a listing broker from liability for the buyer's losses caused by the building and zoning violations which were **suspected to exist** by the broker's listing agent and not known or suspected by the buyer?

No! The seller's broker and listing agent have a **general duty**, owed to all parties in the transaction, to personally conduct a competent visual inspection of the property sold. Based on their inspection, they are to disclose **all known and observable** property conditions which adversely affect the value and desirability of the property which are not already known to the buyer. The breach of this duty by the listing agent's failure to disclose his knowledge or observations about **potential adverse conditions** is not excused by writing an "as-is" disclaimer into the purchase agreement in lieu of factual disclosures. [**Katz** v. **Department of Real Estate** (1979) 96 CA3d 895]

"As is" provisions become unnecessary to explain the condition of the property when information regarding defects is included in the seller's TDS and handed to the buyer. The seller simply discloses the defects, whether he does or does not agree to make repairs.

Further, public policy prohibits the sale of one-to-four unit residential property "as is." All buyers purchase property "as disclosed" by the seller, the seller's broker and the broker's agents, and as actually observed by the buyer **prior to entering** into the purchase agreement, unless negotiations on entering into a purchase agreement call for the seller to correct some or all of the previously disclosed defects. [CC §1102.1(a)]

Controlled and exempt sellers

Unless a seller is *exempt*, sellers of one-to-four unit residential real estate are required to furnish buyers with a statutory Transfer Disclosure Statement filled out by the seller. [CC §1102]

Listing brokers and their agents are never exempt from:

- conducting a **visual inspection** of a one-to-four unit residential property, sold or acquired on behalf of a seller or buyer [CC §2079]; and

- **disclosing their observations and knowledge** about the property on a TDS form or other separate document, whether or not the seller is exempt from using the form. [CC §1102.1]

Transactions which exempt the seller from preparing and delivering the statutory TDS to the buyer include transfers:

- by court order, such as probate, eminent domain or bankruptcy;

- by judicial foreclosure or trustee's sale;

- on the resale of real estate owned property acquired by a lender on a deed-in-lieu of foreclosure, or by foreclosure;

- from co-owner to co-owner;

- from parent to child;

- from spouse to spouse, including property settlements resulting from a dissolution of marriage;

- by tax sale;

- by reversion of unclaimed property to the state; and

- from or to any government agency. [CC §1102.2]

Duty to disclose on exempt sales

A seller who is exempt from the **use and delivery** of the statutory Condition of Property Statement to buyers still has a *common law duty* to prospective buyers to disclose all **known defects**. In exempt transactions, the seller and listing agent can use a separate document to make the disclosures, or they may use the TDS form to list the defects known or suspected by them to exist to avoid deceit. [CC §1102.1(a)]

The best property disclosure tool for exempt sellers is the preparation and delivery of the statutory disclosure form (and a property inspector's report) to prospective buyers or buyer's agents on every type of transaction. If the transaction is exempt or concerns property other than one-to-four residential units, the form should still be used.

Foreclosing lender's silent deceit

Consider a trust deed lender who holds a trustee's foreclosure sale on a one-to-four unit residential property. The lender knows soil defects exist on the property, but does not disclose the defects to the bidders at the trustee's sale — a sale which exempts the seller (lender) from use of the statutory Condition of Property Disclosure Statement. [CC §1102.2(c)]

The high bidder at the trustee's sale later discovers the property's soil defects. The high bidder demands a full return of the sales price from the lender in exchange for return of the property to the lender, a recovery remedy called *rescission and restoration.*

The high bidder claims the lender had a common-law duty to prospective bidders to disclose property defects known to the foreclosing lender which materially affect the value of the property.

The lender claims the exemption of a foreclosing lender's use of the TDS form at a trustee's sale **eliminates any duty** the lender or trustee may have had to disclose defects in the property's condition known to the them. The lender claims the ancient doctrine of *caveat emptor* or "buyer beware" controls the bidding at the foreclosure sale.

Can the high bidder rescind the sale for the lender's failure at the trustee's sale to disclose known material defects in the condition of the property?

Yes! A transaction which exempts sellers from using the statutory TDS form to disclose known defects does not eliminate the foreclosing lender's common-law duty owed to the buyer or immunize the lender from liability for failing to disclose property defects **actually known** to him which affect the property's value and desirability to prospective buyers. [**Karoutas** v. **HomeFed Bank** (1991) 232 CA3d 767]

What is the "as-is" condition?

Since *Karoutas*, legislation states a lender (or trustee) at a trustee's sale is not in violation of law if bidders are advised the property is being sold "as is." Thus, no *contractual warranties* are given by the lender about the property's condition. [CC §2924h(g)]

By announcing the property is being sold "as is," the lender does not warrant the actual condition of the property to the bidders.

Editor's note — However, even with legislation allowing lenders to sell property "as is" at trustee's sales to avoid a contractual warranty, Karoutas *represents a line of reasoning the courts will continue to uphold. A foreclosing lender will not be sheltered from liability for its intentional misrepresentation and deceit at a public sale when the buyer later discovers a material defect the lender knew existed and failed to disclose. The contractual disclaimer stating the property is sold "as is" draws the lender into a web of* **deceit by silence,** *called* intentional misrepresentation by omission.

Announcing the property is sold "as is" does not excuse the lender from his common-law duty to disclose those defects actually known to the lender which affect the value and desirability of the property. A lender selling property at a foreclosure sale does not have the listing broker's duty owed to a buyer to conduct a visual inspection (or a home inspector's duty to conduct a physical examination) of the property and disclose its findings to potential bidders. However, the lender does have and will continue to owe a common-law duty to disclose facts known to him which adversely affect the property's value. Disclosures will remain that way until the legislature states its intention to eliminate the lender's common-law disclosure duty by codifying the reestablishment of the long discredited doctrine of caveat emptor.

Chapter 24

Safety standards for improvements

This chapter discusses the need for the seller and listing agent to make disclosures about the property's noncompliance with current safety standards before acceptance of a buyer's offer.

Disclosing noncompliant improvements

A seller of a one-to-four unit residential property, who is solicited by a listing agent, enters into a listing agreement employing the agent's broker to locate buyers and sell the property.

The seller is asked to fill out a Transfer Disclosure Statement (TDS) and return it to the listing agent. When the TDS is filled out by the seller and picked up by the listing agent, the agent will conduct his own **visual inspection** of the property as mandated. On completion of the inspection, the agent will note any defects he observed on the TDS and sign it. [Calif. Civil Code §2079; see **first tuesday** Form 304]

The seller fills out and signs the TDS and returns it to the listing agent.

The listing agent then conducts his visual inspection of the property to identify components and defects not disclosed by the seller on the TDS. He **observes several safety conditions** which he knows do not meet current building codes. These observations are noted on the seller's TDS in the space provided above the location for the listing agent's signature.

The disclosure statement signed by the seller and listing agent now reveals that the garage door closing mechanism is not equipped with an automatic reversing device, the spa does not have a locking safety cover, the pool does not have barriers restricting access, the water heater is not anchored or braced, and the security bars on the windows in one of the bedrooms do not have a release mechanism — all in violation of current safety standards.

The TDS and all other seller disclosures and property reports are included as part of a listing package the listing agent will hand to prospective buyers and buyer's agents.

At an open house held on the property by the listing agent, a visitor indicates he is interested in possibly buying the property and asks for more information about the property.

By the visitor's request for additional property information, the visitor has begun negotiations. Thus, he has become a *prospective buyer*, entitled to a complete set of disclosures from the seller or the seller's agent before any offer is made.

The listing agent responds to the request by handing the prospective buyer the listing package which includes a copy of the TDS for the buyer's review.

A purchase agreement offer is then prepared and eventually signed by the prospective buyer, acknowledging receipt of the TDS and all other disclosures mandated for the transaction. The purchase agreement offer does not contain a provision calling for the seller to correct any of the **previously disclosed safety defects** or to bring the property up to current building standards.

However, prior to closing, the buyer becomes concerned about the existing safety defects. Also, local ordinances may require the safety defects to be eliminated before issuing the buyer a certificate of occupancy.

The buyer makes a demand on the seller to repair, replace or install an automatic reversing device for the garage door, a locking cover for the spa, barriers to restrict access to the pool, a brace or anchor on the water heater and security bar release mechanisms as necessary to meet current safety standards. The buyer claims the seller must cure the safety defects by meeting current construction standards before the seller can require the buyer to close escrow on the sale.

The seller refuses to cure any of the defects, claiming the buyer must close escrow since the **buyer knew** the defects existed before entering into the purchase agreement and the seller never agreed to correct the defects and bring the property up to current building codes.

Can the seller cancel or enforce the purchase agreement when the buyer refuses to close escrow due to the existence of physical defects in the property known to the buyer before the buyer agreed to purchase the property, which the seller has not agreed to cure?

Yes! The buyer knew the precise condition of the property when he agreed to the price he would pay to purchase the property.

Thus, the buyer agreed to acquire the property "as disclosed" in the seller's TDS. The buyer was **on notice** of the defects prior to his agreement to buy the property and did not bargain for the seller to cure the defects as a condition for paying the agreed price.

Automatic garage doors

All automatic garage doors installed after January 1, 1991 are required to have an automatic reverse safety device which meets code. [Calif. Health and Safety Code §19890(a)]

In addition, garage door openers installed after January 1, 1993 are required to have a sensor which, when garage door movement is interrupted or misaligned, causes a closing door to open and prevents an open door from closing. [Health & S C §19890(b)]

The safety standards for garage doors are designed to prevent children from becoming trapped under closing doors. Property constructed before 1993 probably do not meet current safety standards.

Further, when any residential garage door is serviced, the person servicing the garage door must test whether the door reverses on contact with a two-inch high obstacle placed beneath the door.

If the door does not reverse, the repairman must place a warning sticker on the garage door stating the door does not reverse and is not in compliance with current safety standards. [Health & S C §19890(e)]

Child resistant pool barriers

A construction permit issued after 1997 for a pool at a single-family residence requires the completed pool to comply with **at least one** of the following safety requirements, i.e.,:

- the pool is isolated from access to the house by a surrounding fence or barrier at least 60 inches in height;

- an approved safety cover is installed for the pool;

- all the doors of the residence providing direct access to the pool are equipped with exit alarms;

- all the doors of the residence providing access to the pool are equipped with a self-closing, self-latching device with a release mechanism placed no lower than 54 inches above the floor; or

- some other means of protection as determined to be adequate by the building official in the area where the permit is issued is installed. [Health & S C §115922]

These safety requirements do not apply to hot tubs or spas with locking safety covers.

Condominium and apartment projects are not required to maintain safety barriers for pools and spas as their projects are not classified as single-family residences. Also, pools in condos and apartments are considered public facilities.

However, condo projects and apartment buildings must post signs indicating whether or not lifeguard services are available. Lifeguard services are not required, and if not provided, a sign saying so must be posted. [Health & S C §116045]

Public pools and spas are considered environmental hazards to a user's health if the managers do not operate and maintain them in a sanitary, healthful and safe manner. [Health & S C §116040]

If pools and spas in multiple-housing projects are not operated or maintained in a sanitary, healthful and safe condition, the pools and spas are considered a public nuisance and can be shut down by local health inspectors. [Health & S C §116060]

Water heaters

All existing residential water heaters are to be anchored, braced or strapped to prevent displacement due to an earthquake. [Health & S C §19211(a)]

A residential seller must state whether the water heater is anchored, braced or strapped. [Health & S C §19211(b)]

If the water heater meets safety requirements, the seller notes the compliance by marking the box on the TDS next to "anchored, braced or strapped." No further notice is necessary as it would be redundant and is not required.

If the seller's water heater does not comply, the seller should include a written statement on the TDS disclosing that fact.

When a prospective buyer receives the TDS before entering into a binding purchase agreement, and the TDS notes the water heater is not in compliance with safety standards, the prospective buyer has agreed to accept the property with the defect, unless a provision to the contrary is included in the purchase agreement.

Residential security bars

Security bars on residential property must have release mechanisms for fire safety reasons.

However, the release mechanisms are not required if each bedroom with security bars contains a window or door to the exterior which opens for escape purposes. [Health & S C §13113.9]

Chapter 25

The home inspection report

This chapter introduces the seller's and listing agent's use of a home inspection report to document the present physical condition of the listed property for prospective buyers.

Transparency by design

A seller of a one-to-four unit residential property, on entering into a listing to sell the property, is asked to give the listing agent authority to order out a home inspection report (HIR) from a local home inspection company as part of the seller's cost to market the property for sale.

The listing agent explains the HIR will be used to complete the seller's Condition of Property (Transfer) Disclosure Statement (TDS). The report will then be attached to the seller's TDS.

On receipt of the report, the seller could act to eliminate some or all of the deficiencies noted in the home inspection report. On the elimination of any defects, an updated report would be ordered out for use with the TDS.

The seller's TDS, as reviewed by the listing agent and supplemented with the HIR, will be used to inform prospective buyers about the **precise condition** of the property before they make an offer to purchase. Thus, the seller will not be confronted later with demands to correct defects or to adjust the sales price in order to close escrow. The property will have been purchased by the buyer "as disclosed."

The listing agent's marketing role

The task of gathering information about the condition of the property listed for sale and delivering the information to prospective buyers lies primarily with the listing agent. [Calif. Civil Code §2079]

Further, to retain control throughout the process of marketing, selling and transferring ownership, the listing agent should be the one who requests the HIR (on behalf of the seller). The agent will lose control over the marketing and closing process, and expose himself to claims of misrepresentation, when the buyer or the buyer's agent is the one who first orders the HIR.

As part of the listing agent's management of the home inspection activity, the agent should be present while the home inspector carries out his investigation of the property. The agent can discuss the home inspector's observations and whether his findings are **material** in that they affect the desirability, value, habitability or safety of the property, and thus its value to prospective buyers.

If the listing agent cannot be present, then he should request that the home inspector call the agent before the HIR is prepared to discuss the home inspector's findings and any recommendations he may have for further investigation. On receipt and review of the report by the seller and listing agent, any questions or clarifications they may have on its content should be followed up by a further discussion with the home inspector, and if necessary, an amended or new report.

Home inspector's qualifications

Any individual who holds himself out as being in the business of conducting a home inspection and preparing a home inspection report on his findings during the inspection of a one-to-four unit residential property is a **home inspector**. No licensing scheme exists to set the minimum standard of competency or qualifications necessary to enter the home inspection profession. [Calif. Business and Professions Code §7195(d)]

However, general contractors, structural pest control operators, architects and registered engineers typically conduct home inspections and prepare reports as requested by sellers, buyers and their agents. The **duty of care** expected of licensed members of these professions by prospective buyers who receive and rely on their reports is set by their licensing requirements and professional attributes, i.e., the skill, prudence, diligence, education, experience and financial responsibility normally possessed and exercised by members of their profession. These licensees are experts with a high level of duty owed to those who receive their reports. [Bus & P C §7068]

Those home inspectors who **do not hold** any type of license relating to construction, such as a person who is a construction worker or building department employee, are required to conduct an inspection of a property with the same "degree of care" a reasonably prudent home inspector would exercise to locate material defects during their **physical examination** of the property and report their findings. Prospective buyers who rely on home inspection reports can expect a high level of competence from experts. [Bus & P C §7196]

However, a home inspector who is not a registered engineer cannot perform any analysis of systems, components or structural components which would constitute the practice of a civil, electrical or mechanical engineer. [Bus & P C §7196.1]

Hiring a home inspector

A seller's broker and listing agent can rely on **specific items** in a home inspection report (HIR) to prepare their final TDS. Their reliance on an HIR prepared by an inspector relieves the seller and the listing broker from liability for errors which are unknown to them to exist. However, to rely on the HIR, they must be free of simple negligence in the selection of the home inspector who inspects and prepares the HIR. Thus, the broker must exercise *ordinary care* when selecting the home inspector.

If **care in the selection** of a home inspector is lacking, then reliance on the HIR by the seller and listing agent preparing the TDS will not relieve the broker or the listing agent of liability.

However, use of an HIR by the listing agent does not relieve the agent (or his broker) from conducting their mandatory visual inspection. [CC §1102.4(a)]

Thus, the broker and listing agent must look into or be aware of whether the home inspector who prepares the report is qualified. The home inspector who holds a professional license or is registered with the state as a general contractor, architect, pest control operator or engineer is deemed to be qualified, unless the agent knows of information to the contrary.

When hiring a home inspector, the qualifications to look for include:

- educational training in home inspection related courses;

- length of time in the home inspection business or related property or building inspection employment;

- errors and omissions insurance covering professional liability;

- professional and client references; and

- membership in the California Real Estate Inspection Association, the American Society of Home Inspectors or other nationally recognized professional home inspector associations with standards of practice and codes of ethics.

Remember, the reason for hiring a home inspector in the first place is to assist the seller and his listing agent to better represent the condition of the property to prospective buyers, and hopefully reduce the risk of errors.

Reliance by buyers on the report

A listing agent requesting a home inspection report should advise the home inspector that the seller, broker and all prospective buyers of the property will be relying on the report. This disclosure will avoid later (unenforceable) claims by the home inspector that the report was intended for the sole use of the seller, broker or buyer who signed the home inspector's contract. [CC §1102.4(c)]

Consider a buyer under a purchase agreement who requests a home inspection report on the property being purchased. On receipt of the report, the buyer cancels the purchase agreement. Another prospective buyer receives the same home inspection report from the listing agent and relies on it to acquire the property.

However, the report fails to correctly state the extent of the defects. The second buyer discovers the errors and makes a demand on the home inspector who prepared the report for the first buyer to cover the cost to cure the defects which were the subject of the errors.

The home inspector claims the report was prepared only for use by the buyer who requested the report and no subsequent buyer can now rely on it, as stated in the home inspection contract under which the report was prepared.

Here, the home inspector knew the listing agent also received the report and should have known that the agent would properly provide it to other prospective buyers if the buyer who ordered the report did not complete the purchase. A home inspection report, like an appraisal-of-value report or a structural pest control report, is not a confidential document. Thus, all prospective buyers of the property are **entitled to rely** on the existing home inspection report.

This reliance by other prospective buyers imposes liability on the home inspector for his failure to exercise the level of care expected of a home inspector when examining the property and reporting defects. Liability for the defects is imposed even though the home inspection contract and report contained a provision restricting its use solely to the person who requested it. [**Leko** v. **Cornerstone Building Inspection Service** (2001) 86 CA4th 1109]

The home inspection contract

Provisions in a contract with a home inspector and his home inspection company which purport to limit the dollar amount of their liability for errors, inaccuracies or omissions in their reporting of defects to the dollar amount of the fee they received for the report are unenforceable.

Further, any provision in the home inspection contract or condition in the home inspection report which purports to waive or limit the home inspector's liability for the negligent investigation or preparation of the HIR is unenforceable. [Bus & P C §7198]

Should the buyer discover an error in the HIR regarding the existence or nonexistence of a defect affecting the value or desirability of the property, the buyer has no more than four years after the **date of the inspection** to file a legal action to recover any money losses. [Bus & P C §7199]

Occasionally, a boilerplate provision in the home inspector's contract or the home inspection report will attempt to limit the buyer's period for recovery to one year after the inspection occurred. However, any such limitation the home inspector places on time periods during which the buyer must discover and make a claim is unenforceable. The statutory four-year period is needed to provide time for buyers to realize the home inspector produced a faulty report. [**Moreno** v. **Sanchez** (2003) 106 CA4th 1415]

The home inspector's malpractice insurance

An agent ordering a home inspection report needs to verify the home inspection company has **professional liability insurance coverage** before allowing the company to conduct an investigation and prepare a report.

Should the home inspector fail to detect and report a material defect or the extent of the defect, and the cost to correct it is significant, the buyer will be seriously disadvantaged in any recovery effort against the home inspector and the home inspection company unless insurance is available to pay amounts recoverable by the buyer.

Likewise, if the same defect was also missed by the listing agent due to the agent's failure to observe the defect during the agent's mandatory visual inspection, the broker and the listing agent are also liable to the buyer for the costs of curing the defect — separate from the home inspector's liability.

Here, the broker and listing agent will be able to force the home inspector to contribute to the recovery by an *indemnification claim* made by the broker against the home inspector for payment of all or a portion of the buyer's loss. Unless the home inspector has insurance coverage, the ability of the seller's broker to force the home inspection company to pay the home inspector's share of the responsibility for having failed to observe the same defect the listing agent missed will be limited to the home inspector's personal assets. [Leko, *supra*]

The inspection and report

A home inspection is a **physical examination** conducted on-site by a home inspector. The inspection of a one-to-four unit residential property is performed for a noncontingent fee.

The purpose of the physical examination of the premises is to identify *material defects* in the condition of the structure and its systems and components. **Material defects** are conditions which affect the property's:

- market value;
- desirability as a dwelling;
- habitability from the elements; and
- safety from injury in its use as a dwelling.

Defects are material if they adversely affect the **price** a reasonably prudent and informed buyer would pay for the property when entering into a purchase agreement. As the report may affect value, the investigation and delivery of the home inspection report to a prospective buyer must precede a prospective buyer's offer to purchase to be meaningful. [Bus & P C §7195(b)]

The **home inspection** is to be a *non-invasive examination* of the mechanical, electrical and plumbing systems of the dwelling, as well as the components of the structure, such as the roof, ceiling, walls, floors and foundations. Non-invasive indicates there will not be an intrusion into the roof, walls, foundation or soil by dismantling or taking apart the structure which would disturb components or cause repairs to be made to remove the effects of the intrusion. [Bus & P C §7195(a)(1)]

The **home inspection report** is the written report prepared by the home inspector which sets forth his findings while conducting his physical examination of the property. The report identifies each system and component of the structure inspected, describes any material defects the home inspector found or suspects, makes recommendations about the conditions observed and suggests any further evaluation needed to be undertaken by other experts. [Bus & P C §7195(c)]

The listing agent needs to make sure the report addresses the cause of any defect or code violation found which constitutes a significant defect in the use of the property or cost to remedy the defects. The report should also include suspicions the home inspector might have which need to be clarified by further inspections and reports by others with more expertise.

The agent, or anyone else, may also request that the home inspector conduct an inspection on the energy efficiencies of the property and include his findings in the report. On a request for an **energy efficiency inspection**, the home inspector will report on items including:

- the R-value of the insulation in the attic, roof, walls, floors and ducts;

- the quantity of glass panes and the types of frames;

- the heating and cooling equipment and fans;

- water heating systems;

- the age of major appliances and the fuel used;

- thermostats;

- energy leakage areas throughout the structure; and

- the solar control efficiency of the windows. [Bus & P C §7195(a)(2)]

The home inspector's conflicts of interest

The home inspector who prepares a home inspection report, the company employing the home inspector and any affiliated company may not:

- pay a referral fee or provide for any type of compensation to brokers, agents, owners or buyers for the referral of any home inspection business;

- agree to accept a contingency fee arrangement for the inspection of the report, such as a fee payable based on the home inspector's findings and conclusions in the report or on the close of a sales escrow;

- perform or offer to perform any repairs on a property which was the subject of a HIR prepared by them within the past 12 months; or

- inspect any property in which they have a financial interest in its sale. [Bus & P C §7197]

Chapter 26

Verify property disclosures: retain a home inspector

This chapter reviews the buyer's use of a home inspector to confirm the physical condition of the property, as represented by the seller and listing agent, prior to entering into a purchase agreement.

Protecting the prospective buyer

A buyer, with the assistance of the buyer's agent, locates a one-to-four unit residential property suitable for the buyer to purchase. Both the agent and his buyer walk through the property and confirm the property fits the buyer's needs.

The buyer's agent contacts the listing agent and informs him he has a prospective buyer who is interested in the property. The buyer's agent requests information on the property, including a title profile, a Transfer Disclosure Statement (TDS) and a home inspection report (HIR). The listing agent responds by suggesting the buyer's agent go ahead and submit a purchase agreement offer and that the "necessary disclosures for closing" will be delivered after an offer is accepted by the seller.

The indication the buyer's agent gets is that the listing agent has not prepared a listing package and no information on the property will be made available to prospective buyers until it is time to close escrow.

The buyer agrees with his agent to proceed with an offer at a price and on terms which the agent believes are justified. The agent has checked out comparable sales information provided by the title company, plus he has a working knowledge of properties in the immediate area. They know of no problems presented by the physical condition of the property.

An offer is prepared with contingency provisions regarding the condition of the property. The buyer has no information on the condition of the property except for his walk-through with his agent to determine whether the arrangement of the space within the structure was suitable.

Contingency provisions included in the purchase agreement, among others, call for:

- the seller to furnish a HIR prepared by an insured home inspector showing the land and improvements to be free of material defects [See **first tuesday** Form 150 §11.1(b)];

- the seller and the listing agent to prepare, sign and deliver a condition of property disclosure (TDS) [See **first tuesday** Form 150 §11.2]; and

- the buyer to inspect the property twice — once to initially confirm the condition of the property and once again before closing escrow to confirm maintenance has not been deferred and material defects discovered after entering into the purchase agreement have been corrected or eliminated. [See **first tuesday** Form 150 §11.3]

The offer is submitted and promptly rejected by the seller. Eventually, a purchase agreement is entered into which eliminates the provision calling for the seller to furnish a HIR. No previous offer has been submitted to the seller by other prospective buyers who obtained an HIR on the property.

The buyer authorizes his agent to immediately obtain a HIR, which the buyer's agent orders. The inspection takes place and the HIR is received by the buyer's agent and reviewed with the buyer. The seller and the listing agent have not delivered a TDS or any of the other seller disclosures or inspection reports which both the seller and the listing agent are duty bound to deliver to a prospective buyer. [Calif. Civil Code §§1102, 2079]

The home inspector's written report lists numerous significant defects he has observed during his physical inspection of the property's condition. Repair/replacement costs are estimated at $2,500 to eliminate the defects not disclosed by the seller or observed by the buyer or the buyer's agent on their cursory review of the space within the structure.

The buyer makes a written demand on the seller to cure (repair) the defects discovered by the home inspector based on the terms agreed to in the purchase agreement. [See **first tuesday** Form 150 §11.3; see Form 269 accompanying this chapter]

A copy of the HIR and a contractor's estimate of the cost to cure the defects are attached to the buyer's request for repairs. Thus, the buyer substantiates his demand on the seller to cover previously undisclosed defects.

The seller and his agent prepare a TDS and note all the defects listed in the HIR and on the buyer's notice demanding repairs. The seller then refuses to make any of the corrections, claiming he has disclosed the defects in the TDS as agreed in the purchase agreement. Eventually, the buyer is told to either close escrow or cancel.

Can the buyer require the seller to cure the *material defects* found by the home inspector and close escrow?

Yes! The seller must deliver the property to the buyer as disclosed by the seller and the seller's broker and observed by the buyer **at the time the buyer's purchase agreement offer was accepted**, not in the condition stated in an untimely disclosure made in the seller's TDS during escrow.

The seller's and listing agent's failure to disclose prior to acceptance is an omission of facts, called *negative fraud, deceit* or *misrepresentation by omission.*

The most significant issue arising out of these discoveries concerns the price the buyer agreed to pay in the purchase agreement. The seller and buyer agreed on a price for the property based on the conditions **disclosed and known to the buyer** at the time the offer was accepted.

Thus, the price represents the agreed value of a used, but defect-free property, except for any defects observed by the buyer or disclosed to the buyer prior to entering into the purchase agreement. The price, as it turns out, exceeded the property's fair market value by the amount of the costs which will be incurred to cure the defects and deliver the property "as disclosed" prior to acceptance.

Confirm the seller's disclosures

A seller and his listing broker must disclose to a prospective buyer all known and observable property conditions which adversely affect the value of the property.

A Transfer Disclosure Statement completed by the seller and listing agent, without the benefit of a HIR, typically does not accurately or fully reveal the significant property defects or code violations which actually exist, whether or not known to the seller or listing agent.

When the seller has not obtained or refuses to authorize the preparation of a HIR prior to entering into a purchase agreement, the buyer should always order one on opening escrow to confirm the condition of the property before the expiration of any cancellation period.

A buyer should undertake an inspection in the interest of avoiding:

- after-closing discoveries of defects which require correction; and

- after-closing claims he may make against the seller to recover the value lost or the costs incurred to correct the defects.

PROPERTY INSPECTION
Request for Repairs

DATE:_____, 20_____, at_____, California.

TO SELLER: _____

FACTS:

1. Buyer entered into a purchase agreement with you dated _____, 20_____ agreeing to buy real estate described as: _____

    _____

2. The purchase agreement calls for an **initial inspection** of the real estate by Buyer, or a representative of Buyer.

    2.1   The inspection is to confirm that the condition of the real estate is substantially the condition reasonably expected by Buyer based on observations by Buyer and representations made by Seller or Seller's Agent to Buyer or Buyer's Agent prior to acceptance of the purchase agreement.

3. The purchase agreement calls for Buyer to notify Seller, on completion of Buyer's initial inspection, of any material defects discovered by Buyer which were undisclosed and unknown to Buyer prior to acceptance of the purchase agreement.

4. The purchase agreement further calls for Seller to repair, replace or correct the noticed defects prior to closing the transaction and delivering possession to Buyer.

5. By this notice of material defects in need of repair, replacement or correction, Buyer does not intend to cancel the purchase agreement or avoid Buyer's obligation to perform on the purchase agreement.

    5.1   Buyer will close as scheduled or as soon thereafter as any noticed defects have been eliminated by repair, replacement or correction and completion has been verified by Buyer.

THUS:

6. Buyer hereby confirms the condition of the property on the initial inspection satisfies Buyer's expectations of its physical condition regarding both the land and its improvements, **except** for the following itemized material defects in the condition of the property.

    6.1   Buyer hereby notifies Seller of the material defects in the condition of the property which were undisclosed and unknown to Buyer prior to acceptance of the purchase agreement and makes a demand on Seller to repair, replace or correct the following itemized defects prior to closing:

    _____
    _____
    _____
    _____
    _____
    _____
    _____
    _____
    _____
    _____
    _____
    _____
    _____
    _____

I agree to the terms stated above.	Seller hereby acknowledges receipt of a copy.
Date:_____, 20_____	Date:_____, 20_____
Buyer: _____	Seller: _____
Buyer: _____	Seller: _____

FORM 269   08-01   ©2005 **first tuesday**, P.O. BOX 20069, RIVERSIDE, CA 92516 (800) 794-0494

The buyer's discovery of defects after acceptance of the purchase agreement and **prior to closing**, whether by the buyer's investigation or by the seller's tardy disclosure, does not alter the buyer's right to close escrow, acquire the property and pursue the recovery of costs or the loss of value due to defects known to the seller or the listing agent and not disclosed prior to entering into the purchase agreement.

Armed with a HIR containing findings of material defects not known to the buyer or disclosed at the time the purchase agreement was accepted, the buyer can then make the necessary demands on the seller. Thus, the buyer ensures the property will be delivered in the condition **as disclosed** by the seller on entering into the purchase agreement, whether or not a TDS was received prior to acceptance of the buyer's offer.

The buyer's remedies for deceit

If a home inspection report reveals property defects unknown and previously undisclosed to the buyer, the buyer may:

- make a demand on the seller to correct or eliminate the defects, and refuse to close escrow until the seller has either complied or agreed to an adjusted price [See Form 269];

- refuse to close escrow for lack of seller compliance to the demand for corrections and enforce the agreement and its price correction provisions by *specific performance*; or

- close escrow and make a money demand on the seller for the difference between the purchase price set in the purchase agreement and the price as adjusted for the undisclosed defects as called for in the purchase agreement. [**Jue** v. **Smiser** (1994) 23 CA4th 312]

If the purchase agreement entered into by the seller and buyer contains a price adjustment provision, the buyer can, before closing, enforce a reduction of the purchase price. The price adjustment will be for the amount of the costs necessary to bring the property into the condition as disclosed by the seller or the seller's broker and known to the buyer at the time of acceptance.

Also, by the seller failing to deliver the property in the condition disclosed prior to acceptance, the seller has failed to convey the property as agreed. Thus, the buyer is justified in refusing to close escrow until the seller compensates the buyer for, or corrects, the defects discovered during escrow.

However, if the buyer is made aware of facts about the condition of the property at the time the buyer enters into the purchase agreement, which would cause an ordinary buyer to be put on notice to investigate into their consequences, the buyer has no grounds for claiming a loss for the condition he knew about.

Final pre-closing inspection

A buyer must personally reinspect the property just before close of escrow to confirm:

- the quality of any repairs made by the seller; and

- the general condition and maintenance of the property after entering into the purchase agreement.

The buyer's right to a final pre-closing inspection of the property is agreed to in the purchase agreement. [See **first tuesday** Form 150 §11.3(b)]

On final inspection of the property, the buyer lists any property defects not already addressed, such as equipment and fixture malfunctions or deferred maintenance, on the final walk-through inspection statement. [See **first tuesday** Form 270]

Chapter 27

Natural hazard disclosures by the listing agent

This chapter discusses the use of the Natural Hazard Disclosure (NHD) Statement by sellers and listing agents to fulfill their obligations to inform prospective buyers.

A unified disclosure for all sales

Natural hazards come with the **location** of a parcel of real estate, not with the man-made aspects of the property. Locations where a property might be subject to natural hazards include:

- special flood hazard areas, a federal designation;

- potential flooding and inundation areas;

- very high fire hazard severity zones;

- wildland fire areas;

- earthquake fault zones; and

- seismic hazard zones. [Calif. Civil Code §1103(c)]

The existence of a hazard due to the geographic location of a property affects its value and desirability to prospective buyers. Hazards, by their nature, limit a buyer's ability to develop the property, obtain insurance or receive disaster relief.

Whether a seller markets his property himself or lists the property with a broker, the seller must disclose to prospective buyers any natural hazards **known to the seller**, as well as those **contained in public records**.

To unify and streamline the disclosure by a seller (and his listing agent) about those natural hazards which affect a property, the California legislature created a statutory form entitled the *Natural Hazard Disclosure (NHD) Statement*.

The NHD form is used by a seller and his listing agent for their preparation (or acknowl-edgement of their review of a report prepared by an NHD expert) and disclosure of natural hazard information. The information is both known to the seller and listing agent (and the NHD expert) and available to them as shown on maps in the public records of the local planning department. [CC §1103.2; see Form 314 accompanying this chapter]

Actual use of the NHD Statement by sellers and their agents is **mandated** on the sale of **one-to-four unit residential properties**, called *targeted properties*. Some sellers of targeted properties are excluded from mandatory use of the form, but never their listing agents. Thus, the form, filled out and signed by the seller (unless excluded) and the listing agent, must be included in listing packages handed to prospective buyers on every one-to-four unit residential property.

Editor's note — Any attempt by a seller or listing agent to use an "as-is" provision or otherwise provide for the buyer to agree to waive his right to receive the seller's NHD statement is void as against public policy. [CC §1103(d)]

Regarding excluded sellers and sales of property other than one-to-four unit residential property, use of the statutory NHD Statement by sellers and listing agents is an **optional** method for making their disclosure of natural hazard information to buyers. However, delivery of the information by use of one form or another is not optional. A natural hazard disclosure is mandated on all types of property. [CC §1103.1(b)]

All sellers, and any listing or selling agent involved, have an initial common law duty owed to prospective buyers to disclose conditions on

NATURAL HAZARD DISCLOSURE STATEMENT

DATE:_____, 20_____, at_____, California.

> **Note:** The seller's listing broker (and the seller) of one-to-four residential units shall prepare a NHD form and deliver it to prospective buyers prior to making a purchase agreement offer and indicate compliance in the purchase agreement or a counteroffer. If not so disclosed, the buyer has the right to cancel the purchase agreement within three days of delivery of the disclosure in person. [Calif. Civil Code §1103.3]

This disclosure statement is prepared for the following:

☐ Seller's listing agreement

☐ Purchase agreement

☐ Counteroffer

☐ _____

Dated:_____, 20_____, at_____, California

Entered into by: _____

Regarding property referred to as: _____

Natural Hazard Disclosure Statement

Seller and Seller's Agent(s) or a third-party consultant disclose the following information with the knowledge that even though this is not a warranty, prospective buyers may rely on this information in deciding whether and on what terms to purchase the subject property.

Seller hereby authorizes any agent(s) representing any principal(s) in this action to provide a copy of this statement to any person or entity in connection with any actual or anticipated sale of the property.

> THE FOLLOWING ARE REPRESENTATIONS MADE BY SELLER AND SELLER'S AGENT(S) BASED ON THEIR KNOWLEDGE AND MAPS DRAWN BY THE STATE AND FEDERAL GOVERNMENT. THIS INFORMATION IS A DISCLOSURE AND IS NOT INTENDED TO BE PART OF ANY CONTRACT BETWEEN BUYER AND SELLER.

THIS REAL PROPERTY LIES WITHIN THE FOLLOWING HAZARDOUS AREA(S): (Check appropriate response)

1. A SPECIAL FLOOD HAZARD AREA (Any type Zone "A" or "V") designated by the Federal Emergency Management Agency.

   Yes____ No____ Do not know/information not available from local jurisdiction____

2. AN AREA OF POTENTIAL FLOODING shown on an inundation map pursuant to Section 8589.5 of the Government Code.

   Yes____ No____ Do not know/information not available from local jurisdiction____

3. A VERY HIGH FIRE HAZARD SEVERITY ZONE pursuant to Section 51178 or 51179 of the Government Code. The owner of this property is subject to the maintenance requirements of Section 51182 of the Government Code.

   Yes____ No____

4. A WILDLAND AREA THAT MAY CONTAIN SUBSTANTIAL FOREST FIRE RISKS AND HAZARDS pursuant to Section 4125 of the Public Resources Code. The owner of this property is subject to the maintenance requirements of Section 4291 of the Public Resources Code. Additionally, it is not the state's responsibility to provide fire protection services to any building or structure located within the wildlands unless the Department of Forestry and Fire Protection has entered into a cooperative agreement with the local agency for those purposes pursuant to Section 4142 of the Public Resources Code.

   Yes____ No____

5. AN EARTHQUAKE FAULT ZONE pursuant to Section 2622 of the Public Resources Code.

   Yes____ No____

6. A SEISMIC HAZARD ZONE pursuant to Section 2696 of the Public Resources Code.

   Yes (Landslide Zone)____   Yes (Liquefaction Zone)____
   No____   Map not yet released by state____

THESE HAZARDS MAY LIMIT YOUR ABILITY TO DEVELOP THE REAL PROPERTY, TO OBTAIN INSURANCE OR TO RECEIVE ASSISTANCE AFTER A DISASTER.

THE MAPS ON WHICH THESE DISCLOSURES ARE BASED ESTIMATE WHERE NATURAL HAZARDS EXIST. THEY ARE NOT DEFINITIVE INDICATORS OF WHETHER OR NOT A PROPERTY WILL BE AFFECTED BY A NATURAL DISASTER. BUYER(S) AND SELLER(S) MAY WISH TO OBTAIN PROFESSIONAL ADVICE REGARDING THOSE HAZARDS AND OTHER HAZARDS THAT MAY AFFECT THE PROPERTY.

Check only one of the following:

☐ Seller and their agent represent that the information herein is true and correct to the best of their knowledge as of the date signed by Seller and Seller's Agent.

☐ Seller and their agent acknowledge that they have exercised good faith in the selection of a third-party report provider as required in Civil Code Section 1103.7, and that the representations made in this Natural Hazard Disclosure Statement are based upon information provided by the independent third-party disclosure provider as a substituted disclosure pursuant to Civil Code Section 1103.4. Neither seller nor their agent has independently verified the information contained in this statement and report or is personally aware of any errors or inaccuracies in the information contained on the statement. This statement was prepared by:

Third-Party Disclosure Provider:_____ Date: _____

Date:_____, 20_____   Date:_____, 20_____

Seller: _____   Seller's
Broker:_____

Seller: _____   Agent: _____

Buyer represents that he has read and understands this document. Pursuant to Civil Code Section 1103.8, the representations made in this Natural Hazard Disclosure Statement do not constitutes all of Seller's or Seller's Agent's disclosure obligations in this transaction.

Buyer:_____   Date: _____

Buyer:_____   Date: _____

or about a property which are **known to them** and might adversely affect the buyer's willingness to buy or influence the price and terms of payment he is willing to offer.

Natural hazards, or the lack thereof, irrefutably affect a property's value and desirability to a prospective buyer. If a hazard is known to any agent (as well as the seller) or noted in public records, it must be disclosed to the prospective buyer before he agrees to purchase the property. If not disclosed, the buyer can cancel the transaction, called *termination*. And if the transaction has closed escrow, the buyer may *rescind* the sale and be **refunded** his investment, called *restoration*. [**Karoutas** v. **HomeFed Bank** (1991) 232 CA3d 767]

Therefore, the need to prepare the seller's NHD statement in advance of locating a prospective buyer **must be anticipated** by the seller and listing agent.

If the need is not anticipated, the NHD will not be prepared, signed and available for delivery to prospective buyers before an offer is accepted or a counteroffer is made, all requisites to delivery of the NHD *as soon as practicable*. [Calif. Attorney General Opinion 01-406 (August 24, 2001); CC §1103.3(a)(2)]

Investigating the existence of a hazard

Natural hazard information must be obtained from the public records. If not obtained, the seller and listing agent cannot make their required disclosures.

To obtain the natural hazard information for delivery to prospective buyers, the seller and his listing agent are required to exercise *ordinary care* in gathering the information. They may gather the information themselves or the seller may employ an NHD expert to gather the information. When an expert is employed, he prepares the NHD form for the seller and the listing agent to review, add any comments, sign and deliver to prospective buyers. [CC §1103.4(a)]

Thus, the seller and listing agent may obtain natural hazard information:

- directly from the public records themselves; or

- by employing a natural hazard expert, such as a geologist.

For the seller and the listing agent to rely on an NHD report prepared by others, the listing agent need only:

- **request** a NHD report from a reliable expert in natural hazards, such as an engineer or a geologist who has studied the public records (as some natural hazards clearly do not pertain to engineering or geology);

- **review** the NHD form prepared by the expert and **enter** any actual knowledge the seller or listing agent may possess, whether contrary or supplemental to the expert's report, on the form prepared by the expert or in an addendum attached to the form; and

- **sign** the NHD Statement provided by his NHD expert and **deliver** it with the NHD report to prospective buyers or buyer's agents. [CC §1103.2(f)(2)]

When prepared by an NHD expert, the NHD report must also note whether the listed property is located within 2 miles of an existing or proposed airport, an environmental hazard zone called an *airport influence area* or *airport referral area*. The buyer's occupancy of property within the influence of an airport facility may be affected by noise and restrictions, now and later, imposed on the buyer's use as set by the airport's land-use commission. [CC §1103.4(c)]

Also, the expert's report must note whether the property is located within the jurisdiction of the San Francisco Bay conservation and development commission.

Broker uses experts to limit liability

The Natural Hazard Disclosure scheme, while not making the practice mandatory, encourages brokers and their agents to use natural hazard experts rather than gather the information from the local planning department themselves. The use of an expert, who himself relies on the contents of the public record to prepare his report, relieves the listing agent of any liability for errors not known to the agent to exist.

Neither the seller nor any agent, be he the seller's or the buyer's agent, is liable for the erroneous preparation of a NHD Statement they have delivered to the buyer, if:

- the NHD report and form is prepared by an **expert in natural hazards**, consistent with his professional licensing and expertise; and

- the seller and listing agent used **ordinary care** in selecting the expert and in their review of the expert's report for any errors, inaccuracies and omissions of which they have **actual knowledge**. [CC §§1103.4(a), 1103.4(b)]

Neither the seller nor the listing agent need enter into an *indemnification agreement* with the natural hazard expert to avoid liability for errors. By statute, the expert who prepared the NHD is liable for his errors, not the seller or listing agent who relied on the report of a non-negligently selected expert to fulfill their duty to check the public records.

However, if brokers are sued based on the inaccuracy of the expert's report, an indemnity agreement entered into by the expert, given in exchange for the request to prepare a natural hazard report, will cover the cost of any litigation which might unnecessarily haul the broker into court.

The listing agent's dilatory delivery of an expert's NHD to the buyer or the buyer's agent, after the offer has been accepted, will not pro-tect the broker from liability for the buyer's lost property value due to the nondisclosure before acceptance. If the agent **knew or should have known** of a natural hazard based on the readily available planning department's parcel list, he is exposed to liability. Liability exposure includes costs the buyer may incur to correct or remedy the undisclosed hazardous condition and that portion of the agreed price which exceeds the property's fair market value based on the undisclosed hazard. [CC §1103.13]

Further, the agents, seller and expert are not exposed to liability from **third parties** to the sale transaction who might receive their erroneous NHD Statement and rely on it to analyze the risk they undertake by their involvement. Such third parties include insurance companies, lenders, governmental agencies and others who may become affiliated with the transaction. [CC §1103.2(g)]

Documenting compliance with NHD law

Compliance by the seller and listing agent to deliver the NHD Statement to the buyer is required to be documented by a provision in the purchase agreement. [CC §1103.3(b); see **first tuesday** Form 150 §11.4]

However, should the listing agent fail to disclose a natural hazard and then provide in the purchase agreement for the compliance to be an untimely "in escrow" disclosure, his seller is statutorily penalized. The buyer, on an in-escrow disclosure, is allowed either a three-day right of cancellation should he be handed the NHD Statement, or a five-day right of cancellation should the NHD Statement be mailed to the buyer. [CC §1103.3(c)]

Further, delivery of the NHD after acceptance of an offer, when it could have been previously prepared by the seller or listing agent and timely delivered, imposes liability on the seller and listing agent, but not the buyer's agent. Liability is based on any money losses (including a reduced property value) inflicted on the buyer by the disclosure should the buyer choose not to exercise his right to cancel and instead proceed with the agreement and close escrow. [CC§1103.13; **Jue** v. **Smiser** (1994) 23 CA4th 312]

Delivery of the NHD to the buyer

It is the **buyer's agent** who has the duty to hand the buyer the NHD Statement the buyer's agent receives from the seller or the listing agent, called *delivery*. [CC §1103.12(a)]

The **buyer's agent**, on receiving the NHD form from the listing agent, owes the buyer a special agency duty to care for and protect his buyer's best interest by reviewing the NHD Statement himself for any disclosure which might affect the property's value or its desirability for his buyer. The buyer's agent is then required to deliver the NHD to the buyer and make any recommendations or explanations the buyer's agent may have regarding its content. [CC §§1103.2, 1103.12]

If the buyer does not have a broker, the seller's agent is responsible for delivering the NHD Statement to the prospective buyer.

However, the listing agent is not required to understand the effect hazards have on the property or the buyer. Also, the listing agent has absolutely no duty to voluntarily explain to a prospective buyer the effect a known natural hazard (which is itself disclosed) might have on the property or the buyer. The task of explaining the consequence of living with a natural hazard is the duty of a buyer's agent.

Delivery may be in person or by mail. Also, delivery is considered to have been made if the NHD is received by the spouse of the buyer. [CC §1103.10]

Sellers occasionally act as "For Sale By Owners" (FSBOs) and directly negotiate a sale of their property with buyers in transactions which exclude brokers and agents. Here, the seller is responsible for preparing or obtaining an NHD statement and delivering the NHD Statement to the prospective buyer.

No warranty, just awareness

A seller's NHD Statement is **not a warranty or guarantee** by the seller or listing agent of the natural hazards affecting the property. The NHD Statement is a report of the seller's and listing agent's (or the NHD expert's) knowledge (actual and constructive) of any natural hazards affecting the property.

However, the NHD Statement is relied on by prospective buyers. The NHD is designed to assist them in their decisions as to whether they should buy the property, and if they do decide to buy, at what price and on what terms. These conditions all need to exist before entering into a purchase agreement to avoid misleading the buyer, called *deceit*. [AG Opin. 01-406]

Disclosures concerning the value and desirability of a property, such as an NHD Statement, are **price-sensitive information**. Thus, the statement must be delivered to the prospective buyer before he enters into a purchase agreement in order to accomplish their intended result. If not timely disclosed, the seller and listing agent subject themselves to claims for price adjustments (offsets) which may be made by the buyer either before or after closing. Alternatively, the buyer may cancel the purchase agreement and have his deposit refunded.

Good brokerage practice would deliver the NHD to the prospective buyer on or before he makes an offer or accepts a counteroffer, while he is still the prospective buyer. Disclosures should not be made later when the prospect has become the buyer under a purchase agreement and entitled to ownership of the property at the price and on the terms agreed. Properly, the purchase agreement offer would then include a copy of the seller's NHD Statement as an addendum (along with all other disclosures), noting the transaction is in compliance with NHD law.

As for an **escrow officer** handling a sale in which the listing agent fails to provide the buyer's agent or the buyer with the NHD prior to opening escrow, the escrow officer has no duty to the seller or buyer to prepare, order out or deliver the NHD to the buyer. The obligation remains that of the seller and listing agent. However, escrow may accept instruction to perform any of these activities, in which case escrow becomes obligated to follow the instructions agreed to by the escrow officer. [CC §1103.11]

Excluded sellers, not agents

While all sellers of properties must disclose what is known to them about the natural hazards endemic to a property's location, sellers in some transactions **do not need to use** the mandated NHD form to make their disclosures, such as:

- court-ordered transfers or sales;

- deed-in-lieu of foreclosures;

- trustee's sales;

- lender resales after foreclosure or deed-in-lieus;

- estates on death;

- transfers between co-owners;

- transfers to relatives/spouses; or

- transfers to or by governmental entities. [CC §1103.1(a)]

However, any listing agent involved in an excluded transaction must himself make hazard disclosures, even though he does not need to use the statutory form. [CC §1103.1(b)]

Also, all sellers of any type of property, included or excluded, must, as always, disclose what **they know about any hazards**. Again, the disclosure is best accomplished by use of

the NHD Statement on all sales. The NHD expert will definitely include the statement as part of his report. [CC §1103.2(f)(2)]

On properties not mandated to use the form, the listing agent can comply with his and his seller's duty to disclose by ordering a report from a natural hazard expert. On the listing agent's receipt of the expert's report, he will review the report (preferably with the seller), add what they know about hazards which are not included in the expert's report, sign the NHD statement accompanying the report and hand the entire NHD package to prospective buyers before an offer is submitted or a counteroffer made.

Other disclosure statements distinguished

The NHD Statement handed to a prospective buyer of one-to-four unit residential property is an additional disclosure unrelated to the environmental hazards and physical deficiencies in the soil or improvements located on or about a property as disclosed on Transfer Disclosure Statement (TDS) or in the purchase agreement. [See **first tuesday** Form 304 §C(1)]

The TDS discloses health risks resulting from **man-made** physical and environmental conditions affecting the use of the property. They are limited to facts known to the seller and listing agent without concern for a review of public records on the property at the planning department or elsewhere. The NHD Statement discloses risks to life and property which exist **in nature** due to the property's location and are known and readily available from the public records (planning department).

Other than one-to-four

Use of the statutory NHD form for hazard disclosures by sellers and their agents is mandated only on the sale of non-exempt, targeted one-to-four unit residential property. [CC §1103]

Thus, sellers and listing agents on all other properties do not need to use and deliver the statutory NHD form to prospective buyers of those properties. However, all sellers and their listing agents still have a duty to disclose hazardous conditions known to them to exist.

Sellers and listing agents of **any type of real estate** must disclose whether the property is located in:

- an area of potential flooding;

- a very high fire hazard severity zone;

- a state fire responsibility area;

- an earthquake fault zone; and

- a seismic hazard zone. [CC §1103.2]

Even though use of the form is not mandated for sales of property other than one-to-four residential units, agents best meet their hazard disclosure duty in all transactions by using the NHD Statement to convey their knowledge and information contained in public records. [CC §1103.1(b)]

Editor's note — The following discussion details the different hazards which must be disclosed on the NHD Statement.

Flood zones

Investigating flood problems was facilitated by the passage of the National Flood Insurance Act of 1968 (NFIA).

The NFIA established a means for property owners to obtain flood insurance with the National Flood Insurance Program (NFIP).

The Federal Emergency Management Agency (FEMA) is the administrative entity created to police the NFIP by investigating and mapping regions susceptible to flooding.

Any flood zone designated with the letter "A" or "V" is a *special flood hazard area* and must be disclosed as a natural hazard on the NHD Statement. [See Form 314 §1]

Zones "A" and "V" both correspond with areas with a 1% chance of flooding in any given year, called 100-year floodplains, e.g., a structure located within a special flood hazard area shown on an NFIP map has a 26% chance of suffering flood damage during the term of a 30-year mortgage.

However, Zone "V" is subject to additional storm wave hazards.

Both zones are subject to mandatory flood insurance purchase requirements.

Information about flood hazard areas and zones can come from:

- city/county planners and engineers;

- county flood control offices;

- local or regional FEMA offices; and

- the U.S. Corps of Engineers.

Additional information concerning flood hazard areas can be obtained in the Community Status Book. The book lists communities and counties participating in the NFIP and the effective dates of the current flood hazard maps available from FEMA.

The Community Status Book can be obtained via the web at: http://www.fema.gov/fema/csb.shtm.

Flood Insurance Rate Maps and Flood Hazard Boundary Maps are all available at the FEMA Flood Map store by calling (800) 358-9616 or via the web at: http://msc.fema.gov/.

Another flooding disclosure which must be made on the NHD Statement arises when the property is located in an area of **potential flooding**. [See Form 314 §2]

An area of potential flooding is a location subject to partial flooding if sudden or total **dam failure** occurs. The inundation maps showing the areas of potential flooding due to dam failure are prepared by the California Office of Emergency Services. [Calif. Government Code §8589.5(a)]

Once alerted by the listing agent to the existence of a flooding condition, the buyer's agent must inquire further to learn the significance of the disclosure to the buyer.

Very high fire hazard severity zone

Areas in the state which are subject to significant fire hazards have been identified as *very high fire hazard severity zones*. If a property is located in a very high fire hazard severity zone, a disclosure must be made to the prospective buyer. [See Form 314 §3]

The city, county or district responsible for providing fire protection have designated, by ordinance, very high fire hazard severity zones within their jurisdiction. [Gov C §51179]

The fire hazard disclosure on the NHD form mentions the need to maintain the property. Neither the seller nor the listing agent need to explain the nature of the maintenance required or its burden on ownership. Advice to the buyer on the type of maintenance and the consequences of owning property subject to the maintenance are the duties of the buyer's agent, if they have an agent.

For example, a buyer occupying a residence located in a very high fire hazard severity zone is advised by his agent that as the new owner, the buyer must:

- maintain a firebreak around the structure of a distance of no less than 30 feet or to the property line, whichever is nearer, unless the local agency requires up to 100 feet or more;

- remove tree branches extending within 10 feet of any chimney or stovepipe;

- clear dead or dying wood from trees adjacent to or overhanging the structure;

- remove leaves, needles or other dead vegetative growth from the roof; and

- maintain a screen over the chimney or stovepipe. [Gov C §51182]

State Fire Responsibility Areas

If a property is in an area where the financial responsibility for preventing or suppressing fires is primarily on the state, the real estate is located within a *State Fire Responsibility Area*. [Calif. Public Resources Code §4125(a)]

Notices identifying the location of the map designating State Fire Responsibility Areas are posted at the offices of the county recorder, county assessor and the county planning agency. Also, any information received by the county after receipt of a map changing the State Fire Responsibility Areas in the county must be posted. [Pub Res C §4125(c)]

If the property is located within a **wildland area** exposed to substantial forest fire risks, the seller or his listing agent must disclose this fact. If the property is located in a wildland area, it requires maintenance by the owner to prevent fires. [Pub Res C §4136(a); see Form 314 §4]

In addition, the NHD Statement advises the prospective buyer of a home located in a **wildland area** that the **state has no responsibility** for providing fire protection services to the property, unless the Department of Forestry and Fire Protection has entered into a cooperative agreement with the local agency. No further disclosure about whether a cooperating agreement exists need be made by the seller or listing agent. [See Form 314 §4]

However, if property disclosures place the property in a wildland area, the buyer's agent has the duty to advise the buyer about the need to inquire and investigate into what agency provides fire protection to the property.

Earthquake fault zones

To assist seller's agents in identifying whether the listed property is located in an earthquake fault area, maps have been prepared by the State Geologist.

The State Mining and Geology Board and the city or county planning department have maps available which identify special studies zones, called *Alquist-Priolo Maps*. [Pub Res C §2622]

The maps are used to identify whether the listed property is located within one-eighth of a mile on either side of a fault.

Also, the NHD Statement requires both the seller and the listing agent to disclose to a prospective buyer or the buyer's agent whether they have knowledge the property is in a fault zone. [See Form 314 §5]

Seismic hazards

A *Seismic Hazard Zone* map identifies areas which are exposed to earthquake hazards, such as:

- strong ground shaking;

- ground failure, such as liquefaction or landslides [Pub Res C §2692(a)];

- tsunamis [Pub Res C §2692.1]; and

- dam failures. [Pub Res C §2692(c)]

If the property for sale is susceptible to any of the earthquake (seismic) hazards, the seismic hazard zone disclosure on the NHD Statement must be marked "Yes." [See Form 314 §6]

Seismic hazard maps are not available for all areas of California. Also, seismic hazard maps do not show Alquist-Priolo Earthquake Fault Zones. The California Department of Conservation creates the seismic hazards maps.

The seismic hazard maps which exist are on the web at http://www.consrv.ca.gov/shmp/.

If the NHD indicates a seismic hazard, the buyer's agent must then determine which type of hazard, the level of that hazard and explain the distinction to the buyer, or see to it that someone else does. The listing agent has no such obligation to the buyer.

For example, property located in Seismic Zone 4 is more susceptible to **strong ground shaking** than areas in Zone 3. But which zone the property is located in is a question the buyer's agent must answer. Most of California is in Zone 4, except for the southwest areas of San Diego County, eastern Riverside and San Bernardino Counties, and most of the Northern California Sierra Counties.

Homes in Zone 4 can be damaged even from earthquakes which occur a great distance away.

Ground failure is a seismic hazard which refers to landslides and liquefaction. Liquefaction occurs when loose, wet, sandy soil loses its strength during ground shaking. Liquefaction causes the foundation of the house to sink or become displaced. The condition is prevalent in tidal basins which are fills.

A **tsunami** is a large wave caused by an earthquake, volcanic eruption or an underwater landslide. Coastal areas are the ones at risk for loss of property and life.

Tsunami inundation maps are available from the National Oceanic and Atmospheric Administration (NOAA) led National Tsunami Hazard Mitigation Program (NTHMP) at: http://www.pmel.noaa.gov/tsunami-hazard.

Also, FEMA's Flood Insurance maps consider tsunami wave heights for Pacific coast areas.

Dam failure results in flooding when an earthquake causes a dam which serves as a reservoir to rupture. The city or county planning department has maps showing areas which will be flooded if a local dam fails.

Areas susceptible to inundation due to dam failure caused by an earthquake are also noted on the NHD Statement as a potential flooding area.

Chapter 28

Environmental hazards and annoyances

This chapter presents the environmental conditions located on or in the vicinity of a property which adversely affect occupants of the property due to their injurious effect on the health or sensitivities of humans.

Noxious man-made hazards

Environmental hazards are noxious or annoying conditions which are **man-made hazards**, not natural hazards. As *environmental hazards*, the conditions are classified as either:

- injurious to the health of humans; or

- an interference with an individual's sensitivities.

In further analysis, environmental hazards are either located on the property or originate from sources located elsewhere which affect the occupant in his **use and enjoyment** of the property.

Environmental hazards **located on the property** which pose a direct health threat on occupants due to construction materials, the design of the construction, the soil or its location, include:

- asbestos-containing building materials and products used for insulation, fire protection and the strengthening of materials [Calif. Health and Safety Code §§25915 et seq.];

- formaldehyde used in the composition of construction materials [Calif. Civil Code §2079.7(a); Calif. Business and Professions Code §10084.1];

- radon gas concentrations in enclosed, unventilated spaces located within a building where the underlying rock contains uranium [CC §2079.7(a); Bus & P C §10084.1];

- hazardous waste from materials, products or substances which are **toxic**, **corrosive**, **ignitable** or **reactive** [Health & S C §25359.7; Bus & P C §10084.1];

- hazardous waste from the attempt to manufacture drugs [CC §1102.18];

- toxic mold [Health & S C §§26140, 26147];

- smoke from the combustion of materials, products, supplies or substances located on or within the building [Health & S C §§13113.7, 13113.8];

- security bars which might interfere with an occupant's ability to exit a room in order to avoid another hazard, such as a fire [CC §1102.16; Health & S C §13113.9]; and

- lead. [See Chapter 29]

Environmental hazards **located off the property**, but which have an adverse effect on the use of the property due to noise, vibrations, odors or some other ability to inflict harm, include:

- military ordnance sites within one mile of the property [CC §1102.15];

- industrial zoning in the neighborhood of the property [CC §1102.17];

- airport influence areas established by local airport land commissions [CC §§1103.4(c), 1353; Bus & P C §11010(b)(12)(B)]; and

- ground transportation arteries which include train tracks and major highways in close proximity to the property.

The effect on value and desirability

Environmental hazards have an adverse effect on a property's value and desirability. Thus, they are considered defects which, if known, must be disclosed as *material facts* since the hazards might affect a prospective buyer's decision to purchase the property.

The disclosure of a seller's and listing agent's knowledge of existing environmental hazards is required on the sale, exchange or lease of all types of property.

While the disclosure of an environmental hazard is the obligation of the seller, it is the listing agent who has the agency duty of care and protection owing to his seller to place the seller in compliance with the environmental hazard disclosure requirements.

Further, and more critically, the listing agent also has an additional, more limited duty owed to prospective buyers of the listed property. The listing agent must personally conduct a **visual inspection** of the property for environmental hazards (and other physical defects), and do so with competence in order to advise prospective buyers of his observations (and knowledge) about conditions which constitute environmental hazards. [CC §2079]

To conclude the listing agent's disclosure of environmental hazards and eliminate any further duty to advise the prospective buyer about the environmental hazards, the listing agent delivers, or confirms the buyer's agent has delivered, a copy of the **environmental hazard booklet** approved by the California Department of Health and Safety (DHS) to the buyer. Delivery of the booklet is confirmed in writing by use of a provision in the purchase agreement. [See **first tuesday** Form 150 §11.5]

However, the listing agent might be subjected to an inquiry by either the prospective buyer or the buyer's agent about environmental hazards on or about the property. Here, the listing agent is duty bound to respond fully and honestly to the inquiry.

Method of disclosure

The notice of any environmental hazard to be delivered to a buyer by a seller must be given in writing. No special form exists for giving the buyer notice of environmental hazards, as is provided for natural hazards. Until the real estate industry or the legislature develops one, the Transfer Disclosure Statement (TDS) and the purchase agreement are currently used as the vehicles for written delivery.

Some environmental hazards are the subject of provisions in the TDS, such as a direct reference to hazardous construction materials and waste; window security bars and release mechanisms, and an indirect reference to environmental noise. [See **first tuesday** Form 304 §§C(1), A and C(11)]

All other known environmental hazards can be separately itemized in the TDS. As for environmental hazards emanating from off-site locations, they can be disclosed through provisions in the purchase agreement. [See **first tuesday** Form 150 §11.6]

Editor's note — The environmental hazard booklet is not a disclosure of known defects on the property. The booklet merely contains general information on a few environmental hazards, none of which might actually exist on the property. It is voluntarily delivered to the buyer by an agent, but with no legal mandate to do so.

Regardless of the vehicle of delivery, the seller is to give the environmental hazard disclosures to the prospective buyer as soon as *practicable*, meaning **as soon as reasonably possible**. As with the disclosure of natural hazards, the legislature intended for the environmental hazard disclosures to ideally be made prior to entry into a purchase agreement. [Attorney General Opinion 01-406 (August 24, 2001)]

Need and motivation for disclosure

For the listing agent to properly anticipate the need to have the disclosures available to deliver to prospective buyers, the effort to promptly gather the information from the seller begins at the moment the listing is solicited and negotiated.

The seller and the listing agent have numerous good reasons to fully comply at the **earliest moment** with the environmental hazard disclosures (as well as all other property-related disclosures). The **benefits of a full disclosure**, upfront and before the seller accepts an offer or makes a counteroffer, include:

- the prevention of delays in closing;

- the avoidance of cancellations on discovery under due diligence investigation contingencies;

- the elimination of having to renegotiate the price or offset corrective costs due to the listing agent's dilatory disclosure or the buyer's discovery during escrow;

- the shortening of the time needed for the buyer to complete his due diligence investigation; and

- control by the seller of remedial costs and responsibilities by terms included in the purchase agreement, not by later offsets or demands by the buyer or a court.

The listing agent needs to document in writing (for his file only) the agent's inquiry of the seller about environmental hazards which are known or should be known to the seller. The agent's list should itemize all the environmental hazards which might possibly exist on or about a property and the construction materials which contain them, the age or date of construction to elicit a review of probable hazard-

ous construction materials used at the time of construction, and information known about the property on disclosures the seller received when he purchased the property or were brought to his attention on any renovation of the property.

Also, the listing agent's inquiry into hazardous materials should precede the seller's preparation of the TDS. Thus, the seller is mentally prepared to release information about his knowledge of defects in the condition of the property. Finally, the listing agent's visual inspection should also be conducted before the seller prepares his TDS so his observations may be discussed.

The seller has **no obligation to hire an expert** to investigate and report on whether an environmental hazard is present on or about the property. The seller is also not obligated to remove, eliminate or mitigate an environmental hazard, unless he becomes obligated under the terms of his purchase agreement with the buyer.

It is the seller's and his listing agent's knowledge about the property which is disclosed on the TDS. The off-site environmental hazards which affect the use of the property are generally well known by the buyer's agent for inclusion in the purchase agreement. If not included in the TDS or the purchase agreement, a counteroffer by the seller is necessary to disclose — as soon as practicable — the seller's and the listing agent's knowledge of environmental hazards located both on and off the property.

Asbestos in construction materials

Asbestos is any of a diverse variety of *fibrous mineral silicates* which are commercially mined from natural deposits in the earth. In the 1940's manufacturers began mixing asbestos fibers with substances commonly used to produce materials for the construction of residential and non-residential real estate improvements, such as cement, plastic, stucco, vinyl, insulation and felt roofing materials. Asbestos fibers added greater tensile strength, insulation qualities and fire protection to the construction materials which included them. [Health & S C §25925]

However, asbestos is a known *carcinogen*. As an occupant of a building continues to inhale asbestos fiber, he increases his risk of developing cancer of the stomach and chest lining (mesothelioma), asbestosis of the lungs, and lung cancer.

Construction materials which contain **friable asbestos** are those that can be crumbled, pulverized or reduced to powder by hand pressure when dry. Examples of friable material include:

- the acoustic popcorn ceilings homes, apartments and offices;

- thermal insulation on pipes and hot water heaters;

- wall texturing compounds; and

- sheet rock joint compounds, called "mud."

Construction materials which contain **non-friable asbestos** cannot be crushed by hand pressure. Examples of non-friable material include vinyl, asphalt or cement items, such as stucco plaster, vinyl tiles and asphalt roofing felts. Of course, on the removal of stucco or plaster, the asbestos may **become friable** since the material is disturbed and broken down for removal, creating particles which may become airborne and inhaled.

Asbestos is only harmful to humans when the fibers are inhaled and accumulate in the lungs producing, over time and with continuous exposure, an increased risk of cancer.

Thus, asbestos-containing material used in the construction of a building is best left undisturbed by avoiding renovation or demolition. If the material is in good condition (not crumbling or deteriorating), it is best to leave it in place when redecorating or renovating a property.

The seller of a property constructed with asbestos-containing building materials is under no obligation to investigate or have a survey conducted to determine the existence of asbestos on the property — whether friable or non-friable.

Further, the seller is not obligated to remove or clean up any adverse asbestos condition. However, the condition **must be disclosed**. As a result, a prospective buyer may well condition the purchase of a property containing friable asbestos on its clean up and removal by the seller.

Asbestos fibers have not been used in molded thermal insulation material in spray applications for textured ceilings since 1978.

From 1940 to 1996, some homes were built with materials containing asbestos mixed with other components, such as vinyl floor tiles, backings for linoleum, HVAC duct wrapping, hot water pipe insulation, cement siding and pipes, stucco, plaster, asphalt roofing felts, ceiling and wall insulation, and taping compounds. Any removal of these components requires notification to the local air quality management district and the use of a registered contractor.

Formaldehyde gas emissions

Formaldehyde is a colorless, pungent gas contained in most organic solvents which are used in paints, plastics, resins, pressed-wood fiberboard materials, urea-formaldehyde foam insulation (UFFI), curtains and upholstery textiles. Gas emitted from these materials and products contains formaldehyde.

Formaldehyde is considered a *probable carcinogen* which is likely to cause cancer in humans who inhale the gas emitted by formaldehyde-containing material.

The use of UFFI occurred in construction during the 1970s and was banned in residential property constructed after 1982. However, formaldehyde emissions decrease over time. As a result, properties built during the 1970s and early 1980s with formaldehyde-containing materials give off levels of formaldehyde no greater than newly constructed homes. Over time, emissions decrease to undetectable levels. However, an increase in humidity and temperature will increase the level of emissions.

Radon gas in the soil

Radon is a naturally-occurring radioactive gas. It is not visible, cannot be tasted and has no odor. Detection is by instruments only. Radon gas is located in soils with a concentration of uranium in the rock, e.g., granite or shale, beneath it.

Radon is a known human *carcinogen*. The health risk for humans is lung cancer. For smokers, the risk of cancer is substantially increased by radon gas exposure.

Radon gas enters a building from the soil beneath the structure, be it a home, apartment building or nonresidential improvement. Cracks and openings for plumbing in concrete slabs and the porous nature of concrete block basement walls allow the gas from the soil to enter space at or below ground level. Thus, radon is rare in buildings of two or more floors in elevation, except for the ground floor and underground areas.

Radon is sucked into ground floor residential space by interior heating on cold weather days and the use of exhaust fans in the kitchen and bathrooms since these conditions create a vacuum within the lower area of the structure.

However, California residences rarely experience elevated and harmful levels of radon gas emission. Radon does appear in approximately one percent of housing in California. Proper ventilation avoids the build up of harmful concentrations of radon in a home or other enclosed space, a function of its design and operation.

Hazardous waste on site

Waste is hazardous if it has the potential to harm human health or the environment. Hazardous waste is released into the environment, primarily the soil, by the leaking of underground storage tanks, drum containers, poorly contained landfills or ponds, accidental spills or illegal dumping.

Hazardous waste materials include any product, material or substance which are toxic, corrosive, ignitable or reactive, such as is generated by oil, gas, petrochemical and electronics industries, and dry cleaner and print shops.

Information is available to prospective buyers on their inquiry into the location and status of hazardous waste sites in the vicinity of a home from the "Cortese list" maintained by the California Environmental Protection Agency (EPA).

Mold: the rogue presently in vogue

Mold produces spores which become airborne. The spores are inhaled by humans who enter or occupy the space within the area generating the spores. There are many different kinds of spores, each having differing effects, if any, on humans. Some may be a mere annoyance, irritating the sensitivities of an individual. Others might be a threat to the health of those who inhale them.

The uncertainty of the toxic nature of mold spores has lead to a sort of intellectual moratorium on determining just what kinds of molds have an adverse or harmful effect on humans.

Sellers are under no obligation to investigate whether the improvements contain mold. If it is known the structure does contain mold, the seller has no obligation to determine if the mold is a threat to human health.

The DHS has not yet set any **standards** for disclosures regarding the existence of mold. **Guidelines** for the remediation of mold threats and the approval and distribution of a **consumer-oriented booklet** on mold have also not yet been set by the DHS. Until they are produced, the prospective buyer will, at best, receive a writing from the seller and the listing agent in the form of a TDS advising the buyer of any awareness or knowledge the seller or the listing agent may have that mold exists on the property. No common knowledge exists for sellers or listing agents to visually distinguish between harmful and benign molds.

The DHS is expected to release these standards, guidelines and booklet on or after July 1, 2008 to inform prospective buyers about any harmful molds. These rules will set the permissible exposure limits for humans to various molds and identify those molds which pose a health threat to humans.

In any event, no compulsory investigation need be conducted by a seller into the presence of mold on his property. If the seller is aware of mold, regardless of type, he is to disclose his awareness of the mold's existence, as well as any other reports or knowledge about the variety of mold he may have.

To produce mold standards, guidelines and the consumer-oriented booklet, the DHS must first assemble a panel of advisors as a task force to investigate, review and recommend the content of the standards, guidelines and booklet. But before assembling the task force, the program must be funded ($900,000 plus, and not yet available as of March 1, 2006), a cost which is far less than the results of litigation brought about by the uncertainties of not having standards and guidelines.

The DHS anticipates that once the task force is selected, recommendations will not be forthcoming for two additional years. Then, the standards, guidelines and booklet produced by the task force must be adopted or approved by the DHS. When the DHS does finally act to adopt or approve the rules and booklet, they will not become effective for an additional six to twelve months. Thus, no disclosure based on guidance from the state will likely be available to brokers, agents and sellers to deliver to buyers until well after July 1, 2008.

Chapter 29

Lead-based paint disclosures

This chapter evaluates the lead-based paint hazard disclosure mandatory on the sale of all residential housing built prior to 1978 and the risks of accepting a buyer's purchase agreement offer before disclosure.

Crystal clear transparency

An agent, while soliciting an owner of a residential property to employ the agent's broker to market and locate a buyer for the property, gathers facts about the property, its ownership and its likely market value.

The property profile furnished by a title company confirms the agent's suspicion that the structure was built **prior to 1978**. The agent is now aware the property is the target of separate state and federal environmental protection disclosure programs designed to prevent the poisoning of children by the presence of lead-based paint.

The agent sets up a meeting with the owner to review the requisite listing and marketing requirements laid down by his broker, and the owner's expectations for a listing price and an acceptable sales price. To prepare for the meeting, the agent fills out the listing agreement and attaches all the disclosure forms needed to correctly market and sell the property, called a *listing package*.

Among other informational forms, the agent includes two forms which address **lead-based paint conditions** on the property:

- the Federal Lead-based Paint (LBP) disclosure [See Form 313 accompanying this chapter]; and

- the California Transfer Disclosure Statement (TDS). [See **first tuesday** Form 304]

At the presentation of the listing agreement, the agent explains the **seller's legal obligation**, owed to prospective buyers and their agents, to provide them with all the information known to the owner or known or readily available on an inquiry by the listing agent regarding the property which adversely affects its value.

The objective of the listing agent's marketing effort is to provide prospective buyers with all known or readily available information about the property which may affect its value before the prospective buyer makes an offer. By making the transaction **fully transparent** to prospective buyers from the outset of negotiations, the renegotiation of the purchase agreement, including a demand for a price reduction, cancellation or refund after closing due to further disclosures, is avoided. [**Jue** v. **Smiser** (1994) 23 CA4th 312]

A full disclosure to the prospective buyer about the property by the seller and the listing agent does not entail a review or explanation of the facts disclosed. Application of the facts disclosed and the potential consequences flowing from the facts which may affect the prospective buyer's use, possession or ownership of the property are not among the listing agent's duties of affirmative disclosure.

However, federal LBP rules do require the listing agent to advise the seller of the seller's pre-purchase agreement disclosure requirements. The listing agent must **insure compliance** by or on behalf of the seller before the seller enters into a purchase agreement.

Editor's note — Regarding the LBP disclosures, the owner is properly informed he has no obligation to have his property inspected and have a report prepared on the presence of lead-based paint or any lead-based paint hazards. Also, the owner is advised he does not have to perform any **corrective work** *to clean up or even eliminate the conditions, unless he agrees with the buyer to do so. [24 Code of Federal Regulations §35.88(a); 40 CFR §745.107(a)]*

Thus, the seller needs to cooperate in the LBP disclosure and his agent's marketing efforts by:

- filling out and signing the federal LBP disclosure form required on all pre-1978 residential construction [See Form 313];

- filling out and signing the TDS containing the lead-based paint, environmental and other property conditions [See **first tuesday** Form 304];

- ordering or authorizing the listing agent to order a physical home inspection report to be made available to prospective buyers as an attachment to the TDS form; and

- providing the listing agent with copies of reports or documents known to the seller which contain information about the presence of lead-based paint or lead-based paint hazards on the property.

Lead-based paint and hazards

Lead-based paint was **banned** by the Federal Consumer Product Safety Commission in 1978.

Lead-based paint is defined as paint or other surface coating that contains lead equal to at least 1.0 milligram per square centimeter or 0.5% by weight. [24 CFR §35.86; 40 CFR §745.103]

A **lead-based paint hazard** is any condition that causes exposure to lead from lead-contaminated dust, soil or paint which has deteriorated to the point of causing adverse human health effects. [24 CFR §35.86; 40 CFR §745.103]

Editor's note — A list of statewide laboratories certified for analyzing lead in hazardous material, including paint, is available from the National Lead Information Center at (800) 424-LEAD. Lists are also available on the web at http://www.leadlisting.com/lead.html and http://www.dhs.ca.gov/childlead.

LBP disclosure content

The LBP disclosure form includes the following:

- the **Lead Warning Statement** as written in federal regulations [See Form 313 §1];

- the **seller's statement** disclosing the presence of known lead-based paint hazards or the seller's lack of any knowledge of existing lead-based paint [See Form 313 §2];

- a **list of records** or reports available to the seller which indicates a presence or lack of lead-based paint, which have been handed to the listing agent [See Form 313 §2.2];

- the **buyer's statement** acknowledging receipt of the LBP disclosure, any other information available to the seller and the lead hazard information pamphlet entitled *Protect Your Family From Lead in Your Home* [See Form 313 §3.1];

- the **buyer's statement** acknowledging the buyer has received a 10-day opportunity to inspect the property or has agreed to reduce or waive the inspection period [See Form 313 §3.2];

- the **listing agent's statement** noting the seller has been informed of the seller's disclosure requirements and that the agent is aware of his duty to ensure the seller complies with the requirements [See Form 313 §4]; and

Property address:_____

> **NOTE: For use on the sale of any residential property which was constructed pre-1978.**

1. **Lead Warning:**

    1.1   Every buyer of any interest in residential real property on which a residential dwelling was built prior to 1978 is notified that such property may present exposure to lead from lead-based paint that may place young children at risk of developing lead poisoning. Lead poisoning in young children may produce permanent neurological damage, including learning disabilities, reduced intelligence quotient, behavioral problems, and impaired memory. Lead poisoning also poses a particular risk to pregnant women.

    1.2   The seller of any interest in residential property is required to provide the buyer with any information on lead-based paint hazards from risk assessments or inspections in the seller's possession and notify the buyer of any known lead-based paint hazards.

    1.3   A risk assessment or inspection for possible lead-based paint hazards is recommended prior to purchase.

    Items left blank or unchecked are not applicable.

2. **Seller's Certification:**

    2.1   Presence of lead-based paint and/or lead-based paint hazards:

        a. ☐ Are known to be present in the housing as explained:_____

        _____

        _____

        b. ☐ Are not known to Seller to be present in the housing.

    2.2   Records and reports available to Seller:

        a. ☐ Seller has provided Buyer with all available records and reports listed below pertaining to lead-based paint and/or lead-based paint hazards in the housing: _____

        _____

        b. ☐ Seller has no reports or records pertaining to lead-based paint and/or lead-based paint hazards in the housing.

    Date:_____, 20_____ Seller:_____

    Date:_____, 20_____ Seller:_____

3. **Buyer's Acknowlegement:**

    3.1   Buyer has received:

        a. ☐ Copies of all information listed above.

        b. ☐ The pamphlet *Protect Your Family From Lead in Your Home*.

    3.2   Buyer:

        a. ☐ Will receive a ☐ 10-day or ☐ _____-day opportunity from acceptance of the purchase offer to conduct a risk assessment or inspection for the presence of lead-based paint and/or lead-based paint hazards.

        b. ☐ Waives the opportunity to conduct a risk assessment or inspection for the presence of lead-based paint and/or lead-based paint hazards.

    3.3   I acknowledge that I have read and understood the attached lead warning statement in Section 1 of this form and received all information noted in Section 2 of this form.

    Date:_____, 20_____ Buyer: _____

    Date:_____, 20_____ Buyer: _____

4. **Broker's Certification (When Applicable):**

    4.1   Broker certifies to have informed Seller of his/her obligation under 42 U.S.C. §4852d to disclose to Buyer and Broker all information known to Seller regarding the presence of lead-based paint and lead-based paint hazards within this target housing and that all information known to Broker regarding the presence of lead-based paint and lead-based paint hazards within this target housing has been disclosed to Buyer.

    4.2   Broker further certifies that Buyer has received the lead hazard information pamphlet *Protect Your Family From Lead in Your Home* and that Buyer has or will be given a 10-calendar-day period (unless otherwise agreed in writing) to conduct a risk assessment or inspection for the presence of lead-based paint before becoming obligated under the contract to purchase the housing.

    Date:_____, 20_____ Broker: _____

- the **signatures** of the seller, buyer and listing agent. [24 CFR §35.92(a)(7); 40 CFR §745.113(a)(7)]

The seller and the listing broker must each keep a copy of the disclosure statement for at least three years from the date the sale is completed. [24 CFR §35.92(c); 40 CFR §745.113(c)]

Whether or not the LBP disclosure form is retained does not have an effect on the statute of limitations for the buyer to pursue misrepresentations or alter the buyer's right to post-contract disclosures. [24 CFR §35.92(c)(2); 40 CFR §745.113(c)(2)]

Also, the disclosure form must be in the language of the purchase agreement. For example, if the purchase agreement is in Spanish, then the LBP disclosure must also be in Spanish. [24 CFR §35.92(a); 40 CFR §745.113(a)]

Opportunity to evaluate risk

A prospective buyer must be notified before he makes an offer that he has the opportunity, by way of a **10-day period** after acceptance, to evaluate the hazardous risks involved due to the presence of lead-based paint in residential housing built prior to 1978. The buyer can agree to a **lesser period of time** or can entirely **waive** the right to the federally permitted risk evaluation period. [40 CFR §745.110(a)]

However, disclosures about the property cannot be waived, no matter the nature of the facts, data or information, by the use of an "as-is" sale provision.

Both the mandated lead-based paint disclosures and the notice of the waiveable right to a lead-based paint risk evaluation period are complied with by the use of the Federal LBP disclosure form. [See Form 313]

Pre-contract disclosure avoids cancellation

Consider a prospective buyer who indicates he wants to make an offer to buy pre-1978 residential property. The listing agent hands the prospective buyer a lead-based paint disclosure signed by the owner of the property which discloses that lead-based paint is known to exist on the property.

The prospective buyer is also handed independent reports and documents related to the existence of the lead-based paint on the property.

The prospective buyer enters into a purchase agreement offer, but does not waive the 10-day lead-based paint risk evaluation period, wishing instead to **inspect and confirm** the accuracy of the seller's disclosure since the seller's disclosure of the property condition is not a warranty guaranteeing the actual condition of the property.

After the seller's acceptance of the offer, the buyer has the property inspected. The inspector's report states lead-based paint exists as stated in the seller's disclosure documents. The buyer now seeks to cancel the purchase agreement due to the presence of lead-based paint.

Can the buyer refuse to complete the purchase of the property due to the existence of the lead-based paint as previously disclosed by the seller?

No! The buyer had full knowledge of the presence of lead-based paint and any lead-based paint hazards **prior to the seller's acceptance** of his purchase agreement offer. Thus, the buyer purchased the property **as disclosed** since the purchase agreement did not contain conditions calling for removal or abatement of the lead-based paint. The risk evaluation period only enabled the buyer to cancel had the seller not disclosed the presence of any lead-based paint or lead-based paint hazards prior to acceptance.

Thus, when the buyer entered into the purchase agreement, the buyer was put on notice about the presence of lead-based paint and the buyer could not later use the existence of lead-based paint as justification for cancellation.

Foreclosure sale exemption

Exempt from the Federal LBP disclosures are **foreclosure sales** of residential property. [24 CFR §35.82(a)]

Yet, a foreclosing lender still has a **common law duty to disclose known defects** at the foreclosure sale. Thus, even if the property is purportedly sold "as-is" at a foreclosure sale, a foreclosing lender is not protected from liability for intentional misrepresentation (negative fraud by omission) and deceit should the fore-closing lender have knowledge of a defect in the property and fail to disclose the defect at the time of the sale to the highest bidder. [**Karoutas** v. **HomeFed Bank** (1991) 232 CA3d 767]

However, the foreclosure exemption **does not apply** to the resale of housing previously acquired by the lender at a foreclosure sale, commonly called *real estate owned* (REO) property, or to the resale by a third party bidder who acquired the property at a foreclosure sale.

Thus, if a lender or other bidder who acquired property at a foreclosure sale is reselling it, the resale must comply with the lead-based paint disclosure requirements. [61 Federal Register 9063]

Chapter
30   Marketing condominium units

This chapter presents the listing agent's use of condominium association documents to market a unit listed for sale and to inform prospective buyers about the association and the project.

Managed housing

A buyer seeking to acquire a unit in a condominium project, or in any other residential *common interest development* (CID), is **bargaining for** living restrictions and ownership operating costs unlike those experienced in the ownership of a self-managed, single-family residence (SFR).

Ownership of a unit in a condominium project includes compulsory membership in the homeowners' association (HOA). The HOA is charged with managing and operating the entire project.

As a common owner of the project and a HOA member, use and operating restrictions are placed on most types of conduct, including:

- parking;

- pets;

- guests;

- signs;

- use of the pool, recreational and other like-type common facilities;

- patio balconies;

- care and maintenance of the unit,

- structural alterations; and

- the leasing of the premises.

The bargain implicit in becoming an owner-member is consenting to conform his conduct to meet extensive **use restrictions** in exchange for every other owner-member doing the same. The standards for the conduct consented to are found in the use restriction documents created for the project, such as association bylaws, Covenants, Conditions and Restrictions (CC&Rs) and operating rules.

The HOA has committees and a board of directors, both consisting of owner-members who are appointed to oversee the conduct of all the owner-members and their guests. On a committee's recommendation concerning a member's violation of a restriction, rule or policy of the HOA, the HOA takes steps to enforce compliance, usually by a notice of violation to the offending owner-member.

A fair comparison to the member's occupancy in a multiple-unit housing project, such as a condominium development, is a tenant's occupancy in an apartment complex of equal quality in construction, appearance and location. The behavior of a tenant in an apartment is also controlled by use restrictions, operating rules and policies established by a landlord. However, a landlord is subject to market conditions when establishing guidelines for tenant conduct, unlike a HOA which is ruled by majority vote, committees and directors.

Yet the conduct of tenants is regulated and policed in very much the same way as the conduct of a member of a condo project is policed. In fact, security arrangements required to be implemented and maintained for condo projects and apartment complexes are the same, i.e., the property is to be maintained so its use is safe and secure from dangerous defects and preventable criminal activity. Both the landlord and the board of directors of a HOA are responsible for the safety of the users of their respective multiple-housing projects. Both are managed housing.

Classification of member obligations

The bargain entered into on acquiring a unit in a CID must be understood by the prospective buyer to include a highly involved **socio-economic relationship** with all other members of the project's HOA. A commonality of interest arising out of CID ownership creates a relationship amongst the members built not only on **use restrictions** and operating rules, but also on **financial commitments** to one another.

Financially, all members collectively provide all the revenue the HOA needs to pay the expenses of present and future repairs, restorations, replacements and maintenance of all components of the structures they own in common or through the HOA.

Thus, the obligations undertaken by a prospective buyer who acquires a unit in a CID, and the HOA's documentation of those obligations, fall into two classifications:

- **use restrictions** contained in the association's articles of incorporation, by-laws, recorded CC&Rs, age restriction statements and operating rules; and

- **financial obligations** to pay assessments as documented in annual reports entitled pro forma operating budgets, a Certified Public Accountant's (CPA's) financial review, an assessment of collections and enforcement policy, an insurance policy summary, a list of construction defects, and any notice of changes made in assessments not yet due and payable.

Assessments generate revenue

Two types of assessment charges exist to fund the expenditures of HOAs:

- **regular assessments**, which fund the operating budget to pay for the cost of maintaining the common areas; and

- **special assessments**, which are levied to pay for the cost of repairs and replacements that exceed the amount anticipated and funded by the regular assessments.

Annual increases in the dollar amount levied as **regular assessments** are limited to a 20% increase in the regular assessment over the prior year. An increase in **special assessments** is limited to 5% of the prior year's budgeted expenses. [Calif. Civil Code §1366(b)]

An extraordinary expense brought about by an emergency situation lifts the limits placed on the amount of an increase in regular and special assessments. **Extraordinary expenses** include amounts necessitated:

- by a court order;

- to repair life-threatening conditions; and

- to make unforeseen repairs. [CC §1366(b)]

The schedule for payment of assessments by a member varies depending on the type of assessment. **Regular assessments** are set annually and are due and payable in monthly installments. **Special assessments** are generally due and payable in a lump sum on a date set by the HOA when making the assessment.

To better understand the impact of assessment obligations, a prospective buyer of a unit needs to analyze the assessments based on:

- the present and future **annual operating costs** the HOA will incur; and

- the amounts which must be set aside annually as **reserves** for future restoration or replacement of major components of the improvements.

Should the association's reserves be insufficient to pay for major repairs to components of the structure which were foreseeable, a **special assessment** is used by the association to immediately call for additional funds from members to provide revenues to cover these extraordinary or inadequately reserved expenditures.

Arguably, repairs and replacements for which assessment revenues are needed to cover HOA costs are expenses any owner of a SFR would also incur. However, the difference in a CID is the individual member cannot substitute his time, effort and personal judgment for how much will be paid, when the repairs will take place, how repairs might be financed or exactly what repairs or quality of repairs are appropriate. These decisions are left to HOA committees who hopefully vote based on the same concerns and ability to pay as would the prospective buyer of a unit.

Order in the financial house

To determine if a HOA has its finances in order, a prospective buyer should look to the financial reports held by the seller or readily available from the HOA on the seller's request.

The HOA's current **pro forma operating budget** is the starting point for the prospective buyer's analysis of the financial impact the purchase of a unit in the CID will have on his income. Remember, it is the *regular assessments* which will be increased if reserves are inadequate and a *special assessment* which is levied to cover an immediate expenditure for which insufficient cash reserves exist.

The **pro forma operating budget** makes several mandatory disclosures about the state of the HOA's finances, including, but not limited to:

1. An estimate of the revenues from assessments, paid or delinquent, and the **expenses** the HOA anticipates incurring during the fiscal year covered by the budget. The revenues must exceed expenses since the HOA must set aside cash reserves for the future replacement of major components of the structure.

2. A summary of the HOA's **cash reserves** itemizing:

    - the estimated repair or replacement cost of each major component of the structure owned by the HOA;

    - the amount of cash reserves needed to pay for the repairs or replacements of these major components; and

    - the cash reserves actually on hand and available to pay for these repairs or replacements.

3. Any determination or anticipation of the HOA's board of directors as to whether **special assessments** will be required in the future for reserves, repairs, replacements or maintenance. [CC §1365(a)]

On review of the HOA's pro forma operating budget, the prospective buyer can quickly determine whether cash reserve shortages exist. If they do exist, the only way for the HOA to get the funds into reserves or immediately pay for the repairs or replacements is to increase the regular assessments (which are paid monthly) or call for a special assessment (which will be a lump sum amount due and payable when set).

Thus, when setting the purchase price of a unit, the buyer must consider (the present value of) the amount of **deferred assessments** he will have to pay in the future, assessments which should have been levied and paid by the seller.

Some HOAs initially supply only a **summary** of the pro forma operating budget. In this case, the full budget can be requested and will be delivered without further charge.

Further, the prospective buyer needs to review additional HOA documents to fully **determine** the value (price) of the unit he is interested in purchasing and the **financial impact** assessments will have on the buyer's disposable income.

For example, another financial disclosure issued by the HOA, unless the HOA's revenues are $75,000 or less, is a **CPA's review** of the HOA's financial statement (this is not the pro forma operating budget statement). Look for comments in the CPA's review about deficiencies in reserves or accounting procedures. [CC §1365(b)]

HOA assessment enforcement policy

Also available from the HOA is a statement on the HOA's policies for **enforcing collection** of delinquent payments of assessments. [CC §1365(d)]

At issue for a prospective buyer of a unit is the method used by the HOA to enforce collection of assessments, e.g.,:

- does the HOA record a Notice of Default and proceed with a trustee's foreclosure on the owner's unit, a default which can be cured by the payment of delinquencies and statutorily limited foreclosure costs; or

- does the HOA hire an attorney and file a lawsuit requiring a response, a trial and results in a personal money judgment against the owner, all of which has no limit on the dollar amount of costs and attorney fees to defend or prosecute and, if not paid, becomes an abstract of judgment which is a foreclosable lien on all property owned by the owner and collectible by attaching the owner's wages or salary. [CC §§1367, 1367.1]

Also, if a "list of defects" in the structure or a disclosure of any changes already made to regular and special assessments that are not yet

due and payable exists, it indicates financial inadequacies the HOA is now attempting to cure or cover. [CC §§1368(a)(6), 1368(a)(8)]

The prospective buyer of a unit in a CID needs to review all readily available HOA information with the buyer's agent **before making an offer**. With this information, the property's fundamentals become more **transparent**, allowing the buyer and his agent to better determine the price the buyer should pay for the unit and whether or not he has the ability (and desire) to carry the cost of ownership after acquisition.

HOA documentation

An **association's participation** in a listing agent's efforts to induce a prospective buyer to enter into a purchase agreement and close escrow on the sale of a unit located within the project is limited to:

- **providing the listing agent**, on written request from the owner of the listed unit, with documents which include items, statements and reviews regarding the permissible use of the unit and the financial condition of the HOA [CC §1368(b)(3)];

- **providing escrow**, on written request from the owner of the listed unit, with documents which include notices, statements, lists and disclosures regarding the status of the owner's membership in the HOA; and

- **changing HOA administrative records** to reflect the identification of the new owner should the prospective buyer purchase the unit.

The HOA may charge a **service fee** equal to their reasonable cost to prepare and deliver the documents requested by the owner. A charge in connection with the change of ownership is permitted, but is limited to the amount necessary to reimburse the association for its actual out-of-pocket cost incurred to change its internal records to reflect the new ownership of the unit. [CC §§1366.1, 1368(c)]

Within 10 days after the postmark on the mailing or hand delivery to the HOA of a written request from the owner itemizing the documents sought from the HOA, the **association is obligated** to provide them to the owner. A willful failure to timely deliver up the requested documents subjects the HOA to a penalty of up to $500. [CC §1368(b), 1368(d)]

The association documents regarding use restrictions and financial data should be delivered by the owner's listing agent to a prospective buyer prior to entering into a purchase agreement. When disclosures are received before agreeing to buy, the buyer does not have a valid reason to later use this information to terminate the purchase agreement.

Status documents are also available from the HOA on request (usually by escrow) prior to closing. Using these documents, the buyer confirms the owner's representations in the purchase agreement about the status of his occupancy and the assessments imposed on the unit he is selling.

Escrow's only concern with HOA documents is the receipt of information for the purpose of prorations made necessary by prepaid or delinquent assessments.

The closing documents needed by escrow and the buyer regarding the owner's status with the HOA include:

- the CID's *statement of condition of assessments* in order for escrow to calculate **prorates and adjustments** on closing; and

- any HOA notices to the owner of CC&R violations, a list of construction defects and any assessment charges not yet due and payable in order for the buyer to **confirm** the representations made by the owner in the purchase agreement.

A real estate broker and his agents who provide a copy of the use restriction documents or the covenants, conditions and restrictions (CC&Rs) of a homeowners' association to any person must use a **cover page or stamp** on the first page of the previously recorded CC&Rs. The cover page or stamp must state, in at least 14-point boldface type, the following:

"If this document contains any restriction based on race, color, religion, sex, sexual orientation, familial status, marital status, disability, national origin, source of income as defined in subdivision (p) of Section 12955, or ancestry, that restriction violates state and federal fair housing laws and is void, and may be removed pursuant to Section 12956.2 of the Government Code. Lawful restrictions under state and federal law on the age of occupants in senior housing or housing for older persons shall not be construed as restrictions based on familial status."

However, the requirement to include the above declaration does not apply to documents submitted to the county recorder for recordation.

Listing agent's role

Unless a listing agent is remiss, or simply ignorant of his duties owed to prospective buyers, he knows exactly what information and documents he needs to gather to prepare himself to properly market and disclose to prospective buyers the material facts about a condominium unit he has listed for sale, called *transparency*.

Accordingly, it is at the listing stage that the agent should prepare the **owner's request** to the HOA to deliver up the CID documents concerning use restrictions and HOA finances. The documents are immediately available from the association and will be delivered within 10 days of the posted or hand delivered request. [CC §§1368(a), 1368(b)]

The owner is obligated by statute to ensure the disclosures are handed to prospective buyers as soon as practicable (ASAP). It is quite easy for the owner to request and quickly receive the documents from the association. Thus, the ready availability of the documents confirms the disclosures can, as a practical matter, be made available to a prospective buyer before the owner accepts an offer. [CC §1368(a)]

However, once the owner lists the property, it becomes the **listing agent's obligation**, acting on behalf of the owner, to diligently fulfill the owner's obligation to make the association documents available for delivery to prospective buyers, ASAP.

Chapter 31

Bonded indebtedness due improvement districts

This chapter addresses the minimum factual disclosures a seller and listing agent must make to a prospective buyer about an assessment district lien versus the special agency duty of a buyer's agent to review the assessment lien and advise the buyer.

Costs of subdividing land

The subdivision of property carries with it the need for access roads and facilities, none of which are located on any of the parcels created for sale. The parcels created for sale as lots or condominium units are themselves either improved with structures or unimproved.

All the access roads, streets, bridges, distribution systems for water, electricity, natural gas, phones and sewers, as well as parks or other community service facilities are located on portions of the subdivided lands dedicated to the public, not on the lots and units to be sold. The improvements located on the dedicated portions of the subdivided land are called *off-site improvements* since they are not located on or within the parcels sold.

Off-site improvements are constructed solely for the benefit of the parcels offered for sale. Without right-of-way access and improvements, the parcels held out for sale would have little value. It is the availability of fully improved streets, utilities and community facilities which gives value to the parcels and ultimately sets the price a buyer is willing to pay.

Financially, someone must provide the money needed to make these **long-term capital improvements**. When the developer or subdivider of the land does not have sufficient capital or the access to conventional mortgage financing to fund the construction of the subdivision's infrastructure, the subdivider or developer can establish an assessment district encompassing his subdivided lands.

Once established, the assessment district obtains the funds the subdivider needs to pay for the cost of the infrastructure improvements by selling improvement bonds. The bonds are **secured by a lien** on each of the individual (nonpublic) parcels in the subdivision (district) for a prorata amount of the bonded indebtedness. They are not liens on the dedicated lands which are actually improved by use of the funds.

The lien for the bonds serves the same economic function as a trust deed lien for conventional mortgage financing. It is a debt that can be enforced by a foreclosure sale of the parcel liened if not paid.

The dollar amount of the lien on each parcel represents an allocation of the value of the benefits flowing from the off-site improvements to each parcel. Thus, a lien placed on each parcel to secure the long-term semi-annual repayment of the cost of the improvements on the dedicated lands, which contribute to the parcels' market value, is purchase-assist financing by any accounting technique.

Funding off-site improvements

A subdivider's financing scheme to fund off-site improvements is called **Mello-Roos** and is deceptively entitled a *special tax*. It is **not a tax**. However, the tax collection authority for each county collects the annual installments due on the 20-year amortized payoff of the Mello-Roos bonds. The annual installment payment is called an "assessment." [Calif. Government Code §§53311 et seq.]

The debt secured by each lot to repay the bonds has a principal amount which remains due and unpaid until it is prepaid or fully amortized. The interest rate on the remaining principal due is set by the rate on the bonds. At any time, the lien for the improvement bonds can be **paid off** by the owner and the "special tax" lien **released from title** to the parcel.

These infrastructure improvement bond liens are *junior* to regular property taxes.

An improvement district bonding scheme for adding improvements to the right-of-way infrastructure of an **existing neighborhood**, or in several adjoining neighborhoods, is the *Improvement Bond Act of 1915*. Here, the lots or units do not presently enjoy all the off-site improvements or facilities needed to give the parcels their maximum market value, such as sidewalks, street lighting, sewers, parks, etc. [Calif. Streets and Highways Code §§8500 et seq.]

Thus, the 1915 Improvement Act is a financing arrangement used by parcel owners who now want to upgrade the value of their neighborhoods, and with it the value of their properties.

In a democratic fashion, the owners vote to create a 1915 improvement district. Bonds will be sold to pay for the off-site improvements. If voted in, a lien is imposed on each parcel within the improvement district in a dollar amount equal to each parcel's share of the bonded indebtedness. The bonds are payable in annual amortized installments, including interest on the remaining unpaid balance, until paid.

Of course, solvent owners with available cash can pay their prorata share of the costs (equal to the value of the benefits received by their parcel) and avoid the lien. Once a parcel is encumbered, the owner may pay off the lien at any time.

On rare occasions, a Mello-Roos **servicing district** will be established. Unlike the improvement district bonds which can be paid in full at any time, the **service assessment** is annual and forever, unless scheduled to eventually "sunset." A servicing district assessment for a subdivision is comparable to a homeowners' association (HOA) assessment.

Trust deed lenders and improvement bonds

A purchase-assist lender funding a loan to be secured by a first trust deed lien on a parcel in a Mello-Roos subdivision will be junior, not only to real estate taxes, but also to the "sandwich lien" held by the bondholders who funded the construction of off-site improvements.

Thus, the lender's trust deed lien is junior and second to the lien of the improvement bond with its 20-year amortization. Should the trust deed lender foreclose and the lender acquire title, the title will remain subject to the improvement bond lien. As the new owner, the lender must pay the installments on the bond (or pay it off so the trust deed lender is truly a first/senior lienholder, subject only to regular property taxes).

Of course, the market value of property needs to equal or exceed all debts which are voluntary liens on the property, including property taxes, bonded assessments and the lender's trust deed lien, if all monetary liens are to be supported, or in the case of a foreclosure, satisfied by the property's value. Thus, the **value** of the trust deed lender's secured position on title is the difference between the fair market value of the parcel with its on-site improvements (usually a home) and the amounts remaining due on the bonds (and any property taxes).

Misleading disclosures and improper accounting

The "special tax assessment" misnomer used to label the semi-annual installment payments due on an improvement bond lien leads prospective buyers to believe they are dealing with an annual property tax, which they are not.

As a result, sellers and listing agents, when structuring the terms for payment of the price in a purchase agreement offer, often **ignore the principal** amount of the bonded indebtedness on the property, except to prorate the current principal and interest installment on the lien.

The extensive use by organized agents of trade union purchase agreements has memorialized the financial deception. The amount of the improvement bonds is excluded from the terms and no alternative provisions for payment of the buyer's purchase price are provided. The disclosure of the bonded indebtedness assumed by the buyer is placed within the title conditions as a tax, which it is not.

Escrows officers then perpetuate the concept that the improvement lien is not part of the price to be paid by the buyer by handling the current assessment installment as a prorated item. Accounting for the **remaining principal** amount which is due, but not yet payable, is ignored.

The accounting employed in the trade union's purchase agreement for the buyer's assumption of the bond amount can best be compared to an agreement to prorate the current installment on an assumption of a trust deed note while ignoring the elephantine principal amount remaining unpaid on the note — a monetary debenture not unlike an improvement bond. Both have principal, interest and amortized installments. Both are liens on the property.

Under this disclosure-by-proration approach, the buyer is given insufficient information by the seller or listing agent to make an intelligent decision about assuming the lien for the bond. Alone, the purchase agreement provision probably does not satisfy the listing agent's general duty to give the prospective buyer sufficient information to actually place the buyer on notice of the bonded indebtedness.

On the other hand, it is the **buyer's agent** who has the duty to further advise his buyer about the lack of an accounting for the bond, rather than simply "going along" with the boilerplate purchase agreement pricing and proration arrangements.

Presently, the disclosure of an improvement lien as a proration of taxes has become "standard operating procedure," but remains a contractually deceptive and unacceptable accounting standard.

As a result, the California legislature stepped in during the 1990s with legislation to ensure that prospective buyers of real estate got sufficient information to make an informed decision. Sellers (and thus, their agents) were mandated to give to buyers of Mello-Roos encumbered properties:

- a **notice** of the lien for the bonded debt and an **opportunity** to decide whether or not to assume the debt before entering into a purchase agreement; or

- the **right to renegotiate** the terms for payment of the price if they have already agreed to buy before receipt of the notice.

If fully informed, the buyer (and thus the buyer's agent) would prudently require the bond amount to be credited toward the price paid since its entire principal amount has accrued and cannot be prorated.

Statutory Notice of Assessment

The sale of property comprised of one-to-four residential units and encumbered by a Mello-Roos or 1915 Act improvement bond **requires the seller** to disclose the existence and terms of the bonded indebtedness. To comply, sellers must obtain and deliver to prospective buyers a notice prepared by the improvement district office entitled either *Notice of Assessment* or *Notice of Special Tax*. [Calif. Civil Code §1102.6b]

Anyone can request a Notice of Assessment from the office of the improvement district at any time, which of course includes both the listing agent and the buyer's agent. No particular manner of request is required, be it by phone, fax or mail, since it may be an oral or written request. The district office must deliver the notice to whomever requests it, and do so within five working days of their receipt of the oral or written request. The maximum charge for the service is $10. [Gov C §53754(b)]

The seller, since he has the **primary obligation** to request the notice and deliver it to prospective buyers, should be advised by the listing agent to request the notice when entering into the listing agreement employing the broker's office to sell the property.

If the seller refuses to assist the listing agent by complying with the seller's statutory duty for disclosure of the lien, the listing agent can and should request the Notice of Assessment himself. However requested, the agent needs to include the notice in the **listing package** prepared for disclosing to prospective buyers significant relevant information about the property. Information presented in a listing package is either **mandated**, as is the case with assessment bonds, or **known** to the seller and listing agent to exist.

Occasionally, the listing agent lacks knowledge of the lien's existence, lacks an opportunity to deliver information on the lien to the prospective buyer prior to submission of an offer, or just delays disclosure until after a purchase agreement has been entered into.

However, when the prospective buyer enters into a purchase agreement with the seller before the Notice of Assessment is delivered to the buyer, the buyer has a **statutory contingency** allowing the buyer to cancel the purchase agreement. The buyer has three calendar days after hand delivery (five days after posting by mail) of the Notice of Assessment to cancel the purchase agreement by handing a Notice of Cancellation to the seller or listing agent (not escrow or the buyer's agent). [Gov C §53754(c)]

Differing duties to give notice or advise

Whether a buyer receives a Notice of Assessment before agreeing to buy or after, the contents of the notice, without explanation or additional information, has fulfilled the seller's and his agent's *general statutory duty* owed to the buyer to disclose the existence of the assessment.

On the other hand, a buyer's agent must advise the buyer about the need for further facts regarding the assessment so an evaluation of the financial impact the assessments have on the value, price, carrying costs, etc., can be made. Worse yet, if the listing agent does not actually know if a lien exists, the buyer's broker is obligated to review the **preliminary title report** in order to catch it.

Editor's note — If the purchase agreement does not provide for the assessment lien to remain of record, and the seller and buyer enter into a binding purchase agreement, the seller has agreed to deliver title clear of lien amounts.

The Notice of Assessment (special tax) is a statutory form. However, the contents of the form do not call for the entry of enough data regarding the assessment to sufficiently inform the buyer. Without additional data on the assessment lien, the buyer cannot make an informed decision about the bonded indebtedness. The notice **only includes**:

- the amount of each annual installment (which incidently could be a variable payment due to inflation adjusted bonds); and

- the last year in which an amortized installment will be paid (thus releasing the lien encumbering the lot as fully paid).

The Notice of Assessment does not include three additional elements about the debt which are needed to determine the **extent of the obligation**, and whether the debt is one to be assumed as a credit toward the price or to be satisfied by the seller:

- the **rate of interest** the bonds bear;

- the **current remaining principal** balance due to discharge the debt; and

- whether the bond lien is a **blanket lien** on the entire subdivision or common interest development (CID), and if so, whether a partial release of a lot is available.

Neither the interest nor the principal balance can be calculated from the information provided in the notice from the assessment district's office. Hence, the buyer's agent must step forward and request this additional information from the district, which the district must then deliver.

On receipt of the additional information, the buyer and his agent now have sufficient information to commence an analysis of the bonds and make an intelligent (informed) decision on pricing, terms of payment, assumption of the bonds, etc. In a word, the buyer's agent must provide the buyer with the **transparency** needed to make decisions in the transaction.

Accounting for assessment bonds

With the differing biases expressed by the content and format of purchase agreements from differing sources, so to are the biases for handling of the accounting for bonded assessments on the liens for subdivision improvements.

Some purchase agreements treat the unpaid principal on Mello-Roos or 1915 Act bonds as **additional consideration** paid for the property by the buyer, **over and above the price** agreed to be paid in the offer. For consistency, the current annual installment is then prorated without concern for a breakdown between the installment's principal and interest, or that the buyer assumes several thousands of dollars of principal and interest installments.

Here, the (undisclosed) remaining unpaid principal due on the bonds is not included as part of the stated purchase price the buyer is paying for the property.

Thus, these purchase agreements do not provide for a calculation of the total consideration (price plus bond balance assumed) the buyer is actually paying for the property, called *acquisition costs*. This lack of disclosure is statutorily sanctioned conduct by the seller and listing agent.

However, their duty of limited disclosure does not apply to the buyer's agent under his duty owed to the buyer.

Without advice from a buyer's agent about the true nature of the improvement assessment bonds, the buyer will not begin to understand the nature of the contents of a Notice of Assessment or the payoff aspect. However, the advice of the buyer's agent is logically limited to his actual knowledge about the bond arrangements and any information readily available from the assessment district's office.

On the other hand, other publisher's purchase agreements place the accounting for the bonded indebtedness, if it is not to be paid off by the seller, in the price to be paid for the property. Thus, the buyer assumes the debt as a lien on the property owed by the seller and part of the price paid, which it is.

The treatment of the amount of the **monetary lien** for the bonded indebtedness is fully equivalent to the assumption of a trust deed lien by a buyer. The principal balance on the improvement bond lien is credited to the price to be paid by the buyer as part of the agreed price, which typically is the property's fair market value (FMV). [See **first tuesday** Form 150 §7]

The argument surrounding the two diametrically opposed accounting and disclosure procedures revolves around a determination of the property's FMV.

Would two parcels in the same subdivision improved with identical same-type housing, both have different sales prices simply because of the financing which encumbers them? At first glance, the answer is no.

However, if the buyer is fully advised by his agent about the consequences of both an assumption of the improvement bonds as part of the price paid for the property, or conversely, as an additional amount to be eventually paid but not accounted for as included in the price, then the accounting schemes available to the buyer are both *transparent*. Thus, due to the full disclosure of the buyer' agent:

- if the price offered **includes** an assumption of the bond amounts (or the seller is to clear title of the lien), the price will represent the property's FMV (which by definition is free and clear of monetary liens); or

- if the price offered **excludes** the bond amounts which are assumed, the price offered will be less than the property's FMV by the exact amount of the lien for the balance due on the bond.

Therefore, both offers would, in the final accounting, be paying the same total consideration as the **cost of the acquisition** of identical houses in the same subdivision since both houses are subject to the same amount of bonded indebtedness.

Chapter 32

Prior occupant's use, affliction and death

This chapter discusses the disclosure of a prior occupant's death or affliction with AIDS.

When and when not to disclose

A real estate broker and his listing agent are employed by a seller to locate a buyer for his real estate. The listing agent soon locates a buyer who wants to purchase the property.

Prior to making an offer, the listing agent hands the buyer the seller's Transfer Disclosure Statement (TDS) disclosing the seller's and agent's knowledge about the present **physical condition** of the property. All other mandatory disclosures are made.

The buyer does not inquire into any deaths which might have occurred on the property. Ultimately, the buyer acquires and occupies the property.

Later, a neighbor informs the buyer a prior occupant died on the property from AIDS or HIV. The prior occupant's death occurred **more than three years** before the buyer submitted the offer to purchase the real estate.

The buyer discovers the listing agent knew of the prior occupant's AIDS affliction and death on the property. The buyer claims the listing agent breached his agency duties since the agent had an affirmative duty to voluntarily disclose to the buyer that the prior occupant died on the property and was afflicted with AIDS.

Here, no real estate agent has an affirmative duty to **voluntarily disclose** information to a potential buyer regarding a prior occupant:

- whose death, from any cause, occurred on the real estate **more than three years prior** to the purchase offer; or

- who was afflicted with the HIV virus or afflicted with AIDS. [Calif. Civil Code §1710.2(a)]

*Editor's note — Deaths on the property which occurred **within three years** of the offer are treated differently.*

Disclosure on inquiry

Consider a buyer of real estate who asks the listing agent if any deaths have occurred on the property at any time.

On direct inquiry by the buyer or the buyer's agent, the listing agent must **disclose his knowledge** about whether deaths have occurred on the real estate, no matter when they occurred. [CC §1710.2(d)]

An intentional misrepresentation or concealment by any agent in the real estate transaction after a buyer makes a **direct inquiry** is:

- a breach of the listing agent's *general duty* owed to the buyer to truthfully respond when the listing agent represents the seller exclusively; or

- a breach of the buyer's agent's *agency duty* owed the buyer since the agent is the buyer's representative in the transaction. [CC §1710.2(d)]

Further, an **inquiry** by the buyer into deaths is an indication a death on the premises is a fact which might affect the buyer's use and enjoyment of the property and constitute a *material fact*. Thus, an affirmative duty is imposed on the **buyer's agent** to either investigate or recommend an investigation by the buyer before an offer is made, unless the offer includes a contingency on the subject of death.

An agent who does not know whether a death occurred on the real estate and who, **on inquiry**, discloses he does not know or has limited information which he does disclose, should confirm the disclosure by handing the buyer a memorandum stating:

- the buyer has made an inquiry about deaths on the property;

- the agent has disclosed all his knowledge concerning the inquiry; and

- whether or not the agent will further investigate the occurrence of deaths on the property.

Deaths affecting market value

The duty of each agent in a transaction to disclose facts known to them which may adversely affect the property's value, called *material facts*, is not limited to disclosures of the property's physical condition.

Consider a buyer who enters into a purchase agreement negotiated by an agent, acting either as the buyer's agent or the listing agent. The offer includes the seller's TDS disclosures about the condition of the property as an attachment. However, the buyer is unaware multiple murders occurred on the property more than three years before the buyer's purchase offer.

The agent does not disclose the murders, **concealing his knowledge** of the murders from the buyer. The agent is aware that the notoriety of the murders **adversely affects** the market value of the property, placing its value below the price the buyer is agreeing to pay.

The transaction closes and the buyer occupies the property. The buyer learns of the multiple murders on the property. The buyer sues the agent to collect his price-to-value money losses, claiming the agent had a duty to disclose the deaths since the agent was aware the property's market value, due to the stigma of the deaths, was **measurably lower** than the purchase price paid by the buyer.

The agent claims he does not have a duty to disclose the deaths since the deaths occurred on the property more than three years ago and were not required to be disclosed on the TDS.

Did the agent have an affirmative duty to disclose the deaths?

Yes! The deaths had an **adverse affect** on the property's market value and were facts known to the agent. The deaths were a **material fact** and **intentionally concealed** from the buyer.

Thus, every agent has an affirmative duty owed to a buyer to disclose prior deaths when the death **might affect the buyer's valuation** or desire to own the property. [**Reed** v. **King** (1983) 145 CA3d 261]

Desirability based on prior events

Consider a buyer's agent who is aware a death, from any cause, occurred on the real estate **within three years** of a buyer's purchase offer. The value of the property is **not adversely affected** by the death. Thus, the knowledge is not a material fact about the property which needs to be disclosed.

The buyer does not ask his agent if any deaths have occurred on the property.

After closing, the buyer learns of the death.

The buyer is deprived of the pleasurable use and enjoyment he expected of the property — an **idiosyncracy** of the buyer about death which was unknown to his agent.

The buyer claims the buyer's agent breached his special agency duty by failing to disclose the death since the death interferes with the buyer's intended use of the property by inflicting an intangible harm on the buyer which will not allow the buyer to occupy the real estate.

Here, the buyer's agent probably should have inquired of the buyer to determine if a known death on a property is a fact which might affect the buyer's decision to purchase the property. Since the buyer's agent has a greater agency duty to care for and protect the buyer than does a listing agent, a buyer's agent should disclose any death occurring on the property within three years, especially if he believes the death, no matter when it occurred, is a fact which might affect the buyer's decision to make a purchase agreement offer.

It is the buyer's agent's duty to **investigate and disclose** material facts about the property and the transaction, placing a greater burden on the buyer's agent to know and understand his client, a sort of **know-your-client rule**.

Conversely, the buyer has a duty of care, owed to himself, to **inquire and discover** facts to protect his own personal interests, especially uncommon ones.

However, whether or not a buyer's agent will be subject to any liability or penalties for not disclosing a death which occurred on the property within three years prior to the buyer's purchase offer, when the agent was **unaware of the buyer's idiosyncracy** and the death was not a material fact affecting the value of the property, has yet to be reported.

Chapter 33

Income property operating data

This chapter addresses the data a listing agent needs from a seller on any type of income producing property before the listing agent is able to diligently market the property to prospective buyers.

Fundamentals induce offers

It is said about an income property's operating data that it is both the beginning and conclusion of a transaction.

An income producing property's operating data is gathered and entered on an Annual Property Operating Data (APOD) sheet by the seller or listing agent. The purpose of preparing an APOD is to provide information about the property to prospective buyers or their agents.

By design, the APOD is **intended to induce** prospective buyers to rely on its content to buy the property. Thus, with the presentation of an APOD to a prospective buyer, negotiations have begun.

If negotiations are successful, a prospective buyer enters into a purchase agreement with the seller. The conclusionary act by the buyer and the buyer's agent is the completion of their due diligence investigation into the accuracy of the income data contained in the APOD.

To do so, the buyer's agent reviews the operating expenses, rent rolls, leases and tenant estoppel certificates. If the certificates are substantially the same as the data contained in the APOD and the leases, and the expenses are verified, the transaction closes.

Thus, on close of the transaction, the income and expenses experienced by the property and presented on an APOD by the listing agent have come full circle. The buyer's receipt of the APOD on introduction to the property has been tied to the confirmation of the APOD figures and the transaction has closed.

Honest start equals strong finish

The price an investor will pay for income producing real estate is set by a property evaluation analysis of data based on different appraisal techniques, one of which is the *income approach*. When another evaluation approach sets a value different than set by the income approach, the lesser of the values should greatly influence the investor's decision on pricing.

This chapter is concerned primarily with the income approach to valuation since income is initially used by investors to determine a property's fair market value (FMV) and the ability of the rents to service debt. Here, comparable sales or depreciated replacement cost approaches are of secondary concern.

Rental income and operating expenses produce a property's *net operating income* (NOI). In turn, the property's NOI represents the annual return the property delivers to the owner, which is accounted for as:

- a **return of** the owner's original capital investment, called *depreciation*, (evidenced in part by the principal reduction on purchase-assist loans); and

- a **return on** the owner's capital investment, called a *yield*, (including NOI used to service interest payments on the purchase-assist loans).

Since the NOI represents the investor's annual returns, the information and data entered in an APOD are the **fundamentals** upon which an income property investment is initially judged for setting its market value. Thus, the APOD prepared by the listing agent must contain accurate representations of either:

- **current operations**, as experienced by the seller; or

- an **opinion honestly held** by the agent about future income and expenses which an investor will likely experience as owner of the property.

Thus, a prospective buyer of income property is buying a **future flow** of income (NOI) for which he is willing to pay a price today. This price is the **discounted, present worth** of the property's NOI over the coming years. Further, this is the maximum price the prospective buyer would agree to pay for the property.

By the listing agent's use of an APOD, the prospective buyer is *induced to rely* on the APOD figures to evaluate the property, enter into negotiations, and sign a purchase offer. If the figures hold up under an investigation, the buyer will acquire ownership of the property.

For the listing agent to avoid deceitful and dishonest activities in the inducement, the figures entered in an APOD must have some close relationship to the income and expenses the property actually does or will likely produce. The only known **sources of data** for the APOD figures which the listing agent can draw on are the owner's actual operating records of the property and the operations of comparable properties. Both are readily available to agents on inquiry.

The need for forecasts

Data from comparable properties might demonstrate that the listed property's current operations are producing less rental income and greater expenses than experienced by owners of other properties.

The comparison may justify the preparation of an APOD using figures which are decidedly not reflective of the property's current operat-

ing income and expenses. Instead, the APOD figures represent the listing agent's opinion about the property's probable future operations based on the income and expenses experienced by both the listed property and comparable properties.

Here, the listing agent must have a reasonable basis for developing a **rational opinion** about the property's future potential by estimating the anticipated income and expenses. The estimate is the listing agent's *forecast* of income and expenses which the listing agent **honestly believes** has a reasonable likelihood of actually occurring under new ownership.

Thus, two entirely different NOI estimates could logically be presented to a prospective buyer regarding the listed property:

- one based on **current operations** as continuing without a significant change in anticipated income and expenses, properly called a *projection*; and

- the other being an **opinion** of potential income and expenses likely to be experienced in the future, properly called a *forecast*.

The difference in the NOI produced by these two estimates of the property's future annual operations has a profound financial impact for the property's value. A $10,000 potential increase in annual NOI over the current NOI experienced by the seller converts, by the financial process of *capitalization of income,* into an increase in value ranging from $80,000 to $120,000. The range depends on the rate of return expected in the marketplace at the time of sale. It is in the best interest of the seller for the listing agent to put forward on an APOD the best set of figures which the listing agent honestly believes an owner could actually achieve.

However, the listing agent must be certain the buyer does not rely on the APOD figures as a *warranty* or anything more than the listing agent's **honestly held belief** that the NOI estimated has a reasonable likelihood of occurring. Listing agents must accompany their optimistic forecasts on APODs with a statement indicating the figures are *opinions* and nothing more.

If the buyer receives positive assurances from the listing agent that the APOD figures are **attainable**, the buyer can rely on the APOD as a *guarantee* of what will occur. Then, the buyer may rely on the data unconditionally presented by the listing agent without further investigation to confirm whether or not the assurances will occur. [**In re Jogert, Inc.** (9th Cir. 1991) 950 F2d 1498]

A contingency provision in the purchase agreement calling for the buyer's further approval of the income and expenses would be prudent to demonstrate that the buyer is not relying on the agent's APOD estimates as a guarantee.

Seller's good-faith assistance

To assist a listing agent to marshall information about a property's operations for the preparation of an APOD and determining the property's current NOI, the seller must, *in good faith*, provide the listing agent with printouts of his monthly, year-to-date and past 12 months income and expense statements. Either the seller, the property manager or resident manager have or can generate this operating information for the listing agent.

An owner, having employed a listing agent to market his income property and locate a buyer willing to pay the listed price, owes a duty to the listing agent to make a good-faith effort to cooperate and assist the agent to meet the objectives of the employment. Otherwise, the seller *wrongfully interferes* with the agent's ability to successfully market the property (and earn a fee). Without accurate operating data, income property cannot be honestly marketed to prospective buyers.

In turn, the listing agent's duty as the seller's agent is to deliver to his seller the best business advantage **legally achievable**. This duty is tempered by the listing agent's *general duty* owed to prospective buyers to provide them with accurate factual information about the integrity of the property which may adversely affect the value of the property, and to do so before the buyer enters into a purchase agreement.

To meet this affirmative disclosure duty owed to prospective buyers, the listing agent must provide prospective buyers or their agents with information **known or readily available** to the seller or listing agent about the operations of the property which **might affect** the decisions of a reasonably prudent buyer regarding acquisition of the property. As a result, the listing agent must present known facts to a prospective buyer in a manner which will not mislead or deceive the buyer by omitting factors adversely affecting the property's value.

If the seller or his property manager are the source of the information on the property's operations, and the listing agent has no reason to believe the data is false, the listing agent has no duty to prospective buyers to investigate the truthfulness (accuracy) of the information. However, the **source of the data** must be disclosed.

The APOD

An APOD, prepared by a listing agent and handed to a prospective buyer, provides operating information on the property, including:

- the **estimated NOI**, for setting the price to be paid and the loan amounts which can be serviced by the income generated by the property;

- the **spendable income**, for providing a cash-flow cushion reflected by the amount of the NOI remaining after servicing the mortgage financing (including information on trust deed balances, monthly payments, interest rates and any due dates); and

- the **income tax consequences** the prospective buyer will likely experience during the first year of ownership due to allowable deductions of interest on trust deed loans and standard depreciation schedules.

In the comment's section of the APOD form, the listing agent enters local trends and factors **known to the listing agent** which may not be observable by a prospective buyer or the buyer's agent when viewing the property, or discoverable by them when reviewing the marketing package. Local trends and factors include currently evolving economic or regulatory conditions which might affect the property's future income or expenses, and thus, impact the prospective buyer's decision to buy or use the property.

Economic impacts include:

- population demographics in the location of the property as decreasing, static or increasing in density;

- the local population's future effect on the appreciation or depreciation of the property's value;

- whether the quality and location of the property will, in the future, support the APOD's income and expense analysis; and

- the rents and expenses experienced by comparable property in the area.

Income property expense ratios

Expenses, as a percentage of scheduled income, are calculated on the APOD in the center column. Percentages are obtained by dividing each expense item by the (100%) scheduled income. [See Form 352 accompanying this chapter]

The percentage calculated for each operating expense alerts the prospective buyer and his

agent to data which varies from a range typically experienced by the type of income property involved.

For example, if the percentage allocated to utility expenses is abnormally high compared to other properties, this cost should be evaluated to determine:

- what can be done to bring the utility expenses within the normal percentage range; and

- what effect the expense has on the value of the property, other than reducing the NOI.

Information which needs to be separately disclosed to a prospective buyer so he can determine the property's worth includes recent "spikes" in expense items, such as:

- utilities;

- evictions necessitated by delinquencies;

- security re-evaluations needed due to incidents of crime on the premises;

- loss of a local industry which employs a significant percentage of area tenants;

- assumable or locked-in financing;

- rent control adjustments; and

- loan commitments.

Loan payments

Loan payments entered on the APOD should reflect only the principal and interest payment, separate from any impounded (escrowed) funds deposited with the lender as part of the monthly payment. Impounds, however, should be disclosed elsewhere in the APOD.

Impounds are merely a **reserve** for some of the owner's fixed operating expenses (already figured into the NOI) which the lender will pay on behalf of the owner using the impounded funds, such as property taxes, improvement district assessments and the hazard insurance premium.

Deposits into an impound account are not a loan charge or an operating expense. However, the lender's later disbursements from the impound account represents payment of the owner's operating expenses.

The amount of any monthly impound deposit will change on transfer of the property's ownership, typically due to an increase in property taxes triggered by reassessment due to the change of ownership. The buyer's agent calculates the increase in the impounds and enters the estimated future impound payment on the APOD, not the seller's present impound payment.

Data approved for release

As a service to his seller, a listing agent can prepare the APOD if all the verifiable rents and expenses are made known to the agent by the seller. Unless a seller is willing to "lay open" the books on the property to the listing agent so its operations are sufficiently transparent to provide verifiable data for a prospective buyer, this listing goes nowhere.

Before the listing agent can effectively market the property, the APOD has to be prepared for delivery to prospective buyers. Again, the APOD can be prepared to reflect either:

- the property's **current operations**, which implicitly infers that the figures given will more than likely occur during the following year; or

- the property's **potential future operations**, influenced by income and expenses now experienced by comparable properties and trends in rents and operating expenses in the surrounding area.

When the APOD is completed to the satisfaction of the listing agent and the seller, the seller should **sign a copy** for the listing agent's file. Thus, the seller acknowledges his approval of the contents of the APOD and consents to the release of the figures.

With a seller-approved APOD in the listing file, the APOD becomes the centerpiece of the listing agent's marketing (listing) package to be presented to prospective buyers or buyer's agents.

Duties owed the buyer

A listing agent owes a **general duty** to a prospective buyer and buyer's agent to gather together readily available information on the property and make it available to them without investigation into its accuracy, called **putting the buyer on notice**.

In turn, the **special agency duty** owed the buyer by a buyer's agent is to review the skeletal property information received from the seller and listing agent and advise the buyer as to the inquiry or investigation needed to understand and appreciate the ramifications of the disclosures.

In essence, the seller's listing agent literally hands off to the buyer's agent the decision as to which points raised by the APOD figures need to be checked out to get the remainder of the story and an accurate picture of the property's earning power.

For example, the APOD and rent roll sheets may not give critical details about leases, such as whether or not any leases might include;

- free-rent incentives for a period of time preceding the commencement period stated in the written lease;

- a downward gradation in the amount of rent after a six or eight month occupancy on month-to-month tenancies as an incentive for a tenant to remain in possession; or

ANNUAL PROPERTY OPERATING DATA SHEET
APOD

Date:_____, 20_____, at _____, California

1. PROPERTY TYPE: _____

    1.1 Location: _____

    1.2 APOD figures are estimates reflecting:

        a. ☐ Current operating conditions.

        b. ☐ Forecast of anticipated operations.

        c. Prepared by: _____

			%
2. INCOME:			
2.1 **Scheduled Rental Income**	$_____		**100%**
a. Less: Vacancies, discounts and uncollectibles – $_____			_____%
Credit card charges – $_____			_____%
2.2 **Effective Rental Income**	$_____		_____%
a. Other income + $_____			_____%
2.3 **Gross Operating Income**	$_____		_____%
3. EXPENSES:			
3.1 Electricity	$_____		_____%
3.2 Gas	$_____		_____%
3.3 Water	$_____		_____%
3.4 Rubbish	$_____		_____%
3.5 Insurance	$_____		_____%
3.5 Taxes	$_____		_____%
3.6 Management Fee	$_____		_____%
3.7 Resident Manager	$_____		_____%
3.8 Office expenses/supplies	$_____		_____%
3.9 Advertising	$_____		_____%
3.10 Lawn/Gardening	$_____		_____%
3.11 Pool/Spa	$_____		_____%
3.12 Janitorial	$_____		_____%
3.13 Maintenance	$_____		_____%
3.14 Repairs and Replacements	$_____		_____%
3.15 CATV/phone	$_____		_____%
3.16 Accounting/Legal Fees	$_____		_____%
3.17 _____	$_____		_____%
3.18 _____	$_____		_____%
3.19 **Total Operating Expense**	– $_____		_____%
4. NET OPERATING INCOME:	$_____		_____%

5. **SPENDABLE INCOME** (annual projection):

    5.1 **Net Operating Income** (enter from section 4) . . . . $_____ ___%

5.2 Loan	Principal Balance Amount	Monthly Payment	Rate	Due Date
a. 1st	$_____	$_____	___%	_____
b. 2nd	$_____	$_____	___%	_____
c. 3rd	$_____	$_____	___%	_____

    5.3 Total Annual Debt Service . . . . – $_____ ___%

    5.4 **Spendable Income** . . . . $_____ ___%

6. **PROPERTY INFORMATION:**

    6.1 Price $_____; Loan amounts $_____; Owner's equity $_____

    6.2 Current vacancy rate or vacant space: _____%

    6.3 Assessor's allocations for depreciation schedule:
       Improvements _____%; Land _____%; Personal property _____%.

    6.4 Property disclosures:

       a. ☐ Rent roll available; ☐ need confidentiality agreement.

       b. ☐ Rent control restrictions.

       c. ☐ Condition of improvements available: ☐ by owner, ☐ by inspector.

       d. ☐ Environmental report available.

       e. ☐ Natural hazard disclosure available.

       f. ☐ Soil report available.

       g. ☐ Termite report available.

       h.﹨ ☐ Building specification available.

       i. _____

       j. _____

7. **REPORTABLE INCOME/LOSS** (annual projection): | For Buyer to fill out. |

    7.1 **Net Operating Income** (enter from section 4) . . . . $_____

       a. Annual interest expense . . . . $_____

       b. Annual depreciation deduction (ft Form 354.5) . . $_____

    7.2 Total deductions from NOI . . . . – $_____

    7.3 **Reportable Income/Loss** (annual projection): . . . . $_____

Broker: _____	**I have reviewed and do approve this information.**
Address: _____	Date: _____, 20_____
_____	
Phone: _____ Cell: _____	Owner's name: _____
Fax: _____	Signature: _____
Email: _____	Signature: _____

FORM 352   06-05   ©2006 **first tuesday**, P.O. BOX 20069, RIVERSIDE, CA 92516 (800) 794-0494

- an option to extend the lease at a fixed rate which might be inconsistent with the prospective buyer's expectations of rental income.

Thus, the terms of occupancy, provisions in the leases, discounts, incentives, options or first-refusal rights to additional space, etc., must be part of the buyer's inquiry, triggered by the disclosure of the fact tenants hold leases and rental agreements.

Quite possibly, the buyer's agent, on completion of the inquiry into the facts behind the numbers on the listing agent's APOD, will himself fill out an APOD form to reflect his own belief about the future operating potential of the property. For the buyer's agent, the APOD prepared as his forecast must be presented as his opinion of what likely will be the performance of the property in the hands of the prospective buyer.

No assurances by the agent equals no guarantees. However, the APOD figures given as an opinion must represent a belief, **honestly held** by the buyer's agent, that the figures have a fair chance of actually occurring in the future.

Due diligence by the buyer's agent

Once the listing agent informs the prospective buyer and the buyer's agent about the property's operating facts by delivery of an APOD, issues concerning the rent and expenses need to be investigated and analyzed by the buyer's agent. Thus, the buyer is assisted in a determination of the probability that the APOD figures will actually be experienced in the future. This investigation or recommendation for further inquiry includes:

- a review of any **tenant files**, including lease or rental agreements, application for rent, deposits received, credit report printouts, criminal or other background checks, photocopies of driver's licenses, credit card information for payment of monthly rent and payment history;

- discovering if any units or spaces in the project have a **chronic vacancy** or turnover history requiring a downward adjustment in the price paid for the property;

- a **confirmation of expenses**, by getting quotes if necessary, on what amounts the buyer will be charged, not what the seller has been able to arrange and be charged, for hazard insurance premiums, taxes based on the price to be paid, improvement district assessments, professional management fees, and the management's opinion of APOD projections;

- determining the date of the last **rental increase**, the amount of the increase and the seller's rent increase policy employed during the past few years;

- establishing who has been providing **maintenance**, and what charges can the new owner anticipate (as well as questions on intentionally deferred maintenance);

- a confirmation of the **utilities** paid by the owner and any price fluctuations, past or anticipated;

- a review of any **criminal activity** on the premises as confirmed by the local police department and by inquiry of a few tenants;

- ascertaining the number of **unlawful detainers** (UDs) filed during the past 12 months and why those tenants had to be evicted;

- a review of any **rent control** activity, if the units are locally controlled, and a check with the local agency to determine the property's compliance and the buyer's ability to maintain or attain market rates; and

- a confirmation of any **miscellaneous income** to be received from on-site vending machines, such as laundry room equipment and supplies, food and beverage dispensers and furnishings rented to occupants.

If the buyer's agent is not willing to conduct this due diligence investigation, the buyer needs to be informed of the buyer's agent's knowledge concerning the data, the source of his data and any advice on the investigations the agent believes should be undertaken for the buyer to protect his own interest.

Buyer's homeownership expenses

Consider a prospective buyer of a single-family residence (SFR) who intends to occupy the property as his principal residence. The buyer is not concerned about the rent the property will command in the rental market.

However, the buyer is interested in getting information from the seller about the cost of owning and operating the SFR he will occupy.

The best way for the buyer to get this data is for the buyer's agent to include a provision in the buyer's purchase agreement calling for the seller to prepare and hand the buyer an occupant's property operating cost sheet disclosing the monthly expenses which have been incurred by the seller as the owner of the property. [See **first tuesday** Forms 150 §11.7 and 562]

Chapter 34

Required disclosures on seller carrybacks

This chapter reviews the financing disclosures agents must make to buyers and sellers in carryback transactions.

Mandated notices

A seller is willing to help finance the sale of his one-to-four unit residential real estate by carrying back a note and trust deed, sometimes called an *installment sale* or *credit sale*.

The seller's listing agent locates a qualified prospective buyer. The agent prepares an offer on a purchase agreement form and presents it to the buyer for his approval and signature since the buyer is not represented by an agent.

The terms offered for payment of the purchase price include a note and trust deed, to be signed by the buyer in favor of the seller, for the amount of the price remaining to be paid after the down payment and an assumption of the existing loan on the property.

A **Seller Carryback Disclosure Statement** is attached to the purchase agreement as an addendum. The addendum, prepared by the agent, contains numerous statements on the financial, legal and risk-of-loss aspects of the carryback note and trust deed. [See Form 300 accompanying this chapter]

The information entered in the carryback disclosure statement is based on the terms of the purchase offer, the title conditions, the activities to be undertaken in escrow and information obtained from the buyer.

However, the agent's disclosures regarding other important aspects of the carryback paper which are not addressed in the disclosure form and might affect the transactional decisions of the buyer or the seller do not end on completion and presentation of the carryback disclosure form.

The form contains only the **minimum disclosures** legislatively mandated for inclusion in the carryback disclosure statement.

Both the listing agent and the buyer's agent must be assured their respective clients, in addition to receiving the disclosure statement, understand and appreciate the risks and consequences which rise out of the **financial, legal and tax aspects** of the carryback transaction.

Controlled carryback transactions

All brokered transactions for the purchase of **one-to-four unit residential property** involving seller carryback financing are controlled by statute. For one-to-four unit residential properties, a written carryback disclosure statement is required to be presented to both the buyer and seller for their review and signatures. [Calif. Civil Code §§2956 et seq.]

Even the use of a *masked security device*, such as a land sales contract, lease-option and unexecuted purchase agreement with interim occupancy, requires the written carryback disclosures. The written carryback disclosures inform the buyer and the seller about the seriousness of the risks presented by failing to use grant deeds, notes and trust deeds to evidence an installment sale when the buyer takes possession. [See Form 300 and **first tuesday** Forms 309 and 312]

On a sale, any credit extended by the seller to accommodate the buyer's deferred payment of the purchase price for a one-to-four unit residential property requires a written carryback disclosure statement when the credit extended to the buyer includes:

- interest or other finance charges;

FINANCIAL DISCLOSURE STATEMENT
For Entering a Seller Carryback Note

DATE:_____, 20_____, at _____, California

> **INSTRUCTIONS FOR USE:** This statement is required to be prepared when the seller carries back a note executed by the buyer as part of the sales price for property containing four-or-less residential units. [Calif. Civil Code §2956]
>
> This statement is to be prepared by the broker who obtains the signature of the person who first offers or counteroffers to buy, sell, exchange or option on terms which include a carryback note.
>
> Both the buyer and the seller shall be handed a copy of the statement and sign it to acknowledge they have read and received a copy.

1. This is an addendum to the following agreement:

☐ Purchase agreement ☐ Option to purchase (with or without lease)

☐ Counteroffer ☐ Exchange agreement

    1.1 Dated _____, 20_____.

    1.2 Entered into between _____

    1.3 and _____

2. This addendum was prepared by _____

Items left blank or unchecked are not applicable.

DISCLOSURES:

3. GENERAL INFORMATION CONCERNING THE TERMS OF PAYMENT;

    3.1 The Note to be executed by Buyer is in the original amount of $_____, payable in constant monthly _____ installments of $_____ to include _____% per annum interest; all due and payable with a final/balloon payment on _____, 20_____, in the approximate amount of $_____.

    3.2 The note will be secured by a trust deed on the property described as:_____
_____

    3.3 Should the note contain a FINAL/BALLOON PAYMENT, the debt is not fully amortized. When the remaining balance of the note is due and payable, there can now be no assurance that refinancing, modification or extension of the balloon payment will then be available to Buyer.

    3.4 Unless stated and explained in an attached ARM addendum, the note contains a fixed rate of interest with no variable or adjustable interest rates which would increase payments or result in a negative amortization of the debt. [ft Form 263]

    3.5 Unless otherwise agreed, the original amount of the note will be adjusted by endorsement at close of escrow to reflect differences in the then remaining balance of any underlying trust deed obligation(s) being assumed or obtained.

    3.6 ☐ The note and trust deed to be is carried back by Seller is of the all-inclusive variety, and will contain provisions passing through to Buyer any prepayment penalties, late charges, due-on sale or further encumbrance acceleration and future advances due on the underlying wrapped loans.

4. SPECIAL PROVISIONS AND DISCLOSURES CONCERNING THE CARRYBACK NOTE AND TRUST DEED:

    4.1 ☐ The all-inclusive note and trust deed to be carried back by Seller contains provisions calling for Seller to place the note on contract collection with any institutional lender or real estate broker, other than Seller, and the collection agent will be instructed to first disburse funds on payments due senior encumbrances. **NOTE: Inclusion of this provision may cause adverse income tax consequences for Seller.**

    4.2 A joint protection policy of title insurance will be delivered to Buyer and Seller insuring their interests in title on the close of escrow.

    4.3 The trust deeds and grant deeds to be executed will be recorded with the county recorder at close of escrow.

    4.4 Seller will be named, through escrow, as a loss payee under the hazard and fire insurance obtained by Buyer.

    4.5 A tax reporting service ☐ will, or ☐ will not, be obtained by buyer for Seller. If not obtained, Seller will assure himself that real estate taxes have been paid while he holds the note.

    4.6 ☐ Requests for Notice of Default and Notice of Delinquency under California Civil Code Sections 2924b and 2924e will be recorded and served on behalf of Seller on encumbrancers senior to the carryback.

4.7   Seller is aware that in the event of a default under the carryback note and trust deed, his sole source of recovery is limited to the net proceeds from a foreclosure sale or his subsequent resale of the real estate; and he is not entitled to rental value for Buyer's occupancy or a deficiency money judgment under the note. [Calif. Code of Civil Procedure §580b]

4.8   Buyer ☐ shall, or ☐ shall not, receive net proceeds or cash back upon the close of escrow. Amount to be received $_____; source of funds _____; reason for receipt _____.

4.9   The note shall include the following provision: "This note is subject to Section 2966 of the Civil Code, which provides that the holder of this note shall give written notice to the trustor, or his successor in interest, of prescribed information at least 90 and not more than 150 days before any balloon payment is due."

5. ENCUMBRANCES SENIOR AND PRIOR TO SELLER'S CARRYBACK TRUST DEED AND NOTE:

5.1   Conditions of encumbrances, with priority over Seller's carryback note and trust deed which will remain or be placed of record at time of closing are as follows:

	First Trust Deed	Second Trust Deed
Original balance:	$_____	$_____
Current balance:	$_____	$_____
Interest rate:	_____% ☐ ARM	_____% ☐ ARM
	Type: _____	Type: _____
Monthly payments:	$_____	$_____
Due date:	_____, 20____	_____, 20____
Balloon payment:	$_____	$_____
Current defaults:	$_____	$_____

5.2   If any of the senior encumbrances contain a due date, it may be difficult or impossible to refinance, modify or extend the balloon payment in the conventional mortgage marketplace.

6. BUYER CREDIT INFORMATION (SUPPLIED BY BUYER):

6.1   Buyer to hand Seller a completed credit application on acceptance. [ft Form 302]

6.2   Seller may terminate the agreement within _____ days of receipt of the credit application by delivering to Buyer, Buyer's broker or escrow written Notice of Cancellation based on Seller's disapproval of Buyer's credit. [ft Form 183]

7. BROKER DISCLOSURES:

7.1   Credit data is supplied by Buyer. Broker knows of no falsity or omission concerning Buyer's credit information.

7.2   This statement and its contents are statutorily required disclosures and do not limit Broker's duties to disclose other facts material about Seller to Buyer or Seller about the carryback financing arrangements and which are known to Broker or his agent.

7.3   Buyer and Seller are not to sign this statement until they have read and understood all of the information in it. All parts of the form must be completed before signing below.

7.5   ☐ See attached addendum for additional disclosures which are part of this disclosure. [ft Form 250]

8. OTHER: _____
_____
_____

Date:_____, 20_____   Date:_____, 20_____

Buyer's   Seller's

Broker:_____   Broker:_____

By: _____   By: _____

I have read and received a copy of this statement.   **I have read and received a copy of this statement.**

Date:_____, 20_____   Date:_____, 20_____

Buyer: _____   Seller: _____

Buyer: _____   Seller: _____

FORM 300   1-06   © 2006 **first tuesday**, P.O. BOX 20069, RIVERSIDE, CA 92516 (800) 794-0494

- five or more installments running beyond one year;

- an installment land sales contract;

- a purchase lease-option or lease-option sale;

- credit (note) to adjust equities in an exchange of properties; or

- an all-inclusive note and trust deed (AITD). [CC §2957]

Further, carryback transactions creating straight notes which do not bear interest or include finance charges are **not controlled**. However, the carryback disclosures should be included as a matter of good brokerage practice since the risks and issues for the buyer and seller remain much the same.

Now consider a real estate agent who is acting as a property manager or leasing agent negotiating a lease for the landlord of a single-family residence (SFR).

A prospective tenant makes an offer to lease which contains an option to buy the property. The terms for payment of the price under the proposed option include:

- a carryback note, to be executed on exercise of the purchase option (on expiration of the lease) for the balance of the seller's equity in the property after a down payment; and

- part or all of the lease payments applying as a credit toward the price or down payment.

Here, the tenant's offer to lease under a purchase option **builds up an equity** in the property due to the rent credit to the price. Thus, the agent is required to make the mandated carryback financing disclosures on a written form as an addendum to the lease-option. [See **first tuesday** Form 309]

Who prepares the disclosure

The carryback disclosure statement must be **prepared and submitted** to all parties in a carryback transaction on one-to-four unit residential property by:

- the real estate broker, or his agent, **negotiating** the carryback sales transaction and preparing the buyer's purchase offer on behalf of a buyer or seller for a fee; or

- the buyer or seller if either one is a real estate licensee or attorney, when neither the buyer nor the seller is represented by a broker. [CC §2957(a)(2)]

When both the buyer and seller are represented by different brokers, the carryback disclosure statement is prepared by the broker or his agent who prepared the buyer's offer.

Offer includes disclosures

As a minimum requirement, the carryback disclosure statement is to be signed by the buyer and seller **prior to closing** the carryback sales escrow. [CC §2959]

However, after a purchase agreement has been entered into, and until the carryback disclosure statement is approved by the buyer and seller in a one-to-four unit transaction, a **statutory contingency** exists in favor of the buyer allowing the buyer to cancel the transaction. The contingency does not arise if the carryback disclosure statement is attached as an addendum to the offer or counteroffer.

If the buyer has a reasonable basis for disapproval of the carryback disclosures he receives after entering into a purchase agreement, the buyer may cancel the transaction and terminate his obligation to purchase the property.

However, the buyer may not arbitrarily cancel the sale when he is presented with the carryback disclosure statement for his acknowledgment and approval during escrow. To cancel, the buyer must act in good faith, by showing the carryback disclosures are inconsistent with his **reasonable expectations** when he entered into the purchase agreement.

After closing, the only legal remedy available to the buyer or seller for inadequate or nonexistent financial disclosures is to pursue the broker for any money losses actually incurred as a result of the nondisclosure. The judicial remedy for failure of the broker or his agent to make mandated carryback disclosures would be no less than a return to the injured party of brokerage fees received on the transaction, based on a failure of agency duties.

Thus, the best policy for the **buyer's agent** is to eliminate the need for further approval of the statutory carryback disclosures by preparing and attaching the carryback disclosure statement as an addendum to the purchase agreement. If it is not attached, it would be prudent for the **listing agent** to include it as an addendum to a counteroffer. If neither agent prepares and includes the disclosures as an addendum in the offers, the buyer's agent becomes responsible for preparing the disclosures and obtaining both the buyer's and seller's approval before closing.

Contingency utilized

Consider a buyer and seller of a single-family residence who enter into a purchase agreement. The terms call for carryback financing in the principal amount of $50,000 with an interest rate of 9%, monthly payments on a 30-year amortization and a five-year due date.

The purchase agreement does not state the amount of the balloon payment due on the carryback note at the end of five years. The risks imposed and the consequences of a five-year due date are not discussed.

A carryback financial disclosure statement is not presented to the buyer or seller for their signatures as part of the purchase agreement or counteroffer. Thus, closing is automatically contingent on the buyer's and seller's **further approval** of the financial and legal aspects of the carryback note and trust deed as presented in the carryback disclosure statement.

Prior to closing, the buyer is handed the carryback disclosure statement. He discovers his final balloon payment at the end of five years will be approximately $48,300. The buyer is now concerned about the financial risks of ownership since he has no assurance he will be able to refinance, modify or extend the note, much less have the ability to accumulate funds for payoff of the final/balloon payment.

The buyer cancels the purchase agreement and escrow, claiming he did not previously realize the extent of the financial risk created by the due date in the carryback financing. He is now aware he could be forced, by the due date, to either sell the property or lose it to foreclosure should he be unable to arrange refinancing or an extension of the carryback note.

Can the buyer cancel the transaction prior to closing?

Yes! The buyer did not sign the carryback disclosure statement prior to agreeing to buy — a failure which triggers the **statutory further-approval contingency**. The risk of loss imposed by the amount of the due date payoff is far greater than the buyer realized when entering into the purchase agreement. Thus, the buyer has justification for exercising his right to cancel.

Buyer's ability to pay

A buyer's ability to meet the terms and conditions of the carryback note is of great importance to a seller who is carrying back a note on a sale. Thus, the listing agent must alert his seller to facts about the buyer's financial condition which are known to the broker and not previously disclosed to his seller.

For example, a listing agent locates a buyer willing to purchase his seller's property.

The agent advises the seller that the buyer is financially qualified to handle the large cash down payment, but will require carryback financing for the remainder of the purchase price.

Believing his agent's representations regarding the buyer's financial qualifications, the seller agrees to carry paper to finance the sale.

Before escrow closes, the buyer tells the agent he does not have the cash down payment and will need to obtain a loan. The listing agent does not disclose the buyer's lack of capital to the seller. Further, the listing agent makes the buyer a money loan to help fund the down payment.

Escrow closes and the buyer takes title to the property. Soon the buyer defaults on the carryback note and trust deed held by the seller. The seller suffers a total loss on his carryback note due to a foreclosure sale on the first trust deed.

The seller then discovers his listing agent made a separate loan to the buyer for the down payment. The seller also discovers the agent knew the buyer was financially unstable prior to closing.

Here, the listing agent has an agency duty to advise the seller about the buyer's reduced financial capability to repay the carryback note, a significant fact which came to the agent's attention prior to closing. Thus, the listing agent and the agent's broker are liable to the seller for the seller's money losses on the carryback note since the listing agent failed to disclose his knowledge of the buyer's revised or altered financial status. [**Ziswasser** v. **Cole & Cowan, Inc.** (1985) 164 CA3d 417]

A seller willing to carry back paper needs to know if the prospective buyer will be able to make the payments and pay the operating costs incurred as owner of the property. As carryback financing becomes more prevalent during periods experiencing a declining real estate market or tight mortgage money conditions, more unqualified buyers are produced with whom agents must contend.

As part of the carryback disclosures, the listing agent has an **affirmative duty** to obtain a written financial statement from the buyer and hand it to the seller of one-to-four unit residential property. [See Form 300 §4]

The primary purpose of the carryback disclosure statement is to inform the seller so he understands that owners and lenders are bound by different rules and face different risks based on the respective ownership and security interests they hold in the real estate.

For example, while the buyer is concerned with paying no more than the *fair market value* (FMV) for a property, the carryback seller is concerned with his *loan-to-value (LTV) ratio*, whatever may be the price, since he will become a "financier" on the close of escrow.

Typically, a seller wants to receive the highest sales price negotiable for his real estate. However, the seller as a "carryback lender" wants assurance the buyer's down payment is a large enough percentage of the purchase price to establish adequate equity value in the real estate, over and above the amount of the carryback trust deed note, to allow full recovery of the carryback note from the property in the event of a default which requires the seller to foreclose.

Chapter
35
The seller's net sheet

This chapter reviews the listing agent's use of a checklist to prepare an estimate and disclose the expenses a seller will likely incur to fix up the property for marketing, provide reports to prospective buyers and close a sale.

Financial consequences of a sale

Probably the most pressing concern sellers of real estate have about selling is the amount of money they will receive for their property on a sale since what sellers receive on closing is **not the full amount** of the purchase price, although the amount they will receive is a calculable part of the price.

While a seller may not straight out ask the listing agent what amount escrow will hand him in exchange for conveying his property to a buyer, the serious nature of the unspoken concern the seller has about the amount of money he will carry away from the closing is implicit. Sellers always want to know the amount of money they will **actually receive** as *net sales proceeds* for transferring ownership.

The sole reason for employing an agent is to convert the **seller's equity** into cash by selling the property at the highest possible price.

Significantly, a seller on listing his property for sale has a **motive** which drives his decision to acquire cash, if only for the opportunities cash makes available to him. The motives range from the disposal of real estate no longer of use to the owner or now threatened with loss to foreclosure, to the need for cash to accomplish a personal, business or investment objective, such as acquiring a replacement home or a premises for the operation of a trade or business, investing in the equities, bonds or commodities market, or simply putting the cash into savings.

However, the ordinary seller has little idea how to figure the dollar amount of net proceeds a sale of his property will bring. A seller's initial belief is that the net sales proceeds will be roughly equal to his equity in the property, less a brokerage fee. The notion of retrofitting property and complying with governmental safety regulations, as well as lender payoff penalties or buyer's demands for repairs, is not known to most sellers.

Further, the asking price is unadjusted for the need to fix up the property and to clear the property of structural pests and accumulated defects so the property can be properly marketed. In other words, most sellers who have not sold real estate within the last several years, if ever, are without a clue as to how to estimate their net sales proceeds.

On the other hand, agents routinely sell properties and review closing statements. They have a working understanding of all the expenses a seller is most likely to be confronted with to market, sell and close escrow on a property.

The expertise of an agent is more than sufficient to marshall the information needed to make a reasonable estimate of the likely net sales proceeds on any sale.

The estimate should be first prepared on a **seller's net sheet** at the listing stage and again when reviewing offers or updating the net sheet figures when changes become known.

For a listing agent, a down side always exists when making disclosures regarding net sales figures. The information might cause a prospective client to decide not to sell, or cause a seller of listed property to reject an offer and counter at a price needed by the seller but unacceptable to a buyer. It is for these pricing

SELLER'S NET SHEET
On Sale of Property

This is an estimate of the fix-up, marketing and transaction expenses Seller is likely to incur on a sale, and the likely amount of net sales proceeds Seller may anticipate receiving on the close of a sale under the following agreement:

☐ Seller's listing agreement   ☐ Purchase agreement   ☐ Counteroffer

☐ Escrow instructions   ☐ Exchange agreement   ☐ Option to buy

Entered into by _____

Dated _____, 20_____, at _____, California.

Regarding property at: _____

_____. The day of the month anticipated for closing is _____.

> This net sheet is prepared to assist the seller by providing an estimate of the amount of net sales proceeds the seller is likely to receive on closing, based on the price set in the agreement, the estimated amount for expenses likely to be incurred to market the property and close a sale, and any adjustments and prorates necessitated by the sale.
>
> The figures estimated in the net sheet may vary at the time each is incurred due to periodic changes in charges for professional services, administration fees and work enforcement made necessary by later inspections, and thus constitute an opinion, not a guarantee.
>
> If the property disposed of is IRC §1031 property and the seller plans to acquire replacement property, use a §1031 Recapitulation Form to compute the tax consequences of the seller's §1031 Reinvestment Plan. [ft Form 354]

1. **SALES PRICE:**
   1.1 Price Received . . . . ADD: $_____

2. **ENCUMBRANCES:**
   2.1 First Trust Deed Note . . . . $_____
   2.2 Second Trust Deed Note . . . . $_____
   2.3 Other Liens/Bonds/UCC-1 . . . . $_____
   2.4 TOTAL ENCUMBRANCES: . . . . DEDUCT: $_____

3. **SALES EXPENSES AND CHARGES:**
   3.1 Fix-up Cost . . . . $_____
   3.2 Structural Pest Control Report . . . . $_____
   3.3 Structural Pest Control Clearance . . . . $_____
   3.4 Property/Home Inspection Report . . . . $_____
   3.5 Elimination of Property Defects . . . . $_____
   3.6 Local Ordinance Compliance Report . . . . $_____
   3.7 Compliance with Local Ordinances . . . . $_____
   3.8 Natural Hazard Disclosure Report . . . . $_____
   3.9 Smoke Detector/Water Heater Safety Compliance . . . . . . $_____
   3.10 Owners' Association Document Charge . . . . $_____
   3.11 Mello-Roos Assessment Statement Charge . . . . $_____
   3.12 Well Water Reports . . . . $_____
   3.13 Septic/Sewer Reports . . . . $_____
   3.14 Lead-based Paint Report . . . . $_____
   3.15 Marketing Budget . . . . $_____
   3.16 Home Warranty Insurance . . . . $_____
   3.17 Buyer's Escrow Closing Costs . . . . $_____
   3.18 Loan Appraisal Fee . . . . $_____
   3.19 Buyer's Loan Charges . . . . $_____
   3.20 Escrow Fee . . . . $_____
   3.21 Document Preparation Fee . . . . $_____
   3.22 Notary Fees . . . . $_____

3.23 Recording Fees/Documentary Transfer Tax . . . . $_____

3.24 Title Insurance Premium. . . . . $_____

3.25 Beneficiary Statement/Demand . . . . $_____

3.26 Prepayment Penalty (first). $_____

3.27 Prepayment Penalty (second). . . . . $_____

3.28 Reconveyance Fees . . . . $_____

3.29 Brokerage Fees . . . . $_____

3.30 Transaction Coordinator Fee . . . . $_____

3.31 Attorney/Accountant Fees . . . . $_____

3.32 Misc. Expense _____ . . . $_____

3.33 Misc. Expense _____ . . . $_____

3.34 TOTAL EXPENSES AND CHARGES . . . . DEDUCT: $_____

4. ESTIMATED NET EQUITY . . . . SUBTOTAL: $_____

5. PRORATES DUE BUYER:
    5.1 Unpaid Taxes/Assessments . . . . $_____

    5.2 Interest Accrued and Unpaid . . . . $_____

    5.3 Unearned Rental Income . . . . $_____

    5.4 Tenant Security Deposits . . . . $_____

    5.5 TOTAL PRORATES DUE BUYER . . . . DEDUCT: $_____

6. PRORATES DUE SELLER:
    6.1 Prepaid Taxes/Assessments. . . . . $_____

    6.2 Impound Account Balances . . . . $_____

    6.3 Prepaid Association Assessment . . . . $_____

    6.4 Prepaid Ground Lease . . . . $_____

    6.5 Unpaid Rent Assigned to Buyer . . . . $_____

    6.6 Miscellaneous _____ . . . $_____

    6.7 TOTAL PRORATES DUE SELLER. . . . . ADD: $_____

7. **ESTIMATED PROCEEDS OF SALE** . . . . $_____

    7.1 The estimated net proceeds at Section 7 from the sale or exchange analyzed in this net sheet will be received in the form of:

        a. Cash . . . . $_____

        b. Note secured by a Trust Deed. . . . . $_____

        c. Equity in Replacement Real Estate. . . . . $_____

        d. Other_____ . . . . $_____

I have prepared this estimate based on my knowledge and readily available data.	I have read and received a copy of this estimate.
Date:_____, 20_____	Date:_____, 20_____
Broker:_____	Seller's Name: _____
Agent: _____	Signature: _____
Signature: _____	Signature: _____

FORM 310   11-04   ©2006 **first tuesday**, P.O. BOX 20069, RIVERSIDE, CA 92516 (800) 794-0494

decisions that the net sheet information is a **material fact** requiring an *affirmative disclosure* by the listing agent of the figures which comprise the seller's net sheet and the seller's bottom line.

Costs of sale as a material fact

A **material fact** is information which, if known to a client, might affect the client's decisions, such as a seller's decision to enter into a listing or accept an offer to buy.

If the information, such as sales expenses, closing costs or the net proceeds of a sale, is known to the seller, the listing agent has no obligation to disclose it. However, if the information may affect a decision to be made by the seller and the information about sales costs is not fully known to the seller or is not more readily available to the seller than it is to the listing agent, the costs must be disclosed to the seller to meet the listing agent's obligations under his special agency duties owed to his client.

It is best to prepare and review a net sheet with a seller, regardless of whether or not the seller requests or even declines to receive a net sheet. The time and effort needed to prepare a net sheet is a small premium to pay to assure the agreed fee is not attacked should the seller, at the time of closing, claim he thought he would receive a greater amount as net proceeds.

Analyzing the net sheet estimates

A listing agent prepares a **Seller's Net Sheet, first tuesday** Form 310, to inform his client about the expenses the seller will likely incur on the disposition of his real estate by sale. The sheet lists expenditures typically incurred for most sales of real estate, including expenses for readying the property for marketing, preparing third-party reports on investigations covering the nature and condition of the property, complying with government requirements or buyer demands to correct defects, and for escrow charges on the sales transaction.

The estimates entered on the form by the seller's broker or listing agent must be based on information **known** by them or **readily available** to them on the inquiry of others or on minimal investigation about each item of expense they anticipate the seller will incur. Thus, the figures entered as estimates reflect the listing agent's **honestly held belief** that the amounts estimated will likely be experienced by the seller.

Brokerage events triggering a listing agent's preparation of the net sheet and a review of its contents with the seller for the sale of property include:

- soliciting or entering into a seller's listing agreement;

- submitting a buyer's purchase agreement offer;

- entering into a counteroffer; and

- entering into an exchange agreement offer or acceptance.

The net sheet is used by a listing agent for the purpose of disclosing to the seller the crucial financial information surrounding expenditures required to:

- put the property in a condition attractive to the greatest number of prospective buyers;

- comply with local retrofit ordinances and current safety standards;

- eliminate defects and infestation; and

- provide the listing agent with reports for delivery to prospective buyers which contain information on the physical condition of the property, the nature of the property's location, the expenses of ownership and any other aspects regarding the integrity of the property that have a measurable impact on the property's value.

The Seller's Net Sheet consists of four sections, each serving an entirely separate purpose in the setting of the amount of net proceeds to be received by a seller on a sale. The sections list:

- the **encumbrances** of record, including any improvement district bonds, trust deeds and possible abstracts of judgment or tax liens to be assumed, reconveyed or released;

- the **expenses** of a sale, including repair and renovation expenditures, fees for investigative reports and closing charges paid by the seller;

- **adjustments and prorates** for unpaid or prepaid items and any tenant deposits to be taken over by the buyer; and

- the **net proceeds** remaining after deducting all sales-related expenses, fees and charges, as well as the form of the net proceeds.

Preparing the seller's net sheet

The following instructions are for the preparation and use of the Seller's Net Sheet, **first tuesday** Form 310, with which a seller's agent may prepare an estimate for an analysis of the costs the seller will likely incur in the preparation, marketing and sale of the property. The disclosure of this data to the seller is necessary for the seller to make an informed decision regarding whether to sell, and if so, on what terms and conditions.

Each instruction corresponds to the number given each item in the form.

*Editor's note — **Enter** figures throughout the net sheet in the blanks provided, unless the item is not intended to be included in the final estimate, in which case it is left blank.*

Document identification:

Check the appropriate box to indicate the underlying agreement which is the subject of this disclosure. **Enter** the name(s) of the parties to the underlying agreement, the identification date and place of preparation of the underlying agreement, the address or parcel number identifying the property for sale, and the day of the month on which escrow is to close for prorations and adjustments.

1. Sales price:

1.1 *Price received*: **Enter** the amount of the sales price to be paid by the buyer.

2. Encumbrances:

2.1 *First trust deed note*: **Enter** the dollar amount of the principal balance remaining due on any first trust deed loan of record as noted on loan payment records held by the seller, whether the loan is to be assumed or paid off on closing.

2.2 *Second trust deed note*: **Enter** the dollar amount of the principal balance remaining due on any second trust deed loan of record as noted on loan payment records held by the seller, whether the loan is to be assumed or paid off on closing.

2.3 *Other liens/bonds/UCC-1*: **Enter** the total dollar amount of the principal balance and any accrued unpaid interest on any judgment liens, tax liens and improvement district bond liens encumbering the property, and any UCC-1 liens on any personal property which are part of the sale, whether the liens will be assumed or paid off on closing.

Editor's note — Some purchase agreements, in their provisions for handling improvement district bond liens, omit any accounting on the transfer of title subject to a lien for the balance of an improvement district bond with annual installments. Annual installments on the improvement bond lien are treated in these purchase agreements as prorates of both the principal and interest installment amounts, without concern for an accounting of the principal balance which remains unpaid.

2.4 *Total encumbrances*: **Add** the figures entered in sections 2.1 through 2.3. **Enter** the total as the dollar amount of debts encumbering the property, whether assumed by the buyer or paid off on closing.

3. **Sales expenses and charges:**

3.1 *Fix-up cost*: **Enter** the dollar amount estimated to cover the costs it is anticipated the seller will incur to ready the property for previews by other agents, caravans, walk-throughs by prospective buyers and open house viewings, such as the cost to add color to the landscaping, paint outside trim and any interior walls showing wear and tear, and replace any plumbing or electrical fixtures which are beyond repair or of unacceptable appearance.

3.2 *Structural pest control report*: **Enter** the dollar amount of the fee a pest control operator will charge to conduct a physical inspection and submit a report on his findings and provide an estimate of the costs of repairs necessary to eliminate any infestation and repair any existing damage or condition allowing for infestation. These are property conditions most buyers do not want to acquire.

3.3 *Structural pest control clearance*: **Enter** the dollar amount estimated

to cover the cost it is anticipated the seller will incur for fumigation or to correct damage from an infestation or conditions supporting an infestation. The amount estimated will need to be reviewed and updated on receipt of the structural pest control report.

Also, the amount estimated should be considered when setting any ceiling in a counteroffer on the costs the seller might be willing to incur to correct the adverse condition of his property.

3.4 *Property/home inspection report*: **Enter** the dollar amount of the fee a home inspection company will charge to conduct a physical inspection of the property and submit a report on their observations of defects existing on the property.

3.5 *Elimination of property defects*: **Enter** the dollar amount estimated to cover the cost it is anticipated the seller will incur to eliminate, by repair or replacement, any conditions not up to building or safety codes, such as malfunctioning or defective components, e.g., the roof, electrical wiring, plumbing, heating, the foundation, walls, fences, doors, and appliances. The amount estimated will need to be reviewed and updated on receipt of a property/home inspection report.

Also, the amount estimated should be considered when setting any ceiling in an offer or counteroffer of the amount of costs the seller might be willing to incur to correct the condition of his property for transfer.

3.6 *Local ordinance compliance report*: **Enter** the dollar amount of the fee a local government agency charges to inspect the property and submit a report on its findings and the corrections required to be completed before transfer of ownership and occupancy may occur.

3.7 *Compliance with local ordinances*: **Enter** the dollar amount estimated to cover the cost it is anticipated the seller will incur for retrofitting, curative permits, and any repairs necessary to meet local ordinance standards as a requisite to a change in ownership or occupancy. The amount estimated will need to be reviewed and updated on receipt of the local agency's compliance report.

3.8 *Natural Hazard Disclosure report*: **Enter** the dollar amount of the fee charged by a third party for a review of the county records and the preparation and submission of a report on the natural hazards the property is subjected to due to its location.

3.9 *Smoke detector/water heater safety compliance*: **Enter** the dollar amount of the cost it is anticipated the seller will incur to install smoke detectors and the water heater anchors or bracing which are necessary to comply with safety standards.

3.10 *Owners' association document charge*: **Enter** the dollar amount of the fees charged by any owners' association connected to the property for their delivery of a complete marketing packet of documents comprised of restrictions, operations, budgets, insurance and other documents mandated to be handed to the prospective buyer, and their delivery to escrow of their statement of condition of assessments.

3.11 *Mello-Roos assessment statement charge*: **Enter** the dollar amount of the fee charged for a statement of assessments to be provided by any improvement district which holds a lien on the property to secure the repayment of bonds issued by the improvement district.

3.12 *Well water reports*: **Enter** the dollar amount of the combined fees which will be charged by a licensed well-drilling contractor to test and certify the capacity of any well on the property, and by a licensed water testing lab to test and report on the quality of the water produced by the well.

3.13 *Septic/sewer reports*: **Enter** the dollar amount of the fee charged by a licensed plumbing contractor to test and certify the function of the sewage disposal system, and if it contains a septic tank, whether it is in need of pumping.

3.14 *Lead-based paint report*: **Enter** the dollar amount of the fee charged by an environmental testing company to investigate and report on the lead content of paint on the premises.

3.15 *Marketing budget*: **Enter** the dollar amount of any contribution (to be) made by the seller toward the expenses of marketing the property and locating prospective buyers.

3.16 *Home warranty insurance*: **Enter** the dollar amount of the premium the seller agrees to pay as charged by a home warranty insurance company to issue a policy to the buyer.

3.17 *Buyer's escrow closing costs*: **Enter** the dollar amount of the combined escrow closing costs incurred by the buyer which the seller agrees to pay.

3.18 *Loan appraisal fee*: **Enter** the dollar amount of any loan appraisal fee the seller will agree to pay which will be charged to determine the property's qualification for the purchase-assist loan which will be applied for by the buyer.

3.19 *Buyer's loan charges*: **Enter** the dollar amount of any loan charges the seller will agree to pay which the buyer will incur for the purchase-assist loan needed to fund the price to be paid for the property. These loan charges are also referred to as non-recurring loan charges.

3.20 *Escrow fee*: **Enter** the dollar amount of the charge the seller will incur for escrow services to process the closing of the sale.

3.21 *Document preparation fee*: **Enter** the dollar amount of the charge the seller will incur, usually with escrow, for a third party to prepare the documents necessary for the seller to convey the property, such as grant deeds and bills of sale.

3.22 *Notary fees*: **Enter** the dollar amount of the charge the seller will incur for services provided by a notary to acknowledge the seller's signature on documents which are to be recorded to accomplish the transfer of the property (grant deed, spousal quit claim deed, release of recorded instruments, power-of-attorney, etc.).

3.23 *Recording fees/documentary transfer tax*: **Enter** the dollar amount of the combined recording charges and transfer taxes collected by the county recorder and paid by the seller to convey title.

3.24 *Title insurance premium*: **Enter** the dollar amount of the premium the title insurance company will charge for issuance of a policy of title insurance conveying the seller's conveyance of the property.

3.25 *Beneficiary statement/demand*: **Enter** the dollar amount of the combined fees the trust deed lender of record will charge for delivering a beneficiary statement or payoff demand to escrow which is needed to either confirm the loan balance on an assumption or subject-to transaction, or the amount of a payoff of the loan on closing a sale.

3.26 *Prepayment penalty (first)*: **Enter** the dollar amount of any penalty the first trust deed lender will charge on a payoff of the loan on close of a sale.

3.27 *Prepayment penalty (second)*: **Enter** the dollar amount of any penalty the second trust deed lender will charge on a payoff of the loan on close of a sale.

3.28 *Reconveyance fees*: **Enter** the dollar amount of reconveyance fees and recording fees the trustees on the trust deeds of record will charge to release the trust deed liens from the record title to the property sold.

3.29 *Brokerage fees*: **Enter** the dollar amount of the fees earned by the brokers which will be paid by the seller on the close of escrow for the sale of the property.

3.30 *Transaction coordinator fee*: **Enter** the dollar amount of the fee charged the brokers which the seller will pay for a third party to assist the listing agent in the preparation of the listing package and the sales package to provide all the documentation necessary to close the transaction.

3.31 *Attorney/accountant fees*: **Enter** the dollar amount estimated as the attorney fees and accounting fees the seller will incur as a result of their advice and assistance in the sale.

3.32 *Miscellaneous expense*: **Enter** the name of the further expense. **Enter** the dollar amount of the expense.

3.33 *Miscellaneous expense*: **Enter** the name of the further expense. **Enter** the dollar amount of the expense.

3.34 *Total expenses and charges*: **Add** the figures entered in sections 3.1 through 3.33 **Enter** the total as the dollar amount of the expenses and charges on the sale.

4. **Estimated net equity**: **Subtract** the figures entered in sections 2.4 and 3.34 from the figure entered at section 1.1 **Enter** the difference as the dollar amount of the estimated net equity, an amount against which prorates and adjustments are next made to calculate the estimated net sales proceeds generated by the sale.

5. **Prorates due buyer:**

5.1 *Unpaid taxes/assessments*: **Enter** the dollar amount of those real estate taxes and improvement district bond assessments which have ac-

crued and have not been paid by the seller if they are to be prorated without a credit to the price for the remaining principal due on bonds under section 2.3.

Taxes have not been paid for one of two reasons: they are not yet due to be paid to the tax collector or they are past due and delinquent. If they are not yet due, the taxes which accrued during the seller's ownership will be paid by the buyer at a later date. Thus, taxes are prorated as a credit to the buyer through the **last day prior** to the date of closing. The proration is calculated as a daily amount of the annual tax based on a 30-day month. The current tax bill or, if it is not yet available, the past year's amounts are used (and adjusted for up to 2% inflation, etc.) to arrive at the daily amount of the proration.

Editor's note — For example, if escrow is scheduled to close September 16, the tax billing has not yet been received and (if it has been) it has not been paid. Thus, 75 days of accrued taxes/assessments at the daily rate are credited to the buyer (and charged to the seller).

5.2 *Interest accrued and unpaid*: **Enter** the dollar amount of interest accrued and unpaid on loans assumed under sections 1.1 through 2.3 for the number of days during the month the seller will remain the owner prior to closing. The proration will be calculated as a daily amount of interest paid in monthly installments based on a 30-day month. The daily amount of interest accruing is credited to the assuming buyer for each day of the month prior to the day scheduled for closing since interest on loans is paid after the running of the monthly accrual period. Thus, the current installment will become the obligation of the buyer, unless the installment is disbursed by escrow and charged pro rata to each the seller and the buyer.

5.3 *Unearned rental income*: **Enter** the portion of the dollar amount of rent from the rent rolls, both prepaid and unpaid, which will remain unearned on the day scheduled for closing. The buyer is entitled to a credit of the unearned portion as a proration. The day of closing is the first day of ownership by the buyer and entitles the buyer to unearned rents for the entire day. The proration is calculated as a daily amount of the rent roll earned (accrued) based on a 30-day month.

Editor's note — For example, if the rents are $30,000 monthly, the daily proration for earned rents would be $1,000 and be multiplied by the number of days remaining in the month, beginning with and including the day of closing. If closing is on the 16th, the dollar amount of prorated rents credited to the buyer from funds accruing to the seller's account on closing would be $15,000, the 16th being day one of the remainder of the 30-day month.

For unpaid delinquent rents shown on the rent roll, see section 6.5 for an offset charge to the buyer by an adjustment.

5.4 *Tenant security deposits*: **Enter** the dollar amount of all the security deposits held by the seller (as landlord) which belong to the tenants as disclosed on the seller's rent roll information sheet. This credit is an **adjustment in funds**, not a proration, which is due the seller on closing since the buyer on transfer of ownership will be the landlord (by assignment of the leases and rent agreements) and responsible for the eventual accounting to the tenants for any deposit held by the seller.

Editor's note — Include any interest accrued and unpaid on the security deposits from the date of the seller's receipt of the deposits if mandated by rent control or landlord-tenant law.

5.5 *Total prorates due buyer*: **Add** the figures estimated in sections 5.1 through 5.4. **Enter** the total as the dollar amount of all the "credits" the buyer can anticipate due to prorations and adjustments.

6. **Prorates due seller:**

6.1 *Prepaid taxes/assessments*: **Enter** the dollar amount of real estate taxes and improvement assessments prepaid by the seller which have not yet accrued. The calculations are made in the same manner as explained in section 5.1.

Editor's note — For example, the seller has paid all installments of taxes/assessments for the entire fiscal year (July through June). A closing of the buyer's transaction on January 2 requires a proration charge to be paid by the buyer for one-half year's taxes and assessments since they have been prepaid, but will not accrue until after the buyer closes escrow.

6.2 *Impound account balances*: **Enter** the dollar amount of any impounds held by the lender on loans assumed under sections 2.1, 2.2 or 2.3. The information is readily available as an "escrow account" item on the lender's monthly statement of the loan's condition received by the seller from the lender servicing the loan.

6.3 *Prepaid association assessment*: **Enter** the dollar amount of the prepaid and unaccrued portion of the seller's current installment for any owners' association assessment. The proration charge is based on a 30-day month for those days remaining in the month beginning with the day of closing as day one of the days remaining in the month.

6.4 *Prepaid ground lease*: **Enter** the dollar amount of the prepaid and unaccrued portion of rent the seller has paid on the ground lease if the property interest being purchased is a leasehold interest transferred by assignment, not a fee interest transferred by grant deed.

6.5 *Unpaid rent assigned to buyer*: **Enter** the portion of the dollar amount of delinquent unpaid rents to be charged to the buyer if the seller will not collect the rent before the close of escrow. These unpaid rents belong to the buyer on closing due to the seller's assignment of the leases to the buyer, unless other arrangements are made for an accounting of the uncollected rents. Typically, a closing after the tenth of the month will not experience the need for a delinquent rent adjustment. (Rents have been prorated in section 5.3.)

6.6 *Miscellaneous prorates and adjustments*: **Enter** the name of other items to be prorated or adjusted in the transaction. **Enter** the dollar amount charged to the buyer.

6.7 *Total prorates due seller*: **Add** the figures estimated in sections 6.1 through 6.6. **Enter** the total as the dollar amount of all the "charges" the buyer is likely to experience due to prorations and adjustments.

7. *Estimated proceeds of sale*: **Add** the figures in sections 4 and 6.7, and then **subtract** the figure in section 5.5 from the sum. **Enter** the difference as the total dollar amount of the estimated net proceeds generated by the sale.

7.1. *Form of net sales proceeds*: **Enter** the dollar amount of the net sales proceeds estimated in section 7 allocated to cash, carryback note, equity received in exchange or other form of consideration the seller will be receiving on the sale.

Signatures:

Broker's/Agent's signature: **Enter** the date the seller's net sheet is signed, the broker's name and the agent's name. **Enter** the broker's (or agent's) signature.

Seller's signature: **Enter** the date the seller signs and the seller's name. **Obtain** the seller's signature.

Chapter 36

Cost of acquisition disclosures

This chapter presents the use of a buyer's cost sheet by a buyer's agent to identify, analyze and disclose the funding requirements a buyer undertakes when agreeing to acquire property.

The capital to buy

During every real estate business cycle, a time comes when buyers collectively refuse or become unable to pay ever higher prices. Gone then are the back-up buyers and forgotten are the previously ever-present multi-offer auctions surrounding nearly every fresh listing of property.

Thus begins a three-year descendency of real estate prices. The drop in prices is usually brought about by the end of a cyclical real estate bubble, evidenced by excessive asset inflation and low mortgage rates.

It is during this evolving buyer's market of descending prices and ever more anxious sellers that real estate agents have difficulty attracting buyers, either as clients they will represent or as prospective buyers of properties they have listed. For agents, a **clientele of buyers** becomes financially more rewarding during the transition into a buyer's market than a pile of property listings.

However, buyers are confused and reticent about buying while this corrective phase of the real estate business cycle is taking place. With its soft prices and plentiful supply of inventory for buyers to consider, this period of price correction will eventually reflect sales-to-listing ratios indicating less than 25% of the existing listings are selling each month.

Agents generally face a decline in overall sales activity until prices stabilize and begin to rise. In the interim, the less ingenious and most disconnected agents will fail to maintain a livelihood in real estate sales. They will pursue employment elsewhere.

Disclosures as confidence builders

To reverse the trend in buyer apathy toward acquiring real estate during these corrective transitions, the "sales" approach used by agents needs to be altered. Buyers can no longer be rushed to purchase since they have no sense of urgency when prices are dropping. Valuations placed on properties by seller's now seem pricey to buyers, yet listing agents tend to defend against any thought of a price reduction as though their job was that of a "marketmaker," not "matchmaker."

Buyers under these market conditions will not first jump into a purchase agreement contract and sort out the problems later, conduct typical during the run up to the peak of a real estate sales bubble. They now want the facts first, and will not act until they have them.

To combat an oversold real estate market, sellers and their listing agents must be more forthcoming with property information when placing a property on the market, rather than stalling until they have a buyer in escrow at an agreed price.

Buyer's agents adjust more quickly than listing agents to the cyclical shift from a seller's market long on buyers to a buyer's market long on sellers and inventory. They simply marshall information on a property and analyze it **before making an offer,** rather than doing so later as is too often the case when competition between buyers is keen.

To accommodate individuals who are hesitant about buying now, or to encourage others, such as tenants, who have not previously considered buying real estate, the initial step taken by an agent striving to become a buyer's representative is to **financially qualify** the individual as both a mortgage borrower and prospective buyer.

An individual buyer must have **access to cash** to pay the price and costs of acquiring property. Beyond the cash available in savings or readily liquidated investments (stocks/bonds), arranging purchase-assist mortgage financing is nearly always a requisite to establishing what price and costs of acquisition an individual will be able to pay. With financing comes lender, mortgage banker and loan broker charges to originate the loan, amounts which greatly exceed the costs of all other services required to buy property, except for brokerage fees.

Amount and source of funds

To document the cash a prospective buyer can bring together from all his available sources to fund the purchase of a property, the buyer's agent uses a worksheet, called a *buyer's cost sheet*. The worksheet helps the agent identify and itemize the costs of acquisition and financing, as well as the buyer's sources of funding. The buyer's agent then reviews the completed form with the prospective buyer. [See Form 311 accompanying this chapter]

The maximum price a prospective buyer can offer to pay for a property is determined by the amount of available funds from all sources which remains after deducting the acquisition costs. It is this residual amount of funds available for payment of a property's price which sets the value of a property to the buyer, not the seller's listing price. Sellers tend to ignore this reality as interest rates rise, but take full advantage of the rule when rates fall.

Obviously, the primary source of cash for nearly all buyers of any type of real estate is a purchase-assist loan from a mortgage lender. Before a cost sheet review with the buyer can go beyond identifying the various sources of cash available to the buyer, the agent must arrange a conference with a mortgage banker's representative.

The objective of the mortgage banker conference is two fold:

- to determine the maximum gross dollar amount of purchase-assist, fixed-rate loan funds the buyer is qualified to borrow (if the property qualifies); and

- the lender's (good-faith) cost estimate of the dollar amount of all costs the buyer will incur to originate the maximum fixed-rate loan he is qualified to borrow.

These two dollar amounts (the loan and its costs) are treated as mutually exclusive amounts, separately analyzed on the buyer's cost sheet. The lender's estimated costs of borrowing will be entered on the agent's cost worksheet to document the amount of funds the buyer will need to pay for all transactional and financing costs. Separately, the total amount of the loan the buyer qualifies to borrow will be entered on the buyer's cost worksheet as cash available from a purchase-assist loan source.

During the conference with the mortgage banker, the buyer's agent needs to inquire about any restrictions the lender may place on the loan commitment. For example, a loan-to-value ratio may require a minimum down payment by the buyer of up to 20% of the price paid for a property. Also, limitations might be placed on the seller's payment of the buyer's nonrecurring transactional and financing costs, such as permitting the seller's payment of all, a ceiling amount or none at all.

With knowledge of any lender restrictions, the buyer's agent can structure purchase agreement offers to shift large amounts of transactional and financing charges to the seller. Thus, the charges will be paid by the seller out of funds the seller receives from the buyer, not paid by the buyer, which would reduce the funds he has available to buy property. Here, the buyer can acquire a more valuable property since he will have more funds for payment of the purchase price.

Having determined the prospective buyer's costs of financing and the transactional charges he will incur to acquire a property, a high level of certainty about the price he can pay and the amount of the buyer's nonrecurring acquisition and financing costs he will incur is made known to the buyer. What remains for the buyer's agent to do is locate suitable properties and write up a purchase agreement offer agreeable to the buyer.

Buyers combat declining prices and alleviate their tendency to wait before buying by making an offer at a price they feel comfortable paying for a property. Thus, pricing is based on their knowledge the real estate market is in a descendency, the property's condition, and their capacity to arrange for payment of the negotiated price and bear the costs of financing and closing escrow.

The task of complying with the agent's duty to **care for and protect** the buyer begins with the gathering of data to complete the preparation of the cost sheet. The process ends by making offers to come up with the match the buyer wants.

Cost of carrying property

While a review of the costs of acquisition is under way, many other related disclosure situations will come to the attention of the buyer's agent.

For example, another cost analysis involves the ongoing **operating expenses** any buyer will likely incur as the owner of property. Operating expenses are obtained from the listing agent or compiled by the buyer's agent from data readily available to the seller, and reviewed with the prospective buyer.

Also, a drop in prices is usually a loss in the present worth of a property brought about by an increase in long-term interest rates. Prices and mortgage rates nearly always move in opposite directions. Important to buyers during times of rising long-term interest rates is the understanding that the price paid and costs incurred to acquire property are unalterable in the future once escrow closes on the purchase.

This is not true for interest rates. A high interest rate on a loan required to finance payment of the purchase price of a property can be reduced by refinancing during later periods of cyclically lower interest rates. The original purchase price paid, if too high, is unalterable.

Reducing and shifting the costs

Taxwise, a further source of an additional minimal amount of cash to cover the costs of acquiring property is available to buyers who **itemize deductions** on their federal tax returns. Loan origination fees or points incurred to finance the purchase can be deducted (even if paid by the seller) to reduce the buyer's taxable income (and thus the amount of taxes paid) for the year of purchase. As a result, more funds are freed by a tax refund (or reduced payment).

For example, payment to the lender of 2% of the loan amount for **origination fees** will produce a rebate (or subsidy) to the buyer by way of a reduction in federal income taxes equal to 1/3 to 2/3 of a percent of the purchase price paid for the property. The amount of the refund depends on the buyer's low-income (10%-15%) or high-income (28%-35%) tax bracket status and the amount of the buyer's adjusted gross income.

Also, buyers who finance their purchase under government-insured finance programs can attend **homeownership classes** and earn credits which will cut their costs of acquiring financing. In a buyer's market, potential first-time buyers, such as tenants, can be encouraged to consider homeownership by attending one of these lender-provided classes. The purpose is to learn about the benefits and

BUYER'S COST SHEET
On Acquisition of Property

This is an estimate of acquisition costs and the funds required to close the following transaction:

☐ Purchase agreement ☐ Exchange agreement ☐ Counteroffer ☐ Escrow instructions ☐ Option

Entered into by _____.

Dated _____, 20_____, at _____, California.

Regarding property at: _____

_____.

This cost sheet is prepared to assist the buyer to anticipate the amount of funds likely needed to close, the source of these funds and the estimated total cost of acquisition for this property.

The figures estimated in this cost sheet may vary at the time of closing due to periodic changes in lender demands, escrow fees, other charges and prorates, and thus constitute an opinion, not a guarantee.

If acquiring IRC §1031 replacement property, also use a §1031 Recapitulation Form to compute the income tax consequence of the transaction. [ft Form 354]

EXISTING FINANCING ASSUMED:

1. First Trust Deed of Record . . . . $_____

2. Second Trust Deed of Record . . . . $_____

3. Other Encumbrances/Liens/Bonds . . . . $_____

4. TOTAL Encumbrances Assumed . . . . ADD: $_____

   a. If loan balance adjustments are to be made in cash, the total funds required to close escrow at §50 and §55 will vary.

INSTALLMENT SALE FINANCING:

5. Seller Carryback Financing: . . . . ADD: $_____

NEW FINANCING ORIGINATED:

6. New Loan Amount . . . . ADD: $_____

7. Points/Discount . . . . $_____

8. Appraisal Fee . . . . $_____

9. Credit Report Fee . . . . $_____

10. Miscellaneous Origination Fees . . . . $_____

11. Prepaid Interest . . . . $_____

12. Mortgage Insurance Premium . . . . $_____

13. Lender's Title Policy Premium . . . . $_____

14. Tax Service Fee . . . . $_____

15. Loan Brokerage Fee . . . . $_____

16. _____ . . . . $_____

17. TOTAL New Financing Costs . . . . ADD: $_____

PURCHASE COSTS AND CHARGES:

18. Assumption Fees (First) . . . . $_____

19. Assumption Fees (Second) . . . . $_____

20. Escrow Fee . . . . $_____

21. Notary Fee . . . . $_____

22. Document Preparation Fee . . . . $_____

23. Recording Fee/Transfer Taxes . . . . $_____

24. Title Insurance Premium . . . . $_____

25. Property Condition Reports . . . . $_____

26. Cost of Compliance Repairs . . . . $_____

27. _____ . . . . $_____

28. _____ . . . . $_____

29. TOTAL Closing Costs . . . . ADD: $_____

30. **DOWN PAYMENT ON PRICE** . . . . ADD: $_____

31. **TOTAL ESTIMATED ACQUISITION COST** . . . . $_____
      a. No post-closing repairs or renovation cost are included here.

FUNDS REQUIRED TO CLOSE ESCROW:

32. Down Payment On Price (From line 30) . . . . ADD: $_____

33. Closing Costs (From line 29) . . . . ADD: $_____

34. New Loan Proceeds (From line 6) . . . . ADD: $_____

35. New Financing Costs (From line 17) . . . . ADD: $_____

36. Impounds for New Financing . . . . ADD: $_____

37. Hazard Insurance Premium . . . . ADD: $_____

PRORATES DUE BUYER AT CLOSE:

38. Unpaid Taxes/Assessments . . . . $_____

39. Interest Accrued and Unpaid . . . . $_____

40. Unearned Rental Income . . . . $_____

41. Tenant Security Deposits . . . . $_____

42. TOTAL Prorates Due Buyer: . . . . DEDUCT: $_____

PRORATES DUE SELLER AT CLOSE:

43. Prepaid Taxes/Assessments . . . . $_____

44. Impound Account Balance . . . . $_____

45. Prepaid Homeowners' Assessment . . . . $_____

46. Prepaid Ground Lease Rent . . . . $_____

47. Unpaid Rents assigned to Buyer . . . . $_____

48. _____ . . . . $_____

49. TOTAL Prorates Due Seller: . . . . ADD: $_____

50. **TOTAL FUNDS REQUIRED TO CLOSE ESCROW:** (See §4.a. adjustments) . . . . $_____

SOURCE OF FUNDS REQUIRED TO CLOSE ESCROW:

51. New First Loan Amount (From line 6) . . . . $_____

52. New Second Loan Amount (Net loan proceeds) . . . . $_____

53. Third-Party Deposits . . . . $_____

54. Buyer's Cash . . . . $_____

55. **TOTAL FUNDS REQUIRED TO CLOSE ESCROW:** (Same as line 50) . . . . $_____

I have prepared this estimate based on my knowledge and readily available data.	I have read and received a copy of this estimate.
Date:_____, 20_____	Date:_____, 20_____
Broker:_____	Buyer's Name: _____
Agent: _____	Signature: _____
Signature: _____	Signature: _____

FORM 311   09-03   ©2006 **first tuesday**, P.O. BOX 20069, RIVERSIDE, CA 92516 (800) 794-0494

obligations of owning real estate. The financing costs charged by the lender will be reduced when the prospective buyers decide to purchase after completing such a course.

Sellers, in an effort to maintain price, often are willing to extend credit in some form of **carryback financing,** a method for the buyer to finance the purchase price. For a buyer, seller carryback financing avoids all the costs of new financing.

If the **interest rate** charged by the seller on the carryback is low enough (below market), the price paid can be above market. The buyer's reduced long-term carrying costs arguably justify payment of the above-market price, one offsetting the other based on the dollar amount saved in interest. However, the buyer should always ask for, and hopefully receive, an option to pay off the carryback early and at a discount to keep the purchase price realistic should the buyer later decide to sell or refinance the property.

During the early stages of a buyer's market, and continuing until prices bottom out and become stable, buyers who make offers must be prepared to have their offers rejected. Historically, sellers and listing agents are slow to acknowledge that prices have in fact stopped rising on comparable properties. When sellers finally recognize that market values are declining, they tend to panic by accepting huge price reductions before realizing that buyers are entering the market in increasing numbers and the bottom of the price cycle has arrived.

Once buyers become addicted to the possibilities of price and cost reductions, buyer's agents will need to be ever more creative to keep costs down. One maneuver for shaving a sizeable dollar amount off the price of property is for buyer's agents to track suitable properties by the date the listing expires. On expiration of the listing, an inquiry of the seller by the buyer's agent for the sole purpose of submitting an offer, not for

soliciting a dual agency listing, is likely to open up a price advantage for the buyer.

Here, the advantage for the buyer amounts to a price paid of around 3% less for the property (than the previously listed price). The buyer's agent will still receive the same amount for a fee as he would have received had a higher price been paid under a listing and the brokerage fee been shared with the listing agent (who did not locate a buyer).

Motivating individuals to own

The objective of agents in a buyer's market of declining prices, increasing inventory and fewer sales is to **create buyers**, not sales.

No longer can agents concentrate primarily on listing property and be successful. Primary attention must now be given to potential and prospective buyers, to educate them and demonstrate why they should be represented by a buyer's agent.

Thus, **locating buyers** is no longer best accomplished by listing and marketing property for sale. Individuals who are qualified to be a buyer of real estate must be attracted to the market by inducements other than publishing property listings and holding auctions or open houses.

Most potential buyers are tenants occupying apartments, condominium units or single-family residences. They have a job and thus can qualify for a purchase-assist loan to enter into ownership. These tenants are sought out by agents through business, social, civic, athletic and religious networks.

New arrivals to the community should be contacted by advertisements located in airports, train stations and bus terminals to convert the new arrivals to homeownership. A kiosk in a shopping mall (or airport) manned by an agent might solicit tenants to fill out a homeownership application for the agent to review and advise on the homeownership available to the tenant.

Finally, the issue of the agent's need to enter into an **employment agreement** before the agent undertakes the representation of an individual needs to be addressed.

Whether the need for a written employment is broached with the potential buyer **before making** a thorough loan qualification analysis and a review of the costs of acquisition or **afterward**, when the prospective buyer's financial capability and price range have been established, a buyer's listing agreement certainly should be obtained before commencing a search for qualified properties the buyer might deem suitable to own.

Analyzing the cost sheet estimates

The buyer's cost sheet, **first tuesday** Form 311, is used by buyer's brokers and their agents to inform a prospective buyer about the cost of acquiring a particular parcel of real estate they have located and feel is suitable for acquisition by the buyer. The form contains a checklist of bookkeeping items typical of most purchases, including acquisition costs, financing charges, prorations, funds required for acquisition and the buyer's probable sources for these funds.

The **estimates** entered on the form by the buyer's agent must be based on information about transactional costs and financing charges both known to him or readily available to him on an inquiry of others or on minimal investigation. Thus, the figures entered must reflect the agent's **honestly held belief** that the estimated amount will likely be experienced by the buyer should the buyer acquire the property under consideration.

The cost sheet is used to disclose the crucial **financial information** the buyer needs to know about the acquisition of a property. With it, the buyer's agent provides the buyer with a high level of **transparency** about the costs of acquisition. Thus, the prospective buyer is able to make an informed decision about the financial commitment needed to purchase the property.

The events triggering the buyer's agent's preparation of a cost sheet and a review of the costs with the prospective buyer include:

- entering into a buyer's listing agreement;

- pre-qualifying for a maximum loan amount; and

- entering into a purchase agreement offer or accepting a counteroffer.

The cost sheet is also used to **solicit tenants**, residential or nonresidential, to consider the purchase of property. With it, the agent can demonstrate whether the tenant has the financial capability to occupy a comparable property as an owner instead of as a tenant, be it a home or business premises.

Each section in Form 311 has a separate purpose. The sections cover:

- the **acquisition costs** of the property (cost basis);

- the **closing charges** (including prorations and adjustments); and

- the buyer's **source of funds** (savings, gifts, loans, etc.).

Preparing the buyer's cost sheet

The following instructions are for the preparation and use of the Buyer's Cost Sheet, **first tuesday** Form 311, with which the buyer's broker and his agent can prepare an estimate for an analysis of the buyer's ability to pay the price and all the costs and charges related to the purchase.

Each instruction corresponds to the provision in the form bearing the same number.

*Editor's note — **Enter** figures throughout the cost sheet in the blanks provided, unless the items left blank are not intended to be included in the final estimate.*

Document identification:

Check the appropriate box indicating the underlying agreement which is the subject of this disclosure of costs. **Enter** information to identify the agreement regarding the name(s) of the parties to the agreement, the identification date of the agreement, the place of preparation and an address or parcel number identifying the property involved.

Existing financing assumed:

1. *First trust deed*: **Enter** the dollar amount of the first trust deed loan balance if the buyer is to take over the loan.

2. *Second trust deed*: **Enter** the dollar amount of the second trust deed loan balance if the buyer is to take over the loan.

3. *Other encumbrances/liens/bonds*: **Enter** the dollar amount of the principal balance remaining on any other money obligations which the buyer is to take over, such as liens for improvement district bond assessments (Mello Roos, 1915 Act, etc.), abstracts of judgment, UCC-1 security agreements (on personal property/improvements included in the purchase) or other debts to be assumed by the buyer.

4. *TOTAL encumbrances assumed*: **Add** the figures estimated in sections 1, 2 and 3. **Enter** the total as the dollar amount of the principal balance on debts to be assumed or otherwise taken over by the buyer as part of the price.

    a. *Funds to close escrow will vary*: Each estimated figure may vary by the time of closing, depending on the accuracy of the estimates, principal reduction on existing loans and changing service charges, fees and premiums. Also, if the difference in amounts is to be adjusted into the cash down payment, the amount of funds required to close escrow at sections 50 and 55 will vary. Adjustments into price, such as in an equity purchase transaction, merely adjust the total consideration paid to the seller, not the amount of the down payment or any carryback note and trust deed. Likewise, adjustments for the differences into any seller carryback leaves the price and down payment unaffected, but will alter the amount of the carryback note at section 5 by the time escrow closes.

Installment sale financing:

5. *Seller carryback financing*: **Enter** the dollar amount of the note the buyer is to execute in favor of the seller. This amount will vary if adjustments at closing are to be made into the carryback note, and not into the down payment or the price.

New financing originated:

6. *New loan amount*: **Enter** the dollar amount of the new trust deed loan the buyer is to originate with a lender to provide purchase-assist funds to close escrow. The total amount of the loan is entered without reduction for any lender discounts, costs, fees or charges.

7. *Points/discount*: **Enter** the dollar amount of the points to be paid or the discount charged to originate the new loan, a figure usually calculated as a percentage of the new loan amount.

8. *Appraisal fee*: **Enter** the dollar amount the new lender will charge for an appraisal of the property to be purchased. Upon request, the buyer is entitled to a copy of the appraisal from the lender. [See **first tuesday** Form 329]

9. *Credit report fee*: **Enter** the dollar amount of the credit report fee charged by the lender for ordering the report and analyzing the buyer's creditworthiness.

10. *Miscellaneous origination fees*: **Enter** the total dollar amount of all other fees charged by the lender to process the loan, including fees labelled as escrow set-up fees, administrative fees, processing fees, origination fees, wire fees, document preparation fees, etc., which are **not itemized** in sections 7 through 16.

11. *Prepaid interest*: **Enter** the dollar amount of prepaid interest the new lender will demand for closing before the last day of the calendar month. The interest charge will be a daily amount due for each day following closing through the last day of the month in which the sale closes. This prepayment of interest allows for the first installment on the loan to be due on the first day of the first month falling more than 30 days after closing.

12. *Mortgage insurance premium*: **Enter** the dollar amount of any private mortgage insurance (PMI), mortgage insurance premium (MIP) or other insurance premium to be paid by the buyer to guarantee payment for losses the lender may suffer on a default. The amount is a quote by a corporate or government insurer based on the loan-to-value ratio and the amount of the loan. A further creditworthiness risk review of the buyer is conducted by the insurer, which could alter the premium or the availability of the insurance.

13. *Lender's title policy premium*: **Enter** the dollar amount of the premium charged by the title company to issue a separate lender's policy of title insurance (in addition to the owner's policy at section 24) to cover the existence of the security interest in the property as evidenced by the lender's trust deed lien.

14. *Tax service fee*: **Enter** the dollar amount charged by a separate service company which informs the lender when the buyer has not paid the property taxes.

15. *Loan brokerage fee*: **Enter** the dollar amount of any fees due a loan broker for arranging the new loan for the buyer. Do not include any financial benefit (kickback/referral fee) paid the brokers or sales agents by the lender since they are paid from increased fees or above-market interest rates the lender charges the buyer.

16. *Miscellaneous loan charges*: **Enter** the name of any other loan charge to be incurred by the buyer due to the new loan origination. **Enter** the dollar amount of the charge.

17. *TOTAL new financing costs*: **Add** the figures estimated in sections 7 through 16. **Enter** the total as the dollar amount of all the expenditures anticipated to be incurred by the buyer to originate a new loan.

Purchase costs and charges:

18. *Assumption fees (first)*: **Enter** the dollar amount of the anticipated assumption fees the existing first trust deed lender will likely demand if the lender's consent is required for the buyer to take over the loan.

19. *Assumption fees (second)*: **Enter** the dollar amount of the anticipated assumption fees the existing second trust deed lender will likely demand if the lender's consent is required for the buyer to take over the loan.

20. *Escrow fee*: **Enter** the dollar amount of the service charge the buyer will incur for an escrow to handle the closing of the purchase agreement.

21. *Notary fee*: **Enter** the dollar amount of the charges the buyer will incur for notary services to acknowledge the buyer's signature on documents which are to be recorded to purchase the property (trust deeds, power of attorney, spousal quit claim deeds, declaration of homestead, release of recorded instruments, request for NOD/NODq, UCC-1 filing, etc.).

22. *Document preparation fee*: **Enter** the dollar amount of any additional miscellaneous fees charged by escrow for providing escrow-related services.

23. *Recording fee/transfer taxes*: **Enter** the dollar amount of charges imposed or collected by the county recorder and paid by the buyer for recordings which are necessitated by the transfer.

24. *Title insurance premium*: **Enter** the dollar amount of the title insurance premium the title company will charge for issuing a policy to the buyer if the buyer is to pay the premium. Typically, the seller pays the premium to acquire the insurance which covers the seller's conveyance to the buyer.

25. *Property condition reports*: **Enter** the total dollar amount of fees and charges it is anticipated the buyer will incur to investigate and confirm the condition of the property (its land, improvements and components) as known to the buyer by both the buyer's observations and disclosures made by the seller or the listing agent prior to entering into the purchase agreement.

*Editor's note — The seller's broker or listing agent has a statutory duty, owed to prospective buyers on the sale of one-to-four residential units, to personally conduct a **visual inspection** of the property and enter on the mandated seller's Transfer Disclosure Statement (TDS) any **observations** he may have contrary to the seller's disclosures. The TDS is to be made available to prospective buyers at the earliest opportunity during the negotiating stage. The first opportunity to disclose rarely occurs later than at the time a purchase agreement offer is accepted.*

However, the listing agent too often deliberately delays an investigation or certification of a property's condition until after the buyer has committed himself to purchase the property (in its undisclosed condition). Thus, the buyer, in a effort to confirm the property is all he has been lead to believe it is, must himself obtain the reports and certifications to discover the conditions which were known (or should have been known) and not disclosed by the seller or the listing agent prior to entering into the purchase agreement, a form of fraud called negative deceit.

Such reports, clearances and certificates include pest control reports, local occupancy certificates, sewer/septic certificates, home inspection reports, well water condition certificates, hazard reports, safety compliances, etc. It is the buyer's agent, not the seller's listing agent, who is duty bound to see to it his buyer has been informed about inspections and investigations readily available to the buyer, and explain which he believes the buyer should use to check out the property.

26. *Cost of compliance repairs*: **Enter** the dollar amount of the costs it is anticipated the buyer will incur to correct, retrofit or eliminate defects in the property prior to or immediately after closing, which will not be eliminated by the seller.

27. *Miscellaneous closing costs*: **Enter** the name of any additional costs it is anticipated or believed the buyer will incur to acquire the property prior to or immediately after closing. **Enter** the dollar amount estimated as likely to be incurred.

28. *Miscellaneous closing costs*: See instructions for section 27.

29. *TOTAL closing costs*: **Add** the figures estimated for sections 18 through 28. **Enter** the total as the dollar amount of all costs it is anticipated the buyer will incur to close escrow.

30. *DOWN PAYMENT ON PRICE*: **Enter** the dollar amount of the down payment the buyer has agreed to pay the seller through or outside of escrow, whether the funds are from the buyer's cash reserves, gifts and bonuses from third parties, or a brokerage fee credited to the buyer's account due to the buyer's participation as a licensee in the transaction.

Editor's note — This sum of money for the down payment does not include any loan funds to be paid over to the seller from the new loan under section 6, or charges, prorations and adjustments reflected in section 50.

31. *TOTAL ESTIMATED ACQUISITION COST*: **Add** the figures from sections 4, 5, 6, 17, 29 and 30. **Enter** the total as the approximate dollar amount of monetary commitments in cash or loan amounts which the buyer will be committing himself to pay.

a. *Post-closing repairs*: This cost figure does not include any capital contribution to be made by the buyer to pay for the cost of any renovation, rehabilitation or reconstruction of any part of the property to be incurred immediately after closing, which will become part of the buyer's cost of acquisition for tax reporting purposes.

Funds required to close escrow:

32. *Down payment on price*: **Enter** the dollar amount from section 30.

33. *Closing costs*: **Enter** the dollar amount from section 29.

34. *New loan proceeds*: **Enter** the dollar amount from section 6.

35. *New financing costs*: **Enter** the dollar amount from section 17.

36. *Impounds for new financing*: **Enter** the dollar amount of the deposit of buyer's funds into the lender's loan escrow account the lender will demand if the new loan under section 6 is to be impounded for the future payment of property taxes, assessments and hazard insurance premiums.

Editor's note — When disbursed by the lender, these expenditures from the impound account become the operating expenses of the buyer. They are not, now or then, a cost of acquiring the property (but are nonetheless an out-of-pocket advance made prior to closing).

37. *Hazard insurance premium*: **Enter** the dollar amount of the premium the buyer will be advancing for hazard insurance coverage on the property.

Editor's note — This is not a cost of acquisition. It is an operating expense.

Prorates due buyer at close:

38. *Unpaid taxes/assessments*: **Enter** the dollar amount of those real estate taxes and improvement district bond assessments which have accrued and have not been paid by the seller if they are to be prorated and are not credited to the price under section 3.

They have not been paid for one of two reasons: they are not yet due to be paid to the tax collector or they are past due and delinquent. If they are not yet due, the buyer will at a later date be paying those property taxes which accrued during the seller's ownership. Thus, they are prorated as a credit to the buyer through the last day prior to the date of closing. The proration is calculated as a daily amount of the annual tax and assessment amounts based on a 30-day month. The current tax bill or, if it is not yet available, the past year's amounts are used (and adjusted for inflation, etc.) to arrive at the daily amount of the proration.

Editor's note — If escrow is scheduled to close September 16, the tax billing has not yet been received and the current taxes have not been paid. Thus, 75 days of accrued taxes/assessments at the daily rate are credited to the buyer (and charged to the seller).

39. *Interest accrued and unpaid*: **Enter** the dollar amount of interest accrued and unpaid on loans assumed under sections 1 through 3 for the number of days during the month the seller will remain the owner prior to closing. The proration will be calculated as a daily amount of interest paid in monthly installments based on a 30-day month. The daily amount of interest accrued is credited to the buyer for each day of the month prior to the day scheduled for closing since interest on loans is paid following the month of accrual. Thus, the next installment will become the obligation of the buyer, unless the installment is disbursed by escrow and charged pro rata to the seller and the buyer.

40. *Unearned rental income*: **Enter** the portion of the dollar amount of rent from the rent rolls, both prepaid and unpaid, which remains unearned on the day scheduled for closing. The buyer is entitled to a credit of the unearned portion of rent as a proration. The day of closing is the first day of ownership by the buyer and entitles the buyer to unearned rents for the entire day on which escrow closes. The proration is calculated as a daily amount of the rent roll unearned based on a 30-day month.

Editor's note — If the rents are $30,000 monthly, the daily proration for earned rents would be $1,000, which is multiplied by the number of days remaining in the month, beginning with and including the day of closing. If closing is on the 16th, the dollar amount of prorated rents credited to the buyer from funds accruing to the seller's account on closing would be $15,000, the 16th being day one of the remainder of the 30-day month.

For unpaid delinquent rents shown on the rent roll, see section 47 for an offset charge to the buyer by an adjustment.

41. *Tenant security deposits*: **Enter** the dollar amount of all the security deposits held by the seller (as landlord) which belong to the tenants as disclosed on the seller's rent roll information sheet. This credit is an *adjustment*, not a proration, in funds due the seller since the buyer on transfer of ownership will be the landlord (by assignment of the leases and rent agreements) and responsible for accounting to the tenants for any deposit held by the seller.

Editor's note — Include any interest accrued and unpaid on the security deposits from the date of the seller's receipt of the deposits if mandated by rent control or landlord-tenant law.

42. *TOTAL prorates due buyer at close*: **Add** the figures estimated in sections 38 through 41. **Enter** the total as the dollar amount of all the "credits" the buyer can anticipate due to prorations and adjustments.

Editor's note — The debits charged to the buyer by proration are calculated in the following sections.

Prorates due seller at close:

43. *Prepaid taxes/assessments*: **Enter** the dollar amount of real estate taxes and improvement assessments prepaid by the

seller which have not yet accrued. The calculations are made in the same manner as explained in section 38.

Editor's note — For example, the seller has paid all installments of taxes/assessments for the entire fiscal year (July through June). A closing of the buyer's transaction on December 31 requires a proration charge to be paid by the buyer for one-half year's (180 days') taxes/assessments since they have been prepaid, but will not accrue until after the buyer closes escrow.

44. *Impound account balance*: **Enter** the dollar amount of the impounds held by the lender on each loan assumed under sections 1, 2 or 3. The information is readily available from the monthly accounting of the loan's condition received by the seller from the lender servicing the loan.

45. *Prepaid homeowners' assessment*: **Enter** the dollar amount of the prepaid and unaccrued portion of the seller's current installment for any homeowners' association (HOA) assessment. The proration charge is based on a 30-day month for those days remaining in the month, beginning with the day of closing as day one of the days remaining in the month.

46. *Prepaid ground lease rent*: **Enter** the dollar amount of the prepaid and unaccrued portion of rent the seller has paid on the ground lease if the property interest being purchased is a leasehold interest transferred by assignment and not a fee interest transferred by grant deed.

47. *Unpaid rents assigned to buyer*: **Enter** the dollar amount of delinquent unpaid rents to be charged to the buyer if the seller will not collect the rent before the close of escrow. These unpaid rents belong to the buyer on closing due to the seller's assignment of the leases to the

buyer, unless other arrangements are made for an accounting of the uncollected rents. Typically, a closing after the tenth of the month will not experience the need for a delinquent rent adjustment. (All rents have been prorated in section 40.)

48. *Miscellaneous prorates and adjustments*: **Enter** the name of other prorates or adjustments which may be required. **Enter** the dollar amount charged to the buyer.

49. *TOTAL prorates due seller*: **Add** the figures estimated in sections 43 through 48. **Enter** the total as the dollar amount of all the "charges" the buyer is likely to experience due to prorations and adjustments.

50. *TOTAL FUNDS REQUIRED TO CLOSE ESCROW*: **Add** the figures from sections 32 through 37 and section 49, and then **subtract** the figure from section 42 from the total. **Enter** the difference as the dollar amount of funds the buyer will need to close escrow.

Source of funds required to close escrow:

51. *New first loan amount*: **Enter** the dollar amount of the new loan estimated in section 6.

52. *New second loan amount*: **Enter** the dollar amount of any second trust deed loan to be originated. If the costs of originating the second have not been entered in section 7 through 17, then **enter** only the estimated amount of the net proceeds generated by the second loan here.

53. *Third-party adjustments*: **Enter** the dollar amount of any funds received from third parties which the buyer expects to use to fund the purchase of the property. For example, families make

gifts, employers give bonuses and equity sharing and other co-ownership arrangements contribute cash.

54. *Buyer's cash*: **Subtract** the figures in sections 51 through 53 from the figure in section 50. **Enter** the result as the dollar amount of funds the buyer needs to presently hold or have in reserves (savings/readily convertible securities and certificates) to meet the expenditures anticipated by the estimates in this opinion given by the buyer's broker or his selling agent.

55. *TOTAL FUNDS REQUIRED TO CLOSE ESCROW*: **Add** the figures estimated in sections 51 through 54. **Enter** the total as the amount of funds needed by the buyer to acquire the property.

Editor's note — The amount will be the same as the figure in section 50.

Signatures:

Broker's/Agent's signature: **Enter** the date the cost sheet is signed, the broker's name and the agent's name. **Obtain** the broker's (or agent's) signature.

Buyer's signature: **Enter** the date the buyer signs and the buyer's name. **Obtain** the buyer's signature.

SECTION D

Contract
Law

Chapter 37

Making an offer

This chapter presents the elements of a contract and fully examines the first stage of the real estate purchase agreement process, i.e., the intent of a buyer to make an offer to purchase.

The intent to contract

A **contract** is an agreement between persons binding them to do or not to do something. [Calif. Civil Code §1549]

Persons include individual people and those entities qualified to contract within the state of California.

To form a contract, the agreement must be accompanied by the following elements:

- an **offer**;

- an **acceptance**;

- **consideration** — a bargained-for exchange;

- **capable parties**; and

- a **lawful purpose**. [CC §1550]

While oral agreements are valid contracts, most agreements involving real estate or real estate services must be formalized in a **writing** to be judicially enforceable. [CC §1624]

The elements needed to form an agreement and the numerous rules for contracting must be viewed in light of typical real estate transactions.

For example, a sales transaction involving a broker acting on behalf of a buyer or seller is structured on a variety of contracts, including:

- a **listing agreement** employing the broker;

- a **purchase agreement**, option or exchange agreement documenting the sales transaction;

- **escrow instructions** to close the sales transaction;

- interim or holdover **occupancy agreement** between the buyer and seller;

- a **note and trust deed** executed by the buyer;

- **service agreements** for investigations, reports, repairs and coordinators; and

- **insurance policies** for title, home warranty, hazards and personal liability.

The buyer, seller and broker have separate rights and obligations under the different contracts, in addition to duties owed to themselves and others in the transaction. Also, their obligations to sign or perform one contract, such as escrow instructions and deeds, often depends on having agreed to perform under a prior agreement, such as a purchase agreement.

Life cycle of a contract

The life cycle of a real estate purchase agreement is divided into four stages of activity:

- the **formation** (offer and acceptance) stage;

- the **conditions** (contingencies) stage;

- the **performance** (closing) stage; and

- the **failure of performance** (breach) stage. [See Figure 1 accompanying this chapter]

During the **formation stage**, offers are made between a buyer and a seller. Negotiations commence and eventually, one of the (counter) offers may be accepted.

The acceptance of an offer forms a *binding* agreement. However, the agreement may not be enforceable by actual performance yet due to conditions contained in the agreement.

Actual performance of the agreement cannot be enforced until the second stage, the conditions stage, is completed.

During the **conditions stage**, the contingencies contained in the purchase agreement must be satisfied or waived before the sale can move toward closing. These contingencies are called *conditions precedent*.

Contingencies address the clearance of significant conditions prudent buyers and sellers have regarding the transaction, including:

- financial conditions (mortgage availability, price corroboration by appraisal, etc.);

- operating conditions (expense of ownership, tenant leases/income, etc.);

- title and zoning conditions (Covenants, conditions and restrictions, use ordinances, etc.);

- physical conditions (home inspection/certification, energy efficiency, environmental analysis, utilities, etc.); and

- location-related conditions (ordnances, green belts, neighbors, natural hazards, etc.).

Also, the buyer or seller must complete their **mutual performance** duties, called *conditions concurrent*, during the conditions stage, prior to closing. Mutual performance duties of one party are to be completed independent of and without concern for the other party first performing their mutual performance duties.

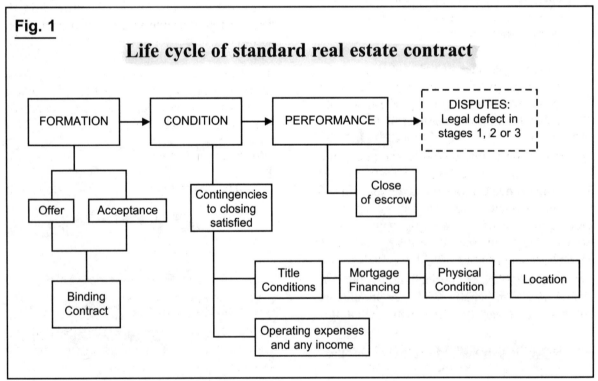

Fig. 1

Life cycle of standard real estate contract

FORMATION → CONDITION → PERFORMANCE → DISPUTES: Legal defect in stages 1, 2 or 3

Offer — Acceptance

Binding Contract

Contingencies to closing satisfied

Close of escrow

Title Conditions — Mortgage Financing — Physical Condition — Location

Operating expenses and any income

For example, a seller's obligation to deliver a deed to escrow is independent of, and not conditioned on, the buyer's obligation to deposit closing funds into escrow.

In contrast, a **condition precedent** calls for the satisfaction or waiver of an act or event by one party before the other party must perform.

A purchase agreement has arrived at the **performance stage** when all the contingencies and independent activities to close escrow have been cleared, i.e., all closing documents have been signed and delivered and funds have been handed to escrow in full performance of the contract by all parties.

Should there be a failure to perform or if a deficiency has arisen in one of the first three stages of the contract's life, the transaction has unfortunately moved into the **breach stage**.

For example, there may be:

- a defect in the contract's formation (e.g., invalid acceptance, incapacity of a person to contract, uncertain terms, lack of essential terms, etc.);

- a failure of one party to eliminate a contingency provision allowing the other party to avoid further performance by cancellation of the contract; or

- a defense to closing has arisen (e.g., misrepresentation of the physical, title or income of the property, untimely performance, etc.).

If the defect in the agreement is serious enough, a compromise, legally called an *accord and satisfaction*, may be negotiated by the broker or his agents between the parties, or the dispute may be resolved by court order.

Disputes are usually resolved through negotiation handled by the brokers and agents.

However, it is this stage that produces the court cases which decide and flesh out our application of real estate contract law.

Forming a contract

A contract is formed when an **offer** to enter into an agreement is made and accepted.

The party who makes the offer is called the *offeror*. The party to whom the offer is directed is called the *offeree*.

In real estate sales transactions, the buyer typically makes an offer to the seller. Thus, the buyer becomes the *offeror*. However, the offeror can be the seller.

For example, a buyer makes an offer which is unacceptable to the seller. The seller counters with an offer to sell on different terms than those offered by the buyer.

Here, the seller has **terminated** the buyer's offer by *rejection*. He has done so by making a *new offer* back to the buyer, called a *counteroffer*. The seller has now become the offeror.

The buyer, as the offeree under the counteroffer, must now decide whether to accept or reject the seller's offer to sell.

To a large extent, the terms *offeror* and *offeree* are useless in practice. The cast of characters in a real estate transaction are better viewed by their more common names, such as:

- buyer and seller;

- landlord and tenant;

- lender and owner; and

- broker and client.

Once each person is identified by the title given their position in a transaction (buyer, seller, etc.), then the offer or acceptance conduct each person engages in sets the rules for their conduct under a purchase agreement offer or counteroffer — as the *offeror* or *offeree*.

What is an offer?

To be valid, an offer must:

- show a serious **intent to enter** into an agreement;

- be **definite and certain** in detailing the essential elements, such as price, terms of payment, property identification and conditions for performance; and

- be **communicated** to the person who can accept the offer.

The buyer's signing of a purchase agreement form which has been properly filled out will satisfy the first two conditions of intent and terms.

However, consider a seller who puts his real estate up for sale without contracting for the services of a listing broker.

A buyer responding to the "For Sale By Owner" sign writes the seller a letter expressing an interest in buying the property, so long as a broker is not used. The buyer asks what price the seller **expects to receive**.

The seller writes back, stating:

"As long as your offer would be in cash, I see no reason why we could not deal directly .... I expect to receive $450,000 for the property. Please let me know what you decide."

The buyer responds:

"Have agreed to buy your real estate on your terms ... would appreciate a contour map as we are desirous of building at once ...."

The seller refuses to convey the property claiming a binding contract was never entered into since his letter to the buyer was a mere invitation for an offer — a *solicitation* by the seller for an offer from the buyer — not a **serious intent** by the seller to enter into a sales agreement.

Does the seller's letter stating the cash price he **expected to receive** constitute an offer to sell which the buyer could accept?

No! The letter did not show a serious intent to contract. Rather, the letter was an **invitation** to the buyer to make an offer. Since the letter lacked words of an offer to sell, a reasonable buyer could not have believed the letter was intended to be an offer capable of acceptance. [**Richards** v. **Flower** (1961) 193 CA2d 233]

Similarly, the following communications with respect to the purchase of real estate are not offers:

- listing agreements;

- offers made in jest [Restatement 2d Contracts §18];

- advertisements;

- letters of intent (LOI) to contract [Rest.2d Contracts §26]; or

- preliminary negotiations or letters of proposal.

Terms and conditions

For an offer to be accepted and a binding contract formed, the offer's terms of payment and conditions of the performance must be **definite and certain**.

Should a breach of an agreement occur and litigation be pursued, a court must be able to glean from the agreement what the parties intended, and whether enough terms exist to enforce performance of the agreement or determine a party's losses.

For example, a landlord and tenant sign a lease giving the tenant the option to renew the lease. The amount of rent due on exercise of the renewal option are to be "agreed on" at the time the option is exercised.

An **option** is an offer which has not yet been accepted. It is irrevocable for a period of time during which it can be accepted, called *exercise*.

Here, the option given the tenant to renew the lease does not specify an essential term (i.e., the rental rate, which is the price to be paid for the use of the property).

Later, the tenant tries to *exercise* (accept) the option (irrevocable offer). The landlord refuses to comply, claiming the option is unenforceable as the rent terms are too vague.

Is the option to renew too vague to be enforced?

Yes! The purported renewal option was merely an "agreement to agree" regarding an intent to change the rent to be charged under the lease, which leaves the option unenforceable. [**Ablett** v. **Clauson** (1954) 43 C2d 280]

To be definite and certain in its terms and conditions for enforcement, an offer must set forth the **essential elements** of the transaction, such as:

- the **identity** of the parties;

- a **description** of the real estate;

- the **price** and the form in which it will be paid; and

- the **time for performance**. [**King** v. **Stanley** (1948) 32 C2d 584; CC §1550]

The offer does not need to be on a standardized form to be enforceable. In fact, an offer can even be made on the back of a business card.

Finally, the offer must be **communicated** to the person who is intended to be able to accept the offer.

The offer can only be accepted by the intended offeree. In real estate transactions, the buyer almost always makes the initial offer to buy on terms set forth in a purchase agreement form signed by the buyer. The offer to buy is intended to be accepted by the owner of the property, a person known but not usually identified by name in the offer.

Regular offers

To be certain an offer exists, brokers and their agents in the real estate industry use regular checklist-type forms to transmit offers between buyers and sellers.

A "Real Estate Purchase Agreement" form is used in the purchase and sale of fee simple and existing leasehold estates, such as ground leases, long-term leases or master leases. [See **first tuesday** Form 150]

The California real estate industry has an extensive variety of *boilerplate contracts* for practically any contractually negotiated real estate situation.

The use of a regular form in lieu of independently drafted forms to make an offer to buy or sell real estate is justified for two reasons.

First, regular forms satisfy the writing requirements mandated by the Statute of Frauds. [CC §1624]

Second, a regular form gives the agreement between the buyer and seller clarity of meaning and more uniformity than typically results from individually drafted contracts.

However, regular forms are not a cure-all. regular merely decreases the potential for error or omission by limiting brokers and their agents to the task of filling in blanks and checking the boxes to indicate the provisions included in the contract.

The phrase "all forms are not created equal" becomes most apparent as each publisher's regular purchase agreement manifests its **inherent prejudice** when the form is put to use.

Purchase agreements at work

Standardized purchase agreements set forth the essential terms and conditions of an offer to make it enforceable, complete and clear in meaning.

Specifically, purchase agreements contain clauses for:

- the identities of the parties;

- the location of the real estate sold, leased or encumbered;

- the time for acceptance and performance;

- the time for opening and closing escrow;

- the price and financing;

- title conditions and vesting;

- the physical condition of the property;

- the property's natural hazards and environmental conditions;

- tax planning; and

- the brokerage fee.

A variety of purchase agreements exist with the terms and contingencies needed for different types of properties and transactions. Thus, a purchase agreement becomes a grand **checklist of provisions** to be considered for inclusion in the final contract by filling in the blanks and checking boxes, or leaving them blank and not a part of the contract.

Chapter 38

Acceptance of an offer

This chapter applies the rules of acceptance and rejection to an offer or counteroffer to buy or sell real estate.

Time and nature of a response

A person making an offer, intending to enter into a binding agreement on the terms in the offer, will not have an agreement until:

- the offer is *submitted* to the person with whom he intends to contract, called the *offeree*; and

- that person indicates his intention to enter into an agreement on the same terms contained in the offer by delivering an *acceptance* to the person who made the offer, called the *offeror*.

An **acceptance** is the response to an offer which agrees, without qualification or condition, to the terms of the offer.

Acceptance of an offer in which rights are created and obligations are imposed between two people forms a **binding contract**, also called an *agreement*. A "meeting of the minds" has occurred based on the terms offered and unconditionally accepted, resulting in the agreement.

When an offer is **received** by a person, called *communicated* or *submitted*, the offer can either be:

- **accepted** prior to its *termination*; or

- **rejected**.

No alternative responses to an offer exist. Thus, any response to an offer must fall into one of these two categories.

The process for an **acceptance** of an offer includes several considerations, such as:

- whether the acceptance called for is a promise to perform an act or the actual performance of the act, distinguished as *bilateral* or *unilateral* agreements, respectively;

- who may accept and their identification;

- what documentation is necessary to formalize an acceptance;

- what method or medium is to be used to deliver the acceptance to the offeror, called *communication*;

- what inquiries of clarification need to be made and included as terms in the offer before acceptance; and

- whether to accept prior to termination of the offer.

The other response to an offer is a **rejection**. When a rejection is submitted to the person making the offer, the offer is **terminated**. Thus, on communication of a rejection, an offer no longer remains to be accepted.

Issues affecting an offer which might terminate the offer by **rejection** include:

- a counteroffer to the offer [See **first tuesday** Form 180];

- formal disapproval or unacceptability of the terms offered [See **first tuesday** Form 184];

- inquiries regarding clarification and the inclusion of terms not rising to a rejection;

- qualifications or conditions imposed on the offer by a purported acceptance;

- whether a rejection has been submitted; and

- an attempt to accept the offer after a rejection.

To give a promise or to act

All offers to enter into a contract fall into one of two categories based on the **manner of acceptance** called for in the offer, i.e.:

- the **giving of a promise** agreeing to perform as stated in the offer, called a *bilateral contract*, which, for example, exists in exclusive listings and purchase agreements; or

- the **performance of the act** called for in the offer, called a *unilateral contract*, which, for example, exists on the exercise of an option to buy and the taking of an open listing.

Offers made by buyers in real estate purchase agreements signed and submitted to the owner of the described properties form **bilateral contracts** when accepted. A purchase agreement offer made by a buyer calls for the real estate owner to accept by merely **promising to transfer** the property to the buyer on terms set out in the offer. The seller's performance of the actual acts of conveying title and delivering possession as promised by the seller on acceptance will not occur until closing.

Conversely, an option to buy real estate is a **unilateral contract**. An option to buy gives a buyer the **power to accept** the seller's irrevocable offer (to sell) contained in the option granted to the buyer by the owner of the described property.

To accept the irrevocable offer to sell, called *exercise of the option*, the buyer must do an act, usually the opening of an escrow and the deposit of all funds necessary to close the purchase. Until exercise of the option, the buyer has not promised to buy the property. After the buyer exercises the option, the only act then remaining to be performed is the conveyance of title and delivery of possession promised by the owner in the option agreement.

The buyer (or assignee of the right to buy) cannot accept the irrevocable offer contained in the option by merely promising to open escrow and deliver funds, as is required to form a bilateral contract. To accept, the buyer must actually perform all acts required to exercise the option agreement.

Submit the offer; relay the acceptance

Real estate purchase agreements identify the buyer making the offer, but rarely name the seller who is the person to whom the offer will be submitted. The offer describes the property on which the offer to purchase is made. Thus, the only person who can accept the offer, though unnamed within the buyer's offer, is the person who can deliver title and possession of the described property. Usually, this person is the vested owner of the property, but it might be someone who holds an option to buy the property.

Real estate agreements are nearly always reduced to a writing and signed by all parties due to the mandates of the Statute of Frauds for their enforcement. Thus, it follows that a buyer seeking to enter into an enforceable agreement with a seller will submit his offer to purchase in a writing signed by the buyer.

Further, pre-printed purchase agreement forms all contain acceptance provisions which are devoid of qualifying or conditional language which would destroy any attempt at an acceptance.

Accordingly, the only documentation required of an owner of real estate who accepts an offer submitted by a buyer is to place his signature in the space provided beneath the acceptance provision on the purchase agreement form without adding to or deleting a word in the purchase agreement.

Once the acceptance provision has been signed by the seller, the acceptance must be **submitted** to the buyer who made the offer, called *communication of the acceptance*. When submitted, the process of the seller's acceptance is complete and a binding contract is formed.

Again, since real estate related agreements are all in writing and nearly all are on pre-printed forms, the authorization to accept the offer contained in the form instructs the person accepting about what he must do to accept. Besides signing the **acceptance statement** at the end of the agreement, the acceptance provision in the purchase agreement requires a copy of the document bearing the acceptance signatures to be *delivered* to the person making the offer, or that person's real estate agent. [See **first tuesday** Form 150 §10.1]

In the case of a seller making an offer which is a counteroffer to an unacceptable offer from a buyer, the buyer begins the process of accepting the seller's offer by signing the acceptance provision in the counteroffer form. Typically, the signed counteroffer is then handed to the buyer's agent. At this point, the process of acceptance is still incomplete — the acceptance has not been communicated to the seller as instructed in the acceptance provision of the counteroffer.

To form a binding contract, a copy of the counteroffer signed as accepted by the buyer must be delivered to the listing broker (or his agent) or the seller himself, if he does not have a broker.

If the buyer's broker is also the seller's listing broker, the counteroffer has been accepted on the buyer's handing the signed acceptance to the broker, unless the acceptance provision requires other steps before acceptance is complete.

If the seller has a listing broker, delivery to the listing broker of a copy of the counteroffer containing the buyer's signature accepting the offer completes the acceptance process and forms a binding contract at that moment, even if the listing broker fails to hand it to the seller, unless the broker is required to do so to form a contract.

If the seller is not represented by a broker, delivery by handing or faxing the seller a copy of the counteroffer signed by the buyer forms a binding contract.

Clarifying or refining the offer

On a seller's review of an offer submitted on the described property, the seller advises his listing agent the offer as written needs clarification or possible changes to contain all the terms desired by the seller. Such items might address the escrow period, the note or trust deed provisions in a carryback, a condition or contingency in the offer, or the inclusion of seller and broker disclosures which should be acknowledged in the offer to eliminate exposure to liability.

Thus, the seller seeks to have the offer "cleaned up" or "redrafted" before he accepts it.

Here, the seller considering an offer which can be accepted within three days could instruct the listing agent to either:

- contact the buyer's agent (or the buyer if he has no agent) and ask if the buyer's offer could be clarified or possibly altered to include the seller's suggestions; or

- prepare a counteroffer containing the suggested alterations or clarifications which the seller signs and submits to the buyer.

Without preparing and submitting a counteroffer, an inquiry can be made into the buyer's willingness to include the suggestions. The inquiry for clarifications or changes is not a counteroffer or any other type of rejection of the buyer's offer which would terminate the offer and make a later acceptance impossible. The seller is merely attempting to get the offer cleaned up, by inducing change or clarification, and doing so apart from and without any disapproval or counteroffer. Should the buyer refuse to clarify or alter his offer, the seller must then decide whether to accept or reject the offer.

However, had an acceptance been attempted which altered the terms of the buyer's purchase agreement offer by *interlineation* prior to signing the acceptance provision, the change of the terms in the offer on acceptance by the seller is a *counteroffer* to perform on different terms. It is a rejection which terminates the offer.

Further, once a rejection (by counteroffer or a change of terms on acceptance) has been communicated by delivery to the buyer, the seller cannot then accept the original offer by signing and delivering a signed copy of the unaltered purchase agreement offer to the buyer — even if the days stated for the acceptance period have not yet expired.

Acceptance period for contracting

An offer is considered revoked:

- by the lapse of time for acceptance stated in the offer; or

- if no time limit exists, by the lapse of a reasonable time without communication of an acceptance. [Calif. Civil Code §1587(2)]

All offers to buy or sell real estate terminate at some point in time, after which the power to create a contract by accepting the offer no longer exists. Thus, an acceptance, if there is to be one, must be *communicated* to the person who made the offer **during the acceptance period** to form a binding contract on the terms offered.

If the time period for acceptance is not entered or checked in a purchase agreement or counteroffer, the acceptance can be submitted any time during a reasonable period after the offer was submitted. A reasonable period could be any time period ranging from a few days to a week or more, depending entirely on the circumstances surrounding the negotiations.

In nearly all real estate purchase agreements or counteroffer situations, a date or the occurrence of an event is given as the expiration of the acceptance period. Thereafter, no offer remains to be accepted.

Should the buyer's purchase agreement offer expire by its terms, such as three days from the date of the offer, and the seller later signs the acceptance provision and delivers a signed copy to the buyer, the buyer may act on the "late-acceptance effort" to form a contract by taking steps to **acknowledge the late acceptance**. With the buyer's acknowledgment of the seller untimely acceptance by the opening of an escrow, the seller becomes bound to the agreement since the buyer's positive response to a late acceptance is considered a *waiver* of the expiration period for acceptance.

However, the buyer is under no obligation to respond to a tardy attempt to accept. No offer remains to be accepted and no obligation can be imposed on the buyer by the late attempt to accept. The provision for expiration of the acceptance period is solely for the benefit of the person (buyer) making the offer.

Consider a seller who contacts a broker to sell his property. The broker's agent locates a buyer who makes an offer to purchase the property.

The offer contains a provision stating the offer will be deemed revoked unless accepted in writing within five days after the date of the offer.

The agent is unable to present the offer to the seller until six days following the date of the offer. The seller signs his acceptance of the buyer's offer and the acceptance is handed to the buyer. The buyer does not respond by a writing "accepting the acceptance."

However, the buyer's agent dictates escrow instructions which are prepared, signed by the buyer and returned to escrow. The seller refuses to sign his copy of the escrow instructions or proceed with the transaction.

The seller claims his signature accepting the offer does not constitute an acceptance since the buyer's offer had expired by its provisions for revocation, and a late acceptance becomes a counteroffer which the buyer never accepted.

Did the seller's untimely submission of his acceptance of the purchase agreement constitute a counteroffer?

No! A counteroffer is an offer which replaces or qualifies a term or condition in the original offer. A late acceptance is not a counteroffer since it does not substitute new or different terms for the terms originally offered. It is just a late acceptance of all the terms and conditions of the offer.

Here, the buyer, by opening escrow, acted to **waive** the acceptance period time limit. Time for acceptance is a condition placed in the offer solely for the benefit of the buyer to eliminate his future exposure to contract liabilities. However, when a buyer acts on a late acceptance by having escrow instructions prepared and signing them, a binding agreement between the buyer and seller is formed. Thus, the seller must close escrow. [**Sabo** v. **Fasano** (1984) 154 CA3d 502]

Events terminating the offer

Other events terminating an offer contained in a purchase agreement or counteroffer include:

- **death** of either person before acceptance;

- **destruction** of the real estate before acceptance;

- **revocation** of the offer by the person who made the offer by sending a *notice of withdrawal* of the offer by mail, phone, fax, email or agent to the person who could accept, and do so before an acceptance is submitted;

- **rejection** of the offer by the person who could accept, such as occurs on a qualified or conditional acceptance by *interlineation* on the purchase agreement or a formal counteroffer, since the communication of these actions terminate the offer which now ceases to exist and cannot be accepted after a rejection; or

- a **prior sale** of the property to another buyer during the acceptance period for the seller's counteroffer, notice of which is either placed in the mail to the buyer (whether or not received) or hand delivered to the buyer before a copy of the buyer's signed acceptance of the seller's counteroffer is submitted to the seller, the listing agent or other authorized agent for acceptance.

Chapter 39

The counteroffer environment

This chapter examines the seller's response to an unacceptable purchase offer by countering with an offer which consists of terms different from the terms of the purchase offer being rejected.

Meeting the seller's objectives

The preparation of a counteroffer is an occasion when a listing agent and seller have an opportunity to take control of negotiations which a prospective buyer has commenced by the submission of a written purchase agreement offer. For the listing agent, the counteroffer is his moment:

- **to care for and protect** the seller by addressing property disclosures to be made by the seller to perfect any agreement the seller may enter into with the prospective buyer; and

- **to clarify** any uncertainties about the buyer's ability to close escrow.

Essentially, a counteroffer allows the listing agent to actually eliminate contingencies regarding disclosures which serve only to cancel or reprice the sale for the seller. At the same time, the listing agent can take steps to establish the buyer's qualifications for any purchase-assist financing and the source of any other funds needed by the buyer to close the transaction.

The environment surrounding the listing agent's analysis of the buyer's offer and the agent's later review of the offer with the seller is nearly always within the control of the listing agent, as it should be.

A prompt, initial review of the offer by the listing agent, alone and before advising the seller it has been received, is necessary to prepare the agent to handle his call to the seller to set an appointment for a review of the buyer's offer.

On hearing the listing agent has received an offer, the seller's first comments generally tend to focus on the price, transactional costs, the buyer's ability to close escrow and when the seller will be handed the net sales proceeds.

Conversely, the listing agent is primarily concerned with:

- the seller's obligation to the prospective buyer to disclose his knowledge about the property which, if disclosed after entering into a purchase agreement contract, may well affect the price the buyer may then be willing to pay for the property, lead to the buyer's cancellation of the purchase agreement, or reduce the seller's net proceeds should the seller have to eliminate undisclosed conditions exposed by a late disclosure which are unacceptable to the buyer; and

- the agent's preparation for his appointment with the seller which will cover information needed to be reviewed by the seller before a decision can be made to accept or reject (by a counteroffer) the buyer's purchase agreement offer.

The diligent listing agent

A listing agent's duty owed to his seller on the submission and review of a prospective buyer's offer includes:

- advice on the seller's obligations to disclose property conditions and obtain clearances or eliminate defects triggered by the buyer's due diligence investigation;

- a review of the agent's concerns about the acceptability or modification of contingency provisions which affect closing;

- disclosure of the likely net sales proceeds the offer will generate; and

- if the property is other than the seller's personal residence, the agent's knowledge about the profit tax liability the seller will most likely incur on the sale.

For example, an agent representing a prospective buyer submits a purchase agreement offer without first obtaining a copy of the listing agent's marketing package on the property. The package contains all the required seller disclosures the seller and listing agent are required to deliver to prospective buyers. Thus, the buyer does not take into consideration the adverse property conditions **disclosed** in the marketing package when the buyer made his decision about the price and terms on which he is willing to buy the property. However, the buyer will discover these conditions when the disclosures are eventually handed over.

Accordingly, the listing agent's advice to the seller on submitting and reviewing the offer is to counter the offer and include as addenda all the required disclosures. The disclosures, at the agent's insistence when listing the property, have already been prepared and are available for the prospective buyer to approve before entering into a purchase agreement.

Thus, the pre-contract disclosures will eliminate most of the contingencies which affect the price, the amount of the seller's transactional expenses and the buyer's ability to cancel the purchase agreement, all of which concern the listing agent.

By a thoughtful analysis of the buyer's offer prior to meeting with the seller, the listing agent prepares himself to advise the seller on the use of a counteroffer to best respond to the offer. Thus, the agent seeks to reduce the uncertainties about the consequences of an unmodified acceptance of an offer.

Various responses to an offer

Several procedures exist for a seller to respond to an unacceptable offer, especially an offer which, with a few minor changes, would be acceptable to the seller, such as changes regarding the selection of the escrow company, the deadline for loan approval, verification of downpayment funds, or the sale or purchase of other property.

The listing agent handling negotiations for a change in the terms of the buyer's purchase offer should reduce the seller's (counter)offer to a writing signed by the seller before it is submitted to the buyer. The seller's signed counteroffer manifests his intent to be bound by his offer to sell, if the buyer accepts.

The seller's counter to an unacceptable purchase agreement offer can be written up by the listing agent and submitted to the buyer using any one of the following formats:

1. Prepare the seller's offer on a **new purchase agreement form**, possibly on a different and more appropriate form for the transaction than the form used by the buyer's agent. No reference is made in the seller's new offer to the rejected purchase agreement offer previously submitted by the buyer. This new original offer prepared by the listing agent will be signed first by the seller and listing agent, then submitted to the buyer for the buyer's acceptance or rejection.

2. Prepare the seller's offer on a **counteroffer form** which includes, by reference, all the terms and conditions of the buyer's offer. Modifications are then entered on the counteroffer form stating the terms and conditions sought by the seller which are different from those in the buyer's offer which are unacceptable to the seller. [See **first tuesday** Form 180]

3. Dictate **escrow instructions** based on an agreement orally negotiated with the buyer (or buyer's agent) to resolve the

seller's dissatisfaction regarding the terms and conditions in the buyer's offer. The instructions are submitted to the seller and buyer for signatures. On receipt by escrow of copies of the instructions containing the signatures of all parties, the escrow instructions then become the only agreement entered into by both the buyer and seller. Here, the escrow company becomes a sort of secretarial service used by agents who do not take the time to prepare a written counteroffer themselves.

4. **Alter the original written offer** the buyer has already signed by deleting unacceptable provisions from the face of the document and entering the differing provisions sought by the seller, a process called *deface and interlineate*. The altered purchase agreement is then signed by the seller in the acceptance provision and returned to the buyer as the seller's counteroffer. This counteroffer and acceptance procedure is called *change and initial*, and is used when a counteroffer form is not made available and prepared by the listing agent.

5. Set up an **auction environment** (if the current market is composed of too many buyers for too little inventory) by calling for the submission of all offers on a date and at a time set for the seller to accept the best offer of all those presented by prospective buyers, or by creating some other auction situation short of the seller signing multiple counteroffers, an awkward (and typically misguided) response to the receipt of multiple purchase offers.

6. **Orally advise** the buyer's agent about the changes required before the buyer's offer will be acceptable to the seller. If the buyer is interested in the property based on those changes, the buyer's agent is asked to prepare and submit a new purchase agreement offer signed by the buyer for the seller to consider. This

situation requires the buyer to "negotiate with himself," while the seller remains uncommitted to sell on any terms. Here, either the listing agent does not take the time to prepare a counteroffer stating the terms and conditions on which the seller will sell or the seller wants to remain uncommitted.

7. Let the **offer expire**, then resume negotiations with the buyer and his agent if the buyer still has an interest in the property.

The counter is an offer

The rules for preparing and submitting a counteroffer and those for accepting a counteroffer which will form a binding contract to buy and sell real estate are the same rules which are applied to determine whether an offer made by a seller has been submitted to the buyer or an acceptance by the buyer has occurred to form a binding contract.

Real estate agents instinctively consider submitting written offers from a buyer to a seller to comply with the rule requiring a written agreement, signed by the buyer and seller to form a real estate contract. Likewise, they should automatically submit written counteroffers from sellers to buyers when the seller will not accept the buyer's offer.

For example, on the buyer's receipt of a seller's counteroffer, the buyer may be unwilling to accept the terms stated, but be willing to submit another offer. In essence, this is a counter to the counter. The buyer's agent may also use a counteroffer form to prepare the buyer's new offer. The buyer's counteroffer, by reference, includes all the terms and conditions of the seller's counteroffer (which itself may reference and include all the provisions in the buyer's original offer), as modified by entry on the counteroffer form of terms and conditions contrary to those sought by the seller. Alternatively, the buyer's agent could draft an entirely fresh purchase agreement offer setting forth the terms agreeable to the buyer.

Forms for entering into agreements usually are flexibly worded for the signatories to merely reflect, "I agree to the terms stated above." The wording eliminates concern about whether the buyer or seller must first sign the document to make an offer or counteroffer.

Defacing a signed document

Listing agents sometime delete terms or provisions in a signed purchase agreement they have received by lining them out with a pen or covering them with white-out, called *defacing*. The agent then adds copy to the document to replace the deleted material, called *interlineation*. The seller then signs the altered document agreeing to the terms of the offer as modified, a counteroffer technique called *change and initial*. However, it is improper conduct for anyone to in any way alter the contents of an original document once it has been signed.

Consider the plight of a buyer's agent who is industriously working to locate unimproved land for a client. He contacts the owners of several suitable properties by mail, soliciting information as to whether they will consider selling their property. One absentee owner who responds indicates he would entertain an offer from the agent's buyer.

The agent prepares an offer which his buyer signs, agreeing to purchase the land on an installment sale arrangement payable over a ten-year period. The signed purchase agreement is sent to the absentee seller. On receipt, the seller calls the buyer's agent to discuss some changes he wants by way of an increase in price and an earlier payoff. The terms discussed are acceptable to the buyer.

The buyer's agent prepares another purchase agreement offer reflecting the changes sought by the seller, which the buyer signs as a fresh, new offer. The offer is sent to the seller. On his receipt, the seller calls the buyer directly. They orally negotiate a cash price payable in 20 days.

To write up the new terms, the seller makes extensive changes to the buyer's second purchase agreement offer by **striking out** the price, terms of payment, closing date, title changes, due diligence investigation contingency provision, etc. On the face of the document, the seller then enters the terms and conditions which replace the strickened ones.

The seller signs the purchase agreement indicating he "agrees to all the terms stated" and returns it to the agent. The changes correctly reflect the changes the buyer agreed to by phone. To accept the modified purchase agreement, the buyer then **initials** all the significant changes made by the seller, but does not initial every minute and minor entry made by the seller. No changes or additions to the document are made by the buyer. The buyer does not re-sign the original purchase agreement in addition to his initializing the changes.

The purchase agreement with the buyer's initials throughout is returned to the seller, who receives it. The agent dictates escrow instructions which are prepared reflecting the final terms as agreed to in the changed-and-initialed counteroffer. The buyer signs and returns his copy of the instructions; the seller does not.

The agent calls the seller asking him to sign and return the escrow instructions and the deed. The seller says they have no deal since the buyer did not initial each and every entry made by the seller on the purchase agreement. The seller claims the failure to initial each minute change he made was a *qualified acceptance* which did not form a binding agreement.

Here, the seller and buyer did enter into a binding and enforceable purchase agreement. The **essential terms** needed as a minimum to provide the certainty and clarity required to establish an enforceable real estate purchase agreement between them existed and were initialled. Further, and significantly, the buyer did not make any changes or add any wording, and by returning the initialed and unaltered counteroffer intended to accept of the seller's (counter)offer as submitted by the seller.

Also, the failure to initial minor and nonessential provisions was inadvertent and not necessary to determine the performance required of the seller to deliver a deed in exchange for cash. [**Kahn** v. **Lischner** (1954) 128 CA2d 480]

In retrospect, had the buyer's agent been directly involved in the final counter-proposal made by the seller, he would have prepared yet another new original purchase agreement offer. It would have been signed by the buyer and sent to the seller to sign and return.

However, the seller did commit himself in his counteroffer to sell on terms which were certain. The buyer should have again signed his name at the end of the agreement and dated it to demonstrate he "agreed to the terms stated above," which on signing would have included all the changes made by the seller on the face of the document.

Had the seller been represented by an agent, his agent properly would have prepared the counteroffer on either a counteroffer form or a new purchase agreement form for the seller to sign. The prepared form would have contained those terms the seller entered by interlineation into the buyer's original purchase agreement offer. Then, the buyer's acceptance of the counter would have been simple. He would agree to buy on the terms stated in the seller's counteroffer by simply signing the seller's (counter)offer and delivering the counteroffer with the signed acceptance.

Chapter 40

Contingency provisions

This chapter reviews the inclusion of contingency provisions in purchase agreements to allow buyers and sellers to either confirm their expectations and meet objectives or avoid closing the transaction.

Conditioning the close of escrow

The contents of a purchase agreement is a collection of provisions generally called terms and conditions. While **terms** focus on the price and the (terms for) payment of the price, **conditions** address:

- the performance of **acts** by the buyer and seller respectively; and

- **events** which are to occur in the process of closing escrow on the transaction.

Thus, each condition addressed in a provision must either be shown to exist or come into existence, by its occurrence or approval, before the purchase agreement can be enforced and escrow closed. Alternatively, the condition can be *waived* as though never part of the purchase agreement.

Thus, all purchase agreements contain one or more provisions "conditioning" closing on the "elimination of a contingency."

When conditions are the subject of *contingency provisions*, the conditions are initially distinguished by whether they:

- do **occur** (events and activities), called *event-occurrence contingencies*; or

- are **approved** (information, data, documents and reports), called *further-approval* or *personal-satisfaction contingencies*.

These **contingency provisions** grant the buyer or seller, or both, the *power to terminate* any further performance of the purchase agreement should an identified activity or event fail to occur or a condition be disapproved.

Also, provisions containing **conditions** are further classified by the sequence or order in which they will be performed by the buyer or seller. Thus, the occurrence or approval called for is either:

- a *condition precedent* to the performance of an activity by the other person; or

- a *condition concurrent* to be performed without concern for the other person's activities.

Categorizing conditions still further, some conditions **must be performed**, making the failure to perform them and close escrow a *breach* of the purchase agreement. Other conditions are the subject of contingency provisions and **might not occur or be approved**, in which case the failure of one or both parties to further perform and close escrow is *excused*.

Thus, under any type of contingency provision, the buyer or seller benefitting from the contingency holds an **option** to "do away with" any further performance of the purchase agreement and escrow instructions, called *cancellation*.

Conditions precedent and concurrent

While all contingency provisions are conditions, it must be well understood that not all conditions agreed to in the provisions of a purchase agreement are contingencies. Contingency provisions authorize the cancellation of the purchase agreement and *excuse* any further performance. Other conditions must be met since they are not contingencies, in which case a failure becomes a *breach*.

For analysis, the two classifications of conditions which exist in purchase agreements, distinguished by whether or not the other person must perform or is excused due to the failure of the identified event to occur or condition (information) to be approved, are:

1. *Conditions precedent*, which consist of contingency provisions calling for the occurrence or approval of an event or condition which **may or may not occur**. Examples include the buyer obtaining a written loan commitment, the recording of a purchase-assist loan, approving due diligence investigations, etc. Here, the contingency provision may be *eliminated* and the transaction can proceed toward closing. Alternatively, if the event or approval is not forthcoming, the person authorized to cancel may *exercise* his right to terminate the transaction, doing away with any **further performance** of the purchase agreement and escrow instructions, called *cancellation*; and

2. *Conditions concurrent*, which consist of noncontingent, mandatory performance provisions calling for the buyer or seller to perform some activity which **must occur**. If the activity does not occur, the purchase agreement has been *breached* by the person who promised to perform or was obligated to cause the activity or event to come about. Examples include the failure of the seller to produce promised information, data, documents and reports on the property or deliver a clearance, grant deed or title insurance policy as agreed. The failure to deliver is a *breach* which allows the other person to either terminate the transaction by notice of cancellation or pursue specific performance of the purchase agreement.

Before escrow can proceed on to closing, contingency provisions must be *eliminated*. Contingency provisions (conditions precedent) included in purchase agreements are **eliminated** by either:

- *satisfaction* of the condition by either an **approval** of the data, information, documents or reports identified as the subject of the provision by the person holding the right to terminate the transaction, or by the **occurrence** of the event called for in the provision; or

- *waiver* (or expiration) of the right to cancel the transaction by the person authorized to cancel, if the identified condition or event has not been satisfied by its approval or occurrence.

Thus, the buyer or seller who has not been granted the power to terminate the transaction under a noncontingency provision, and thus cannot immediately cancel escrow to avoid his further performance, must perform all obligations of his remaining on the contract to be completed, called *conditions concurrent*. He must act without concern for the other person's performance under the purchase agreement, unless the other person must first perform some activity before he is able to comply, such as the seller providing a Natural Hazard Report before the buyer can review it and approve its contents. [See **first tuesday** Form 150 §11.4b]

The obligation of a buyer or seller to complete noncontingent (concurrent) activities required of him to close escrow exists in spite of the fact the other person may not have yet fully performed, or that the other person has a right to later cancel the purchase agreement. Examples include the inability of a buyer to originate a purchase-assist loan after the seller has fully performed by delivering all closing documents to escrow. [See **first tuesday** Form 150 §10.2]

Content of a contingency provision

Regardless of the type of contingency involved, agents must make sure the contingency provision is in writing, even though oral contingencies are generally enforceable. Written contingencies avoid confusion over content, enforceability and forgetfulness.

Specifically, a written contingency should include:

- a description of the event addressed in the contingency (i.e., what is to be approved or verified);

- the time period in which the event called for in the contingency provision must occur;

- who has the right to cancel the purchase agreement if the event does not occur (i.e., whether the buyer, the seller or both can enforce the contingency provision by canceling the transaction);

- any arrangements to avoid cancellation if the contingency is not satisfied or waived (i.e., offsets to the price or time to cure the failure or defect); and

- the method for service of the notice of cancellation on the other person.

Provisions for uncertainties

An agent includes contingency provisions in a purchase agreement in an effort to protect his client from agreeing absolutely to do or cause something to occur which might not occur, or from being forced to accept a situation inconsistent with the client's expectations or ability to accomplish it at the time he enters into the purchase agreement.

Without authority to terminate the agreement on the failure of the client's expectations, such as the buyer's inability to record a purchase-assist loan or to confirm the seller's representations, the client's inability or refusal to continue to further perform under the purchase agreement and close escrow would be a *breach* of the purchase agreement by the client. Thus, the client would be liable to the other person, unless the client's nonperformance was justified by some pre-contract misrepresentation (or omission) of facts which led to the client's lost expectations, called *deceit*.

To avoid a **breach** and be **excused** from closing escrow when events and conditions develop during escrow which do not meet the expectations or anticipations of the client, his agent *conditionalizes* the client's continued performance by including contingency provisions in the purchase agreement. Due to the inclusion of a contingency provision, the client is authorized to terminate the agreement and avoid closing escrow on failure of the identified event to occur or the unacceptability of data, information, documents or reports. [See **first tuesday** Form 159 §11]

But before lacing a purchase agreement with contingency provisions, or allowing the client to enter into one, a prudent agent will first attempt to clear uncertainties the client may have about the property or the transaction.

Use of contingency provisions

It is the buyer's agent who, along with buyers, is the primary user of contingency provisions in purchase agreements. From a buyer's point of view, and thus the buyer's agent's perspective, every activity, event or condition which is the responsibility of the buyer to review for approval or cause to occur so escrow can close should be the subject of a contingency provision in the purchase agreement.

Also for buyers, the period for exercise of the right to cancel should be as long as possible. Thus, the right to cancel should be structured to expire no earlier than the date scheduled for the close of escrow. The possibility always exists that the event or approval needed by the buyer to close escrow may never occur. These conditions range, for example, from applying for purchase-assist financing or retaining consultants for advice on the value or integrity of the property, to making the down payment or providing personal identity information to the title insurance company.

When preparing the purchase agreement, the buyer's agent must rely on his experience to decide which events and approvals the buyer is responsible for and thus need to be the subject matter of a contingency provision. Then, if the event does not occur, such as the recording of mortgage financing, or are unacceptable, such as the failure of the property on a due diligence investigation to meet expectations, the buyer may cancel and be excused from proceeding. Thus, he can act to avoid closing and not be in default (breach) on the purchase agreement (or end up in a dispute claiming he has been misled by the seller or the listing agent).

There are many events and disclosures which are the subject of contingency provisions contained in stock forms used by agents. [See **first tuesday** Form 159 §11]

However, the boilerplate wording of pre-printed contingency provisions varies greatly regarding:

- the time for the gathering and delivery of data, information, documents and reports;

- the time period for review of the material received or the occurrence of an event (such as a loan commitment or sale of other property);

- the date set for expiration of the right to cancel the transaction after failure of the event or approval to occur;

- whether a written waiver is to be delivered evidencing the elimination of the contingency provision, without which the other party may then cancel;

- the requirement of a written notice of cancellation should the right to cancel be exercised on failure of an event or condition; and

- the time period for the other person's response to a notice of cancellation to cure the defect or failure, and thus avoid a termination of the purchase agreement.

Typically, several contingency provisions are included in a purchase agreement. Thus, a **uniform method** for terminating the agreement is

employed. Termination provisions call for a written notice of cancellation, and how and to whom it is to be delivered, including instructions to escrow. [See **first tuesday** Form 150 §10.3]

Also, approval notices or waiver of contingency provisions need not be called for in purchase agreements. Contingency provisions are considered to be the grant of an **option to terminate** a transaction by exercise of the right to cancel prior to the *expiration* of the option period. Therefore, if the person authorized to cancel or who otherwise benefits from the inclusion of the contingency provision does not intend to use the provision to cancel, he does not need to do anything. He simply allows the "option period" for cancellation to expire. [See **first tuesday** Form 150 §8.5]

The contingency is eliminated by the expiration of the right to cancel. Thus, a need never exists to approve or waive the contingency in order to do away with the right to cancel and proceed to close escrow, unless the purchase agreement wording states an approval or waiver is required to keep the contract alive. [**Beverly Way Associates** v. **Barham** (1990) 226 CA3d 49]

Conditions not contingent

The condition of the property, namely the physical integrity of the land and improvements, is frequently not disclosed to the buyer before entering into a purchase agreement. Most delayed disclosures fail to comply with the statutory mandates imposed on sellers and listing agents to hand the information to prospective buyers as soon as reasonably possible.

The listing agent has a mandated duty, owed to the public, to visually inspect the listed property and note his observations and awareness of property conditions adversely affecting the value on the seller's statutory disclosure document, called a Condition of Property or Transfer Disclosure Statement (TDS).

Not only is it **reasonably possible** for the listing agent to deliver the TDS before his seller enters into a purchase agreement with a buyer, it is mandated by case law and the economic imperatives of *transparency* to deliver property disclosures before a price is set in property transactions.

However, some stock purchase agreement forms convert the failure of the listing agent to deliver a TDS before the acceptance of an offer into a contingency, the result of a statutorily imposed penalty placed on the seller for his tardy disclosures. As the subject matter of a contingency, the buyer is granted the right to cancel the transaction when the TDS is belatedly received.

If on review of the tardy disclosures the property conditions do not meet the expectations held by the buyer at the time he entered into the purchase agreement, the buyer may cancel the purchase agreement all due to the dilatory and misleading conduct of the listing agent, a type of fraud called *deceit*.

If not cancelled, the buyer would become the owner of property which is not in the condition and of the value he was lead to believe and to think existed when he entered into the purchase agreement.

Now applying the same disclosure facts, consider a diametrically opposed purchase agreement provision designed to handle the listing agent's dilatory delivery of the TDS by not establishing a contingency, and therefore avoiding the need to cancel. Rather, the provision calls for the buyer to review the seller's and listing agent's post-acceptance property disclosures. The provision grants no one the authority to cancel should the property's conditions be unacceptable or less than expected when entering into the purchase agreement. Instead, it requires performance by all.

On the buyer's review of the TDS after entering into the purchase agreement, if defects or other significant discrepancies in the property's condition are disclosed (which affect its value) and were not observed or known to the buyer before entering into the purchase agreement, the buyer is **authorized to notify** the seller of the defects and discrepancies and make a demand on the seller to cure them by repair, replacement or correction. If the buyer fails to give notice, he has let his right expire to demand the correction of previously undisclosed defects noted in the TDS and must proceed to close escrow. [See **first tuesday** Form 269]

However, if the buyer makes a demand on the seller to cure those defects first discovered by the buyer on his in-escrow review of the TDS, the seller is required to make the corrections before closing or suffer a reduction in the price equivalent to the cost to cure the noticed defects. Of course, the disclosure of the property's condition before the purchase agreement is accepted relieves the seller (and the buyer) of the need to activate this performance provision regarding repairs. [See **first tuesday** Form 150 §11.2]

Of course, the time set for delivery of data, information, documents and reports under a contingency provision so they can be approved or disapproved, as well as the date set for delivery of a notice of cancellation given for any valid reason, is always subject to *time-essence rules*. [**Fowler** v. **Ross** (1983) 142 CA3d 472]

Failure to close is a breach, unless excused

Frequently, a contingency provision calls for two events to occur in tandem, i.e., a condition concurrent, which **must occur**, followed by a condition precedent (approval), which **may or may not occur**.

For example, a seller of a condominium is to first provide documents on the homeowners' association (HOA) to the buyer (the condition concurrent) for what then becomes the buyer's review (the condition precedent). Here, the seller **must deliver** the documents as a prerequisite to the buyer's review of their content for approval or disapproval. The seller must obtain the documents or otherwise cause them to be handed to the buyer. If he does not, the seller has *breached* the provision and the purchase agreement. [See **first tuesday** Form 150 §11.8]

As for the buyer who receives the documents, he must then enter upon a *good-faith review* of their content under his further-approval portion of the contingency provision. After the review and completion of any further inquiry or investigation into their content, the buyer is to either express his approval by waiving or letting the right to cancel expire, or, if he has good reason and an honest belief that he cannot approve of their content, disapprove the documents by canceling the transaction.

Here, the seller is obligated to get the documents and deliver them to the buyer without concern for what steps the buyer may or may not be taking to perform any of his obligations under the purchase agreement, such as applying for a loan, providing a credit report or approving disclosures he has received. In practice, disclosures should be handed to the buyer for review and approval before entering into a purchase agreement since the information may adversely affect value requiring thier disclosure by the seller and the listing agent.

Consider another **tandem-events provision** in which the buyer will execute a promissory note in favor of the seller in a carryback transaction. The buyer, in a *further-approval contingency provision*, agrees to prepare and hand the seller a credit application. On receipt, the seller is to review and then approve, or cancel the transaction if the seller has a reasonable basis for disapproving the buyer's creditworthiness.

The buyer's obligation to deliver the credit application is a compulsory event he is required to perform. The failure to deliver is a *breach* of the provision since the buyer's delivery of the application is not conditioned on anyone first doing something. [See **first tuesday** Form 150 §8.4]

On the other hand, the seller on receipt of the credit application is required to review the buyer's creditworthiness. However, he is not required to approve the buyer's creditworthiness, and if disapproved based on reasonable grounds, the seller is *excused* from closing escrow by canceling the transaction. [See **first tuesday** Form 150 §8.5]

Act to close without concern

Other contingency provisions require one person, such as the buyer, to first enter upon an activity (such as signing and returning escrow instructions) without concern for whether the other person, such as the seller, is performing his required obligations, such as obtaining a pest control clearance, an occupancy certificate, the release or reconveyance of liens on title, etc.

For example, a purchase agreement contains a contingency provision calling for the buyer to obtain and record a purchase-assist loan. Should the buyer fail to originate the loan as anticipated, the buyer may cancel the transaction and be *excused* from further performing. However, the buyer is obligated to promptly initiate the loan application process without concern for whether the seller has commenced any performance of the seller's obligations, such as signing and returning the seller's escrow instructions, providing a deed or ordering out inspections and reports required to be obtained by the seller. [**Landis** v. **Blomquist** (1967) 257 CA2d 533]

A person's performance of an activity which **must occur**, versus his undertaking to bring about an event or approve a condition which **may or may not occur**, is an important distinction to be made. One is a *breach* of the purchase agreement should the activity not occur; the other *excuses* any further performance by cancellation should the described event not occur. Both failures permit the purchase agreement to be canceled by the opposing party, but a breach carries with it **litigation and liability exposure**.

For example, the buyer of a nonresidential income property is willing to purchase the property only if the seller cancels a disadvantageous lease held by a tenant. The buyer's agent prepares a purchase agreement with a provision calling for the seller to deliver title and assign all existing leases except the one the buyer is unwilling to accept.

While the seller believes he can negotiate a cancellation of the lease, the listing agent does not want his seller committed to delivering title and then fail to be able to negotiate the cancellation of the lease. To accept the purchase agreement with the provision calling for delivery of the title clear of the lease would place the seller in breach if he could not negotiate a cancellation of the lease. Thus, the seller would be exposed to liability for the decrease in the value of the property resulting from the lease remaining as a defect (i.e., an unapproved encumbrance) on the title.

Here, the seller should submit a counteroffer prepared by the listing agent calling for the delivery of title to be contingent on the seller's termination of the lease, an **event-occurrence contingency provision**. Thus, the seller will only become obligated to make a good-faith effort to negotiate the cancellation of the lease. Should he fail to be able to deliver title clear of the lease, he may cancel the transaction and be *excused* from any further performance, and, importantly, be free of any liability for the failure to deliver title as agreed.

Performing without concern

Many contingency provisions authorize the buyer to exercise his right to cancel at any time up to and including the date scheduled for closing should the identified condition or event fail to occur. In the interim, the seller must fully perform all of his obligations to deliver to escrow all documents needed from the seller to close. After the seller has fully performed, the buyer, at the time of closing, may then cancel on failure of the condition or event.

The only rights a seller has in the buyer's contingency provision is the assurance that the buyer must act on any cancellation before the right to cancel expires, and that the cancellation is reasonable and the result of a good-faith effort by the buyer to satisfy the contingency so the transaction can close.

Consider a purchase agreement with terms for the payment of the purchase price which include having the buyer obtain a purchase-assist loan. The close of escrow is contingent on the buyer recording the loan since the buyer has the right to cancel if payment of the price cannot be funded by a purchase-assist loan. [See **first tuesday** Form 150 §10.3]

However, the seller has not handed escrow any of the documents or information requested by escrow, the receipt of which is needed to close escrow. The buyer then refuses to submit his loan application and fees to his lender until the seller has fully performed all his obligations for escrow to close. The buyer claims it is futile for him to proceed if the seller has not performed.

In turn, the seller cancels the transaction, claiming the buyer has breached his duty to make a good-faith effort to eliminate the loan contingency by applying for the loan.

Here, the buyer's obligation to take steps to satisfy the loan contingency and the seller's obligation to deliver deeds, termite clearances, etc. to escrow are independent obligations called *conditions concurrent*. Thus, the buyer and seller must each perform their part of the closing activities without concern for whether the other person has or is performing.

Also, the seller must, prior to the date scheduled for close of escrow, have fully performed all the acts required of the seller for escrow to close, and perform them in a timely manner for escrow to close on the date scheduled. The seller must comply even though the buyer's right to terminate the transaction can be exercised by canceling the escrow as late as the date scheduled for closing. [Landis, *supra*]

Sellers who agree to loan contingency provisions for buyers often require a separate and specific time-essence contingency provision to assure themselves that the buyer will act promptly to arrange a loan. In the provision, the buyer authorizes the seller to cancel the transaction if the buyer does not produce a loan commitment or a statement from a qualified lender by a specific date demonstrating that the buyer is qualified for a loan in the amount sought. [See **first tuesday** Form 150 §6.1]

Now, if the buyer fails to timely act on an application to negotiate a loan and arrange for a statement of his creditworthiness to be handed to the seller by the deadline for satisfaction of the condition, the seller may cancel the transaction.

Purchase agreement as binding

The existence of an oral or written contingency provision in a purchase agreement does not render the agreement *void*, as though it were a mere illusory contract which never was binding.

On the contrary, when an offer is accepted, a *binding agreement* is formed. The overriding issue on forming a binding purchase agreement which contains a contingency provision is whether the purchase agreement will ever **become enforceable** by the elimination of contingencies as satisfied or waived.

For example, the board of directors of a corporation decides the company needs to purchase a warehouse to store inventory. To meet the corporate objectives, the president, on behalf of his corporation, employs a broker who locates a suitable building. It appears the property will be sold to another person before board approval can be obtained authorizing the corporation to enter into a purchase agreement to acquire it.

As the agent authorized to bind the corporation to perform under a purchase agreement, the president, on behalf of the corporation, submits a signed purchase agreement offer to the listing agent agreeing to buy the real estate, conditioned on the **further approval** of the board of directors within 20 days of acceptance.

The seller accepts the offer after his listing agent explains the purchase agreement will not be enforceable until the board of directors approves the purchase, and thus *eliminates* the contingency.

The corporation, based on the offer submitted by its president and the seller's acceptance, has effectively taken the seller's property off the market while the president completes his due diligence investigation. Further, the board gets a "free look" by controlling the property before deciding on the property's suitability as a warehouse, or whether the terms of the purchase agreement are acceptable.

Here, the seller has a binding commitment from the corporate buyer to purchase the real estate, subject to presenting the purchase agreement and the property selection to the board for approval or rejection and cancellation under the contingency provision. [**Moreland Development Company** v. **Gladstone Holmes, Inc.** (1982) 135 CA3d 973]

However, the officers and board of directors of any corporate buyer or seller must act in *good faith* when exercising a contingency provision by cancellation. Accordingly, the officers need to submit the purchase agreement transaction to the board. The board then needs to review the purchase agreement. If conditions are unacceptable, the board should reject the purchase agreement in a resolution so the officers can show a reasonable basis exists for exercising the corporation's rights under the contingency provision to disapprove of the property selection or the terms of purchase and cancel the transaction. [**Jacobs** v. **Freeman** (1980) 104 CA3d 177]

Now consider a corporate owner of real estate who agrees to sell contingent on the **further approval** of the transaction by its board of directors prior to close of escrow. The corporate officers deliberately fail to submit the agreement for board approval since they no longer want to sell the property to this buyer. They cancel the sales transaction, believing they can do so for lack of board approval.

The buyer demands the corporation close escrow on the purchase agreement, claiming the agreement was breached by the failure to deliver a deed to the property when the agreement was never presented to the board of directors for approval as required by the contingency provision in the agreement.

The corporate seller claims the purchase agreement was properly cancelled since the board of directors did not approve the sale.

Here, the corporation cannot use the lack of board approval as a basis for canceling the purchase agreement. The board never disapproved the purchase agreement since the corporate officers failed to submit the purchase agreement to the board for approval. However, the cancellation would be valid if the corporate officers could show why submitting the agreement to the board for approval would have been futile. [**Jacobs** v. **Tenneco West, Inc.** (1986) 186 CA3d 1413]

In a real estate syndication context, consider a manager of a limited liability company (LLC) who submits a purchase agreement offer on behalf of his LLC to buy property (or accept an offer to sell), contingent on the further approval of the terms of the purchase agreement by the LLC members as required by the LLC operating agreement.

As a further-approval contingency, the LLC's inclusion of the provision in the purchase agreement offer is comparable to the situations calling for a corporate officer to act in good faith and submit the purchase agreement to their board of directors for approval (or disapproval). Thus, if the purchase agreement offer is accepted, the manager will submit the binding agreement to the members for a vote. If the members vote to disapprove, the manager will cancel the transaction rendering the purchase agreement unenforceable.

Chapter 41

The elimination of contingencies

This chapter discusses conditions which must be eliminated before a purchase agreement becomes enforceable.

Occur, approve, waive or exercise

As a result of negotiations over the content of a purchase agreement, buyers and sellers frequently include provisions in the agreement which place **conditions** on their duty to close escrow, called *contingencies*. Contingency provisions placed in a purchase agreement grant the authority, which may only be **used for good cause**, to terminate the buyer's duty to pay the purchase price or the seller's duty to deliver title.

Contingencies describe an **event or condition** which the buyer or seller feels must occur or be approved before the purchase agreement transaction can proceed to closing. These contingencies need to be *eliminated* before a binding purchase agreement becomes fully enforceable, obligating the buyer and seller to close the transaction.

Contingency provisions contained in purchase agreements are eliminated by either:

- *satisfaction* of the contingency provision by the occurrence of an event or by someone's approval of the conditions contained in information, data, documents or a report; or

- *waiver* or *expiration* of the contingency provision.

On the occurrence or approval as described in a contingency provision, the condition is said to be *satisfied*, such as the buyer's receipt of a loan commitment or approval of disclosures.

If a condition is not satisfied, the **person authorized in writing or benefitting** from the contingency can either:

- *cancel* the transaction by serving the other person with a Notice of Cancellation [See Form 183 accompanying this chapter]; or

- *waive* the contingency and proceed with the transaction by notifying the other person the contingency has been waived or by allowing the time period for cancellation to expire. [See Form 182 accompanying this chapter]

If the **event or approval** called for in the contingency provision does not come about, the person with the right to cancel may *waive* the contingency provision or allow it to expire and proceed to closing. If the contingency provision is not waived or allowed to expire on failure of the event or approval to occur, the purchase agreement transaction can be terminated by the person with the right to cancel.

The person with the right to cancel may only *exercise* the right if they have a **reasonable basis** for the cancellation. If a reasonable basis exists, they can avoid enforcement of the purchase agreement by the other person. To exercise the right to cancel, a notice of cancellation must be delivered to the other person during the period for timely exercise of the right to cancel, and in the manner set out in the cancellation provision. [See **first tuesday** Form 150 §10.5]

Colorful jargon in the real estate industry has tagged contingency provisions with such titles as "weasel clauses," "escape clauses" or "back-door provisions." These titles suggest a misunderstanding of the ability to use contingency provisions to cancel and avoid buying or selling the property should the person wishing to cancel merely have a change of heart about proceeding with the transaction.

He who benefits may waive bye-bye

Consider a buyer who agrees to purchase property for a price acceptable to the seller. The terms for payment call for the buyer to fund part of the price by obtaining a purchase-assist loan at a particular interest rate with a specific monthly amortization schedule, until paid, e.g., a loan amount of no less than $200,000 at a fixed rate no greater than 6.5% amortized by monthly payments over a 30-year period.

Included in the purchase agreement is a provision stating the close of escrow is "contingent on" the buyer obtaining the purchase-assist loan, an event-occurrence contingency provision. [See **first tuesday** Form 150 §10.3]

The buyer discovers that mortgage lenders are raising rates, encouraged by a national monetary policy aimed at dampening an *asset inflation* bubble reflected in fast rising property values. As a result, one loan commitment received by the buyer comes in at a higher fixed rate of interest and a lesser loan amount than sought. Another is for the amount sought, but with a variable rate of interest. Neither commitment falls within the parameters of the terms set for the purchase-assist loan in the purchase agreement. [See **first tuesday** Form 150 §6]

The seller is advised the loan commitments do not satisfy the terms called for in the purchase agreement. At the same time, the buyer either hands the seller a notice of waiver of the contingency or lets the right to cancel expire, as called for in the loan contingency provision.

When the seller receives confirmation the loan commitments do not satisfy the contingency provision, the seller cancels the transaction. The seller claims the failure of the loan commitments to meet the conditions set for the loan gives him the power to terminate any further performance of the purchase agreement or escrow.

However, the power to cancel a transaction due to the failure of a contingent event can only be exercised by the person who **benefits** from the inclusion of the contingency provision in the purchase agreement.

Here, the seller has agreed to a **cash transaction**. On closing, the seller will receive net proceeds consisting of cash; nothing else. Thus, while the loan will help the buyer fund the sales price, the existence or nonexistence of the purchase-assist loan has no effect on the seller's ability to perform or the seller's net proceeds. The loan contingency does not benefit the seller.

If financing is not available and the buyer could not otherwise fund the close of escrow, the buyer would be in breach of the purchase agreement, unless he had the right to cancel the transaction and be excused from closing. Thus, the event-occurrence contingency provision calling for the recording of a purchase-assist loan was solely for the benefit of the buyer.

Accordingly, only the buyer held the right to cancel the transaction or waive the contingency. The buyer did neither. He did not exercise his right to cancel by **stating he disapproved** of the loan commitment or by delivering a notice of cancellation (as required by the contingency provision). The seller's attempt to usurp the benefits of the provision by canceling had no legal effect on the continued enforceability of the purchase agreement. [**Wesley N. Taylor, Co.** v. **Russell** (1961) 194 CA2d 816]

Mutually beneficial further-approval contingencies

Now consider a buyer who agrees to **purchase and develop** real estate.

The seller agrees to carry back a purchase-money note secured by a trust deed which is *subordinate* to a construction loan the buyer is to originate to fund his development of the property. It is agreed the loan is to be approved and insured by the Federal Housing Authority (FHA). Neither the seller nor the

NOTICE OF CANCELLATION

Due to Contingency or Condition

DATE:_____, 20_____, at _____, California.

TO: _____

Items left blank or unchecked are not applicable.

FACTS:

This is a notice of cancellation and termination of the following contract:

☐ Purchase agreement

☐ Escrow instructions

☐ Exchange agreement

☐ Counteroffer

☐ Other:_____

Dated:_____, 20_____, at _____, California

Entered into by you and the undersigned, regarding real estate referred to as: _____

_____

CANCELLATION AND TERMINATION:

The above referenced contract and any underlying agreements are hereby cancelled and terminated.
This cancellation is based on:

1. _____
    _____

2. _____
    _____

3. _____
    _____

4. And further, is cancelled for any other legally sufficient grounds not here mentioned.

5. If approved by all parties, the real estate broker(s) and escrow agent(s) are hereby instructed to return all
    instruments and funds to the parties depositing them. _____
    _____
    _____
    _____
    _____
    _____
    _____
    _____

I agree to this notice and instructions.

Date:_____, 20_____, at _____, California

Signature:_____

Signature:_____

RECEIPT AND CONSENT TO CANCELLATION

**I acknowledge receipt of a signed copy of this notice, and agree to this
cancellation and instructions.**

Date:_____, 20_____, at _____, California

Signature:_____

Signature:_____

FORM 183   09-96   ©2006 **first tuesday**, P.O. BOX 20069, RIVERSIDE, CA 92516 (800) 794-0494

buyer are given the written right to cancel if the approval is not forthcoming, although closing is contingent on recording the loan.

The FHA fails to approve the development project for mortgage insurance. As an alternative, the buyer obtains financing for the project elsewhere and notifies the seller he *waives* the FHA-approval contingency. [See Form 182]

On receipt of the buyer's notice of waiver of the FHA further-approval contingency, the seller hands escrow a notice of cancellation and refuses to close escrow. The seller claims the failure to obtain FHA approval excuses the seller's performance as he did not waive his right to an FHA approval.

Can the seller enforce his cancellation of the purchase agreement and escrow instructions when the buyer's application for FHA approval was rejected?

Yes! Here, the FHA approval benefits both the carryback seller and the buyer. Thus, one or the other can cancel the transaction on the failure of the FHA approving the project since the contingency provision did not note who had the right to waive the provision or cancel on failure of the event to occur. Thus, each party who benefits from the inclusion of a contingency provision has the power to exercise the right of cancellation.

The buyer benefits under the contingency since FHA insurance will induce a lender to make a construction loan so he can fund the project.

However, the seller also benefits. An FHA-approved and insured project is additional security (protection) and provides a reduced risk of loss for his subordinated carryback trust deed note.

Thus, the contingency was included for the **mutual benefit** of both the buyer and seller, and cannot be waived — except by mutual consent — and either the buyer or seller may cancel on failure of the buyer to obtain FHA approval. [**Spangler** v. **Castello** (1956) 147 CA2d 49]

Waiver implied by conduct

When a buyer's **conduct** leads a seller to believe a contingency benefitting the buyer has been waived and the seller then relies on the buyer's indications by taking steps to complete his performance under the purchase agreement, the contingency is deemed to have been *waived*.

For example, a buyer enters into a purchase agreement with a builder to buy a lot on which the builder will construct a single-family residence (SFR) for the buyer. The purchase agreement contains a provision conditioning the close of escrow on the sale of the buyer's current residence, an *event-occurrence contingency provision*.

However, the buyer does not want to market his current residence for sale and locate a buyer until just before the completion of construction, as he has no other place to live.

The buyer instructs the builder to begin construction based on plans and specifications approved by the buyer for the new home. During construction, the buyer continually reviews the progress of the construction with the builder. Also, the buyer orders changes in the plans and specifications during construction, with which the builder complies. The buyer never tells the builder to stop construction, nor does he advise the builder his current residence has not yet been sold.

On completion of construction, the builder makes a demand on the buyer to fund and close escrow.

The buyer then cancels the purchase agreement and refuses to perform. The buyer claims the contingency provision calling for the sale of other property has not been satisfied, which triggers his right to cancel since the sale of the current residence has not occurred.

The builder claims the buyer's conduct constituted a *waiver* of the contingency, which now requires the buyer to perform.

WAIVER OF CONTINGENCY

DATE:_____, 20_____, at _____, California

TO: _____

Items left blank or unchecked are not applicable.

FACTS:

This waiver pertains to contingencies in the following contract:

☐ Purchase agreement

☐ Exchange agreement

☐ Counteroffer

☐ Escrow

Dated _____, 20_____, at _____, California

Entered into between: _____

And_____

Regarding real estate referred to as: _____

_____

_____

_____

AGREEMENT:

The undersigned hereby waives the following contingency: _____

_____

_____

_____

_____

_____

_____

_____

_____

_____

_____

_____

_____

_____

_____

I agree to perform the agreement on its remaining terms and conditions.

Date:_____, 20_____

Signature:_____

Signature:_____

RECEIPT OF WAIVER:

I acknowledge receipt of a copy of this waiver.

Date:_____, 20_____

Signature:_____

Signature:_____

FORM 182   09-96   ©2006 **first tuesday**, P.O. BOX 20069, RIVERSIDE, CA 92516 (800) 794-0494

Here, the buyer, by his conduct in changing the construction specifications and remaining silent concerning the lack of activity on the sale of his current residence during his inspections into the progress of construction, *reasonably induced* the builder into believing the "sale-of-other property" contingency had been considered by the buyer to be waived. Thus, the buyer's failure to close the transaction was a breach of the purchase agreement since the power to exercise the right of cancellation authorized by the sale-of-other property contingency provision no longer existed after the waiver. [**Noel** v. **Dumont Builders, Inc.** (1960) 178 CA2d 691]

Satisfaction by occurrence or approval

Events or **conditions** identified in contingency provisions, which if not forthcoming allow the transaction to be terminated, fall into two categories:

- those which are satisfied by *occurrence*, consisting of event-occurrence contingency provisions which are dependent on the existence, completion or outcome of an activity or event for their elimination; and

- those satisfied by *approval*, consisting of further-approval and personal-satisfaction contingency provisions calling for the receipt and review of information, data, documents and reports as the conditions to be approved, waived or disapproved by others or by the person authorized to terminate the transaction.

Event-occurrence contingencies

Event-occurrence contingency provisions address the **occurrence** of activities and events, such as:

- the sale or acquisition of other property or the cancellation of a prior sale;

- the recording (or approving) of a lot split or subdivision map;

- rezoning;

- the issuance of a use permit or a variance;

- the approval of building permits;

- the issuance of subdivision reports;

- the documentation from off-record spouses;

- the availability of utilities;

- the availability of hazard/fire insurance;

- the elimination of title conditions, or the release of encumbrances, such as liens or leases;

- building permit compliance;

- providing warranties on appliances;

- a loan commitment;

- the recording of a loan; and

- the deposit of equity financing funds for the down payment.

Further-approval contingencies

Further-approval contingency provisions address the right of a party to the purchase agreement or a third party to cancel the transaction should they disapprove or find the following unacceptable:

- disclosures and inspection reports concerning the physical integrity and natural and environmental hazards of the property sold;

- due diligence investigative reports;

- title reports;

- leases and estoppel certificates;

- rent control restrictions;

- service contracts;

- operating income and expense statements;

- the financial suitability of a carryback note;

- credit reports;

- appraisals;

- tax aspects;

- surveys;

- utilities, well water and sewage conditions;

- use feasibility reports;

- engineering reports on land use;

- existing plans and specifications for building;

- ingress and egress;

- loan commitments; and

- the availability of equity financing.

The buyer or seller with the right to cancel based on a further-approval contingency has a duty to fairly evaluate the condition to be approved or disapproved prior to canceling the transaction, called *acting in good faith*.

The buyer or seller who tries to terminate a purchase agreement under a right-to-cancel contingency without first acting to satisfy the contingency would be exercising an unfair advantage since to do so would allow them to terminate the transaction "at will," simply because a contingency existed in their agreement.

Personal-satisfaction contingencies

A personal-satisfaction contingency allows the buyer or seller to avoid performance of the purchase agreement if they are not personally satisfied with an aspect of the transaction referenced in the contingency provision.

Personal-satisfaction contingencies are identical to further-approval contingencies, except the buyer or seller is the one who approves or disapproves the subject matter of the contingency — **not a third party**.

Since the personal-satisfaction contingencies are essentially the same as the further-approval contingencies, they are judged by the same reasonableness standard when used to cancel a transaction.

Thus, a buyer or seller must have a reasonable basis for disapproving a personal-satisfaction contingency before a cancellation of the agreement is permitted.

Approval by waiver

The objective of a buyer's agent when he includes a contingency provision in a purchase agreement for the benefit of his buyer is to provide the buyer with the ability to cancel the transaction should the **event** fail to occur or the **condition** be disapproved.

If the contingency is to be eliminated by approval (waiver) or expiration of the right to cancel, or exercised by cancellation of the purchase agreement prior to the date scheduled for the close of escrow, the buyer is to act by giving the **appropriate notice** to the seller as called for in the purchase agreement.

If the condition reviewed is acceptable or the event occurs, the buyer's agent may be required by the wording of the provision to prepare a **notice of waiver** to eliminate the contingency. It is then signed by the buyer and handed to the seller, escrow or the seller's agent, as called for in the contingency provision. [See Form 182]

The buyer may also *waive* the right to cancel and, while neither approving nor disapproving the situation, *eliminate* the contingency provision as called for in the purchase agreement. Here, the buyer's agent uses the same notice of waiver form used for an unequivocal approval, if the buyer is required by the purchase agreement to notify the seller of the buyer's intention not to cancel, but to continue with the further performance and closing of the transaction. [See Form 182]

Chapter 42

Cancellation excuses further performance

This chapter reviews the conduct of a buyer or seller under a contingency provision in a purchase agreement which cancels their transaction and excuses any further performance of the agreement.

Exercising the option to terminate

Consider a seller who has agreed to carry back a note which is secured by a second trust deed junior to the existing trust deed note the buyer is to assume. The purchase agreement entered into with the buyer contains a **further-approval contingency provision** which grants the right to cancel the transaction to:

- the seller if the buyer's creditworthiness is unacceptable to the seller [See **first tuesday** Form 150 §8.5]; and

- both the buyer and the seller if either one disapproves of the existing trust deed lender's terms for an assumption of the loan by the buyer should the terms exceed the loan parameters agreed to in the purchase agreement. [See **first tuesday** Form 150 §§8.6 and 10.3]

On the seller's receipt of the buyer's credit application form, the listing agent orders and receives a report on the buyer's creditworthiness from a credit reporting agency.

The seller, on review of the information with his agent, expresses concern about the buyer's payment history. The listing agent asks the buyer for more information regarding the buyer's income and net worth. Specifically, the agent asks for a **balance sheet** listing assets and liabilities and an end-of-year **financial statement** on the buyer's income and expenses for the past two calendar years.

The buyer promptly supplies the additional financial data. Meanwhile, the listing agent learns the buyer is going to use a line of credit at a bank to finance the down payment called for in the purchase agreement. As this informa-tion may affect the carryback seller's decision to exercise his right to cancel the transaction under the credit approval contingency, the listing agent relays the information to the seller.

With all the relevant credit information readily available and known to the listing agent now in the hands of the seller, the seller determines he has *justification* for exercising his option to terminate the purchase agreement transaction and cancel escrow. However, the seller has not yet decided what to do about allowing the transaction to continue.

The listing agent is mindful of the upcoming expiration date of the seller's right to cancel and of his duty to protect the interests of the seller. Seeing his client's inaction, the agent advises the seller that if he does nothing to cancel by the expiration of his right he will have lost his ability to be *excused* from completing the transaction, whether or not the buyer's credit is acceptable. The seller understands he must serve a notice of cancellation on the buyer before the expiration date set in the contingency provision, unless he intends to let the period for cancellation expire and proceed to close escrow.

On the expiration date of the seller's right to cancel, he decides to do nothing. The seller is willing to undertake the additional risks, including the possible need to foreclose, presented by the buyer's insufficient creditworthiness.

In the meantime, the lender has processed the buyer's application to assume the loan and forwarded assumption documents to escrow for the buyer to sign and return. The terms for an assumption demanded by the lender include a modification of the interest rate, a new amortization schedule for payments and a due date not previously included in the note. However, these terms exceed and are more financially burdensome than the loan assumption parameters agreed to in the purchase agreement.

The buyer promptly signs the loan documents and returns them to escrow, together with the assumption fee demanded by the lender. Thus, the buyer, by conduct inconsistent with his right to cancel granted him by the loan assumption contingency provision, has *waived* his right to cancel the transaction. The buyer now no longer has the authority to terminate the purchase agreement for failure of the terms for an assumption to fall within the parameters agreed to in the purchase agreement. [See **first tuesday** Form 150 §10.3]

Conversely, the seller, on learning that the terms for assumption and modification of the existing first trust deed note exceeded the parameters of the loan assumption terms agreed to in the purchase agreement, has his listing agent prepare a notice of cancellation to terminate the transaction and escrow. The notice is immediately signed by the seller and delivered to the buyer and escrow.

Here, the risks of loss presented by the loan modification accompanying the assumption agreement is greater than the risks presented by the terms agreed to in the purchase agreement. Thus, the seller has a valid reason for refusing to subordinate to terms which would put his carryback note at a greater risk of loss of his security than agreed.

The seller's cancellation now allows the seller (as well as the buyer) to avoid any *further performance* of the purchase agreement or escrow since all obligations to close escrow have been *excused*.

An authorized unilateral cancellation

Cancellation of a real estate purchase agreement and escrow is due either to a *breach* of the agreement by the other party or the *failure* of an event to occur or a condition to be approved as called for in a contingency provision. The act of canceling is a *unilateral agreement* since the cancellation of the purchase agreement is undertaken by one person only. Cancellation **does away with** whatever remains to be performed under the purchase agreement, called *termination of the contract.*

Terminated is the right to buy or sell the property and close escrow by enforcing the further performance of the agreement. Thus, a cancellation affects the future enforcement of the agreement from the moment of cancellation. However, the cancellation of a purchase agreement does not affect the legal consequences and liabilities for activities and events which preceded the cancellation.

Conversely, *rescission* of either an unexecuted purchase agreement (escrow has not yet closed) or of a completed real estate transaction (escrow has closed) is a *bilateral agreement* in which the buyer and seller **retroactively annul** the purchase agreement as of the moment it was entered into by the buyer and seller, not later when the transaction is rescinded.

While a **cancellation** merely brings a purchase agreement to a standstill, a **rescission** returns the buyer and seller to their respective positions **prior to entering into** the purchase agreement, as though they had never agreed to the transaction. The retroactive return to their former, pre-contract positions is called *restoration.*

Both the buyer and seller enter into a rescission agreement, and the **restoration** of the buyer and seller to their pre-contract positions eliminates all claims they may have had against each other for conduct which occurred in performance of the purchase agreement before it was rescinded. A rescission is voluntarily accomplished as part of a mutual agreement to eliminate the purchase agreement, called a *release and waiver agreement.*

Distinguished from a cancellation of the purchase agreement is the unilateral or mutual cancellation of only the **escrow instructions**, without including any reference to cancellation of the purchase agreement. Often, due to a dispute or failure of a contingency, escrow will not close. Here, escrow will issue instructions calling for the return of funds and documents to the party who deposited them in escrow.

These cancellation-of-escrow instructions, signed by both the buyer and seller, need not also call for a cancellation of the purchase agreement. If the purchase agreement is not also canceled, the cancellation instructions handed escrow do not interfere with any rights the parties may have to enforce the purchase agreement. Escrow instructions are a separate contract from the purchase agreement.

The purchase agreement remains intact to be enforced to buy, sell or recover money losses. [Calif. Civil Code §1057.3(e)]

Cancellation for a valid reason

A seller or buyer who refuses to hand escrow the instruments (funds and documents) needed to close the transaction or otherwise comply with the escrow instructions has breached the agreement, unless his nonperformance is *excused*.

Nonperformance is **excused**, and the refusal to act is not a breach of the purchase agreement, if:

- a contingency provision exists authorizing the buyer or seller or the person benefitting from the contingency to terminate the purchase agreement on the failure of an event to occur or on disapproval of data, information, documents or reports;

- the event fails to occur or the condition reviewed is disapproved; and

- the person authorized or benefiting from the contingency provision acts to terminate the agreement by delivering a notice of cancellation prior to the expiration of his right to cancel.

When a **valid reason** exists which triggers the buyer's or seller's right to *exercise* their option to cancel, and they choose not to serve a notice of cancellation on the other party, their option to be *excused* from further enforcement **expires**.

Conduct less than disapproval

Consider a buyer who has entered into a purchase agreement and later receives a property operating cost sheet from the seller for his review and approval, called an *income and expense statement* or an *Annual Property Operating Data* (APOD) sheet. Receipt commences a **period of review** by the buyer to determine whether to exercise his right of disapproval and cancellation of the purchase agreement under a contingency provision. [See **first tuesday** Form 159 §11]

The data tends to confirm the general information received by the buyer before making the offer. However, the breadth and depth of the information seems inadequate for a large, long-term investment. Thus, the seller is asked by the buyer's agent to supply additional data and information, including access to all supporting documentation regarding the property's operating history. [See **first tuesday** Form 159 §§11.1, 11.2 and 11.8]

The seller claims the information he has already handed over sufficiently discloses the property's operating history and the buyer's request for more data and documents constitutes a disapproval of the information and acts as a cancellation. Thus, the seller says the deal is dead.

Has the buyer, by seeking additional information, disapproved of the condition of the income and expenses, and thus exercised his right to terminate the agreement?

No! The buyer's request for additional data on the property's operations is an expression of concern, not a disapproval. Implicit in a request for more information is the notion that a decision of any type has not yet been made.

Further, the seller has not fulfilled his obligation to deliver sufficient information to allow the buyer to complete his review and make an informed decision about the acceptability of the property's operations.

Before an agreement is terminated by a buyer under a contingency provision, the buyer's conduct must rise to the level of an *unequivocal disapproval* of the condition presented by the data, information, documents and reports supplied by the seller.

To accomplish a termination of the purchase agreement, the buyer must either deliver a notice of cancellation, as called for to exercise the right granted to terminate the agreement, or otherwise communicate an *unequivocal rejection* of the disclosed condition to the seller.

Any inadequacy of information perceived by the buyer may result in the buyer's inquiry into the apparent failure or possible unacceptability of the conditions disclosed. A request for more information is to be complied with by the seller as his obligation under the contingency provision.

If the seller does not comply with a reasonable request for more information made in good faith by the buyer to assist the buyer in the decision making process of approval or disapproval of the condition under review, the seller has failed to meet his obligation agreed to in the contingency provision to hand over data, information, documents and reports. Thus, the seller has **defaulted** on his obligations, a *breach* which excuses the buyer's further performance until the seller complies with the requests. Further, the seller's breach of the provision allows the buyer to either cancel the agreement or pursue enforcement by a *specific performance* suit.

Post-cancellation waiver attempt

Consider a prospective buyer of nonresidential property who includes a further-approval contingency in his purchase agreement offer calling for his approval of a survey to be furnished by the seller. The seller accepts the offer and a survey is conducted. The surveyor's observations are delivered to the buyer as agreed in the contingency provision. On the buyer's review of the survey and accompanying report, the buyer discovers the location of structures does not conform to building permits. Thus, the buyer has a reasonable basis for exercising his right to cancel the transaction under the contingency provision.

However, the buyer's agent does not prepare a notice of cancellation form for the buyer to sign and deliver to the seller as required by the purchase agreement for a termination of the transaction. Instead, the buyer advises the seller of his disapproval of the survey in letter form. However, the buyer does not state he is canceling the transaction due to his disapproval.

The seller does not respond to the buyer's disapproval letter in an effort by the seller to work out the discrepancies found in the survey and resolve the differences by an approval of the survey or a waiver of the contingency.

Prior to the date originally scheduled for escrow to close, the buyer's agent prepares a notice of waiver of the further-approval contingency which the buyer signs. On the seller's receipt of the notice of waiver, the seller has escrow prepare unilateral cancellation instructions which the seller signs and hands escrow. The buyer then demands a conveyance of the property as agreed in the purchase agreement, which the seller rejects.

The seller claims the letter disapproving the survey *terminated* the transaction and *excused* the seller (and the buyer) from further performing on the purchase agreement or escrow.

The buyer believes his communication did not cancel the transaction, but merely disapproved of the survey without exercising the contingency provision which has now been waived and no longer affects the enforceability of the purchase agreement.

Here, the buyer **unequivocally disapproved** the conditions disclosed by the survey. As a result, his rejection of the survey by the disapproval was itself an *exercise* of the buyer's right under the contingency provision to terminate the purchase agreement and escrow, as though he had signed a notice of cancellation and delivered it to the seller. Thus, on disapproval of the survey, the buyer terminated the purchase agreement and is left without any contract rights with which he may later attempt to waive the right to cancel and close escrow. [**Beverly Way Associates** v. **Barham** (1990) 226 CA3d 49]

Chapter
43
<h1 style="text-align:right">Time to Perform</h1>

This chapter looks into the enforceability of one person's right to cancel a transaction when the other person fails to perform by an appointed date.

Default and cancellation

The short, seemingly harmless time-is-of-the-essence provision stands alone amongst the boilerplate provisions of some, but not all, stock purchase agreement forms used to buy and sell real estate in California. By its plain words, the existence of a time-essence provision **gives notice** to the buyer and seller that their compliance by the date scheduled for an event to occur or a condition to be met as called for in the purchase agreement or escrow instructions is **essential to the continuation** of the transaction.

Thus, the bargain built into the purchase agreement by the presence of the time-essence provision gives the buyer or seller the right to **immediately cancel** the transaction on the failure of an event to occur or the other person to approve a condition by the appointed date. By virtue of the multiple number of tasks a typical buyer undertakes to close a transaction, contrasted with the very few tasks imposed on a seller to close, the time-essence clause "stacks the odds" of losing a transaction against the buyer, even though the buyer and all the third parties involved on their behalf may have acted with diligence at all times.

Further, for a vast majority of agents who work diligently to clear conditions and close a transaction, the time-essence clause places a **risk of cancellation** on a transaction which is not helpful. Foreseeable delays in closing a transaction exist in all real estate sales. Worse yet, the time-essence clause has, over the years, consistently demonstrated an ability to **produce litigation** over rights to money or ownership which have been lost or forfeited by a cancellation that is typically initiated by the seller.

*Editor's note — **first tuesday** purchase agreement forms do not contain a time-essence clause. Instead, the purchase agreements authorize agents to extend performance dates by up to one month. [See **first tuesday** Form 150 §10.2]*

Purpose of the time-essence provision

The "common understanding" said to exist as the purpose for including a time-essence clause in a purchase agreement is to **protect the seller from delays** in the buyer's payment of the sales price. Delays "tie up" both the seller's ownership of the real estate and receipt of the net sales proceeds beyond the date or period fixed for the transfer of ownership.

Another less logical theory for enforcing appointed dates as deadlines for the occurrence of events or the approval of the conditions called for in agreements containing a time-essence clause is the purported inability of courts to estimate the compensation owed a seller for losses resulting from a delay in the close of escrow due to the buyer's failure to perform.

However, delays in closing of a few days or even a few weeks or more, while inconvenient, rarely cause any compensable loss of money, property value, rights or property for the person attempting to cancel due to the passing of a performance deadline. Typically, the cancellation by a seller is motivated not by time, but by greater profits to be had elsewhere, i.e., "money is of the essence."

Even if a money loss is incurred due to a delay in performance, the loss is usually sustained by the seller and is easily calculable. Seller losses typically consist of lost rental value (or carrying costs of the property) for the period beyond the appointed closing date to the actual date of closing. An infrequent exception which occurs and causes the seller an incalculable (and uncollectible) loss arises out of the seller's actions in different transactions, such as the seller's reliance on the closing of a sale (not his entry into the sale) to complete some other transaction.

As for the buyer, his losses on a seller's default usually arise out of a missed closing deadline which he needed to meet in order to receive tax benefits or a locked-in (low) interest rate loan.

Termination of rights

An effective **Notice of Cancellation** interferes with the completion of a transaction as initially envisioned by the buyer and seller at the time they entered into the purchase agreement and escrow instructions. On a proper cancellation, the person terminating the purchase agreement transaction **does not need to further perform** any act called for, including the close of escrow. Further, the transaction has been terminated and the obligations of both the buyer and seller to further perform no longer exist. [See **first tuesday** Form 183]

For example, the person who properly cancels a purchase agreement has the unfettered right:

- **in the case of a seller**, to retain ownership or resell the property to other buyers at a higher price; and

- **in the case of a buyer**, to keep his funds or use them to purchase other property on a better bargain.

These rights to act, free of purchase agreement and escrow obligations, are the very objectives met by canceling the purchase and escrow agreements. The alternative to canceling both agreements is an attempt to keep the transaction together by determining the additional time reasonably needed by the other person to perform as originally contemplated, and then granting an extension of time in which to do

so. Should the "grace period" of additional time be granted, and then expire without compliance, a cancellation for failure to then perform is most understandable by all involved, and enforceable. [**Fowler** v. **Ross** (1983) 142 CA3d 472]

Still, an effective cancellation by one person *forfeits the rights* held by the other to close the transaction and receive the benefits bargained for on entering into the purchase agreement. Further, on an effective cancellation, the agents, escrow, lender and title company are all adversely affected by the cancellation's ripple effects since they all lose the time and effort they invested to get the transaction closed.

For example, when a seller cancels, the buyer loses, by *forfeiture*, his contract right to become the owner of the property. Conversely, if the buyer cancels, the seller loses the right to receive funds and be relieved of the obligation of ownership. Thus, a cancellation by either the buyer or the seller, if proper and enforceable, is the "final moment" in the life of a purchase agreement and escrow. Cancellation spells the end to all expectations held by everyone directly or indirectly affiliated with the sale who would have benefitted by the closing of the transaction.

Editor's note — For simplicity's sake, the following discussion will mostly refer to the timing of a seller's cancellation. However, the discussion fully applies to a buyer's cancellation as well.

Cancellation factors

For a seller to successfully cancel an escrow based on the failure of an event to occur or a condition to be approved, the purchase agreement or escrow instructions should contain:

- a clear description of the **event** which is to occur or the **condition** to be approved;

- an appointed **date** or expiration of a time period by which the event or approval described is to occur; and

- a written provision stating in clear and unmistakable wording, understandable to the buyer, that the seller has the **right to cancel** the transaction as the consequence of a failure of the event or the approval to occur by the appointed date.

If provisions in the purchase agreement or escrow instructions meet all of the above criteria, then the seller will **only be allowed to cancel if**:

- the seller has **performed all acts which must precede**, by agreement or necessity, the event or approval triggering the cancellation (in other words, the seller cannot be in default);

- the event or approval **fails to occur** by the appointed date; and

- the seller performs or **stands ready, willing and able to perform** all other acts necessary on the part of the seller to close the transaction on the appointed date for the failed event or approval.

The notice given by the existence of the time-essence provision advises the buyer that his performance of the event which is to occur or be brought about by the date scheduled is **critical to the continuation** of the purchase agreement and escrow instructions. Thus, the time-essence provision sets the buyer's reasonable expectations of the consequences of his failure to perform, i.e., the risk that the seller may cancel the transaction and the buyer's right to buy the property will be forfeited.

However, the consequences of the failure of the buyer to perform or for an approval or event to occur depend upon the type of **time-related provision** contained in the purchase agreement and escrow instructions. The different provisions which might be included are:

- a **time-essence** provision, which gives the seller the right to cancel should the event

or approval of a condition called for not occur by an appointed date;

- a **seller-may-cancel** contingency provision, which authorizes the seller to cancel should the condition or event not occur, whether or not a time-essence clause exists;

- an **authorization-to-extend** provision, which grants the agents the power to extend performance dates up to 30 days (or other wording indicating an accommodation for delays), whether or not a time-essence clause or a seller-may-cancel clause exists [See **first tuesday** Form 150 §10.2]; and

- an **extension of time granted by the seller**, typically in supplemental escrow instructions, with wording imposing strict adherence to the new performance deadlines and authorizing the seller to cancel on expiration of the extension should the event or approval not be forthcoming.

Elements of a default

Before either a buyer or seller can effectively cancel a transaction, they must "place the other person in default." Thus, in order for a person to exercise the right to cancel, that person cannot also be in default themselves on the date scheduled for the other person's performance or the event to occur.

For the buyer or seller to place the other in default, three transactional facts must exist:

1. a **date crucial to the continuation** of the transaction must have passed;

2. the condition called for in the purchase agreement **did not occur** by the scheduled date; and

3. the person canceling must have **fully performed** all activities required of him in order for the other person to perform by the scheduled date, called *conditions*

precedent, and have performed or **be ready, willing and able to perform**, at the time of cancellation, all activities he was obligated to perform in order to close escrow, called *conditions concurrent*.

Was the cancellation timely

The **setting of a time** for an act or event to occur does not, by itself, automatically allow a purchase agreement transaction to be terminated by one person when the appointed date has passed and the other person has not yet performed.

To permit a cancellation immediately following the expiration of the appointed time for performance, the purchase agreement or escrow instructions must clearly state it is the intention of both parties that the failure by one or the other person to perform by the appointed day will subject his contract rights to forfeiture.

Thus, clear cut wording throughout the purchase and escrow documents must consistently manifest an intent to **make time for performance crucial** to the continued existence of the transaction. If not so worded, the appointed date has insufficient significance to justify instant cancellation.

For example, sometimes the only wording regarding any right to cancel a transaction appears in the escrow instructions. Escrows are nearly always instructed to close at any time after the date scheduled for closing if escrow is in a position to do so, provided escrow has not yet received instructions to cancel escrow and return documents and funds.

Thus, in this example, neither the purchase agreement nor the escrow instructions contain a clause stating "time is of the essence in this agreement." Further, no clear, unequivocal or unmistakable wording in any contingency provision shows an intent on the part of the buyer and seller to make time of the essence, such as

wording giving the seller or buyer the "right to cancel" on the failure of either the other person to perform a described activity or for an event to occur by a scheduled date.

Under these examples, which lack time-essence provisions, the time appointed for the delivery of such items as loan commitments, termite reports, funds for closing or clearance of encumbrances from title is merely a "target date" **preliminary to establishing the right to cancel**.

To **establish** the right to cancel when time is not stated or established in the purchase agreement or escrow instructions as crucial, the person in default must be given notice that the date set as the "new deadline" will be **strictly adhered to**. Further, the person in default must be given a realistic opportunity (period of time) after being given a notice to perform before any cancellation would be effective. Continued nonperformance past the new deadline date will be treated as a **default** and escrow can be immediately canceled.

For example, a purchase agreement calls for a buyer to close escrow within 45 days after acceptance. No time-essence clause, cancellation provisions (other than the *implied right* to cancel exercisable on a failure of the other person to perform) or agent authorization to extend performance dates exists. [See **first tuesay** Form 150 §12.2]

The seller agrees with the buyer's request to extend the date of performance (closing) an additional 30 days during which the buyer is to complete his arrangements to close escrow. Two days after the extension expires, the seller cancels the transaction.

Is the seller's cancellation of the transaction effective?

Yes! The 30-day extension was a **reasonable amount of time** for the buyer to perform before the seller *exercised* his right to cancel. A further unilateral extension of time is not needed for the cancellation to be reasonable and effective. [Fowler, *supra*]

Now, consider an example of strict compliance with performance dates as "deadlines," after which the purchase agreement and escrow can be terminated by cancellation for failure of the described activity or event to take place. The **purchase agreement** contains a simple time-essence clause. Authority is not granted to the agents to extend performance dates should the appointed date for performance prove to be an inadequate amount of time for either the buyer or seller to complete or bring about all of their closing activities.

Consistent with the time-essence clause in the purchase agreement, **escrow instructions** provide for an interference with closing of the escrow after the date initially targeted for closing. The instructions authorized escrow to close at anytime after expiration of the escrow period, unless escrow received instructions calling for the return of documents and funds.

One day after the passing of the date scheduled for closing, the buyer cancels escrow. Twelve days later, the seller, using diligence at all times, is able to clear title and close. The seller challenges the buyer's cancellation as premature and ineffective, claiming the buyer is required to grant him the additional time needed to close escrow before the buyer can *forfeit the seller's right* to enforce the buyer's promise to purchase the property.

Is the seller entitled to the additional time he needs to close escrow?

No! The seller was **on notice** by the existence of the time-essence clause in the purchase agreement and the wording of the escrow instructions that the buyer had the right to cancel on failure of escrow to close by the date scheduled. No provision in any document expressed an intent which was contrary to the time-essence provision in the purchase agreement.

Thus, the buyer's cancellation, one day after the appointed closing date, was in accordance with the **intent stated** in the purchase agree-ment and escrow instructions, i.e., that timely performance was essential to the continuation of the agreement, and that escrow was authorized to return the money and instruments on the demand of either the buyer or seller should the closing not occur on or before the date set for closing. Thus, the buyer was not required to grant the additional time reasonably necessary for the seller to close the transaction. [**Ward** v. **Downey** (1950) 95 CA2d 680]

Intent in conflict with time-essence clause

Consider a sale under a purchase agreement (or escrow instructions) which contains a provision **authorizing the agents to extend** the time for performance of any act for a "period not to exceed one month." The purchase agreement also includes a boilerplate provision that "time is the essence of this agreement." Escrow is for a 60-day period, the end of which is the appointed date for closing the transaction. As usual, the escrow instructions state escrow may close at any time after the date scheduled for closing, unless instructions to the contrary have been received.

On the date scheduled for closing, escrow is not in a position to close due to the buyer's inability to immediately record his purchase-assist loan. The seller immediately cancels escrow in an attempt to terminate the transaction, claiming time was of the essence by agreement.

Can the seller cancel without giving an extension of time when both a time-essence and an authority-to-extend provision exist?

No! The bargain struck by the conflicting provisions controlling performance dates did not contemplate time for the occurrence of activities or events by their appointed dates to be so essential that the transaction could be canceled on the mere passing of the appointed date. The use of a purchase agreement (or escrow instructions) containing wording that "time is of the essence" does not allow for the forfeiture of contract rights on a failure to perform within the agreed time period when **other provisions exist expressing an intent contrary** to the time-essence provision.

When logically possible, courts ignore boilerplate time-essence clauses and enforce the original bargain, if no financial harm results from the delay.

Here, the purchase agreement (or escrow instructions) gave the agents the unconditional right to extend performance dates. Thus, being able to close by the date set for closing escrow could hardly be considered crucial to the continued viability of the transaction. Accordingly, the seller must give the buyer a **reasonable amount of time** to close escrow, i.e., the additional days needed for the agent to record the buyer's loan, before the buyer's failure to perform justified exercising any cancellation rights.

Editor's note — The fact the agents do not exercise the authority granted them to extend the time for performance is of no concern. It is the mere existence of the agents' unrestricted right to extend performance dates by up to 30 days which requires the person canceling to allow the other person a reasonable, additional time period in which to perform before cancellation can occur.

Default needed to justify cancellation

Before a buyer or seller may consider canceling a transaction, the other person must have *defaulted* on his completion of an activity or an event has failed to occur.

For example, a seller cancels a 30-day escrow the day after the date it is scheduled to close. The purchase agreement granted the agents authorization to extend performance dates, including the date for closing, up to 30 days. [See **first tuesday** Form 150 §10.2]

Thirty-three days later, for a total of 63 days from the date of acceptance, the buyer, using diligence in the pursuit of a loan, obtains final loan approval and has all the funds needed to close escrow.

Is the seller's cancellation effective without first giving an extension of additional time for closing when the buyer has not performed by the date scheduled for the close of escrow?

No! The buyer is not yet in default. Sixty-three days is a reasonable period of time for the buyer to obtain the purchase-assist mortgage funds agreed to in the purchase agreement. Most importantly for the buyer and agents, time for closing was not made crucial to the continuation of the agreement. Thus, a reasonable period of time must pass before the buyer is in default. Only when the buyer is in default may the seller *exercise* his right to cancel. [**Henry** v. **Sharma** (1984) 154 CA3d 665]

Now, consider an agent who prepares a purchase agreement and inadvertently fails to set a fixed time period for the opening of escrow. However, the purchase agreement does state an appointed date for closing escrow as 60 days from the date the purchase agreement was entered into.

The buyer fails to sign and return escrow instructions to open escrow.

The seller cancels the transaction 12 days after the date escrow was scheduled to close.

Was the buyer in default at the time of cancellation?

Yes! The buyer was in default for his failure to sign and return escrow instructions. The buyer had an obligation to open escrow within an unstated period of time. Since the time for opening escrow was not agreed to, a **reasonable period of time** for opening escrow is allowed.

A reasonable period for opening escrow is a date sufficiently in advance of the date set for the close of escrow to give escrow enough time to perform its tasks by the date scheduled for closing. The cancellation 12 days after the closing date was effective to terminate the transaction since a reasonable period for the buyer to open escrow ended well before the scheduled closing date. The buyer, having failed to open escrow before the closing date, was in default on the closing date. Thus, the buyer lost his right to buy the property since he did not cure the default by opening escrow before the seller canceled. [**Consolidated World Investments, Inc.** v. **Lido Preferred Ltd.** (1992) 9 CA4th 373]

However, a one day delay by a buyer before signing and delivering instructions to open escrow does not allow a (remorseful) seller to cancel the transaction and avoid closing escrow. Reasonably, a **one day delay in opening escrow** is not a default at all, even when time is unequivocally declared to be of the essence in the purchase agreement.

To cancel you must first perform

Consider a seller who wants to cancel a transaction since the buyer is in default under the purchase agreement or escrow instructions. Before the seller may cancel, the seller must:

- perform all acts and cause all events to occur which, by agreement or necessity, are the seller's obligation and **must occur before** the buyer becomes obligated to perform or can perform, called *conditions precedent*, such as delivering disclosures, reports, etc., or completing repairs requiring the buyer's approval;

- fully perform all activities and obligations imposed on the seller which are to **occur at the same time** as the buyer's performance, without concern for whether the buyer has performed, called *conditions concurrent*, such as handing escrow a grant deed and all other information and items required of the seller for escrow to clear title and close; and

- perform or **demonstrate he can perform** all other activities or bring about events

which are the obligation of the seller for closing the transaction, whether or not the buyer ever performs, called *conditions subsequent*, such as meeting any requirements of the buyer's lender for repairs or clearances.

Thus, while the buyer may have failed to perform by the time agreed, the seller may not cancel until the seller has performed or stands ready, willing and able to perform under the above three conditions (precedent, concurrent and subsequent), conditions which exist in most purchase agreements and escrow instructions.

When failure to fund is not a default

On the date set for the close of escrow, buyers often have not deposited their down payment funds into escrow as called for in the purchase agreement and escrow instructions. When the deposit of closing funds or the lender's wire of loan funds does not occur as scheduled, the buyer clearly has not yet performed his obligation to close escrow. However, the failure to fund does not necessarily mean the buyer is in default.

The question which arises for a seller who is attempting to cancel when time has been established as essential and the buyer or the buyer's lender has not delivered closing funds, is whether the buyer is either in **default** or is **not yet obligated** to deposit funds.

Escrow, as a matter of custom, will not call for a wire of closing funds from the mortgage lender or the buyer until **escrow is in a position to close**. Escrows, as an entirely practical matter, do not want closing funds sitting in an escrow which is not yet ready to close.

Specifically, before escrow calls for closing funds, the seller must have already fully performed by providing documents (deeds, releases, reconveyances, title clearances, etc.) so the conveyance of title can be insured and property clearances, prorates and adjustments can be delivered and accounted for as called for in the escrow instructions. If the seller has not delivered instruments so escrow can be in a position to close by the date scheduled for closing, escrow will not make a demand on the buyer (or lender) for funds. The deposit of closing funds would be premature since escrow cannot yet close.

Further, when the closing is contingent on the buyer recording a purchase-assist loan, escrow, as a matter of *commercial necessity,* does not call for the buyer's funds until the lender is ready to fund.

Thus, the buyer has no obligation to deposit any money into escrow and is not in default until escrow has received the lender's documents and requests the buyer's funds, which the buyer **then fails to deliver**. Until the buyer is in default due to a failure to timely respond to escrow's request for funds, any attempt by the seller to cancel is premature and ineffective.

Escrow instructions usually state the buyer is to deposit funds for use by escrow **provided the seller has performed**. Thus, the obligation of the buyer to deposit closing funds is subject to the seller first performing, called a *condition precedent* to the buyer's performance. Therefore, the buyer's "failure" to deposit funds before escrow is in a position to close is *excused*. The seller has failed to hand escrow documents and information sufficiently in advance of the scheduled closing date for escrow to close by the appointed date. [See **first tuesday** Form 150 §12.2]

Consider a seller who is unable to convey title to a buyer and deliver a title insurance policy by the closing date called for in the purchase agreement and escrow instructions. The title company cannot issue a policy as ordered due to encumbrances affecting title, such as abstracts, trust deeds, leases, tax liens, assessments, etc., which have not been released and the amounts needed for discharge and payoff have not yet been determined.

Here, the time for closing has arrived and the seller cannot deliver a marketable title as agreed. Thus, until the seller obtains title insurance for his deed, the buyer is not in default for not yet depositing his funds.

Cancellation right waived by conduct

Even when the date scheduled for a buyer or seller to perform is established as crucial, thus allowing one person to immediately cancel on the other's default, **inconsistent conduct** by the person entitled to cancel constitutes a *waiver* of his right to cancel. Once the right to immediately cancel has been waived, the person who failed to perform by the agreed deadline is **no longer in default**. Until the person who failed to perform is placed in default again, the right to cancel cannot be exercised.

For example, the date set for escrow to close arrives. The seller has not yet handed escrow (or the buyer) clearances which are required before escrow may close.

A few days after escrow is scheduled to close, the seller deposits the clearances with escrow. The buyer then deposits his closing funds on a call from escrow.

Two days later, the seller cancels escrow, claiming the buyer was in default since he failed to deposit his funds by the appointed date.

Here, the cancellation is ineffective and the buyer is entitled to close escrow. The seller *waived his right* to cancel, time having been of the essence, by conducting himself without concern for the passing of the appointed date for closing. The seller failed to deliver up documents or information sufficiently in advance for escrow to meet the deadline. [**Katemis** v. **Westerlind** (1953) 120 CA2d 537]

However, a **waiver by inaction** does not occur simply because a person's right to cancel the transaction is not immediately exercised on the failure of the other person to perform or an event to occur. **Affirmative conduct must occur** by the person entitled to cancel, not just mere inaction, before the right to cancel under a time-essence situation is waived.

After a waiver of a date scheduled for approval of a condition or occurrence of an event, time must be **reinstated as crucial** to the continuance of the transaction, or a reasonable, additional period of time must have passed after waiver of the right to cancel, before the transaction can be canceled.

Time is best reinstated as essential to the continuation of the transaction by notifying the person who needs to perform that he must perform by the end of an additional period of time, set with sufficient duration as is needed to provide him with a realistic opportunity to perform.

If performance is not forthcoming during the additional period of time, the transaction may be promptly canceled since *strict compliance* with the extension is now enforceable.

Chapter 44

Cancellation, release and waiver

This chapter discusses the use of cancellation agreements containing release and waiver of rights provisions as a method of eliminating future liability exposure in disputes arising out of listings and purchase agreements.

Known and unknown claims

The vocation of providing real estate brokerage services to members of the public is, in the long run, a rewarding profession. Inevitably, however, the occupational hazard of a dispute with a client or another party to a transaction will eventually surface. Disputes arise even though the licensed brokers and sales agents have fulfilled all of their agency duties, acted diligently and cooperated fully with the client and other parties.

Unless the conflict with the client or other party is resolved at the earliest possible moment, the continuing aggravation will take a toll on the agent's time and effort, and possibly on his cash reserves as well.

Also, disputes with a client tend to make the continued representation of the client less effective. At some point in an extended dispute, the broker or agent may well be rendered incapable of logically making normal discretionary decisions in the course of fulfilling agency obligations owed the client.

The unreasonable interference of an uncompromising client, who either claims to have all the right answers or is listening to other advisors who are not privy to the circumstances surrounding the dispute, creates a stressful condition which can easily lead to errors in an agent's judgment.

As always, disputes need to be put to rest quickly, lest they turn into correspondence with attorneys or worse, litigation. When a settlement is not promptly worked out and the agency relationship clarified so the employment can continue on sound footing, the relationship should be terminated.

To terminate an agency relationship due to a dispute, a *release and waiver* must be entered into by all concerned to put an end to an otherwise unresolvable disagreement.

Agency disputes arise during one of three periods in the representation of a client, i.e.:

- the **marketing period** beginning on the agent's entry into an authorization to sell, locate, finance, lease or manage a property and ending on the client's entry into an agreement to sell, buy, finance or lease the property in question;

- the **escrow period** beginning on the client's entry into a purchase agreement, loan agreement or lease and ending on the close of escrow, the transfer of possession or the failure of the transaction to close; or

- the **post-closing period** following the closing of the purchase agreement, loan or lease transaction.

Marketing period disputes

Misunderstandings sometimes occur regarding the extent of the marketing services a client expects out of his broker and the broker's agents. The client's extraordinary expectations might have existed before entering into the employment agreement or have come about when the agent explained what will be done to market or locate property. Also, outside influences during the marketing period, by others or by a change in the real estate market, may cause the client to believe the agent should be doing more.

Conversely, a seller may become uncooperative in the marketing of the property or simply refuse to hand over property information needed by the listing agent to succeed in his effort to locate a buyer willing to make an offer to buy the property.

For example, a listing agent's **marketing efforts** to present the current status and integrity of a property to prospective buyers, such as providing home inspection reports, natural hazard disclosures, common interest development documents, local ordinance compliances, property operating expense sheets and rental income data, are interfered with when the **seller refuses to cooperate** or make them available. Without proper disclosures, prospective buyers cannot readily, if ever, ascertain the value of the property and distinguish it from other properties they are considering.

To resolve disputes when a compromise has been attempted and is unattainable, it becomes prudent to consider terminating the agency. If the client decides to unilaterally withdraw the property from the market, cancel the employment (listing/management) or continue to interfere in the sales effort, the client owes the broker the fee called for in the employment agreement. Of course, the listing agent must have diligently performed the brokerage services owed the seller under the listing, whether or not a buyer has been found.

Here, a cancellation agreement form should be prepared and entered into to end the relationship forever. The broker might agree to a mutual cancellation of the listing in exchange for the client's payment of the brokerage fee. The consideration for cancellation ranges from payment of the entire fee to some lesser arrangement. For example, the client might agree to pay a fee should the client relist the property with another broker or sell the property, lease it, etc., during a fixed period of months after the mutual cancellation of the listing. [See **first tuesday** Form 121]

Further, the broker, on entering into a cancellation, release and waiver agreement, eliminates his exposure to future claims based on a purported failure of agency duties.

Escrow period disputes

After opening a sales escrow for the purchase of real estate, disputes which arise do so under two types of conditions. Either one may ultimately require the termination of relationships. One set of disputes is of the type classified as *agency disputes*. Agency disputes arise between the agent and his client after the client has entered into a purchase agreement. The agency, if the dispute cannot be resolved and the representation continued, is terminated in the same manner as the listing period disputes discussed in the previous section.

The other set of disputes is classified as *principal disputes*. They develop between the buyer and seller and result in a refusal of one or the other to act further to close escrow. The refusal to proceed with the transaction might be excused, justified or constitute a breach of the purchase agreement.

Negotiations to resolve the misunderstandings or differences and close escrow might not be successful. If the escrow dispute becomes unresolvable, the agents should consider recommending that the buyer and seller terminate the purchase agreement. At the same time the buyer and seller cancel the transaction, they should release each other from any claims they may have against one another, by entering into a *cancellation, release and waiver agreement*. [See **first tuesday** Form 181]

As for the agent's concern about his liability exposure for any type of claim the disgruntled buyer or seller may assert against each other or the broker, the cancellation, release and waiver agreement entered into by the buyer and seller also **releases everyone involved** in the transaction. Thus, any liability exposure the agents and client may have due to the transaction is eliminated.

Post-closing disputes

After closing a transaction, brokers and their agents are occasionally brought into *annoyance disputes* by buyers disgruntled over the condition of the property, its improvements, the neighborhood, hazards of the location, zoning, easements held by neighbors, fence locations, operating expenses, tenant problems, etc. The expectations of a buyer are always high, as with any new owner of property. The condition of a property is almost never as rosy as it appeared before taking possession.

Buyers, believing they have gotten less than they bargained for, often attempt to **shift responsibility** for payment of expenses they have incurred to cure typically insignificant obsolescence, deterioration, wear and tear or inadequacies in electrical or plumbing needs. Worse yet, they may seek to recover a portion of the purchase price on a claim the property value received was measurably less than the price they paid.

In context, the listing broker is not the guarantor of any obligation the seller may owe the buyer for defects. However, it usually is the broker who is the first person put upon by a disgruntled buyer to "cure the problem."

Brokers and agents often pay some of these claims to permanently remove themselves from the disputed purchase. However, on the first payment by anyone in a settlement to resolve a dispute in a closed transaction, the broker should demand a *release and waiver agreement*. Once the buyer has "raided the cookie jar," he may well be back for more. This agreement puts an end to it. [See **first tuesday** Form 540]

The documentation

A mutual **cancellation agreement**, which does not include a release of claims or a waiver of rights, merely serves to *terminate* any further activity under the existing agreement or agency relationship. Thus, all parties are *excused* from further performing since the agreement and relationship have been terminated.

In essence, the cancellation "does away with" the remainder of the purchase agreement that has not yet been performed. A cancellation, by itself, does not affect the responsibilities of the buyer, seller, brokers or agents, for their activities which proceeded the cancellation.

Conversely, a *rescission and restoration* agreement returns the parties to the respective positions they held before entering into the terminated agreement, more commonly called a *release and waiver of rights*.

A *release agreement*, signed by all parties to a transaction as part of a cancellation agreement, retroactively extinguishes all **known claims** in disputes the parties have between themselves. Thus, the release agreement is general in that it ends all liability between the parties for those claims **actually known** to the parties to exist in the dispute.

However, a **general release** does not affect unknown claims later uncovered. [Calif. Civil Code §1541]

Thus, a category of claims remain unresolved, i.e., those which might exist, come into existence or be later established and are unknown to the parties on entering into a general release, called *unknown and unsuspected claims*. To eliminate these unknown claims, a **waiver** of the right to later pursue these claims must be included with a general release and made part of the mutual cancellation agreement. [CC §1542]

A written, signed release agreement does not require new consideration to be paid for the cancellation, release and waiver to be enforceable as a bar to further claims. [CC §1541]

Waiving unknown claims

A *release* is the relinquishment of a known right. Rights or claims unknown at the time of a release are not extinguished by a general release agreement. [CC §1541]

To protect oneself from **unknown claims** and prevent further disputes, an agent must use a *release and waiver of rights agreement* to eliminate all future claims arising out of the canceled purchase agreement or agency relationship.

A **waiver of rights** to unknown claims bars recovery on later and different claims arising out of the same transaction or agency relationship.

A person involved in a real estate dispute may waive his right to sue on truly unknown claims he may have against an agent which exist in the transaction and later come to his attention. [**San Diego Hospice** v. **County of San Diego** (1995) 31 CA4th 1048]

For a client or party to a purchase agreement to waive their rights to assert unknown claims which later come to their attention, the person signing the waiver of rights must be aware of the legal consequences of what he is agreeing to in the waiver.

To meet this awareness test, the *waiver of rights agreement* should include copy from the statutory release law as a provision agreed to in the waiver agreement. [See **first tuesday** Form 540]

Chapter
45
The seller's breach

This chapter illustrates the conduct of a seller which constitutes a breach of the purchase agreement and imposes liability on the seller for any increase in property value, the buyer's expenses and interest on the amounts recovered.

Failure to act or timely act

On occasion, a buyer's agent in a real estate sales transaction will be confronted with conduct by the seller which interferes with the close of escrow. The seller's conduct is inconsistent with or contrary to those activities the seller is required to perform before escrow can close.

Examples of **seller interference** with a buyer's acquisition of property include the seller's failure to (timely):

- return escrow instructions;

- deliver closing documents;

- provide escrow with information on the existing lenders so payoff demands, beneficiary statements or assumption papers can be ordered on existing loans;

- deliver seller identification information for title insurance purposes;

- eliminate agreed-to defects and previously undisclosed property defects known by the seller and unacceptable to the buyer;

- arrange or permit inspection of the property by the buyer, appraiser, home inspector, city inspector, etc.; or

- close escrow.

Thus, the seller is not fulfilling the objectives of the purchase agreement he entered into with the buyer to **voluntarily perform** under the escrow instructions. As a result, the buyer is ei-

ther unable to proceed toward closing or has fully performed (or his further performance is excused due to a cancellation by the buyer), and escrow cannot close due to a failure on the part of the seller to act.

Typically, the seller's refusal or failure to timely act under the purchase agreement and close escrow arises during dramatic increases in the value of the type of property he has just agreed to sell to the buyer. Thus, a better bargain can be had by the seller with other buyers since the seller has either agreed to a below market price or the market value was or has risen dramatically above the price agreed to in the purchase agreement.

As a result, "seller remorse" has set in, manifested by his efforts to trigger a default by the buyer which will justify terminating the purchase agreement.

Faced with the failure of escrow to close, due to the seller's nonperformance or obstruction of the buyer's efforts to close escrow and the inability of the buyer and agents to induce the seller to **voluntarily close escrow**, the buyer must make a pivotal decision regarding his bargained-for ownership of the property.

The decisions available to the buyer, called *remedies,* when the seller breaches the purchase agreement or escrow instructions include:

- **abandoning the transaction** by entering into a mutual cancellation of the purchase agreement and escrow instructions with the seller, agreeing to do nothing further to enforce the right to purchase the property or seek a money recovery from the seller, other than a return of the buyer's good-faith deposit;

- **acquiring the property** by pursuing enforcement of the purchase agreement and escrow instructions;

- **pursuing the recovery of money** when the buyer **wants to acquire** the property but cannot now do so due to the seller's conveyance of the property for a measurably higher price to another person who was unaware of the pre-existing purchase rights held by the buyer; and

- **pursuing the recovery of money** when the buyer can, but **no longer wants to acquire** the property, and the value of the property was measurably higher on the date the seller canceled escrow than the price the buyer agreed to pay.

An unsuspecting buyer who acquires the ownership of real estate without actual knowledge or recorded notice (constructive knowledge) of a pre-existing enforceable purchase agreement held by another buyer regarding the same property is referred to as a *bona fide purchaser* (BFP). As a BFP, the buyer pays consideration for the acquisition of property and takes title without knowledge of a claim to the property held by the other buyer. [Calif. Civil Code §3395]

Economic motives

Market conditions surrounding a seller's refusal to voluntarily cooperate with a buyer and transfer property under a purchase agreement usually consist of:

- seller pricing power (due to too little inventory for too many prospective buyers);

- cyclically moderate to low mortgage interest rates; and

- a generally recognized trend in price increases, commonly referred to as a "hot (seller's) real estate market."

It is during these economic "boom" or "bubble" periods of fast upward movement in real estate prices that sellers often agree to sell property before checking out their property's value.

The failure to ascertain the value of the property before the seller enters into a purchase agreement sometimes results in his later discovery (prior to closing) that the sales price agreed to is significantly below the present worth of the property. It is then that the seller determines additional money can be had by simply canceling what is now viewed as a "bad bargain" and reselling the property to another buyer at a higher price.

The end game for all sellers of real estate is to net the most money possible on a sale under current market conditions. However, when a seller decides to cancel a sale so he can position himself to resell the property at the higher market value, he merely encourages the buyer to pursue the same end game for himself, i.e., the recovery of money from the seller equal to the increase in price received on a resale by the seller.

Thus, if the seller is pursued by the buyer for the difference in price, the seller will be unable to retain the financial advantage he sought to attain by breaching and reselling at a higher price.

Consider an owner of nonresidential real estate who lives out of the area. The absentee owner is solicited by a buyer's agent seeking to locate properties suitable for his buyer. The owner responds indicating he will sell the property, but does not know its value. He requests an indication of its value from the buyer's agent.

The owner is a sophisticated and intelligent individual capable of understanding that the buyer and the buyer's agent are his adversaries in negotiations.

After phone calls and correspondence exchanging information about the property, the buyer's agent states he does not want to express an opinion of value on someone else's property, but has shown his buyer **similar properties** offered at $200,000. The owner does not indicate what he believes the value of his property might be, but acknowledges he knows the market value of nonresidential property is on the rise.

The buyer's agent prepares a purchase agreement offer for a cash price of $250,000. The buyer signs the offer and it is faxed to the owner.

The owner accepts the offer and the buyer's agent promptly dictates escrow instructions, which the buyer signs and returns. The buyer, on receiving and reviewing the preliminary title report, advises escrow he will place the balance of the cash price into escrow when escrow calls for funds. The owner does not return escrow instructions or the deed for conveyance of the property.

The owner then visits the community where his property is located. For the first time, the owner inquires into the worth of his property by contacting some local agents. On his initial superficial inquiry, the owner finds that the property is worth considerably more than the price he has agreed to receive.

The owner quickly determines he has entered into an extremely bad bargain concerning the price the buyer has agreed to pay. Another buyer is located and a price of $750,000 is agreed to. Escrow is opened with the new buyer and closed immediately.

Meanwhile, the original buyer is involved in a futile attempt to close his escrow with the owner. When asked by escrow to sign and return the escrow instructions and the deed, the owner claims the agreement he entered into with the buyer was never a binding contract due to the buyer's **misrepresentation of the property's value** and the owner's reliance on the valuation to set the sales price. Thus, he explains, they have no deal.

The original buyer decides he no longer wants the property (or will not pursue acquiring it since the new buyer is a BFP).

Aware he has lost his ability to buy the property under the purchase agreement, the original buyer makes a demand on the owner for $500,000, the difference between the price agreed to and its worth on the owner's breach based on the price the seller received on the resale of the property.

The owner refuses to pay the demand claiming his refusal to close escrow at the agreed price was *justified* since the property's value was known to the buyer and the buyer's agent, but not to the owner. Thus, he claims, they took advantage of his ignorance of the property's true value, called *misrepresentation.*

Here, the owner owes the buyer the difference between the price agreed to with the buyer and the value of the property on the date the seller breached ($500,000).

Ordinarily, misrepresentation of a property's value by a prospective buyer and his agent does not, by itself, justify the owner's cancellation of the purchase agreement. Estimates of value made by prospective buyers and their agent's are usually mere expressions of their opinion, not facts to be relied upon by sellers since the buyer and the buyer's agent are **known adversaries** of any seller.

More importantly, the owner here was neither induced or persuaded by the buyer or the buyer's agent to forego an independent investigation into his property's value, nor was the owner in a situation where he could not reasonably undertake an investigation into value.

For a representation of value by the buyer or his agent to be deceitful, the representation made to the owner must be coupled with some other misfeasance, bad action or false representation. Further, the owner was neither gullible or ignorant, nor unable to protect and care for himself as against the buyer or agent who he claims took unconscionable advantage of his ignorance of the property's value. Thus, his reliance on their expressions of value to set an acceptable price did not justify his cancellation.

The owner should have taken the opportunity, as he later did, to retain a broker (and pay him a fee) to determine the value of the property before agreeing to accept a price. [**Kahn** v. **Lischner** (1954) 128 CA2d 480]

Recover money, not the property

A buyer who seeks to recover money from a breaching seller, in lieu of title to the property, does so based on **monetary claims** which must fall within three categories of money losses:

- *general damages*, being money **directly expended** in the transaction;

- *consequential or special damages*, being money **collaterally lost** due to the seller's breach; and

- *prejudgment interest* on all monies recovered. [CC §3306]

General damages are monetary losses incurred by the buyer due to his expenditures and loss of value (price increase) that were **directly related** to his acquisition of the property, which he will not now acquire, including:

- **money advanced** by the buyer toward the price of the property, such as deposits held by the agent or escrow, or previously released to the seller;

- **expenses incurred** examining title conditions, inspecting the property, verifying operating income and expenses, and obtaining financing, escrow services, engineering and improvement plans, etc., all called *transactional expenses*;

- **move-in expenses incurred** preparing the property to take possession; and

- the **price-to-value difference** between the price agreed to in the breached purchase agreement and the value of the property on the date of the seller's breach.

Value-over-price on date of breach

Consider a buyer of real estate who enters into a purchase agreement to acquire one of two adjacent lots held by the owner. The purchase agreement contains a provision granting the buyer a *right of first refusal* to acquire the adjacent lot, also called a *preemptive right to buy*.

The right-of-first-refusal provision sets the price of the adjacent lot at $400,000, but does not state an expiration date for the right to buy it. Thus, the buyer believes he has the right to buy the adjacent lot should the owner decide to sell it at anytime during the owner's lifetime. A further, more formal, memorialization of the right of first refusal is not entered into. No memorandum of the right is recorded. The transaction closes.

Many years later, the owner conveys the adjacent lot to another person for $880,000. The person who acquires the adjacent lot has no knowledge of the outstanding right of first refusal which was triggered by his purchase. Thus, the buyer holding the right of first refusal is unable to exercise his preemptive right and acquire ownership of the adjacent lot. The person who acquired the adjacent lot is a *bona fide purchaser* (BFP), barring any recovery of the lot by the buyer.

The buyer claims the owner has breached the right-of-first-refusal provision in their purchase agreement. Thus, the buyer makes a demand for the monetary value of the lost right to buy since he no longer has the ability to acquire the adjacent lot. The buyer's demand on the owner is for the sum of $480,000, the difference between the price set in the right of first refusal provision and the *value of the property* on the

date of the breach, plus interest at 10% (the legal rate) on the demand from the date of the breach until the demand is paid.

The owner refuses to pay the demand claiming the right of first refusal he granted at the time of the purchase of the first lot *expired* prior to the owner's sale of the lot since the provision did not contain an expiration date and a reasonable period of time for the right to continue in existence has long ago passed.

Can the buyer recover money equal to the **price-to-value difference** several years later at the time of the sale of the lot covered by the right of first refusal?

Yes! The right of first refusal which the owner granted did not express a date of expiration. Thus, the date of expiration becomes the date of the death of the owner who granted the right.

More importantly, the right to buy held by the buyer had not previously been triggered. Thus, the right could not have been exercised by the buyer until the owner triggered the right to buy by deciding to sell the property. It is the owner's decision to sell that provides the buyer, on notice of the decision (which he did not get), with his first *opportunity to exercise* the right by deciding to buy the property at the price and on the terms stated in the provision granting him the preemptive right to buy.

It is the length of the period **following the notice** of the owner's intent to sell which controls the buyer's actions. Delivery of the notice sets the period during which the buyer may *exercise* his right to buy. If this period for exercise is not stated in the right-of-first-refusal provision, it is limited to a **reasonable period** of time which begins to run when the buyer receives notice from the owner of his decision to sell.

Thus, it is the period **after the notice** which expires, not the grant of the right to buy, unless the right-of-first-refusal provision limits the term of the grant.

Accordingly, the buyer's money recovery of the value-over-price is the difference between:

- the **value** of the property on the date of the breach, here set by the price the owner received for the property on the resale (the event which triggered the right to buy); **less**

- the **price** agreed to in the right of first refusal provision as the amount the buyer was to pay for the property on exercise of the right to buy. [**Mercer** v. **Lemmens** (1964) 230 CA2d 167]

Preparing to take possession

Consider a buyer who enters into a purchase agreement with a builder to construct a new home. The buyer purchases appliances and upgrades the fixtures, which the builder installs.

Later, the builder substantially alters the construction plans for the exterior without the buyer's approval. The buyer demands the builder complete construction under the plans and specifications as agreed. The builder refuses since he has prospective buyers for the property at a significantly higher price.

The buyer decides he no longer wants the new home due to his conflict with the builder. He cancels the purchase agreement since the builder has breached the agreement. The buyer now seeks to recover money from the builder, not the property.

Here, the actual **money losses** the buyer may recover from the builder include:

- funds advanced toward the purchase price, including good-faith deposits and monies released to the seller;

- the value-over-price difference between the price the buyer agreed to pay in the purchase agreement and the resale value of the property at the time of the builder's breach;

- expenses incurred to prepare the property for possession (to the extent they exceed the value-over-price difference), i.e., the expenditures made by the buyer for the additional appliances and upgraded fixtures; and

- interest from the date of the breach on all amounts of money recovered.

A buyer is allowed to recover expenditures incurred to prepare a property so he can take possession. The buyer and seller must intend for the expenditures to be incurred by the buyer as a condition in their purchase agreement. Recovery of construction costs advanced by a buyer for upgrades and additions gives the buyer the *benefit of the bargain* contemplated by both the buyer and seller when they entered into their agreement. However, the buyer cannot enjoy a double recovery for the upgrades he paid for when the price-to-value increase exceeds the cost of the upgrades.

Excluded from recovery are any expenditures by the buyer to purchase furnishings for the new home. The recovery of these expenses are typically not agreed to under a purchase agreement and are not related to the acquisition of real estate. Also, a seller cannot reasonably foresee these **collateral expenses** for home furnishings as becoming his obligation should he breach the purchase agreement.

Consequential damages, naturally

A buyer whose seller has breached their purchase agreement is also entitled to recover expenses incurred by the buyer **after the breach**, if the expenditures are the **natural result** of the seller's breach, called *consequential damages*.

For the buyer to recover post-breach expenditures, the seller on entry into the agreement must have known or should have known the expenses would be incurred by the buyer as a **natural and unavoidable result** of the seller's breach of the purchase agreement.

For example, a buyer enters into an agreement to purchase a lot from a builder. The builder also agrees to complete the construction of improvements on the lot and convey the property by an agreed-to date.

Before the builder enters into the purchase agreement agreeing to sell the property and construct improvements, the builder is informed of the adverse tax consequences the buyer will be subjected to if the construction is not completed and the property conveyed by the date scheduled for closing. Thus, **time for performance** by completion of construction and close of escrow is known by the builder on entering into the agreement to be a prerequisite to the buyer's avoidance of profit taxes.

The buyer has sold real estate he used in his trade or business and needs to acquire ownership of a replacement property within 180 days after the sale closed. The time constraint must be met to qualify the sale as an IRC §1031 exempt transaction and avoid reporting profits and incurring state and federal tax liability for the tax on the profits.

However, the builder fails to complete construction and convey the property prior to the date set for closing. Thus, due to the builder's breach, the buyer is unable to avoid payment of the profit tax on the sale of his business property. Also, the buyer is forced to rent another property (and incur moving expenses) until the construction is completed.

Here, the **consequential damages** recoverable by the buyer in the form of a money award include:

- the full amount of the profit tax the buyer paid;

- the rent paid for the temporary facilities until the improvements were completed (plus the cost of additional moving expenses); and

- interest at 10% from the date the amounts of rent and profit tax were paid by the buyer. [**Walker** v. **Signal Companies, Inc.** (1978) 84 CA3d 982]

Interest

A buyer who recovers money losses is also entitled to recover **interest** at the **(legal) rate of 10%**, commencing on the date of the seller's breach, on amounts recovered for:

- the value-over-price money differential recovered;

- money paid toward the purchase price, whether held by the seller or as a deposit in escrow, until the date released to the buyer;

- funds expended on title examination and other transaction expenses incurred preparing to take title;

- expenses incurred preparing the property to take possession; and

- *consequential losses,* but only accruing from the date of their disbursement. [**Al-Husry** v. **Nilsen Farms Mini-Market, Inc.** (1994) 25 CA4th 641]

Consider a buyer who enters into a purchase agreement with a seller. The buyer opens escrow and deposits funds in accordance with the purchase agreement.

Meanwhile, the seller has received a better offer from another buyer. The seller conveys the property to the second buyer.

The first buyer, whose purchase agreement has now been breached by the seller's conveyance to another person, is entitled to recover:

- the increased value of the property on the date of the breach over his purchase price, with **interest on the difference** at the legal rate (10%) from the date of the breach; and

- the refund of his deposits held either in escrow or by the seller, plus **interest on the deposits** from the date of the breach to the date the deposits are returned to the buyer. [**Rasmussen** v. **Moe** (1956) 138 CA2d 499]

Nonrecoverable losses

A buyer's expenses and losses which are unrelated to the real estate and not intended to be incurred by the buyer based on the buyer's entry into the purchase agreement are not the responsibility of the breaching seller. Losses and expenses **too remote and speculative** to be foreseen by the seller when entering into the purchase agreement as his obligations should he breach are **not recoverable** from the seller.

For example, a buyer enters into a purchase agreement to acquire an unimproved parcel of commercial property. The seller knows the buyer plans to develop the property. Before escrow closes, the seller determines he can get a higher price for the property from other prospective buyers and cancels escrow.

Here, the buyer can recover any increase in the value of the land on the date of breach over the agreed-to purchase price, as may be reflected by the seller's resale of the property. However, the buyer is **not entitled** to recover the **profits** he would have earned had he been able to acquire and develop the land. Lost profits for the **anticipated use** of the property to be purchased are unrelated to the sale and too speculative to be recoverable by the buyer. [**Stewart Development Co.** v. **Superior Court for County of Orange** (1980) 108 CA3d 266]

Also, lost income from rents a buyer would have received had he acquired property subject to a long-term lease are not recoverable. The recovery of rents is barred on a different legal theory from consequential losses since rents are related to the property.

Rent produced by income property is a factor used to establish the property's **present value**.

To allow the buyer to collect future rents from a breaching seller when the buyer does not buy the property and the buyer is awarded a money recovery for the increase in the resale value (which by definition is established by the future flow of rents) would be double recovery, i.e., present value of the future flow of rent, plus those future rents. Thus, the buyer would be improperly placed in a **better position** than had the seller performed by conveying the property.

Further, interest serves the same economic function as rents. Both are a *return on capital*. Thus, when a buyer receives interest on the amount of his recovery, the further receipt of future rent would also be an **impermissible double recovery**. [**Stevens Group Fund IV** v. **Sobrato Development Co.** (1992) 1 CA4th 886]

Commercial reality of a call for funds

Consider a buyer and seller who enter into a purchase agreement which sets the date scheduled for the close of escrow. However, the purchase agreement does not contain a performance date by which the seller is to deliver documents to escrow. Escrow is opened.

The buyer obtains a commitment letter from a lender for a purchase-assist loan. The lender issuing the commitment informs escrow it will prepare loan documents and fund escrow within five days after its receipt of an estimated closing statement from escrow.

On the day scheduled for closing, escrow is still not in a position to prepare an estimated closing statement, much less call for closing funds from the lender or the buyer. The seller has not yet submitted a current rent roll statement which is needed by escrow to prepare the estimated closing statement for the lender.

Later on the same day, the seller submits a current rent roll statement to escrow, completing his performance of all conditions imposed on the seller by the date set for closing. Then, on learning that the buyer has not yet deposited his funds into escrow, the seller hands escrow a written notice of cancellation.

The buyer makes a demand on the seller to convey title as soon as the lender is in a position to fund the loan. The buyer claims his failure to fund escrow by the closing date is excused due to the seller's **untimely delivery** of the rent roll statement to escrow.

Here, the buyer's failure to fund escrow when he had otherwise fully performed was *excused* by the seller's dilatory delivery of closing document to escrow. The seller must now allow escrow to close.

Escrow is a process which depends on the orderly receipt of documents to close the transaction, a process the seller must honor. Thus, as a matter of *commercial reality*, escrow will not call for closing funds from either the buyer or the lender until escrow is in a position to close. In turn, neither the buyer nor the lender will deposit or wire funds until they receive a call from escrow for funds.

Since escrow was not in a position to call for funds due to the seller's untimely performance, the buyer's delivery of funds by the date scheduled for closing was excused and the seller must allow escrow to close. [**Ninety Nine Investments, Ltd.** v. **Overseas Courier Service (Singapore) Private, Ltd.** (2003) 113 CA4th 1118]

The seller's obligation to deliver documents and the buyer's obligation to fund escrow are considered mutually exclusive *concurrent conditions*. Thus, they must be independently performed by the buyer and seller on or before the date scheduled for closing. However, in actual practice, escrows require receipt of all documents needed by escrow to close before they will **call for funds**.

Even with all the buyer's and seller's documents in hand, lenders generally need five to seven days to prepare, forward and receive signed loan documents before they will fund.

While a provision might not exist in a purchase agreement calling for the seller to deliver documents to escrow prior to the date set for closing, the existence of an *implied covenant of good faith and fair dealing* does call for the **timely advance occurrence** of events or actions to be taken by the seller to avoid frustrating the buyer's right to receive the benefits of the contract, i.e., time for the buyer and his lender to fund escrow and for the buyer to receive title to the property. [See **first tuesday** Form 150 §12.2]

Chapter 46

The breaching buyer's liabilities

This chapter digests a buyer's liabilities to a seller, arising out of the buyer's breach of a purchase agreement, for property value decreases, operating and carrying costs, and losses on a resale.

First, there must be a money loss

Consider a prospective buyer of a residence who is informed the seller has already entered into a purchase agreement to acquire a replacement residence. The seller is relying on the sale of his current residence to fund his purchase of the replacement residence.

The prospective buyer makes a written offer agreeing to pay cash for the seller's equity and assume the existing trust deed loan, called a *cash-to-loan transaction*. The seller accepts the offer. Escrow instructions are prepared and signed, and the buyer's good-faith deposit is placed in escrow.

Later, as agreed, the buyer deposits additional funds in escrow. Although escrow is not yet ready to close, the buyer agrees to release some of the downpayment money held in escrow so the seller can close his purchase of the replacement residence. The funds are released and the seller acquires his new residence.

The seller vacates the old residence he has *sold* and moves his family and belongings into the new residence.

To consent to the buyer's application to assume the seller's existing loan, the lender demands a modification of the interest rate and payment schedule, and an assumption fee. The buyer refuses to proceed with the loan assumption and cancels escrow.

The buyer makes a demand on the seller to return all funds the buyer deposited into escrow, which the seller rejects.

The seller then makes a demand to be paid the funds remaining in escrow. The seller claims the buyer has *forfeited* all funds since he breached the purchase agreement by not assuming the loan.

The seller promptly relists the property and it is **resold** for the same price, but on terms calling for payoff of the existing loan, requiring the seller to pay a prepayment penalty. The seller also agrees to pay the new buyer's non-recurring closing costs and one point on new financing to be obtained by the new buyer. On closing the resale transaction, the seller's net proceeds are less than he would have received on the sale to the original buyer under the breached purchase agreement.

Can the seller recover any money from the original buyer by either:

- retaining all the funds deposited by the buyer; or

- accounting for offsets against the buyer's deposits for the seller's losses?

Here, the seller is entitled to recover his losses. However, he must **account for his actual money losses** caused by the buyer's breach since a forfeiture of deposits is not allowed, no matter the wording or initialing of the forfeiture provisions. Depending on the amount of the seller's **total recoverable losses** on the resale, the buyer's deposit will be partially or totally offset by the amount of the seller's losses caused by the breaching buyer. [**Allen v. Enomoto** (1964) 228 CA2d 798]

Recoverable seller losses

A seller's **total recoverable losses**, summarized here and analyzed in detail in this chapter, include:

- the **operating and carrying costs** of trust deed interest payments, taxes, insurance, maintenance and utilities, which were incurred by the seller during the period between the date of the breach and the date escrow closed on the resale;

- the **increased closing costs** due to the seller's payment of the new buyer's non-recurring closing costs and financing fees on the resale which reduced the seller's net proceeds compared to the net proceeds the seller would have received from the breaching buyer;

- the **additional resale costs** of the prepayment penalty demanded by the lender on the loan payoff; and

- **interest** on the seller's net equity from the date escrow was to close to the date of closing on the resale.

Resell or retain the property

A seller of real estate who is faced with a breaching buyer and the loss of the sales transaction must first decide whether to:

- **enforce** the purchase agreement and have a court order the buyer to close escrow, called *specific performance*;

- **remarket** the property for sale promptly and diligently seek to locate a buyer; or

- **retain the property** and postpone or entirely forego any resale effort.

Editor's note — This chapter illustrates money losses recoverable by the seller who chooses either to retain the property or resell it. Thus, the specific performance remedy is not considered here.

Only a money loss is recoverable

A buyer, due to his breach of the purchase agreement, owes the seller **actual money losses**, called *damages*, which are classified as:

- **general damages**, also called *normal damages*, being the dollar amount of any decline in the property's fair market value as of the date of the buyer's breach below the price agreed to in the purchase agreement;

- **special damages**, also called *consequential damages*, being 1) transactional costs incurred by the seller while preparing to close under the breached purchase agreement, 2) marketing expenses, increased closing costs, and ownership and operating costs incurred to remarket and sell the property, and 3) any further drop in property value after the buyer's breach for so long as the buyer interferes and stalls the seller's resale effort; and

- **interest** from the date of the buyer's breach to the closing date of a resale of the property on all money and any carryback note the seller was to receive [Calif. Civil Code §3307]; less

- **offsets or credits** due the buyer for 1) any rent received from tenants or the *implicit rent* for the owner's use of the property, 2) the amount of any price increase on the resale, and 3) the amount of any reduction in the seller's expenses on the resale, so the seller will not be placed in a better financial position than he would have been in had the breaching buyer fully performed. [**Smith** v. **Mady** (1983) 146 CA3d 129]

Price-to-value as a money loss

When a seller decides to resell the property after the buyer breaches their purchase agreement and the property's value has declined below the price set in the purchase agreement, the seller has incurred a **loss in value** which is recoverable from the buyer. However, the amount of future value decline recoverable after the buyer's breach is limited to two time periods:

- the initial decline in value below the purchase price during the period **before the breach**, which is recoverable as *general damages* or more commonly called a *price-to-value loss*; and

- any further decline in value **after the breach**, which is recoverable only if the buyer **interferes** with the seller's resale effort, also called *special damages* or more commonly called *additional damages*, damages being money. [CC §3307]

The price-to-value loss on the date of breach is recoverable by the seller whether the property is retained, remarketed or resold by the seller.

During periods of reduced regional economic activity, the boom-bust cyclical nature of real estate sales typically causes California property values to drop dramatically below the price the buyer agreed to pay just a few months earlier. Further, the intangible impacts on a property's market value, due to its "shop-worn" listing status and the "fall-out syndrome" of a lost sale, give the property an aura in the local real estate market which negatively affects some buyers and their brokers. This aura is often reflected in a further dampening of the property's value on the date of breach. [**Bouchard** v. **Orange** (1960) 177 CA2d 521]

To limit the breaching buyer's liability, the seller's loss on a resale at a price lower than the price agreed to by the breaching buyer is limited to the amount of the value decline which occurs by the date of the buyer's breach, not the date of resale. Any further decline in value after the date of breach to the date of resale (or trial, if the property is not yet resold) is recoverable only if the buyer interferes with the seller's diligent resale efforts.

Same or greater price on resale

When property is resold for the same price agreed to by a breaching buyer, or more, and the net proceeds from the resale are the same or the cash equivalent, or more, the price-to-value decline on the date of breach is no longer recoverable. With equal or greater net proceeds on a resale, the seller incurs no money loss, called *general damages*, since he has no loss of value to recover.

To set the dollar amount of the price-to-value loss on the date of breach, any "noncash" terms for payment of the purchase price by the breaching buyer and any "noncash" terms for payment of the resale price are adjusted to their **cash equivalency**.

For example, if terms for payment of a sale price include a seller carryback note, the principal amount of the carryback note is adjusted downward to reflect any discount required to convert the carryback paper to its cash equivalent, i.e., its present worth in cash.

Interfering with the resale

A seller might **diligently remarket** the property and still be unable to resell it due to interference from the breaching buyer. Buyer interference with resale efforts usually consists of filing a *specific performance action* and recording a *Notice of Lis Pendens*, or taking possession and refusing to vacate.

When the breaching buyer interferes with the resale, the seller recovers any decline in the property's value after the date of breach until the buyer stops interfering with the seller's resale efforts.

For example, a buyer sues a seller seeking specific performance of the purchase agreement. The seller claims the buyer breached the purchase agreement by failing to satisfy contingencies as scheduled. The buyer claims the seller breached when he canceled, thus *excusing* the buyer from further performing. The buyer sues to recover the property and records a **Notice of Lis Pendens**, which clouds the marketability of title.

Ultimately, the buyer is held to have breached the agreement and the lis pendens is removed from the record, called *expungement*.

A seller, whether he attempts to resell the property or retains it, generally bears the risk of any fluctuation in the value of the property after the buyer breaches. The breach is the cutoff date for recovery of a decline in value, unless the buyer later interferes.

However, the risk of loss due to a decline in value after the date of breach is shifted to the buyer until the date title is cleared of the recorded lis pendens if the recording interferes with the seller's prompt and diligent efforts to resell the property. [**Askari** v. **R & R Land Company** (1986) 179 CA3d 1101]

Natural-consequence expenses

A seller who takes the property off the market or is not prompt and diligent in his efforts to remarket and resell it after the buyer's breach is limited in his recovery of money to his **actual transactional expenses** and any **operating expenses** incurred to fulfill the seller's performance under the purchase agreement up to the time of the buyer's breach.

Recoverable money losses the seller might incur as **transactional expenditures** include:

- escrow and title charges;

- lender charges for beneficiary statements or payoff demands;

- lender or carryback seller charges to process the buyer's credit clearance, loan application or loan assumption; and

- other expenses and property reports incurred in reasonable reliance on the buyer's full performance of the purchase agreement.

However, **ownership and operating expenses** incurred by a seller who chooses to either retain the property or delay reselling the property are not recoverable. The seller, as the owner of the property, remains responsible for the expenses of carrying and maintaining the property since these expenses are not incurred by the seller due to a buyer's agreement to purchase or a breach by the buyer. These expenses are incurred because the seller owns the property.

However, some operating losses incurred by a seller due solely to his **compliance** with the terms of a purchase agreement are recoverable, including:

- the seller's relocation expenses to reoccupy the property if he vacated after all contingencies allowing the buyer to cancel were eliminated;

- rental income lost after the breach on units left vacant or vacated by the terms of the purchase agreement;

- a crop revenue loss due to the planting season having passed at the time of the buyer's breach; and

- a price drop on the late harvest of a crop due to the buyer's breach. [**Wade** v. **Lake County Title Company** (1970) 6 CA3d 824]

Replacement property

Consider a buyer who enters into a purchase agreement knowing the seller intends to acquire replacement real estate with the net proceeds from the sale. After all the buyer's contingencies are eliminated and no uncertainties remain about the buyer's full performance, the seller enters into a purchase agreement to buy replacement property without conditioning his purchase on the "sale of other property."

The buyer then breaches and the seller is unable to complete his purchase of the replacement property. The seller incurs expenses and losses to avoid liability for having unconditionally agreed to purchase the replacement property.

Expenses incurred on the replacement property transaction are recoverable since:

- the buyer knew when he entered into the purchase agreement that the seller intended to contract to purchase replacement property based on the buyer's agreement to purchase; and

- the seller agreed to purchase other property in reasonable reliance on his buyer closing the sales escrow since all contingencies had been removed and no obstacles to closing existed, except for the breach. [**Jensen** v. **Dalton** (1970) 9 CA3d 654]

Operating losses during the resale period

A seller who, after his buyer breaches, promptly takes steps to diligently remarket the property for sale may recover his operating expenses and carrying costs of the property incurred **after the date of breach**, subject to offsets for rent credit, owner's use, etc.

Recoverable operating losses and carrying costs are limited to those the seller incurs during the period beginning on the buyer's breach and ending on the earlier of:

- the date a **resale closes**;

- the **trial** judgment on the breach; or

- the date of **withdrawal** of the property from the resale market.

The seller who decides to promptly resell the property and then recover any losses from the buyer has a duty to the breaching buyer to limit the operating and ownership losses, called *mitigation of damages*. To do so, the seller must take immediate steps to market the property for resale within the shortest possible time. [**Spurgeon** v. **Drumheller** (1985) 174 CA3d 659]

To begin calculating the seller's net loss, the seller's costs of maintaining his ownership are totalled. However, the recoverable operating expenses and carrying costs of the property incurred by the seller during the resale period are limited to operating and ownership expenses understood by the buyer to exist at the time he entered into the purchase agreement.

However, the buyer is **due a credit** for the rental value of the seller's occupancy, called *implicit rent,* and any rental income received by the seller from the property after the buyer's breach.

Thus, for a seller to recover on-going losses incurred to carry the ownership of the property before resale or trial, a full accounting of income, expenses and the carrying costs of financing is required. [See **first tuesday** Form 352]

Interest on recovered losses

A seller is also **entitled to interest** on the losses and expenditures he recovers for the decline in the property's value, expenses of the breached transaction, resale related expenses and the carrying costs of the property during the resale effort. [CC §3307]

Unless the purchase agreement states otherwise, the interest is collectable at the legal annual rate of 10%, accruing from the date the recoverable loss or expenditure was incurred, called *prejudgment interest.* [CC §3289(b)]

If the seller **retains the property**, no property operating or value losses after the breach are recoverable on which interest can accrue.

For the seller who **diligently remarkets** the property for resale, recoverable resale costs and out-of-pocket carrying costs of the property not offset by rental income or the rental value of the seller's use of the property accrue interest from the date of each expenditure.

Had the buyer performed and closed escrow, the seller would no longer own the property.

The seller would have received the net sales proceeds for his equity in the property.

Since escrow did not close and the seller did not receive the net sales proceeds for his equity, the question of whether he is entitled to interest on his **net equity** turns on the seller's use of the property at the time the purchase agreement was entered into.

For example, a **seller's use** of the subject property falls into one of two categories:

- **income-producing property** used as the seller's residence or to house the seller's trade or business (implicit rent) or held out as a residential or nonresidential rental; or

- **nonincome-producing property**, such as vacant land or the seller's vacant residence.

Rents received from income producing property are the **economic equivalent** of interest on the dollar amount of the equity. Thus, for the seller to also receive interest on his equity in income-producing property until it resells would be a nonrecoverable windfall, a double recovery on his equity in the form of interest and rent, which are economic equivalents. Should the seller occupy the property until it is resold, the value of his use is *implicit rent* and the amount is an offset against all money recoverable from the breaching buyer, including interest on the seller's equity.

For vacant unused land or the seller's vacant residence, a breach by the buyer again fails to convert the seller's equity into cash or cash equivalent. Thus, the seller temporarily retains ownership of the equity, which may be increasing, decreasing or remaining the same depending on price fluctuations for the property's market value until it is resold.

Since the resale seller cannot recover his equity in vacant property from the breaching buyer (except by specific performance), can interest be collected on the equity?

First, any interest due on the dollar amount of the net equity can only accrue from the **scheduled closing date** of the breached contract — the date the benefits from the breached sale in the form of cash for the seller's net equity would have been received by the seller — up to and ending on the **date of resale or trial**. Any interest due accrues at the legal rate of 10%. However, if the seller agreed to an installment sale, the note rate for the carryback paper would be the controlling rate.

Next, if the breached purchase agreement contains a provision limiting the dollar amount of losses the seller can collect, the losses recoverable would be controlled by the agreed-to limit, except for the accrual of interest which would be an additional amount. [See **first tuesday** Form 150 §10.7]

Thus, when the buyer breaches an agreement to purchase vacant, nonincome-producing property, interest is due on the net sales proceeds the seller would have received on the sale, until the property is resold.

Chapter 47

Liquidated damages provisions

This chapter is a survey of the unenforceability of liquidated damages provisions in real estate purchase agreements and the limitation on a breach to recovery of actual losses.

Windfalls and responsibility for losses

Everyone, by the time they reach the age of capacity to contract, understands the fundamental premise that when you wrongfully cause another person to lose money, you are responsible for *repayment* of the loss. This moral concept was codified for real estate transactions in 1872 and remains intact today. [Calif. Civil Code §3307]

However, an equally fundamental premise holds that windfalls are abhorred by all since they are unearned.

These two precepts are frustrated by the inclusion of a *liquidated damages provision* in a purchase agreement. Use of a liquidated damages provision is an attempt:

- to limit a buyer's responsibility for payment of losses he inflicts on another; and

- to provide the seller with a windfall at the buyer's expense.

The contractual liquidated damages provision creates aberrations in the natural expectations held by everyone in the transaction.

For instance, a seller expects to lose nothing of value in exchange for what is the buyer's good-faith deposit should the buyer fail to close the transaction. However, the buyer expects a refund of his good-faith deposit if he does not acquire the property. Ironically, the listing agent looks at the liquidated damages provision in the purchase agreement as a way to be paid a small fraction of the fee he earned since he has not bargained for a full fee should the buyer breach the purchase agreement. All of these expectations are without concern for the amount of money the seller and agents lost or that the breaching buyer caused the losses and should reimburse them.

A **listing agent**, being charged with a *duty of care* for his seller, needs to understand the contractual and financial nature of his seller's position under a purchase agreement so he can properly advise the seller when the purchase agreement is breached by a buyer. When the buyer breaches and the seller cancels the purchase agreement, the seller still owns the property, although with no further claim by the buyer of a right to acquire it.

Also, the good-faith deposit, even if released to the seller after contingencies have been removed, is the buyer's money until:

- the buyer receives consideration (the property); or

- the deposit is offset by reimbursement to the seller for his **actual money losses** suffered due to a breach by the buyer.

The seller's purported loss of prospective buyers and prior market synergies and the infliction of seller frustration and inconvenience, all due to the buyer's breach, are not money losses. Thus, these ancillary or collateral situations leave the seller with nothing to collect.

However, the seller's agent properly focuses on **resolving a breached** and failed sales transaction by immediately turning his attention to assisting his client to "clear out" the transaction so the property can be remarketed to another prospective buyer. The listing agent is still obligated to locate buyers under the seller's exclusive right-to-sell agreement, unless it has expired.

Thus, cancellation instructions need to be given to escrow to terminate the breached purchase agreement and escrow instructions, unless the resale value of the property has dropped or the seller has reason to pursue a specific performance action and forego reselling or retaining the property. [See Chapter 46]

Money losses reimbursed

What is the listing agent to do about a buyer's good-faith deposit when the buyer breaches a purchase agreement?

While a listing agent's knee-jerk reaction may well be to get the buyer's funds to the seller so half of the deposit will be earned as a brokerage fee, the first reasonable step to be taken by the agent is to analyze the extent of the seller's loss of money now that the sales escrow is dead. The buyer owes the seller the seller's actual money losses since they are expenditures which will not be reimbursed by a resale. Thus, the seller has a *claim* on the buyer's good-faith deposit as the **primary source for recovery** of the losses.

Fortunately for all, the seller's recoverable losses are quite straightforward for calculating the amount of the demand to be made on the buyer. Getting all the figures for the demand will take time and effort. Presuming, as the listing agent must, that the seller will not interfere with the listing and allow the agent to locate a new prospective buyer, the property will be resold in the near future.

A seller's net sheet used to lay out the net proceeds received on the closing of a **resale**, when compared to a seller's net sheet estimating the net proceeds the seller would have received on the **canceled sale**, will present a fairly accurate representation of the money losses the seller incurred due to a decline in property value and the transactional costs not reimbursed by the resale.

The ongoing operating and carrying costs, if the property remains **rented or used** by the owner prior to resale, generally are not recov-

erable expenses. The actual or implicit rent usually exceeds the operating expenses and carrying costs of the property until the closing of the resale. Also, operating income and expenses usually are not altered due to the terms of the purchase agreement. Hence, little loss, if any, exists for the seller to recover on his continued ownership of the property.

Demands, challenges and limitations

The seller making a demand on a breaching buyer for the deposit is confronted with a decision as to when to make the demand. The seller may make a demand for all or a portion of the good-faith deposit at either:

- the time of the breach; or

- after closing a resale of the property when a loss, if any, is known.

To analyze the demand process, first look to the provisions of the purchase agreement used for the sale of a **one-to-four unit residential property** to a **buyer-occupant**. If a liquidated damages (forfeiture) provision is included in the purchase agreement and the buyer and seller both initialed the provision, they have actually agreed that the buyer's good-faith deposit is to be forfeited to the seller on a breach by the buyer.

However, liquidated damages provisions are initially enforceable by a seller only to **set the limit** of the buyer's liability to the seller by placing a ceiling on the seller's recovery at the amount of the deposit agreed to be forfeited.

For example, if the buyer demands the deposit be refunded, the seller becomes obligated to provide an accounting showing his losses **equaled or exceeded** the amount of the deposit in order to keep the entire deposit. Should the losses be **less**, the seller is not entitled to the entire deposit. Thus, the seller can recover the money he has lost up to the total amount of the deposit referenced in the agreed liquidated damages provision, no matter the amount of the deposit.

Thus, when a liquidated damages provision exists, the proper initial reaction of the seller and the listing agent is to make a demand on the buyer for the entire good-faith deposit if it does not exceed 3% of the price since this amount of forfeiture is *presumed valid*.

Once the demand for the forfeiture has been made on the buyer — and it will be made without concern for the actual money losses the seller may have experienced or will experience on a resale — the seller merely waits for the buyer's response. If it is positive and the funds are released to the seller, the seller has won the war. Hopefully for the seller, the buyer will not later realize that the seller's actual money losses were less than the amount released and then make a demand for a refund.

However, if the buyer's agent and the buyer are as well informed as the seller and listing agent, the buyer will **challenge** the liquidated damages provision as *voidable* and demand a return of his deposit. Thus, the provision as a forfeiture is unenforceable since the provision's validity is a *rebuttable presumption*.

The seller must have sufficient losses to justify his retention of the entire liquidated damages deposit. In other words, the amount of the deposit, always being arbitrary in amount and coincidental to the price paid, has no relationship to the losses the seller might suffer on the buyer's breach.

The seller, confronted with the buyer's challenge that the liquidated damages provision is **voidable,** is back to square one. Namely, the seller must now calculate his losses on the resale and his permissible interim operating and carrying costs of the property prior to a resale as though:

- no liquidated damages provision existed in the purchase agreement;

- the amount of the deposit for liquidated damages was more than 3% and thus initially presumed invalid;

- the liquidated damages or liability limitation provision placed a ceiling on the buyer's liability for the seller losses; and

- no provision limiting recovery existed in the purchase agreement restricting the seller's right to recover all his losses.

Under any of the above scenarios, the seller is to itemize his money losses, which include:

- any decline in the property's value by the time of the buyer's breach;

- the seller's transactional costs incurred on the lost sale which are not recoverable on a resale; and

- any increased operating costs or rent losses caused by the purchase agreement with the buyer and incurred prior to the resale.

The buyer will cover these itemized losses from the good-faith deposit up to any dollar limitation set by a liquidated damages or liability limitation provision in the purchase agreement.

The seller who seeks to recover losses caused by the breaching buyer when the buyer asserts his right to pay only the seller's actual money losses, needs to:

- proceed to resell and close a resale of the property rather than retain the property;

- calculate the total amount of the price-to-value loss, lost transactional expenses and the loss of nonvalue-added improvements or repair expenditures;

- make a demand on the buyer for the amount of the itemized money losses; and

- if not paid, pursue collection of the lost money and a release of the amount from the buyer's deposit, subject, of course, to any agreed limitation on the dollar amount of the buyer's liability for his breach.

Challenging the validity of a forfeiture

A buyer and his agent, when the seller demands any of the buyer's good-faith deposit, need to understand:

- the funds belong to the buyer until escrow closes, which will not occur due to the buyer's breach;

- the seller has a claim against the deposit for recoverable losses; and

- the buyer is to make a demand on the seller for an itemized statement of the seller's losses before the buyer will pay any compensable losses incurred by the seller.

Thus, when a liquidated damages provision exists on the sale of a one-to-four unit residential property which is initialed by both the seller and buyer, the buyer's demand for an itemization of the seller's money losses constitutes a *legal challenge* which rebuts the presumed validity of a forfeiture provision for deposits not exceeding 3% of the purchase price.

On making the request of the seller for an accounting, the buyer awaits the seller's response. If the seller fails to respond with an accounting, he either did not incur a recoverable loss or waived any claim he may have to recover his losses.

Limiting the breaching buyer's liability

Without a liquidated damages provision or contract liability limitation provision in the purchase agreement, a seller is entitled to recover the entire amount of his money losses caused by the buyer's breach.

Conversely, the seller is limited in his recovery to the amount of the forfeitable deposit should the purchase agreement (for the sale of one-to-four residential units to a buyer-occupant) include an initialed liquidated damages provision or a contract liability limitation provision.

In either case, if an accounting is sought by the buyer for the seller's recoverable money losses, the seller must present an accounting in order to be reimbursed for them.

When an initialed liquidated damages provision is included in a purchase agreement, the breaching buyer avoids the forfeiture called for by challenging the *presumed validity* of any amount **up to 3%** of the purchase price.

However, for the seller to enforce a forfeiture of any portion of a deposit **exceeding 3%** of the purchase agreement price, the seller must challenge the *presumed invalidity* of the excess by demonstrating in an accounting that his losses on the sale exceeded 3% of the purchase price.

Thus, the liquidated damages provision has a "split-personality" aspect. The responsibility for challenging the *presumed validity* of a forfeiture of 3% or less is the buyer's, and the responsibility for challenging the *presumed invalidity* of a forfeiture of more than 3% is the seller's.

In general, liquidated damages provisions agreed to by a buyer and seller of real estate, other than on the sale of one-to-four residential units to a buyer-occupant, are presumed to be *valid*. However, they are classified as *forfeitures* and are unenforceable if they do not provide an amount which bears some **reasonably close relationship** to the actual losses the seller will incur due to harm inflicted by the buyer on a default.

When the amount of the forfeiture exceeds the seller's losses, the buyer can **void** the provision as unreasonable. Thus, the liquidated damages provision is *voidable* as it is only presumed to be valid if the amount is reasonably close to actual losses.

Liability ceiling or forfeiture

If a buyer and seller do not agree to either a liquidated damages provision or a contract liability limitation provision, then the buyer who enters into such a purchase agreement and breaches will be liable for an **unlimited amount of losses** incurred by the seller due to the buyer's breach. In the economic environment of a stable resale market for homes or one of generally rising or fast rising prices little risk is taken by a buyer when entering into a purchase agreement without a ceiling on his liability exposure.

However, it is for buyers in a static market or one following a peak in prices when mortgage rates rise that the buyer's agent needs to take *utmost care* to explain the need for a ceiling on liability exposure.

As for the listing agent, he should advise his seller in times of weak or weakening pricing power to avoid agreeing to a ceiling on the buyer's liability and to get a huge deposit.

Seller breach by refusal to refund

Consider a buyer of a single family residence who has entered into a purchase agreement containing an initialed, liquidated damages provision.

Prior to closing, the buyer waives all contingencies and releases his original and additional good-faith deposit to the seller in an amount in excess of 3% of the agreed price. At the time of closing, the buyer decides not to close escrow on the purchase of the property.

The seller promptly remarkets the property, accepts an offer and quickly closes a resale of the property, but at a slightly lower price. The buyer then makes a demand on the seller to return that portion of the deposit now held by the seller which exceeds the seller's losses. The breaching buyer is willing to cover the seller's loss due to the reduced amount of net proceeds on the resale.

The seller rejects the buyer's demand for a refund, claiming the funds released were option money which he is entitled to keep as consider-

ation for his *irrevocable offer* to sell the property to the buyer, which the buyer did not exercise by closing escrow.

However, the liquidated damages provision in the purchase agreement indicates the agreement is bilateral. The purchase agreement called for a forfeiture of the deposit should the buyer fail to close escrow, the antithesis of an option agreement which is unilateral and by its nature contains no forfeitures. Thus, the seller's defense for keeping the buyer's deposits as option money consideration for granting an option is a non-starter.

Also, the seller did not attempt to show that his losses caused by the buyer's breach equaled or exceeded the buyer's deposits. The seller did not produce closing statements for either the lost sale or the resale, lost transactional expenses, nonvalue-adding expenditures for repairs or maintenance, or any recoverable operating costs for carrying the property or lost rental value until the close of the resale.

Here, the liquidated damages provision becomes a **promise by the seller** to refund the portion of the deposit which exceeds the seller's recoverable losses, due to either:

- a buyer's challenge of the forfeiture's reasonableness; or

- the forfeiture amount being in excess of 3% of the purchase price.

Thus, the seller's failure to refund (or release) the amount exceeding his losses is a **breach by the seller** of the liquidated damages provision and the purchase agreement. [**Allen** v. **Smith** (2002) 94 CA4th 1270]

Had the purchase agreement not contained a liquidated damages provision or other contractual liabilities limitation, the seller would still have been **limited to collecting** no more than his actual losses. Thus, the excess amount of the buyer's deposit over the seller's losses must always be refunded by the seller or released from escrow to the buyer.

Court-ordered forfeiture not enforced

Consider a buyer and seller of a one-to-four unit residential property who enter into a court-ordered settlement agreement to resolve a dispute over their purchase agreement by agreeing to close escrow. The settlement agreement contains a forfeiture provision calling for the release of the buyer's good-faith deposit to the seller if the buyer does not complete the sale as agreed.

However, the buyer is unable to secure purchase-assist financing and cancels escrow, a breach of the settlement agreement since closing escrow was not contingent on his obtaining a loan.

The seller seeks to recover the buyer's good-faith deposit. However, the seller has incurred no loss due to the buyer's failure to perform.

The buyer claims the seller cannot enforce the forfeiture provision in the court-ordered settlement agreement since any provision agreeing to the forfeiture of the good-faith deposit is limited by contract law to a provable loss.

The seller claims the forfeiture provision is enforceable without a proof of loss since the provision is contained in a court-ordered settlement agreement between the buyer and seller, not in a privately negotiated real estate purchase agreement.

Here, as in all forfeitures of money arising out of any real estate transaction, the seller may not enforce the forfeiture provision and recover the buyer's good-faith deposit without a showing of his actual money losses. The court-approved settlement agreement is a contract agreed to by the buyer and seller and contract law prohibits the enforcement of liquidated damages provisions in real estate purchase agreements, unless the seller incurs a loss. [**Timney** v. **Lin** (2003) 106 CA4th 1121]

Chapter 48

Arbitration: the independent beast

This chapter presents the adverse impacts created by agreeing to a binding arbitration clause in a real estate listing or purchase agreement.

Rights to correct a decision lost

The trend among real estate agents regarding dispute resolution, encouraged since 1978 by trade unions, arbitration associations and the courts, has been to avoid the California court system by agreeing to resolve disputes involving the purchase or leasing of real estate and agency relationships through *binding arbitration*. The wisdom of this trend in real estate related contracts is under increasing attack.

Many pre-printed brokerage and purchase agreements include a boilerplate **arbitration provision**. The arbitration provision included in a purchase agreement, listing or lease agreement **forms a contract** with an arbitrator. Thus, the provision forms an agreement between the person who initials the provision and the arbitrator, an agreement separate from the purchase agreement which contains the provision. [**Prima Paint Corporation** v. **Flood & Conklin Mfg. Co.** (1967) 388 US 395]

To be enforceable, the arbitration provision must be initialed by the person against whom the provision is being enforced. Thus, an arbitration provision is enforceable against any person who initials the provision, even if the person is the only one to initial it. [**Grubb & Ellis Company** v. **Bello** (1993) 19 CA4th 231]

*Editor's note — **first tuesday's** purchase agreements and addenda do not contain either an arbitration provision or an attorney fee provision as a matter of policy to reduce disputes by making them less economically feasible.*

An **arbitration provision** in a real estate purchase agreement, listing or lease:

- is an arbitration agreement between the arbitrator and each person who agrees to be bound by the provision; and

- defines the arbitrator's powers and the limitations on those powers. [Calif. Code of Civil Procedure §1297.71]

The rights of the person agreeing to arbitration are established by the incorporation in the provision of arbitration statutes, applicable law limitations and discovery policies. Also controlling are the rules adopted by the arbitrator named in the provision, such as the American Arbitration Association.

Unless the arbitration provision states an arbitration award is "subject to judicial review," the award resulting from arbitration brought under the clause is **binding and final**. Without judicial review of an award in an arbitration action, the parties cannot be assured the award will be either **fair or correct**.

Arbitration's hype

Arbitration proceedings are reputed to be swifter and less costly than trials. Also, arbitrating disputes rather than litigating them eases the burden on the court system, and thus the taxpayer. Further, a public airing of "dirty laundry" produced in court filings and proceedings is avoided.

However, arbitration does not always live up to its reputation for being inexpensive or expedient. Filing fees for arbitration are high compared to filing fees for litigation. Unlike judges who are paid by the taxpayer, the arbitrator's charges must be paid by the loser. Additionally, the winner's attorney fees are paid by the loser when an attorney fee provision exists in the purchase agreement, lease or listing agreement involved.

Arbitration proceedings draw out for years when the dispute becomes complicated, just as in litigation. Also, a legitimate disagreement with the arbitrator's award as inconsistent with controlling California law, when called for in the powers granted the arbitrator by the arbitration provision, frequently leads to litigation in an effort to get the result attainable had the action been filed in a court of law in the first place.

Bizarre results not correctable

Consider a seller who contacts a brokerage office to list his property for sale. The sales activity is delegated to the broker's agent who procured the listing, customarily called the *listing agent*.

The seller and listing agent sign a listing agreement containing a provision calling for disputes to be submitted to binding arbitration — no judicial oversight permitted.

A buyer is located and an offer is obtained by another agent employed by the same broker, customarily called the *selling agent*. Both the agents and the broker are aware the buyer is financially unstable and may encounter difficulties closing the transaction. However, confirmation of the buyer's creditworthiness and net worth are not made the subject of a contingency provision by the selling agent who prepared the offer for the buyer. A contingency would have authorized the seller to cancel the purchase agreement if the buyer's credit had been found to be unsatisfactory.

When the listing agent, acting alone, submits the buyer's offer to the seller, the buyer's financial status is not discussed or disclosed, orally or in writing. The supervising broker fails to catch or correct the oversight.

The seller accepts the purchase agreement offer which provides for payment of a fee to the broker. Each agent will receive a share of any fee their broker may receive on the sale. Each agent's share is based on formulas agreed to in their respective written employment agreements with the broker.

Later, the buyer fails to close the transaction due to his disabling financial condition. The seller discovers that the listing agent, broker and selling agent all knew of the buyer's financial condition and failed to advise him of this fact. The seller makes a demand on the broker and both agents for his losses on the failed transaction, claiming the buyer's financial condition was a material fact in the transaction which the agents and broker knew about and failed to disclose.

The dispute is submitted to binding arbitration since a court action is barred by the arbitration provision in the listing agreement.

The arbitrator awards money damages to the seller based on the professional misconduct of the listing agent and employing broker for failure to disclose their knowledge of the buyer's unstable financial status — the broker being *vicariously liable* as the employer of the listing agent who failed to disclose.

Further, the arbitrator issues the seller a money award against the selling agent ruling the selling agent and the listing agent were "partners" since they would share in the fee the broker was to receive on the transaction. Thus, the selling agent is held *liable as a partner* of the listing agent for the seller's money damages resulting from the misconduct of the listing agent.

The selling agent then seeks to vacate the portion of the arbitration award holding him liable as a "partner" of the listing agent, claiming the arbitrator incorrectly applied partnership law to a real estate agency and employment relationship.

Can the award against the selling agent be corrected by a court since the arbitrator wrongfully applied partnership law?

No! An arbitrator's award, based on an erroneous application of law, is **not subject to judicial review** since a judicial review of the arbitrator's award was not included as a condition of an award in the arbitration provision. The arbitrator acted within his powers granted by the arbitration provision, even though he applied the wrong law and produced an erroneous result.

A court of law confronted with a binding arbitration agreement cannot review the arbitrator's award for **errors of fact or law** even if the error is obvious and causes substantial injustice. [**Hall** v. **Superior Court** (1993) 18 CA4th 427]

Grounds for correction

Any defect in an arbitrator's award resulting from an error of fact or law, no matter how flagrant, is neither reviewable nor correctable, unless:

- the arbitrator exceeded his authorized powers;

- the arbitrator acted with fraud or corruption;

- the arbitrator failed to disclose grounds for his disqualification;

- the award was procured by corruption, fraud or other misconduct; or

- the refusal of the arbitrators to postpone the hearing substantially prejudiced the rights of the party. [CCP §1286.2]

An arbitrator, unlike a judge in a court of law, is not bound by the rules of law when arbitrating a dispute. Even when the arbitrator agrees to follow applicable California law, his erroneous award, unlike an award of a court, cannot be corrected by any judicial review. The arbi-

trator's award is final and binding on all parties, unless:

- the parties have agreed the arbitrator's award is subject to "judicial review;" or

- the arbitrator applied the wrong law and in so doing exceeded his powers which had been limited to applicable law by the arbitration provision.

Otherwise, no judicial oversight exists, by petition or appeal, to correct an arbitrator's erroneous award.

The arbitrator's award

Consider a buyer and seller of real estate who enter into a purchase agreement on a form which contains an arbitration clause. They both initial the provision.

Prior to closing, the seller discovers the property has significantly greater value than the price the buyer has agreed to pay in the purchase agreement, a condition brought about by a sharply rising real estate market.

Motivated by his belief the property's value will continue to rise to price levels other buyers will be willing to pay, the seller refuses to close the sale.

The buyer files a "demand for arbitration" with the arbitrator, claiming the seller breached the purchase agreement. The buyer seeks only to recover his **money losses** amounting primarily to the difference between the purchase price he agreed to pay for the property and the increased value of the property on the date of the seller's breach, called *money damages*.

The buyer no longer wants the property and does not seek specific performance of the purchase agreement, even though the seller still owns the property.

Prior to completion of the arbitration hearings, the value of the property drops significantly due to a cyclical local economic downturn.

The arbitrator then issues an award in favor of the buyer.

However, the arbitrator does not award the buyer his money losses as asked for by the buyer. The arbitrator is aware the property's current value has fallen below the sales price agreed to in the purchase agreement and the increased value at the time of the seller's breach.

Instead of the requested money award, the arbitrator's award grants the buyer the right to purchase the property for a price equal to its current fair market value.

The buyer now petitions the court to vacate the arbitration award and remand the case for a money award as requested in the arbitration. The buyer claims the arbitrator exceeded his powers by awarding a result not contemplated by the purchase agreement nor sought by the parties, i.e., the right to acquire the property at a different price even though the buyer does not want to acquire the property.

Did the arbitrator exceed his powers, act corruptly or prejudice the rights of the parties by awarding an *equitable remedy* (specific performance) which was in conflict with the purchase agreement (different price) and beyond any expectations of either the buyer or the seller?

No! The arbitrator was not corrupt and did not exceed his powers in awarding the buyer the right to purchase the property at its current market value. The erroneous award was drawn from the arbitrator's (mis)interpretation of the purchase agreement and the law.

Basically, the remedy awarded a buyer by an arbitrator in binding arbitration is not reviewable by a court of law, as long as the remedy has "some remotely conceivable relationship" to the contract. [**Advanced Micro Devices, Inc.** v. **Intel Corporation** (1994) 9 C4th 362]

When individuals enter into a purchase agreement, each person has expectations about his and the other person's performance as defined by the terms of the agreement and set by existing law.

Yet by agreeing in the purchase agreement to binding arbitration, not only is a person forced to accept an arbitrator's incorrect application of law, he is forced to proceed with arbitration and accept an award impossible to predict.

As the dissent in *Advanced Micro Devices, Inc.* points out, a bizarre interpretation by an arbitrator of the agreement underlying a dispute, coupled with a blatant error of law, might result in an arbitration award "ordering the marriage of the disputing parties' first-born children."

An arbitrator has great latitude in making decisions since he may use his own discretion and does not need to follow the mandates of regulations, case decisions and codes.

Arbitrator's authority to enforce

Consider two partners in a real estate venture whose partnership agreement contains a boilerplate arbitration clause stating any dispute arising out of the agreement will be submitted to binding arbitration without judicial review.

On dissolution of the partnership, a dispute arises regarding disposition of the property, which is arbitrated. On issuing the award, the arbitrator includes the appointment of a receiver to supervise the sale of the partnership's property, rather than an award limited to calling for the property to be sold.

One of the partners seeks to vacate the arbitration award claiming the arbitrator exceeded his powers by appointing a receiver to sell the partnership's property.

Did the arbitrator exceed his powers by appointing a receiver to enforce his award?

Yes! The portion of the arbitration award appointing the receiver is invalid. An arbitrator lacks authority to **enforce his award** for the sale of the property, which is what the appointment of the receiver is designed to do.

The arbitration award must first be reduced to a court-ordered judgment before enforcement. On issuing an award, the person receiving the award files a petition with the court to **confirm** the award. On confirmation at a hearing on the petition, judgment is entered in conformance with the award.

It is the **judgment** which is enforced, not the arbitrator's award.

Although an arbitrator is not bound to follow the law when issuing an award, an arbitrator **exceeds his powers** when he attempts to also enforce his award — conduct reserved for a court of law after the award has been reduced to a judgment by the court. [**Marsch** v. **Williams** (1994) 23 CA4th 238]

An arbitrator also exceeds his powers when he **imposes fines** on a party to an arbitration for failure to comply with the arbitration award. An arbitrator does not have the power to impose **economic sanctions,** such as penalties and fines.

However, had the arbitration agreement authorized the arbitrator to appoint a receiver or impose fines, the arbitrator then has the power to do so, despite the general prohibition barring arbitrators from enforcing their awards. [**Mastrobuono** v. **Shearson Lehman Hutton, Inc.** (1995) 514 US 52]

Attorney fees as a power

Now consider a buyer and seller who enter into a real estate purchase agreement containing both an arbitration provision and an attorney fee provision. The attorney fee provision entitles the buyer or seller who prevails in an action to be awarded his attorney fees.

The buyer terminates the purchase agreement and seeks to recover all his transactional costs, claiming the seller has breached the agreement. As agreed, the dispute is submitted to binding arbitration. The arbitrator rules in favor of the seller, but denies the seller's request for attorney fees as called for under the attorney fee provision in the purchase agreement.

The seller seeks a correction of the arbitration award in a court of law claiming the arbitrator exceeded his powers by denying an award of attorney fees as agreed in the purchase agreement.

Here, the arbitrator did exceed his powers by failing to award attorney fees. The seller as the prevailing party was entitled to an award of attorney fees by a provision in the purchase agreement which was the subject of the arbitration. If the agreement underlying the dispute contains an attorney fee provision, the arbitrator must award attorney fees to the prevailing party. [**DiMarco** v. **Chaney** (1995) 31 CA4th 1809]

The attorney fee dilemma has a flip side. Not only must the arbitrator award attorney fees to the winner if the recovery of fees is called for in the purchase agreement, the arbitrator must determine the amount of the attorney fees to be awarded, an amount which is not subject to court review. [DiMarco, *supra*]

Avoiding arbitration

Consider a broker or agent who becomes a member of a local trade association. As part of the membership agreement, he agrees to binding arbitration for disputes arising between himself and other association members.

The arbitration panel who hears and decides disputes between members is composed of other members of the local association who have little to no legal training.

These local arbitration panels frequently base their decisions on moral or social beliefs and local customs they have personally adopted, rather than on controlling legal principles. Preference and bias towards a particular member of the association is more likely since the members of the arbitration panel are acquainted with or know about the members involved in the dispute. Yet, these panels are to consist of "neutral" arbitrators.

The panels are also very much aware the decisions they render are not appealable or reversible. Their award is final and binding.

However, the primary problem with arbitration proceedings heard by a local association's arbitration panel is the feeling held by most brokers and agents who are compelled to arbitrate that they are being railroaded through a process that disregards their rights, whether or not they are violated.

Further, by becoming a member of a local trade association, brokers and agents are forced to relinquish their rights to a court trial and an appeal to correct an erroneous decision rendered in disputes with other members.

However, brokers and agents employed by a broker who is an association member can avoid the complications imposed on them by membership. To do so and still comply with their broker's need to satisfy the local trade association's annual monetary demands arising out of their association with the broker, they can pay "nonmember dues" and become "paid nonmembers." [**Marin County Board of Realtors, Inc.** v. **Palsson** (1976) 16 C3d 920]

SECTION E

Purchase Agreements

Chapter
49   The purchase agreement

This chapter covers the use and preparation by an agent of a written purchase agreement entered into by buyers and sellers of real estate to document the terms and conditions of their transaction.

Types and variations

A newcomer's entry as a real estate agent into the vocation of soliciting and negotiating real estate transactions typically begins with the marketing and locating of single-family residences (SFRs) as listing and selling agents.

However, an agent often branches out and begins handling other types of property and interests.

Other properties the agent may begin handling include one-to-four unit residential properties, apartments and other nonresidential income properties like office buildings, commercial units, industrial space or unimproved parcels of land.

Interests which might be negotiated by the agent include leasehold tenancies when acting as a property manager or leasing agent of the landlord or prospective tenant, or financing arranged as a loan broker for an owner, buyer or tenant.

For sales, the primary document used to negotiate the transaction between a buyer and seller is a purchase agreement form. As different types of properties exist, so too do different types of purchase agreements exist, each with the provisions necessary to negotiate the sale of that particular type of property.

Three basic categories of purchase agreements exist for the documentation of real estate sales. The categories are influenced primarily by legislation and court decisions addressing the handling of the disclosures and due diligence investigations in the marketing of properties. The three categories of purchase agreements are for:

- one-to-four unit residential property sales transactions;

- other than one-to-four unit residential property sales transactions, such as for residential and nonresidential income properties and owner-occupied business/farming properties; and

- land transactions.

Within each category of purchase agreements, several variations exist. The variations cater to the specialized use of some properties or to specific conditions which affect a property, particularly within the one-to-four unit residential property category.

For example, purchase agreement variations for **one-to-four unit residential sales** transactions include purchase agreements for:

- negotiating the conventional financing of the purchase price [See Form 150 accompanying this chapter];

- negotiating the government insured financing (FHA/VA) of the purchase price [See **first tuesday** Forms 152 and 153];

- negotiating the sale of an owner-occupied residence-in-foreclosure to an investor, called an *equity purchase agreement* [See **first tuesday** Form 156];

- direct negotiations between principals (buyers and sellers) without either party being represented by a real estate agent;

- negotiating highly specialized transactions using a "short-form" purchase agreement which does not contain

One-to-Four Residential Units
(with escrow instructions)

DATE:_____, 20_____, at_____, California.

Items left blank or unchecked are not applicable.

FACTS:

1. Received from Buyer(s)_____
    and_____ the sum of $_____,
    evidenced by ☐ personal check, or ☐ _____,
    payable to _____,
    to be held undeposited until acceptance of this offer as a deposit toward acquisition of property situated in
    the City of _____, County of _____, California, described as:
    Real property: _____
    Personal property:_____

2. This agreement is comprised of this four-page form and _____ pages of addenda/attachments.

TERMS: Buyer to pay the purchase price as follows:

3. Cash down payment through escrow, including deposits, in the amount of. . . . . $_____
    3.1 Other consideration paid through escrow _____ . . . . $_____

4. ☐ Take title subject to, or ☐ assume, an existing first trust deed note held by
    _____ with an unpaid principal balance of . . . . $_____
    payable $_____ monthly, including interest not exceeding _____%,
    ☐ ARM, type _____, plus a monthly tax/insurance impound
    payment of $_____. _____
    4.1 At closing, loan balance differences per beneficiary statement(s) to be adjusted
         into: ☐ cash, ☐ carryback note, or ☐ sales price.
    4.2 The impound account to be transferred: ☐ charged, or ☐ without charge, to Buyer.

5. ☐ Take title subject to, or ☐ assume, an existing second trust deed note held by
    _____ with an unpaid principal balance of . . . $_____
    payable $_____ monthly, including interest not exceeding _____%,
    ☐ ARM, type _____, due _____, 20 _____.

6. Buyer to obtain a ☐ first, or ☐ second, trust deed loan in the amount of . . . . $_____
    payable approximately $_____ monthly for a period of _____ years.
    Interest on closing not to exceed _____%, ☐ ARM, type _____.
    Loan points not to exceed _____.
    6.1 ☐ Unless Buyer, within _____ days after acceptance, hands Seller satisfactory
         written confirmation Buyer is qualified for the financing of the purchase price,
         Seller may terminate the agreement. [**ft** Form 183]

7. Assume a tax bond or assessment lien with an unpaid principal balance of . . . . $_____

8. Note for the balance of the purchase price in the amount of. . . . . $_____
    to be executed by Buyer in favor of Seller and secured by a trust deed on the property
    junior to any above referenced financing, payable $_____ monthly, or more,
    beginning one month after closing, including interest at _____% from closing, due
    _____ years after closing.
    8.1 This note and trust deed to contain provisions to be provided by Seller for:
         ☐ due-on-sale; ☐ prepayment penalty; ☐ late charges; ☐ _____.
    8.2 A Carryback Disclosure Statement is attached as an addendum. [**ft** Form 300]
    8.3 Buyer to provide a Request for Notice of Delinquency to senior encumbrancers.
         [**ft** Form 412]
    8.4 Buyer to hand Seller a completed credit application on acceptance. [**ft** Form 302]
    8.5 Within _____ days of receipt of Buyer's credit application, Seller may terminate
         the agreement based on a reasonable disapproval of Buyer's creditworthiness.
    8.6 Seller may terminate the agreement on failure of the agreed terms for priority
         financing. [**ft** Form 183]
    8.7 As additional security, Buyer to execute a security agreement and file a UCC-1
         financing statement on any property transferred by Bill of Sale. [**ft** Form 436]

9. **Total Purchase Price is** . . . . $_____

— — — — — — — — — — — — — — — *PAGE ONE OF FOUR — FORM 150* — — — — — — — — — — — — — — — — — — —

10. ACCEPTANCE AND PERFORMANCE:

10.1   This offer to be deemed revoked unless accepted in writing ☐ on presentation, or ☐ within _____ days after date, and acceptance is personally delivered or faxed to Offeror or Offeror's Broker within this period.

10.2   After acceptance, Broker(s) are authorized to extend any performance date up to one month.

10.3   On failure of Buyer to obtain or assume financing as agreed by the date scheduled for closing, Buyer may terminate the agreement.

10.4   Buyer's close of Escrow is conditioned on Buyer's prior or concurrent closing on a sale of other property, commonly described as: _____.

10.5   Any termination of the agreement shall be by written Notice of Cancellation timely delivered to the other party, the other party's broker or Escrow, with instructions to Escrow to return all instruments and funds to the parties depositing them. [ft Form 183]

10.6   Both parties reserve their rights to assign and agree to cooperate in effecting an Internal Revenue Code §1031 exchange prior to close of escrow, on either party's written notice. [ft Forms 171 or 172]

10.7   Should Buyer breach the agreement, Buyer's monetary liability to Seller is limited to ☐ $_____, or ☐ the deposit receipted in Section 1.

11. PROPERTY CONDITIONS:

11.1   Seller to furnish prior to closing:

    a.   ☐ a structural pest control inspection report and certification of clearance of corrective measures.

    b.   ☐ a home inspection report prepared by an insured home inspector showing the land and improvements to be free of material defects.

    c.   ☐ a one-year home warranty policy:
        Insurer:_____
        Coverage: _____

    d.   ☐ a certificate of occupancy, or other clearance or retrofitting, required by local ordinance for the transfer of possession or title.

    e.   ☐ a certification by a licensed contractor stating the sewage disposal system is functioning properly, and if it contains a septic tank, is not in need of pumping.

    f.   ☐ a certification by a licensed water testing lab stating the well supplying the property meets potable water standards.

    g.   ☐ a certification by a licensed well-drilling contractor stating the well supplying the property produces minimum of _____ gallon(s) per minute.

    h.   ☐ _____

    i.   ☐ _____

11.2   Seller's Condition of Property (Transfer) Disclosure Statement (TDS) [ft Form 304]

    a.   ☐ is attached; or

    b.   ☐ is to be handed to Buyer on acceptance for Buyer's review. Within ten days after receipt, Buyer may either cancel the transaction or deliver to Seller or Seller's Broker a written notice itemizing any material defects in the property disclosed by the statement and unknown to Buyer prior to acceptance [ft Form 269]. Seller to repair, replace or correct noticed defects prior to closing.

    c.   On Seller's failure to repair, replace or correct noticed defects under §11.2b or §11.3a, Buyer may tender the purchase price reduced by the cost to repair, replace or correct the noticed defects, or close escrow and pursue available remedies. [ft Form 183]

11.3   Buyer to inspect the property twice:

    a.   An **initial property inspection** is required on acceptance to confirm the property's condition is substantially the same as observed by Buyer and represented by Seller or Seller's Agents prior to acceptance, and If not substantially the same, Buyer to promptly notify Seller in writing of undisclosed material defects discovered [ft Form 269]. Seller to repair, replace or correct noticed defects prior to closing; and

    b.   A **final walk-through inspection** is required within five days before closing to confirm the correction of any noticed defects under §11.2b and §11.3a and maintenance under §11.11. [ft Form 270]

11.4   Seller's Natural Hazard Disclosure Statement [ft Form 314] ☐ is attached, or ☐ is to be handed to Buyer on acceptance for Buyer's review. Within ten days of receipt, Buyer may terminate the agreement based on a reasonable disapproval of hazards disclosed by the Statement and unknown to Buyer prior to acceptance. [ft Form 182 and 183]

11.5   Buyer acknowledges receipt of a booklet and related seller disclosures containing ☐ *Environmental Hazards: A Guide for Homeowners, Buyers, Landlords and Tenants* (on all one-to-four units), ☐ *Protect Your Family from Lead in Your Home* (on all pre-1978, one-to-four units) [ft Form 313], and ☐ *The Homeowner's Guide to Earthquake Safety* (on all pre-1960, one-to-four units). [ft Form 315]

11.6   The property is located in: ☐ an industrial use area; ☐ a military ordnance area; ☐ an airport influence area; ☐ _____.

11.7 On acceptance, Seller to hand Buyer the following property information for Buyer's review:
☐ Property Operating Cost Sheet [ft Form 352 or 562]; ☐ Rental Income Statement. [ft Form 380]

    a.   Within ten days of receipt, Buyer may terminate the agreement based on a reasonable disapproval of the property information received.

11.8 If an **Owner's Association** is involved, ☐ Buyer has received and approves, or ☐ Buyer on acceptance to be handed, copies of the Association's Articles, Bylaws, CC&Rs, collection and lien enforcement policy, operating rules, operating budget, CPA's financial review, insurance policy summary and any age restriction statement.

    a.   No association claims for defects or changes in regular or special assessments are pending or anticipated. Current monthly assessment is $_____.

    b.   Seller is not in violation of CC&Rs, except_____.

    c.   Seller to pay association document and transfer fees.

    d.   Buyer to approve Association's statement of condition of assessments and confirm representations in §11.8a as a condition for closing escrow.

    e.   Within ten days of Buyer's post-acceptance receipt of the association documents, Buyer may terminate the agreement based on a reasonable disapproval of the documents. [ft Form 183]

11.9 Smoke detector(s) and water heater bracing exist in compliance with the law, and if not, Seller to install.

11.10 Possession of the property and keys/access codes to be delivered: ☐ on close of escrow, or ☐ as stated in the attached Occupancy Agreement. [ft Forms 271 and 272]

11.11 Seller to maintain the property in good condition until possession is delivered.

11.12 Fixtures and fittings attached to the property include, but are not limited to: window shades, blinds, light fixtures, plumbing fixtures, curtain rods, wall-to-wall carpeting, draperies, hardware, antennas, air coolers and conditioners, trees, shrubs, mailboxes and other similar items.

11.13 Notice: Pursuant to Section 290.46 of the Penal Code, information about specified registered sex offenders is made available to the public via an Internet Web site maintained by the Department of Justice at www.meganslaw.ca.gov. Depending on an offender's criminal history, this information will include either the address at which the offender resides or the community of residence and ZIP code in which he or she resides.

12. CLOSING CONDITIONS:

12.1 This transaction to be escrowed with _____.
Parties to deliver instructions to Escrow as soon as reasonably possible after acceptance.

    a.   ☐ Escrow holder is authorized and instructed to act on the provisions of this agreement as the mutual escrow instructions of the parties and to draft any additional instructions necessary to close this transaction. [ft Form 401]

    b.   ☐ Escrow instructions, prepared and signed by the parties, are attached to be handed to Escrow on acceptance. [ft Form 401]

12.2 Escrow to be handed all instruments needed to **close escrow** ☐ on or before _____, 20_____, or ☐ within _____ days after acceptance. Parties to hand Escrow all documents required by the title insurer, lenders or other third parties to this transaction prior to seven days before the date scheduled for closing.

    a.   Each party to pay its customary escrow charges. [ft Forms 310 and 311]

12.3 Buyer's title to be subject to covenants, conditions, restrictions, reservations and easements of record.
_____.

12.4 Title to be vested in Buyer or Assignee free of encumbrances other than those set forth herein. Buyer's interest in title to be insured under an ALTA form policy issued by _____
as a(n) ☐ Homeowner(s) policy (one-to-four units), ☐ Residential ALTA-R policy (vacant or improved residential parcel), ☐ Owner's policy (other than one-to-four units), ☐ CLTA Joint Protection policy (also naming Carryback Seller or purchase-assist lender), or ☐ Binder (to insure resale or refinance within two years).

    a.   Endorsements: _____

    b.   ☐ Seller, or ☐ Buyer, to pay the title insurance premium.

12.5 Buyer to furnish a new fire insurance policy covering the property.

12.6 Taxes, assessments, insurance premiums, rents, interest and other expenses to be **prorated** to close of escrow, unless otherwise provided.

12.7 Bill of Sale to be executed for any **personal property** being transferred.

12.8 If Seller is unable to convey marketable title as agreed, or if the **improvements** on the property are materially damaged prior to closing, Buyer may terminate the agreement. Seller to pay all reasonable escrow cancellation charges. [ft Form 183]

13. BROKERAGE FEE:

13.1 Parties to pay the below-mentioned Broker(s) a fee now due of _____ as follows: Seller to pay the brokerage fee on the change of ownership. The party wrongfully preventing this change of ownership to pay the brokerage fee.

13.2 Seller's Broker and Buyer's Broker, respectively, to share the brokerage fee _____:_____.

13.3 Attached is the Agency Law Disclosure. [ft Form 305]

13.4 Broker is authorized to report the sale, its price and terms for dissemination and use of participants in brokerage trade associations or listing services.

14. _____

_____

_____

_____

_____

_____

_____

_____

_____

_____

_____

Buyer's/
Selling Broker:_____

By: _____

Is the agent of: ☐ Buyer exclusively.
☐ Both Seller and Buyer.

Seller's/
Listing Broker:_____

By: _____

Is the agent of: ☐ Seller exclusively.
☐ Both Seller and Buyer.

I agree to the terms stated above.

Date:_____, 20_____

Buyer: _____

Buyer: _____

Signature: _____

Signature: _____

Address: _____

Phone:_____

Fax: _____

Email: _____

I agree to the terms stated above.

Date:_____, 20_____

Seller: _____

Seller: _____

Signature: _____

Signature: _____

Address: _____

Phone:_____

Fax: _____

Email: _____

REJECTION OF OFFER

Undersigned hereby rejects this offer in its entirety. No counteroffer will be forthcoming.

Date:_____, 20_____

Name: _____

Name: _____

Signature: _____

Signature: _____

boilerplate provisions setting forth the terms for payment of the price, which allows the agent to attach specialty addenda to set the terms for payment (a carryback ARM or equity sharing addenda) [See **first tuesday** Form 155]; and

- offers to enter into a lease-option sale or a land sales contract. [See **first tuesday** Forms 164 and 167]

Variations among purchase agreements used in **income property** and **owner-occupied business property** sales transactions include purchase agreements for:

- the conventional financing of the purchase price [See **first tuesday** Form 159];

- the downpayment note financing of the purchase price [See **first tuesday** Form 154];

- the reciprocal sale and purchase of different properties by their owners [See **first tuesday** Form 171]; and

- an offer to grant an option to provide the buyer with an owner's irrevocable offer to enter into a purchase agreement on the buyer's exercise of the option. [See **first tuesday** Form 160]

Escrow instructions provide yet another variation on the purchase agreement. A buyer and seller who have entered into escrow instructions without first entering into a real estate purchase agreement are bound by the escrow instructions as though it was a purchase agreement. [See **first tuesday** Form 401]

Attached to all these various purchase agreements are one or more addenda, regarding:

- disclosures about the property;

- the financing of the price paid for the property;

- agency relationship law; and

- special provisions called for by the needs of the buyer or seller.

However, the focus here is limited to the needs of the newly licensed agent who will be negotiating single-family real estate sales. Thus, this chapter discusses the purchase agreement used in SFR sales transactions structured for the conventional financing of the purchase price.

Analyzing the purchase agreement

The conventional purchase agreement, **first tuesday** Form 150, is used to prepare and submit the buyer's **written offer** to purchase one-to-four unit residential property. Terms for payment of the price are limited to conventional financing, an assumption of existing loans and a carryback note. Form 150 is also properly used by sellers in a counteroffer situation to submit their **fresh offer** to sell the real estate.

The purchase agreement offer, if accepted, becomes the binding written contract between the buyer and seller. Its terms must be complete and clear to prevent misunderstandings so the agreement can be judicially enforced. Thus, Form 150 is a comprehensive "boilerplate" purchase agreement which serves as a **checklist**, presenting the various conventional financing arrangements and conditions a prudent buyer would consider when making an offer to purchase.

Each section in Form 150 has a separate purpose and need for enforcement. The sections include:

1. *Identification*: The date of preparation for referencing the agreement, the name of the buyer, the amount of the good-faith deposit, the description of the real estate, an inventory of any personal property included in the transfer and the number of pages contained in the agreement and its addenda are set forth in sections 1 and 2 to establish the facts on which the agreement is negotiated.

2. *Price and terms*: All the typical variations for payment of the price by conventional purchase-assist financing or an assumption of existing financing are set forth in sections 3 through 9 as a checklist of provisions. On making an offer (or counteroffer), the terms for payment and financing of the price are selected by checking boxes and filling blanks in the desired provisions.

3. *Acceptance and performance*: Aspects of the formation of a contract, excuses for nonperformance and termination of the agreement are provided for in section 10, such as the time period for acceptance of the offer, the broker's authorization to extend performance deadlines, the financing of the price as a closing contingency, procedures for cancellation of the agreement, a sale of other property as a closing contingency, cooperation to effect a §1031 transaction and limitations on monetary liability for breach of contract.

4. *Property Conditions*: The buyer's confirmation of the physical condition of the property as disclosed prior to acceptance is **confirmed** as set forth in section 11 by the seller's delivery of reports, warranty policies, certifications, disclosure statements, an environmental, lead-based paint and earthquake safety booklet, any operating cost and income statements, and any homeowners' association (HOA) documents not handed to the buyer prior to entry into the purchase agreement, as well as by the buyer's initial inspection, personally or by a home inspector, and final inspection at closing to confirm the seller has eliminated defects known, but not disclosed, prior to acceptance.

5. *Closing conditions*: The escrow holder, escrow instruction arrangements and the date of closing are established in section 12, as are title conditions, title insurance, hazard insurance, prorates and loan adjustments.

6. *Brokerage and agency*: The release of sales data on the transaction to trade associations is authorized, the brokerage fee is set and the delivery of the agency law disclosure to both buyer and seller is provided for as set forth in section 13, as well as the confirmation of the agency undertaken by the brokers and their agents on behalf of one or both parties to the agreement.

7. *Signatures*: The seller and buyer bind each other to perform as agreed in the purchase agreement by signing and dating their signatures to establish the date of offer and acceptance.

Preparing the purchase agreement

The following instructions are for the preparation and use of the Purchase Agreement, **first tuesday** Form 150. Form 150 is designed as a checklist of practical provisions so a broker or his agent can prepare an offer for a prospective buyer who seeks to purchase conventionally financed, one-to-four unit residential property located in California.

Each instruction corresponds to the provision in the form bearing the same number.

*Editor's note — **Check** and **enter** items throughout the agreement in each provision with boxes and blanks, unless the provision is not intended to be included as part of the final agreement, in which case it is left unchecked or blank.*

Document identification:

Enter the date and name of the city where the offer is prepared. This date is used when referring to this purchase agreement.

Facts:

1. *Buyer, deposit and property*: **Enter** the name of each buyer who will sign the offer.

Enter the dollar amount of any good-faith, earnest money deposit. **Check** the appropriate box to indicate the form of the good-faith deposit. **Enter** the name of the payee (escrow, title company or broker).

Enter the name of the city and county in which the property is located.

Enter the legal description or common address of the property, or the assessor's parcel number (APN).

Enter the description of any personal property included, or **enter** words of reference, such as "see attached inventory," and **attach** an itemized list of the inventory. The seller's trade fixtures to be purchased by the buyer must be listed as inventory if they are to be acquired by the buyer. [See **first tuesday** Form 250]

2. *Entire agreement*: **Enter** the number of pages comprising all of the addenda, disclosures, etc., which are attached to the purchase agreement.

Terms for payment of the purchase price:

3. *Cash down payment*: **Enter** the dollar amount of the buyer's cash down payment toward the purchase price.

    3.1 *Additional down payment*: **Enter** the description of any other consideration to be paid as part of the price, such as trust deed notes, personal property or real estate equities (an exchange). **Enter** the dollar amount of its value.

4. *First trust deed note*: **Check** the appropriate box to indicate whether the transfer of title is to be "subject-to" an existing loan or by an "assumption" of the loan if the buyer is to take over an existing first trust deed loan. **Enter** the lender's name. **Enter** the remaining bal-

ance, the monthly principal and interest (PI) payment and the interest rate on the loan. **Check** the box to indicate whether the interest is adjustable (ARM), and if so, **enter** the index name. **Enter** any monthly impound payment made in addition to the PI payment. **Enter** any due date or other terms unique to the loan.

4.1 *Loan balance adjustments*: **Check** the appropriate box to indicate the financial adjustment desired for loan balance differences at the close of escrow.

4.2 *Impound balances*: **Check** the appropriate box to indicate whether the impound account transferred to the buyer will be with or without a charge to the buyer.

5. *Second trust deed note*: **Check** the appropriate box to indicate whether the transfer of title is to be "subject-to" an existing loan or by an "assumption" of the loan if the buyer is to take over an existing second trust deed loan. **Enter** the lender's name. **Enter** the remaining balance, the monthly PI payment and the interest rate on the loan. **Check** the box to indicate whether the interest is adjustable (ARM), and if so, **enter** the index name. **Enter** the due date for payment of a final/balloon payment.

6. *New trust deed loan*: **Check** the appropriate box to indicate whether any new financing will be a first or second trust deed loan. **Enter** the amount of the loan, the monthly PI payment, the term of the loan and the rate of interest. **Check** the box to indicate whether the interest will be adjustable (ARM), and if so, **enter** the index name. **Enter** any limitations on loan points.

6.1 *Buyer's loan qualification*: **Check** the box to indicate the seller is authorized to cancel the agreement if the buyer is to obtain a new loan and fails to deliver documentation from a lender indicating he has been qualified for a loan. **Enter** the number of days the buyer has after acceptance to deliver written confirmation of his qualification for the loan.

7. *Bond or assessment assumed*: **Enter** the amount of the principal balance remaining unpaid on bonds and special assessment liens (such as Mello-Roos or 1915 improvement bonds) which will remain unpaid and become the responsibility of the buyer on closing.

*Editor's note — Improvement bonds are obligations of the seller which may be assumed by the buyer in lieu of their payoff by the seller. If assumed, the bonded indebtedness becomes part of the consideration paid for the property. Some purchase agreements erroneously place these bonds under "property tax" as though they were **ad valorem taxes**, and then fail to prorate and charge the unpaid amount to the seller.*

8. *Seller carryback note*: **Enter** the amount of the carryback note to be executed by the buyer as partial payment of the price. **Enter** the amount of the note's monthly PI payment, the interest rate and the due date for the final/balloon payment.

8.1 *Special carryback provisions:* **Check** the appropriate box to indicate any special provisions to be included in the carryback note or trust deed. **Enter** the name of any other special provision to be included in the carryback note or trust deed, such as impounds, discount options, extension provisions, guarantee arrangements or right of first refusal on the sale or hypothecation of the note.

8.2 *Carryback disclosure*: **Fill out** and **attach** a Seller Carryback Disclosure Statement as an addendum. [See **first tuesday** Form 300]

Editor's note — Further approval of the disclosure statement in escrow creates by statute a buyer's contingency allowing for cancellation until time of closing on any purchase of one-to-four unit residential property.

8.3 *Notice of Delinquency*: **Requires** the buyer to execute a Request for Notice of Delinquency and pay the costs of recording and serving it on senior lenders since they will have priority on title to the trust deed securing the carryback note.

8.4 *Buyer creditworthiness*: **Requires** the buyer to provide the seller with a completed credit application.

8.5 *Approval of creditworthiness*: **Enter** the number of days within which the seller may cancel the transaction for reasonable disapproval of the buyer's credit application and report.

8.6 *Subordination*: **Provides** for the seller to terminate this transaction if the parameters agreed to for financing by an assumption or origination of a trust deed loan with priority on title to the carryback note are exceeded.

8.7 *Personal property as security*: **Requires** the buyer on the transfer of any personal property in this transaction to execute a security agreement and UCC-1 financing statement to provide additional security for any carryback note.

9. *Purchase price*: **Enter** the total amount of the purchase price as the sum of lines 3, 3.1, 4, 5, 6, 7 and 8.

10. Acceptance and performance periods:

10.1 *Delivery of acceptance*: **Check** the appropriate box to indicate the time period for acceptance of the offer. If applicable, **enter** the number of days in which the seller may accept this offer and form a binding contract.

Editor's note — Acceptance occurs on the return delivery to the person making the offer (or counteroffer) or to his broker of a copy of the unaltered purchase agreement offer containing the signed acceptance.

10.2 *Extension of performance dates*: **Authorizes** the brokers to extend the performance dates up to one month to meet the objectives of the agreement — time being of a reasonable duration and not the essence of this agreement as a matter of policy. This extension authority does not extend to the acceptance period.

10.3 *Loan contingency*: **Authorizes** the buyer to cancel the transaction at the time scheduled for closing if the financing for payment of the price is not obtainable or assumable.

10.4 *Sale of other property*: If the closing of this transaction is to be contingent on the buyer's receipt of net proceeds from a sale of other property, **enter** the address of the property to be sold by the buyer.

10.5 *Cancellation procedures*: **Provides** the method of cancellation required to terminate the agreement when the right to cancel is triggered by other provisions in the agreement, such as contingency or performance provisions.

10.6 *Exchange cooperation*: **Requires** the parties to cooperate in an IRS §1031 transaction on further written notice by either party. **Provides** for the parties to assign their interests in this agreement.

10.7 *Liability limitations* **Provides** for a dollar limit on the buyer's liability for the buyer's breach of the agreement. **Check** the first box and **enter** the maximum dollar amount of money losses the seller may recover from the buyer or **check** the second box to indicate the buyer's monetary liability is limited to the good-faith deposit tendered with the offer to buy.

Editor's note — Liability limitation provisions avoid the misleading and unenforceable forfeiture called for under liquidated damage clauses included in most purchase agreement forms provided by other publishers of forms.

11. Property Conditions:

11.1 *Seller to furnish*: **Check** the appropriate box(es) within the following subsections to indicate the items the seller is to furnish prior to closing.

a. *Pest control*: **Check** the box to indicate the seller is to furnish a structural pest control report and clearance.

b. *Home inspection report*: **Check** the box to indicate the seller is to employ a home inspection company and furnish the buyer with the company's home inspection report.

c. *Home warranty*: **Check** the box to indicate the seller is to furnish an insurance policy for home repairs. **Enter** the name of the insurer and the type of coverage, such as for the air conditioning unit, etc.

d. *Local ordinance compliance*: **Check** the box to indicate the seller is to furnish a certificate of occupancy or other clearance required by local ordinance.

e. *Sewer or septic certificate*: **Check** the box to indicate the seller is to furnish a certificate of the condition of the sewage disposal system stating it is functioning properly.

f. *Potable well water*: **Check** the box to indicate the seller is to furnish a certificate stating the well supply meets water standards.

g. *Well water capacities*: **Check** the box to indicate the seller is to furnish a certificate stating the amount of water the well supplies. **Enter** the number of gallons per minute the well is expected to produce.

h. *Other terms*: **Check** the box and **enter** any other report, certification or clearance the seller is to furnish.

i. *Other terms*: **Check** the box and **enter** any other report, certification or clearance the seller is to furnish.

11.2 *Property condition(s)*: **Check** the appropriate box within the following subsections to indicate the status of the Transfer Disclosure Statement (TDS).

a. *Attached TDS*: **Check** the box to indicate the seller's TDS has been prepared and handed to the buyer, and if so, **attach** it to this agreement. Thus, the property's condition is accepted by the buyer upon entering into the purchase agreement offer.

*Editor's note — Use of the TDS form is mandated on one-to-four unit residential property. [See **first tuesday** Form 304]*

b. *Later delivered TDS*: **Check** the box to indicate the TDS is to be **delivered later** to the buyer to confirm the condition of the property is as disclosed prior to entry into the purchase agreement. On receipt of the TDS, the buyer may either cancel the transaction for failure of the seller or the listing agent to disclose known property defects prior to acceptance of the purchase agreement (or counteroffer), or give notice to the seller of the defects known and not disclosed prior to acceptance and make a demand on the seller to correct them prior to closing.

c. *Repair of defects*: **Authorizes** the buyer to either cancel the transaction or adjust the price should the seller fail to correct the defects noticed under sections 11.2b or 11.3a.

11.3 *Buyer's inspection*: **Authorizes** the buyer to inspect the property twice during the escrow period to verify its condition is as disclosed by the seller prior to the time of acceptance.

a. *Initial property inspection*: **Requires** the buyer to inspect the property immediately after acceptance to put the seller on notice of material defects to be corrected by the seller prior to closing. [See **first tuesday** Forms 269]

b. *Final walk-through inspection*: **Requires** the buyer to inspect the property again within five days before closing to confirm repairs and maintenance of the property have occurred. [See **first tuesday** Form 270]

11.4 *Seller's Natural Hazard Disclosure (NHD) Statement*: **Check** the appropriate box to indicate whether the NHD statement disclosing the seller's knowledge about the hazards listed on the form has been prepared and handed to the buyer. If it has been received by the buyer, **attach** a copy to the purchase agreement. If the NHD will be handed to the buyer after acceptance, the buyer has ten days after the buyer's receipt of the NHD statement in which to approve it or cancel.

Editor's note — Disclosure by the seller is mandated on one-to-four unit residential property. [Calif. Civil Code §1103]

11.5 *Hazard disclosure booklets*: **Check** the appropriate box(es) to indicate which hazard booklets have been received by the buyer, together with the seller's prepared and signed disclosures accompanying each booklet.

11.6 *Other property disclosures*: **Check** the appropriate box(es) to indicate other disclosures made by the seller regarding the location of the property. **Enter** a reference to any local (option) ordinance disclosure statement attached as an addendum

to the purchase agreement and **attach** it. [See **first tuesday** Form 307]

11.7 *Operating costs and rents*: **Check** the appropriate box(es) to indicate the information the seller is to disclose regarding the operating expenses of ownership and any rents.

a. *Disclosure approval*: **Authorizes** the buyer to cancel the purchase agreement and escrow if the operating expenses and income disclosures are unacceptable.

11.8 *Homeowners' association (HOA)*: **Check** the appropriate box to indicate whether the HOA documents have been or are to be delivered to the buyer.

a. *Monthly payments*: **Enter** the dollar amount of the monthly payments assessed by the HOA.

b. *CC&Rs*: **Enter** the nature of any violation of the CC&Rs by the seller.

c. *HOA charges*: **Provides** for the seller to pay all HOA charges on the transaction.

d. *Condition of assessments*: **Provides** for the buyer to approve the HOA's condition of assessments statement prior to closing.

e. *Disapproval of HOA documents*: **Authorizes** the buyer to terminate this purchase agreement within ten days after his receipt of HOA documents when the disclosures are made after entering into the purchase agreement. Disclosure of HOA conditions in escrow trigger a statutory contingency allowing the buyer to cancel the purchase agreement.

11.9 *Safety compliance*: **Requires** smoke detectors and water heater bracing to exist or be installed by the seller.

11.10 *Buyer's possession*: **Check** the appropriate box to indicate when possession of the property will be delivered to the buyer, whether at closing or under an **attached** buyer's interim occupancy or seller's holdover agreement. [See **first tuesday** Forms 271 and 272]

11.11 *Property maintenance*: **Requires** the seller to maintain the present condition of the property until the close of escrow.

Editor's note — See section 11.3b for the buyer's final inspection to confirm maintenance at closing.

11.12 *Fixtures and fittings*: **Confirms** this agreement includes real estate fixtures and fittings as part of the property purchased.

Editor's note — Trade fixtures are personal property to be listed as items on an attached inventory at section 1.

11.13 *Sex offender disclosure*: **Complies** with requirements that the seller disclose the existence of a sex offender database on the sale (or lease) of one-to-four residential units.

Editor's note — By the existence of the disclosure in the form, the seller and brokers are relieved of any duty to make further disclosures regarding registered sex offenders.

12. **Closing conditions:**

12.1 *Escrow closing agent*: **Enter** the name of the escrow company handling the closing.

   a. *Escrow instructions*: **Check** the box to indicate the purchase agreement is to also serve as the mutual instructions to escrow from the parties. The escrow company will typically prepare supplemental instructions they will need to handle and close the transaction. [See **first tuesday** Form 401]

   b. *Escrow instructions*: **Check** the box to indicate escrow instructions have been prepared and are attached to this purchase agreement. **Prepare** and **attach** the prepared escrow instructions to the purchase agreement and **obtain** the signatures of the parties. [See **first tuesday** Form 401]

12.2 *Closing date*: **Check** the appropriate box to indicate the method to be used to set the date on which escrow is scheduled to close. Following the checked box, **enter** the specific date for closing or the number of days anticipated as necessary for the parties to perform and close escrow. Also, prior to seven days before closing, the parties are to deliver all documents needed by third parties to perform their services by the date scheduled for closing.

   a. *Escrow charges*: **Requires** each party to pay their customary escrow closing charges, amounts any competent escrow officer can provide on inquiry.

12.3 *Title conditions*: **Enter** wording for any further-approval contingency provision the buyer may need to confirm that title conditions set forth in the preliminary title report will not interfere with the buyer's intended use of the property, such as "closing contingent on buyer's approval of preliminary title report."

12.4 *Title insurance*: **Provides** for title to be vested in the name of the buyer or his assignee. **Enter** the name of the title insurance company which is to provide a preliminary title report in anticipation of issuing title insurance. **Check** the appropriate box to indicate the type of title insurance policy to be issued on closing.

   a. *Policy endorsements*: **Enter** any endorsements to be issued with the policy.

   b. *Payment of premium*: **Check** the appropriate box to indicate whether the buyer or seller is to pay the title insurance premium.

12.5 *Fire insurance*: **Requires** the buyer to provide a new policy of hazard insurance.

12.6 *Prorates and adjustments*: **Authorizes** prorations and adjustments on the close of escrow for taxes, insurance premiums, rents, interest, loan balances, service contracts and other property operating expenses, prepaid or accrued.

12.7 *Personal property*: **Requires** the seller to execute a bill of sale for any personal property being transferred in this transaction as called for in section 1.

12.8 *Property destruction*: **Provides** for the seller to bear the *risk of loss* for any casualty losses suffered by the property prior to the close of escrow. Thus, the buyer may terminate the agreement if the seller is unable to provide a marketable title or should the property improvements suffer major damage.

13. Brokerage fee:

13.1 *Fee amount*: **Enter** the total amount of the fee due all brokers to be paid by the seller. The amount may be stated as a fixed dollar amount or a percentage of the price.

Editor's note — The defaulting party pays all brokerage fees and the brokerage fee can only be altered or cancelled by mutual instructions from the buyer and seller.

13.2 *Fee sharing*: **Enter** the percentage share of the fee each broker is to receive.

Editor's note — The percentage share may be set based on an oral agreement between the brokers, by acceptance of the listing broker's MLS offer to a selling office to share a fee, or unilaterally by an agent when preparing the buyer's offer.

13.3 *Agency law disclosures*: **Attach** a copy of the Agency Law Disclosure addendum for all parties to sign.

Editor's note — The disclosure is mandated to be acknowledged by the buyer with the offer and acknowledged by the seller on acceptance as a prerequisite to the brokers enforcing collection of the fee when the property involved contains one-to-four residential units. [See **first tuesday** *Form 305]*

13.4 *Disclosure of sales data*: **Authorizes** the brokers to report the transaction to trade associations or listing services.

14. *Other terms*: **Enter** any special provision to be included in the purchase agreement.

Agency confirmation:

Buyer's broker identification: **Enter** the name of the buyer's broker. **Obtain** the signature of the buyer's broker or the selling agent acting on behalf of the buyer's broker. **Check** the appropriate box to indicate the agency which was created by the broker's (and his agents') conduct with the parties.

Seller's broker identification: **Enter** the name of the seller's broker. **Obtain** the signature of the seller's broker or the listing agent acting on behalf of the seller's broker. **Check** the appropriate box to indicate the agency which was created by the broker's (and his agents') conduct with the parties.

Signatures:

Buyer's signature: **Enter** the date the buyer signs the purchase agreement and each buyer's name. **Obtain** each buyer's signature on the purchase agreement and on each attachment which requires his signature. **Enter** the buyer's address, telephone and fax numbers, and email address.

Seller's signature: **Enter** the date the seller signs the purchase agreement and each seller's name. **Obtain** each seller's signature on the purchase agreement and on each attachment which requires his signature. **Enter** the seller's address, telephone and fax numbers, and email address.

Rejection of offer:

Should the offer contained in the purchase agreement be rejected instead of accepted, and the rejection will not result in a counteroffer, **enter** the date of the rejection and the names of the party rejecting the offer. **Obtain** the signatures of the party rejecting the offer.

Observations

As a policy of the publisher, this purchase agreement **does not contain** clauses which tend to increase the risk of litigation or are generally felt to work against the best interests of the buyer, seller and broker. Excluded provisions include:

- an *attorney fee provision*, which tends to **promote litigation** and inhibit contracting;

- an *arbitration clause*, which, if included and initialed, absolutely **waives** the buyer's and seller's right to a fair and correct decision by trial and appeal; and

- a *time-essence clause*, since future performance (closing) dates are, at best, estimates by the broker and his agents of the time needed to close and are too often **improperly used** by sellers in rising markets to cancel the transaction before the buyer or broker can reasonably comply with the terms of the purchase agreement.

Chapter 50

An owner's residence in foreclosure

This chapter examines the equity purchase restrictions which must be known and applied by all investors buying owner-occupied, one-to-four unit residential property during foreclosure.

The equity purchase sales scheme

An equity purchase (EP) transaction takes place when an owner-occupied, one-to-four unit residential property in foreclosure is acquired for rental, investment or dealer purposes by a buyer, who is called an *EP investor*. Conversely, an EP transaction does not occur and the EP rules do not apply if the buyer acquires the property for use as his personal residence.

Equity purchase statutes apply to all buyers who are EP investors regardless of the number of EP transactions the investor completes. The investor does not need to be in the business of buying homes in foreclosure for the statutes to apply to him. [**Segura** v. **McBride** (1992) 5 CA4th 1028]

Both the EP investor and his agent must comply with EP law or be subject to drastic penalties.

Also, all agents need to be aware that the EP agreement signed by an EP investor must be printed in **bold type**, ranging from at least 10-point to 14-point font size, and be in the **same language** used during negotiations with the seller-in-foreclosure. [Calif. Civil Code §§1695.2, 1695.3, 1695.5]

Thus, the EP investor and all the agents involved in the transaction must use a written agreement containing statutory EP notices. Failure to use the correct forms subjects the EP investor and the agents to liability for all losses incurred by the seller-in-foreclosure, plus harsh penalties. [Segura, *supra*]

*Editor's note — **first tuesday's** Equity Purchase Agreement, Form 156, complies with all* statutory requirements and properly sets forth the right of the seller-in-foreclosure to cancel. *[See Form 156 accompanying this chapter]*

Cancellation within five business days

Prior to closing a sale, a seller-in-foreclosure has a **statutory five-business-day right to cancel** the EP agreement he has entered into with an EP investor. Thus, the seller can avoid the sale entirely, with or without cause.

The EP investor's compliance with the requirement of a written purchase agreement incorporating the EP rules grants the EP seller the automatic five-business-day right to cancel the agreement before a closing can take place. If the seller cancels within the period, the sale under the purchase agreement cannot be closed.

When the notice of the seller-in-foreclosure's cancellation rights are properly contained in the EP agreement, the seller's **cancellation period ends** at:

- midnight (12:00 a.m.) of the **fifth business day** following the day the seller enters into any type of purchase agreement with an EP investor; or

- 8:00 a.m. of the day scheduled for the **trustee's sale**, if it is to occur first. [CC §1695.4(a)]

The seller-in-foreclosure's five-business-day right to cancel does not begin to run until proper notice of the cancellation period is given to the seller. [CC §1695.5]

The first and proper time for giving the seller-in-foreclosure the notice is in the EP agreement. Failure to do so allows the seller to

EQUITY PURCHASE AGREEMENT *

DATE:_____, 20_____, at _____, California.

NOTICE: For use by buyers of one-to-four residential units which are owner-occupied and in foreclosure, when the buyer does not intend to occupy the property. [Calif. Civil Code §1695]

Items left blank or unchecked are not applicable.

FACTS:

1. This agreement is for the purchase of property situated in the City of_____,
   County of _____, California, described as:
   Real property: _____
   _____
   Personal property: ☐ See attached inventory;
   _____

2. This agreement is comprised of this six-page form and _____ pages of addenda/attachments.

TERMS: Buyer to pay the purchase price as follows:

3. Cash down payment through escrow in the amount of......................... $_____

4. Take title subject to an existing first trust deed note held by
   _____ with an approximate unpaid amount of........... $_____
   payable $_____ monthly until paid, including interest not exceeding
   _____%, ☐ ARM, type _____, plus a monthly tax/insurance
   impound payment of $_____.

   4.1 The unpaid amount includes delinquent payments and foreclosure costs to
       be cured by Buyer in the amount of $_____, representing
       monthly payments due beginning with the month of _____,
       20_____.

   4.2 The impound account to be transferred without charge.

5. Take title subject to an existing second trust deed note held by
   _____ with an approximate unpaid amount of........... $_____
   payable $_____ monthly, including interest not exceeding _____%,
   ☐ ARM, type_____, due _____, 20_____.

   5.1 The unpaid amount includes delinquent payments and foreclosure costs to
       be cured by Buyer in the amount of $_____, representing
       monthly payments due beginning with the month of _____,
       20 _____.

6. At closing, loan balance differences disclosed by beneficiary statement(s) to be
   adjusted into the purchase price, but if the balance exceeds the amount stated,
   the difference to be adjusted into the cash down payment.

7. Buyer to obtain a ☐ first, or ☐ second, trust deed loan in the amount of .... $_____
   payable approximately $_____ monthly for a period of _____ years.
   Interest on closing not to exceed _____%, ☐ ARM, type _____.

8. Assume a tax bond or assessment lien with an unpaid principal balance of........... $_____

9. Note for the balance of the purchase price in the amount of .... $_____
   to be executed by Buyer in favor of Seller and secured by a trust deed on the
   property junior to any above referenced financing, payable $_____
   monthly, or more, beginning one month after closing, including interest at
   _____% per annum from closing, due _____, 20_____.

   9.1 This note and trust deed will not contain provisions for due-on-sale,
       prepayment penalty or late charges.

   9.2 A Carryback Disclosure Statement is attached as an addendum. [ft Form 300]

10. TOTAL PURCHASE PRICE IS... $_____

— — — — — — — — — — — — — — — — *PAGE ONE OF SIX — FORM 156* — — — — — — — — — — — — — — — —

11. ACCEPTANCE AND PERFORMANCE:

    11.1 This offer to be deemed revoked unless accepted in writing ☐ on presentation, or ☐ within _____ days after date, and acceptance is personally delivered or faxed to Offeror or Offeror's Broker within this period.

    11.2 After acceptance, Broker(s) are authorized to extend any performance date up to one month.

    11.3 On failure of Buyer to obtain or assume financing as agreed by the date scheduled for closing, Buyer may terminate the agreement.

    11.4 Buyer's close of escrow is conditioned on Buyer's prior or concurrent closing on a sale of other property, commonly described as: _____.

    11.5 Any termination of the agreement shall be by written Notice of Cancellation timely delivered to the other party, the other party's broker or Escrow, with instructions to Escrow to return all instruments and funds to the parties depositing them. [ft Form 183]

    11.6 Both parties reserve their rights to assign and agree to cooperate in effecting an Internal Revenue Code §1031 exchange prior to close of escrow, on either party's written notice. [ft Forms 171 or 172]

    11.7 Should Buyer breach the agreement, Buyer's monetary liability to Seller is limited to $_____.

12. PROPERTY CONDITIONS:

    12.1 Seller to furnish prior to closing:

        a. ☐ a structural pest control inspection report and certification of clearance of corrective conditions.

        b. ☐ a home inspection report prepared by an insured home inspector showing the land and improvements to be free of material defects.

        c. ☐ a one-year home warranty policy:
            Insurer: _____
            Coverage: _____

        d. ☐ a certificate of occupancy, or other clearance or retrofitting, required by local ordinance for the transfer of possession or title.

        e. ☐ a certification by a licensed contractor stating the sewage disposal system is functioning properly, and if it contains a septic tank, is not in need of pumping.

        f. ☐ a certification by a licensed water testing lab stating the well supplying the property meets potable water standards.

        g. ☐ a certification by a licensed well-drilling contractor stating the well supplying the property produces a minimum of _____ gallon(s) per minute.

        h. ☐ _____

        i. ☐ _____

    12.2 Seller's Condition of Property (Transfer) Disclosure Statement (TDS) [ft Form 304]

        a. ☐ is attached; or

        b. ☐ is to be handed to Buyer on acceptance for Buyer's review. Within ten days after receipt, Buyer may either cancel the transaction or deliver to Seller or Seller's Broker a written notice itemizing any material defects in the property disclosed by the statement and unknown to Buyer prior to acceptance [ft Form 269]. Seller to repair, replace or correct noticed defects prior to closing.

        c. On Seller's failure to repair, replace or correct noticed defects under §12.2b or §12.3a, Buyer may tender the purchase price reduced by the cost to repair, replace or correct the noticed defects, or close escrow and pursue available remedies. [ft Form 183]

    12.3 Buyer to inspect the property twice:

        a. An initial property inspection is required on acceptance to confirm the property's condition is substantially the same as observed by Buyer and represented by Seller or Seller's Agents prior to acceptance, and if not substantially the same, Buyer to promptly notify Seller in writing of undisclosed material defects discovered [ft Form 269]. Seller to repair, replace or correct noticed defects prior to closing; and

        b. A final walk-through inspection is required within five days before closing to confirm the correction of any noticed defects under §12.2b and §12.3a and maintenance under §12.11. [ft Form 270]

    12.4 Seller's Natural Hazard Disclosure Statement [ft Form 314] ☐ is attached, or ☐ is to be handed to Buyer on acceptance for Buyer's review. Within ten days of receipt, Buyer may terminate the agreement based on a reasonable disapproval of hazards disclosed by the Statement and unknown to Buyer prior to acceptance. [ft Forms 182 and 183]

12.5 Buyer acknowledges receipt of a booklet and related seller disclosures containing ☐ *Environmental Hazards: A Guide for Homeowners, Buyers, Landlords and Tenants* (on all one-to-four units), ☐ *Protect Your Family from Lead in Your Home* (on all pre-1978, one-to-four units) [ft Form 313], and ☐ *The Homeowner's Guide to Earthquake Safety* (on all pre-1960, one-to-four units). [ft Form 315]

12.6 The property is located in:
☐ an industrial use area; ☐ a military ordnance area; ☐ an airport influence area;
☐ _____.

12.7 On acceptance, Seller to hand Buyer the following property information for Buyer's review: ☐ Property Operating Cost Sheet [ft Form 352 or 562]; ☐ _____

a. Within ten days of receipt, Buyer may terminate the agreement based on a reasonable disapproval of the property information received.

12.8 If an Owner's Association is involved, ☐ Buyer has received and approves, or ☐ Buyer on acceptance to be handed, copies of the Association's Articles, Bylaws, CC&Rs, collection and lien enforcement policy, operating rules, operating budget, CPA's financial review, insurance policy summary and any age restriction statement.

a. No association claims for defects or changes in regular or special assessments are pending or anticipated. Current monthly assessment is $_____.

b. Seller is not in violation of CC&Rs, except _____.

c. Seller to pay association document and transfer fees.

d. Buyer to approve Association's statement of condition of assessments and confirm representations in §12.8a as a condition for closing escrow.

e. Within ten days of Buyer's post-acceptance receipt of the association documents, Buyer may terminate the agreement based on a reasonable disapproval of the documents. [ft Form 183]

12.9 Smoke detector(s) and water heater bracing exist in compliance with the law, and if not, Seller to install.

12.10 Possession of the property and keys/access codes to be delivered: ☐ on close of escrow, or ☐ as stated in the attached Occupancy Agreement. [ft Forms 271 and 272]

12.11 Seller to maintain the property in good condition until possession is delivered.

12.12 Fixtures and fittings attached to the property include, but are not limited to: window shades, blinds, light fixtures, plumbing fixtures, curtain rods, wall-to-wall carpeting, draperies, hardware, antennas, air coolers and conditioners, trees, shrubs, mailboxes and other similar items.

12.13 Notice: Pursuant to Section 290.46 of the Penal Code, information about specified registered sex offenders is made available to the public via an Internet Web site maintained by the Department of Justice at www.meganslaw.ca.gov. Depending on an offender's criminal history, this information will include either the address at which the offender resides or the community of residence and ZIP code in which he or she resides.

13. CLOSING CONDITIONS:

13.1 This transaction to be escrowed with _____.
Parties to deliver instructions to Escrow as soon as reasonably possible after acceptance.

a. ☐ Escrow holder is authorized and instructed to act on the provisions of this agreement as the mutual escrow instructions of the parties and to draft any additional instructions necessary to close this transaction. [ft Form 401]

b. ☐ Escrow instructions, prepared and signed by the parties, are attached to be handed to Escrow on acceptance. [ft Form 401]

13.2 Escrow to be handed all instruments needed to close escrow ☐ on or before _____, 20_____, or ☐ within _____days after acceptance. Parties to hand Escrow all documents required by the title insurer, lenders or other third parties to this transaction prior to seven days before the date scheduled for closing.

a. Each party to pay its customary Escrow charges. [ft Forms 310 and 311]

13.3 The amount of any taxes, liens, bonds, assessments or other encumbrances on the property not referenced are, at Buyer's option, to remain of record and be deducted first from the cash down payment and then from any carryback note.

13.4 Buyer's title to be subject to covenants, conditions, restrictions, reservations and easements of record. _____.

13.5 Title to be vested in Buyer or Assignee free of encumbrances other than those set forth herein. Buyer's interest in title to be insured under an ALTA form policy issued by _____ as a(n) ☐ Homeowner(s) policy (one-to-four units), ☐ Residential ALTA-R policy (vacant or improved residential parcel), ☐ Owner's policy (other than one-to-four units), ☐ CLTA Joint Protection policy (also naming Carryback Seller or purchase-assist lender), or ☐ Binder (to insure resale or refinance within two years).

    a. Endorsements: _____

    b. ☐ Seller, or ☐ Buyer, to pay the title insurance premium.

13.6 Buyer to furnish a new fire insurance policy covering the property.

13.7 Taxes, assessments, insurance premiums, rents, interest and other expenses to be prorated to close of escrow, unless otherwise provided.

13.8 Bill of Sale to be executed for any personal property being transferred.

13.9 If Seller is unable to convey marketable title as agreed, or if the improvements on the property are materially damaged prior to closing, Buyer may terminate the agreement. Seller to pay all reasonable escrow cancellation charges. [ft Form 183]

14. BROKERAGE FEE:

14.1 Parties to pay the below-mentioned Broker(s) a fee now due of _____ as follows: Seller to pay the brokerage fee on the change of ownership. The party wrongfully preventing this change of ownership to pay the brokerage fee.

14.2 Seller's Broker and Buyer's Broker, respectively, to share the brokerage fee _____:_____.

14.3 Attached is the Agency Law Disclosure. [ft Form 305]

14.4 Broker is authorized to report the sale, its price and terms for dissemination and use of participants in brokerage trade associations or listing services.

15. ☐ Buyer's Broker hereby confirms he is a licensed real estate broker and holds a bond issued by a security insurer for more than twice the property's fair market value.

16. CANCELLATION PERIOD:

16.1 Seller has the below noticed right to cancel this agreement until midnight of the fifth business day following the day Seller signs this agreement, or until 8 a.m. on the day scheduled for a trustee's foreclosure sale of the property, whichever occurs first.

NOTICE REQUIRED BY CALIFORNIA LAW:

Until your right to cancel this contract has ended,

_____(Buyer)

or anyone working for

_____(Buyer)

CANNOT ask you to sign or have you sign any deed or any other document.

You may cancel this contract for the sale of your house without any penalty or obligation at any time before _____:_____, _____.m. on _____, 20_____.

See attached Notice of Cancellation form for an explanation of this right.
(To be filled out by Buyer)

Buyer's/
Selling Broker: _____

By:_____

Is the agent of: ☐ Buyer exclusively.

             ☐ Both Seller and Buyer.

I agree to the terms stated above.

Date:_____, 20_____

Buyer: _____

Buyer: _____

Signature:_____

Signature:_____

Address:_____

_____

Phone: _____

Fax: _____

Email: _____

Seller's/
Listing Broker: _____

By:_____

Is the agent of: ☐ Seller exclusively.

             ☐ Both Seller and Buyer.

I agree to the terms stated above.

Date:_____, 20_____

Seller: _____

Seller: _____

Signature:_____

Signature:_____

Address:_____

_____

Phone: _____

Fax: _____

Email: _____

— — — — — — — — — — **NOTICE OF CANCELLATION** — — — — — — — — — — —
(To be filled out by Buyer)

Seller signed the Equity Purchase Agreement on _____, 20_____.

You may cancel this contract for the sale of your house, without any penalty or obligation, at any time before
_____:_____, _____.m. on _____, 20_____.

To cancel this transaction, personally deliver a signed and dated copy of this cancellation notice, or send
a telegram to _____ (Buyer)

at _____(Business Address)

NOT LATER THAN _____:_____, _____.m. on _____, 20_____.

I hereby cancel this transaction.

Date _____, 20_____

Seller's Signature:_____

Seller's Signature:_____

— — — — — — — — — NOTICE OF CANCELLATION — — — — — — — — — —
(To be filled out by Buyer)

Seller signed the Equity Purchase Agreement on _____, 20_____.

You may cancel this contract for the sale of your house, without any penalty or obligation, at any time before _____:_____, _____.m. on _____, 20_____.

To cancel this transaction, personally deliver a signed and dated copy of this cancellation notice, or send a telegram to _____ (Buyer)

at _____ (Business Address)

NOT LATER THAN _____:_____, _____.m. on _____, 20_____.

I hereby cancel this transaction.

Date _____, 20_____

Seller's Signature:_____

Seller's Signature:_____

FORM 156   01-06   ©2006 **first tuesday**, P.O. BOX 20069, RIVERSIDE, CA 92516 (800) 794-0494

cancel the sales agreement and escrow, even to *rescind* the sale after closing, until the notice is ultimately given and the five business days have run without cancellation.

A **business day** is any day except Sunday and the following business holidays: New Year's Day, Washington's Birthday, Memorial Day, Independence Day, Labor Day, Columbus Day, Veterans' Day, Thanksgiving Day and Christmas Day. Thus, Saturday is considered a business day under EP law, unless it falls on an enumerated holiday. Many state holidays are not included as holidays. [CC §1695.1(d)]

Until expiration of the right of the seller-in-foreclosure to cancel the transaction, the EP investor may not:

- **accept or induce a conveyance** of any interest in the property from the seller;

- **record any document** regarding the residence signed by the seller with the county recorder;

- **transfer an interest** in the property to a third party;

- **encumber any interest** in the residence; or

- **hand the seller** a "good-faith" deposit or other consideration. [CC §1695.6(b)]

However, escrow can be opened on acceptance, and deeds and funds deposited with escrow, since the seller-in-foreclosure is not delivering a conveyance (to the buyer) and will not receive funds until the close of escrow.

In negotiations with the seller-in-foreclosure, the EP investor, as with any buyer or agent, may not make false representations or misleading statements about:

- the value of the property in foreclosure;

- the net proceeds the seller will receive on closing escrow [See **first tuesday** Form 310];

- the terms of the purchase agreement or any other document the EP investor uses to induce the seller to sign; or

- the rights of the seller in the EP transaction. [CC §1695.6(d)]

Cancellation of the purchase agreement by the seller-in-foreclosure is **effective on delivery** of the signed written notice of cancellation to the EP investor's address in the purchase agreement. [CC §1695.4(b)]

When the EP investor receives the seller-in-foreclosure's written notice of cancellation, he must return, without condition, any original contract documents, such as the EP agreement bearing the seller's signature, to the seller within ten days following receipt of the notice. [CC §1695.6(c)]

Accordingly, the EP investor should not place funds in escrow before expiration of the cancellation period and a request for funds is made by escrow since an EP investor is not permitted to couple the release of funds to the return of documents on cancellation.

When the cancellation period expires for lack of a cancellation, the purchase agreement becomes enforceable and escrow can be closed, unless other contingencies exist.

Requirements for every EP investor

A homeowner defaults on a note secured by a trust deed on his principal residence, a one-to-four unit residential property. A Notice of Default (NOD) is recorded under a power-of-sale provision in the trust deed.

A private lender, who has **no knowledge** of equity purchase (EP) laws, orally agrees to refinance the property on the condition the owner transfers the property's title to the private lender. The private lender agrees to take title and refinance the existing loan on the property since he has good credit.

The owner will **remain in possession** and make monthly payments to the private lender. The owner will **recover title** when he pays off the private lender and assumes the refinancing.

The private lender is a real estate licensee, but at no time acts as an agent in the transaction. The private lender (erroneously) believes he is purchasing ownership to the real estate since he will receive a grant deed and remain the vested owner of the property until it is "repurchased and reconveyed" to the homeowner.

Without a written purchase agreement or escrow instructions to document the terms of the transaction, the **owner conveys title** to the private lender by a grant deed which is immediately recorded.

Concurrent with the conveyance, the owner enters into a written sale-leaseback agreement with the private lender, calling for the payment of "monthly rent." The lease agreement includes an "option" allowing the owner to repurchase title to the property on his payment of a fixed sum of money, being the balance due the private lender. The **sale-leaseback and option** agreement also states the private lender reserves the right to sell the property on the owner's default.

The owner receives no funds for his equity at any time. On acquiring title, the private lender pays off the existing trust deed loan with his own funds.

The private lender then **transfers** the property's title to himself and his spouse. The couple then **refinance** the property to recover their funds by obtaining a new first trust deed loan secured by the property. The private lender pays all costs relating to the new loan, including title insurance premiums, escrow fees and loan charges.

Later, the private lender **again refinances** the property when interest rates drop to increase his cash flow under the sale-leaseback and option agreement. Prepayment penalties are incurred on the payoff, as well as origination costs for the new loan.

The owner then defaults on the monthly payments due on the lease. A 3-day notice to pay rent or quit is served on the owner. Eventually, the owner is evicted from the property.

The private lender then **sells the property** to a buyer who is unaware of the owner's option rights to repurchase the property, called a *bona fide purchaser* (BFP). No sales proceeds remain after the loan is paid off, due to a decline in the property's value after taking title and the addition of two sets of refinancing charges. The owner receives no money from the sale.

The owner makes a demand on the private lender to recover the value of his **equity in the property** based on the property's value at the time of the sale-leaseback transaction.

Is the owner entitled to recover the amount of his equity from the lender?

Yes! The owner is entitled to recover money equal to the fair market value of his equity at the time he conveyed title to the private lender, less any funds he received from the private lender, which were none.

Recovery of the owner's lost equity is allowed since the **private lender violated** the EP laws by each of the following events:

- **acquiring recorded title** to the owner's principal residence, consisting of a one-to-four unit residential property in foreclosure, without first entering into a written purchase agreement which conforms to EP statutes [CC §1695.6(a)];

- **failing to document** in writing (a note) the terms for repayment of the loan [CC §1695.3(c), 1695.3(d)]; and

365

- further **transferring title** to the property (to the spouse and again to the resale buyer) without the written consent of the owner. [**Boquilon** v. **Beckwith** (1996) 49 CA4th 1697; CC §1695.6(e)]

Editor's note — The private lender in our facts should have structured the transaction as a conventional loan, evidenced by a note and secured by a trust deed on the property. Note and trust deed documentation of the loan would have avoided compliance with EP laws and the penalties for failure to comply due to the transfer of title. Title does not transfer when a trust deed lien is used to secure the repayment of a loan.

Brokers limited to listing property

Equity purchase (EP) legislation regulates brokers when they act as a **buyer's agent** for EP investors who attempt to buy an owner-occupant's home that is in foreclosure.

The broker **representing an EP investor** must, when negotiating an EP transaction, deliver to the seller-in-foreclosure a written **EP disclosure statement** that the buyer's agent representing the EP investor is:

- a **licensed** real estate broker; and

- **bonded** by a surety insurer for twice the property's fair market value. [CC §1695.17(a)]

If the buyer's agent fails to deliver the EP disclosure statement to the seller-in-foreclosure, directly or through the seller's listing broker, the EP agreement is **voidable** at the discretion of the seller any time before escrow closes. [See **first tuesday** Form 156 §16]

Also, the EP investor is liable to the seller-in-foreclosure for any **losses arising** out of the buyer's agent's nondisclosure of licensing and bonding requirements. [CC §1695.17(b)]

However, the EP investor would be entitled to *equitable indemnity* from his agent, a reimbursement for the seller's losses caused by the agent's nondisclosure. Equitable indemnity is available to the EP investor who, without active fault on his part, is forced by legal obligation to pay for losses created by his agent's nondisclosure. [**San Francisco Examiner Division, Hearst Publishing Company** v. **Sweat** (1967) 248 CA2d 493]

For the buyer's broker, obtaining a surety bond is generally economically prohibitive. Due to bonding requirements, licensed real estate brokers have essentially been removed from representing EP investors who want to locate and purchase owner-occupied, one-to-four unit residential property in foreclosure for EP investors.

Thus, EP investors are learning to "go it alone," now (and in the future), without brokerage assistance.

Further, sellers-in-foreclosure are denied the full assistance of their listing broker. The EP statutes, while restricting brokers who represent EP investors, have effectively wiped out the listing broker's ability to bring in one of his investors as a buyer and be a **dual agent** in an EP transaction.

Broker as principal

The EP legislation does not restrict the ability of an individual, who may coincidentally be licensed as a broker or sales agent, to act solely as a **principal** purchasing property as an investor in an EP transaction.

Thus, a licensed real estate broker or agent may himself be the EP investor, eliminating use of the agency law disclosure as well as avoiding licensee disclosure and bonding requirements. The licensed real estate broker or agent, acting solely as an EP investor, is a buyer who merely happens to hold a real estate license — a fact which does not need to be disclosed to the seller-in-foreclosure since the licensee is not also acting as an agent for anyone in the transaction.

Conversely, if a real estate broker **employed** as the listing broker by a seller-in-foreclosure decides to directly or indirectly buy his client's property, he **must disclose** to his seller-client that he is **also acting as a principal** in the transaction. [Calif. Business and Professions Code §§10176(d), 10176(g), 10176(h)]

Representing the seller

Prudent brokers and agents are inclined not to solicit or accept an exclusive right-to-sell listing from a seller-in-foreclosure. Property in foreclosure must be sold and escrow closed before the date of the trustee's foreclosure sale to have fully performed the employment and be entitled to a fee.

Unless the delinquent loan is brought current prior to five business days before the trustee's sale or paid in full before the sales date, the home will be sold at the trustee's sale. [CC §§2924c(e), 2903]

The listing agent for a seller-in-foreclosure usually needs extra time to find a buyer and close escrow since the frequency of foreclosures is inversely related to the volume of sales. The time constraints imposed on the listing agent by a trustee's sale date, before which the listing agent must close any sale of the property, place extra pressure on the broker employed under an exclusive listing agreement to locate a buyer.

As always, the listing agent acting under an exclusive listing must perform his agency duties owed the seller by properly marketing the property with care and diligence. As a further complication, the seller-in-foreclosure expects the broker to save his equity by negotiating a sale of the property and closing escrow before the property is lost to the foreclosing lender.

If the insolvent seller loses his equity, he may claim a lack of due diligence or unprofessional conduct on the part of the broker to locate a buyer and close an escrow — a risk the broker and his agents take when listing a home which is in foreclosure.

Other EP agents

The agent placing a listing of an owner-occupied residence in a **multiple listing service (MLS)** when the residence is in foreclosure should advise participating buyer's agents that:

- the property is an owner-occupied residence which is in foreclosure; and

- the participating agent is to represent a buyer-occupant or be bonded if representing an EP investor.

Although purchase transactions by buyer-occupants are not controlled by EP law, buyer-occupants are frequently **unwilling to purchase** property in foreclosure since the property is often:

- **physically damaged or unattractive** due to deferred maintenance; and

- **improperly encumbered** since either the buyer cannot assume or will not assume the loan on the terms demanded, or the property cannot be refinanced for an amount sufficient to pay off the existing loan and the lender will not agree to a short payoff.

Thus, the property is attractive primarily to an investor-type buyer who is willing to take these risks. The property must be rehabilitated and financing and operating costs carried until the property is resold or rented — at a profit or a loss.

Two-year right of rescission

A Notice of Default (NOD) is recorded on a homeowner's personal residence after several months of unpaid installments.

The homeowner, now in foreclosure, is willing to sell on almost any terms to salvage his remaining credit and equity in the property.

The property is listed with a broker. The broker's listing agent markets the property primarily to buyers who will occupy the property as their personal residence.

However, an offer is submitted directly to the seller-in-foreclosure by an EP investor, acting on his own account, without broker representation. Under the EP offer, the seller-in-foreclosure will receive cash for his equity. Additionally, the EP investor will cure the seller's loan delinquencies.

The seller-in-foreclosure contacts his listing broker who, after reviewing the offer, recommends the seller accept the EP investor's offer and, if an acceptable backup offer is received within the cancellation period, accept the backup offer and cancel the EP agreement.

The agent advises his client he has five business days after his acceptance of the EP offer to cancel the sale since the sale involves the seller's home, which is in foreclosure.

The seller-in-foreclosure accepts the EP investor's offer. The five-day cancellation period expires without receiving a backup offer and escrow is opened on the EP agreement. The EP transaction is later closed and the property conveyed.

Does the EP investor receive good title when he accepts the grant deed?

No! The EP investor's title remains subject to the seller-in-foreclosure's *right of rescission* for two years after closing. If at any time during the two years following the close of escrow and the recording of the grant deed conveyance the seller believes the **EP investor's conduct** and the **price paid** gave the EP investor an *unconscionable advantage*, the seller may attempt to rescind the transaction and recover the home he sold. [CC §1695.14]

The unconscionable advantage

The two-year rescission period only allows a seller-in-foreclosure to recover property if he can demonstrate the EP investor took *unconscionable advantage* of him when negotiating the purchase of the property.

Showing the existence of an unconscionable advantage in the **EP investor's conduct** is problematic for both the seller-in-foreclosure and the EP investor. The legislature has not defined what exactly constitutes an act of unconscionable advantage by the buyer.

What was a reasonable sales price under the circumstances surrounding the seller-in-foreclosure when the transaction was entered into might appear to be unconscionable to the seller in the future due to market factors and inflation, not the conduct of the EP investor. Thus, an EP investor assumes the risk that a rising economy may provoke the seller into attempting to rescind (for the wrong legal reason).

If real estate values rise rapidly and significantly, the "greed factor" may set in, turning a formerly desperate seller-in-foreclosure into an astute rescinding seller.

However, any **increase in the value** of the property after acceptance of the EP investor's offer may not be considered. The test of unconscionable advantage is not based on events occurring after the seller-in-foreclosure enters into the purchase agreement.

Market circumstances existing at the time of the negotiations or when the parties entered into the agreement are the economic considerations which form one of the two elements for testing unconscionable advantage. [**Colton** v. **Stanford** (1890) 82 C 351]

Unconscionability has two aspects:

- the lack of a **meaningful choice** of action for the seller-in-foreclosure when negotiating to sell the home to the EP investor, legally called *procedural unconscionability*; and

- a purchase price or method of payment which is **unreasonably favorable** to the EP investor, legally called *substantive unconscionability*.

The **price paid**, like any other provision in a purchase agreement, can be considered unconscionable. When determining the unconscionability of the purchase price, justification for the price at the time of the sale and the terms of payment will be examined.

An **unconscionable method of payment** could include:

- carryback paper with an unreasonably low interest rate, long amortization or a due date on the note that bears no relationship to current market rates and payment schedules; or

- an exchange of worthless land, stock, gems or zero coupon bonds at face value with a 20-year maturity date.

A form of payment which is uncollectible, unredeemable and with no present value would be unconscionable.

However, the existence of unreasonable pricing and payment alone is not enough to show the unconscionable advantage needed to rescind a closed transaction. Both the lack of a meaningful choice and unreasonably favorable (advantageous) terms must exist to show unconscionability existed.

The un-American low price

Any procedures used or conduct employed by an EP investor as a misfeasance or misrepresentation made to deprive the seller-in-foreclosure of a reasonable choice between the EP investor's offer and offers from other buyers must exist to establish the lack of a meaningful choice or alternative to the EP investor's offer.

An unconscionable advantage occurs if the EP investor **exploits** an element of **oppression or surprise** in exacting an unreasonably low and favorable purchase price or terms of payment.

Oppression by the EP investor exists when the inequality in bargaining power between the investor and the seller-in-foreclosure results in

no real negotiations between them — a "take it or leave it" environment deliberately removed from competing buyers. The foreclosure environment itself often presents a one-sided bargaining advantage for the EP investor to exploit should be decide he does not want his offer "shopped around" and used to solicit a better deal from other buyers during the five-business-day cancellation period.

Surprise occurs due to the post-closing discovery of terms which are hidden in the lengthy provisions of the agreement. The price and how it will be paid is not a surprise. The price is well known to the seller-in-foreclosure and, on any rescission action by the seller, will likely be the only term of the agreement contested by the seller.

The greater the marketplace oppression or post-closing surprise discovery in the transaction, the less an unreasonably favorable price paid by an EP investor will be tolerated. [**Carboni** v. **Arrospide** (1991) 2 CA4th 76]

Structuring the EP agreement

An investor, not intending to be an owner-occupant buyer, wants to purchase single family residences (SFRs) for investment purposes.

The investor locates an owner-occupied SFR encumbered by a trust deed on which a Notice of Default (NOD) has been recorded, commencing a trustee's foreclosure.

Because the seller occupies the residential property and an NOD has been recorded, the **investor realizes** he must comply with California's EP laws when preparing and submitting an offer to purchase the property.

The EP investor is willing to purchase the SFR for a price of $140,000 on the following terms:

- **pay** $10,000 cash to the seller-in-foreclosure for his equity in the property;

- **take over** the existing loan with a total of $130,000 due the lender in unpaid principal, delinquent installments and foreclosure costs; and

- **pay** the delinquent installments of principal, interest, taxes and insurance (PITI) and the foreclosure costs of approximately $7,400 — all of which are included in the $130,000 owed the lender on the loan.

The EP agreement calls for a $10,000 cash down payment.

Also, the EP investor will take title to the property "subject to" the existing first trust deed with a 28-year amortization remaining.

The conditions of the trust deed note are:

- $122,600 of remaining principal (after the delinquent payments have been brought current);

- 6.5% interest;

- $802.30 monthly principal and interest payments;

- $150 monthly taxes/insurance impounds payments;

- current five month delinquencies on PITI of $4,761.50; and

- foreclosure costs of $1,316.80.

The first trust deed is a loan insured by the Federal Housing Administration (FHA) subject to the Department of Housing and Urban Development (HUD) due-on-sale rules controlling investor purchases. However, only HUD, not the lender, has the right to call a HUD-insured loan. The likelihood of HUD calling any loan which is kept current is remote. Thus, the loan may be taken over by the EP investor "subject to" with minimal interference from the lender, i.e., assumption fees and loan modification are avoided.

Editor's note — As of the date of this text, FHA is suffering a 12% delinquency rate on its insured loans.

The seller-in-foreclosure will not be carrying back a portion of the purchase price since this is a cash-to-loan transaction. As an alternative method for payment of the purchase price, negotiations could have included provisions for the seller to carryback paper in the EP transaction.

The seller-in-foreclosure is five months delinquent in payments. The EP investor will bring the $4,761.50 in delinquent PITI payments current, which includes $326.66 in principal reduction.

Taxwise, the payment of the delinquent principal and interest (PI) payments (not the impounds) is part of the EP investor's original **costs of acquisition**. The interest paid by the EP investor which accrued **before acquiring** the property is an expense of the seller-in-foreclosure, not the EP investor. Thus, the payment of the seller's debts must be capitalized by the EP investor as part of his *cost basis* in the property. [Internal Revenue Code §1012]

The EP investor's cost basis on acquisition of the property will be the purchase price of approximately $140,000, which includes the seller-in-foreclosure's delinquent (PI) installments, foreclosure costs and the principal balance on the loan, less the impound account balance.

A prudent EP investor will determine the total cash funds needed to close escrow before making an offer. Cash expenditures of the EP investor on closing include:

- a down payment of $10,000.00;

- delinquent principal, interest, taxes and impounds of $4,761.50;

- foreclosure costs of $1,316.80;

- escrow fees and charges of $300.00; and

- a total cash investment of **$16,378.30**.

Analyzing the EP agreement

The equity purchase (EP) agreement, **first tuesday** Form 156, is used to prepare a written offer to be submitted by an investor or dealer to purchase a one-to-four unit residential property which is occupied by the owner as his principal residence and is in foreclosure. As required by EP law, the form contains bold print, minimum size type and the statutory notice of the five-business-day right of cancellation, as well as the actual Notice of Cancellation for use by the seller who chooses to cancel the agreement.

A purchase of the owner-occupied residence in foreclosure by a buyer who will occupy the property as his residence does not require the use of an EP agreement as the purchase is not subject to EP law. However, an equity purchase requiring the use of an EP agreement does occur when a buyer is acquiring the property for business, rental, investment or dealer purposes.

The terms for payment of the price are structured to include a lump sum amount of cash to be paid to the seller for his equity in the property. Thus, all adjustments, prorations, credits and offsets are formulated to deliver to the seller this lump sum amount unchanged since it is based on the seller's representations of sums owing on all encumbrances affecting title to the property.

Each section in Form 156 has a separate purpose and need for enforcement. The sections include:

1. *Identification*: The date of preparation, the real estate and any personal property to be purchased, and the number of pages comprising the entire agreement, including addenda, arc set forth in sections 1 and 2.

2. *Price and terms of payment*: All the typical variations for payment of the price

are set out in sections 3 through 10 as a "checklist of provisions." The EP investor selects the terms of purchase by checking boxes and filling blanks in the desired provisions. While the subject matter of the various provisions is typical, the terms each contain are not. All financial aspects are biased in favor of the buyer, such as prorates and adjustments, since EP transactions are structured as the payment of a lump sum for the conveyance.

3. *Acceptance and performance*: Aspects of the formation of a contract, excuses for nonperformance and termination of the agreement are provided for in section 11, such as the time period for acceptance of the offer, the broker's authorization to extend performance deadlines, the financing of the price as a closing contingency, procedures for cancellation of the agreement, a sale of other property as a closing contingency, cooperation to effect a §1031 transaction and limitations on monetary liability for breach of contract.

4. *Property conditions*: The EP investor's confirmation of the physical condition of the property as disclosed prior to acceptance is provided for in section 12 by the seller's delivery of reports, warranty policies, certifications, disclosures statements, an environmental, lead-based paint and earthquake safety booklet, any operating cost and income statements, and any homeowners' association (HOA) documents not handed to the EP investor prior to entry into the purchase agreement, as well as by thc EP investor's initial inspection, personally or by a home inspector, and final inspection at closing to confirm the seller has eliminated defects known, but not disclosed, prior to acceptance.

5. *Closing conditions*: The escrow holder, escrow instruction arrangements and the date of closing are established in section 13, as are title conditions, title insurance, hazard insurance, prorates and loan adjustments.

6. *Brokerage and agency*: The release of sales data on the transaction to trade associations is authorized, the brokerage fee is set, and the delivery of the agency law disclosure to both EP investor and seller and the disclosure of compliance with bonding requirements is provided for as set forth in sections 14 and 15, as well as the confirmation of the agency undertaken by the brokers and their agents on behalf of one or both parties to the agreement.

7. *Seller's right to cancel*: Mandated by law, the notice to the owner-occupant seller whose home is in foreclosure (NOD has been recorded) is set forth in section 16, disclosing the seller' right to cancel the entire transaction within five business days after he enters into this agreement. The notice is one of two major additions imposed on standard purchase agreements by EP law. The other is the Notice of Cancellation used by the seller to implement the right to cancel during the five-business-day period following the seller's acceptance.

8. *Signatures*: The seller and EP investor bind each other to perform as agreed in the purchase agreement by signing and dating their signatures to establish the date of offer and acceptance.

9. *Cancellation notice*: Separate from the actual EP purchase agreement is the form completed by the EP investor, in duplicate, that the seller will use if he chooses to cancel the agreement. By signing and delivering one of the easily detachable cancellation forms to the EP investor at any time before midnight of the fifth business day after the date the seller signs the agreement, the seller effectively cancels the entire EP purchase agreement, with or without reason.

Preparing the EP purchase agreement

The following instructions are for the preparation and use of the Equity Purchase Agreement, **first tuesday** Form 156. Form 156 is designed to comply with EP law when used by an investor to purchase a one-to-four unit, owner-occupied residential property which is in foreclosure.

Each instruction corresponds to the provision in the form bearing the same number.

*Editor's note — **Check** and **enter** items throughout the agreement in each provision with boxes and blanks, unless the provision is not intended to be included as part of the final agreement, in which case it is left unchecked or blank.*

Document identification:

Enter the date and name of the city where the offer is prepared. This date is used when referring to this purchase agreement.

Facts:

1. *Property identification*: **Enter** the name of the city and county in which the property is located.

   Enter the legal description or common address of the property, or the assessor's parcel number (APN).

   Enter the description of any personal property included, or **enter** words of reference, such as "see attached inventory," and **attach** an itemized list of the inventory. The seller's trade fixtures to be purchased by the buyer must be listed as inventory if they are to be acquired by the buyer. [See **first tuesday** Form 250]

2. *Entire agreement*: **Enter** the number of pages comprising all of the addenda, disclosures, etc., which are attached to the purchase agreement.

Terms for payment of the purchase price:

3. *Cash down payment*: **Enter** the dollar amount of the buyer's cash down payment toward the purchase price. The down payment represents the amount of cash the seller-in-foreclosure will receive on closing, less any adjustments, escrow charges and fees.

4. *First trust deed note*: **Check** the appropriate box to indicate whether the transfer of title is to be "subject-to" an existing loan or by an "assumption" of the loan if the buyer is to take over an existing first trust deed loan. **Enter** the lender's name. **Enter** the remaining balance, the monthly principal and interest (PI) payment and the interest rate on the loan. **Check** the box to indicate whether the interest is adjustable (ARM), and if so, **enter** the index name. **Enter** any monthly impound payment made in addition to the PI payment. **Enter** any due date or other terms unique to the loan.

    4.1 *Delinquencies*: **Enter** the dollar amount required to cure all defaults on the loan. **Enter** the date the loan payments became delinquent.

    4.2 *Impound balances*: **Authorizes** the impound account to be transferred without charge to the EP investor.

5. *Second trust deed note*: **Check** the appropriate box to indicate whether the transfer of title is to be "subject-to" an existing loan or by an "assumption" of the loan if the buyer is to take over an existing second trust deed loan. **Enter** the lender's name. **Enter** the remaining balance, the monthly PI payment and the interest rate on the loan. **Check** the box to indicate whether the interest is adjustable (ARM), and if so, **enter** the index name. **Enter** the due date for payment of a final/balloon payment.

    5.1 *Delinquencies*: **Enter** the dollar amount required to cure all defaults on the loan. **Enter** the date the loan payments became delinquent.

6. *Loan balance adjustments*: **Authorizes** any adjustments due to differences between the loan balances stated in the agreement and actually existing at the time of closing to be made into the purchase price. However, if the balance on the loans exceeds the amount stated in the purchase agreement, the difference is subtracted from the cash down payment.

7. *New trust deed loan*: **Check** the appropriate box to indicate whether any new financing will be a first or second trust deed loan. **Enter** the amount of the loan, the monthly PI payment, the term of the loan and the rate of interest. **Check** the box to indicate whether the interest will be adjustable (ARM), and if so, **enter** the index name. **Enter** any limitations on loan points.

8. *Bond or assessment assumed*: **Enter** the amount of the principal balance remaining unpaid on bonds and special assessment liens (such as Mello-Roos or 1915 improvement bonds) which will remain unpaid and become the responsibility of the buyer on closing.

Editor's note — Improvement bonds are obligations of the seller which may be assumed by the EP investor in lieu of their payoff by the seller. If assumed, the bonded indebtedness becomes part of the consideration paid for the property. Some purchase agreements errone-

*ously place these bonds under "property tax" as though they were **ad valorem taxes**, and then fail to prorate and charge the unpaid amount to the seller.*

9.   *Seller carryback note*: **Enter** the amount of the carryback note to be executed by the EP investor as partial payment of the price. **Enter** the amount of the note's monthly PI payment, the interest rate and the due date for the final/balloon payment.

   9.1   *Special carryback provisions*: No transfer restrictions or charges for early payoff or late payment will be included in the carryback note and trust deed.

   9.2   *Carryback disclosure*: **Fill out** and **attach** a Seller Carryback Disclosure Statement as an addendum. [See **first tuesday** Form 300]

Editor's note — Further approval of the disclosure statement in escrow creates by statute a buyer's contingency allowing for cancellation until time of closing on any purchase of one-to-four unit residential property.

10.   *Purchase price*: **Enter** the total amount of the purchase price as the sum of lines 3, 4, 5, 7, 8 and 9.

11.   **Acceptance and performance periods:**

   11.1   *Delivery of acceptance*: **Check** the appropriate box to indicate the time period for acceptance of the offer. If applicable, **enter** the number of days in which the seller may accept this offer and form a binding contract.

Editor's note — If "on presentation" is used, the seller still has a statutory period of five business days to cancel the agreement after the seller's acceptance.

11.2   *Extension of performance dates*: **Authorizes** the brokers to extend the performance dates up to one month to meet the objectives of the agreement — time being of a reasonable duration and not the essence of this agreement as a matter of policy. This extension authority does not extend to the acceptance period.

11.3   *Loan contingency*: **Authorizes** the EP investor to cancel the transaction at the time scheduled for closing if the financing for payment of the price is not obtainable or assumable.

11.4   *Sale of other property*: If the closing of this transaction is to be contingent on the EP investor's receipt of net proceeds from a sale of other property, **enter** the address of the property to be sold by the EP investor.

11.5   *Cancellation procedures*: **Provides** the method of cancellation required to terminate the agreement when the right to cancel is triggered by other provisions in the agreement, such as contingency or performance provisions.

11.6   *Exchange cooperation*: **Requires** the parties to cooperate in an IRS §1031 transaction on further written notice by either party. **Provides** for the parties to assign their interests in this agreement.

11.7   *Liability limitations* **Provides** for a dollar limit on the EP investor's liability for the EP investor's breach of the agreement. **Enter** the maximum dollar amount of money losses the seller may recover from the EP investor.

12. Property Conditions:

12.1 *Seller to furnish*: **Check** the appropriate box(es) within the following subsections to indicate the items the seller is to furnish prior to closing.

   a. *Pest control*: **Check** the box to indicate the seller is to furnish a structural pest control report and clearance.

   b. *Home inspection report*: **Check** the box to indicate the seller is to employ a home inspection company and furnish the buyer with the company's home inspection report.

   c. *Home warranty*: **Check** the box to indicate the seller is to furnish an insurance policy for home repairs. **Enter** the name of the insurer and the type of coverage, such as for the air conditioning unit, etc.

   d. *Local ordinance compliance*: **Check** the box to indicate the seller is to furnish a certificate of occupancy or other clearance required by local ordinance.

   e. *Sewer or septic certificate*: **Check** the box to indicate the seller is to furnish a certificate of the condition of the sewage disposal system stating it is functioning properly.

   f. *Potable well water*: **Check** the box to indicate the seller is to furnish a certificate stating the well supply meets water standards.

   g. *Well water capacities*: **Check** the box to indicate the seller is to furnish a certificate stating the amount of water the well supplies. **Enter** the number of gallons per minute the well is expected to produce.

   h. *Other terms*: **Check** the box and **enter** any other report, certification or clearance the seller is to furnish.

   i. *Other terms*: **Check** the box and **enter** any other report, certification or clearance the seller is to furnish.

12.2 *Property condition(s)*: **Check** the appropriate box within the following subsections to indicate the status of the Transfer Disclosure Statement (TDS).

   a. *Attached TDS*: **Check** the box to indicate the seller's TDS has been prepared and handed to the buyer, and if so, **attach** it to this agreement. Thus, the property's condition is accepted by the EP investor upon entering into the purchase agreement offer.

   b. *Later delivered TDS*: **Check** the box to indicate the TDS is to be **delivered later** to the EP investor to confirm the condition of the property is as disclosed prior to entry into the purchase agreement. On receipt of the TDS, the EP investor may either cancel the transaction for failure of the seller or the listing agent to disclose known property defects prior to acceptance of the purchase agreement (or counteroffer), or give notice to the seller of the defects known and not disclosed prior to acceptance and make a demand on the seller to correct them prior to closing.

c. *Repair of defects*: **Authorizes** the EP investor to either cancel the transaction or adjust the price should the seller fail to correct the defects noticed under sections 12.2b or 12.3a.

12.3 *EP investor's inspection*: **Authorizes** the EP investor to inspect the property twice during the escrow period to verify its condition is as disclosed by the seller prior to the time of acceptance.

a. *Initial property inspection*: **Requires** the EP investor to inspect the property immediately after acceptance to put the seller on notice of material defects to be corrected by the seller prior to closing. [See **first tuesday** Form 269]

b. *Final walk-through inspection*: **Requires** the EP investor to inspect the property again within five days before closing to confirm repairs and maintenance of the property have occurred. [See **first tuesday** Form 270]

12.4 *Seller's Natural Hazard Disclosure (NHD) Statement*: **Check** the appropriate box to indicate whether the NHD statement disclosing the seller's knowledge about the haz-

ards listed on the form has been prepared and handed to the EP investor. If it has been received by the EP investor, **attach** a copy to the purchase agreement. If the NHD will be handed to the EP investor after acceptance, the EP investor has ten days after the EP investor's receipt of the NHD statement in which to approve it or cancel.

Editor's note — Disclosure by the seller is mandated on one-to-four unit residential property. [Calif. Civil Code §1103]

12.5 *Hazard disclosure booklets* **Check** the appropriate box(es) to indicate which hazard booklets have been received by the EP investor, together with the seller's prepared and signed disclosures accompanying each booklet.

12.6 *Other property disclosures*: **Check** the appropriate box(es) to indicate other disclosures made by the seller regarding the location of the property. **Enter** a reference to any local (option) ordinance disclosure statement attached as an addendum to the purchase agreement and **attach** it. [See **first tuesday** Form 307]

12.7 *Operating costs and rents*: **Check** the appropriate box(es) to indicate the information the seller is to disclose regarding the operating expenses of ownership.

a. *Disclosure approval*: **Authorizes** the EP investor to cancel the purchase agreement and escrow if the operating expense disclosure is unacceptable.

12.8 *Homeowners' association (HOA)*: **Check** the appropriate box to indicate whether any HOA documents have been or are to be delivered to the EP investor.

a. *Monthly payments*: **Enter** the dollar amount of the monthly payments assessed by the HOA.

b. *CC&Rs*: **Enter** the nature of any violation of the CC&Rs by the seller.

c. *HOA charges*: **Provides** for the seller to pay all HOA charges on the transaction.

d. *Condition of assessments*: **Provides** for the EP investor to approve the HOA's condition of assessments statement prior to closing.

e. *Disapproval of HOA documents*: **Authorizes** the EP investor to terminate this purchase agreement within ten days after his receipt of HOA documents when the disclosures are made after entering into the purchase agreement. Disclosure of HOA conditions in escrow trigger a statutory contingency allowing the EP investor to cancel the purchase agreement.

12.9 *Safety compliance*: **Requires** smoke detectors and water heater bracing to exist or be installed by the seller.

12.10 *Buyer's possession*: **Check** the appropriate box to indicate when possession of the property will be delivered to the EP investor, whether at closing or under an **attached** buyer's interim occupancy

or seller's holdover agreement. [See **first tuesday** Forms 271 and 272]

12.11 *Property maintenance*: **Requires** the seller to maintain the present condition of the property until the close of escrow.

Editor's note — See section 12.3b for the buyer's final inspection to confirm maintenance at closing.

12.12 *Fixtures and fittings*: **Confirms** this agreement includes real estate fixtures and fittings as part of the property purchased.

Editor's note — Trade fixtures are personal property to be listed as items on an attached inventory.

12.13 *Sex offender disclosure*: **Complies** with requirements that the seller disclose the existence of a sex offender database on the sale (or lease) of one-to-four residential units.

Editor's note — By the existence of the disclosure in the form, the seller and brokers are relieved of any duty to make further disclosures regarding registered sex offenders.

13. **Closing conditions:**

13.1 *Escrow closing agent*: **Enter** the name of the escrow company handling the closing.

a. *Escrow instructions*: **Check** the box to indicate the purchase agreement is to also serve as the mutual instructions to escrow from the parties. The escrow company will typically prepare supplemental instructions they will need to handle and close the transaction. [See **first tuesday** Form 401]

b. *Escrow instructions*: **Check** the box to indicate escrow instructions have been prepared and are attached to this purchase agreement. **Attach** the prepared escrow instructions to the purchase agreement and **obtain** the signatures of the parties. [See **first tuesday** Form 401]

13.2 *Closing date*: **Check** the appropriate box to indicate the method to be used to set the date on which escrow is scheduled to close. Following the checked box, **enter** the specific date for closing or the number of days anticipated as necessary for the parties to perform and close escrow. Also, prior to seven days before closing, the parties are to deliver all documents needed by third parties to perform their services by the date scheduled for closing.

a. *Escrow charges*: **Requires** each party to pay their customary escrow closing charges, amounts any competent escrow officer can provide on inquiry.

13.3 *Undisclosed lien adjustments*: At the EP investor's option, adjustments for liens not disclosed in the agreement will be made first into the down payment and then into any carryback note for any amounts remaining.

13.4 *Title conditions*: **Enter** wording for any further-approval contingency provision the EP investor may need to confirm that title conditions set forth in the preliminary title report will not interfere with the EP investor's intended use of the property, such as "closing contingent on EP investor's approval of preliminary title report."

13.5 *Title insurance*: **Provides** for title to be vested in the name of the EP investor or his assignee. **Enter** the name of the title insurance company which is to provide a preliminary title report in anticipation of issuing title insurance. **Check** the appropriate box to indicate the type of title insurance policy to be issued on closing.

a. *Policy endorsements*: **Enter** any endorsements to be issued with the policy.

b. *Payment of premium*: **Check** the appropriate box to indicate whether the EP investor or seller is to pay the title insurance premium.

13.6 *Fire insurance*: **Requires** the EP investor to provide a new policy of hazard insurance.

13.7 *Prorates and adjustments*: **Authorizes** prorations and adjustments on the close of escrow for taxes, insurance premiums, rents, interest, loan balances, service contracts and other property operating expenses, prepaid or accrued.

13.8 *Personal property*: **Requires** the seller to execute a bill of sale for any personal property being transferred in this transaction at section 1.

13.9 *Property destruction*: **Provides** for the seller to bear the *risk of loss* for any casualty losses suffered by the property prior to the close of escrow. Thus, the EP investor may terminate the agreement if the seller is unable to provide a marketable title or should the property improvements suffer major damage.

14. Brokerage fee:

14.1 *Fee amount*: **Enter** the total amount of the fee due all brokers to be paid by the seller. The amount may be stated as a fixed dollar amount or a percentage of the price.

Editor's note — The defaulting party pays all brokerage fees and the brokerage fee can only be altered or cancelled by mutual instructions from the EP investor and seller.

14.2 *Fee sharing*: **Enter** the percentage share of the fee each broker is to receive.

Editor's note — The percentage share may be set based on an oral agreement between the brokers, by acceptance of the listing broker's MLS offer to a selling office to share a fee, or unilaterally by an agent when preparing the buyer's offer.

14.3 *Agency law disclosures*: **Attach** a copy of the Agency Law Disclosure addendum for all parties to sign. The disclosure is mandated to be acknowledged by the EP investor with the offer and acknowledged by the seller on acceptance as a prerequisite to the brokers enforcing collection of the fee when the property involved contains one-to-four residential units. [See **first tuesday** Form 305]

14.4 *Disclosure of sales data*: **Authorizes** the brokers to report the transaction to trade associations or listing services.

15. *Bonding disclosure*: **Check** the box to indicate whether the EP investor is represented by a licensed real estate broker, exclusively or as a dual agent, and the broker possesses the bond required to represent the EP investor.

16. Cancellation period:

16.1 *Statutory cancellation period*: The seller has the **right to cancel** the EP agreement until midnight (12 a.m.) of the fifth business day (Monday through Saturday, excluding specified holidays) following the day the EP agreement is accepted or until 8 a.m. on the day scheduled for a trustee's foreclosure sale of the property, whichever occurs first. [CC §1695.4(a)]

Notice of right to cancel

Enter the EP investor's name and the appropriate time and date for the expiration of the seller's cancellation period of five business days after acceptance.

Editor's note — See explanations for time and date given in section 16.1 above and in the Notice of Cancellation section below.

Agency confirmation:

Buyer's broker identification: **Enter** the name of the buyer's broker. **Obtain** the signature of the buyer's broker or the selling agent acting on behalf of the buyer's broker. **Check** the appropriate box to indicate the agency which was created by the broker's (and his agents') conduct with the parties.

Seller's broker identification: **Enter** the name of the seller's broker. **Obtain** the signature of the seller's broker or the listing agent acting on behalf of the seller's broker. **Check** the appropriate box to indicate the agency which was created by the broker's (and his agents') conduct with the parties.

Signatures:

Buyer's signature: **Enter** the date the buyer signs the purchase agreement and each buyer's name. **Obtain** each buyer's signature on the purchase agreement and on each attachment which requires his signature. **Enter** the buyer's address, telephone and fax numbers, and email address.

Seller's signature: **Enter** the date the seller signs the purchase agreement and each seller's name. **Obtain** each seller's signature on the purchase agreement and on each attachment which requires his signature. **Enter** the seller's address, telephone and fax numbers, and email address.

Notice of Cancellation:

*Editor's note — The Notice of Cancellation is not part of the actual EP agreement. It is the notice the seller-in-foreclosure signs and delivers to cancel the transaction. It must be filled out, **in duplicate**, by the **buyer** and handed to the seller with the EP agreement.*

Enter the date the seller signs his acceptance of the EP agreement. **Enter** the time (12 a.m. or 8 a.m.) and the date on or before which the seller may cancel the agreement (five business days after acceptance or the date set for the trustee's sale, if earlier).

Enter the EP investor's name and the address where the Notice of Cancellation is to be delivered if the seller-in-foreclosure chooses to cancel the EP agreement by signing it. **Enter** the time (12 a.m. or 8 a.m.) and the date by which the seller may cancel the agreement (five business days after acceptance or the date set for the trustee's sale, if earlier).

The EP investor is to also **complete** the second, duplicate Notice of Cancellation which follows.

Editor's note — The Notices of Cancellation at the end of the EP agreement are not dated or signed by the seller on acceptance. The seller will later sign and deliver a Notice of Cancellation to the EP investor only if the seller actually decides to cancel the transaction.

Chapter 51

Income property acquisitions

This chapter distinguishes the purchase agreement used for acquiring income property from purchase agreements used for other purposes and reviews its use as a checklist for due diligence investigations.

Investigating a property's worth

At an investment property marketing session, an agent looking for properties to acquire on behalf of his client picks up a mini-package on a property listed for sale by another agent. The package contains an Annual Property Operating Data (APOD) sheet. On review of the APOD, the property appears to match the income property requirements of his client.

The client is contacted. Both the agent and the client drive by the property. The building's exterior appearance is acceptable. The area surrounding the property looks stable. The property seems properly located for a project of its size and type. It is agreed the agent will gather more information on the property.

The agent obtains a profile on the property from a title company. The title is consistent with information received from the listing agent regarding trust deeds and vesting.

To begin an analysis of the property, the agent contacts the listing agent for more **fundamentals** on the property, asking him to produce:

- a **rent roll** spread sheet covering each unit (type, size, tenant, commencement of occupancy, expiration of lease, rent amount and any discount/free rent, payment history, furnishings, etc.);

- a two-year **occupancy history** on each unit;

- information regarding **security arrangements** and criminal activity on or around the property during the past year;

- a **property manager** or resident manager who is available for an interview;

- information regarding **maintenance procedures** and the repair services used;

- a copy of schedule "B" (CC&R exclusions) to the owner's policy of **title insurance**;

- the lender's name and the balance, payments, interest rates and due date on each **existing loan**; and

- any available information relating to the integrity of the **property's condition** and the nature of the property's location which might adversely affect the property's value.

The prospective buyer's agent asks for all this information knowing the seller and the listing agent **owe a duty** to all prospective buyers and their agents to inform them of all facts about the property that are known or readily available to them which might have an adverse impact on its market value. Hopefully, the listing agent has already gathered all the fundamental property information and has it ready in a complete listing or marketing package.

If the listing agent has not yet gathered the facts which are available to him, he will likely insist the information is not necessary for a prospective buyer to submit an offer. However, price negotiations should not commence until disclosures of **all readily available** property data and information have been handed over by the seller or his listing agent since the confirmation of the veracity of these disclosures is what due diligence investigations prior to closing are all about.

The prospective buyer is advised the seller or the seller's agent may insist he enter into a confidentiality agreement before some of the information requested of the seller's agent will be released. Thus, the buyer may need to identify himself to the seller before the seller will release information on the tenants, their leases and property operations, which the buyer needs to determine the property's worth and set the price and terms, before making an offer.

When the information is received and reviewed, if it warrants a further investigation into the suitability of the property for acquisition, the buyer's agent and prospective buyer will then personally inspect the premises and any vacant units, and thoroughly discuss operations with those who manage the property.

After receiving these initial disclosures and conducting a minimal investigation, the buyer's agent will prepare a purchase agreement if the property still appears to be suitable to the prospective buyer. By submission of the purchase agreement offer, they will commence negotiations on the price to be paid and the conditions which must be met so the prospective buyer can complete a due diligence investigation to confirm his initial expectations about the property. Any counteroffer by the seller will sort out the seller's willingness to permit the prospective buyer to corroborate the property's worth.

Analyzing the income property purchase agreement

The income property purchase agreement, **first tuesday** Form 159, is used to prepare and submit the buyer's **written offer** to purchase income property, excluding one-to-four unit residential property. Terms for payment of the price are limited to conventional financing, an assumption of existing loans and a carryback note. Form 159 is also properly used by sellers in a counteroffer situation to submit their **fresh offer** to sell the real estate. [See Form 159 accompanying this chapter]

The purchase agreement offer, if accepted, becomes the binding written contract between the buyer and seller. Its terms must be complete and clear to prevent misunderstandings so the agreement can be judicially enforced. Thus, Form 159 is a comprehensive "boilerplate" purchase agreement which serves as a **checklist**, presenting the various conventional financing arrangements and conditions a prudent buyer would consider when making an offer to purchase.

Each section in Form 159 has a separate purpose and need for enforcement. The sections include:

1. *Identification*: The date of preparation for referencing the agreement, the name of the buyer, the amount of the good-faith deposit, the description of the real estate, an inventory of any personal property included in the transfer and the number of pages contained in the agreement and its addenda are set forth in sections 1 and 2 to establish the facts on which the agreement is negotiated.

2. *Price and terms*: All the typical variations for payment of the price by conventional purchase-assist financing or an assumption of existing financing are set forth in sections 3 through 9 as a checklist of provisions. On making an offer (or counteroffer), the terms for payment and financing of the price are selected by checking boxes and filling blanks in the desired provisions.

3. *Acceptance and performance*: Aspects of the formation of a contract, excuses for nonperformance and termination of the agreement are provided for in section 10, such as the time period for acceptance of the offer, the broker's authorization to extend performance deadlines, the financing of the price as a closing contingency, procedures for cancellation of the agreement, a sale of other property as a closing contingency, cooperation to ef-

fect a §1031 transaction and limitations on monetary liability for breach of contract.

4. *Due diligence contingencies*: Contingencies for the buyer's due diligence investigations into income and expense records, rental income statements, hazard disclosures, property condition disclosures, and other relevant information to be delivered by the seller are set forth in section 11.

5. *Property Conditions*: The buyer's confirmation of the physical condition of the property as disclosed prior to acceptance is **confirmed** as set forth in section 12 by the seller's delivery of reports, warranty policies and certifications not handed to the buyer prior to entry into the purchase agreement.

6. *Closing conditions*: The escrow holder, escrow instruction arrangements and the date of closing are established in section 13, as are title conditions, title insurance, hazard insurance, prorates and loan adjustments.

7. *Brokerage and agency*: The release of sales data on the transaction to trade associations is authorized, the brokerage fee is set and the delivery of the agency law disclosure to both buyer and seller is provided for as set forth in section 14, as well as the confirmation of the agency undertaken by the brokers and their agents on behalf of one or both parties to the agreement.

8. *Signatures*: The seller and buyer bind each other to perform as agreed in the purchase agreement by signing and dating their signatures to establish the date of offer and acceptance.

Preparing the income property purchase agreement

The following instructions are for the preparation and use of the Income Property Purchase Agreement, **first tuesday** Form 159. Form 159 is designed as a checklist of practical provisions so a broker or his agent can prepare an offer for a prospective buyer who seeks to purchase conventionally financed, other than one-to-four unit, income property located in California.

Each instruction corresponds to the provision in the form bearing the same number.

*Editor's note — **Check** and **enter** items throughout the agreement in each provision with boxes and blanks, unless the provision is not intended to be included as part of the final agreement, in which case it is left unchecked or blank.*

Document identification:

Enter the date and name of the city where the offer is prepared. This date is used when referring to this purchase agreement.

Facts:

1. *Buyer, deposit and property*: **Enter** the name of each buyer who will sign the offer.

   Enter the dollar amount of any good-faith, earnest money deposit. **Check** the appropriate box to indicate the form of the good-faith deposit. **Enter** the name of the payee (escrow, title company or broker).

   Enter the name of the city and county in which the property is located.

   Enter the legal description or common address of the property, or the assessor's parcel number (APN).

   Enter the description of any personal property included, or **enter** words of reference, such as "see attached inventory," and **attach** an itemized list of the inventory. The seller's trade fixtures to be purchased by the buyer must be listed as inventory if they are to be acquired by the buyer. [See **first tuesday** Form 250]

PURCHASE AGREEMENT

Income Property other than One-to-Four Residential Units
Conventional Financing Provisions

DATE:_____, 20_____, at _____, California.

Items left blank or unchecked are not applicable.

FACTS:

1. Received from Buyer(s) _____ and
   _____ the sum of $_____,
   evidenced by ☐ personal check, or ☐ _____,
   payable to _____,
   to be held undeposited until acceptance of this offer as a deposit toward acquisition of property situated in
   the City of _____, County of _____, California, described as:
   Real property: _____
   Personal property: _____

2. This agreement is comprised of this four-page form and _____ pages of addenda/attachments.

TERMS: Buyer to pay the purchase price as follows:

3. Cash down payment through escrow, including deposits, in the amount of . . . . $_____
   3.1 Other consideration paid through escrow _____ . . . . $_____

4. ☐ Take title subject to, or ☐ assume, an existing first trust deed note held by
   _____ with an unpaid principal balance of . . . . $_____
   payable $_____ monthly, including interest not exceeding _____%,
   ☐ ARM, type _____, plus a monthly tax/insurance impound
   payment of $_____. _____

   4.1 At closing, loan balance differences per beneficiary statement(s) to be adjusted
   into: ☐ cash, ☐ carryback note, or ☐ sales price.

   4.2 The impound account to be transferred: ☐ charged, or ☐ without charge, to Buyer.

5. ☐ Take title subject to, or ☐ assume, an existing second trust deed note held by
   _____ with an unpaid principal balance of . . . $_____
   payable $_____ monthly, including interest not exceeding _____%,
   ☐ ARM, type _____, due _____, 20 _____.

6. Buyer to obtain a ☐ first, or ☐ second, trust deed loan in the amount of . . . . $_____
   payable approximately $_____ monthly for a period of _____ years.
   Interest on closing not to exceed _____%, ☐ ARM, type _____.
   Loan points not to exceed _____.

   6.1 ☐ Unless Buyer, within _____ days after acceptance, hands Seller satisfactory
   written confirmation Buyer is qualified for the financing of the purchase price,
   Seller may terminate the agreement. [**ft** Form 183]

7. Assume a tax bond or assessment lien with an unpaid principal balance of . . . . $_____

8. Note for the balance of the purchase price in the amount of. . . . . $_____
   to be executed by Buyer in favor of Seller and secured by a trust deed on the property
   junior to any above referenced financing, payable $_____ monthly, or more,
   beginning one month after closing, including interest at _____% from closing, due
   _____ years after closing.

   8.1 This note and trust deed to contain provisions to be provided by Seller for:
   ☐ due-on-sale; ☐ prepayment penalty; ☐ late charges; ☐ _____.

   8.2 ☐ A Carryback Disclosure Statement is attached as an addendum. [**ft** Form 300]

   8.3 ☐ Buyer to provide a Request for Notice of Delinquency to senior encumbrancers.
   [**ft** Form 412]

   8.4 Buyer to hand Seller a completed credit application on acceptance. [**ft** Form 302]

   8.5 Within _____ days of receipt of Buyer's credit application, Seller may terminate
   the agreement based on a reasonable disapproval of Buyer's creditworthiness.

   8.6 Seller may terminate the agreement on failure of the agreed terms for priority
   financing. [**ft** Form 183]

   8.7 As additional security, Buyer to execute a security agreement and file a UCC-1
   financing statement on any property transferred by Bill of Sale. [**ft** Form 436]

9. **Total Purchase Price is** . . . . $_____

— — — — — — — — — — — — — — *PAGE ONE OF FOUR — FORM 159* — — — — — — — — — — — — — — — — —

10. ACCEPTANCE AND PERFORMANCE:

10.1 This offer to be deemed revoked unless accepted in writing ☐ on presentation, or ☐ within _____ days after date, and acceptance is personally delivered or faxed to Offeror or Offeror's Broker within this period.

10.2 After acceptance, Broker(s) are authorized to extend any performance date up to one month.

10.3 On failure of Buyer to obtain or assume financing as agreed by the date scheduled for closing, Buyer may terminate the agreement.

10.4 Buyer's close of escrow is conditioned on Buyer's prior or concurrent closing on a sale of other property, commonly described as: _____ .

10.5 Any termination of the agreement shall be by written Notice of Cancellation timely delivered to the other party, the other party's broker or Escrow, with instructions to Escrow to return all instruments and funds to the parties depositing them. [ft Form 183]

10.6 Both parties reserve their rights to assign and agree to cooperate in effecting an Internal Revenue Code §1031 exchange prior to close of Escrow on either party's written notice. [ft Forms 171 or 172]

10.7 Should Buyer breach the agreement, Buyer's monetary liability to Seller is limited to ☐ $_____, or ☐ the deposit receipted in Section 1.

11. DUE DILIGENCE CONTINGENCIES:

Within _____ days after receipt or occurrence of any of the following conditions, Buyer may terminate the agreement based on Buyer's reasonable disapproval of the condition.

11.1 Income and expense records, leases, property management and other service contracts, permits or licenses affecting the operation of the property, which Seller will make available to Buyer on acceptance.

11.2 A Rental Income Statement itemizing, by unit, the tenant's name, rent amount, rent due date and delinquencies, deposits, rental period and expiration, and any rental incentives, bonuses or discounts, signed by Seller and handed to Buyer on acceptance. [ft Form 380]

11.3 Seller's Natural Hazard Disclosure Statement to be signed by Seller and handed to Buyer on acceptance. [ft Form 314]

11.4 A Seller's Condition of Property (Transfer) Disclosure Statement to be signed by Seller and Seller's Broker and handed to Buyer on acceptance.

11.5 Itemized inventory of the personal property included in the sale to be handed to Buyer on acceptance.

11.6 Inspection of the property by Buyer, his agent or consultants within _____ days after acceptance for value and condition sufficient to justify the purchase price.

11.7 Preliminary title report for the policy of title insurance, which Seller will cause Escrow to hand Buyer as soon as reasonably possible after acceptance.

11.8 An estoppel certificate executed by each tenant affirming the terms of their occupancy, which Seller will hand Buyer prior to seven days before closing. [ft Form 598]

11.9 Criminal activity and security statement prepared by Seller setting forth recent criminal activity on or about the property relevant to the security of persons and their belongings on the property, and any security arrangements undertaken or which should be undertaken in response.

12. PROPERTY CONDITIONS:

12.1 Seller to furnish prior to closing:

    a. ☐ a structural pest control inspection report and certification of clearance of corrective conditions.

    b. ☐ a home inspection report prepared by an insured home inspector showing the land and improvements to be free of material defects.

    c. ☐ a one-year home warranty policy:
        Insurer: _____
        Coverage: _____

    d. ☐ a certificate of occupancy, or other clearance or retrofitting, required by local ordinance for the transfer of possession or title.

    e. ☐ _____

    f. ☐ _____

12.2 Smoke detector(s) and water heater bracing exist in compliance with the law, and if not, Seller to install.

12.3 Seller to maintain the property in good condition until possession is delivered.

12.4 Fixtures and fittings attached to the property include, but are not limited to: window shades, blinds, light fixtures, plumbing fixtures, curtain rods, wall-to-wall carpeting, draperies, hardware, antennas, air coolers and conditioners, trees, shrubs, mailboxes and other similar items.

12.5 New agreements and modifications of existing agreements to rent units, or to service, alter or equip the property, will not be entered into by Seller without Buyer's prior written consent, which will not be unreasonably withheld.

13. CLOSING CONDITIONS:

13.1 This transaction to be escrowed with _____.
Parties to deliver instructions to Escrow as soon as reasonably possible after acceptance.

    a. ☐ Escrow holder is authorized and instructed to act on the provisions of this agreement as the mutual escrow instructions of the parties and to draft any additional instructions necessary to close this transaction. [ft Form 401]

    b. ☐ Escrow instructions, prepared and signed by the parties, are attached to be handed to Escrow on acceptance. [ft Form 401]

13.2 Escrow to be handed all instruments needed to close escrow ☐ on or before _____, 20_____, or ☐ within _____ days after acceptance. Parties to hand Escrow all documents required by the title insurer, lenders or other third parties to this transaction prior to seven days before the date scheduled for closing.

    a. Each party to pay its customary escrow charges. [ft Forms 310 and 311]

13.3 Title to be vested in Buyer or Assignee free of encumbrances other than those set forth herein. Buyer's interest in title shall be insured by _____ Title Company under a(n) ☐ CLTA standard, ☐ ATLA owner's, or ☐ ALTA binder, policy of title insurance.

    a. Endorsements:_____

    b. ☐ Seller, or ☐ Buyer, to pay the title insurance premium.

13.4 Buyer to furnish a new fire insurance policy covering the property.

13.5 Taxes, assessments, insurance premiums, rents, interest and other expenses to be prorated to close of escrow, unless otherwise provided.

13.6 Bill of Sale to be executed for any personal property being acquired.

    a. ☐ A UCC-3 Condition of Title Report to be ordered from the Secretary of State and approved by Buyer prior to close of Escrow.

13.7 Seller to assign, and title to be subject to, all existing leases and rental agreements. [ft Form 595]

    a. Seller to notify each tenant of the change of ownership on or before the close of escrow. [ft Form 554]

13.8 Security deposits held by Seller to be handed to Buyer on close of escrow. Seller to notify each tenant of the transfer of the security deposit on close of escrow, with a copy of each notice to Buyer through escrow. [ft Form 586]

13.9 Delinquent unpaid rent to be treated as paid. Any recovery by Buyer of Seller's portion of delinquent rent and prorated delinquent rent credited to Buyer shall be refunded to Seller on collection by Buyer.

13.10 Service and equipment contracts to be assumed by Buyer include: _____
_____

    a. Contracts assumed by Buyer to be prorated to close of escrow.

13.11 Possession of the property and keys/access codes to be delivered on close of escrow.

13.12 If Seller is unable to convey marketable title as agreed, or if the improvements on the property are materially damaged prior to closing, Buyer may terminate the agreement. Seller to pay all reasonable escrow cancellation charges. [ft Form 183]

14. BROKERAGE FEE:

14.1 Parties to pay the below mentioned Broker(s) a fee now due of _____ as follows: Seller to pay the brokerage fee on the change of ownership. The party wrongfully preventing this change of ownership to pay the brokerage fee.

14.2 Seller's Broker and Buyer's Broker, respectively, to share the brokerage fee _____:_____.

14.3 ☐ Attached is the Agency Law Disclosure. [ft Form 305]

14.4 Broker is authorized to report the sale, its price and terms for dissemination and use of participants in brokerage trade associations or listing services.

15. _____
_____
_____
_____
_____
_____
_____
_____
_____
_____
_____

Buyer's/
Selling Broker: _____

By: _____

Is the agent of: ☐ Buyer exclusively.
                 ☐ Both Seller and Buyer.

Seller's/
Listing Broker: _____

By: _____

Is the agent of: ☐ Seller exclusively.
                 ☐ Both Seller and Buyer.

I agree to the terms stated above.

Date:_____, 20_____

Buyer: _____

Buyer: _____

Signature: _____

Signature: _____

Address: _____

_____

Phone:_____

Fax: _____

Email: _____

I agree to the terms stated above.

Date:_____, 20_____

Seller: _____

Seller: _____

Signature: _____

Signature: _____

Address: _____

_____

Phone:_____

Fax: _____

Email: _____

REJECTION OF OFFER

Undersigned hereby rejects this offer in its entirety. No counteroffer will be forthcoming.

Date:_____, 20_____

Name: _____

Name: _____

Signature: _____

Signature: _____

FORM 159   08-05   ©2006 **first tuesday**, P.O. BOX 20069, RIVERSIDE, CA 92516 (800) 794-0494

2. *Entire agreement*: **Enter** the number of pages comprising all of the addenda, disclosures, etc., which are attached to the purchase agreement.

Terms for payment of the purchase price:

3. *Cash down payment*: **Enter** the dollar amount of the buyer's cash down payment toward the purchase price.

   3.1 *Additional down payment*: **Enter** the description of any other consideration to be paid as part of the price, such as trust deed notes, personal property or real estate equities (an exchange). **Enter** the dollar amount of its value.

4. *First trust deed note*: **Check** the appropriate box to indicate whether the transfer of title is to be "subject-to" an existing loan or by an "assumption" of the loan if the buyer is to take over an existing first trust deed loan. **Enter** the lender's name. **Enter** the remaining balance, the monthly principal and interest (PI) payment and the interest rate on the loan. **Check** the box to indicate whether the interest is adjustable (ARM), and if so, **enter** the index name. **Enter** any monthly impound payment made in addition to the PI payment. **Enter** any due date or other terms unique to the loan.

   4.1 *Loan balance adjustments*: **Check** the appropriate box to indicate the financial adjustment desired for loan balance differences at the close of escrow.

   4.2 *Impound balances*: **Check** the appropriate box to indicate whether the impound account transferred to the buyer will be with or without a charge to the buyer.

5. *Second trust deed note*: **Check** the appropriate box to indicate whether the transfer of title is to be "subject-to" an existing loan or by an "assumption" of the loan if the buyer is to take over an existing second trust deed loan. **Enter** the lender's name. **Enter** the remaining balance, the monthly PI payment and the interest rate on the loan. **Check** the box to indicate whether the interest is adjustable (ARM), and if so, **enter** the index name. **Enter** the due date for payment of a final/balloon payment.

6. *New trust deed loan*: **Check** the appropriate box to indicate whether any new financing will be a first or second trust deed loan. **Enter** the amount of the loan, the monthly PI payment, the term of the loan and the rate of interest. **Check** the box to indicate whether the interest will be adjustable (ARM), and if so, **enter** the index name. **Enter** any limitations on loan points.

   6.1 *Buyer's loan qualification*: **Check** the box to indicate the seller is authorized to cancel the agreement if the buyer is to obtain a new loan and fails to deliver documentation from a lender indicating he has been qualified for a loan. **Enter** the number of days the buyer has after acceptance to deliver written confirmation of his qualification for the loan.

7. *Bond or assessment assumed*: **Enter** the amount of the principal balance remaining unpaid on bonds and special assessment liens (such as Mello-Roos or 1915 improvement bonds) which will remain unpaid and become the responsibility of the buyer on closing.

Editor's note — Improvement bonds are obligations of the seller which may be assumed by the buyer in lieu of their payoff by the seller. If assumed, the bonded indebtedness becomes part of the consideration paid for the property. Some purchase agreements erroneously place *these bonds under "property tax" as though they were **ad valorem taxes**, and then fail to prorate and charge the unpaid amount to the seller.*

8. *Seller carryback note*: **Enter** the amount of the carryback note to be executed by the buyer as partial payment of the price. **Enter** the amount of the note's monthly PI payment, the interest rate and the due date for the final/balloon payment.

    8.1 *Special carryback provisions*: **Check** the appropriate box to indicate any special provisions to be included in the carryback note or trust deed. **Enter** the name of any other special provision to be included in the carryback note or trust deed, such as impounds, discount options, extension provisions, guarantee arrangements or right of first refusal on the sale or hypothecation of the note.

    8.2 *Carryback disclosure*: **Fill out** and **attach** a Seller Carryback Disclosure Statement as an addendum. [See **first tuesday** Form 300]

Editor's note — Further approval of the disclosure statement in escrow creates by statute a buyer's contingency allowing for cancellation until time of closing on any purchase of one-to-four unit residential property.

    8.3 *Notice of Delinquency*: **Requires** the buyer to execute a Request for Notice of Delinquency and pay the costs of recording and serving it on senior lenders since they will have priority on title to the trust deed securing the carryback note.

    8.4 *Buyer creditworthiness*: **Requires** the buyer to provide the seller with a completed credit application.

    8.5 *Approval of creditworthiness*: **Enter** the number of days within which the seller may cancel the transaction for reasonable disapproval of the buyer's credit application and report.

    8.6 *Subordination*: **Provides** for the seller to terminate this transaction if the parameters agreed to for financing by an assumption or origination of a trust deed loan with priority on title to the carryback note are exceeded.

    8.7 *Personal property as security*: **Requires** the buyer on the transfer of any personal property in this transaction to execute a security agreement and UCC-1 financing statement to provide additional security for any carryback note.

9. *Purchase price*: **Enter** the total amount of the purchase price as the sum of lines 3, 3.1, 4, 5, 6, 7 and 8.

10. **Acceptance and performance periods:**

    10.1 *Delivery of acceptance*: **Check** the appropriate box to indicate the time period for acceptance of the offer. If applicable, **enter** the number of days in which the seller may accept this offer and form a binding contract.

Editor's note — Acceptance occurs on the return delivery to the person making the offer (or counteroffer) or to his broker of a copy of the unaltered purchase agreement offer containing the signed acceptance.

    10.2 *Extension of performance dates*: **Authorizes** the brokers to extend the performance dates up to one month to meet the objectives of the agreement — time being of a reasonable duration and not the essence of this agreement as a matter of policy. This extension authority does not extend to the acceptance period.

10.3 *Loan contingency*: **Authorizes** the buyer to cancel the transaction at the time scheduled for closing if the financing for payment of the price is not obtainable or assumable.

10.4 *Sale of other property*: If the closing of this transaction is to be contingent on the buyer's receipt of net proceeds from a sale of other property, **enter** the address of the property to be sold by the buyer.

10.5 *Cancellation procedures*: **Provides** the method of cancellation required to terminate the agreement when the right to cancel is triggered by other provisions in the agreement, such as contingency or performance provisions.

10.6 *Exchange cooperation*: **Requires** the parties to cooperate in an IRS §1031 transaction on further written notice by either party. **Provides** for the parties to assign their interests in this agreement.

10.7 *Liability limitations* **Provides** for a dollar limit on the buyer's liability for the buyer's breach of the agreement. **Check** the first box and **enter** the maximum dollar amount of money losses the seller may recover from the buyer or **check** the second box to indicate the buyer's monetary liability is limited to the good-faith deposit tendered with the offer to buy.

Editor's note — Liability limitation provisions avoid the misleading and unenforceable forfeiture called for under liquidated damage clauses included in most purchase agreement forms provided by other publishers of forms.

11. Due Diligence Contingencies:

Approval period: **Enter** the number of days the buyer has to approve or disapprove and cancel this agreement after the buyer's receipt of each item listed below. This section calls for the buyer to complete a due diligence investigation to confirm the representations of the seller and the seller's broker and the pre-contract expectations of the buyer about the property. If the buyer is unable to confirm his expectations, he may waive the requirements or cancel the transaction.

11.1 *Operating records*: **Requires** the seller to make income and expense records and supporting documents available to the buyer for inspection as soon as possible after acceptance of the offer.

11.2 *Rents and deposits*: **Requires** the seller to prepare a detailed rent roll profile on each occupancy and deliver it to the buyer as soon as possible after acceptance.

11.3 *Natural Hazard Disclosure (NHD) Statement*: **Requires** the seller to prepare and deliver to the buyer a NHD Statement disclosing the seller's knowledge of the hazards listed on the form.

11.4 *Condition of property*: **Requires** the seller to prepare and deliver a statement disclosing the physical condition of the property as known to the seller.

11.5 *Inventory*: **Requires** the seller to prepare and deliver an itemized list of all personal property being transferred to the buyer on closing.

11.6 *Valuation inspection*: **Enter** the number of days after acceptance in which the buyer is to investigate the market value of the property to confirm its value justifies the price the buyer has agreed to pay.

11.7 *Title report*: **Requires** the seller to deliver a preliminary title report to the buyer for review to confirm the condition of title allows the buyer to use the property as he intended.

11.8 *Tenant Estoppel Certificate*: **Requires** the seller to produce Tenant Estoppel Certificates prior to seven days before the date scheduled for closing to confirm the tenants' acquiescence to the terms stated in the certificate.

11.9 *Tenant security*: **Requires** the seller to prepare and deliver a statement disclosing criminal activity affecting individuals on the property and any crime prevention undertaken or which should be undertaken.

12. Property Conditions:

12.1 *Seller to furnish*: **Check** the appropriate box(es) within the following subsections to indicate the items the seller is to furnish prior to closing.

a. *Pest control*: **Check** the box to indicate the seller is to furnish a structural pest control report and clearance.

b. *Home inspection report*: **Check** the box to indicate the seller is to employ a home inspection company and furnish the buyer with the company's home inspection report.

c. *Home warranty*: **Check** the box to indicate the seller is to furnish an insurance policy for home repairs. **Enter** the name of the insurer and the type of coverage, such as for the air conditioning unit, etc.

d. *Local ordinance compliance*: **Check** the box to indicate the

seller is to furnish a certificate of occupancy or other clearance required by local ordinance.

e. *Other terms*: **Check** the box and **enter** any other report, certification or clearance the seller is to furnish.

f. *Other terms*: **Check** the box and **enter** any other report, certification or clearance the seller is to furnish.

12.2 *Safety compliance*: **Requires** smoke detectors and water heater bracing to exist or be installed by the seller.

12.3 *Property maintenance*: **Requires** the seller to maintain the present condition of the property until the close of escrow.

12.4 *Fixtures and fittings*: **Confirms** this agreement includes real estate fixtures and fittings as part of the property purchased.

Editor's note — Trade fixtures are personal property to be listed as items on an attached inventory at section 1.

12.5 *Leasing and lease modifications*: **Requires** the seller to obtain the buyer's consent (which will not be unreasonably withheld) to any new tenancies or modifications of existing tenancies entered into during the escrow period.

13. Closing conditions:

13.1 *Escrow closing agent*: **Enter** the name of the escrow company handling the closing.

a. *Escrow instructions*: **Check** the box to indicate the purchase agreement is to also serve as the mutual instructions to escrow from the parties. The escrow company will typically prepare supplemental instructions they will need to handle and close the transaction. [See **first tuesday** Form 401]

b. *Escrow instructions*: **Check** the box to indicate escrow instructions have been prepared and are attached to this purchase agreement. **Attach** the prepared escrow instructions to the purchase agreement and **obtain** the signatures of the parties. [See **first tuesday** Form 401]

13.2 *Closing date*: **Check** the appropriate box to indicate the method to be used to set the date on which escrow is scheduled to close. Following the checked box, **enter** the specific date for closing or the number of days anticipated as necessary for the parties to perform and close escrow. Also, prior to seven days before closing, the parties are to deliver all documents needed by third parties to perform their services by the date scheduled for closing.

a. *Escrow charges*: **Requires** each party to pay their customary escrow closing charges, amounts any competent escrow officer can provide on inquiry.

13.3 *Title insurance*: **Provides** for the title to be vested in the name of the buyer or their assignee. **Enter** the name of the title insurance company which is to provide a preliminary title report in anticipation of issuing title insurance. **Check** the

appropriate box to indicate the type of title insurance policy to be issued.

a. *Policy endorsements*: **Enter** any endorsements to be issued with the policy.

b. *Payment of premium*: **Check** the appropriate box to indicate whether the buyer or seller is to pay the title insurance premium.

13.4 *Fire insurance*: **Requires** the buyer to provide a new policy of hazard insurance.

13.5 *Prorates and adjustments*: **Authorizes** prorations and adjustments on the close of escrow for taxes, insurance premiums, rents, interest, loan balances, service contracts and other property operating expenses, prepaid or accrued.

13.6 *Personal property*: **Requires** the seller to execute a bill of sale for any personal property being transferred in this transaction at section 1.

a. *Personal property report*: **Check** the box to indicate escrow is to order a UCC-3 from the Secretary of State on any personal property located on the real estate which is to be transferred by bill of sale to the buyer.

13.7 *Assignment of leases*: **Requires** the seller to assign all leases and rental agreements to the buyer on closing. [See **first tuesday** Form 595]

a. *Ownership notice*: **Requires** the seller to notify each tenant of the change of ownership. [See **first tuesday** Form 554]

13.8 *Tenant security deposits*: **Requires** the seller to credit or pay the buyer on the close of escrow for security deposits held by the seller under the existing occupancies. **Requires** the seller to notify each tenant of the transfer of the security deposit. [See **first tuesday** Form 586]

Editor's note — Proper notice to the tenant regarding the security deposit transfer to the buyer eliminates all future liability the seller may have had due to the seller's original receipt of the deposits.

13.9 *Rent due and unpaid at closing*: **Treats** delinquent unpaid rent as paid for purposes of prorations. The buyer is credited for his share of paid and unpaid rents for the month of the closing. On any later recovery by the buyer of delinquent prorated rent, the buyer is to forward the entire amount received to the seller.

13.10 *Service contracts*: **Enter** the name of the providers of services under contracts the buyer is to assume.

 a. *Prorations*: **Authorizes** the proration of amounts prepaid or unpaid on the service contracts.

13.11 *Buyer's possession*: **Requires** the seller to deliver possession of the property to the buyer on the close of escrow.

13.12 *Property destruction*: **Provides** for the seller to bear the *risk of loss* for any casualty losses suffered by the property prior to the close of escrow. Thus, the buyer may terminate the agreement if the seller is unable to provide a marketable title or should the property improvements suffer major damage.

14. **Brokerage fee:**

 14.1 *Fee amount*: **Enter** the total amount of the fee due all brokers to be paid by the seller. The amount may be stated as a fixed dollar amount or a percentage of the price.

Editor's note — The defaulting party pays all brokerage fees and the brokerage fee can only be altered or cancelled by mutual instructions from the buyer and seller.

 14.2 *Fee sharing*: **Enter** the percentage share of the fee each broker is to receive.

Editor's note — The percentage share may be set based on an oral agreement between the brokers, by acceptance of the listing broker's MLS offer to a selling office to share a fee, or unilaterally by an agent when preparing the buyer's offer.

 14.3 *Agency law disclosures*: **Attach** a copy of the Agency Law Disclosure addendum for all parties to sign. The disclosure is mandated to be acknowledged by the buyer with the offer and acknowledged by the seller on acceptance as a prerequisite to the brokers enforcing collection of the fee when the property involved contains one-to-four residential units. [See **first tuesday** Form 305]

 14.4 *Disclosure of sales data*: **Authorizes** the brokers to report the transaction to trade associations or listing services.

15. *Other terms*: **Enter** any special provision to be included in the purchase agreement.

Agency confirmation:

Buyer's broker identification: **Enter** the name of the buyer's broker. **Obtain** the signature of the buyer's broker or the selling agent acting on behalf of the buyer's broker. **Check** the appropriate box to indicate the agency which was created by the broker's (and his agents') conduct with the parties.

Seller's broker identification: **Enter** the name of the seller's broker. **Obtain** the signature of the seller's broker or the listing agent acting on behalf of the seller's broker. **Check** the appropriate box to indicate the agency which was created by the broker's (and his agents') conduct with the parties.

Signatures:

Buyer's signature: **Enter** the date the buyer signs the purchase agreement and each buyer's name. **Obtain** each buyer's signature on the purchase agreement and on each attachment which requires his signature. **Enter** the buyer's address, telephone and fax numbers, and email address.

Seller's signature: **Enter** the date the seller signs the purchase agreement and each seller's name. **Obtain** each seller's signature on the purchase agreement and on each attachment which requires his signature. **Enter** the seller's address, telephone and fax numbers, and email address.

Rejection of offer:

Should the offer contained in the purchase agreement be rejected instead of accepted, and the rejection will not result in a counteroffer, **enter** the date of the rejection and the names of the party rejecting the offer. **Obtain** the signatures of the party rejecting the offer.

Observations

As a policy of the publisher, this purchase agreement **does not contain** clauses which tend to increase the risk of litigation or are generally felt to work against the best interests of the buyer, seller and broker. Excluded provisions include:

- an *attorney fee provision*, which tends to **promote litigation** and inhibit contracting;

- an *arbitration clause*, which, if included and initialed, absolutely **waives** the buyer's and seller's right to a fair and correct decision by trial and appeal; and

- a *time-essence clause*, since future performance (closing) dates are, at best, estimates by the broker and his agents of the time needed to close and are too often **improperly used** by sellers in rising markets to cancel the transaction before the buyer or broker can reasonably comply with the terms of the purchase agreement.

Chapter 52

The formal exchange agreement

This chapter presents an exchange agreement form used to initiate a §1031 transaction where the ownership of properties is exchanged between two persons.

Structuring a comprehensible transaction

An **exchange of properties** is an arrangement structured as an agreement and entered into by owners of two or more parcels of real estate who agree to transfer the ownership of their properties between themselves in consideration for the value of the equity in the properties received. Economic adjustments are made for any difference in the valuations given to the equities in the properties exchanged.

Thus, the owners of real estate, on entering into a written exchange agreement, agree to **sell and convey** their property to the other party. However, unlike a sale under a purchase agreement, the down payment is not in the form of cash. Instead, the down payment is the **equity in property** each owner will receive. The dollar amount of the down payment is the value given to the equity in the property to be received in exchange.

In an exchange of equities, as in the sale of property with a cash down payment, the **balance of the price** agreed to must be paid in some form of consideration. If a sales price is to be paid in cash, the balance of the price after the down payment is typically funded by a purchase-assist loan.

Conversely, in a sale calling for a cash down payment and an assumption of the loan of record, any balance remaining to be paid on the price is usually deferred, evidenced by a carryback note. The carryback note in a cash down payment sale presents no different a situation than the carryback note in an "equity down payment" situation, such as occurs in an exchange of an equity in one property as a down payment toward the purchase of a larger equity in another property, called an *adjustment* or *balancing of equities*.

Also, unlike a cash sale which "frees up" the capital investment in real estate by converting the equity to cash proceeds on closing, an exchange is a clear manifestation of the owner's desire to **continue his investment** in real estate. In an exchange, the owner disposes of a property he no longer wants.

The owner might use his equity in an estate building plan to move up into property of greater value (and greater debt leverage), or simply to consolidate several properties the owner has that he exchanges to acquire a single, more efficiently operated property.

The **hallmarks of an exchange transaction**, in contrast to the common features of a sales transaction, include:

- the **exchange of equities** in real estate in lieu of a cash down payment;

- no **good-faith deposit** as cash is rarely used in an exchange of equities, except for prorations, adjustments (such as security deposits), transactional expenditures or as a "sweetener" to encourage an acceptance of the exchange offer, since the signature of each party binds them to perform on the exchange agreement and is the only consideration needed from each party to form a contract;

- a take-over of **existing financing** by an assumption of the loans or a transfer of title subject to the loans, rather than refinancing and incurring expenses that greatly increase the cost of reinvesting in real estate;

- **adjustments** brought about by the difference in the value of the equities exchanged, a balancing that requires the owner with the lesser valued equity to cover the difference in cash installments evidenced by the execution of a promissory note or the contribution of additional personal property or real estate of value;

- joint or **tandem escrows**, interrelated due to the conveyance of one property as consideration for the conveyance of the other property, similar in effect to a cash sale of a property when the closing is contingent on the sale of other property to obtain the funds needed to close escrow, a contingency that does occur in some delayed §1031 reinvestment plans;

- two sets of **brokerage fees**, one for each property involved in the exchange, rather than the receipt of a single fee as occurs in a cash-out sale of property;

- one party simultaneously selling and buying, a **coupling of two properties** consisting of a sale of one and purchase of the other, motivated primarily by the tax compulsion to remain invested in business or investment real estate, called *like-kind properties*, rather than cash out on the sale of one and later separately locate, analyze and purchase a replacement property with the cash proceeds of the sale, as occurs in a delayed "sell now/buy later" §1031 reinvestment plan; and

- **tax advice** from a real estate broker counseling on the profit tax avoidance of a coordinated, simultaneous reinvestment of the owner's equity in business or investment category real estate in a replacement property, thus avoiding the need to first locate a cash buyer to convert the equity to cash and then scramble to locate replacement property so the sales proceeds can be reinvested within a specific time period while avoiding receipt of the proceeds.

Commonality with a sale

The **common features** found in the acquisition of real estate by either a cash purchase or an exchange of equities include:

- a **disclosure** by the owner and listing broker of the conditions known to them about the property improvements, title, operation and natural hazards of the location which adversely affect the property's market value or the buyer's intended use of the property; and

- a **due diligence investigation** by the buyer acquiring title concerning his ownership, use and operation of the property.

As in all real estate transactions, a form is used to **prepare the offer** and commence written negotiations. The objective of a written agreement is to provide a comprehensive checklist of boilerplate provisions for the parties to consider in their offer, acceptance and counteroffer negotiations.

Also, the terms of an exchange agreement must be sufficiently complete and clear in their wording to prevent a misunderstanding or uncertainty over what the parties have agreed to do should the agreement require enforcement by one or the other party.

Once the brokerage process of locating a suitable replacement property has produced a property the owner is willing to acquire in exchange for the property he wants to dispose of, the broker prepares an exchange agreement on a preprinted or computer generated form. When prepared, the terms are reviewed with the owner, signed by the broker and the owner, and submitted to the owner of the replacement property for acceptance. [See Form 171 accompanying this chapter]

An exchange agreement form will only be used when an owner's equity in a property is offered as a **down payment** in exchange for replacement property. An owner who has already en-

EXCHANGE AGREEMENT

(Other than One-to-Four Residential Units)

DATE:_____, 20_____, at _____, California

Items left blank or unchecked are not applicable.

PROPERTIES TO BE EXCHANGED:

1. The FIRST PARTY, _____ will deliver
the FIRST PROPERTY, located in the City of _____
County of _____, State of _____
described as _____.

   1.1   The equity valuation for the property is. . . . .$_____

   1.2   The loans of record presently encumbering the property total . . . .$_____

         a. A first loan of $_____ payable $_____ monthly
including _____% interest ☐ ARM, due _____, 20_____.

         b. A second loan of $_____ payable $_____ monthly
including _____% interest ☐ ARM, due _____, 20_____.

   1.3   The market value of the First Property is . . . .$_____

   1.4   The market value includes delivery of personal property described as:

_____

2. The SECOND PARTY, _____will deliver
the SECOND PROPERTY, located in the city of_____
County of _____, State of _____,
described as _____.

   2.1   The equity valuation for the property is. . . . .$_____

   2.2   The loans of record presently encumbering the property total . . . .$_____

         a. A first loan of $_____ payable $_____ monthly
including _____% interest ☐ ARM, due _____, 20_____.

         b. A second loan of $_____ payable $_____ monthly
including _____% interest ☐ ARM, due _____, 20_____.

   2.3   The market value of the Second Property is. . . . .$_____

   2.4   The market value includes delivery of personal property described as:

_____

3. **TERMS OF EXCHANGE:**

   3.1   The First Party to acquire the **Second Property** on the following terms:

         a. Transfer the First Property with an equity valuation in the amount of . . . .$_____

         b. Payment of cash, as an adjustment for the First Party's receipt of a larger equity
in the Second Property, in the amount of . . . .$_____

         c. Payment of additional cash, to fund the payoff by the Second Party of the loans
of record on the Second Property, in the amount of . . . .$_____

         d. ☐ Take title subject to, or ☐ assume, the loans of record encumbering
the Second Property in the amount of. . . . .$_____

         e. Execution of a note in favor of the Second Party in the amount of. . . . .$_____
Secured by a trust deed on the Second Property, junior to the loans of record,
payable $_____ monthly, or more, beginning one month after
closing of escrow and including interest at _____% from closing, due _____
years after closing. This note to include terms and conditions set out in § 3.3.

         f. Deliver additional property with an equity value in the amount of. . . . .$_____
described as_____,
encumbered by a loan in the amount of $_____, payable_____
_____.

         g. Receipt of consideration from the Second Party provided for in §3.2b, §3.2e
and §3.2f.
as compensation for First Party conveying a larger equity, for an offset of . . . . . . (-)$_____

         h. **TOTAL CONSIDERATION** given the Second Party as the market value paid
by the First Party for the Second Property is the amount of. . . . .$_____

i. Obtain a ☐ first or ☐ second trust deed loan to be secured by the Second Property in the amount of $_____, payable approximately $_____ monthly including interest not to exceed _____%, ☐ ARM, type_____, with a due date of _____ years or more.

3.2 The Second Party to acquire the **First Property** on the following terms:

a. Transfer the Second Property with an equity valuation in the amount of . . . . $_____

b. Payment of cash, as an adjustment for the Second Party's receipt of a larger equity in the First Property, in the amount of . . . . $_____

c. Payment of additional cash, to fund the payoff by the First Party of the loans of record on the First Property, in the amount of. . . . . $_____

d. ☐ Take title subject to, or ☐ assume, the loans of record encumbering the First Property in the total amount of. . . . . $_____

e. Execute a note in favor of the First Party in the amount of . . . . $_____ secured by a trust deed on the First Property, junior to the loans of record, payable $_____ monthly, or more, beginning one month after close of escrow and including interest at _____% from closing, due _____years after closing. This note to include terms and conditions set out in §3.3.

f. Deliver additional property with an equity value in the amount of. . . . . $_____ described as_____, encumbered by a loan in the amount of $_____, payable_____ _____.

g. Receipt of consideration from the First Party provided for in §3.1b, §3.1e and §3.1f as compensation for Second Party conveying a larger equity, for an offset of . . . . (-)$_____

h. **TOTAL CONSIDERATION** given the First Party as the market value paid by the Second Party for the First Property is the amount of. . . . . $_____

i. Obtain a ☐ first or ☐ second trust deed loan to be secured by the First Property in the amount of $_____, payable approximately $_____ monthly including interest not to exceed _____%, ☐ ARM, type_____, with a due date of _____ years or more.

3.3 The terms and conditions of any note and trust deed executed by one party in favor of the other under sections §3.1e or §3.2e include:

a. ☐ Grantor/payee's carryback disclosure statement attached as an addendum to the agreement. [**ft** Form 300]

b. Provisions to be provided by the grantor/payee for ☐ due-on-sale, ☐ prepayment penalty, ☐ late charges, ☐ _____.

c. ☐ Grantee/payor to provide a request for notice of delinquency to senior encumbrances. [**ft** Form 412]

d. ☐ Grantee/payor to hand Grantor/payee a completed credit application on acceptance. [**ft** Form 302]

e. Within _____ days of receipt of Grantor/payee's credit application, Grantor/payee may terminate the agreement based on a reasonable disapproval of Grantor/payee's creditworthiness. [**ft** Form 183]

f. Grantor/payee may terminate the agreement on failure of agreed terms for priority financing. [**ft** Form 183]

g. As additional security, Grantee/payor to execute a security agreement and file a UCC-1 financing statement on any personal property Grantee/payor acquires under this agreement by Bill of Sale.

4. ACCEPTANCE AND PERFORMANCE:

4.1 This offer to be deemed revoked unless accepted in writing within _____ days after date, and the acceptance is personally delivered or faxed to the First Party or the First Party's Broker within the period.

4.2 After acceptance, Brokers are authorized to extend any performance date up to one month.

4.3 On the failure of either party to obtain or assume financing as agreed by the date scheduled for closing, that party may terminate the agreement.

4.4 Any termination of the agreement shall be by written Notice of Cancellation timely delivered to the other party, the other party's broker or Escrow with instructions to Escrow to return all instruments and funds to the parties depositing them. [**ft** Form 183]

4.5 Both parties reserve their rights to assign and agree to cooperate in effecting an Internal Revenue Code §1031 exchange prior to close of escrow on either party's written notice. [**ft** Forms 172 or 173]

4.6 Should either party breach this agreement, that party's monetary liability to the other party is limited to $_____.

5. DUE DILIGENCE CONTINGENCIES:

5.1 Prior to accepting delivery of the First Property, the Second Party may, within _____ days after receipt or occurrence of any of the following checked items, terminate this exchange agreement based on the Second Party's reasonable disapproval of the checked item.

    a. ☐ Income and expense records, leases, property management and other service contracts, permits or licenses affecting the operation of the property, which documents First Party will make available to Second Party on acceptance.

    b. ☐ A Rental Income Statement itemizing, by unit, the tenant's name, rent amount, rent due date, delinquencies, deposits, rental period and expiration and any rental incentives, bonuses or discounts signed by First Party and handed to Second Party on acceptance. [ft Form 380]

    c. ☐ Seller's Natural Hazard Disclosure Statement to be signed by First Party and handed to Second Party on acceptance. [ft Form 314]

    d. ☐ A Seller's Condition of Property (Transfer) Disclosure to be signed by First Party and First Party's Broker and handed to Second Party on acceptance.

    e. ☐ Itemized inventory of the personal property included in the sale to be handed to Second Party on acceptance.

    f. ☐ Inspection of the property by Second Party, his agent or consultants within _____ days after acceptance for value and condition sufficient to justify the purchase price.

    g. ☐ Preliminary title report for the policy of title insurance, which report First Party will cause escrow to hand Second Party as soon as reasonably possible after acceptance.

    h. ☐ An estoppel certificate executed by each tenant affirming the terms of their occupancy, which certificates First Party will hand Second Party prior to seven days before closing. [ft Form 598]

    i. ☐ Criminal activity and security statement prepared by the First Party and setting forth recent criminal activity on or about the First Property relevant to the security of persons and their belongings on the property and any security arrangements undertaken or which should be undertaken in response.

    j. ☐ Submission of the exchange agreement, escrow instructions and any other documentation related to this transaction to the Second Party's attorney or accountant within _____ days after acceptance for their further approval of this transaction as qualifying, in its entirety or partially, as an IRC §1031 tax exempt transaction reportable by the Second Party.

    k. ☐ _____

5.2 Prior to accepting delivery of the Second Property, the First Party may, within _____ days after receipt or occurrence of any of the following checked items, terminate this exchange agreement based on the First Party's reasonable disapproval of the checked item.

    a. ☐ Income and expense records, leases, property management and other service contracts, permits or licenses affecting the operation of the property, which documents Second Party will make available to First Party on acceptance.

    b. ☐ A Rental Income Statement itemizing, by unit, the tenant's name, rent amount, rent due date, delinquencies, deposits, rental period and expiration and any rental incentives, bonuses or discounts, signed by Second Party and handed to First Party on acceptance. [ft Form 380]

    c. ☐ Seller's Natural Hazard Disclosure Statement to be signed by Second Party and handed to First Party on acceptance. [ft Form 314]

    d. ☐ A Seller's Condition of Property (Transfer) Disclosure to be signed by Second Party and Second Party's Broker and handed to First Party on acceptance.

    e. ☐ Itemized inventory of the personal property included in the sale to be handed to First Party on acceptance.

    f. ☐ Inspection of the property by First Party, his agent or consultants within _____ days after acceptance for value and condition sufficient to justify the purchase price.

    g. ☐ Preliminary title report for the policy of title insurance, which report Second Party will cause escrow to hand First Party as soon as reasonably possible after acceptance.

    h. ☐ An estoppel certificate executed by each tenant affirming the terms of their occupancy, which certificates Second Party will hand First Party prior to seven days before closing. [ft Form 598]

    i. ☐ Criminal activity and security statement prepared by the Second Party and setting forth recent criminal activity on or about the Second Property relevant to the security of persons and their belongings on the property and any security arrangements undertaken or which should be undertaken in response.

    j. ☐ Submission of the exchange agreement, escrow instructions and any other documentation related to this transaction to the First Party's attorney or accountant within _____ days after acceptance for their further approval of this transaction as qualifying, in its entirety or partially, as an IRC §1031 tax exempt transaction reportable by the First Party.

    k. ☐ _____

6. PROPERTY CONDITIONS ON CLOSING:

Prior to closing, each party with regard to the property they are conveying, will comply with or furnish the other party the following items:

6.1 ☐ A structural pest control report and clearance.

6.2 ☐ A one-year property warranty policy.
   Insurer: _____
   Coverage: _____

6.3 A certificate of occupancy, or other clearance or retrofitting, required by local ordinance for the transfer of possession or title.

6.4 Smoke detector(s) and water heater bracing in compliance with the law.

6.5 Maintain the property in good condition until possession is delivered.

6.6 Fixtures and fittings attached to the property include but are not limited to: window shades, blinds, light fixtures, plumbing fixtures, curtain rods, wall-to-wall carpeting, draperies, hardware, antennas, air coolers and conditioners, trees, shrubs, mailboxes and other similar items.

6.7 New agreements and modifications of existing agreements to rent space or to service, alter or equip the property will not be entered into without the other party's prior written consent, which will not be unreasonably withheld.

6.8 _____
   _____.

7. CLOSING CONDITIONS

7.1 This transaction to be escrowed with _____.
   Parties to deliver instructions to Escrow as soon as reasonably possible after acceptance.
   a. ☐ Escrow holder is authorized and instructed to act on the provisions of this agreement as the mutual escrow instructions of the parties and to draft any additional instructions necessary to close this transaction. [ft Form 401]
   b. ☐ Escrow instructions, prepared and signed by the parties, are attached to be handed to Escrow on acceptance. [ft Form 401]

7.2 Escrow to be handed all instruments needed to close escrow ☐ on or before _____, 20_____, or ☐ within _____ days after acceptance. Parties to hand Escrow all documents required by the title insurer, lenders or other third parties to this transaction prior to seven days before the date scheduled for closing.
   a. Each party to pay its customary escrow charges. [ft Forms 310 and 311]

7.3 Title to be vested in Grantee or Assignee free of encumbrances other than convenants, conditions and restrictions, reservations and easements of record and liens as set forth herein.

7.4 Each Grantee's interest in title to all real estate conveyed to be insured by _____ under a ☐ CLTA or ☐ ALTA from policy of the title insurance.
   a. Endorsements: _____
   b. Title insurance premium to be paid by Grantor.

7.5 Taxes, assessments, insurance premiums, rents, interest and other expenses to be prorated to close of escrow, unless otherwise provided.

7.6 Any difference in the principal amounts remaining due on loans taken over or assumed as stated in this agreement and as disclosed by beneficiary's statements is to be adjusted into: ☐ cash, ☐ carryback note or ☐ market value.

7.7 Each party to assign to the other party all existing lease and rental agreements on the property they convey. [ft Form 595]
   a. Each party assigning leases and rental agreements to the other to notify each tenant of the change of ownership on or before close of escrow. [ft Form 554]

7.8 Bill of sale to be executed by Grantor for any personal property being transferred by Grantor.
   a. ☐ A UCC-3 request for the conditions of title to the personal property transferred by bill of sale to be obtained by escrow and approved by the party taking title.

7.9 Grantees to furnish a new fire insurance policy on the property acquired.

7.10 Possession of the property and keys/access codes to be delivered on the close of escrow.

7.11 If one party is unable to convey marketable title as agreed or if the improvements on the property are materially damaged prior to closing, the other party may terminate the agreement. The party unable to convey or owning the damaged property to pay all reasonable escrow cancellation charges. [ft Form 183]

8. **Brokerage fees:**

   8.1 First Party to pay $_____ on closing to _____.

   8.2 Second Party to pay $_____ on closing to_____.

   8.3 On wrongful prevention of the change of ownership's by either party, such party to then pay the brokerage fees.

   8.4 The brokerage fees due may be shared by the brokers.

   8.5 Brokers may report the transaction, pricing and terms to brokerage trade associations and listing services for dissemination and use by their participants.

   8.5 ☐ Attached is the Agency Law Disclosure (Mandated on transactions involving four or less residential units.) [ft Form 305]

9. _____

   _____

   _____

   _____

   _____

   _____

First Party's Broker: _____	Second Party's Broker: _____
By: _____	By: _____
Is the agent of: ☐ First Party exclusively. ☐ Both parties.	Is the agent of: ☐ Second Party exclusively. ☐ Both parties.

I agree to the terms stated above. | **I agree to the terms stated above.**

Date:_____, 20_____	Date:_____, 20_____
First Party: _____	Second Party:_____
First Party: _____	Second Party:_____
Signature: _____	Signature: _____
Signature: _____	Signature: _____
Address: _____	Address: _____
_____	_____
Phone:_____	Phone:_____
Fax: _____	Fax: _____
Email: _____	Email: _____

REJECTION OF EXCHANGE OFFER

The Second Party hereby rejects this offer in its entirety. No counteroffer will be forthcoming.

Date:_____, 20_____

Second Party's Name: _____

Second Party's Name: _____

Signature: _____

Signature: _____

FORM 171   01-06   ©2006 **first tuesday**, P.O. BOX 20069, RIVERSIDE, CA 92516 (800) 794-0494

tered into a purchase agreement to sell his property to a cash buyer will make a separate offer to purchase a replacement property by using a purchase agreement form to reinvest the proceeds from his sale.

Locating properties for exchange

Taxwise, a client making an offer to exchange *like-kind* real estate usually plans to complete a fully qualified §1031 reinvestment. Thus, he will acquire real estate with **greater debt** and **greater equity** than exists in the property he now owns, a *trade-up* arrangement for estate building, not a piecemeal liquidation of his asset for a partial §1031 exemption.

When the exchange is a fully qualified §1031 reinvestment, all the profit in the property sold or exchanged is tax exempt.

Thus, the profit on the sale of the property is literally transferred, untaxed, to the replacement property since the entire cost basis in the property exchanged is always carried forward to the replacement property acquired in the exchange.

In the quest to locate suitable replacement properties for a client, the listing broker marketing the client's property needs to locate properties which are owned by a person who will consider acquiring the client's property. In essence, the broker attempts to arrange a transaction which will **match two owners** and their properties, a somewhat daunting task requiring a constant search for properties whose owners are willing to take other property in exchange.

To locate such an exchange-minded owner who is willing to consider owning the client's property, the listing broker is nearly always limited to those owners known to the broker to have acceptable replacement property or have listed their properties with other brokers. Hopefully, the other brokers have **counseled their clients** on an exchange of properties.

The most productive environment for locating owners of qualifying properties who have an interest in acquiring the client's property seems to exist at marketing sessions attended by many brokers and agents. At these meetings, they "pitch" their listings and advise attendees about the types of property their clients will accept in an exchange.

Multiple listing service (MLS) printouts, websites and large brokerage firms with income property sales sections also help in the process of locating qualifying properties. However, the agent considering an exchange usually needs to make a personal contact with the agent who represents the owner of suitable property to determine the likelihood of that owner entering into an exchange.

To get an initial response from other brokers and agents regarding the inclination of their owners to exchange, a preliminary inquiry about a **possible match up** of properties and owners can be made in the form of a written proposal. The proposal should precede any analysis or investigation into the property listed by the other broker, and include only its type, size and location to qualify it as a potential match for the client.

Prudently, an offer to exchange would not be prepared and submitted before getting a reading on the other owner's willingness to consider an exchange of properties, and more particularly, an exchange for a property of the type owned by the client.

To inquire of another broker or agent into the possibility of an exchange and at the same time document the inquiry for further reference, a **preliminary proposal form** is often prepared and personally handed or faxed to the other broker or agent. The proposal will note the type of properties involved, their equities and debt, and arrange for the exchange of information or a discussion between the agents before preparing an exchange agreement. [See Form 170 accompanying this chapter]

DATE:_____, 20_____, at _____, California

TO: _____Profile#_____ _____ _____ Email: _____ Phone:_____Fax: _____ Cell: _____	FROM: _____Profile#_____ _____ _____ Email: _____ Phone:_____Fax: _____ Cell: _____

1. **MY PROPERTY:** _____
   _____

   Location: _____
   _____
   _____

1.1 **Equity: $** _____

   Loan 1:_____
   _____

   Loan 2:_____
   _____

2. **YOUR PROPERTY:** _____
   _____

   Location: _____
   _____
   _____

2.1 **Equity $**_____

   Loan 1:_____
   _____

   Loan 2:_____
   _____

3. **TERMS:** _____
   _____
   _____
   _____

4. **REMARKS:** _____
   _____
   _____

5. **Agent Accord:**

   5.1   Data on the properties is attached.

   5.2   Any additional property data requested will be promptly submitted.

   5.3   This proposal is subject to further approval by my client, and client's inspection of the property and its operating data.

   5.4   Terms to be detailed in further agreements or in escrow instructions.
   a. ☐ I see this as a 2-way transaction.   b. ☐ I see this as a multiple transaction.

6. **Let's get together and talk:**
   ☐ I'll contact you within _____days.   ☐ I'm in room _____.
   ☐ Please send me a back-up package.   ☐ Other_____

I respectfully submit this proposal for consideration by you and your client.

Submitting Agent's Signature: _____

Response: _____
_____
_____

Responding Agent's Signature: _____ Date:_____, 20_____

The preliminary proposal is not an offer and does not contain contract wording. The clients are not involved in the proposal, only the brokers. Their effort is to locate properties to be submitted to their clients for exchange consideration. Only after the probability of actually entering into an exchange is established will an exchange agreement offer be prepared, signed by the client and submitted for acceptance.

Equity valuation adjustments

Once replacement property is located and its owner has indicated a willingness to consider an exchange of properties, the dollar amount of the market value of each property must be established. Once the market value of each property is established, the value of the equity in each can be set. **Valuation** is the single most important task in negotiating an agreement to exchange.

Until a consensus exists between the owners about the value of the equity in each owner's property, negotiations tend not to go forward. Without an agreement on valuation, it follows that the amount of the **adjustment** for any difference between the equities in each property to the exchange cannot be set. Property disclosures and due diligence investigations tend to fall in place only when the values of the equities have been agreed to.

The broker begins negotiations to set the dollar amount of equity each owner has in his property by preparing an **exchange agreement offer**. The offer is based on the owner's and the broker's analysis of valuations, including:

- the **market value** (price) of each property to be exchanged [See Form 171 §1.3 and 2.3];

- the **loan amounts** encumbering each owner's property, whether or not they are to remain of record; and

- the **equity valuations** calculated as the market value of each property less the amount of loans of record.

Having stated the present value of the equity in each property (as viewed by the owner), adjustments need to be entered in the offer to cover the difference between the equity valuations in each property.

Since the equities in properties exchanged rarely are of the same dollar amount, adjustments will nearly always have to be negotiated. Thus, a contribution of **money** (cash or carryback promissory notes) or **other property**, collectively called *cash boot*, must be given by the owner of the property with the lesser amount of equity value, a consideration paid in a process called *adjusting* or *balancing the equities*.

Thus, the owner of the property with the larger amount of equity will receive one or more **cash items** as consideration for the adjustment, including:

- cash;

- carryback note; or

- other property, either real or personal, with a dollar amount of value.

Regarding the existence of financing which encumbers the properties being exchanged, negotiations may call for the loans to remain of record or be paid off and reconveyed.

Refinancing of the replacement property may be necessary to generate cash funds for the payoff and reconveyance of the loans now encumbering the property. A contingency provision for new financing is needed if additional cash for the payoff of loans is required.

Cultivating an exchange environment

Consider an agent who has a working knowledge of income property transactions in the region surrounding his office. The agent regularly attends marketing sessions and visits with brokers and agents whose clients have properties they would like to convert to cash or exchange for other properties.

An investor who is an acquaintance of the agent is known to the agent to be unhappy with the management aspect of a smaller residential rental property he owns. The investor would prefer to own a single-user property requiring little of his time to oversee maintenance and repairs.

Discussions the agent has with the investor about selling the units and locating a more suitable property to meet the investor's ownership objectives culminates in a listing of the property with the agent (on behalf of his broker).

A *reinvestment provision* is included in the listing calling for the location and acquisition of replacement property to provide the continuing investment in real estate required to qualify the sale for the Internal Revenue Code (IRC) §1031 exemption from any profit tax. The investor has owned the property for quite some time and his basis is low compared to the property's present market value.

Soon the agent locates an industrial property which is owned by a businessman whose company occupies the entire building. The property is listed with another broker who explains his client would be willing to lease back the property from the buyer rather than move to other premises. The businessman's broker knows his client's objective is to reduce his debt so he can enlarge the credit line for his business.

On inquiry as to whether the businessman would take residential income units (with a much smaller loan) in exchange for his property, the agent gets a positive response. It happens the businessman owns other residential properties and their management does not pose a problem for him.

Information on the properties is exchanged. The investor's units are priced at $600,000 with a debt of $200,000 and an equity valued at $400,000. The industrial building belonging to the businessman is listed at $1,200,000 subject to a loan of $700,000 with an equity of $500,000.

When data on the industrial property is reviewed with the investor as a probable replacement property under a net lease with the owner/occupant, the investor indicates it is just the situation he is looking for. He will be acquiring a property with a higher value to add to his investment portfolio and the demands on management will be minimal. The flow of rental income will cover payments on the loan and generate spendable income. The agent then conducts preliminary investigations into the property and the loan encumbering it.

The agent prepares an exchange offer. Besides the routine due diligence investigation into each property and typical contingencies and closing provisions, the agent needs to negotiate the **adjustment** for the $100,000 difference between the equities in the two properties and the **terms of a lease** for the businessman's continued occupancy of the industrial building.

Thus, the consideration the investor will offer to pay the price of $1,200,000 for the industrial property includes:

- the $400,000 equity in his residential units;

- an assumption of the $700,000 loan on the industrial building; and

- execution of a $100,000 note in favor of the businessman, the adjustment necessary to balance the equities between the two properties exchanged.

Thus, the total consideration offered by the investor to buy the industrial building is $1,200,000.

Conversely, the consideration the investor wants from the businessman in exchange for the investor's residential units and the investor's execution of a carryback note in favor of the businessman includes:

- the $500,000 equity in the industrial property;

- an assumption of the $200,000 loan on the residential units; and

- a $100,000 **offset** by the investor's execution of a carryback note to be secured by the industrial property.

Thus, the total consideration the businessman will pay for the residential units on acceptance of this offer is $600,000.

The **leaseback arrangements** offered by the investor are based on the market value of the industrial property and rents paid for comparable properties. The terms of the lease are set out in an addendum attached to the exchange agreement offer.

The offer is submitted to the broker representing the businessman. In turn, a counteroffer is submitted to the investor based on all the terms of the exchange agreement, modified as follows:

- the carryback note provision is deleted; and

- the amount of $100,000 in cash is to be paid to adjust the equities.

Ultimately, escrow is opened based on an adjustment in the amount of $90,000; comprised of a $50,000 note and $40,000 in cash and a price reduction for the $10,000 difference.

Analyzing the exchange agreement

The exchange agreement, **first tuesday** Form 171, is used to prepare and submit a property owner's offer to acquire other real estate in exchange for property he owns, neither property being a one-to-four unit residential property.

The exchange agreement offer, if accepted, becomes the binding written contract between each owner. Its terms must be complete and clear to prevent misunderstandings so the agreement can be judicially enforced.

Each section in Form 171 has a separate purpose and need for enforcement. The sections include:

1. *Identification*: The date of preparation for referencing the agreement, the names of the owners, the description of the properties to be exchanged and each property's fair market value, equity valuation and loan encumbrances are set forth in sections 1 and 2 to establish the facts on which the agreement is negotiated.

2. *Terms of exchange*: The total consideration each owner is to deliver to the other owner, such as the transfer of their equity and adjustments in the form of cash, carryback note, loan assumptions or value in additional property, and any new financing required to generate the cash needed to acquire the replacement property are set forth in section 3.

3. *Acceptance and performance*: Aspects of the formation of a contract, excuses for nonperformance and termination of the agreement are provided for in section 4, such as the time period for acceptance of the offer, the broker's control over enforcement of performance dates, the financing of the price as a closing contingency, procedures for cancellation of the agreement, cooperation to effect a §1031 transaction and limitations on monetary liability for breach of contract.

4. *Property conditions*: Each owner's confirmation of the physical condition of the property received as disclosed prior to acceptance is **confirmed** as set forth in sections 5 and 6 by each owner's delivery of information on their property for

the other party's due diligence review and approval, such as rental income, expenses and tenant estoppels, natural and environmental hazards, physical conditions of improvements, title condition, security from crime, as well as providing certification of their property's condition on transfer, such as structural pest control, compliance with local occupancy ordinances and safety standards.

5. *Closing conditions*: The escrow holder, escrow instructions and the date of closing are established in section 7, as are title conditions, title insurance, hazard insurance, prorates and loan adjustments.

6. *Brokerage and agency*: The release of sales data on the transaction to trade associations is authorized, the brokerage fee is set and the delivery of the agency law disclosure to both parties is provided for as set forth in section 7, as well as the confirmation of the agency undertaken by the brokers and their agents on behalf of one or both parties to the agreement.

7. *Signatures*: Both parties bind each other to perform as agreed in the exchange agreement by signing and dating their signatures to establish the date of offer and acceptance.

Preparing the exchange agreement

The following instructions are for the preparation and use of the Exchange Agreement, **first tuesday** Form 171. Form 171 is designed as a checklist of practical provisions so a broker or his agent can prepare an offer for an owner to exchange properties located in California that do not include one-to-four unit residential property.

Each instruction corresponds to the provision in the form bearing the same number.

*Editor's note — **Check** and **enter** items throughout the agreement in each provision with boxes and blanks, unless the provision is not intended to be included as part of the final agreement, in which case it is left unchecked or blank.*

*To alter the wording of a provision or to delete or add a provision, use addendum **first tuesday** Form 250. On it, reference the section number in the exchange agreement to be altered or deleted. If altered, enter the copy that is to supersede the boilerplate provision referenced.*

Document identification:

Enter the date and name of the city where the offer is prepared. This date is used when referring to this exchange agreement.

Properties to be exchanged:

1. *First party and his property*: **Enter** as the first party the name of the owner who is initiating this offer to exchange properties.

   Enter the city, county and state in which the first property is located. **Enter** the legal description or common address of the property, or the assessor's parcel number (APN). If more than one like-kind property is being exchanged by the first party, include the description, financing and equity of the additional property in an addendum. [See **first tuesday** Form 250]

   1.1 *Equity valuations*: **Enter** the dollar amount of the equity in the first property, calculated as the property's fair market value minus the principal balance on the loans of record.

   1.2 *Existing loans*: **Enter** the total amount of the principal debt outstanding on the loans encumbering the first property.

      a. *First trust deed*: **Enter** the amount of the unpaid principal, monthly principal and interest (PI) payment and the interest rate on the first trust deed loan encumbering the first property. **Check** the box to indicate whether the interest is adjustable (ARM). **Enter** the due date for any final balloon payment due on the loan. **Enter** any unique loan conditions such as impounds, alienation restraints, prepayment penalties, guarantees, etc.

b. *Second trust deed*: **Enter** the amount of the unpaid principal, monthly PI payments and the interest rate on the second trust deed loan encumbering the first property. **Check** the box to indicate whether the interest is adjustable (ARM). **Enter** the due date for any final balloon payment due on the loan. **Enter** any unique loan conditions such as impounds, alienation restraints, prepay penalties, guarantees, all-inclusive trust deed (AITD) provisions, etc.

1.3 *Market value*: **Enter** the total dollar amount of the first property's fair market value, i.e., the "price" the first party is to receive in exchange for his property.

Editor's note — The market value set for the first property determines the amount of title insurance, sales and transfer taxes and reassessment for property taxes, as well as fixes the price the first party is paying (and taxable profit) for any non-§1031 property he may be receiving in exchange for his property.

1.4 *Personal property included*: **Enter** the description of any personal property or inventory the first party is to transfer as part of the total property value. If an itemized list is available, **attach** it as an ad-

dendum to the exchange agreement and **enter** the words "see attached inventory."

2. *Second party and his property*: **Enter** as the second party the name of the owner of the **replacement property** sought to be acquired in the exchange.

Enter the city, county and state in which the replacement property is located. **Enter** the legal description or common address of the replacement property, or the APN. If the first party is to acquire more than one like-kind property as a replacement in this exchange, include the description, financing and equity of the additional property in an addendum. [See **first tuesday** Form 250]

2.1 *Equity valuation*: **Enter** the dollar amount of the equity in the replacement property, calculated as the property's fair market value minus the principal balance on the loans of record.

2.2 *Existing loans*: **Enter** the total amount of the principal debt outstanding on the loans encumbering the replacement property.

a. *First trust deed*: **Enter** the amount of the unpaid principal, monthly PI payments and the interest rate on the first trust deed loan encumbering the replacement property. **Check** the box to indicate whether the interest is adjustable (ARM). **Enter** the due date for any final balloon payment due on the loan. **Enter** any unique loan provisions such as impounds, alienation restraints, prepay penalties, guarantees, etc.

b. *Second trust deed*: **Enter** the amount of the unpaid principal, monthly PI payments and the interest rate on the second trust deed loan encumbering the replacement property. **Check** the box to indicate whether the interest is adjustable (ARM). **Enter** the due date for any final balloon payment due on the loan. **Enter** any unique loan provisions such as impounds, alienation restraints, prepay penalties, guarantees, AITD provisions, etc.

2.3 *Market value*: **Enter** the total dollar amount of the replacement property's fair market value, i.e., the "price" the first party is to pay in exchange for the replacement property.

Editor's note — The market value set for the replacement property determines the amount of title insurance, sales and transfer taxes and reassessment for property taxes, as well as fixes the price the second party is paying (and taxable profit) for any non-§1031 property the first party may be contributing in exchange for the replacement property.

2.4 *Personal property included*: **Enter** the description of any personal property or inventory the first party is to receive as part of the total replacement property value. If an itemized list is available, **attach** it to the exchange agreement and **enter** the words "see attached inventory."

3. **Terms of the exchange:**

3.1 *Acquisition of the replacement property*: **Details** the total consideration the first party will **deliver** to the second party to acquire the replacement property.

*Editor's note — The consideration given by the first party for the replacement property includes the **equity value** in the first property and **adjustments** in the form of cash, carryback note or additional property to reflect the difference between the lesser equity value in the first property than the equity value in the replacement property. Also, **financial** provisions for the first party's take-over or refinancing of the loans of record on the replacement property are included.*

a. *Equity value in first property*: **Enter** the dollar amount of the equity value set at section 1.1.

b. *Cash adjustment*: **Enter** the dollar amount of any cash payment to be made by the first party to adjust for any difference due to a lesser amount of equity value in the first property than the equity value in the replacement property.

Editor's note — Only one of the parties will add cash, if at all, to adjust for the differences in equity amounts. Cash for loan payoffs is handled separately at sections 3.1c and 3.2c.

c. *Additional cash payment*: **Enter** the amount of the principal balance remaining due on the loans of record encumbering the replacement property as set at section 2.2 if the first party will not be taking over the loans of record on the replacement property (section 3.1d) and the second party is to pay off and reconvey these loans. Funding for this payoff will be provided by the first party refinancing or further encumbering the replacement property.

d. *Loan take-over*: **Check** the appropriate box to indicate whether the first party will take title to the replacement property subject to the loans of record or will assume the loans if the loans are to remain of record on the replacement property. **Enter** the amount of the principal balance remaining on the loans of record on the replacement property as set forth at section 2.2.

*Editor's note — This boilerplate provision for loan takeover does not include the alternative of a **novation agreement** between both parties and the lender that would terminate the second party's liability on the loan and, unlike an assumption, would shift all loan liability to the first party.*

e. *Promissory note adjustment*: **Enter** the dollar amount of any carryback note and trust deed the first party will execute in favor of the second party to adjust for differences in equity valuations due to a lesser equity value in the first property than in the replacement property. **Enter** as the terms for payment of the carryback note the amount of the monthly payment, the interest rate and the number of years after close of escrow to set the due date for a final balloon payment.

f. *Additional property as adjustment*: **Enter** the dollar amount of the equity in any additional property the first party is to contribute to this exchange to adjust for the difference in the larger equity he will receive in the replacement property. The equity in the additional property is calculated as the difference between its fair market

value and any debt encumbering it. **Enter** the description of the additional property. **Enter** the amount of any debt.

g. *Offset for adjustments received*: **Enter** the dollar amount of any cash boot (money, carryback note or other property) the first party is to receive as compensation for the difference between the greater value of the equity in the first property and the lesser equity value in the replacement property. This amount is the sum of any amounts entered in section 3.2b, e and f. The first party's receipt of an adjustment is subtracted to determine the total consideration the first party will pay to acquire the replacement property.

h. *Total consideration*: **Enter** the total dollar amount of all consideration to be paid by the first party to acquire the replacement property as the sum of the amounts entered in this section 3.1 at subsections a, b, c, d, e and f, less the amount entered at subsection g.

i. *New financing for replacement property*: **Check** the appropriate box to indicate whether any new financing to be originated by the first party on the replacement property will be a first or second trust deed loan. **Enter** the amount of the loan, the monthly payment and the interest rate limitations on the loan. **Check** the box to indicate whether the interest rate will be adjustable. If so, **enter** the index name controlling the

ARM. **Enter** the number of years the loan is to run until it will be due on a final balloon payment.

3.2 *Disposition of the first property*: This section details the total consideration the first party will receive from the second party in exchange for the first property.

*Editor's note — The consideration to be received by the first party on the transfer of his property includes the **equity value** in the replacement property and **adjustments** made by the second party in the form of cash, carryback note or additional property to reflect the difference between the lesser equity value in the replacement property than the equity value in the first property. Also, **financial** provisions for the second party's take-over or refinancing of the loans of record on the first property are included.*

a. *Equity value in the replacement property*: **Enter** the dollar amount of the equity value set at section 2.1.

b. *Cash adjustment*: **Enter** the dollar amount of any cash payment to be made by the second party to adjust for any difference due to a lesser amount of equity value in the replacement property than the equity value in the first property.

c. *Additional cash payment*: **Enter** the amount of the principal balances remaining due on the loans of record encumbering the first property as set at section 1.2 if the second party will not be taking over the loans of record on the first property (section 3.2d) and the first party is to pay off and reconvey these loans. Funding

for this payoff will be provided by the second party refinancing or further encumbering the first property.

d. *Loan takeover*: **Check** the appropriate box to indicate whether the second party will take title to the first property subject to the loans of record or will assume the loans if the loans are to remain of record on the first property. **Enter** the amount of the principal balance remaining on the loans of record on the first property as set forth at section 1.2.

*Editor's note — This boilerplate provision for loan take-over does not include the alternative of a **novation agreement** between both parties and the lender that would terminate the first party's liability on the loan and, unlike an assumption, would shift all loan liability to the second party.*

e. *Promissory note adjustment*: **Enter** the dollar amount of any carryback note and trust deed the second party will execute in favor of the first party to adjust for the difference in equity valuations due to a lesser equity value in the replacement property than in the first property. **Enter** as the terms for payment of the carryback note the amount of the monthly payment, the interest rate and the number of years after close of escrow to set the due date for a final balloon payment.

f. *Additional property as adjustment*: **Enter** the dollar amount of the equity in any additional property the second party is to contribute to this exchange to adjust for the difference in the larger equity he will receive in the first property. The equity in the additional property is calculated as the difference between its fair market value and any debt encumbering it. **Enter** the description of the additional property. **Enter** the amount of any debt.

g. *Offset for adjustment received*: **Enter** the dollar amount of any cash boot (money, carryback note or other property) the second party is to receive as compensation for the difference between the greater value of the equity in the second property and the lesser equity value in the first property. This amount is the sum of any amounts entered in section 3.1b, e and f. The second party's receipt of adjustment is subtracted to determine the total consideration the second party will pay to acquire the first property.

h. *Total consideration*: **Enter** the total dollar amount of all consideration to be paid by the second party to acquire the first property as the sum of the amounts entered in this section 3.2 at subsections a, b, c, d, e and f, less the amount entered at subsection g.

i. *New financing for first property*: **Check** the appropriate box to indicate whether any new financing to be originated by the second party on the first property will be a first or second trust deed loan. **Enter** the amount of the loan, the monthly payment and the interest rate limitations on the loan. **Check** the box to indicate whether the interest rate will be adjustable. If so, **enter** the index name controlling the ARM. **Enter** the number of years the loan will run until it will be due on a final balloon payment.

3.3 *Carryback note conditions*: **Provides** for any carryback note and trust deed, executed to adjust for the equity differences between the properties, to include or be subject to the term and conditions of this section, in addition to the terms for payment of the note established by either section 3.1e or 3.2e.

a. *Financial disclosure statement*: **Check** the box to indicate a carryback disclosure statement is to be prepared and handed to the party executing the note, as is mandated in one-to-four unit residential transactions. If so, **attach** a completed carryback disclosure statement to the exchange agreement for signatures. [See **first tuesday** Form 300]

b. *Special provisions*: **Check** the appropriate box to indicate any special provisions to be included in the carryback note or trust deed. **Enter** the name of any other unlisted special provisions, such as impounds, discount options, extension clauses, guarantee arrangements or right of first refusal on a sale or hypothecation of the note.

c. *Notice of delinquency*: **Check** the box to indicate the party executing the note is also to execute a request for notice of delinquency and pay the cost of recording and serving it on senior lenders. [See **first tuesday** Form 412]

d. *Creditworthiness analysis*: **Check** the box to indicate the party executing the note is to provide the other party with a completed credit application. [See **first tuesday** Form 302]

e. *Approval of creditworthiness*: **Enter** the number of days in which the party carrying back the note may cancel the transaction based on his reasonable disapproval of the other party's creditworthiness. [See **first tuesday** Form 183]

f. *Subordination of trust deed*: **Authorizes** the party carrying back the note and trust deed to terminate the transaction should the terms arranged for the origination or assumption of loans, secured by trust deeds with priority on title and senior to the trust deed securing the carryback note, fall outside the parameters for amount, payments, interest rate and due dates agreed to in this agreement.

g. *UCC-1 for additional security*: **Requires** a security agreement and UCC-1 financing statements to be completed and the UCC-1 to be filed with the Secretary of State to *perfect* a security interest in any personal property being transferred by the party carrying back the note and trust deed.

4. **Acceptance and performance periods:**

4.1 *Authorized acceptance*: **Enter** the number of days in which the second party may accept this exchange offer and form a binding contract.

4.2 *Extension of performance dates*: **Authorizes** the brokers to extend performance dates up to one month to meet the objectives of this exchange agreement, time being a reasonable period of duration and not of the essence in the initially scheduled performance of this agreement.

4.3 *Loan contingency*: **Authorizes** the party taking title to a property to cancel the transaction at the time scheduled for closing if the new financing or loan assumption arrangements agreed to fail to occur.

4.4 *Cancellation procedures*: **Provides** for termination of the agreement when the right to cancel is triggered by other provisions in the agreement, such as contingency and performance provisions. The method for any cancellation of this exchange agreement is controlled by this provision.

4.5 *Exchange cooperation*: **Requires** the parties to cooperate with one another in an IRS §1031 transaction on further written notice by either party. **Provides** for the parties to assign their interests in this agreement.

4.6 *Liability limited on breach*: To limit the liability of either party due to their breach of this agreement, **enter** the dollar amount representing the maximum amount of money losses the other party may recover due to the breach.

Editor's note — Liability limitation provisions avoid the misleading and unenforceable forfeiture called for under liquidated damage clauses included in most purchase agreement forms provided by other publishers of forms.

5. **Due diligence contingencies:**

    5.1 *Satisfaction or cancellation*: **Enter** the number of days in which the second party may terminate the exchange agreement after receipt of data on the first property that is unacceptable to the second party.

        a. *Operating documentation*: **Check** the box to indicate the first party is to make his income and expense records and all supporting documentation available for inspection by the second party.

        b. *Rental rolls*: **Check** the box to indicate the first party is to provide an itemized spreadsheet detailing all aspects of each tenancy in the property. [See **first tuesday** Form 380]

        c. *Natural hazard disclosure (NHD) statement*: **Check** the box to indicate the first party is to prepare and provide the second party with an NHD statement disclosing the first party's knowledge about the hazards listed on the form. [See **first tuesday** Form 314]

        d. *Physical condition of the property*: **Check** the box to indicate the first party is to prepare and provide the second party with a disclosure of the first party's knowledge about the physical conditions of the land and improvements which may have an adverse effect on the value of the first property.

        e. *Personal property inventory*: **Check** the box to indicate the first party is to prepare an itemized list of the personal property he is to transfer with the first property.

        f. *Buyer's inspection*: **Check** the box to authorize the second party to carry out an inspection of the first property, himself or by his agents or consultants, to confirm the property's value. **Enter** the number of days after acceptance in which the second party is to carry out the inspection.

        g. *Title conditions*: **Check** the box to indicate the first party is to cause escrow to order out a preliminary title report for purposes of issuing a policy of title insurance on the first property and deliver the preliminary report to the second party as soon as possible.

        h. *Tenant estoppel certificates*: **Check** the box to indicate the first party will prepare, mail and collect estoppel certificates from all his tenants to be delivered to the second party.

        i. *Tenant personal security*: **Check** the box to indicate the first party will prepare a criminal activity and security statement disclosing his knowledge of crimes that affect the tenants' use and occupancy of the property, and the steps he has taken or should take to provide personal security for the tenants.

        j. *Qualifying for §1031 exemption*: **Check** the box to indicate the closing of the transaction is subject to the further approval of the second party's tax advisors that the transaction qualifies for §1031 treatment.

k. *Additional disclosures or investigations*: **Enter** copy addressing any further information the second party wants in order to confirm expectations about the first property not covered in the boilerplate provisions of this form, such as investigations into zoning, use plans, permits or other governmental and private activities which may affect the property's value to the second party.

5.2 *Satisfaction or cancellation*: **Enter** the number of days in which the first party may terminate the exchange agreement after receipt of data on the replacement property that is unacceptable to the first party.

a. *Operating documentation*: **Check** the box to indicate the second party is to make his income and expense records and all supporting documentation available for inspection by the first party.

b. *Rental rolls*: **Check** the box to indicate the second party is to provide an itemized spreadsheet detailing all aspects of each tenancy in the property. [See Form 380]

c. *Natural hazard disclosure (NHD) statement*: **Check** the box to indicate the second party is to prepare and provide the first party with an NHD statement disclosing the sec-

ond party's knowledge about the hazards listed on the form. [See Form 314]

d. *Physical condition of the property*: **Check** the box to indicate the second party is to prepare and provide the first party with a disclosure of the second party's knowledge about the physical conditions of the land and improvements which may have an adverse effect on the value of the replacement property.

e. *Personal property inventory*: **Check** the box to indicate the second party is to prepare an itemized list of the personal property he is to transfer with the replacement property.

f. *Buyer's inspection*: **Check** the box to authorize the first party to carry out an inspection of the replacement property, himself or by his agents or consultants, to confirm the property's value. **Enter** the number of days after acceptance in which the first party is to carry out the inspection.

g. *Title conditions*: **Check** the box to indicate the second party is to cause escrow to order out a preliminary title report for purposes of issuing a policy of title insurance on the replacement property and deliver the preliminary report to the first party as soon as possible.

h. *Tenant estoppel certificates*: **Check** the box to indicate the second party will prepare, mail and collect estoppel certificates from all his tenants to be delivered to the first party.

    i. *Tenant personal security*: **Check** the box to indicate the second party will prepare a criminal activity and security statement disclosing his knowledge of crimes that affect the tenants' use and occupancy of his property, and the steps he has taken or should take to provide personal security for the tenants.

    j. *Qualifying for §1031 exemption*: **Check** the box to indicate the closing of the transaction is subject to the further approval of the first party's tax advisors that the transaction qualifies for §1031 treatment.

    k. *Additional disclosures or investigations*: **Enter** copy addressing any further information the first party wants in order to confirm expectations about the replacement property not covered in the boilerplate provisions of this form, such as investigations into zoning, use plans, permits or other governmental and private activities which may affect the property's value to the first party.

6. *Property conditions on closing:* **Provides** for the first and second parties to deliver up their properties at closing in a condition commonly expected of all properties bought and sold in California. These items are not those generally necessary to be confirmed as part of a due diligence investigation by the party acquiring title.

6.1 *Structural pest control*: **Check** the box if each party is to provide a report and certified clearance by a structural pest control operator on the property he conveys.

6.2 *Improvement warranty policy*: **Check** the box if each party is to furnish an insurance policy on the property he conveys for emergency repairs to components of the structures which are improvements on the property. **Enter** the name of the insurer who is to issue the policy. **Enter** the type of coverage desired, such as air conditioning units, water heaters, etc.

6.3 *Local ordinance compliance*: **Provides** for each party to furnish a certificate of occupancy or other clearances required by local ordinances on the property he conveys.

6.4 *Safety law compliance*: **Provides** for each property to meet smoke detector placement and water heater bracing required by state law.

6.5 *Property maintenance*: **Requires** each party to maintain the present condition of his property until the close of escrow.

6.6 *Fixtures and fittings*: **Confirms** this exchange includes real estate fixtures and fittings as part of the property acquired.

6.7 *Further leasing and contracting*: **Requires** each party to submit for approval (consent) by the other party all new or modified tenancy arrangements, service contracts and improvement alterations or equipment installation contracts relating to the property he is conveying.

6.8 *Additional affirmative conditions*: **Enter** any other conditions on or about the properties each party is expected to comply with prior to closing, such as obtaining permits, eliminating property defects, certification regarding components of the improvements on the properties, etc.

7. **Closing conditions:**

7.1 *Escrow closing agent*: **Enter** the name of the escrow company handling the closing.

    a. *Escrow instructions*: **Check** the box to indicate the exchange agreement is to also serve as the mutual instructions to escrow from the parties. Typically, escrow companies will (or the broker will) prepare supplemental instructions needed to handle and close the transaction. [See **first tuesday** Form 401]

    b. *Escrow instructions*: **Check** the box to indicate escrow instructions have been prepared and are attached to this purchase agreement. **Attach** the prepared escrow instructions to the purchase agreement and **obtain** the signatures of the parties. [See **first tuesday** Form 401]

7.2 *Closing date*: **Check** the appropriate box to indicate the manner for setting the date on which escrow is scheduled to close. Following the box checked, **enter** as appropriate the specific date for closing or the number of days anticipated as necessary for the parties to perform and close escrow. Note that prior to seven days before closing, the parties are to deliver all documents regarding the property they are conveying that are needed by third parties to perform their services by the date scheduled for closing.

    a. *Escrow charges*: **Provides** for each party to pay their customary closing costs and charges, amounts any competent escrow officer can provide on inquiry. [See **first tuesday** Forms 310 and 311]

7.3 *Title conditions*: **Provides** for title to be vested in the name of the party acquiring the respective properties, or their assignees, subject to covenants, conditions and restrictions (CC&Rs) of record and mortgage liens agreed to in this exchange agreement.

Editor's note — The inclusion of the preliminary title policy contingency at section 5.1g or 5.2g will control the CC&Rs to remain of record at closing, subject to exercise of the right to cancel the transaction if they are unacceptable to the party acquiring title.

7.4 *Title insurance*: **Enter** the name of the title company which will provide a preliminary title report and issue the title insurance policy. **Check** the appropriate box to indicate the type of policy to be issued.

    a. *Policy endorsements*: **Enter** any endorsements to be issued with the policy of title insurance.

    b. *Insurance premium*: **Provides** for the owner of each property to pay the premium for the policy insuring his conveyance.

7.5 *Prorates and adjustments*: **Authorizes** prorations and adjustments on close of escrow for taxes, rents, interest, loan balances, service contracts and other property operating expenses, prepaid or accrued.

7.6 *Loan balance adjustments*: **Check** the appropriate box to indicate the financial adjustment desired for loan balance adjustments brought about by any difference between the principal balance as stated in the exchange agreement at sections 1.2 and 2.2 and the amount stated in beneficiary statements from the lender on the date escrow closes.

Editor's note — Often the parties will treat the equities as fixed and not subject to adjustments for variances in the balances of loans taken over by the new owner. Thus, loan balances adjustments are made into the "market value" of the property encumbered. More typically, the loan balance adjustments are made into any carryback note created in the exchange. Thus, the equity in encumbered property is adjusted to reflect a greater or lesser loan balance on the beneficiary's statement than as stated in the exchange agreement. Adjustment into cash is seldom agreed to in exchanges.

7.7 *Lease assignments*: **Provides** for all leases and rental agreements to be assigned to the new owner on closing. [See **first tuesday** Form 595]

a. *Change of ownership notice*: **Requires** each party assigning lease and rental agreements to notify each tenant of the change of ownership. The notice eliminates any further liability to the tenants of the party assigning the agreements. [See **first tuesday** Form 554]

7.8 *Personal property transferred*: **Provides** for a bill of sale to be executed on any personal property to be transferred with the property.

a. *UCC-3 clearance*: **Check** the box if escrow is to order a UCC-3 condition of title report from the Secretary of State on the personal property being transferred by a bill of sale for approval by the party taking ownership of the personal property.

7.9 *Fire insurance*: **Requires** the party taking title to provide a new policy of fire insurance.

7.10 *Possession*: **Provides** for possession of the property to be transferred to the party acquiring title on the close of escrow.

7.11 *Title failure and property destruction*: **Provides** for the cancellation of the exchange agreement by the party taking title if marketable title cannot be delivered or the property improvements suffer major damage.

8. **Brokerage fees:**

8.1 *Fees paid by first party*: **Enter** the dollar amount of fees to be paid by the first party to his broker. **Enter** the name of the first party's broker. If the fees are to be paid under a separate agreement, **enter** the words "per separate agreement" in lieu of the broker's name.

8.2 *Fees paid by second party*: **Enter** the dollar amount of fees to be paid by the second party to his broker. **Enter** the name of the second party's broker. If the fees are to be paid under a separate agreement, **enter** the words "per separate agreement" in lieu of the broker's name.

8.3 *Fees on default*: **Provides** for the defaulting party to pay all brokerage fees due to be paid the brokers under section 8.

8.4 *Fee-sharing arrangements*: **Authorizes** the brokers to share the fees due them.

8.5 *Transaction data disclosure*: **Authorizes** the brokers to release information on the price of the properties and terms of the exchange to trade organizations and multiple listing services.

8.6 *Agency Law Disclosure*: **Check** the box to indicate an Agency Law Disclosure addendum is attached to the exchange agreement. **Attach** a copy of the addendum for all parties to sign if the addendum is to made a part of the exchange agreement. The disclosure is mandated on one-to-four unit residential transactions for enforcement of fee provisions by the brokers. [See **first tuesday** Form 305]

Agency confirmation:

First party's broker: **Enter** the name of the broker who represents the owner of the first property making the offer to exchange. **Obtain** the signature of the broker or the agent acting on behalf of the first party's broker. **Check** the appropriate box to indicate the nature of the agency created with the parties by the conduct of the broker and his agent.

Second party's broker: **Enter** the name of the broker who represents the owner of the replacement property to whom this exchange agreement offer will be submitted for acceptance (or rejection). **Obtain** the signature of the broker or the agent acting on behalf of the second party's broker. **Check** the appropriate box to indicate the nature of the agency created with the parties by the conduct of the broker and his agent.

Signatures:

First party's signature: **Enter** the date the first party making the offer signs the exchange agreement. **Obtain** the signature of each of the persons who are the owners of the first property. **Enter** the first party's name, address, telephone and fax numbers, and email address. **Confirm** that the parties signing this exchange agreement also sign all the attachments requiring their signatures.

Second party's signature: **Enter** the date second party signs the exchange agreement offer. **Obtain** the signature of each of the persons who are the owners of the replacement property. **Enter** the second party's name, address, telephone and fax numbers, and email address. **Confirm** that the parties signing this exchange agreement also sign all the attachments requiring their signatures.

Rejection of offer:

Should the offer contained in the exchange agreement be rejected by the second party instead of accepted, and the rejection will not result in a counteroffer, **enter** the date of the rejection and the names of the second party. **Obtain** the signatures of the second party.

Observations:

As the policy of the publisher, this exchange agreement **does not contain** clauses which tend to increase the risk of litigation or are generally felt to work against the best interests of the buyer, seller and broker. Excluded provisions include:

- an *attorney fee provision*, which tends to **promote litigation** and inhibit contracting;

- an *arbitration clause*, which, if included and initialed, absolutely **waives** the buyer's and seller's right to a fair and correct decision by trial and appeal; and

- a *time-essence clause*, since future performance (closing) dates are, at best, estimates by the broker and his agent of the time needed to close and are too often **improperly used** by sellers in rising markets to cancel the transaction before the buyer or broker can reasonably comply with the terms of the purchase agreement.

Chapter 53

Real estate purchase options

This chapter discusses the use and effect of option-to-buy agreements in real estate sales.

An irrevocable offer to sell

A real estate syndicator searching for investment-grade, income-producing real estate locates a property which appears to be financially suitable for a group investment, called *syndication*.

However, the syndicator will not commit himself to the purchase of the property until he has **fully investigated** the condition of the improvements, the property's operations and the availability of financing, an effort called *due diligence*.

Further, on completing his due diligence investigation, and if conditions are found to be acceptable, the syndicator will need additional time to prepare an **investment memorandum** and to **locate investors**. The memo will contain his narrative report on the significant information he has gathered concerning the worth of the property. The report will be circulated among equity investors as a solicitation to form a group to fund the acquisition of the property.

First, before the syndicator begins his in-depth analysis of the property, he needs to enter into an enforceable purchase agreement with the seller. Without an agreement to acquire the property, the property may be sold to someone else before he can complete his investigation and determine the property is suitable for acquisition.

To acquire the right to buy the property without unconditionally committing himself to purchase the property, the syndicator submits an offer which calls for the occurrence of several events before he becomes committed to the purchase of the property in provisions called *contingency provisions*.

The **contingency provisions** include approval of the property's physical condition, its leasing income and operating expenses, available mortgage financing, title and zoning restrictions on use, and the existence of equity investors to fund the closing.

The seller fully understands the contingencies are designed primarily to enable the syndicator to confirm his understanding of the property's condition as represented by the seller and to obtain the mortgage and equity financing needed to fund the close of escrow. However, the seller is concerned the syndicator's inability to satisfy and remove the contingencies could interfere with the seller's ability to promptly cancel the agreement should the syndicator fail to close or cancel the transaction by the date scheduled for closing.

The seller decides not to accept the syndicator's purchase offer due to uncertainty regarding the syndicator's timely performance.

However, the seller is willing to grant the syndicator an **option to buy** the property at the same price and for the same time period sought by the syndicator in his offer to purchase. Thus, the seller counters the offer.

Here, a counteroffer form will not be used to respond to the syndicator's offer. A counteroffer would incorporate the terms of the syndicator's purchase offer, subject to any modifications stated in the counteroffer.

In this situation, the seller simply prepares and hands the syndicator an **offer to grant an op-**

tion, which is attached to the seller's offer. Thus, the seller *rejects* the syndicator's offer in its entirety. [See **first tuesday** Form 160]

The seller's offer to grant an option requires the syndicator to accept the offer and the terms of the proposed option agreement before the seller is bound to deliver the signed option agreement. To accept the seller's offer to grant an option, the syndicator must sign the acceptance provision in the offer and return it to the seller. Of course, the acceptance must occur before expiration of the seller's offer to grant the option.

For the syndicator, his purchase of an option to buy property imposes no obligation on him to open escrow and purchase the property. Unlike a real estate purchase agreement, the buyer holding an option to buy has **no obligation to purchase** the property.

Conversely, the option contains the seller's irrevocable offer which **obligates the seller to sell** the property on the terms stated in the option agreement should the syndicator decide to buy the property within a set period of time, called the *option period*. The syndicator only agrees to buy the property when he **timely accepts** the seller's irrevocable offer to sell, an acceptance called *exercising the option*.

In exchange for the seller granting an option on the property, the syndicator will pay the seller *option money*. The amount of option money is the price the syndicator pays to **buy the option** and "tie up" the property by removing it from the market. [See **first tuesday** Form 160]

Thus, the option agreement allows the syndicator to control the property without committing himself to purchase it until he exercises the option, if ever. His completion of the property analysis and solicitation of investors will indicate whether he will exercise the option or not.

However, when the syndicator exercises the option, a *bilateral sales contract* is automatically formed, no differently than had he ac-

cepted an offer from the seller to sell the property under a purchase agreement containing nearly identical terms. Thus, on exercise, both parties become obligated to perform as agreed and must proceed with closing the sale since no contingencies exist. [**Caras** v. **Parker** (1957) 149 CA2d 621]

Should the syndicator let the option period expire without exercising the option, the seller will be able to sell the property to another buyer, unaffected by the option since the seller's irrevocable offer to sell represented by the option has expired.

In an option agreement, the owner is referred to as the *optionor* and the potential buyer is referred to as the *optionee*. They become the seller and buyer, respectively, on exercise of the option.

Editor's note — An option granted to a buyer is to be distinguished from an exclusive right-to-sell listing granted to a broker. On entering into a listing, the seller incurs no obligation to sell the property to anyone. The owner has only employed the broker as his agent to find a buyer and represent the seller in negotiations. The broker has not received the power-of-attorney authority needed to commit the seller to a sale of the property and the listing is not an offer to sell anything.

Benefits for opposing positions

An option agreement provides benefits for both buyer and seller.

A **buyer** should consider acquiring an option when:

- he does not yet want to commit himself to buy;

- he is speculating in a depressed market that values will soon rise;

- he needs time to investigate and determine whether the property will operate profitably;

- he needs time to do promotional work such as syndicating, subdividing, rezoning, obtaining permits or loan commitments, or to complete a §1031 reinvestment; or

- he is a tenant and may want to own the leased premises some day.

A **seller** should consider granting an option when:

- he wants to retain ownership rights to the property for a fixed period into the future (for tax purposes);

- he wants to sell at a price based on higher future market values;

- he needs to provide an incentive to induce a prospective tenant to lease the property; or

- he wants to give a promoter incentive to work up a marketing or use plan and buy the property.

Multiple option periods

Developers require a longer initial option period, or the right to extend the option period, to provide time in which to study a property, obtain government clearances and locate financing for development. If these objectives are met, the developer will be able to purchase the property on a previously agreed set of terms.

Thus, it is foreseeable a developer may need **additional time** beyond the initial option period to complete his due diligence and approval process before committing himself to the purchase of the "optioned" property. Here, the option agreement should include the right to buy one or more extensions of the option period on the payment of additional option money before the expiration of the preceding option period.

The developer who determines he will be unable to develop or to successfully market a development of the property will simply not exercise the option.

Lease with option

The other significant use of an option to buy relates to residential and nonresidential leasing arrangements. Prospective tenants might want the ability to later acquire ownership of the property they will be occupying.

Tenants often need to invest substantial dollar amounts in tenant improvements to tailor the property to the tenant's needs. Whether contracted for by the tenant or the landlord, the tenant pays for the improvements either by a lump sum, upfront expenditure or by payments amortized over the initial life of the lease as part of the monthly rent.

Also, installation of racks, cabinets, shelving, trade fixtures, lighting and other interior improvements will be needed to make the premises fully compatible for the tenant's occupancy. These too will be paid for by the tenant. Always, a degree of "goodwill" is built up with customers due to the location of the business on the property. Thus, the location becomes part of the value of the tenant's business so long as he remains at the location.

All these opportunities will be lost if the landlord refuses to extend the lease or his demands for increased rent under an option to extend the lease compels the tenant to relocate. A tenant with even a small degree of insight into his future operations at the location will attempt to negotiate some sort of option to purchase the property. At least an option to renew at lesser rental rates should be negotiated, as the tenant improvements (TIs) have been paid for by the tenant and the landlord has fully recovered any costs he may have incurred.

A lease with an option to purchase must be distinguished from the purchase rights held by a tenant under a right of first refusal agreement or a buyer under a lease-option sales arrangement.

Need for consideration

An option agreement is not enforceable unless a seller receives some sort of consideration. Unless the seller is given something in exchange for the right he has *surrendered* to revoke his offer to sell or to sell the property to others, the option fails for *lack of consideration*. Without the payment of consideration, the agreement is merely an offer to sell which may be **withdrawn at any time** by the seller. [**Kowal** v. **Day** (1971) 20 CA3d 720]

While consideration is needed to create an option agreement which is binding on the seller, the amount of the consideration paid for an option may be a minimal amount. An enforceable option can be created for as little as 25 cents paid by a buyer.

Also, the consideration given for the option does not need to be in cash. For instance, when an option to purchase is granted to a tenant who enters into a lease, the consideration given for the grant of the option rights is the tenant's signature obligating the tenant to perform on the lease.

In the case of a syndicator or developer using an option to control property he is not yet certain he wants to purchase, the consideration is the option money paid to the seller to grant the irrevocable offer to sell. The option money is typically set at an amount which will compensate the seller for the time the property is kept off the market, similar to a payment of rent or interest (less any actual and implicit income produced for the owner by the property).

Often a small amount of option money is paid for a short initial option period, sometimes called a "free-look" period. The term of the free-look option may be twenty to thirty days, granted on the payment of a small amount of option money, such as $100.

If the buyer is given extensions to continue the option after the free-look period, he usually is required to put up a more substantial amount of option money.

Any number of additional option periods may be agreed to, one following the expiration of another. The number of extensions depends only on the seller's willingness to grant the extensions and the buyer's willingness to put up more option money to pay for those extensions.

Exercising the option

Unless a particular manner for exercising the option is specified in the option agreement, any communication from a buyer to a seller of his intention to exercise the option is sufficient. [**Riverside Fence Co.** v. **Novak** (1969) 273 CA2d 656]

However, if the option agreement requires the buyer to take specific steps to exercise the option, the buyer must follow the conditions set in order to exercise the option and acquire the property. [**Palo Alto Town & Country Village, Inc.** v. **BBTC Company** (1974) 11 C3d 494]

For instance, an option agreement should require a buyer to sign escrow instructions and deposit cash in escrow to exercise the option. If the instructions are not signed, or if signed and the deposit is not made, the option has not been exercised. Thus, the buyer has not exercised his right to acquire the property.

Proposed escrow instructions should be prepared and attached as an addendum to the option agreement to avoid any conflict over the content of the instructions required to be entered into to exercise the option. The instructions will remain unnumbered, undated and unsigned until exercise of the option. [See **first tuesday** Form 401]

The escrow opened to exercise an option should call for escrow to close within a short period of time, i.e., the number of days required to prepare documents, order title reports and close. Unless an option agreement requires the buyer to sign escrow instructions, deposit funds and close escrow within a short period of time, the buyer's exercise of the option merely creates an enforceable bilateral purchase agreement with no escrow, funds or clear closing date.

Recording the option

When a purchase option or memorandum of the option is recorded, it becomes part of the property's chain of title, imparting *constructive notice* of the outstanding option rights to anyone later obtaining an interest in the property. A buyer, lender or tenant acquiring an interest in the property with **actual or constructive notice** of the existence of an option to purchase the property takes his interest in the property **subject to** the buyer's option rights.

Conversely, a buyer, lender or tenant who does not have actual knowledge of an unrecorded and unexpired option, takes his interest in the property **free of** the option.

For example, a seller grants a buyer an option to purchase property. Before the option is recorded or the buyer takes possession, the seller conveys the property to a second buyer. The second buyer did not have actual knowledge of the first buyer's option on the property.

The buyer who was granted the option later exercises the option by depositing the full amount of the purchase price into an escrow he has opened as agreed in the option agreement.

However, the seller who granted the option is no longer the owner of the property. Thus, he has no interest in the property to convey. Also, the option agreement is not enforceable against the second buyer since the second buyer, who is now the owner of the property, had no knowledge of the first buyer's option when he acquired ownership.

Thus, the conveyance of the property to the second buyer without notice of the unexpired option wiped out the first buyer's right to buy the property under the option. [**Utley** v. **Smith** (1955) 134 CA2d 448]

A recorded option **ceases to constitute constructive notice** of a buyer's option rights when:

- six months have run after the expiration date stated in the recorded option agreement or memorandum without the prior recording of an *exercise* or *extension* of the option; or

- six months have run after the option or memorandum was recorded should the expiration date not be stated in the recorded option agreement or memorandum. [Calif. Civil Code §884.010]

The purpose for the extinguishment of the recorded option from title is to protect buyers and sellers of property from old, unexercised and expired option rights which are of record. No such statutory scheme exists for the "outlawing" of unrecorded options which have expired.

SECTION F

Vesting

Chapter
54
Vesting the ownership

This chapter presents the various vestings for holding title, the ownership rights reflected by the vestings and their termination by any right of survivorship on death of a co-owner.

Possession and transfer rights

All parcels of real estate have a recorded history. California's real estate history began with its admittance into the Union, when the United States of America became the initial owner of all the land. Titles were "proven up" by individuals in federal courts or with government agencies who issued certificates of title based on comparable rights held by the individuals under prior Spanish, Mexican or California sovereign law. This is how the recorded history of title to each parcel in California began. Parcels are now identified by the assessor of each county by a parcel number.

A conveyance by the vested owner of a parcel effectively transfers title to the next owner if the person conveying "title" holds title under a prior conveyance transferring title into his name. Thus, for each parcel a linkage exists in title from the beginning of the state of California to the present. The "chain of title" for a parcel reflects a conveyance by each person who previously took title to the property, from themselves to the next vested owner of title, and on to the present holder of title.

The initial focus for an analysis of a transfer of title in a sales transaction is on the person who is conveying title, not the new owner who is taking title. If the person conveying does not hold a good and marketable (insurable) title to the property and have the authority to convey it, the transfer to the new owner is defective, if not ineffective.

Today, the ability of the current owner to transfer title is the concern of the title companies. Title insurers issue policies covering the risk regarding whether the transfer of the ownership interest bargained for by the new owner has occurred. Title company analysis of this conveyancing risk is based on the nature and validity of the present owner's vesting, usually established when that owner took title.

The vesting used to take title when a person acquires ownership establishes the rules controlling his later conveyance of an interest in the property to another.

Thus, the text of this chapter focuses on the vesting used to acquire an interest in real estate under a deed, lease or trust deed.

For example, consider a buyer who has entered into a purchase agreement and escrow instructions. The purchase agreement states the buyer will take title in the condition agreed and as insured by a title insurer under a policy of title insurance. The precise vesting the buyer will use does not need to be stated in the purchase agreement.

However, escrow will include the exact wording of the vesting to be used by the buyer in the mutual instructions signed by both the seller and buyer.

The vesting chosen by the buyer is never a condition of the purchase agreement or escrow. The vesting on conveyance may be chosen (or unilaterally altered) by the buyer at any time prior to closing (but in sufficient time for preparation of the deed, signature by the sellers and acknowledgement by a notary prior to the date scheduled for closing).

Escrows prefer to draft the deed to be signed by the seller when escrow instructions are prepared. Thus, an early decision by the buyer about his vesting is necessary to accommodate the escrow process.

Hence, the buyer's agent needs to possess a working **knowledge of vestings** to be able to advise the buyer on the vestings available to the buyer so the agent is able to aid in the selection of the vesting desired before dictating instructions to escrow.

A person or persons take title

Real estate is owned by a *person* or *persons*, who by definition is either an individual (or individuals) or an entity, such as a corporation, limited liability company (LLC) or partnership. Trusts are not entities in California unless they have been qualified as a corporation by the Department of Corporations. Thus, the beneficiary of the trust relationship, be it an individual or an entity, is the *owner* of the real estate in spite of the vesting being in the name of a third person as trustee.

Further, ownership by an individual or entity is classified as either:

- a **sole ownership**, legally called an *ownership in severalty* [Calif. Civil Code §681]; or

- a **co-ownership** of two or more persons.

Sole ownership is reflected by use of a vesting naming an individual or entity as the one person entitled to ownership of the entire property described in the conveyance transferring title to that person. The one person named in this vesting context could be a married individual who owns property as the separate property of the married individual.

Co-ownerships exist for individuals in two fashions:

- as vested co-owners on title; or

- as co-owners of an **entity**, which is itself the vested owner holding title to the property.

Co-owners vest title in their individual names under one of only four types of ownership available for property located in California:

- as joint tenants;

- as tenants in partnership;

- as tenants in common; and

- as community property, with or without the right of survivorship. [CC §§682, 683]

No other co-ownership vesting exists for individuals. Thus, the trust vestings which exist provide for one person as *trustee* to hold title for the true owner(s) who are named as beneficiary(ies) under a title holding agreement with the trustee. The trust agreement spells out ownership arrangements which are either the same as one of the four co-ownership interests provided by the vestings listed above or distinguishable from them, such as a subordinated ownership interest, priority distributions, allocation of tax benefits, etc., typical of co-ownership arrangements for an entity.

Finally, **community property ownership** has two available vestings:

- husband and wife as community property; and

- husband and wife as community property with the right of survivorship.

The community property vestings are only available to married couples.

Possessory rights of co-owners

Every co-owner of property has the right to:

- **possess** the entire property himself, to the extent it is not already possessed or leased to others by another co-owner;

- **lease** his possessory right to occupy and use the entire property to a tenant, except for community property since the lease is subject to being set aside by a nonconsenting spouse within one year after its commencement;

- **sell** his ownership interest in the property without the need for prior notice to or the consent of the other co-owners, except for community property or a co-owner who has agreed to the contrary; and

- **encumber** his ownership interest in the property without the consent of his co-owners, except for community property or when prohibited by a co-ownership agreement.

On the other hand, a co-owner has obligations to other co-owners not to:

- exclude other co-owners from their right to possession of any part of the property [**Oberwise** v. **Poulos** (1932) 124 CA 247]; or

- create an easement on the property against a co-owner.

Tenancy in common

Should the type of vesting not be stated when two or more persons take title to real estate, the co-owners are presumed to be *tenants in common*, a sort of **default vesting** attributed to their ownership. However, if the co-owners are husband and wife and title is not vested as a tenancy in common, the property is presumed to be *community property*. Also, if the conduct of the co-owners is in fact that of partners, the property ownership is subject to the rights of a tenancy in partnership. [CC §686]

Thus, a tenancy-in-common vesting is the form of ownership used by two or more persons, with an **equal or disproportionate share** of ownership in the property as the separate property of each, when they do not intend their relationship to be that of joint tenants on death or of partners for profit. Further, the property is not acquired as a community property asset. [CC §685]

If the fractional co-ownership interest held by each co-owner was transferred to them at the same time, by the same deed and in equal shares, e.g., 1/3, 1/3 and 1/3, on the recording of one deed, then the only distinction between vesting the co-ownership as a tenancy in common or a joint tenancy is the right of survivorship attached to the joint tenancy vesting.

Thus, the person vested as a tenant in common **retains control** over the destiny of his ownership interest on death. The control is exercisable by will or by vesting the co-owner's interest in the name of his inter vivos trust. The survivors in an ownership arrangement vested as tenants in common will not take the deceased's interest as would have occurred on their death under a joint tenancy vesting.

As tenants in common, co-owners retain the ability on death to transfer their interests in real estate to individuals other than the remaining co-owners of the property. Children jointly taking property on the death of a parent or relative will typically be designated as tenants in common or automatically be classified as tenants in common for failure of the will or trust agreement to state the nature of their co-ownership.

Tenancy in partnership

Groups of investors numbering just a few individuals often acquire property as co-owners, to hold and operate as income-producing property. They often take title to the real estate as tenants in common. However, the venture necessitates a joint effort for the collective benefit of all the individual co-owners. Thus, a *tenancy in partnership* exists for ownership purposes and a California partnership has been formed for operating purposes. [CC §682(2); Calif. Corporations Code §§16202(a), 16204(c)]

The group, as co-owners of property which requires day-to-day management, jointly operate a business venture. The management is conducted either directly by one or more of the co-owners in a coordinated effort or indirectly through a property manager. However, to be common-law tenants in common, the co-owners must intend not to act as a group, an issue for avoiding tax partnership treatment.

Property vested in the names of **profit-sharing, co-venturing co-owners** as tenants in common is property owned by their "partnership," not property fractionally owned and separately managed and operated by each co-owner individually. [Corp C §16203]

Thus, even though title is vested in all the individual co-owners as tenants in common, each co-owner actually holds title as a *trustee* on behalf of their **informal partnership** since the property's operation requires a coordinated or **centralized-management** effort. [Corp C §16404(b)(1)]

Nature of a joint tenancy

Although most joint tenancies are created between a husband and wife, a joint tenancy can be created between persons other than a married couple, such as between other family members. In contrast, the community property vestings, of which there are two, are only available to a married couple.

Also, the number of joint tenants holding title is not limited to two, as is the case for a married couple's ownership of community property. Any number of co-owners can, under one deed, take title to real estate as joint tenants so long as they share equally in ownership.

The joint tenancy vesting has been and is an estate planning tool used for the orderly transfer of ownership between family members on death. The vesting is rarely used in a business environment, except for community-owned enterprises or investments.

Traditionally, the creation of a joint tenancy requires the conveyance of *four unities*:

- *unity of title*, meaning the joint tenants take title to the real estate through the **same instrument**, such as a grant deed;

- *unity of time*, meaning the joint tenants receive their interest in title at the **same time**;

- *unity of interest*, meaning the joint tenants own **equal shares** in the ownership of the property; and

- *unity of possession*, meaning each joint tenant has the **right to possess** the entire property.

Today, a joint tenancy is loosely based on these four unities. For example, a joint tenancy is defined as ownership by two or more persons in **equal shares**. Thus, the joint tenancy co-ownership incorporates the unity of interest into the statutory definition. [CC §683]

Similarly, a joint tenancy must be created by a **single transfer** to all those who are to become joint tenants. Thus, the historic unity of title (same deed) and unity of time (simultaneous transfers) required under common law have been retained in one event, typically being the recording of the conveyance transferring title to the joint tenants.

A joint tenancy ownership in real estate may be created by any of the following transfers, each being a single conveyance to all joint tenants, if the conveyance states the co-owners take title "as joint tenants":

- a transfer by grant deed, quitclaim deed or assignment, from an owner of the fee, leasehold or life estate, to himself and others;

- a transfer from co-owners vested as tenants in common to themselves; or

- a transfer from a husband and wife holding title as community property, tenants in common or separately, to themselves. [CC §683]

For the small percentage of joint tenants who are not husband and wife, typically family members or life-long friends, a valid joint tenancy is created when all co-owners take title under the same deed as joint tenants, without stating their **fractional interest** in ownership. Their actual fractional ownership, if severed or transferred to others, is a function of the number of individuals who took title as joint tenants.

Joint tenant's right of survivorship

The **sole advantage** of a joint tenancy vesting for co-owners is the *extinguishment* of a co-owner's entire co-ownership interest in the property on his death. On death, the interest of the deceased co-owner is **absorbed** by the surviving joint tenant(s). Thus, the ownership interest previously held by the deceased co-owner avoids probate procedures since no interest remains to be transferred.

The same results occurs on death if a married couple uses the community property with right of survivorship vesting to hold title to real estate or personal property.

Other than the right of survivorship, a joint tenancy vesting neither adds nor diminishes the legal or tax aspects of the ownership interest held in the real estate by each co-owner.

For example, whether the interests held by the co-owners are separate property or community property, a joint tenancy vesting neither enlarges nor reduces the nature of the ownership interest, until death.

Thus, the right of survivorship is the distinguishing feature of a joint tenancy vesting and is legally referred to a *jus accrescendi*. The right of survivorship is a doctrine developed by case law and now codified in California.

The right of survivorship only becomes operative at the time of the death of a joint tenant. On death, the right of survivorship extinguishes the deceased's interest and leaves the remaining joint tenant(s) with the entire ownership of the property to share equally among the surviving joint tenants.

Ultimately, on the death of all other joint tenants, the last surviving joint tenant becomes the sole owner of the property originally owned by all the joint tenants.

Ownership overlay

Joint tenancy rights and community property rights held by married couples **overlap** in California law when community property is placed in a joint tenancy vesting. This overlap is a by-product of California legal history.

Joint tenancy, with its inherent right of survivorship, arises out of the English common law, and is called a *common law estate*.

Community property, with its implicit partnership aspect, is a creation of Spanish civil law, dating from the time California was a Spanish colony.

Older cases treated community property and joint tenancy as mutually exclusive, i.e., holding real estate as community property meant it could not be held in a joint tenancy vesting and retain its community property status. Thus, a *transmutation* from community property to the separate property of each the husband and wife occurred by a transfer into a joint tenancy, comparable to vesting community property in a tenancy in common vesting today. [**Tomaier** v. **Tomaier** (1944) 23 C2d 754]

However, this "mutually exclusive" rule, which controlled legal results by the type of vesting and not by the community nature of the ownership by husband and wife, was eliminated in 1975.

Today, a joint tenancy vesting is **merely a vesting** used by co-owners solely to avoid probate. The joint tenancy vesting provides no other advantage to the co-owners. The underlying community or separate property character of the real estate is not affected when a husband and wife vest their co-ownership as joint tenants.

For instance, a husband and wife who take title as joint tenants do not by the vesting *transmute* their community property into separate property owned 50:50 by the husband and wife.

However, a joint tenancy vesting allows a husband and wife to **renounce the community property presumption** should they claim they intended the joint tenancy vesting to establish separate property interests in the real estate. Thus, the community property presumption can be rebutted by either spouse, and is occasionally exercised by the husband and wife to deter creditors. [**Abbett Electric Corporation v. Storek** (1994) 22 CA4th 1460]

A similar result altering community property rights occurs in federal **bankruptcy** proceedings when a husband and wife hold title as joint tenants. The interest of each spouse vested as a joint tenant is treated in bankruptcy as separate property in order to attain the objective of federal bankruptcy law to free individuals of onerous debt. Thus, a spouse's one-half interest in community property vested as joint tenants is not liable under bankruptcy for debts which were incurred solely by the other spouse and not on behalf of the community. [**In re Pavich** (1996) 191 BR 838]

If the couple does not intend by the joint tenancy vesting to transmute their community property into separate property, but take title to their community assets as joint tenants for the sole purpose of avoiding probate — as is the case in nearly all joint tenancy vestings — the property is **presumed** to be a community asset without concern for the joint tenancy vesting.

Conveying community property

Both spouses must consent to the sale, lease for more than one year, or encumbrance of the community real estate no matter how it is vested. [Calif. Family Code §1102]

If one spouse, without the consent of the other, sells, leases for more than one year or encumbers community real estate, the nonconsenting spouse may either *ratify* the transaction or have it *set aside*. The nonconsenting spouse has **one year** from the recording of the nonconsented-to transaction to file an action to set the transaction aside.

However, if the other party to the transaction — the buyer, tenant or lender — has no notice of the marriage, actual or constructive, the transaction cannot be set aside by the nonconsenting spouse who has failed to make the community interest known. [Fam C §1102]

Conveying community property as joint tenants

The ability of a married joint tenant to sell, lease or encumber his interest in the real estate depends on whether the real estate interest vested in the individual is his *separate property* or the *community property* of the individual's marriage.

When community real estate is vested in joint tenancy, both spouses' signatures are required to execute an enforceable purchase agreement or trust deed lien, or to enter into a lease agreement with a term exceeding one year. [Fam C §1102]

Thus, a sale, long-term lease or encumbrance of the community property executed by only one spouse is *voidable* since the transaction may be set aside by the nonconsenting spouse if acted upon within one year after commencement.

Further, a purchase agreement for the sale of community property entered into by only one spouse may not be enforced in any part by the buyer through an action for specific performance.

Thus, a purchase agreement entered into by one spouse to sell only his one-half interest in the community property is unenforceable unless consented to by the other spouse since **no interest** in community property may be conveyed, leased or encumbered without the consent of both spouses. [**Andrade Development Company** v. **Martin** (1982) 138 CA3d 330]

However, if record title to the community real estate is in the name of one spouse only, a sale, lease or encumbrance executed by the title-holding spouse alone is presumed valid if the buyer, tenant or lienholder has no actual or constructive knowledge of the marriage. This includes any knowledge of the agent representing the buyer, landlord or lender, about the owner's marital status. [Fam C §1102(c)]

Separate property joint tenancy vestings

When real estate held in a joint tenancy vesting is the **separate property** of each joint tenant, such as three siblings or a parent and child, each joint tenant can sell or encumber his interest in the real estate **without the consent** of the other joint tenants.

Also, when the real estate owned by a joint tenant is his separate property, the joint tenant may **lease** out the entire property since a lease is a transfer of possession, and each joint tenant has the *right to possession* of the entire property.

However, consider a husband and wife who own real estate which is **community property**. They hold title as joint tenants. The husband enters into an agreement to lease the property to a tenant for a term of over one year. The wife does not enter into the lease agreement with the tenant.

Under joint tenancy rules, any joint tenant alone may lease the entire property to a tenant. However, under community property rules (which apply to property acquired during the marriage with community assets), both spouses must execute a long-term lease agreement for the tenant to avoid challenges to set aside the lease for failure of both the husband and wife to sign the lease.

This one-spouse leasing scenario is an example of the misunderstanding created by the overlay and superiority of community property rights when community property is placed in a joint tenancy vesting.

Although no case or statute addresses this set of leasing facts, existing case law suggests the joint tenancy vesting should be viewed as controlling the landlord-tenant relationship, thus allowing the joint-tenant husband or wife to lease the property. Also, the *doctrine of ratification* would influence the result (in favor of the tenant) if the nonconsenting spouse knowingly enjoyed the benefits of the lease before attempting to set the lease aside. [CC §2310]

The agent's role

A broker and his agents who represent a married person in the sale, lease or financing of community real estate must know whether the performance by the married person of a promise to pay a fee under a listing or to close escrow on a purchase agreement can be legally avoided by asserting community property defenses, thereby inflicting a loss on the broker.

For example, a broker obtains an exclusive right-to-sell listing signed only by the wife. The real estate listed is vested in the name of the husband and wife either as community property or as joint tenants.

During the listing period, the couple acting independent of the broker sell the property without the payment of a fee to the listing broker. The listing entitles the broker to a fee, payable by the person who signed the listing, if the property is sold by anyone during the listing period. [See **first tuesday** Form 102]

The broker claims both the husband and wife are liable for the brokerage fee since the actions of the wife committed the community to the payment of a fee and the property was sold during the listing period.

The wife claims the listing is entirely unenforceable without the husband's signature since no part of the property listed can be sold and conveyed without her husband's written consent.

Is the broker entitled to his fee?

Yes! The wife, separate from the husband, is liable for the fee since she signed the listing agreement **employing the broker**. The broker can enforce collection of his fee due under the listing in an action for money against the wife. However, the husband, who did not sign the listing agreement, is not personally liable for the brokerage fee. [**Tamimi** v. **Bettencourt** (1966) 243 CA2d 377]

Further, on recording the broker's abstract of the judgment against the wife for the brokerage fee, the judgment becomes a lien on all community real estate owned by the couple. The husband's separate property, however, is not liened and remains unaffected by the abstract which attaches as a lien to both the wife's separate property and their community property.

In contrast to a listing employing a broker to locate a buyer, an action for specific performance by a buyer to enforce a real estate purchase agreement signed only by the wife will not be successful since an **agreement to sell** community real estate requires both spouses' signatures. Management and control is in both, not just one co-owner, when the property is community real estate, no matter how vested.

Severing a right of survivorship

A husband and wife are the vested owners of a parcel of real estate which is community property. The vesting provides for the right of survivorship under either a community property with right of survivorship vesting or a joint tenancy vesting.

However, every co-owner vested as a joint tenant or community property with right of survivorship has the right to *unilaterally sever*

the right of survivorship. The severance by a co-owner *terminates* the right of survivorship in that co-owner's interest, whether his interest in the real estate is separate or community property. The separate or community property nature of the co-owner's interest in the property remains the same after severing the right of survivorship from the co-owner's interest.

A co-owner terminating the right of survivorship in his interest is not required to first give notice or seek consent from the other co-owner(s). [**Riddle** v. **Harmon** (1980) 102 CA3d 524]

To *sever* the vesting, the co-owner prepares and signs a deed from himself "as a joint tenant" or "as community property with right of survivorship," back to himself. On recording the deed, the right of survivorship is severed by having merely *revested* the co-owner's interest. The deed revesting title should include a statement noting that the transfer is intended to sever the prior vesting. [CC §683.2(a)]

Alternatively, the co-owner could transfer title to himself as trustee under the co-owner's revocable inter vivos (living) trust agreement. The conveyance into the trust vesting would also sever the right of survivorship. By the conveyance, the trust vesting would also avoid the probate process while gaining control over succession of the co-owner's interest on death. Again, community property remains community property even though vested in the living trust of the individual husband or wife.

Further, any transfer of a joint tenant's interest in the joint tenancy property to a third party, such as from a joint tenant parent to a child, **automatically severs** the joint tenancy.

Termination of interest on death

Again, when the co-ownership of property is vested as joint tenants or community property with right of survivorship, the death of a co-owner *automatically extinguishes* the deceased co-owner's interest in the real estate.

Thus, the surviving co-owner(s) becomes the sole owner(s) of the property.

However, **title** to the deceased co-owner's interest in the property must be cleared away before the surviving co-owner(s) will be able to properly sell, lease or encumber the property as the owner(s).

The enlarged ownership interest of a surviving joint tenant, clear of the deceased's interest, is documented by simply recording an *affidavit*, signed by anyone, declaring the death of a joint tenant who was a co-owner and describing the real estate. [Calif. Probate Code §210(a); see **first tuesday** Form 460]

Likewise, the half interest in **community property** held by the deceased spouse at the time of death vested "as community property with right of survivorship" is *extinguished* by the same affidavit procedure used to eliminate the interest of a joint tenant, except that the surviving spouse (or the surviving spouse's representative) is the only one authorized to make the declaration. [See **first tuesday** Form 461]

Judgment against a spouse

Now consider a husband who encumbers community property with a trust deed, executed by the husband alone and without the consent of the wife. The trust deed secures a note which evidences a debt or other monetary obligation undertaken by the husband.

Later, the trust deed lien is set aside in a judicial action by the wife since the wife did not consent to the encumbrance of the community property.

The husband defaults on the now unsecured loan. The lender obtains a money judgment against the husband individually and records an abstract of the judgment naming only the husband as the judgment debtor.

On recording the abstract, the judgment debt attaches as a lien to all community property in which the husband presently has an interest, as well as the husband's separate property interests in other real estate. The wife's separate property is unaffected by the recorded abstract.

Now, the same community property which had been previously encumbered by the judicially voided trust deed lien is now encumbered by the judgment which attached as a lien by recording the abstract.

Later, the couple's marriage is dissolved and the wife is awarded sole ownership of the community property, now her separate property.

The wife claims the money judgment lien did not attach to the property since the debt which became the money judgment had been secured by the same property under a trust deed the court declared void.

Here, the recording of the abstract of judgment against the husband created a **valid lien** on all community property owned by the couple, including the property which later became property solely owned by the wife. The judgment attached to the property while it was still community property, before a property settlement conveyed the property or the marriage had been dissolved. [**Lezine** v. **Security Pacific Financial Services, Inc.** (1996) 14 C4th 56]

Joint tenancy tax aspects

Taxwise, the main question raised for a husband and wife when the surviving spouse becomes the sole owner of what was community property at the time of death, no matter how vested by them, is: What is the surviving spouse's **cost basis** in the property as the sole owner on the death of the spouse?

The surviving spouse who becomes the sole owner of community real estate on the death of a spouse receives a "fully" stepped-up cost basis to the property's fair market value on the date of the death which terminated the community.

Thus, the surviving spouse is entitled to a fully stepped-up basis in real estate previously owned by the community without concern for whether the **community property** was vested as community property, as joint tenants or in a revocable inter vivos trust. State law controls how marital property will be characterized for federal tax purposes. Federal law is unconcerned with "... the form in which title is taken" to community property. [IRS Revenue Ruling 87-98]

By California law, all property acquired by a husband and wife during marriage is community property, regardless of the vesting, if it is acquired, managed and operated as a community asset by the couple. [Fam C §760]

Thus, the real estate owned by a husband and wife (unless vested as tenants in common) is community property for federal income tax purposes. Accordingly, the surviving spouse on receiving the property receives a cost basis stepped-up to the property's **fair market value** on the date of death, the result of becoming the sole owner of property previously owned by the community.

Chapter 55

Preliminary title reports

This chapter examines the use of a preliminary title report by a buyer to review the condition of title to eliminate contingency provisions, and by escrow to prepare closing documents.

An offer to issue title insurance

An investor enters into an agreement to purchase real estate from a financially distressed seller.

Closing of the transaction is contingent on the investor's receipt and review of a preliminary title report (prelim) to confirm the property is subject only to the loans and other liens disclosed by the seller. Any taxes or monetary liens of record which are not disclosed in the purchase agreement are to remain of record. However, the amount of any undisclosed lien will be deducted from the cash down payment.

Escrow is opened with instructions to order a prelim from a title insurance company for approval of the condition of title by the investor. To keep acquisition costs to a minimum, escrow is instructed to close without obtaining a policy of title insurance.

The prelim received by escrow indicates the title is clear of all encumbrances, except those disclosed by the seller. Believing the title condition is as represented by the seller, the investor waives the further-approval contingency regarding approval of the prelim. Escrow closes on receiving a "date-down" on the prelim from the title company — without the issuance of a policy of title insurance.

However, the preliminary title report failed to disclose a recorded abstract of judgment against the seller which had attached to his title as a judgment lien. Later, the judgment creditor enforces the judgment lien by commencing a foreclosure on the property.

The investor clears title of the lien and makes a demand on the title company for the amount of the payoff since they prepared an erroneous prelim. The investor claims the title company is liable for his losses since it failed to disclose the judgment lien on the preliminary title report, a misrepresentation of title.

Can a buyer, escrow officer, broker or agent rely on a prelim as assurance the title condition is "as represented" in the preliminary title report?

No! A preliminary title report is not a representation of the condition of title or a policy of title insurance. Unlike an *abstract of title*, a prelim cannot be relied on by anyone. A title insurer has no duty to accurately report title defects and encumbrances on the preliminary title report (shown as exceptions in the proposed policy). [**Siegel** v. **Fidelity National Title Insurance Company** (1996) 46 CA4th 1181]

A preliminary title report is no more than an **offer to issue** a title insurance policy based on the contents of the prelim and any modifications made by the title company before the policy is issued. [Calif. Insurance Code §12340.11]

Use of the prelim

A preliminary title report typically discloses the current vesting, as well as the general and special taxes, assessments and bonds, covenants, conditions and restrictions (CC&Rs), easements, rights of way, encumbrances, liens and any interests of others which may be reflected on the public record as affecting title, collectively called *encumbrances*.

The closing of many purchase escrows is conditioned on the buyer's approval of the prelim. The buyer, his agent and escrow review the report on its receipt for defects and encumbrances on title inconsistent with the terms for the seller's delivery of title in the purchase agreement and escrow instructions.

Buyer's agents in a sales transaction check the prelim prior to closing for title conditions. Buyers' agents are looking for title conditions which might interfere with any **intended use or change in the use** of the property contemplated by the buyer. Interferences could be in the form of unusual easements or use restrictions which obstruct the buyer's announced plans to make improvements.

Finally, escrow relies on the preliminary report to carry out its instructions to record grant deeds, trust deeds, leaseholds or options which will be insured.

Typically, escrow instructions call for closing when the deed can be recorded and insured, subject only to taxes, CC&Rs and other encumbrances specified in the instructions.

Ultimately, it is the escrow officer who, on review of the prelim, must advise the seller of any need to eliminate defects or encumbrances on title which interfere with closing as instructed.

The prelim and a last-minute *date-down* of title conditions are used by escrow to reveal any title problems to be eliminated before closing and, as instructed, obtain title insurance for the documents being recorded (deeds, trust deeds, etc.).

Should the date-down of the prelim reveal defects or liens not previously reported in the prelim, either by error or by later recording, the title company can **withdraw its offer** under the prelim and issue a new prelim — a different offer to issue a policy on different terms.

Prelim vs. abstract of title

Title companies have long been aware of the public's reliance on the prelim. This reliance was consistently reinforced by the California courts which held title companies liable for their erroneous reports. However, legislation drafted by the title insurance industry was introduced and enacted in 1981 to eliminate liability for their preparation of faulty preliminary title reports.

Prelims were once compared to abstracts of title. An **abstract of title** is a written statement which may be relied on by those who order them as an accurate, factual representation of title to the property being acquired, encumbered or leased. [Ins C §12340.10]

An abstract of title is a **statement of facts** collected from the public records. An abstract is not an insurance policy with a dollar limit on liability set by the policy. Since the content of an abstract is intended by the insurance company to be relied upon **as fact**, the insurer is liable for all money losses of the policy holder flowing from a failure to properly prepare the abstract. [**1119 Delaware** v. **Continental Land Title Company** (1993) 16 CA4th 992]

In an effort to shield title companies from an *abstractor's liability* on the issuance of a defectively prepared prelim, the prelim has been legislatively redefined as being neither an abstract of title nor a representation of the condition of title. The prelim is now defined as a report furnished in connection with **an application** for title insurance. [Ins C §12340.11]

The prelim has become and is simply an **offer** by a title company to issue title insurance. The prelim is merely a statement of terms and conditions on which the title company is willing to issue a policy — subject to last minute changes prior to issuing the policy of title insurance.

Chapter 56

Title insurance

This chapter discusses title insurance and the different types of policies available.

Identifying an actual loss

A policy of title insurance is the means by which a title insurance company *indemnifies* — reimburses or holds harmless — a person who acquires an interest in real estate against a monetary loss caused by an **encumbrance on title** that:

- is not listed in the policy, which if listed is called an *exception*; and

- the insured was unaware of when the policy was issued. [Calif. Insurance Code §12340.1]

A policy of title insurance is issued on one of several forms which are the prototypes used by the entire title insurance industry in California. The policies are typically issued to **buyers** of real estate, **tenants** acquiring long-term leases and **lenders** whose loans are secured by real estate.

As an **indemnity agreement**, a title policy is a contract. The terms of coverage in the policy set forth the extent of the title insurance company's obligation, if any, to indemnify the named insured for a *money loss* caused by an **encumbrance on title** which is not listed in the policy's exceptions. [Ins C §12340.2]

An insured lender or buyer cannot recover a **reduction in profits** due to an unlisted defect in title as lost profits are not covered by title insurance. The title policy only indemnifies the insured against a **reduction in the value** of the property below the policy limits, not a reduction in future profits on either a foreclosure or resale of the property. [**Karl** v. **Commonwealth Land Title Insurance Company** (1993) 20 CA4th 972]

Encumbrances, unknown and undisclosed

Almost all losses due to the reduction in value of real estate below the policy limits arise out of an encumbrance. An encumbrance is any condition which affects the ownership interest of the insured, whether the interest insured is a fee, leasehold, life estate or the security interest of a lender.

The word encumbrance is all encompassing. Any right or interest in real estate held by someone other than the owner which diminishes the value of the real estate is an encumbrance.

Encumbrances on title include:

- covenants restricting use;

- restrictions on use;

- reservations of a right of way;

- easements;

- encroachments;

- trust deeds or other security devices;

- pendency of condemnation; and

- leases. [**Evans** v. **Faught** (1965) 231 CA2d 698]

Use of property not covered

Physical conditions on the property itself are not encumbrances affecting title since they are uses which exist and are visible (open and notorious) on the property, such as:

- canals;

- highways;

- irrigation ditches; and

- levees.

Accordingly, title policies do not insure against observable physical conditions which exist on the property. Observable physical conditions are not encumbrances. A buyer is always presumed to have contracted to acquire property subject to physical conditions on the property which impede its use or impair its value. In the case of encumbrances, recorded or not, no such presumption exists.

A buyer under a purchase agreement contracts to acquire title from the seller free of all encumbrances except those agreed to in the purchase agreement. Even if the buyer has notice of an encumbrance affecting title and he has not agreed in the purchase agreement to take title subject to the encumbrance, the seller is liable to the buyer for its removal, extinguishment or compensation.

However, for title insurance purposes only, the buyer's knowledge of an encumbrance affecting title at the time of closing **removes the known encumbrance** from coverage. Thus, the insured buyer assumes the risk of loss due to the known encumbrance.

Underwriting conditions

A title insurance policy is not an *abstract of title*. Thus, a policy of title insurance does not *warrant* or *guarantee* the nonexistence of title encumbrances, as does an abstract. Instead, the insured is *indemnified*, up to the policy's dollar limits, against a money loss caused by a title condition not listed as an exception or exclusion in the policy.

Under a title insurance policy, the title company only assumes (covers) the risks of a **monetary loss** caused by an encumbrance which is not listed as an exception to coverage, and was unknown to the insured buyer or lender at the time of closing. The title company has no obligation to clear title of the encumbrance.

Consider an owner who discovers the size of an easement was understated in the title policy.

Due to the actual dimensions of the easement, the owner cannot develop the property.

The owner makes a claim on the title company for the **lost value** of the property based on its potential for development as allowed by the understated easement, not for his loss of value on the price he paid for the property (which is the dollar amount of the title policy limits).

Instead, the title company only pays the owner an *inflation adjusted price* based on the price the owner paid for the property — an amount set by the policy limits and the inflation endorsement.

The owner claims the title company's *negligence* in the disclosure of the easement caused a loss in property value equal to the difference between the purchase price paid and the potential value of the property for development.

However, the title company is not liable under a policy for lost profits in the unrealized potential value of the property. It was the easement that caused the loss of profits, not the issuance of a title insurance policy. [**Barthels** v. **Santa Barbara Title Company** (1994) 28 CA4th 674]

Introduction to title policy forms

Title insurance is bought to assure real estate buyers, tenants and lenders the **interest in title** they acquire is what they bargained for from the seller, landlord or borrower. While title insurance is not a guarantee of the condition of title acquired, it does provide a **monetary recovery** up to the policy's dollar limits for the conveyance of any lesser interest due to unlisted exceptions than the interest insured.

On closing a real estate transaction, a policy of title insurance is issued on one of several forms used throughout the entire title insurance industry in California. The policies are typically issued to **buyers** of real estate, **tenants** acquiring long-term leases and **lenders** whose loans are secured by the real estate.

Two basic forms exist which are the industry prototypes for:

- insuring the condition of record title only, accomplished by the issuance of a *California Land Title Association (CLTA) policy*; and

- insuring both the record title and observable on-site activities which affect title, accomplished by the issuance of an *American Land Title Association (ALTA) policy*.

In analysis, a **policy of title insurance** is broken down into six operative sections, including:

- the risks of **loss covered**, called *insuring clauses*, which are based on the unencumbered title at the time of the insured transfer;

- the risks of **loss not covered**, comprised of encumbrances arising after the transfer or known to or brought about by the insured, called *exclusions*, which are a boilerplate set of title conditions;

- **identification** of the insured, the property, the vesting, the estate in the property, the dollar amount of the coverage, the premium paid and the policy (recording) date for the conveyance insured, called *Schedule A*;

- the **recorded interests**, i.e., any encumbrances affecting title and any observable on-site activities which are **listed as risks** agreed to and assumed by the insured and not covered by the policy, called *excep-*

tions, which are pre-printed for CLTA coverage and itemized for all types of coverage in *Schedule B*;

- the **procedures**, called *conditions*, for **claims made** by the named insured and for *settlement* by the insurance company on the occurrence of a loss due to any encumbrance on title which is not an exclusion or exception to the coverage granted by the insuring clauses; and

- any **endorsements** for additional coverage or removal of exclusions or pre-printed exceptions from the policy.

Insuring clauses

The coverage under the broadly worded **insuring clauses** of a policy of title insurance indemnifies the named insured for risks of loss **related to the title** due to:

- anyone making a claim against title to the real estate interest;

- the title being unmarketable for sale or as security for financing;

- any encumbrance on the title; and

- lack of recorded access to and from the described property.

Exclusions from coverage

All title insurance policies, in their **exclusions section**, excludes from coverage those losses incurred by the insured buyer, tenant or lender due to:

- **use ordinances** or (zoning) laws;

- **unrecorded claims known** to the insured, but not to the title company;

- encumbrances or adverse **claims created** or attaching **after** the date of the policy;

- claims arising out of **bankruptcy** laws or due to a **fraudulent conveyance** to the insured;

- police power and **eminent domain**; and

- **post-closing events** caused by the insured.

Schedule A data

All policies of title insurance in their Schedule A set forth:

- the property interest the insured acquired (fee simple, leasehold, life estate, security, etc.);

- the legal description of the insured property;

- the date and time the insured conveyance or lien recorded and coverage began;

- the premium paid for the policy; and

- the maximum total dollar amount to be paid for all claims settled.

Exceptions to coverage

In addition to the policy exclusions, a policy's coverage under its "no-encumbrance" insuring clause is further limited by Schedule B exceptions in the policy. The **exceptions section** contains an itemized list of recorded and unrecorded encumbrances which are known to the title company and affect the insured title. While the existence of these known encumbrances are insured against in the insuring clauses, they are removed by Schedule B as a basis for recovery under the policy.

In addition to the itemized **list of exceptions**, a CLTA policy includes a set of pre-printed exceptions setting forth risks assumed by the insured buyer, tenant or lender, which include:

- taxes, assessments, liens, covenants, conditions and restrictions (CC&Rs), or any other interests, claims or encumbrances

which have not been recorded with the county recorder or tax collector on the date of closing;

- any unrecorded and observable on-site activity which includes conflicts regarding boundary lines, encroachments or any other facts which a correct survey would disclose;

- unpatented mining claims; and

- all water rights.

Claims and settlements

Lastly, a policy of title insurance includes a **conditions section** which outlines the procedures the named insured must follow when making a claim for recovery under the policy. Also set forth are the settlement negotiations or legal actions available to the title company before they must pay a claim.

Owner's policies for buyers

Several types of title coverage are available for a buyer to choose from when entering into a purchase agreement with the seller, including:

- a CLTA standard policy;

- an ALTA owner's extended coverage policy;

- an ALTA residential (ALTA-R) policy; and

- an ALTA homeowner's policy.

When making an offer, a prospective buyer is informed by his agent about the coverage each type of policy provides. The buyer's need for title coverage must be reviewed when the buyer enters into a purchase agreement since the agreement's title insurance provision calls for the buyer to designate the type of title insurance policy on closing and states who will pay its premium.

The CLTA standard policy

The CLTA standard policy is purchased solely by buyers, carryback sellers and private lenders, not institutional lenders or builders who generally need extended coverage.

The CLTA standard policy insures against all encumbrances affecting title to the property which can be discovered by a search of **public records** prior to issuance of the policy. Any encumbrance not recorded, whether or not observable by an **inspection or survey** of the property, is not covered due to the CLTA policy exclusions and standard exceptions.

Public records include those records which impart *constructive notice* of encumbrances affecting title to the property.

For example, a deed conveying a parcel of real estate which is actually **recorded and indexed** by the county recorder's office imparts constructive notice to buyers and lenders who later acquire an interest in the property. [Calif. Civil Code §1213]

Also, the CLTA standard policy (as well as the ALTA policy) protects the buyer against:

- the unmarketability of title or the inability to use it as security for financing;

- lack of ingress and egress rights to the property; and

- losses due to the ownership being vested in someone other than the buyer.

All title insurance policies provide coverage forever after the date and time the policy is issued, limited in recovery to the dollar amount of the policy, which is generally adjusted for inflation. Coverage is further limited by the **exclusions, exceptions and conditions on claims**.

The CLTA standard policy (as well as the ALTA policy) contains Schedule A *exclusions to coverage* which bar recovery by the buyer or joint protection carryback seller for losses due to:

- zoning laws, ordinances or regulations restricting or regulating the **occupancy, use or enjoyment** of the land;

- the character, dimensions or location of any **improvement erected** on the property;

- a **change in ownership** or a parceling or combining of the described property by the insured buyer;

- **police power**, eminent domain or violations of environmental protection laws, unless a notice or encumbrance resulting from the violation was recorded with the county recorder before closing;

- encumbrances **known** to the insured buyer or lender which are not recorded or disclosed to the title company;

- encumbrances which do not result in a **monetary loss**;

- encumbrances which are created or become encumbrances **after issuance** of the policy;

- encumbrances resulting from the buyer's payment of **insufficient consideration** for the property or delivery of improper security to the lender also insured under the policy; and

- the unenforceability of the insured trust deed lien due to the lender's **failure to comply** with laws regarding usury, consumer credit protection, truth-in-lending, bankruptcy and insolvency.

The CLTA standard policy contains **pre-printed exceptions** listed in the policy as Schedule B, also called *standard exceptions* or *regional exceptions*. It is the inclusion of these pre-printed boilerplate exceptions which makes the CLTA policy a standard policy. An ALTA owner's policy does not contain pre-printed exceptions, only the typewritten exceptions listing the encumbrances which are known to the title company and affect title to the property.

The **pre-printed standard exceptions** in Schedule B of the CLTA standard policy eliminate coverage for losses incurred by the buyer due to:

- taxes or assessments not shown as existing liens in the records of the county recorder, the county tax collector or any other agency which levies taxes on real property;

- unrecorded rights held by others which the buyer could have discovered by an inspection of the property or inquiry of persons in possession;

- easements or encumbrances which are not recorded and indexed by the county recorder;

- unrecorded encroachments or boundary line disputes which would have been disclosed by a survey; and

- recorded or unrecorded, unpatented mining claims or water rights.

A lower premium is charged to issue a CLTA policy since the title company undertakes a lower level of risk for indemnified losses due to the CLTA pre-printed exceptions as compared to the extended risks covered by the more expensive ALTA owner's policy.

The ALTA owner's policy

Most policies issued today are of the ALTA variety. The CLTA policy format with pre-printed standard exceptions does not provide protection for **unrecorded encumbrances or claims** to title.

The ALTA owner's policy provides greater coverage (and premiums) than the CLTA pol-

icy since the exceptions in Schedule B do not include the pre-printed standard exceptions. If the pre-printed exceptions are included in Schedule B and attached to the ALTA policy, the policy becomes an ALTA standard policy, comparable in cost and coverage to the CLTA standard policy since unrecorded encumbrances will not be covered.

The ALTA owner's policy covers **off-record matters** not covered under the CLTA standard policy. As a result, the title company may require the parcel to be surveyed, and those in possession to be interviewed or estopped, before the title company will issue an ALTA policy. Unrecorded interests in title are most often observable by an on-site inspection of the property.

Typewritten exceptions for existing encroachments or boundary conflicts are occasionally added to the ALTA policy (Schedule B) based on the survey.

The ALTA residential policy

For buyers of parcels containing one-to-four residential units, an ALTA residential (ALTA-R) policy is available in lieu of the ALTA owner's or homeowner's policies. Parcels insured include lots and units in common interest developments (CIDs), such as condominiums.

The ALTA-R is referred to by the title companies as the "plain language" policy. The ALTA-R is written using wording which avoids legalese. The policy is structured and written to be easily read and understood by the buyer. The ALTA-R form policy contains a **table of contents** and an **owner's information sheet** which outlines the policy's features.

The coverage, exclusions and exceptions in the ALTA-R policy are similar to the ALTA owner's policy. In addition, the ALTA-R policy covers losses due to:

- mechanic's liens incurred by someone other than the buyer; and

- the inability of the buyer to occupy the property should the single family residence violate the CC&Rs listed in the Schedule B exceptions in the policy or existing zoning.

The premium for an ALTA-R form policy is priced lower than the premium for an ALTA owner's policy since the policy is usually issued only on parcels in an existing subdivision or CID which has no known problems with easements, encroachments or access.

The ALTA homeowner's policy

A homeowner's policy now exists to provide **more coverage** than the ALTA owner's or the ALTA-R policies. In addition to the risks covered by the ALTA owner's and ALTA-R policies, the homeowner's policy covers several risks to ownership which could arise **after closing**, including:

- the **forging** of the buyer's signature on a deed in an attempt to sell or encumber the buyer's property;

- the construction on an adjoining parcel of a structure which **encroaches** onto the buyer's property, excluding a boundary wall or fence;

- the recording of a document which prevents the buyer from obtaining a secured loan or selling the property;

- claims of **adverse possession** or **easement by prescription** against the buyer's property; and

- claims by others of a right in the buyer's property arising out of a lease, contract or option **unrecorded and unknown** to the buyer at the time of closing.

The ALTA homeowner's policy also covers losses arising out of a lack of vehicular and pedestrian access to and from the property. Other owner's policies only cover losses resulting from the lack of a legal right to access, not a practical means of access which is covered by the ALTA homeowner's policy.

Also covered by the ALTA homeowner's policy are losses incurred due to many other risks which may exist at the time of closing, including:

- the correction of any pre-existing violation of a CC&R;

- the inability to obtain a building permit or to sell, lease or use the property as security for a loan due to a pre-existing violation of a subdivision law or regulation;

- the removal or remedy of any existing structure on the property if it was built without obtaining a building permit, excluding a boundary wall or fence;

- damage to existing structures due to the exercise of a right to maintain or use an easement;

- damage to improvements due to mineral or water extraction;

- the enforcement of a discriminatory CC&R;

- the assessment of a supplemental real estate tax due to construction or a change of ownership or use occurring before closing;

- an incorrect property address stated in the policy; and

- the map attached to the policy showing the incorrect location of the property.

Binders

An investor who buys property and plans on reselling the property within two years after his purchase should be advised by the buyer's agent to consider a binder, also called a *commitment to issue.*

A binder entitles the buyer to title insurance coverage until the buyer requests a policy be issued to a new buyer on resale of the property or to a new lender on a refinance, such as occurs when a relocation agent (broker) temporarily takes title to a residence before it is resold to the ultimate buyer.

With a binder, the resale policy will be at no further charge, except for additional liability coverage requested for any increase in the resale price.

Lender's policies

The CLTA and ALTA form title policies available to insure the priority of the lien a lender holds to secure their loan, include:

- a CLTA standard joint protection (JP) policy; and

- an ALTA loan policy.

The CLTA standard JP policy

A lender or a seller who carries back a note and trust deed for part of the sales price has options when calling for title insurance.

The lender or carryback seller can either:

- be named as an additional insured on a CLTA standard JP title insurance policy with the buyer; or

- request a separate ALTA loan policy as a sole named insured.

The JP policy enables one or more individuals or entities to be named as insured.

However, the JP policy is only available under a CLTA standard policy. If either the buyer or

the lender in a cash-to-new-loan transaction requests ALTA coverage, a separate ALTA loan policy will be issued to each at approximately double the cost.

The ALTA lender's policy

An institutional lender will usually require its trust deed lien on a parcel of real estate to be insured under an ALTA loan policy as a condition for making a loan secured by real estate.

The ALTA loan policy insures against money losses incurred by lenders and carryback sellers due to the loss of priority of the insured trust deed lien, unless listed in the exceptions, to encumbrances such as:

- a mechanic's lien, if the work was commenced prior to recording the trust deed (which is the same date and time as the date of the policy) and the trust deed did not secure a loan to pay for the construction;

- a mechanic's lien arising out of work financed by proceeds from the construction loan secured by the insured trust deed, if no part of the construction work was commenced before the trust deed was recorded; and

- assessments (Mello-Roos) for street improvements under construction or completed prior to recording the trust deed.

The ALTA loan policy comes at a higher (and separate) premium than the CLTA standard JP policy due to the extended mechanic's lien and assessment coverage. The buyer who borrows to finance his purchase usually pays the premium for the lender's policy.

Endorsements

Endorsements of great variety can be added to the form policies to provide coverage for title conditions and use or economic conditions not covered by the proto-typical policies. Endorsements are usually issued only to lenders, though modified endorsements can be used in owner's policies as well, particularly for developers and builders.

Endorsements cover losses incurred due to violations of CC&Rs, damage from extraction of water or minerals, mechanic's liens, encroachments (conditions covered in an ALTA-R policy) and the effects of inflation. Endorsements are also issued to remove an exclusion or exception which is an unwanted boilerplate provision in a policy.

SECTION G

Escrow

Chapter 57

Going to escrow

This chapter reviews the use by agents of checklists and pre-printed instructions to better prepare for opening escrow.

The process of closing a purchase agreement

Escrow is a process employed to facilitate the closing of a real estate transaction entered into between two parties, such as a buyer and a seller, who have agreed to the transfer of real estate, typically under a primary agreement, e.g., a purchase agreement. An **escrow consists of**:

- one person, such as a seller of real estate, who delivers written instruments or money to an escrow company for the purpose of the person fully performing his obligations owed another person under an agreement previously entered into for the sale, encumbrancing or leasing of real estate; and

- the escrow company, who delivers the written instruments and money to the other person, such as the buyer, on the occurrence of a specified event or the performance of prescribed conditions, such as the issuance of title insurance. [Calif. Financial Code §17003(a)]

For an individual to engage in the business of acting as an escrow agent, he must himself be licensed and employed by a corporation also licensed by the California Commissioner of Corporations, unless exempt.

Individuals exempt from the escrow licensing requirements include:

- a licensed real estate broker, either individual or corporate, who represents a party to a transaction in which the broker will perform escrow services;

- a licensed attorney who is not actively engaged in conducting (holding himself out as) an escrow agency;

- a bank, trust company, savings and loan association (thrift) or insurance company; and

- a title insurance company whose principal business is preparing abstracts or making searches of title used for issuing title insurance policies.

Duties of an escrow officer include:

- collecting necessary documents, such as appraisals, disclosure statements and title reports called for in escrow instructions;

- preparing documents necessary for conveyancing, encumbrancing and evidencing the creation of debts required for escrow to close;

- calculating prorations and adjustments; and

- disbursing funds or transferring documents when all conditions for their release have been met.

Opening escrow

Consider a buyer and seller who enter into a purchase agreement for the sale of the seller's one-to-four unit residence. As agreed, escrow now needs to be opened to handle the closing of the transaction.

In modern real estate practice, **opening escrow** simply means establishing a depository for the deed, the money and other items, called *instru-*

ments, with accompanying instructions signed by all necessary parties authorizing escrow to transfer or hand those items to the parties or others on closing.

Before accepting any instruments as an escrow holder for a transaction, the escrow officer will need to be informed, i.e., *dictated instructions,* by an agent of one of the parties regarding precisely when and under what circumstances the documents and monies deposited with escrow are to change hands.

Any number of details (preparation, receipt and transfer of monies and documents) must be attended to, by the escrow holder before the transaction can be completed, called a *closing or settlement.*

As a checklist for "going to escrow," a worksheet helps to organize the collection of facts and any supporting papers the escrow officer will need to immediately draw instructions and be able to clear the conditions necessary to close. [See Form 403 accompanying this chapter]

The documents work together

Modern real estate sales transactions depend on both the purchase agreement and the escrow instructions working in tandem to close a transaction.

Both the purchase agreement and the escrow instructions are *contracts* regarding interests in real estate. To be enforceable under the Statute of Frauds, both documents must be **in writing**. [Calif. Civil Code §1624; Calif. Code of Civil Procedure §1971]

A purchase agreement sets forth the sales price and terms of payment, together with conditions to be met before closing.

Escrow instructions constitute an additional agreement between the buyer and seller which is entered into with an escrow company, but it **does not replace the purchase agreement.**

Escrow instructions are merely directives which an escrow agrees to comply with to carry out the terms of the purchase agreement by coordinating a closing on behalf of both the buyer and the seller.

However, escrow instructions occasionally add exactness and completeness, providing the enforceability sometimes lacking in purchase agreements as prepared by brokers or their agents.

The purchase agreement is the primary underlying document in a real estate sales transaction and is considered the original contract. All further agreements, including the escrow instructions, must comply with the primary document, unless **intended to modify** the original agreement.

The agents negotiating a transaction, and their brokers, are responsible for ensuring the escrow instructions, whether prepared or dictated by themselves or others, conform to the purchase agreement.

To provide for a smoother, timely closing, the agent dictating instructions needs to collect and hand escrow, at his earliest opportunity, all of the information the escrow officer needs to prepare the instructions and documents. The agent should use a **checklist** to mark off the items and information escrow might need in order to process the transaction.

The escrow officer will prepare the instructions from information provided by the agent. Thus, the agent dictates the instructions.

Of note, an escrow officer does not have an obligation to notify the parties of any suspicious fact or circumstance detected by the officer before close of escrow, unless the fact **affects closing**. However, as is the policy of many an escrow officer selected by the agent to handle the closing, the officer will alert the agent to potential problems that lie outside the escrow instructions which have been brought to the at-

SALES ESCROW WORKSHEET

For Use on Seller-Occupied SFR Properties

1. PARTIES, PROPERTY AND PRICE:

1.1 Date escrow to close: _____

1.2 Property address: _____

_____

Parcel Number: _____

City:_____ County: _____, California

1.3 Price: $_____

Down payment: $_____

Initial deposit into escrow: $_____

Loan amount on closing: $_____

1.4 Seller's Name:_____

Address: _____

_____

Phone:_____ Fax:_____ E-mail:_____

Seller's Broker: _____

1.5 Buyer's Name:_____

Address: _____

_____

Phone:_____ Fax:_____ E-mail:_____

Buyer's Broker: _____

2. ENCUMBRANCES OF RECORD:

	First Trust Deed	Second Trust Deed
Original amount:	$_____	$_____
Current balance:	$_____	$_____
Interest rate:	_____% ☐ ARM	_____% ☐ ARM
	Type: _____	Type: _____
Monthly payments:	$_____	$_____
Due date:	_____	_____
Assumed or reconveyed:	_____	_____
Lender/Loan Number:	_____	_____

Lender's address: _____

_____

2.1 Bond or assessment lien balance: $_____

Annual payment: _____

Interest rate: _____%

2.2 New Trust Deed loan in amount of $_____, payable approximately $_____ monthly, including interest at the annual rate of _____% ☐ fixed; ☐ VIR.

Loan charges to be paid by: _____

2.3 Seller Carryback Note and Trust Deed: $_____ payable $_____ monthly, or more, including annual interest of _____% all due _____ years from close.

First payment due: _____, 20_____.

☐ Contract collection clause

☐ 90-day balloon payment notice provision

☐ Late charge of $_____ after _____ days.

☐ Prepayment penalty

☐ Due-on-sale clause

☐ All-inclusive note and trust deed addendum

☐ Tax reporting service charge to be paid by:_____

☐ Request for Notice of Default/Delinquency on senior trust deed

3. DISCLOSURES YET TO BE MADE TO BUYERS:

3.1 Lead-based paint disclosure for pre-1978 residences — right to inspect/waiver. [**first tuesday** Form 313]
- ☐ Buyer's receipt
- ☐ Buyer's Broker acknowledgment
- ☐ Seller's compliance
- ☐ Listing Broker acknowledgment

3.2 Condition of property statement (TDS) — three-day right to cancel. [**ft** Form 304]
- ☐ Buyer's receipt
- ☐ Buyer's Broker acknowledgment
- ☐ Seller's compliance
- ☐ Listing Broker acknowledgment

   a. Environmental Hazards Guide for Homeowners and Buyers.
- ☐ Buyer's receipt

   b. Home Energy/Rating Information Booklet.
- ☐ Buyer's receipt
- ☐ Buyer's Broker acknowledgment
- ☐ Seller's compliance
- ☐ Listing Broker acknowledgment

3.3 Natural Hazard Disclosure Statement — three-day right to cancel. [**ft** Form 314]
- ☐ Buyer's Receipt
- ☐ Seller's compliance
- ☐ Listing Broker acknowledgment

   a. Homeowner's Guide to Earthquake Safety (pre-1960 housing, woodframe, no slab). [**ft** Forms 315 and 316]
- ☐ Buyer's receipt
- ☐ Seller's 9A Report

   b. Commercial Guide to Earthquake Safety for pre-1975 housing (unreinforced masonry, woodframe roof or floors).
- ☐ Buyer's receipt
- ☐ Buyer's Broker acknowledgment
- ☐ Seller's 9A Report
- ☐ Listing Broker acknowledgment

3.4 Mello-Roos bond conditions — Notice of Special Tax [District _____].
- ☐ Buyer's receipt

3.5 Ordnance location disclosure.
- ☐ Buyer's receipt
- ☐ Seller's written notice

3.6 Industrial use/zoning affecting residential property.
- ☐ Buyer's receipt
- ☐ Seller's written notice

3.7 Tax withholding disclosures (CA/Fed). [**ft** Form 301 and FTB Form 593C]
- ☐ Buyer's receipt
- ☐ Seller's compliance

3.8 Homeowners' association (CID) documentation: articles, by-laws, CC&Rs, current and approved/additional assessments, unenforceable age restrictions, operating budget, operating rules, CPA's financial statements, insurance policy summary, and collection and lien enforcement policies.
- ☐ Buyer's receipt
- ☐ Seller's compliance

3.9 Seller carryback financing disclosure. [**ft** Form 300]
- ☐ Buyer's receipt
- ☐ Buyer's Broker acknowledgment
- ☐ Seller's compliance
- ☐ Listing Broker acknowledgment

3.10 Estimated closing statement — approved prior to closing.
- ☐ Buyer's approval
- ☐ Seller's approval

3.11 Local option disclosure: city occupancy report, water conservation, etc. [**ft** Form 307]
- ☐ Buyer's receipt
- ☐ Buyer's Broker acknowledgment
- ☐ Seller's compliance
- ☐ Listing Broker acknowledgment

3.12 Property operating data. [**ft** Forms 352 and 562]
- ☐ Buyer's receipt
- ☐ Seller's compliance

4. SELLER COMPLIANCE:

4.1 ☐ Termite report and clearance

4.2 ☐ Water heater strapping/bracing installed

4.3 ☐ Smoke detector — installed/operative

4.4 ☐ Home warranty policy
insurer: _____
coverage:_____

4.5 ☐ Payoff demand/beneficiary statement approval [**ft** Form 429]

4.6 ☐ Bill of sale on personal property sold [**ft** Form 434]

4.7   Holdover occupancy agreement [**ft** Form 272]
      ☐ Buyer's receipt   ☐ Seller's receipt
4.8   ☐ Release of recorded lien [**ft** Form 409]
4.9   Other: _____
      _____

5. **BUYER COMPLIANCE**:
   5.1   ☐ Preliminary title report approval
   5.2   New financing approval:
         ☐ Buyer's receipt   ☐ Seller's receipt
   5.3   Interim occupancy agreement (pre-closing occupancy). [**ft** Form 271]
         ☐ Buyer's receipt   ☐ Seller's receipt
   5.4   Submission of credit application for carryback note. [**ft** Form 302]
         ☐ Seller Approval
   5.5   ☐ Beneficiary statement approval on loan takeover or assumption
   5.6   ☐ Fire/hazard insurance agent_____
         ☐ Carryback seller as loss payee
   5.7   ☐ Appraisal of property's fair market value approval
   5.8   ☐ Home inspector's report approval
   5.9   ☐ Final pre-closing "walk-through" inspection
   5.10 Other: _____
         _____

6. **PRORATES, ADJUSTMENTS AND MISC. INSTRUCTIONS**:
   6.1   Impound account on loan takeover to be:
         ☐ Charged to buyer and credited to seller
         ☐ Transferred without adjustments
   6.2   Prorates and credits from ☐ date of closing or ☐ other date _____:
         ☐ Property taxes and Mello-Roos   ☐ Rents/Security deposits
         ☐ Balance/Interest on loan takeover   ☐ Association assessments
   6.3   Other: _____
         _____

7. **TITLE POLICY**:
   7.1   Seller's vesting: _____
   7.2   Buyer's vesting: _____
         Taking title as: ☐ Community property with right of survivorship
         ☐ Joint tenants   ☐ Community property   ☐ Tenants in common
         ☐ Separate property   ☐ An individual   ☐ An unmarried person
   7.3   Title company:_____
   7.4   Title policy: _____
         ☐ ALTA   ☐ CLTA   ☐ Abstract   ☐ Binder
         ☐ ALTA-R   ☐ Homeowner(s) (one-to-four units) ☐ Owners (other than one-to-four units)
         ☐ Joint protection   ☐ Lenders
         Premium to be paid by:_____
   7.5   Other title conditions: _____
         _____
         _____
         _____

8. BROKERAGE FEES: ☐ in instructions   ☐ in supplement
   $_____ to _____ paid by _____
   $_____ to _____ paid by _____

Agent: _____   Date:_____, 20_____

FORM 403   04-00   ©2006 **first tuesday**, P.O. BOX 20069, RIVERSIDE, CA 92516 (800) 794-0494

tention of the escrow officer or been observed by the officer. [**Lee** v. **Title Insurance and Trust Company** (1968) 264 CA2d 160]

To avoid confusion when dictating instructions, the broker must consider the type of transaction (sale, loan, exchange or lease) which is being escrowed, scheduled dates for the elimination of any contingencies the escrow officer must act upon and the final date scheduled for close of escrow.

If the escrow instructions drafted and signed are vague or incomplete on any point, the underlying purchase agreement must be analyzed by the agents and the parties before dictating amended instructions. The **terms of the purchase agreement supersede** any inconsistencies between the purchase agreement and the escrow instructions not intended to be a modification of the original purchase agreement.

If the point in dispute is not addressed in the purchase agreement, then it is not part of the contract and must, if agreeable, be added to the escrow instructions by amendment.

Naturally, amended instructions adding terms which are modifications of the purchase agreement should note they modify the purchase agreement.

Escrow instructions which **modify** the intentions stated or implied in the purchase agreement must be **written, signed and returned** to escrow by both parties. Proposed modifications signed by some but not all parties are **not binding on a party** who has not agreed to the modifications.

If, before closing escrow, an agent discovers any aspect of the escrow instructions which is in conflict with the intentions expressed in the purchase agreement or the expectations of the buyer or seller, the agent is duty-bound to immediately bring these discrepancies to the attention of the escrow officer and his client. On notification of an error in instructions or a need for clarification, the escrow officer must hold up the close of escrow until the discrepancy is clarified and corrective escrow instructions have been prepared, signed by the buyer and seller, and returned to escrow. [**Diaz** v. **United California Bank** (1977) 71 CA3d 161]

Required escrow disclosures

All written escrow instructions signed by a buyer or seller **must contain a statement**, in not less than 10-point type, which includes the licensee's name and the name of the department issuing the license or granting the authority under which the person conducting the escrow is operating.

In addition, all escrow transactions for the purchase of real estate where a **policy of title insurance will not be issued** to the buyer must include an **advisory notice** prepared in a separate document and signed by the buyer. The notice must state:

"IMPORTANT: IN A PURCHASE OR EXCHANGE OR REAL PROPERTY, IT MAY BE ADVISABLE TO OBTAIN TITLE INSURANCE IN CONNECTION WITH THE CLOSE OF ESCROW SINCE THERE MAY BE PRIOR RECORDED LIENS AND ENCUMBRANCES WHICH AFFECT YOUR INTEREST IN THE PROPERTY BEING ACQUIRED. A NEW POLICY OF TITLE INSURANCE SHOULD BE OBTAINED IN ORDER TO ENSURE YOUR INTEREST IN THE PROPERTY THAT YOU ARE ACQUIRING." [CC §1057.6]

Finally, escrow has a duty to advise the buyer in writing of the Franchise Tax Board requirements for withholding 3 1/3% of the price paid the seller, unless the seller certifies he is exempt from state income tax withholding. [Calif. Revenue and Taxation Code §18662(e)(3)(B)]

Use of the escrow worksheet

In practice, the sales escrow worksheet, **first tuesday** Form 403, is used as a checklist to assist agents in gathering the information and documents needed to dictate instructions to the escrow officer. It is used again to check the completed instructions for compliance with the terms of the purchase agreement. Thus, the agent who dictates the instructions keeps control of the events which must take place to close the transaction.

As with all checklists, the sales escrow worksheet is designed to address activities which are to be considered, but may or may not be applicable to the transaction at hand. Since it is a checklist, the form is not to be used to create an agreement between the buyer and seller. Also, the worksheet serves as the agent's personal control sheet (or that of his transaction coordinator) and is to be maintained in the client's file to act as a reminder of those activities yet to be completed to close the transaction.

Preparing the sales escrow worksheet

The following instructions are for the preparation and use of the sales escrow worksheet, **first tuesday** Form 403. Form 403 is for an agent to make entries and notations in preparation for dictating escrow instructions to close a sale he has negotiated.

Each instruction corresponds to the provision in the form bearing the same number.

1. Parties, property and price:

1.1 **Enter** the date escrow is scheduled to close.

1.2 **Enter** the address, assessor's parcel number (APN) and location of the property sold.

1.3 **Enter** the sales price, down payment, any deposits toward the price/closing costs and the amount of the loan to be assumed or originated by the buyer for the balance of the purchase price.

1.4 **Enter** the name, address, telephone and fax numbers, and email address for each seller. **Enter** the name of any broker representing the seller.

1.5 **Enter** the name, address, telephone and fax numbers, and email address for each buyer. **Enter** the name of any broker representing the buyer.

2. Encumbrances of record: **Enter** the loan amount and terms for payment of each existing loan if the loan will remain of record. **Enter** the words "paid off" or "assumed" to note whether an existing trust deed loan is to be reconveyed or is to remain of record. **Enter** the lender's name, address and loan number.

2.1 *Bonded indebtedness*: **Enter** the remaining balance, the payment schedule and interest rate on any bonded improvement liens, such as Mello-Roos bonds.

2.2 *New loan*: **Enter** the amount, the limitations on the terms of any new loan to be recorded by the buyer and who is to bear the loan charges.

2.3 *Seller carryback*: **Enter** the amount of the principal, payment, interest, due date and the first payment date for any carryback note to be executed by the buyer. **Check** the applicable boxes for special provisions to be included in the note or trust deed. **Check** whether a tax reporting service or request for Notice of Default/Delinquency has been agreed to.

3. Disclosures to buyers: **Check** the appropriate box(es) to indicate the items listed in Section 3 which have yet to be prepared, reviewed or received by a principal or a broker.

3.1 *Lead-based paint*: If the residence was constructed before 1978, **check** the box(es) indicating the principals and agents who have not yet prepared, reviewed or received the disclosure. [See **first tuesday** Form 313]

Editor's note — If the buyer does not receive the disclosure before his offer is submitted, he may cancel and renegotiate the purchase agreement. [40 Code of Federal Regulations §745.107]

3.2 *Condition of Property (TDS)*: If this disclosure has not yet been given to the buyer, **check** the box(es) indicating the principals or agents who have not yet prepared, reviewed or received the disclosure. [See **first tuesday** Form 304]

Editor's note — If the buyer does not receive this disclosure before his offer is accepted, he may cancel the purchase agreement at any time prior to three days after delivery in person of the disclosure or five days after delivery by deposit in the mail. [CC §1102.3]

a. *Environmental Hazards Booklet*: If this booklet has not yet been given to the buyer, **check** the box calling for the buyer's receipt.

Editor's note — The seller and listing agent must disclose in the Condition of Property Statement any environmental hazards known to them to exist on the property. However, delivery of the booklet eliminates any affirmative duty of the seller or listing agent, but not the buyer's agent, to give additional information on environmental hazards. [CC §2079.7]

b. *Home Energy Booklet*: If this booklet has not yet been given to the buyer, **check** the box(es) indicating the principals who have not yet prepared, reviewed or received the disclosure.

Editor's note — The seller and agents must disclose in the Condition of Property Statement any home energy programs known to them which might affect the property. However, delivery of the booklet to the buyer eliminates any affirmative duty of the seller or agents to give additional energy rating information. [CC §2079.10]

3.3 *Natural Hazard Disclosure Statement*: If this disclosure has not yet been given to the buyer, **check** the box(es) indicating the principals or agents who have not yet prepared, reviewed or received the disclosure.

Editor's note — If the buyer does not receive this disclosure before his offer is submitted, he may cancel the purchase agreement at any time prior to three days after delivery in person of the disclosure or five days after delivery by deposit in the mail. [CC §1103.2]

a. *Homeowner's Earthquake Safety Guide*: If the guide has not been given to the buyer, **check** the box(es) indicating the principals or agent who have not yet prepared, reviewed or received the disclosure.

Editor's note — The seller and agent must disclose in the Natural Hazard Disclosure Statement any earthquake hazards known to them which affect the property. Delivery of the guide to the buyer eliminates any duty of the seller or listing agent, but not of the buyer's agent, to provide additional earthquake information. [CC §2079.8]

b. *Commercial Earthquake Safety Guide*: If this guide has not been given to the buyer on the purchase of an unreinforced masonry residence consisting of a woodframe roof or floors,

check the box(es) indicating the principals or agents who have not yet prepared, reviewed or received the guide.

Editor's note — The seller and listing agent must disclose in the Natural Hazard Disclosure Statement any earthquake hazards known to them which might affect the (masonry) property. Delivery of the guide eliminates any duty of the seller or listing agent to provide additional earthquake information. [CC §2079.9]

3.4 *Mello-Roos bond*: If the property is subject to a Mello-Roos bonded assessment lien and the buyer has not been given a Notice of Special Taxes issued by the assessment district, **enter** the name of the district and **check** the box calling for the buyer's receipt of the notice.

Editor's note — The seller and listing agent must disclose in the purchase agreement, as the assumption of bonded indebtedness (or tax obligations), any Mello-Roos liens known to them.

3.5 *Ordnance location*: If the buyer has not been given a written notice of the location of any "former federal or state ordnance locations" within one mile of the property that may contain potentially explosive munitions, **check** the box(es) indicating the principals who have not yet prepared or received the notice. [CC §1102.15]

3.6 *Industrial use or zoning*: If the buyer has not been given a written notice of surrounding industrial use which "affects" the property or the industrial zoning of the property purchased, **check** the box(es) indicating the principals who have not yet prepared or received the notice. [CC §1102.17]

3.7 *Tax withholding disclosure*: If the buyer and seller have not given each other their federal residency declarations for the seller's exemption, and the buyer has not been given the seller's Federal Tax Board's (FTB's) real estate withholding certificate exempting the buyer from tax withholding (from the seller's funds through escrow), **check** the box(es) indicating the principals who have not yet prepared or received the declarations and certificates. [Internal Revenue Code §1445; Rev & T C §18662]

3.8 *Homeowners' association (HOA) documentation*: If a common interest development (CID) or condominium is being acquired and the buyer has not been given copies of all the mandated disclosures, statements and documents, **check** the box(es) indicating the principals who have not yet prepared, delivered or received the documents and **circle** the items not yet delivered. [CC §1368]

3.9 *Seller carryback financing:* If the buyer or seller have not been given a carryback disclosure statement prepared by the agent who obtained the buyer's offer, **check** the box(es) indicating the principals and agents who have not yet prepared, reviewed or received the agent's disclosures. [CC §2956]

3.10 *Estimated closing statement*: If the buyer or seller wants to or should review an estimate of the closing debits and credits prior to closing to confirm their financial expectations on the purchase agreement, **check** the box(es) indicating the principals who have to approve the statement prior to closing.

3.11 *Local option disclosures*: If local ordinances or conditions surrounding the property require additional information to be provided to the buyer by the seller or the agents, and the disclosures have not been made, **check** the box(es) indicating the principals and agents who have not yet prepared, reviewed or received the disclosures. [See **first tuesday** Form 307]

3.12 *Property operating data*: If the seller is to disclose the operating costs incurred in the ownership of the property, **check** the box(es) indicating the principals who have not yet prepared or received the disclosure.

4. **Seller compliance**: This section lists the conditions to be satisfied, approved or waived by the seller prior to closing. **Check** the box(es) indicating each activity to be performed by the seller before escrow can close.

Editor's note — The seller is required to install or make operable smoke detectors on the sale of the property. [Calif. Health and Safety Code §13113.8]

Also, the water heater must be strapped, braced or anchored on the sale of the property. [Health & S C §19211]

5. **Buyer compliance**: This section lists the conditions to be performed, approved or waived by the buyer prior to closing. **Check** the box(es) indicating each activity the buyer must perform or approve before escrow can close.

6. **Prorates and adjustments**: This section **accounts** for the debits and credits called for in the purchase agreement to be made by escrow on closing.

6.1 *Impound account*: If the existing loan on the property is being as-

sumed by the buyer or taken over "subject to," **check** the box which conforms to the purchase agreement.

6.2 *Prorates*: **Check** the box to indicate the date for making miscellaneous prorates and adjustments — usually the date scheduled for "close of escrow", but if not, **enter** a date — and **check** the box(es) indicating each item to be accounted for by escrow.

7. **Title policy information**: This section **addresses** the vestings and title policy on the transfer of the property.

7.1 *Seller's vesting*: **Enter** the current vesting for the seller. Alternatively, provide escrow with a copy of the recorded conveyance transferring title to the seller. The deed is part of a "title profile" report prepared by a title company without charge.

7.2 *Buyer's vesting*: **Enter** the name(s) of the buyer(s) as they are to appear of record on acquisition. **Check** the box to indicate the type of vesting.

Editor's note — The purchase agreement allows the buyer to assign the purchase rights to a substitute buyer, in which case the name and vesting should reflect the assignee's preferences.

7.3 *Title company*: **Enter** the name of the title company who is to insure the conveyance.

7.4 *Title policy*: **Check** the box(es) to indicate the type of policy to be issued to the buyer, carryback seller or new lender, and **enter** who is to pay the premium.

8. **Brokerage fee**: **Check** the box to indicate whether the disbursement provisions

for the brokerage fees are to be located in the mutual instructions signed by all principals or in a supplemental instruction signed only by the principal who is paying the fees. **Enter** the amount of the fee paid to each broker involved, and who is to pay the fee.

Preparer:

Enter the name of the agent who prepared this worksheet and date it.

Use of the escrow instructions

The sales escrow instructions, **first tuesday** Form 401, contains all the typical provisions expected in a set of instructions prepared by an independent escrow company for a sales transaction.

The instructions may be used as an addendum to the purchase agreement for the sales transaction. Both the escrow instructions and the purchase agreement are to be prepared by the agent and signed by each party at the same time. Thus, the need to dictate instructions to the escrow officer and wait for it to be prepared before it can be submitted to the seller and buyer for signatures is avoided. [See Form 401 accompanying this chapter]

Preparing the sales escrow instructions

The following instructions are for the preparation and use of the sales escrow instructions, **first tuesday** Form 401. Form 401 is designed so it can be prepared by an escrow officer, the buyer or the broker or agent who negotiated the sales transaction.

Each instruction corresponds to the provision in the form bearing the same number.

Identification:

Enter the escrow number and the date the instructions are prepared. The date and escrow number are used when referring to this document.

Enter the name of the escrow company, the escrow's licensing agency, its license number, the escrow officer, the address of the escrow company and the escrow officer's phone and fax numbers.

Enter the name of each buyer and each seller.

Terms of Sale:

Enter the price to be paid by the buyer as the total consideration the seller is to receive.

Enter the terms for payment of the price, i.e., the assessment bond balance, the trust deeds of record to be taken over by the buyer, the trust deeds to be recorded by the buyer to assist in funding the price, and the cash or other consideration paid as a down payment on the price by the buyer.

Editor's note — The terms of sale entered here are general and for the escrow's use only to reference the financing of the price. The specific terms of the price and conditions for its payment follow.

1. **Instructions to Escrow**:

   1.1 **Enter** the dollar amount of the buyer's deposit accompanying the purchase agreement offer and handed to escrow.

   1.2 **Enter** the closing date set for the buyer to make any additional deposit agreed to in the purchase agreement, the dollar amount of the deposit and the total deposit escrow is to receive (prior to requesting any further funds needed for closing).

   1.3 **Obligates** the buyer to deliver funds and instructions required by escrow to close.

   1.4 **Authorizes** escrow to close any time after the date set for the buyer to fully perform, unless instructions have been received to the contrary.

Escrow number: _____ Dated:_____, 20_____

Escrow/brokerage company: _____

Licensed by the Department of _____, State of California, license # _____

Escrow officer: _____

Address: _____

_____

Phone number:_____ Fax: _____

Buyer:_____

Seller: _____

TERMS OF SALE: (for escrow use only)

$_____	Total Consideration Seller to receive from Buyer
$_____	Assessment Bond paid with property taxes
$_____	1st Trust Deed of Record
$_____	2nd Trust Deed of Record
$_____	Trust Deed to record
$_____	Trust Deed to record
$_____	Cash through Escrow
$_____	Other Consideration

Items left blank or unchecked are not applicable.

1. **You, the escrow officer, are authorized and instructed as follows:**

    1.1 Buyer deposits herewith the sum of $_____.

    1.2 On or before _____, 20_____, the date set for closing, Buyer will deposit with You on Your request the additional sum of $_____, to make a total deposit of $_____.

    1.3 Buyer will deliver to You prior to the date set for closing any additional funds and instruments required which You request.

    1.4 You may thereafter use these funds and instruments until such time as You have received written instruction not to do so. Brokers are authorized to extend any performance date up to one month.

    1.5 Close of escrow is the date instruments are recorded.

2. Upon the use of these funds and instruments, You are to obtain the following policy of title insurance, with the usual title company exceptions, in the following checked type and form:

    Title to be vested in Buyer or Assignee free of encumbrances other than those set forth herein. Buyer's interest in title to be insured under an ALTA form policy issued by _____ as a(n) ☐ Homeowner(s) policy (one-to-four units), ☐ Residential ALTA-R policy (vacant or improved residential parcel), ☐ Owner's policy (other than one-to-four units), ☐ Joint Protection policy (also naming the Carryback Seller or Purchase-assist Lender), or ☐ Binder (to insure resale or refinance within two years).
    Endorsements: _____

    _____

    2.1 With title insurance in the amount of $_____ covering the following described real property, commonly known as:_____
    and legally described as: _____

    _____

    _____

    _____

    2.2 Showing title vested in:_____

    2.3 Subject to the following only:

    a. All General and Special taxes for the _____ fiscal year, including any special district taxes or personal property taxes collected with the ad valorem taxes.

    b. Assessments and Bonds with an unpaid balance of $_____

c. Any covenants, conditions, restrictions, reservations, rights, right of ways and easements of record, or in deed to record, and EXCEPTIONS of water, minerals, oil, gas, and kindred substances, on or under said real property, now of record, or in deed to record.

d. First encumbrance now of record with an unpaid balance of $_____, payable $_____ monthly, including interest of _____% per annum. ☐ ARM

e. Second encumbrance now of record with an unpaid balance of $_____, payable $_____ monthly, including interest of _____% per annum, all due and payable _____, 20_____.

f. Deed of Trust to record in the amount of $_____.
Execution of loan documents under §2.3f or §2.3g shall be Buyer's approval of their terms. Should Seller carryback under §2.3h, You are to obtain Seller's written approval of the loan terms for any Deed of Trust to record.

g. Deed of Trust to record in the amount of $_____.

h. Purchase money Deed of Trust with Assignment of Rents on standard form, executed by Buyer securing a note for $_____ in favor of Seller as their interests appear on the preliminary title report, with interest at _____% per annum from close of escrow, principal and interest payable in installments of $_____, or more, each on the same day of every calendar month, beginning one month from ☐ close of escrow, or ☐ _____, 20_____, and continuing until _____.

You, as escrow holder, are instructed to prepare the note and deed of trust and insert the correct principal amount and correct first payment date, interest accrual date and due date as soon as they can be determined. The address for deliver of note payments is: _____

3. You are to obtain at Seller's expense beneficiary statements on the Deeds of Trust (or mortgage) now of record (§2.3d and §2.3e above). If the principal balances shown by the statements are more or less than the amount shown above, You are to make adjustments as checked below:

☐ cash through escrow; ☐ total consideration; ☐ purchase-money Deed of Trust.

3.1 You are to deliver to Buyer for Buyer's approval prior to close of escrow a copy of the beneficiary statement for each Deed of Trust to remain of record on closing.

3.2 You are to deliver to Seller prior to close of escrow, any payoff demand necessary to eliminate encumbrances so you can comply with conditions in §2.3 for title insurance.

4. You are to obtain at Seller's expense a UCC-3 clearance on the following described personal property:
_____
_____
_____

and cause title thereto to be vested in Buyer subject to the following UCC-1 financing statements:

a. A UCC-1 obligation in the approximate amount of $_____, payable $_____ per month, including an annual percentage rate of _____%, all due and payable _____, 20_____.

b A UCC-1 form in favor of Seller at Buyer's expense as additional security for any note carried back under §2.3h above.

5. Prior to close of escrow, Buyer is to hand You a sufficient hazard insurance policy. In the event Seller carries back under §2.3h above, then Seller is to be named as additional loss payee. The policy is to be in an amount sufficient to cover all lien balances or the coverage demanded by the new lender if greater in amount.

6. ☐ Prior to the close of escrow and at Seller's expense, Seller to hand You a structural pest control clearance on the subject property.

7. ☐ Prior to close of escrow and at Seller's expense, You are to obtain a one-year policy of homeowner's warranty issued by _____, in favor of Buyer, covering _____.

8. Prior to the close of escrow and at Seller's expense, You are to obtain from the homeowners' association of any common interest development which includes the described property the following checked items for Buyer's approval:

8.1 ☐ A statement of condition of assessments;

8.2 ☐ Copies of the association's articles, bylaws, CC&Rs, collection and lien enforcement policies, operating budget, operating rules, CPA's financial review, insurance policy summary and any age restriction statement;

8.3 ☐ Copies from the association of any notice to Seller of CC&R violations, any list of construction defects, and any assessment charges not yet payable.

9. ☐ You are authorized and instructed to prepare assignments for all existing lease/rental agreements.

10. The following checked prorations and adjustments shall be computed by You on a monthly basis of 30 days as of ☐ close of escrow, or ☐ _____, 20_____, on which date Buyer is to be treated as the owner for the entire day:

    a. ☐ Taxes, based on latest tax statement available and Seller warrants that no reassessment or reassessment activity has since occurred

    b. ☐ Hazard (fire) insurance premium

    c. ☐ Interest on existing note(s) and Deed(s) of Trust

    d. ☐ Rents and deposits based on rental statement handed to You and approved by Buyer and Seller prior to close of escrow

    e. ☐ Impounds, under §2.3d or §2.3e above, together with an assignment of these impounds to Buyer through escrow

    f. ☐ Association assessments for any common interest development which includes the property

    g. ☐ Other:_____

    10.1 You are to account for the above prorations and adjustments into the item checked below:
    ☐ cash through escrow; ☐ total consideration; ☐ purchase money trust deed.

11. You are to promptly obtain and hand Buyer a preliminary title report on the property from title company for Buyer's approval or disapproval and cancellation of this transaction within _____ days of receipt by Buyer or Buyer's Broker of the report.

12. The grant deed to state the tax statements are to be mailed to:_____

_____

    at _____.

13. Escrow is herewith handed a purchase agreement dated _____, 20_____ and (a) counteroffer(s) dated _____, 20_____ and _____, 20_____, entered into by Buyer and Seller regarding the sale of the property which authorizes and instructs escrow to act on the provisions of the agreement as mutual escrow instructions to close this transaction.

    13.1 Any inconsistencies between the provisions in the purchase agreement and provisions in the instructions prepared by escrow shall be controlled by the instructions prepared by escrow.

14. The close of escrow and disbursement of funds can be affected based on the form of the deposit with escrow. Funds deposited in cash or by electronic payment allow for closing and disbursement on or after the business day of deposit with the escrow's financial institution. Funds deposited by cashier's check allow for closing and disbursement on or after two business days after deposit with the escrow's financial institution. All other forms of deposit cannot be disbursed and thus, the closing cannot occur until the funds are made available to escrow by the escrow's financial institution.

15. Buyer is required to withhold 10% of each Seller's share of the sales price for payment of Seller's federal income taxes on this transaction, unless Seller meets one of the following conditions:

    15.1 Each Seller provides Buyer with their taxpayer identification number and declares under penalty of perjury to be a citizen of the United States or a resident alien [**first tuesday** Form 301];

    15.2 Buyer declares under penalty of perjury the property will be used as their residence and the sales price is $300,000 or less [**ft** Form 301]; or

    15.3 Seller requests and obtains a withholding certificate from the Internal Revenue Service (IRS) authorizing a reduced amount or no amount be withheld.

16. Buyer is required to withhold 3⅓% of each Seller's share of the sales price for payment of Seller's California income taxes on this transaction, unless one of the following exemptions exists:

    16.1 Seller executes a real estate withholding certificate, FTB form 593-C, declaring the sale is exempt due to:

        a. The property sold is or was last used as Seller's principal residence;

        b. The property sold was the decedent's principal residence;

        c. The property was sold as part of an IRC §1031 exchange;

        d. The property was taken by involuntary conversion and will be replaced under IRC §1033;

        e. The property was sold at a taxable loss.

    16.2 Buyer is also exempt from withholding 3⅓% of Seller's share of the sales price if:

        a. The property was sold for less than $100,000;

        b. Buyer is acquiring the property by a deed-in-lieu of foreclosure;

        c. Seller is a bank acting as a trustee under an agreement other than a deed of trust.

    16.3 On an installment sale, Buyer may agree to withhold on each payment on the carryback note and thus defer withholding. [FTB Forms 593-I and 597]

17. In the event You become involved in litigation between Buyer and Seller arising out of this transaction, Buyer and Seller shall pay a reasonable fee for attorney services which You may be required to incur.

18. You are authorized to use Seller's instruments when You hold and can deliver to Seller the money and instruments to be delivered to Seller under these instructions.

    18.1 You are authorized to pay and charge Seller for the following checked items:

        a. ☐ Bonds, assessments, taxes and other liens of record to show title as called for.

        b. ☐ Documentary transfer taxes as required.

        c. ☐ Brokerage fees: $_____ to _____
                                    $_____ to _____
                                    $_____ to _____

        d. ☐ Transaction coordinator's fees: _____
                                    $_____ to _____
                                    $_____ to _____

        e. ☐ Title insurance premium on the policy to be issued to Buyer.

        f. ☐ Costs of recording Seller's Grant Deed.

        g. ☐ Escrow fees for your services and any charges incurred by escrow on Seller's behalf.

        h. ☐ Payables submitted to escrow for payment by Seller or Seller's agent.

        i. ☐ Attorney fees: $_____ to _____

        j. ☐ _____

19. You are authorized to pay and charge Buyer for the following checked items:

        a. ☐ Escrow fees for your services and any charges incurred by escrow on Buyer's behalf.

        b. ☐ Costs of and lender's charges for recording or assuming any Deed of Trust, including a policy of title insurance for any new lender.

        c. ☐ Attorney fees: $_____ to _____

        d. ☐ Brokerage fees: $_____ to _____

        e. ☐ Title insurance premium on the policy to be issued to Buyer.

        f. ☐ _____

20. _____

_____

_____

_____

_____

_____

_____

_____

_____

I hereby agree to perform all acts called for above to be performed by Seller.	I hereby agree to perform all acts called for above to be performed by Buyer.
Date:_____, 20_____	Date:_____, 20_____
Seller: _____	Buyer: _____
Seller: _____	Buyer: _____
Signature: _____	Signature: _____
Signature: _____	Signature: _____
Address: _____	Address: _____
_____	_____
Phone: _____	Phone: _____
Fax: _____	Fax: _____
Email:_____	Email:_____

FORM 401   02-05   ©2006 **first tuesday**, P.O. BOX 20069, RIVERSIDE, CA 92516 (800) 794-0494

1.5 **States** escrow is considered closed on the date the instruments are recorded.

2. **Title conditions**: **Enter** the name of the title insurance company agreed to in the purchase agreement to issue the buyer's title insurance policy. **Check** the appropriate box to indicate the type of title policy to be issued. **Enter** any endorsements to be issued with the policy.

2.1 *Coverage*: **Enter** as the dollar amount of title insurance coverage the total dollar amount of consideration the buyer is paying for the property. **Enter** the common address and the legal description for the property.

2.2 *Vesting*: **Enter** the names of the individuals or entities who will be taking title, the type of vesting and the percentages of ownership, if applicable.

2.3 *Title insurance*: **Authorizes** title insurance is to be issued reflecting the following title conditions.

a. **Enter** the fiscal year for any taxes assumed by the buyer.

b. **Enter** the dollar amount of any specific assessment bonds to be assumed by the buyer.

c. **States** title is to be subject to covenants, conditions and restrictions (CC&Rs) of record.

d. **Enter** the dollar amount of any first trust deed of record to be assumed by the buyer, its monthly payment and the rate of interest on the note. **Check** the box to indicate whether the interest is adjustable (ARM).

e. **Enter** the dollar amount of any second trust deed of record to be assumed by the buyer, its monthly payment, the rate of interest on the note and any due date.

f. **Enter** the dollar amount of any first trust deed loan to be recorded by the buyer.

g. **Enter** the dollar amount of any second trust deed loan to be recorded by the buyer.

h. **Enter** the dollar amount of any note and trust deed to be executed by the buyer in favor of the seller, the note's interest rate, the amount of the monthly installments, the date for payment of the first installment and the date the note is due. **Enter** the address to which the buyer is to send the installments.

3. *Beneficiary statement*: **Check** the appropriate box to indicate whether adjustments on any loan assumption for differences in the loan balance between the amounts stated in the purchase agreement and the beneficiary statements are to be made into cash, price or the carryback trust deed.

3.1 **Authorizes** the buyer's further-approval of the beneficiary statement. A buyer assuming the loan needs to confirm the loan conditions before closing.

3.2 **Requires** escrow to submit any lender demand for payoff of an existing loan to the seller. The seller needs to review the demand for accuracy.

4. *Personal property lien*: **Enter** the description of any personal property being transferred to the buyer. Escrow is to obtain a title clearance on the personal property.

a. **Enter** the dollar amount of any note to be assumed by the buyer that is secured by a UCC-1 financial statement on personal property to be transferred to the buyer, the amount of monthly installments, the note's interest rate and the due date.

b. **States** any carryback trust deed note to be executed by the buyer in favor of the seller is to be additionally secured by any personal property to be transferred to the buyer.

5. *Hazard insurance policy*: **Requires** the buyer to provide coverage for the property transferred.

6. *Pest control clearance*: **Check** the box to indicate whether the seller is to provide a structural pest control clearance on the property prior to closing.

7. *Home warranty policy*: **Check** the box to indicate whether the seller is to provide the buyer with a home warranty policy. **Enter** the name of the insurance company issuing the policy and the coverage agreed to in the purchase agreement.

8. *Homeowners' association (HOA) documents*:

   8.1 **Check** the box to indicate whether the buyer is to further approve a statement of condition of assessments from any HOA involved.

   8.2 **Check** the box to indicate whether the buyer is to further approve the documents listed and to be obtained from any HOA involved.

   8.3 **Check** the box to indicate whether the buyer is to further approve any HOA Notice of Violation by the seller, construction defects and any charges in assessments not yet payable.

9. *Tenant leases transferred*: **Check** the box to indicate the existence of tenants and to instruct escrow to prepare assignments of the leases to the buyer.

10. *Prorations and adjustments*: **Check** the box or **enter** the date for escrow to compute adjustments and prorates. **Check** the appropriate box(es) for subparagraphs a. through f. to indicate the prepaid or accrued taxes, premiums, interest, rents/deposits, loan impounds, etc. on obligations taken over by the buyer.

    10.1 **Check** the appropriate box to indicate whether the adjustments and prorates are to be made into the down payment, the price or a carryback note.

11. *Preliminary title report*: **Enter** the number of days after the buyer's receipt of a preliminary title report during which the buyer may approve or disapprove the condition of title.

12. *Mailing address*: **Enter** the name of the buyer(s) and the address of the buyer(s) to which the grant deed is to be mailed.

13. *Purchase agreement instructions*: **Enter** the date of the purchase agreement and any counteroffers entered into by the buyer and seller if the purchase agreement also contains instructions to escrow.

    13.1 *Modification of the purchase agreement*: **Provides** that any inconsistencies between escrow instructions and purchase agreement provisions are to be controlled by the instructions as a modification of the purchase agreement.

14. *Form of deposit*: **Advises** the buyer about the time periods needed after escrow's receipt of various forms of funding before escrow can close.

15. *Federal withholding*: **Discloses** the federal IRS income tax withholding required by the buyer (handled by escrow) on transactions with non-resident, alien sellers who have not obtained an IRS withholding certificate.

16. *California withholding*: **Discloses** the California FTB income tax withholding of the seller's sales proceeds required by the buyer (handled by escrow) on all transactions, unless an exemption exists among those listed in sections 16.1, 16.2 and 16.3.

17. *Attorney fees provision:* **States** escrow is entitled to attorney fees they may incur due to any future litigation between the seller and the buyer.

18. *Authority to close*: **Authorizes** escrow to use the seller's deed when all monies and instruments due the seller as called for in the instructions can be delivered to the seller.

    18.1 **Check** the appropriate box(es) and **enter** the dollar amount(s) and to whom they will be paid for sub-paragraphs a. through j. to indicate whether the items are to be charged to the seller by escrow on closing.

19. *Buyer's charges*: **Check** the appropriate box(es) and **enter** the dollar amount(s) and to whom they will be paid for sub-paragraphs a. through f. to indicate whether the items are to be charged to the buyer by escrow on closing.

20. *Additional provisions*: **Enter** any additional provisions.

Signatures:

Seller's signature: **Enter** the date the seller signs the escrow instructions and each seller's name. **Obtain** each seller's signature on the escrow instructions. **Enter** the seller's name, address, telephone and fax numbers, and email address.

Buyer's signature: **Enter** the date the buyer signs the escrow instructions and each buyer's name. **Obtain** each buyer's signature on the escrow instructions. **Enter** the buyer's name, address, telephone and fax numbers, and email address.

Chapter 58

Funds in a failed escrow

This chapter discusses the return of the buyer's deposit on the failure of escrow to close, the penalties for a bad-faith refusal to permit a refund and the use of an interest-bearing account when funds are not released.

First clear out the deposits

The day before escrow is to close, a buyer hands escrow instructions calling for the return of his entire deposit and the **cancellation of both** the escrow instructions and the purchase agreement. The buyer's cancellation is **not excused**, due to the exercise of a contingency provision, or **justified** due to a misrepresentation of facts or the failure of an agency. Thus, the buyer's instructions constitute a *breach* of the purchase agreement with the seller (and, for the agents, a wrongful interference with payment of their fees).

A copy of the cancellation instructions is forwarded to the seller to sign and return to escrow. No funds will be released from escrow without mutual, conforming instructions from both the buyer and seller.

However, the seller is unwilling to sign the instructions. The seller believes he is entitled to the buyer's deposit and wants the funds released to him:

- as compensation for the time, effort and resale opportunities he has lost;

- in exchange for his consent to a cancellation of the purchase agreement; and

- as provided by the liquidated damages provision agreed to in the purchase agreement for forfeiture.

The listing agent, not wishing to spend time on a dead deal, redirects his energies to locating a prospective buyer for the property. However, the lack of a cancellation of an outstanding sales transaction on the property looms as a potential problem should the buyer who cancelled decide to pursue acquisition of the property or otherwise interfere with title to the property.

The seller is adamant about enforcing the purchase agreement's liquidated damages provision which states he is entitled to the entire deposit now held in escrow. However, the listing agent informs the seller the liquidate damages provision is applicable only if the buyer **voluntarily releases** the deposit to the seller. If the buyer is unwilling to release the funds to the seller, the seller is entitled to the funds only to the extent necessary to reimburse the seller for **actual money losses** he has incurred and any decline in property value he has experienced prior to cancellation of escrow.

A quick review with the seller demonstrates that the seller has not incurred any money losses as a result of the buyer's breach of the purchase agreement. The expenditures he has made to ready the property for closing will be fully recovered on a resale of the property to another buyer. Further, the property value now equals or exceeds the price the buyer agreed to pay since property values have not yet fallen.

When the buyer makes a claim for the release of his deposit, the buyer implicitly challenges the seller's right to the deposit under the liquidated damages provision. It then becomes incumbent upon the seller to "prove up" his *out-of-pocket money losses* brought about by the buyer's failure to complete the transaction if the seller is to recover any money. Here, the seller will be unable to provide proof of money losses as he has none.

The listing agent further informs the seller he could become liable to the buyer for a *money penalty* of up to $1,000, in addition to the deposit, if he wrongfully interferes with the return of the buyer's good-faith deposit for a period beyond 30 days after the buyer demands its return since the property involved is a one-to-four unit residential property. [Calif. Civil Code §1057.3(b)(2)]

The release-of-deposit scheme

The sale of property containing one-to-four residential units is subject to numerous legislative schemes intended to limit or enlarge the existing contract rights of the respective parties and to alleviate burdens which regularly arise in real estate transactions and need a uniform procedure for their resolution.

One set of rights and burdens has as its subject matter the troublesome nature of failed real estate sales escrows which hold funds. When a buyer and seller cannot agree on a mutually acceptable disbursement of the funds on the cancellation of escrow, escrow cannot close out its trust account and avoid further responsibility to account for the funds.

The failed escrow scheme sets up a **deadline** for the buyer and seller, or their agents, to work out an acceptable disbursement. If the deadline is not met with a release of funds and the cancellation of escrow, a monetary penalty (and attorney fees) is imposed on the seller or buyer who interfered with the release and did not have a good-faith, reasonable legal basis for making a claim on the funds.

Also, the scheme clarifies the right of the buyer and seller to cancel escrow instructions without losing any rights to pursue claims they may have against one another under the purchase agreement which remains uncancelled.

Consider a sales escrow which does not close on the date scheduled for closing. The purchase funds of the buyer are on deposit with escrow. A demand is made on escrow by the buyer for a return of the deposit, followed by a demand on the funds by the seller.

Within a period of 30 days after the first demand received by escrow for the funds, the buyer and seller are obligated to determine who is entitled to the funds and hand escrow **cancellation and release of funds** instructions which will clear the deposits out of escrow. If they fail to do so, the person entitled to the funds is to be awarded a penalty and attorney fees for enforcing his right to receive the funds.

As in any transaction which has failed to close, the person entitled to the funds may file a lawsuit to enforce a refund or release of the deposit and the payment of a bad-faith penalty of not more than $1,000. When litigation exists on the transaction, escrow deposits all funds held in the escrow account with the court, less escrow cancellation charges. The deposit by escrow with the court terminates any further responsibility of escrow to account for the funds. On conclusion of the lawsuit, the prevailing party is entitled to attorney fees — and the funds.

Good-faith dispute

Consent by a seller to a return of the buyer's deposit is not required if a legitimate, good-faith dispute exists over the seller's entitlement to the funds. Neither the buyer nor the seller will be entitled to the penalty or statutory attorney fees on court resolution of a *good-faith dispute*. The good-faith standard for an individual's refusal to release escrowed funds requires a **reasonable belief honestly held** by the individual about his right to the funds. [CC §1057.3(f)(2)]

For example, a seller of any type of real estate cannot reasonably believe he is entitled to the buyer's deposit when a mere cursory review of the liquidated damages forfeiture codes indicates he has no right to compensation. The liquidated damages codes apply in spite of forfeiture wording in the purchase agreement to the contrary. Unless the seller has **actually sus-**

tained out-of-pocket money losses on transaction-related expenditures or experienced a decline in the property's value by the date of the buyer's breach, he is making a demand without legal basis. [CC §§1671 et seq.]

It is important for a seller to understand that a buyer who breaches the purchase agreement is entitled to a refund of his entire good-faith deposit, undiminished, so long as no money losses are incurred by the seller. Conversely, the seller who refuses to release the buyer's deposit based solely on the fact the buyer breached, has himself failed to act in good faith.

Thus, a seller's unjustified adverse and hostile reaction to a buyer's breach subjects the seller to the civil money penalty and attorney fees for not instructing escrow to refund the buyer's deposits, after first deducting and reimbursing the seller for his out-of-pocket money losses incurred on the failed transaction which will not be recovered on a resale of the property.

The seller's recovery

Consider a seller who **incurs money losses** due to a buyer's breach of their purchase agreement. Money losses include lost rent, a decline in the property's value, transactional expenses and other expenditures directly related to the transaction which will go uncompensated (on a resale or retention of the property) if the buyer does not close escrow.

On the buyer's breach, the seller sends escrow instructions authorizing escrow to release to the seller a portion of the buyer's deposit equal in amount to the seller's out-of-pocket money losses. Any funds remaining after escrow deducts its cancellation charges are to be returned to the buyer.

The seller promptly provides the breaching buyer with an **itemized accounting** of his money losses incurred in the transaction prior to the breach. The buyer is requested to sign

the disbursement instructions which includes a cancellation of escrow, but not a cancellation of the purchase agreement.

The buyer refuses to sign the instructions due to the reduction in the amount refunded. Instead, the buyer demands the seller sign conflicting instructions releasing the entire deposit to the buyer and calling for cancellation of both escrow and the purchase agreement.

More than 30 days after the seller instructed escrow to disburse the buyer's funds, the seller makes a demand on the buyer for his losses and files a money action for:

- the release of the portion of the deposit necessary to reimburse the seller for his itemized money losses;

- a civil penalty of up to $1,000 against the buyer for wrongfully interfering with the release of funds; and

- attorney fees incurred in the action to recover the funds. [CC §1057.3(b)]

However, the buyer defends his conduct, claiming neither the penalty nor the attorney fees can be awarded since a **good-faith dispute** exists over the seller's entitlement to the funds.

The seller claims the buyer acted in bad-faith since the seller provided complete documentation of his losses and sought the release of only the amount of his losses.

Is the seller entitled to the penalty and attorney fees under the escrow refund statute?

Yes! The buyer's (unreasonable) belief that he is entitled to a full refund of his deposit was entirely without legal foundation. Thus, the buyer's demand for a full refund was **unreasonable**.

Here, the buyer received itemized documentation of the seller's uncompensated losses stemming solely from the buyer's breach, neither of which were in dispute. The seller's performance under the purchase agreement alone necessitated the transactional expenditures the seller now seeks to recover. Thus, the buyer acted in bad faith for lack of an *honestly held belief* about his entitlement to a full refund and cannot avoid liability for the penalty and the seller's attorney fees.

However, the seller **must document his money losses** should the buyer challenge a forfeiture of his funds before the buyer can be reasonably expected to agree to release compensating funds to the seller. If the seller does not provide documentation of his actual money losses, the buyer will likely escape penalties and attorney fees by claiming he acted in good faith when he disputed the release of the funds demanded by the seller.

The purchase agreement remains (but the escrow file is closed)

The primary purpose of the release-of-funds statute is to distance escrow from buyer-seller disputes over funds held in escrow.

The cancellation of escrow and the release of funds **do not cancel the underlying purchase agreement** or alter the rights of either party to litigate any past or future performance of the purchase agreement since the purchase agreement is not the subject of the cancellation instructions. [CC §1057.3(e)]

For example, a buyer's cancellation of escrow due to the seller's nonperformance does not affect the buyer's right to pursue specific performance of the purchase agreement since the purchase agreement remains in effect, unless it too is cancelled. Also, if the funds are withheld by escrow due to a wrongful claim on them by the seller, a *purchaser's lien* on the property is available to the buyer. The lien can be foreclosed to collect the funds withheld. [CC §§3050; 3375 et seq.]

However, the seller, and (especially) his listing broker, do not want the property tied up by a buyer during an on-going attempt to recover funds in a lawsuit.

A listing agent's best advice to his seller is for the seller to consider *rescinding* the underlying purchase agreement at the same time escrow is cancelled — a moment when the buyer is most apt to rescind the entire transaction in exchange for the release of his funds.

The incentive for the seller and his agent to rescind the purchase agreement is to eliminate any claims the dissatisfied buyer may later attempt to advance against the seller, the property or the agent. On eliminating the buyer's claims, the agent is free to move on to the ultimate objective of locating a prospective buyer who is ready, willing and able to purchase the property.

In a declining real estate market, a seller's losses will include the difference between the price agreed to by the buyer and the lower value of the property at the time of the buyer's breach. This amount could easily exceed the amount of the escrow deposit. The seller may want to consider retaining the purchase agreement uncancelled to go after the buyer for losses caused by the buyer's breach.

Finally, a buyer's cancellation of escrow and the release of the escrow deposit to the seller without also entering into a mutual cancellation of the purchase agreement leaves intact the seller's right to enforce specific performance of the sale or the collection of the remainder of his losses (money and any price-to-value decline) brought about by the buyer's breach. [CC §1057.3(e)]

An interest-bearing account offsets losses

Consider a buyer and seller who enter into a purchase agreement regarding property other than one-to-four residential units. The escrow instructions state the buyer's deposit will be placed in a non-interest-bearing trust account.

While in escrow, the buyer and seller get into a dispute and the seller cancels escrow. The buyer makes a demand on the seller to close escrow, which is rejected. The buyer files an action for specific performance of the purchase agreement seeking to acquire ownership of the property.

In the meantime, the funds on deposit in escrow will remain unproductive in the non-interest-bearing trust account or on deposit with the court.

Can the buyer and seller avoid losing interest on deposits held by escrow when a dispute arises and the funds are not released?

Yes! The buyer and seller can agree and instruct escrow to deposit the funds into an interest-bearing account. [10 Calif. Code of Regulations §1737(b)]

The interest-bearing trust account allows escrowed funds to realize their earning power in a savings account instead of allowing the funds to remain dormant during the extended escrow period. The consent of both the seller and buyer is needed to authorize the placement of the funds into an interest-bearing account.

Further, without mutual instructions from the buyer and seller, the escrow agent has no duty to redeposit the funds into interest-bearing accounts. An escrow holder is a *limited agent* who follows instructions, not a trustee with discretionary authority to act. [**Hannon** v. **Western Title Insurance Company** (1989) 211 CA3d 1122]

On occasion, a buyer or seller may refuse to reach an agreement to place the deposit in an interest-bearing account. However, the party entitled to the funds is then also entitled to interest on the funds from the party who wrongfully refuses to allow the funds to be released, or who refuses to authorize placement of the funds in an the interest-bearing account.

SECTION H

Taxes

Chapter 59

Tax aspects advisory

This chapter clarifies the extent of an agent's duty to inform his client about the tax aspects of a proposed real estate transaction.

Disclosure of known consequences

Consider an owner of an income-producing parcel of improved real estate who intends to hire a brokerage office to market his property and locate a buyer. The owner interviews a few brokers and sales agents to determine who he will employ to list the property for sale.

The owner's primary concern is to hire an agent who is most likely to produce a prospective buyer who will purchase the property. Thus, the owner's interviews include an inquiry into:

- the contents of the listing package the agent will prepare to market the property;

- the scope of the advertising the agent will provide to locate prospective buyers; and

- the professional relationship the agent has with other brokers, agents and property owners.

One agent interviewed by the owner inquires about the owner's intended use of the proceeds from the sale. The owner indicates he would like to reinvest the funds in developable land, to hold for profit on a later resale to a subdivider or builder. On further inquiry, the owner provides the agent with data on the price he paid for his property, the debt now encumbering the property and his depreciated cost basis remaining in the property. These three key pieces of data are needed for an agent to assist the owner in his tax planning for a sale.

The agent does some quick math (sales price minus basis equals profit) to approximate the amount of profit the owner will realize on a sale. He immediately determines the owner

would pay profit taxes at *recapture* (25%) and *long-term* (15%) rates that will equal nearly one fifth of his net proceeds from a sale (plus one twelfth for state taxes). The owner is informed of the agent's initial opinion about the owner's tax liability on a sale.

The agent then informs the owner he can **avoid reporting his profit** and paying income taxes on the sale by buying the land he would like to acquire now. Thus, the sale of his income property and his purchase of land can be linked together to form a **continuing investment** in real estate.

Also, the agent informs the owner that the purchase agreements entered into for the sale of the income property and the purchase of the land should contain **contingency provisions** conditioning the closing of the sale on the owner's purchase of other property.

So as not to mislead the owner about the extent of the agent's experience handling §1031 reinvestment plans for clients, the agent informs the owner he has not personally handled a §1031 transaction. However, he lets the owner know he has taken courses on §1031 transactions and has discussed §1031 funding procedures with brokers and escrow officers who do have experience handling §1031 reinvestments.

The agent tells the owner he believes he can properly market the property and locate suitable land for the owner's reinvestment, as well as follow up on procedures for §1031 tax avoidance should the property be listed with his broker.

Conversely, another agent contacted by the owner is reticent about becoming involved in a review of the tax aspects of selling property.

This agent hands the owner a written statement attached to a proposed listing agreement advising the owner that the agent:

- has disclosed the extent of his knowledge of the tax consequences on the sale of real estate;

- is unable to give further tax advice on the rules and procedures involved in a §1031 transaction; and

- has advised the owner to seek the advice of his accountant or tax attorney on how to properly avoid the tax on profit from the sale and purchase of real estate.

Did both agents comply with their agency duty to make proper disclosures to the owner about their knowledge and willingness to give tax advice?

Yes! Both agents met the **agency duty** undertaken when soliciting employment since each agent:

- **determined the tax consequences** of the sale might **affect** the owner's handling of the sales transaction, called a *material fact*;

- **disclosed the extent of his knowledge** regarding the possible tax consequences of the sale; and

- **advised on the need for a professional** who would further investigate and advise on the §1031 tax aspects.

The question then remains, "Must a broker, employed by a seller of real estate, give tax advice to the seller?"

The answer lies in the type of real estate involved and the client's intended use of the sales proceeds.

An affirmative duty to advise

Consider a listing agent who determines that information about the tax aspects of a sale is *material* to a sales transaction entered into by his client since tax information might affect the client's handling of the transaction. Accordingly, the agent has a duty owed to his client to disclose the extent of his knowledge on the transaction's tax aspects, called an *agency duty* or *fiduciary duty*.

Further, a concerned listing agent will go beyond disclosure of mere tax information and assist his client in structuring the sales arrangement to achieve the best possible tax consequences available.

However, a **statutory exception** to the disclosure duties exists. On one-to-four unit residential dwellings, a listing agent has **no duty to disclose** his knowledge of possible tax consequences, even if the tax consequences are known by the agent to affect the client's decision on how to handle the sale of his property, unless the topic becomes the subject of the client's inquiry. [Calif. Civil Code §2079.16]

Advice and disclosure exception

Consider a seller of a one-to-four unit residential property who enters into a client-agent relationship with a broker, employing the broker (and his agents) to sell the property under a listing agreement.

The listing agreement form used by the broker contains a boilerplate clause stating a real estate licensee is a person qualified to advise on real estate, a statement that is consistent with the training and knowledge of brokers and agents. However, the clause goes on to state that if the seller desires legal or tax advice, he should consult an appropriate professional. [CC §2079.16]

The broker also hands the seller a statutorily mandated **agency law disclosure** form that states: "A real estate agent is a person qualified to advise about real estate. If legal or tax advice is desired, consult a competent professional."

Neither disclaimer requires the broker and his agents to provide tax advice or obligates the seller to employ the other professional to advise on the tax aspects of the transaction before closing escrow. [CC §2079.16]

The broker then locates a buyer who enters into a purchase agreement with the seller to buy the property. The purchase agreement also states the seller should consult his attorney or accountant for tax advice.

Prior to closing the sale of the seller's property, the broker also negotiates the seller's purchase of another one-to-four unit residential property, which involves the broker's preparation of a purchase agreement.

Before the separate escrows close on the sale and purchase transactions, the seller asks the broker about the number of days he has after the sale closes to purchase the replacement property and avoid paying profit tax on the sale. The seller has never been involved in a §1031 reinvestment.

The broker informs the seller he is not sure of the number of days and orally advises the seller to consult a tax accountant. The seller does not do so.

Ultimately, the seller is taxed on the profit from the sale, but not because of the time constraints on his closing of escrow that he inquired about. The profit is taxed because the seller failed to avoid actual and constructive receipt of the sales proceeds by either directly transferring the sales proceeds to the purchase escrow or impounding the sales proceeds with a third-party facilitator until the proceeds were needed to fund the purchase escrow for the replacement property.

The seller seeks to recover his losses from the broker. He claims the broker breached the agency duty owed to the seller by failing to disclose that the structure of the seller's transfer of net sales proceeds from the sales escrow to the purchase escrow for the replacement property might result in adverse tax consequences due to his actual receipt of the reinvestment funds.

The broker claims he has no duty to advise the seller on the tax consequences of the one-to-four unit sale since the listing agreement, the agency law disclosure and the purchase agreement all clearly stated:

- the broker did not advise on tax matters; and

- the seller should look to other professionals for tax advice.

Did the listing broker (or his agents) have a duty to advise the seller on the tax consequences of the sale as known to the broker (or his agents)?

No! On the sale of one-to-four unit residential property, sellers (and buyers) are expected, as a matter of public policy, to obtain tax advice from competent professionals other than the real estate brokerage office handling the transaction. [CC §2079.16]

Further, a broker has no duty to voluntarily disclose any tax aspects surrounding the sale of a one-to-four unit residential property, even if the information is known to the broker or the sales agent, so long as the listing agreement specifies the broker and his agents **do not undertake the duty** to advise the seller on the tax aspects of the transactions. However, on a **direct inquiry** from the seller (or buyer), the agent must **respond honestly** and to the best of his knowledge. [**Carleton** v. **Tortosa** (1993) 14 CA4th 745]

The agency law disclosure addendum attached to listing agreements and purchase agreements eliminates the duty of a broker and his agents to disclose their knowledge about the tax aspects of a sale when a one-to-four unit residential property is involved.

The irony of mandated disclosures

The tax consequences of sales transactions involving the subsequent purchase of replacement property are as material to a seller as is the structuring of carryback financing. Carryback financing arrangements require an agent to make extensive mandated disclosures regarding documentation of the carryback and the rights of the carryback seller. However, carryback arrangements are less frequently encountered than §1031 reinvestment opportunities.

Further, the financial damage of avoidable taxation often exceeds the risk of loss on an improperly structured carryback note and trust deed transaction. Unlike the agency duty of a broker (and his agents) in §1031 transactions, the agency duty a broker (and his agents) owes to his carryback seller includes full disclosure of information necessary for the seller to make an informed decision about the **financial suitability** of a carryback sale before the seller enters into the transaction. [**Timmsen** v. **Forest E. Olson, Inc.** (1970) 6 CA3d 860]

Avoiding misleading disclaimers

The boilerplate statement included in some listing agreements and purchase agreements used by unionized real estate brokers and their agents incorrectly implies that they are not qualified to give tax advice.

If a broker or agent is not fully qualified to handle the sale and purchase aspects of a §1031 transaction, he is at least aware of its beneficial tax aspects available to a seller of property.

Further, real estate brokers and their agents with tax knowledge are duty-bound to advise their client about their knowledge concerning the tax consequences of the real estate transaction their client is about to enter into — unless a one-to-four unit residential property subject to agency law disclosure statutes is involved.

However, a savvy broker or agent **capitalizes** on the tax knowledge he has spent time acquiring by advising clients on the tax results of their real estate transactions, regardless of the type of property involved. When a broker or agent uses his knowledge to **voluntarily counsel** his client on the transaction's tax consequences, the decision made by the client will be the result of more relevant information.

However, the broker or agent who advises a client on a transaction's tax consequences has a duty to not mislead the client by intentional or negligent misapplication of the tax rules. [**Ziswasser** v. **Cole & Cowan, Inc.** (1985) 164 CA3d 417]

To avoid misleading the client, the broker or agent should disclose to his client:

- the full extent of his tax knowledge regarding the transaction;

- how he acquired his tax knowledge; and

- whether the broker or agent intends to further investigate the matter or whether the client should seek further advice from other professionals.

When a broker or agent does give tax advice, he should take steps to involve the client's other advisors in the final decision. Input from others who know the client help the broker eliminate future claims arising out of adverse tax consequences due to the **client's reliance** on the agent's (incorrect) opinion. The most practical (and effective) method for shifting reliance to others or to the client himself when the broker gives a client his opinion on a transaction's tax consequences, is to insert a *further-approval contingency* in the purchase offer or counteroffer.

The contingency requires the client to initiate his own investigation by obtaining additional tax advice and further approval of the transaction's tax consequences from his attorney or accountant before allowing escrow to close. An oral or written warning, or general advice to further investigate, is not sufficient since it does not require the client to act nor does it explain why the broker or agent believes the client should act to protect himself. [**Field** v. **Century 21 Klowden-Forness Realty** (1998) 63 CA4th 18]

Tax advisor's further approval

In an exchange agreement (or purchase agreement), the purpose for including a further approval contingency regarding the transaction's tax consequences is to allow a client to confirm that the transaction does qualify for §1031 tax-exempt status as represented by his agent. If the tax status cannot be confirmed, the client may terminate the transaction by delivery of a notice of cancellation. [See **first tuesday** Form 171 §5.2j]

In other words, the client is **not relying** on the agent's opinion if he decides to enter into an exchange agreement with the intent to close escrow only after he has further confirmation of the tax consequences.

However, a purchase agreement or exchange agreement that contains a written contingency provision calling for a third party's approval of some aspect of the transaction, such as the transaction's qualification as an Internal Revenue Code (IRC) §1031 reinvestment plan, also contains an unwritten *implied covenant* provision. Under the implied covenant provision, before a client can cancel a transaction, he is required to "act in good faith and with fairness" in his efforts to obtain a third party's approval, such as submitting data on the transaction for confirmation from his attorney or accountant.

Thus, the implied covenant provision compels the client to actually submit documentation on

the transaction to the third party, and to do so within the time period called for after the date of acceptance.

Here, the client's agent usually steps into the chain of events by contacting the third party and providing the paperwork sought to review the transaction for its §1031 tax-exempt status. On review, procedural changes may need to be made to meet the client's objectives and satisfy the objections of the third party. In response, the agent sees to it the changes are made, unless the changes would be inconsistent with the intent of his client regarding his acceptance of the replacement property.

Since fair dealing and reason are implied in every agreement and applied to the conduct of all parties, a termination of the exchange agreement due to the disapproval of an activity or occurrence subject to a contingency provision must be based on a **justifiable reason**.

On a potential disapproval and possible termination due to reasons expressed by the client or his advisor, the agent may well be able to cure the defect that gave rise to the reason for disapproval or to demonstrate that the third party's concern is unfounded, i.e., if it is, in fact or in law, an erroneous conclusion. [**Brown** v. **Critchfield** (1980) 100 CA3d 858]

Tax aspects: a material fact

All real estate in the hands of a seller is classified as either his principal residence, like-kind (§1031) property or dealer property.

An inquiry as to what the seller of property other than a personal residence or dealer property intends to do with the sales proceeds often opens a window of opportunity, allowing the agent to review his tax knowledge with the seller.

When representing sellers of real estate that, on a sale, would qualify for the §1031 profit reporting exemption, an agent should use a purchase agreement containing a §1031 cooperation provision. [See **first tuesday** Form 159 §10.6]

A §1031 cooperation provision is not an advisory disclaimer by which a broker or agent attempts to relieve himself of his responsibility to give tax advice. Instead, the provision puts the seller on notice he is able to avoid profit reporting on the sale and has bargained for the buyer's cooperation should the seller decide to act to qualify his profit for a §1031 exemption.

Again, an agent who is not knowledgeable about the handling required for a §1031 reinvestment can initially avoid a discussion of tax aspects by including the §1031 cooperation provision in the purchase agreement. The §1031 cooperation provision conveys to the seller the seller's need to consider, plan for and inquire about the tax consequences of the sale.

Knowledge of basic tax aspects

Technical questions posed by a seller that go beyond a listing agent's knowledge or expertise requires a truthful response from the agent. In response, the listing agent has several ways he can respond, including:

- disclosing the extent of his knowledge to the seller and advising the seller to seek any further advice they may want from another source;

- associating with a more knowledgeable broker, a tax attorney or accountant who provides the seller with the advice; or

- learning how to handle §1031 reinvestments and giving the advice himself.

Escrow officers are of great assistance to an agent who is aware he has a potential §1031 transaction. Some escrow officers and agents advertise their expertise in handling §1031 tax-deferred reinvestments to broadcast their competitive advantage over other escrow officers and agents.

Ideally, every broker and agent handling the sale of real estate used in the seller's business or held for investment (like-kind property) should, as a **matter of basic competency**, possess an understanding of several fundamental tax concepts, such as:

- the principal residence owner-occupant's $250,000 profit exclusion;

- the separate income and profit categories for each type of real estate;

- the §1031 profit reporting exemption;

- interest deductions on real estate loans;

- depreciation schedules and deductions;

- the $25,000 deduction and real-estate-related business adjustments for rental property losses;

- the tracking of rental income/losses separately for each property;

- profit and loss spillover on the sale of a rental property;

- standard and alternative reporting and tax bracket rates; and

- installment sales, deferred profit reporting.

All of these tax aspects are basic to the sale or ownership of real estate commonly listed and sold by agents. When applicable, they have significant financial impact on sellers and buyers of real estate. Any agent with a working knowledge of the tax aspects of real estate can and should consider offering a wider range of services, including tax advice, when competing to represent buyers and sellers.

Also, giving a seller tax advice concerning a §1031 reinvestment plan when the seller follows the advice always leads to a second fee for negotiating the purchase of the replacement property and coordinating the transfer of funds.

Chapter 60

Home loan interest deductions

This chapter reviews the home loan interest deduction for reporting the tax consequences of financing first and second homes.

Two deductions, two residences

The federal government has a long-standing policy of encouraging residential tenants to **become homeowners**. The incentive the government offers to tenants is in the form of a significant reduction in the income taxes tenants will pay when they buy a home which will be their principal residence and finance the purchase.

For a tenant considering his income taxes, the monthly payment on a purchase-assist home loan is not just a substitute for his monthly rent payment, it also reduces his combined state and federal taxes by an amount equal to 20% to 30% of the monthly loan payment.

Real estate agents handling the sale or purchase of single-family residences must be able to intelligently discuss this tax reduction incentive with tenants to convert them into homeowners.

Due to the special **home loan interest deduction** rule for income tax reporting, the interest **accrued and paid** on loans is deductible from income as an *itemized expense* if:

- the loans **funded the purchase price** or paid for the **cost of improvements** for the owner's principal residence or second home; and

- the loans are **secured** by either the owner's principal residence or second home.

Only loans secured by either the **first or second home** come under the home loan interest deduction rules. [Internal Revenue Code §163(h)(4)(A)(i)]

Without the home loan interest deduction rule, interest paid on a loan which funded the purchase or improvement of a principal residence or second home is not deductible since the loan funded a *personal expense*, not the acquisition of a business or investment.

Also, interest paid on **equity loans** secured by the first or second residence is deductible under the home loan interest deduction rules, regardless of whether the loan's net proceeds were used for personal or investment/business purposes.

The first/second home loan interest deduction reduces taxable income as an *itemized deduction* under both the standard income tax (SIT) and alternative minimum tax (AMT) reporting rules. In contrast, the real estate **property tax deduction** on the first and second homes applies only to reduce the owner's SIT, not his AMT.

Two categories of loans exist to allow the deduction of interest paid on any loans secured by the first or second home:

- interest on **purchase or improvement loan** balances up to a combined principal amount of $1,000,000; and

- interest on all other loan amounts up to an additional $100,000 in principal, called **home equity** loans.

Purchase/improvement loans

Interest paid on money loans and carryback credit sales originated to **purchase or substantially improve** an owner's first or second home, if secured by either home, is **fully deductible** on:

- combined loan balances up to $1,000,000 for an individual and for couples filing a joint return; and

- $500,000 for married persons filing separately.

Thus, if the loan funds used to acquire, construct or further improve a principal residence or second home collectively exceed $1,000,000, only the interest paid on $1,000,000 of the purchase and improvement loan balances is deductible as purchase/improvement interest. However, interest paid on the excess loan amounts, up to an additional $100,000, qualifies for the interest deduction as a home equity loan.

To qualify home improvement loans for the interest deductions, the new improvements must be *substantial*. Improvements are substantial if they:

- **add** to the residence's market value;

- **prolong** the residence's useful life; or

- **adapt** the property to residential use.

Loan funds spent on repairing and maintaining the residence to keep it in good condition do not qualify as funding for substantial improvements. [IRC §163(h)(3)(B)(i)]

Refinancing limitations

Should an owner refinance a purchase/improvement loan, the portion of the **refinancing** used to fund the payoff qualifies as a purchase/improvement loan for interest deductions. However, interest may be written off only on the amount of refinancing funds used to pay off the **principal balance** on the existing purchase/improvement loan.

For example, an owner borrows $200,000 to fund the purchase of his principal residence. The loan balance is later paid down to $180,000. The owner refinances the residence, paying off the original purchase/improvement

loan. However, the new loan is for a greater amount than the payoff demand on the old loan.

Here, interest on only $180,000 of the refinancing is deductible as interest paid on a purchase or improvement loan, **unless**:

- the excess funds generated by the refinance are **used to improve** the residence; or

- the excess loan amount **qualifies as a home equity loan** under its separate ceiling of $100,000 in principal.

$100,000 home equity loans

Interest on loan amounts secured by the first or second home may not qualify for the purchase/improvement home loan interest deduction, due either to a different use of the loan proceeds or the $1,000,000 loan limitation. However, the interest on loan amounts which do not qualify as purchase/improvement loans is deductible by individuals and those couples filing joint returns as interest paid on additional or other loan amounts up to $100,000 in principal, called *home equity loans*.

For married persons filing separately, the cap for the principal amount of equity loans on which interest can be deducted is limited to $50,000. [IRC §163(h)(3)(C)(ii)]

Home equity loans are typically junior encumbrances, but also include proceeds from a refinance which are not used to improve the proeprty or remain after a pay off of an existing purchase/improvement loan.

The proceeds from home equity loans may be used for **any purpose**, including personal uses unrelated to the property.

Property value ceiling

Interest paid on any portion of loan balances which exceeds the *fair market value* of the residence is not deductible. In practice, the fair market value rule applies to home equity loans and any refinancing which is greater than the amount needed to pay off an existing purchase/improvement loan. [IRC §163(h)(3)(C)(i)]

The **fair market value** of each residence is *presumed* to be the original amount of the purchase and improvement costs. Thus, any future **drop in property value** below the balance remaining on purchase-assist loans does not affect the interest write-off.

Editor's note — Consistent with its policy under codes such as Internal Revenue Code (IRC) §1031, the Internal Revenue Service (IRS) wants to stay out of the appraisal business. Thus, the IRS has substituted the easily computable original cost of purchase and improvements for the "fair market value" limitation established by Congress. However, an owner who takes out a home equity loan which, when added to the other loan balances on the residences exceeds his purchase and improvement costs of the property, can rebut the IRS fair market value presumption of cost with a current fair market value appraisal provided by the lender.

*Thus, on a refinance or origination of an equity loan, it is advisable to request and receive a copy of the lender's appraisal to later corroborate the property's increased value at the time the financing is originated. [See **first tuesday** Form 329]*

Qualifying the first/second home

To qualify for the home loan interest deduction, the loans must be secured by the owner's principal residence or his second home.

A **principal residence** is an individual's home, defined as a dwelling where the homeowner's immediate family resides a majority of the year, which is close to the homeowner's place of employment and banks handling the homeowner's accounts, and is the address used for tax returns.

The **second home** is any residence selected from year to year by the owner, including mobile homes, recreational vehicles and boats.

If the second home is **rented out** during portions of the year, the interest on purchase/improvement loans encumbering the second home qualifies for the home loan interest deduction if the owner occupied the home for more than 14 days or 10% of the number of days the residence was rented, which ever is greater. [IRC §280A(d)(1)]

If the owner does not rent out his second home at any time during the year, it qualifies for the home loan interest deduction whether or not he occupies it. [IRC §163(h)(4)(A)(iii)]

The rental income on the second home is *investment/portfolio income* if the home qualifies for the interest deduction since the owner's occupancy exceeded the 10%/14-day rule.

When the second home has been rented, but the owner's family has occupied the property for so many days as to qualify the home for the loan interest deduction, the owner is not allowed to treat the property as an investment. Thus, the owner cannot depreciate the home. [IRC §§163(h)(4)(A)(i)(II); 280A(d)(1)]

A second home, when purchased for personal use and held for a profit on resale, also qualifies as investment (like-kind) property for exemption from profit taxes under IRC §1031. [IRC §1221; IRS Private Letter Ruling 8103117]

Taking the deductions

Interest deductions on home loans are only allowed for interest which has **accrued and been paid**, called *qualified interest*. [IRC §163(h)(3)(A)]

Interest on first and second home loans is deducted from the owner's **adjusted gross income** (AGI) as an *itemized deduction*, which also has further limitations on the total amount of all deductions. Conversely, business, rental or investment interest are adjustments that reduce the AGI. Thus, the two first/second home loan interest deductions directly reduce the amount of the owner's taxable income, if the interest paid is not limited by ceilings on itemized deductions.

The inability to reduce the AGI by use of the home loan interest makes a difference. The higher an owner's AGI, the lower the amounts allowed for some rental deductions, the itemized deduction phaseout (starting at an AGI of $142,700 for 2004), and any tax credits available to the owner.

Consider a homeowner who wants to generate funds for use as a down payment to purchase business, rental or investment real estate. His only substantial asset is the $300,000 equity in his home.

If the owner further finances (with a home equity loan) or refinances the existing loan to net $200,000 in loan proceeds, he will be paying interest which is only partially deductible. The non-purchase/improvement loan amount exceeds the $100,000 home equity loan cap. The interest the owner pays on the portion of home equity loan balance in excess of $100,000 is not deductible under the home loan interest deduction rules.

The home as additional security

Consider a homeowner who encumbers the equity in his home to secure a note he executes as the down payment, or to borrow funds for a down payment, on the purchase of investment property.

The homeowner wants to avoid the home loan interest deduction limitations and be able to write off all of the interest paid on the note against future income from the rental or portfolio property purchased. Accordingly, the homeowner negotiates with the lender or carryback seller for the note to be secured by **two separate trust deeds**, one as a lien on the home and the other as a lien on the property purchased.

The lender or carryback seller is satisfied with the financial risk regarding the loss of principal. The lender or the carryback seller receives a trust deed on the home, which he views as his primary source of recovery on the note.

However, the note is also secured by the property purchased in order to justify writing off the entire interest accrued and paid on the loan against income from the property purchased. Here, the home is merely **additional security** under a separate trust deed.

Chapter 61

The principal residence profit exclusion

This chapter presents the tax scheme for excluding profits from taxation on the sale of a residential property presently or recently used as the owner's principal residence.

Tax-free sale up to $250,000 per person

Consider a seller of a residential property who presently occupies or recently occupied a portion or all of the property as his principal residence. The price sought is far greater than the combined amount of the price the seller paid for the property several years ago and the costs he has incurred to renovate and improve the property, collectively called the seller's *cost basis* in the property.

The seller's listing agent is aware of the tax benefits available to an owner-occupant of a residential property when the property is sold and the seller takes a profit due to the increase in its sales price over the amounts the seller paid to buy and improve the property.

Interested in the tax aspect of the sale, the listing agent reviews information contained in the property profile provided to him by his title company in order to determine the number of years the seller has owned the property and whether the seller has a homeowner's exemption for property taxes.

Upon questioning the seller, the listing agent further determines the seller has used the property as his principal residence for at least two years during the past five years.

The seller is informed that each owner-occupant is entitled to receive up to $250,000 in profit on the sale tax free if he occupied a portion or all of the property as his principal residence for at least two years during his last five years of ownership, whether or not:

- the seller now rents the property to tenants;

- the seller has taken depreciation deductions as his home office (or rental property);

- the seller now occupies the property, but originally acquired it as a rental; or

- the property consists of two or more residential or business units.

The listing agent reviews the tax issues relative to the seller's qualifying for the $250,000 exclusion of profit, as well as any §1031 exemption for profits which would be allocated to a home office (business use) or separate rental space (investment property) in or about the residence, or due to the property's present status solely as a rental. Questions the agent should consider include:

1. Does the property qualify as the owner's **principal residence**? [Internal Revenue Code §121(a)]

2. Who among the co-owners qualifies as an **owner and occupant** for periods totaling two years during the five years preceding the close of the sale? [IRC §121(a)]

3. If only one spouse is the vested owner, does the **non-vested spouse** qualify as an owner by having occupied the property as a principal residence for periods totaling two years during the five years prior to closing? [IRC §§121(b)(2), 121(d)(1)]

4. Did the homeowner **disqualify himself** by having taken a profit exclusion on the sale of a different principal residence

which closed within two years before the close of the sale on his current residence? [IRC §121(b)(3)]

5. Will the current property sell prior to completing two full years of ownership and occupancy, or within two years after taking a profit exclusion on the sale of a prior principal residence and taking a profit exclusion, under circumstances allowing for a **partial exclusion** as a result of *personal difficulties*? [IRC §§121(c)(1), 121(c)(2)]

6. Did the homeowner originally acquire his residence as a rental property to replace other property he sold (or exchanged) in a §1031 reinvestment plan, and then later convert it to his residence, in which case a **five-year holding period** on ownership must pass before the §121 profit exclusion is allowed?

7. Does the homeowner **presently depreciate** a portion of the residence or the property as his home office or as a rental (duplex etc.) and is the owner considering using some or all of the net sales proceeds to purchase like-kind §1031 property?

8. Did the homeowner take any **depreciation deductions** for his use of the home as an office or rental after May 6, 1997 which must be reported as *unrecaptured gain* (25% tax), unless avoided by acquiring a replacement home office or rental in a §1031 reinvestment plan? [IRC §121(d)(6)]

9. Is the owner an unmarried surviving spouse who has not owned and occupied the property for the two-year period who can still qualify by **tacking** the deceased spouse's period of ownership and occupancy to the surviving owner's? [IRC §121(d)(2)]

10. Can the owner who is now in a government-licensed facility because he has become physically or mentally incapable of caring for himself and who previously resided in the home for periods totaling at least one year during the past five years, qualify by **tacking** the time spent in the facility during his ownership of the property to establish the two-year ownership and occupancy requirements? [IRC §121(d)(7)]

Principal or second residence

Occasionally, a couple will have two or three residences that they occupy at different times during the year (a summer residence on the lake, a desert retreat, a residence in a prestigious community, etc.). On the sale of one of the residences at a profit, the question arises as to which home is the *principal residence*.

Identifying one of two or more residences as the principal residence is based initially on whether the owner seeking the $250,000 per person profit exclusion uses the property a majority of the time during the year.

Other factors taken into consideration when two or more residences exist is whether the claimed principal residence is:

- located near the owner's employment:

- used as the address listed on state and federal tax returns; and

- relatively close to banks and professional services used by the owner.

Profit exclusion for single individuals and co-owners

The amount of profit (or loss) taken on a sale of real estate is set by subtracting the seller's cost basis in the property from the net sales price he receives — a formula of "price minus basis equals profit." Profit taken by an individual on the sale of his principal residence may qualify for the $250,000 profit exclusion.

To qualify for the profit exclusion, an individual must **own and occupy** the residence sold for at least two of the five years prior to closing the sale. [IRC §§121(a), 121(b)(1)]

Thus, **each individual** who owns a principal residence, solely or with others, and who has occupied it for periods totaling two of the five years before closing the sale, can exclude up to $250,000 from his share of the profit on the sale of the property.

Consider an individual who occupies a property as his principal residence for one year. He then moves out, but retains ownership and rents the property.

More than four years after vacating the property, the individual reoccupies the property as his principal residence for one year before closing a sale of the residence at a profit.

Does the individual qualify for the profit exclusion since he occupied the property as his residence for two years?

No! The individual did not occupy the property for a total of two years **within the five-year period** immediately preceding the sale. Both time period limitations must be met to exclude the profit from taxes. Thus, he cannot use the $250,000 exclusion to avoid taxes on the profit from the sale of the property. [IRC §121(a)]

Principal residence exclusion for married couples

A married couple who owns and occupies a property as their principal residence for at least two of the five years prior to the sale can, unless disqualified, exclude an **aggregate amount** of up to $500,000 in profit taken on the sale, i.e., $250,000 per person. [IRC §121(b)(2)(A)]

For a husband and wife to qualify for the **combined $500,000** profit exclusion on the sale of a principal residence:

- either the husband or the wife may **solely own** the residence as separate property or they may be **co-owners** since ownership by one spouse alone is **imputed** to the non-owner spouse;

- **both must occupy** the property during the ownership for time periods totaling two years or more within the five years prior to the sale;

- the couple must file a **joint return** as a married couple for the year of the sale; and

- **neither** spouse may have taken the $250,000 profit exclusion on another principal residence within two years prior to the sale. [IRC §121(b)(2)]

However, should either spouse be **individually disqualified** for having taken the principal residence profit exclusion on the sale of another residence which closed within the two-year period prior to closing the sale of the current residence, the other spouse, owner or non-owner qualifies for an individual $250,000 profit exclusion. [IRC §121(b)(2)(B)]

Consider a husband who is the **sole owner** of a residence as his separate property. The husband and his wife **both occupy** the property as their principal residence during his ownership. They do so for a total of more than two years during the five years immediately preceding their sale of the property.

Neither spouse has been disqualified by having taken a $250,000 exclusion on the sale of a principal residence which closed escrow during the two-year period prior to closing. The couple files a joint return for the year of the sale.

Does each spouse qualify for the exclusion allowing the couple to exclude up to $500,000 of profit taken on the sale of the residence?

Yes! The spouse who holds no ownership interest in the residence is an imputed owner qualifying for the $250,000 exclusion since the other spouse owns the property. Both occupied for the minimum two years within five years of closing the sale.

Now consider a husband and wife who each owned and occupied separate principal residences prior to their marriage. The wife sold her prior residence after they married.

During the five-year period prior to the sale of the wife's separate property, the wife occupied the property as her principal residence for at least two years. For the year of the sale of the wife's residence, the husband and wife filed a joint return.

Can the couple take a $500,000 profit exclusion since the property was sold during the marriage?

No! Only a $250,000 exclusion from profit is allowed since only the wife qualifies. The husband does not qualify for an additional $250,000 profit exclusion since he did not also occupy (for two years) the residence his wife owned and sold.

Both spouses must occupy the residence for a period totaling two years for each to qualify for a $250,000 profit exclusion, whether one spouse or both own the property.

No marital taint to disqualify

Consider a husband and wife who each independently owned and occupied separate principal residences for two consecutive years prior to their marriage.

On marriage, both the husband and wife vacate their prior residences and relocate to a newly acquired property as their residence. Each spouse now needs to sell their prior residences.

The husband sells his prior residence at a profit. The couple files a joint return for the year of the sale.

Does the couple, now married, qualify for a total exclusion of $500,000?

No! Only the husband qualifies to take the $250,000 profit exclusion on the couple's joint tax return. While the wife did not need to be a vested owner of the husband's residence, she did have to occupy the property as her principal residence for two of the five years prior to his sale of the property to also qualify for a $250,000 exclusion.

Further, and within two years after the husband closes the sale on his prior residence, the wife closes the sale of her prior residence at a profit. The wife, having owned and occupied her residence for two of the past five years, qualifies for a $250,000 profit exclusion. The husband and wife file a joint return for the year the wife sold her residence and claim the wife's $250,000 profit exclusion.

Here, the wife is qualified to take the individual $250,000 profit exclusion on the couple's joint return — even though the husband sold and took a $250,000 profit exclusion within two years of her sale. [IRC §121(b)(3)(A)]

In contrast, consider a man who, either prior to or after getting married, closes escrow on the sale of his principal residence and takes a profit.

The man owned and occupied the principal residence for time periods totaling more than two years during the five years prior to closing the sale. A $250,000 profit exclusion is taken on the sale.

Since his marriage, both the man and his wife have occupied as their principal residence the wife's separate property for periods totaling at least two years within the past five years.

Less than two years after the husband closed the sale on which he took the $250,000 profit exclusion, the residence owned by his wife is sold and escrow closed.

Can the couple file a joint return and qualify for the $500,000 profit exclusion by reason of their marriage, the wife's separate ownership and their shared occupancy of the residence?

No! Only the wife qualifies for a $250,000 profit exclusion on their joint return.

Even though the husband met the (imputed) ownership and (actual) occupancy requirements for the property sold by his wife, the husband took a $250,000 profit exclusion on the sale of his prior principal residence which closed within the two-year period preceding the closing of the sale of the wife's residence. Thus, the couple does not qualify for the combined $500,000 profit exclusion. [IRC §121(b)(3)(A)]

Similarly, had the second residence sold been community property and not separately owned by the wife, only the wife would have been allowed to take a $250,000 profit exclusion on their joint return.

Closing the sale of the residence they both occupied should have been delayed to a date more than two years after the sale closed on the husband's residence. If the close of escrow on the second sale had been delayed, the couple would have qualified for the combined $500,000 profit exclusion.

Unoccupied at time of sale

An individual or married couple **need not occupy** a property as a principal residence when the property is purchased or at the time of the sale to qualify for the $250,000 or combined $500,000 profit exclusion.

Consider a married couple who acquires a property and occupies it continuously as their principal residence for over two years.

Later, the couple buys another home and moves in, occupying it as their principal residence. The couple rents the old residence to a tenant, converting it into a depreciable rental property.

Within three years after moving out of their prior residence, the couple closes a sale on the prior residence and takes a profit. The couple files a joint tax return for the year of the sale.

Here, the couple may properly take a $500,000 profit exclusion on the sale even though they did not occupy the property at the time of the sale. The couple **owned and occupied** the prior residence as their principal residence for at least two of the last five years.

An orderly liquidation and §1031

Now consider a married couple who has occupied a home as their principal residence for over two years. They also own, either separately or as community property, several single-family residential rental properties.

The couple sells their principal residence and takes a profit of $300,000 on the sale. They file a joint tax return for the year of the sale and take the $500,000 profit exclusion — avoiding any tax on the $300,000 profit.

The couple then moves into one of the residential rental units they co-own, converting it into their principal residence.

Two years after occupying the residential rental unit as their principal residence, the couple sells the unit and takes a profit. The couple files a joint tax return for the year of sale and claims the $500,000 profit exclusion to avoid taxes on the profit.

Thus, by repeating the two-year occupancy of single-family residences they own as their principal residence, the couple is able to:

- liquidate their real estate holdings; and

- avoid paying tax on the profit taken on the sales.

Should the couple **carry back** a note and trust deed on the sale of one of the properties, the profit allocated to the principal in the note will be declared in the year of sale and excluded from taxation as part of the $500,000 exclusion of profit on the sale.

However, if any property now occupied as the principal residence was acquired as a rental in a §1031 reinvestment plan after October 22, 2004, then later converted into the principal residence of the owner, a holding period of five years is required to qualify for the $250,000 §121 residential exclusion. However, the two-year period for owner-occupancy remains unchanged. [IRC §121(d)(10)]

For example, an individual or couple who acquires a residence for rental or portfolio property purposes after October 22, 2004 as replacement property in a §1031 reinvestment plan and later converts it into their principal residence by occupying the home (for the necessary two years), must retain ownership of the residence for five years after taking title before a sale of the property will qualify for the $250,000 exclusion available to each co-owner.

Occasionally, the homeowner will establish a home office within the residence or in a space separate from the residence, such as a granny flat, maids' quarters or other rentable space on the same parcel as the residence. The home office area is allocated its pro rata share of the cost basis, and depreciation deductions are reported.

On a sale of the property, the §121 $250,000 profit exclusion is always applied first to the profit taken on the residential portion of the cost basis in the property, that portion of the profit and basis not allocated to the depreciable portion used as the home office.

If the home office is **within the space** of the residence, not separate from the residence in other quarters, the §121 profit exclusion applies to the home office space as well, called a *spillover*, except for the depreciation taken on the home office space. Not so for the home office located in **space separate** from the resi-

dence. Either way, the depreciation portion of the profit is taxed at the 25% maximum *unrecaptured gain* rate.

Also, the depreciable portion of the property used as the home office (or a separate rental) at the time of sale is §1031 property, entitled to have its pro rata share of net sales proceeds reinvested in a §1031 plan. [Rev. Proc. 2005-14]

Personal difficulties compel the sale

Even if an individual or couple **cannot fully meet** the two-year ownership and occupancy requirements, they may still qualify to exclude all (or a portion) of their profit under a *partial exclusion* available to owners who sell due to **personal difficulties**.

The **partial exclusion** is a prorated portion of the $250,000 profit exclusion, not a pro rata portion of the profit taken on the sale. The proration sets the maximum dollar amount of the partial exclusion available to cover profits based on the fraction of the two years they have occupied the property.

To qualify for a partial exclusion, a personal difficulty must arise and be the **primary reason for sale** of the property, which includes:

- a **change in employment**, based on occupancy of the residence at the time of the job relocation and the financial need to relocate for the employment;

- a **change in health**, such as advanced age-related infirmities, severe allergies or emotional problems; or

- **unforeseen circumstances**, such as natural or man-made disasters, death and divorce. [IRC §121(c)(2)(B); Temporary Revenue Regulations §1.121-3T]

Thus, when a homeowner must sell because of personal difficulties, all profit is excluded from taxation, limited to the ceiling amount of the partial exclusion set by that **fraction of two years** the owner actually owned and occupied the property as his principal residence. [IRC §121(c)(1)]

However, if the principal residence for which the owner seeks a partial exclusion was a rental acquired as a replacement property to complete a §1031 transaction using §1031 money or in exchange, the five-year holding period applies and is required for use of the §121 residential profit exclusion.

Factors used to determine whether the primary reason for the sale is a **change in circumstances** which qualifies the sale for a partial exclusion include whether:

- the sale of the principal residence and the need compelling the homeowner to relocate are close in time;

- a material change makes the property unsuitable as the principal residence;

- the homeowner's financial ability to carry the residence requires the residence be sold;

- the need to relocate arises during the occupancy of the residence sold; and

- the need to relocate was not foreseeable by the homeowner when he acquired and first occupied the principal residence sold. [Revenue Regulations §1.121-3(b)]

For example, a change in employment may qualify the homeowner for the partial exclusion without first owning and occupying his principal residence for the full two-year period.

Employment compelling the homeowner to relocate can be based on a required job relocation by his current employer, the commencement of employment with a new employer, or if the homeowner is self-employed, the relocation of the place of business or the commencement of a new business.

A sale is deemed to be by reason of a change in employment if:

- the new job location is more than 50 miles farther than the old job was from the principal residence that was sold; or

- if the seller was formerly unemployed, the job location is at least 50 miles from the residence sold. [Rev. Regs. §1.121-3(c)]

For example, a homeowner is forced by his employment to relocate out of the area.

The homeowner has owned and occupied his principal residence for one year and six months — 75% of the necessary two-year occupancy period.

The homeowner sells his residence, taking a $40,000 profit.

When filing his tax return, the homeowner will be able to exclude the entire $40,000 profit from taxation since the entire profit is less than the $187,500 partial exclusion (75% of the $250,000 full exclusion). The same ratio would apply to a couple's $500,000 profit exclusion under the same circumstances. [IRC §121(c)]

Health issues of a chronic nature, which compel the homeowner to sell may qualify the sale for partial exclusion.

To qualify for reasons of health, the owner seeking the exclusion must need to sell in order to obtain, provide or facilitate the diagnosis, cure, mitigation or treatment of a disease, illness or injury, or obtain and provide medical or personal care, for any of the following persons:

- the owner himself;

- the owner's spouse;

- a co-owner of the residence;

- a co-occupant residing in the owner's household as his principal place of abode; or

- close relatives, generally those descendent of the owner's grandparents.

The owner's sale is also deemed to be due to health reasons if a physician recommends a change of residence (relocation). [Rev. Regs. §1.121-3(d)]

Unforeseen circumstances may arise and provide the primary reasons for the sale of the owner's principal residence, permitting use of the partial §121 exclusion of profit from taxation. Events which occur and are classified as unforeseen circumstances do not include events which could have been reasonably anticipated by the owner before he owned and occupied the residence.

Also, the **mere preference** of the owner to buy another property to own and occupy as his principal residence or the **financial improvement** of the owner permitting acquisition of another more affluent appearing residence does not qualify the sale for the partial §121 exclusion of profit.

However, the owner's sale is deemed to be due to **unforeseen circumstances** if:

- the residence is taken by an involuntary conversion; or

- disaster (natural or man-made) or acts of war/terrorism cause a casualty loss to the residence.

Further, the homeowner's sale is deemed to be due to unforeseen circumstances if the following events occur to the owner, owner's spouse, co-owners, co-occupants who are residents and members of the owner's household and close relatives:

- death;

- loss of employment resulting in unemployment compensation;

- inability to pay housing costs and basic living expenses for the owner's household;

- divorce or separation by court decree; or

- a pregnancy with multiple births. [Rev. Regs. §1.121-3(e)]

Chapter 62

1099-S on the sale of a principal residence

This chapter discusses the requirements for filing a 1099-S on the completion of a sale.

Seller certification eliminates 1099-S

The **closing agent** for every real estate sales transaction, except **seller-certified exclusions** of a principal residence, files a 1099-S information return with the Internal Revenue Service (IRS), which includes:

- the name and address of both the seller and the buyer; and

- the amount of the gross sales proceeds. [Internal Revenue Code §6045(a)]

A copy of the 1099-S must also be provided to the seller and buyer by the escrow agent. [IRC §6045(b)]

The 1099-S contains no disclosure of the brokerage fee paid through escrow.

The closing agent who files the 1099-S is called the "real estate reporting person" by the IRS. Typically, escrow is the real estate reporting person who files the 1099-S, also known in the industry as a "snitch sheet."

When a formal escrow is not used, such as frequently occurs in an equity purchase, land sales contract or lease-option sale, the agent who is handling disbursements on closing the transaction is the one who is required to file the 1099-S. [IRC §6045(e)(2)]

However, a 1099-S does not need to be filed when the sales price of the seller's principal residence is less than the $250,000 per person **profit exclusion**. A sales price of up to $500,000 exempts a home owned and occupied by a couple for the two-year period. [IRC §6045(e)(5)]

Seller's principal residence exclusion certification

A 1099-S is not filed by escrow on a sale of a principal residence when the seller hands escrow a **written certification**, signed by the seller under penalty of perjury, which states:

- the seller has occupied the principal residence for a **minimum of two years** during the five-year period prior to closing the sale;

- the seller has **not sold another principal residence** within the two years prior to the sale;

- no portion of the residence has been reported as **used for business** or rental purposes by the seller or the seller's spouse; and

- the sales price of the residence **does not exceed the exclusion amount** the seller(s) qualifies for. [Revenue Procedure 98-20 §4.02]

Escrow must file a 1099-S if the seller reported the use of a portion of the residence as his **place of business** or as a **rental**, such as in the case of a home office or an owner-occupied, two-or-more unit residential property.

The seller's written certification handed to escrow must also indicate which one of the following applies to the sale, whether:

- the sales price of the residence was $250,000 or less;

- the seller is married, the sales price of the residence was $500,000 or less, and the profit taken on the sale was $250,000 or less; or

- the sales price was $500,000 or less, the seller is married and intends to file a joint return for the year of the sale, the seller's spouse also occupied the residence as his or her principal residence for periods totaling at least two of the five years prior to the sale, and neither the seller nor the seller's spouse has taken a principal residence exclusion for a sale which closed within two years prior to the sale. [Rev. Proc. 98-20 §4.02]

Thus, a "snitch sheet" is required to be filed if the sales price of the principal residence **exceeds the profit exclusion** for which the seller and the spouse qualify.

Receipt of certification

As a practical matter, the certificate will be part of the escrow instructions covering the 1099-S reporting. If escrow does not ask for a seller certification, the listing agent as the representative of the seller responsible for protecting the seller's interests should.

Typically, the seller will fill out the certificate and return it to escrow prior to closing — a service provided by escrow officers for no additional fee.

If the residence is sold by more than one person, including spouses, a separate written certification must be provided by each seller who qualifies for an exclusion. [Rev. Proc. 98-20 §4.01]

An escrow that relies on a seller's certification meeting IRS guidelines and does not file a 1099-S is not subject to penalties for failure to file, unless the escrow officer knows the certification is incorrect. [Rev. Proc. 98-20 §7]

Escrow must keep the certification on file for at least **four years** after the year of the sale or exchange. [Rev. Proc. 98-20 §6.01]

Brokers file 1099-S

When obtaining a listing, the agent should review with the seller those tax forms the seller will encounter during escrow, such as the seller certification form.

The disclosure is a courtesy to the seller and prepares the seller for closing a sale without unnecessary surprises.

Tax advice to the seller regarding the 1099-S is comparable to the state and federal withholding tax advice brokers and agents now give to all sellers and buyers of any type of property in California.

However, when the broker is the closing agent, such as occurs when a buyer takes possession of the seller's personal residence under a land sales contract or lease-option agreement which is not formally escrowed, the broker is also the reporting agent. Thus, the broker should obtain the certification form signed by the seller to avoid the requirement for filing a 1099-S.

Chapter
63

Profit tax
withholding on a sale

This chapter describes the federal and state tax withholding requirements for a sale of real estate by a nonresidential foreigner and the exemptions available for sales in a §1031 reinvestment plan.

Qualifying as an exempt §1031 sale

On the sale of real estate by a nonresident foreigner, a duty is imposed on the buyer to instruct escrow to **withhold** and **forward** 10% of the purchase price paid to the Internal Revenue Service (IRS), unless the transaction is *exempt*. [Internal Revenue Code §1445]

Further, when the real estate purchased is located in California, an additional duty is imposed on the buyer to instruct escrow to **withhold** and **forward** 3.33% of the price paid for the real estate to the Franchise Tax Board (FTB), unless the transaction is *exempt*. [Calif. Revenue and Taxation Code §18662]

The sole purpose for the federal withholding scheme is to collect a profit tax at the close of escrow on *all non-resident foreigners* who sell a parcel of real estate other than a residence sold for less than $300,000 that the buyer promises to occupy. A nonresident foreigner's §1031 reinvestment plan requires IRS written approval to avoid withholding.

For the California withholding scheme, the sole purpose is to tax *every individual* who sells business or investment property at a profit, unless the sale is exempt as part of a §1031 reinvestment plan (or other exemption).

The state and federal withholding schemes are completely separate from one another. Each requires **separate** withholding forms to be filed, and different withholding exemptions apply.

California withholding exemptions

A buyer is exempt and not required to withhold 3.33% of the sales price he pays for the property, if:

- the sales price is less than $100,000;

- the property is acquired at a nonjudicial (trustee's) or judicial foreclosure sale;

- the property is acquired by a deed in lieu of foreclosure;

- the seller is a bank acting as a trustee other than as a trustee of a trust deed; or

- escrow fails to provide a written notification of the withholding requirements to the buyer. [Rev & T C §18662(e)(3)]

The buyer is also exempt from California withholding requirements if the buyer receives the seller's written **real estate withholding certificate**, declaring under penalty of perjury that:

- the property sold is or was last used as the **seller's principal residence**, the price being of no concern;

- the property sold was the **decedent's principal residence**;

- the sale is part of the **seller's §1031 reinvestment plan**;

- the property has been **involuntarily converted**, (by destruction, seizure, condemnation, etc.) and the seller intends to acquire similar property to qualify for nonrecognition of gain under Internal Revenue Code (IRC) §1033;

- the property was sold at a **taxable loss** for the seller — a price less than the seller's remaining cost basis, a declaration that further requires the seller to prepare and execute a computation of his estimated gain or loss on the sale;

- the seller is a **Limited Liability Company (LLC)** or a **tax partnership**, but not a common law tenant-in-common co-ownership; or

- the seller is a corporation that maintains and staffs a permanent place of business in California. [Rev & T C §18662(e)(3)(D)]

If the replacement property in a §1031 reinvestment plan is not identified within the 45-day identification period or if identified, not acquired within the 180-day acquisition period, the profit on the sale fails to qualify for §1031 treatment. Here, the buyer (or buyer's trustee) must notify the FTB in writing within 10 days of the transaction's failure to qualify under §1031 rules and forward to the FTB the withholding amount. [Rev & T C §18662(e)(3)(D)(ii)(III)]

Installment sales require separate handling to avoid California withholding on the amount of the carryback note. Two steps are involved and both must be completed:

1. The seller makes his declaration on FTB Form 593-C indicating he has an exempt installment sale.

2. The buyer agrees to withhold on each principal payment by his signed declaration on the FTB form real estate withholding installment sales agreement.

If the buyer agrees, a seller will be able to require the buyer to withhold only as each installment is paid, not in a lump sum of 3.33% of the total purchase price on close of escrow. The listing agent in a carryback sale needs to **include a provision** in either the purchase agreement or a counteroffer calling for the buyer to comply with FTB deferred withholding on installment sales.

Conflicting exemptions for nonresident foreigners

It is possible for a transaction to be exempt from California withholding requirements, but still subject to the federal withholding requirements, or vice versa.

For example, both the state and federal rules provide the buyer with an exemption based on the price paid. The California price paid exemption covers properties purchased at a price "less than $100,000," without concern for the type of property it is or the buyer's use of the property.

Conversely, the federal rules provide for a "$300,000 or less" exemption used solely by nonresident foreigners. However, the price-paid exemption applies only to the purchase of a residence the buyer intends to occupy. Thus, if the seller is a non-resident foreigner and the price paid for the property is between $100,000 and $300,000, California rules require withholding, but the federal rules exempt the purchase when the buyer occupies the property.

For all sales in California priced at $100,000 or more, California requires withholding unless the seller provides the exemption. For another example of the California and federal contrasts, a California property which is sold by a non-resident foreigner for "less than $100,000," is exempt in California. However, no exemption applies federally unless the buyer occupies the property as his residence.

The federal withholding scheme

Federal tax laws require a buyer of real estate to withhold on all purchases from a nonresident foreign seller unless the seller fills out, signs and hands the buyer a **residency declaration form** stating the seller's qualifications for a federal exemption.

Typically, the real estate broker preparing a purchase agreement will prepare and include a federal residency declaration for the seller and the buyer to sign as one of the addenda to the purchase agreement.

If the seller is a **United States citizen** or a **resident foreigner**, the sale is exempt from withholding 10% for the IRS. No federal withholding is required unless a non-resident foreigner is the seller.

For the sale to qualify for the federal residency exemption, the seller must supply the buyer with a **declaration** stating he is either a U.S. citizen or a resident foreigner. [See Form 301 accompanying this chapter]

Brokers are under a duty, imposed by federal law, to notify the buyer of any falsities in the seller's declaration regarding citizenship or alien residency status, falsities known to the broker that would require withholding.

Failure to advise the buyer of a known, false declaration imposes a liability on the broker for taxes unpaid on the sale by the nonresident foreign seller. The broker's liability to the IRS is limited to the amount of the broker's compensation on the sale. [IRC §1445(d)]

The buyer must retain the seller's declaration with his tax return for _five_ years. [Revenue Regulations §1.1445-2(b)(3)]

Resident foreign sellers and the IRS

A foreign seller is considered a U.S. resident and the **sale is exempt** from federal withholding if:

- the foreign seller was present in the U.S. at least 31 days during the calendar year of the sale; and

- the number of days present in the U.S. in the current calendar year, plus one-third of the days present in the preceding year, plus one-sixth of the days present in the preceding two years, equals or exceeds 183 days. [IRC §7701(b)(3)(A)]

The foreign seller may **not** count as residency days, those days spent in the U.S. during which the seller:

- was present due to a medical condition that arose while visiting the U.S.;

- was a foreign government-related individual;

- was a teacher, trainee or student; or

- was a professional athlete temporarily in the U.S. to compete in a charitable event. [IRC §§7701(b)(3)(D)(ii), 7701(b)(5)(A)]

Should the foreign seller not meet the residency requirement for federal tax purposes, the sale is still exempt from federal withholding by the buyer if the property is:

- purchased for a price of $300,000 or less; and

- used as a residence by the buyer. [Rev. Regs. §1.1445-2(d)(1)]

The property is considered used as a residence if the buyer or a family member **plans to reside** on the property for at least 50% of the total number of days the property is occupied by anyone, including tenants, during each of the two 12-month periods following closing. The number of days the property is vacant (unused by anyone) is not taken into account in determining the number of days the property is used. [Rev. Regs. §1.1445-2(d)(1)]

The buyer makes his declaration for the use of the property as his residence in the **residency declaration** signed by both the buyer and the seller. No form or other documentation is to be filed with the IRS for the buyer to use the $300,000 residence exemption to avoid withholding.

However, the buyer or a family member might not **actually reside** on the property for the minimum 50% of all days the property is occupied. Because escrow was not instructed to withhold on the nonresident foreign seller, the buyer is liable to the IRS for the taxes on the sale should the foreign seller fail to pay taxes on his profit. [Rev. Regs. §1.1445-2(d)(1)]

Withholding for IRS in the §1031

Consider a **nonresident foreigner** who enters into an agreement with a broker to list a parcel of California real estate for sale.

The nonresident foreign seller will complete a §1031 reinvestment plan by purchasing replacement property in the United States.

When the broker lists the property for sale, the seller is handed a federal residency declaration to fill out and sign.

Because of the seller's nonresident foreign residency status, 10% of the sales price will be withheld on the sale of the real estate, unless the federal tax is *waived* by the IRS.

However, the non-resident seller intends to complete a tax-exempt §1031 reinvestment.

Does the fact that the nonresident foreign seller intends to complete a §1031 reinvestment change the federal withholding requirements?

Yes! Under federal tax law, the nonresident foreign seller can reduce or eliminate the amount required to be withheld in his §1031 reinvestment plan by requesting and receiving a **withholding certificate** from the IRS.

Further, if the price paid for the non-resident foreigner's real estate was below $300,000 and the buyer planned to reside in the property as his personal or family residence, the buyer need not comply with federal withholding requirements.

If a withholding certificate is not sought from the IRS and the seller is a non-resident foreigner subject to the federal withholding requirements, the buyer must withhold 10% of the purchase price and forward it to the IRS by the 20th day after closing escrow on the sale. [Rev. Regs. §1.1445-1(c)]

The withheld amounts are handled by escrow and filed with the IRS Center in Philadelphia, Pennsylvania.

Under California withholding requirements, the sale will be exempt since the seller can prepare an FTB real estate withholding certificate form and declare that he will use the net sales proceeds in a §1031 reinvestment plan.

The federal withholding certificate

A withholding certificate issued by the IRS to a non-resident foreign seller prior to his close of escrow notifies the buyer whether or not any withholding is required.

Either the buyer or the nonresident foreign seller may submit the application to the IRS for issuance of a withholding certificate. As a result of negotiations, the purchase agreement between the parties may contain a provision requiring the buyer to submit the application as a condition for closing the sale.

The IRS will act on an application for a withholding certificate no later than the 90th day after receipt of an application containing all information necessary for the IRS to make a decision. [Rev. Regs. §1.1445-3(a); Treasury Decision 9082]

Requesting an IRS withholding certificate

If the nonresident foreign seller submits the application for the **withholding certificate** to the IRS on or before the date the sales escrow closes, the seller must notify the buyer of the application.

The notice to the buyer must include:

- the seller's name, address and taxpayer identification number;

- a description of the property on which the withholding certificate is sought; and

DATE:_____, 20_____, at _____, California

Items left blank or unchecked are not applicable.

FACTS:

> **NOTE:** If the declarations differ for individual Sellers, then each Seller must fill out a separate form.

1. This declaration complies with Section 1445 of the United States Internal Revenue Code regarding the Seller's status as a citizen or resident of the United States or otherwise, and is for reliance by the broker and any buyer.

    1.1 Seller:_____

        U.S. Tax Identification Number (or Social Security Number):

        Seller:_____

    1.2 U.S. Tax Identification Number (or Social Security Number):_____

2. Regarding the proposed sale of real estate described as: _____
_____

SELLER'S DECLARATION:

3. Seller hereby declares:

    3.1 ☐ I am a citizen of the United States of America;

    3.2 ☐ I am a resident alien of the United States of America; my resident status is established by the following:

        a. ☐ I have been declared a permanent legal resident of the United States by the U.S. Immigration and Naturalization Service. Resident Alien registration number:
_____, or;

        b. ☐ I have resided at least 31 days in the United States during the current calendar year, and my days of residence in the United States over the last three years are as follows:

Current calendar year . . . . _____ X 1	=	_____
Last calendar year . . . . _____ X 0.334 =		_____
Second preceding year . . . . _____ X 0.167 =		_____
TOTAL DAYS		_____

        Since the total days equals or exceeds 183 days, I meet the substantial presence test of Internal Revenue Code §7701(b)(3).

> **Exclusions:**
>
> Residency does not include days during which the seller:
>
> - remained in the U.S. due to a medical condition which arose while he was visiting;
> - was in transit between two points outside the U.S.;
> - worked for an agency of a foreign government;
> - was a teacher or trainee, or was a student; or participated as a professional athlete in a charitable event.

4. ☐ I am neither a United States citizen nor a resident alien as defined in item 3, above; and

    4.1 Unless I obtain a "qualifying statement" [IRC §1445(b)(4)], or other special permission from the Internal Revenue Service, I authorize the Buyer of the above-referenced real estate to deduct and withhold 10% of the sales price for the federal government. I further authorize escrow holder to deduct these amounts from funds due me at close of escrow, and to deposit it as a tax deposit in an authorized commercial bank.

5. I consent to the reliance on this declaration of the brokers, agents, escrow-holder, and Buyer in any transaction regarding this real estate.

6. Note: This transaction is exempt from IRC §1445 withholding if the sales price is $300,000 or less and the Buyer will use the real estate as his residence.

BUYER'S ACKNOWLEDGMENT:

7. I have read and received a copy of this Seller's Residency Declaration.

8. ☐ I hereby declare I will use the real estate as my residence. If the final sales price is $300,000 or less, I consent to reliance on this declaration by brokers, agents, escrow holder and the nonresident alien Seller.

I declare under penalty of perjury that the foregoing is true and correct.	I declare under penalty of perjury that the foregoing is true and correct.
Date:_____, 20_____	Date:_____, 20_____
Seller:_____	Buyer: _____
Date:_____, 20_____	Date:_____, 20_____
Seller:_____	Buyer: _____

- the date on which the application was submitted. [Rev. Regs. §1.1445-1(c)(2)(i)(B)]

However, even though an application for a withholding certificate is submitted to the IRS, if a withholding certificate is not received from the IRS prior to closing the buyer must still withhold the 10% required by federal law.

On receipt of the IRS withholding certificate, the amount to be withheld need not be reported and paid to the IRS until the 20th day following the IRS's **final decision** on the withholding certificate, which could be as long as 90 days after closing, depending on when the application was filed. [Rev. Regs. §1.1445-1(c)(2)(i)]

A final decision is considered made when the withholding certificate or notification denying the request is delivered by mail from the IRS.

The amount the IRS requires to be withheld may be less than the 10% retained in escrow after closing and while awaiting receipt of the IRS withholding certificate. Prior to closing, the nonresident foreign seller must ensure escrow has mutual instructions to transfer the amount remaining to the §1031 trustee established in the delayed reinvestment plan.

Any funds withheld and paid to the IRS or FTB in a §1031 transaction will be considered cash boot received by the nonresident seller.

Calculating the maximum tax on a sale

To establish the reason for the claimed exemption, the maximum federal tax that may be imposed on the property must be calculated. The nonresident foreign seller lists the tax as the maximum amount he could be required to pay on the sale of the real estate.

Profit on the individual's sale of real estate is subject to the capital gains tax rates of 15% and 25%. [Rev. Regs. §1.1445-3(c)(2)(v)]

The amount of the maximum tax is then adjusted for the following:

- the effect of IRC §1031 on the transaction;

- any reportable losses on the seller's previous disposition of other real estate interests during the taxable year;

- any amount that is treated as ordinary income on the sale, due to the recapture of excess depreciation (a type of gain that expires in 2005); and

- any other amounts that will increase or decrease the amount of tax. [Rev. Regs. §1.1445-3(c)(2)]

Also, any unpaid federal tax liability of the nonresident foreign seller must be included in the maximum tax amount. This unpaid amount of taxes may be disregarded if either:

- the amount is satisfied by a payment accompanying the application for a withholding certificate; or

- an agreement for the payment of the tax is entered into with the IRS. [Rev. Regs. §1.1445-3(c)(3)]

Further, if no previous tax liability exists for the nonresident foreign seller, evidence that the seller has no tax liability must be submitted with the application. The seller may show that he has had no previous tax liability by using any one of the following documents:

- a document showing the seller acquired the real estate prior to January 1, 1995;

- a copy of IRS Form 8288 which was filed by the seller and proof of payment of the amount due;

- a copy of the withholding certificate the seller received on acquisition of the property, plus a copy of Form 8288 and proof of any payment of the amount required to be withheld;

- a copy of the resident foreigner declaration of the person from whom the seller purchased the real estate;

- evidence the seller purchased the real estate being sold for $300,000 or less and the property was the seller's personal residence;

- evidence the previous owner of the property paid his taxes;

- a notice of nonrecognition provided to the seller by the previous owner of the real estate; or

- a statement, signed by the seller under penalty of perjury, on why the seller believed no withholding was required when the property was purchased. [Rev. Regs. §1.1445-3(c)(3)(ii)]

Cases

Federal Codes

Topical Index